Music transcriptions by David Stocker

ISBN 978-1-4234-3348-4

7777 W. BLUEMOUND RD. P.O. BOX 13819 MILWAUKEE, WI 53213

In Australia Contact:
Hal Leonard Australia Pty. Ltd.
4 Lentara Court
Cheltenham, Victoria, 3192 Australia
Email: ausadmin@halleonard.com.au

Visit Hal Leonard Online at
www.halleonard.com

Through the Fire and Flames

Words and Music by Herman Li, ZP Theart, Sam Totman and Vadim Pruzhanov

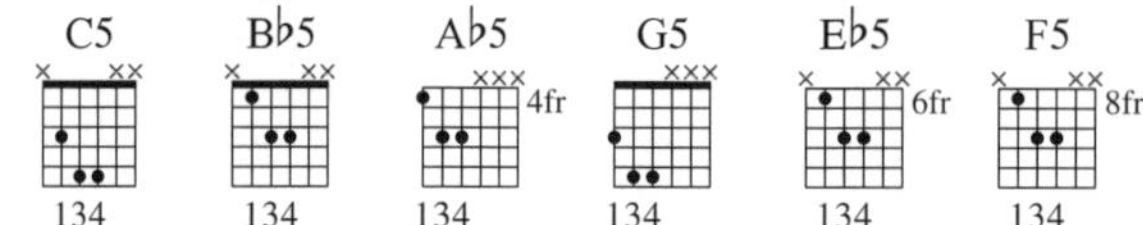

Intro

Very fast ♩ = 200

C5

Gtrs. 1 & 2 (elec.)

f

w/ dist.

(cont. in notatio

Riff A

Gtr. 3 (acous.)

End Riff

mp

w/ fingers

let ring throughout

T A B

8 10 10 10 8 10 10 10 8 10 10 10 8 10 10 10 8 10 9 10 10 10 | 11 10 8 10 9 10 10 10 8 10 10 8 10 10 10 7 10

Riff A1

Gtr. 4 (acous.)

End Riff A

mp

w/ fingers

let ring throughout

T A B

10 10 7 10 8 10 10 10 7 10 8 10 10 10 8 10 | 8 10 8 10 10 10 7 10 8 10 10 10 7 10 8 10

Riff A2

Gtr. 4a (acous.)

End Riff A1

8va

mp

w/ fingers

let ring throughout

T A B

17 17 19 17 20 17 17 17 19 17 20 17 18 17 20 17 | 20 17 20 17 18 17 19 17 20 17 17 17 19 17 20 17

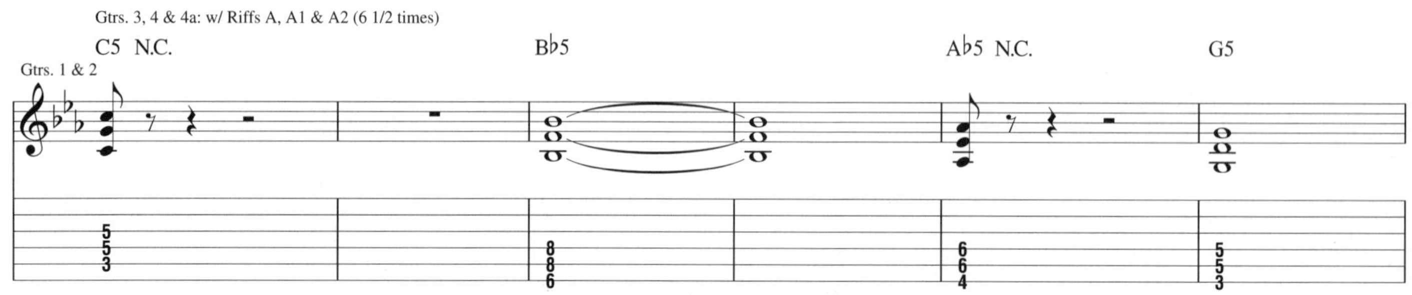

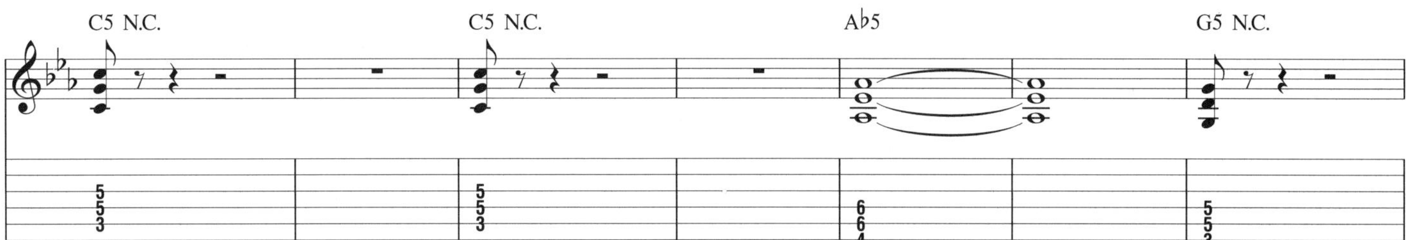

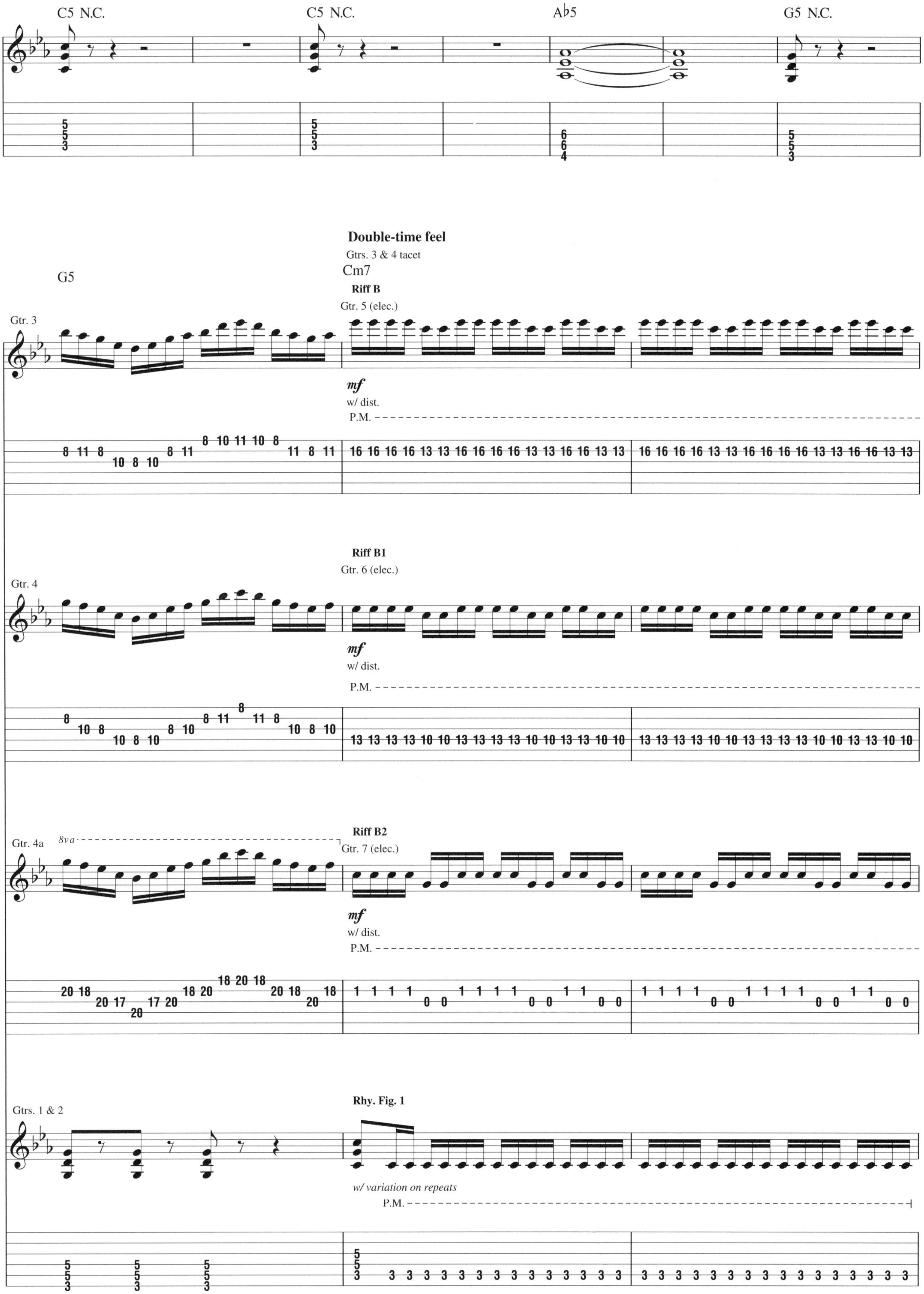

Double-time feel

Gtrs. 3 & 4 tacet

G5

Cm7

Riff B

Gtr. 5 (elec.)

Gtr. 3

mf

w/ dist.

P.M.

8 11 8 10 8 10 8 11 8 10 11 10 8 11 8 11 | 16 16 16 16 13 13 16 16 16 16 13 13 16 16 13 13 | 16 16 16 16 13 13 16 16 16 16 13 13 16 16 13 13

Riff B1

Gtr. 6 (elec.)

Gtr. 4

mf

w/ dist.

P.M.

8 10 8 10 8 10 8 10 8 11 8 11 8 10 8 10 | 13 13 13 13 10 10 13 13 13 13 10 10 13 13 10 10 | 13 13 13 13 10 10 13 13 13 13 10 10 13 13 10 10

Riff B2

Gtr. 7 (elec.)

Gtr. 4a

8va

mf

w/ dist.

P.M.

20 18 20 17 20 17 20 18 20 18 20 18 20 18 20 18 | 1 1 1 1 0 0 1 1 1 1 0 0 1 1 0 0 | 1 1 1 1 0 0 1 1 1 1 0 0 1 1 0 0

Rhy. Fig. 1

Gtrs. 1 & 2

w/ variation on repeats

P.M.

5 5 3 5 5 3 5 5 3 | 5 5 3 3 3 3 3 3 3 3 3 3 3 3 3 3 3 3 | 3 3 3 3 3 3 3 3 3 3 3 3 3 3 3 3

*Chord symbols reflect overall harmony.

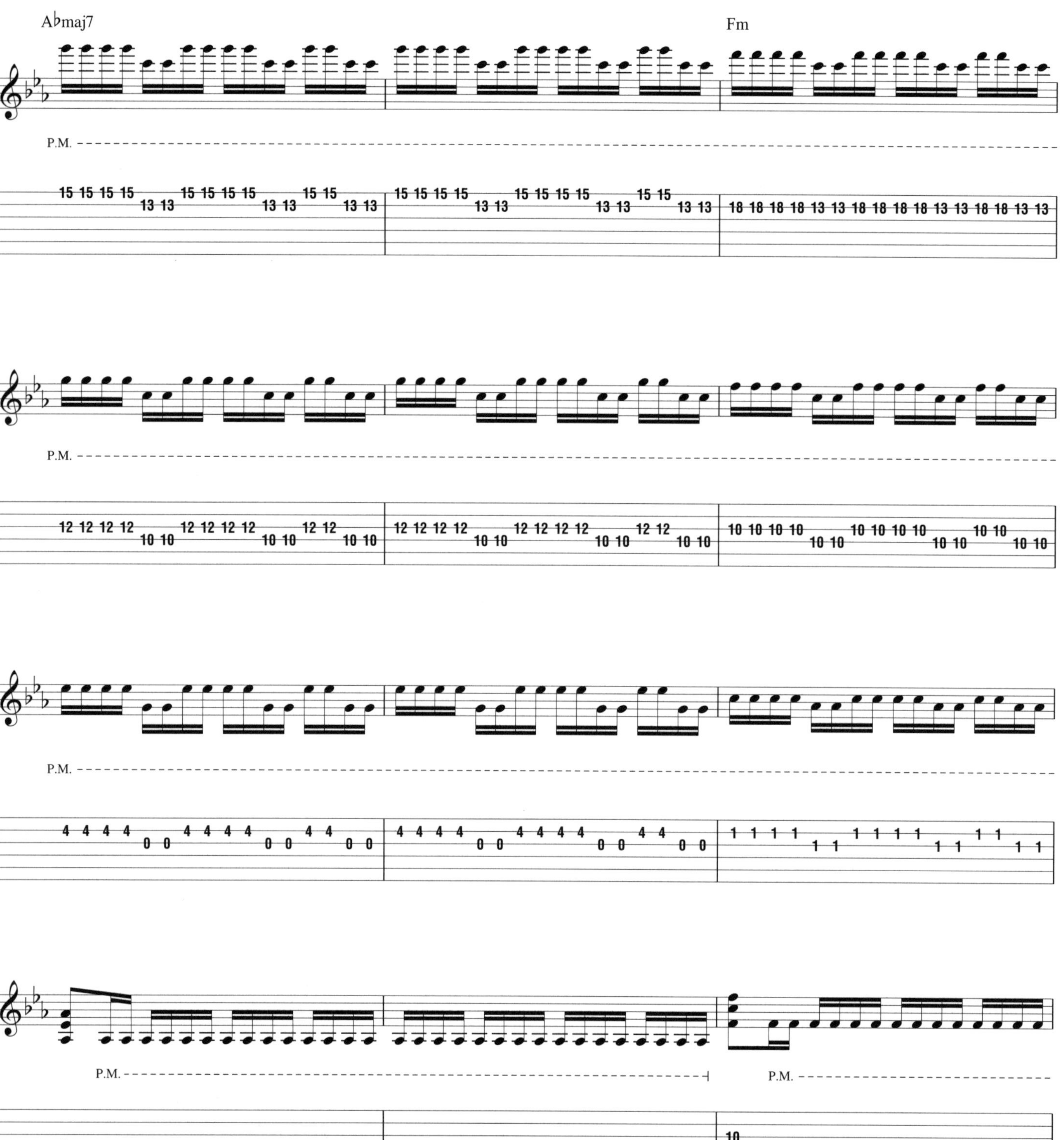
A♭maj7
Fm
P.M.
P.M.
P.M.
P.M.
P.M.

A♭maj7
G7
End Riff B
P.M.
End Riff B1
P.M.
End Riff B2
P.M.
End Rhy. Fig. 1
P.M.
Gtrs. 1 & 2: w/ Rhy. Fig. 1
Gtrs. 5, 6 & 7: w/ Riffs B & B1
Cm7
A♭maj9
Riff C
Gtr. 8 (elec.)
mf
w/ dist.
P.M.
Fm
End Riff C
P.M.

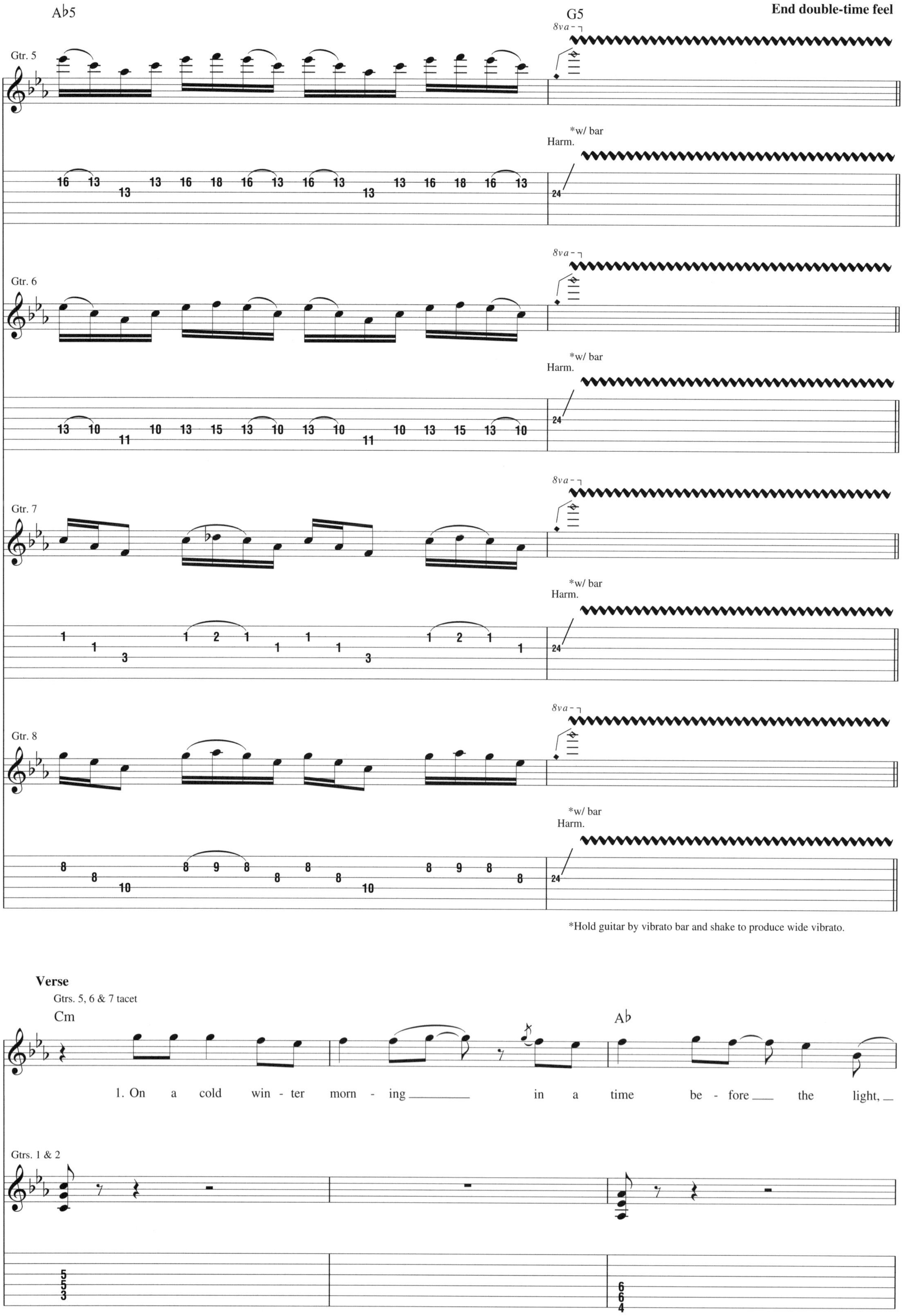

A♭5 G5 **End double-time feel**

Gtr. 5

8va

*w/ bar
Harm.

Gtr. 6

8va

*w/ bar
Harm.

Gtr. 7

8va

*w/ bar
Harm.

Gtr. 8

8va

*w/ bar
Harm.

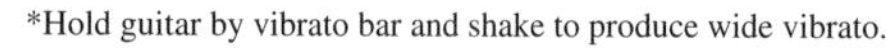
*Hold guitar by vibrato bar and shake to produce wide vibrato.

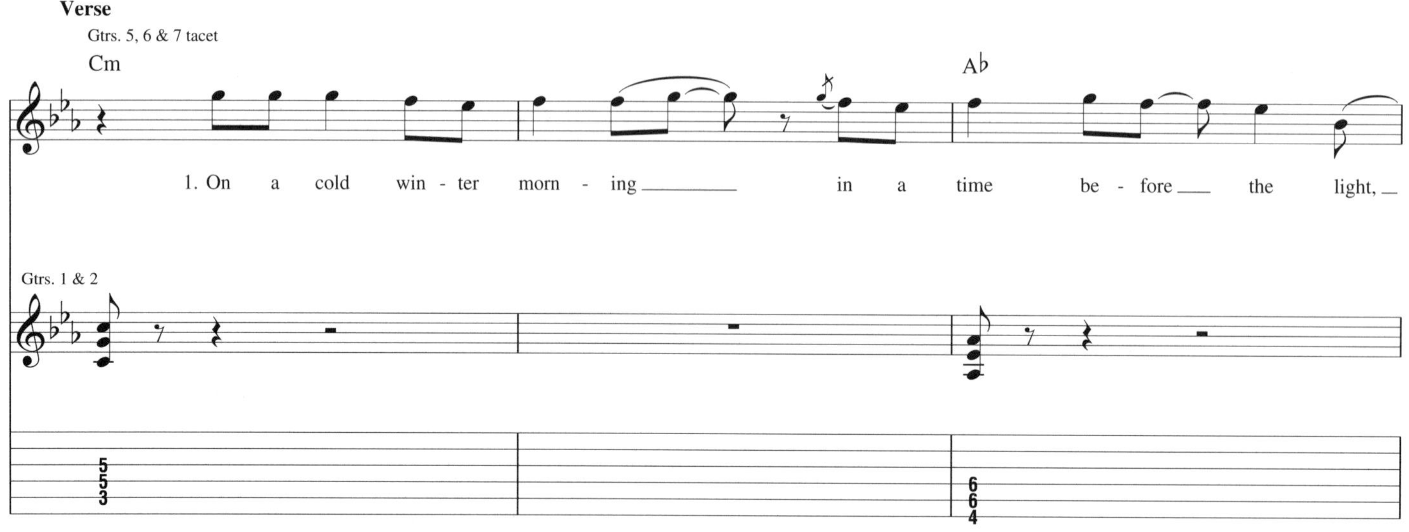
Verse
Gtrs. 5, 6 & 7 tacet
Cm
A♭
1. On a cold win - ter morn - ing in a time be - fore the light,
Gtrs. 1 & 2

B♭
in flames of death's e - ter - nal reign, we
Double-time feel
Cm
C5
ride to - wards the fight.
When the dark - ness has
Gtr. 1
Rhy. Fig. 2
P.M.
P.M.
w/ variation on repeats
P.M.
Gtr. 2
P.M.
P.M.
w/ variation on repeats
P.M.
B♭5 A♭5
fall - en down and the times are tough al - right, the
Gtrs. 1 & 2
P.M.
P.M.
B♭5
C5
sound of e - vil laugh - ter falls a - round the world to -
P.M.
P.M.
P.M.

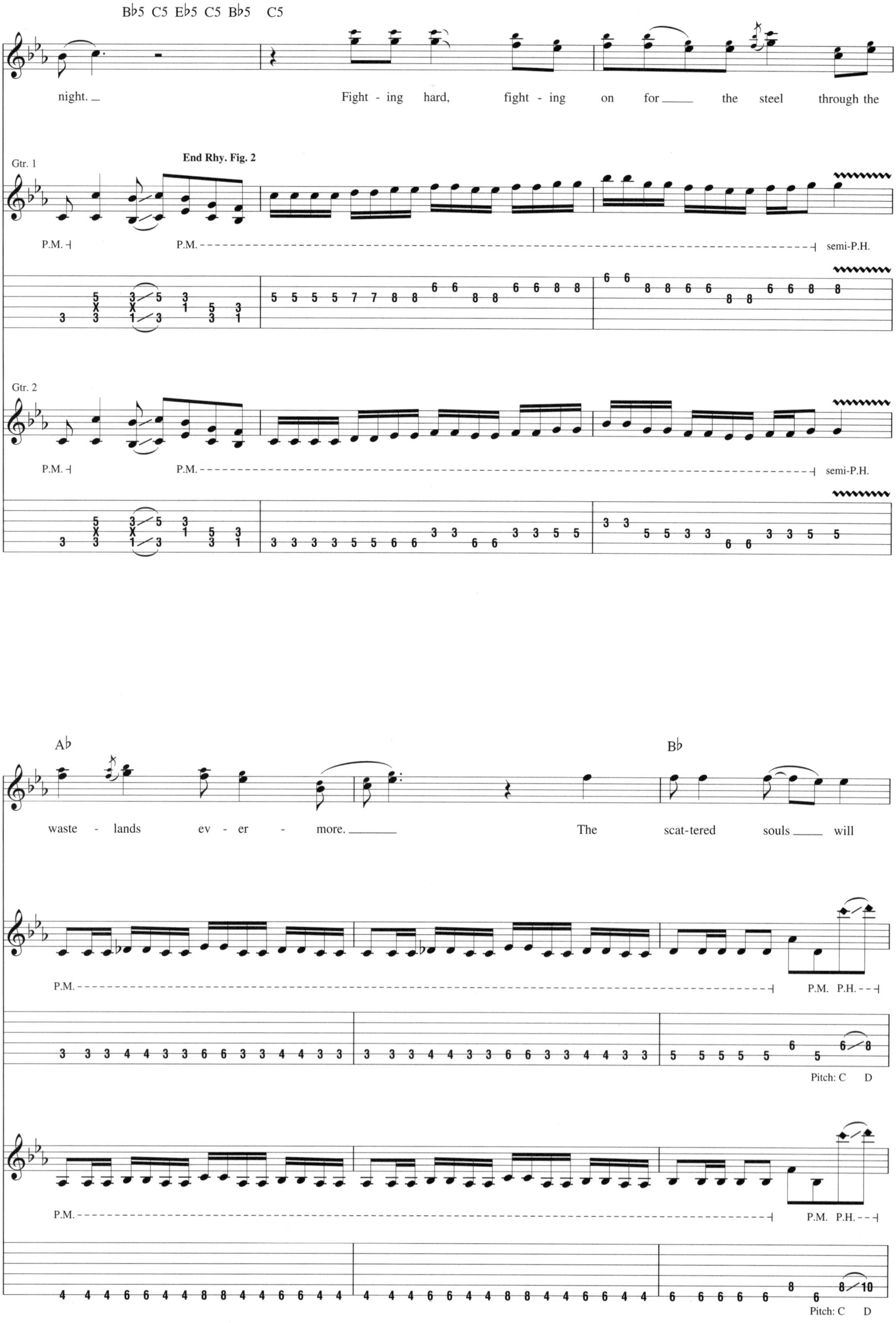

A♭ B♭

waste - lands ev - er - more. The scat-tered souls will

P.M. P.M. P.H.

Pitch: C D

P.M. P.M. P.H.

Pitch: C D

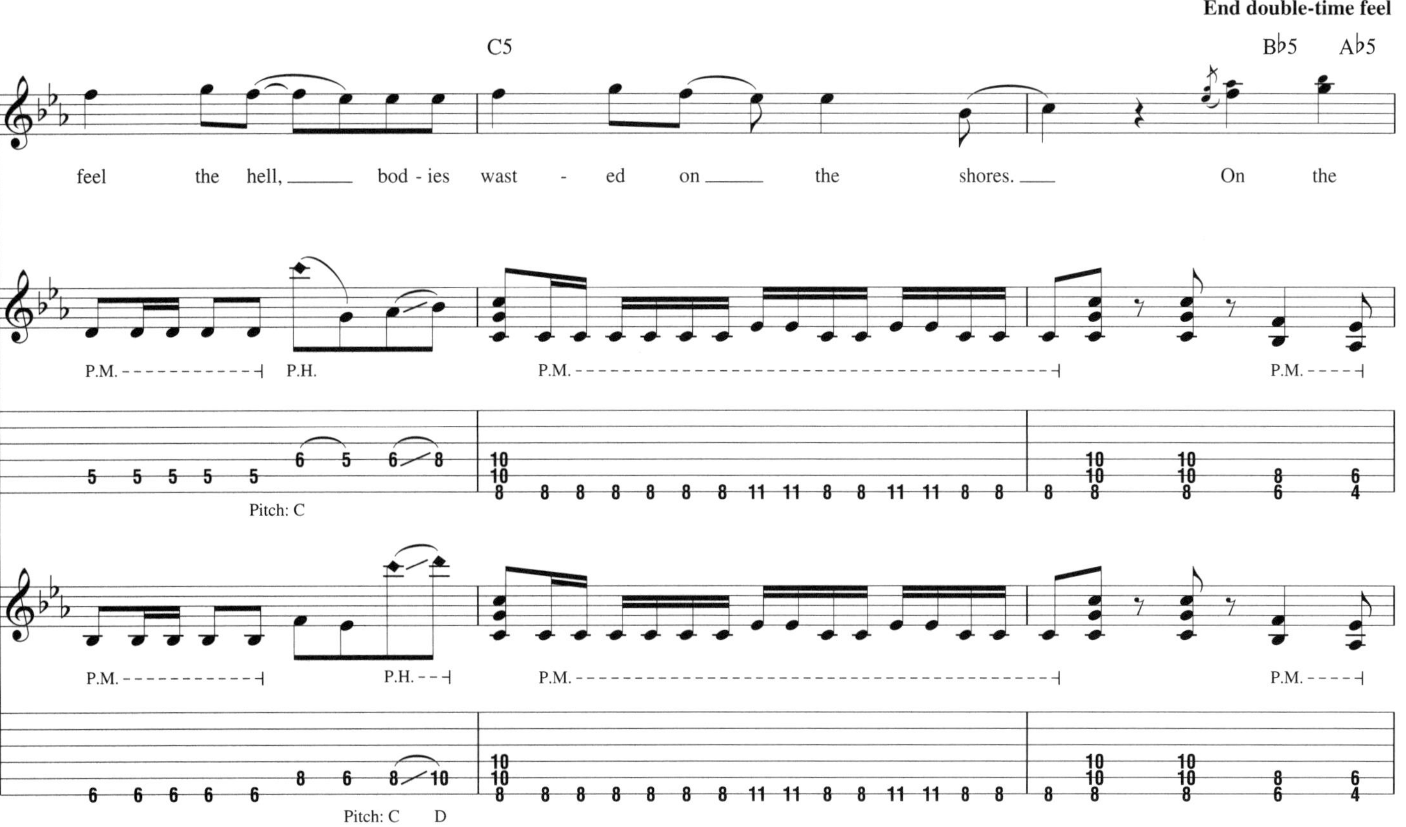

Fm Cm7

black - est plains in hell's do - main we watch them as we

Gtr. 5

P.M. P.M. P.M. P.M. P.M. P.M.

Gtr. 6

P.M. P.M. P.M. P.M. P.M. P.M.

Rhy. Fig. 3

Gtrs. 1 & 2

w/ variation on repeats

P.M. P.M. P.M. P.M. P.M. P.M. P.M.

A♭

go. In fire and pain now

P.M. P.M. P.M.

P.M. P.M. P.M.

P.M. P.M. P.M. P.M. P.M.

B♭ A♭5 B♭5

once a - gain we know. So now we

P.M. P.M. P.M.

w/ slide

P.M. P.M. P.M.

w/ slide

End Rhy. Fig. 3

P.M. P.M. P.M. P.M.

Pre-Chorus
Double-time feel
Gtrs. 5 & 6 tacet
Eb5
Bb5
C5
Bb5
Ab5
fly ev - er free, we're free be - fore the
(Fly ev - er free, ah.
Rhy. Figs. 4 & 4A
Gtrs. 1 & 2
w/ variation on repeats
P.M.
thun - der - storm. On to - wards the wild - er - ness, our
On to - wards the wild - er - ness,
Gtr. 2
End Rhy. Fig. 4A
semi-P.H.
Gtr. 1
8va
loco
End Rhy. Fig. 4
P.H.
Pitch: G
quest car - ries on. Far be - yond the
ah.)
Rhy. Fig. 5

A♭5 C5 B♭5 C5 E♭5

sun - down, far be - yond the moon - light.

Gtr. 6

P.M. P.M. P.M.

8 10 10 8 10 10 8 10 | 8 8 8 8 8 8 9 9 11 11 9 9 8 8 8 8

Gtr. 5

P.M. P.M. P.M.

10 10 10 10 10 10 10 10 | 8 8 10 10 8 8 10 10 8 8 10 10 8 8 10 10

Gtrs. 1 & 2

P.M. P.M.

6 6 4 | 10 10 8 10 8 10 8 10 10 8 10 8 10 8 8 6 10 8 | 8 8 6

F5

Deep in - side our hearts and all our

P.M.

9 9 9 9 11 11 9 9 13 13 9 9 11 11 13 13 | 9 9 9 9 11 11 9 9 13 13 9 9 11 11 13 13

P.M.

10 10 10 10 8 8 10 10 9 9 10 10 8 8 9 9 | 10 10 10 10 8 8 10 10 9 9 10 10 8 8 9 9

P.M. P.M. P.M. P.M.

10 10 8 8 8 8 8 10 10 8 8 8 8 8 8 8 8 8 | 10 10 8 8 8 8 8 10 10 8 8 8 8 8 8 8 8 8

B♭5
N.C.
souls.
So far a -
15ma
P.M.
w/ slide
steady gliss.
***Hypothetical fret location above pickups.
†Hypothetical fret location above pickups.
End Rhy. Fig. 5
Chorus
Gtrs. 5 & 6 tacet
A♭5
C5
way, we wait for the day. For the
Rhy. Fig. 6
Gtrs. 1 & 2
B♭5
G5
lives all so wast - ed and gone.

2nd time, Gtrs. 1 & 2: w/ Fills 1 & 2

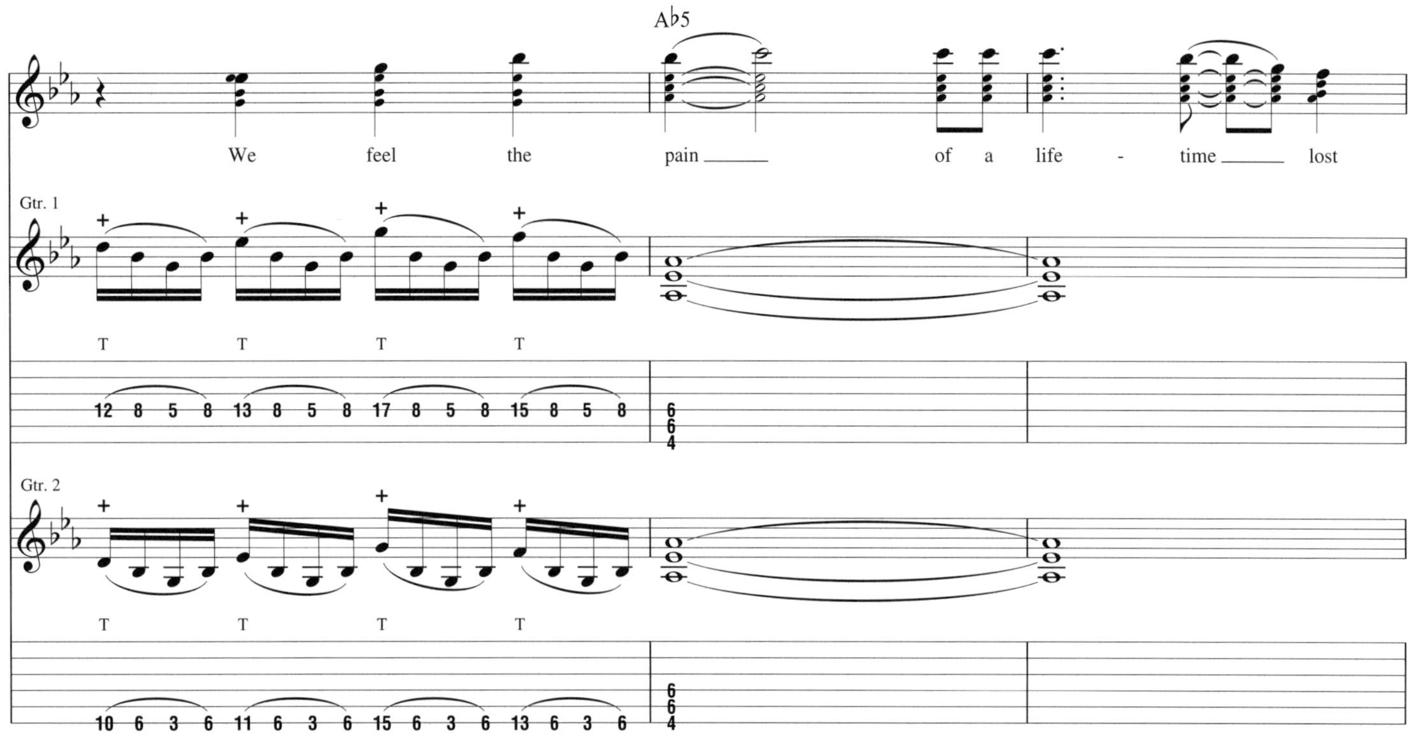

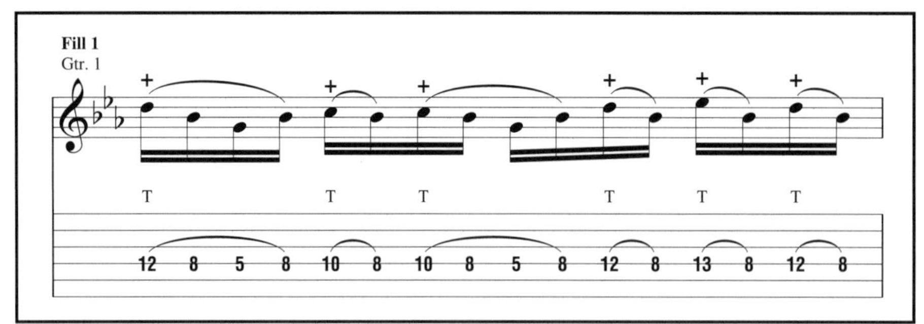

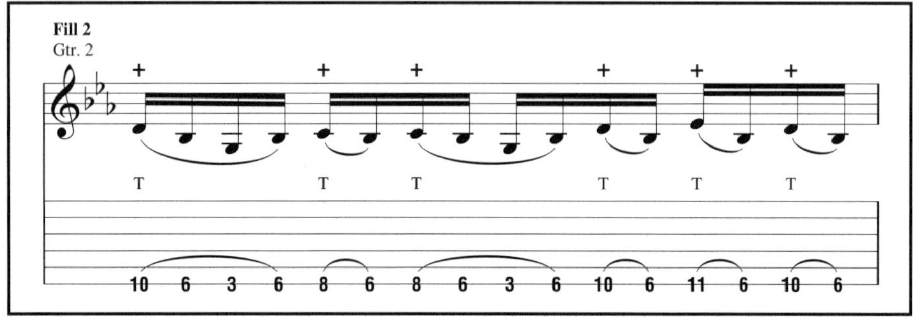

Interlude

C5 A♭5

on.

Gtr. 6

w/o slide

P.M.

Gtr. 5

w/o slide

P.M.

Rhy. Fig. 7

Gtrs. 1 & 2

w/ variation on repeats

P.M.

B♭5 A♭5 B♭5 C5

15ma

loco

8va

P.H.

P.M.

Pitch: B♭

8va

loco

P.H.

P.M.

Pitch: F

P.M.

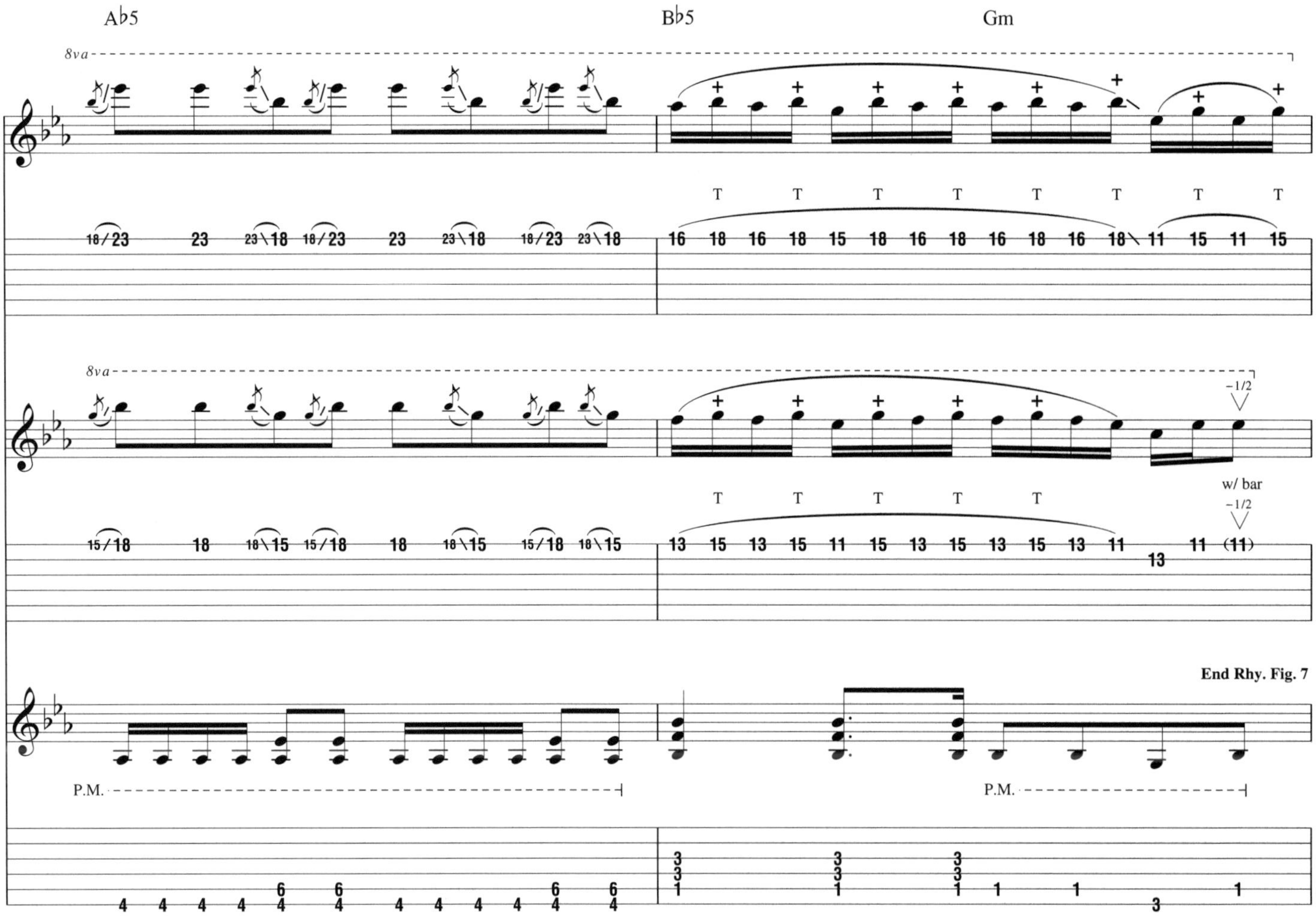

A♭5 B♭5 Gm

8va

T T T T T T T T

8va

T T T T T

w/ bar

−1/2

End Rhy. Fig. 7

P.M.

P.M.

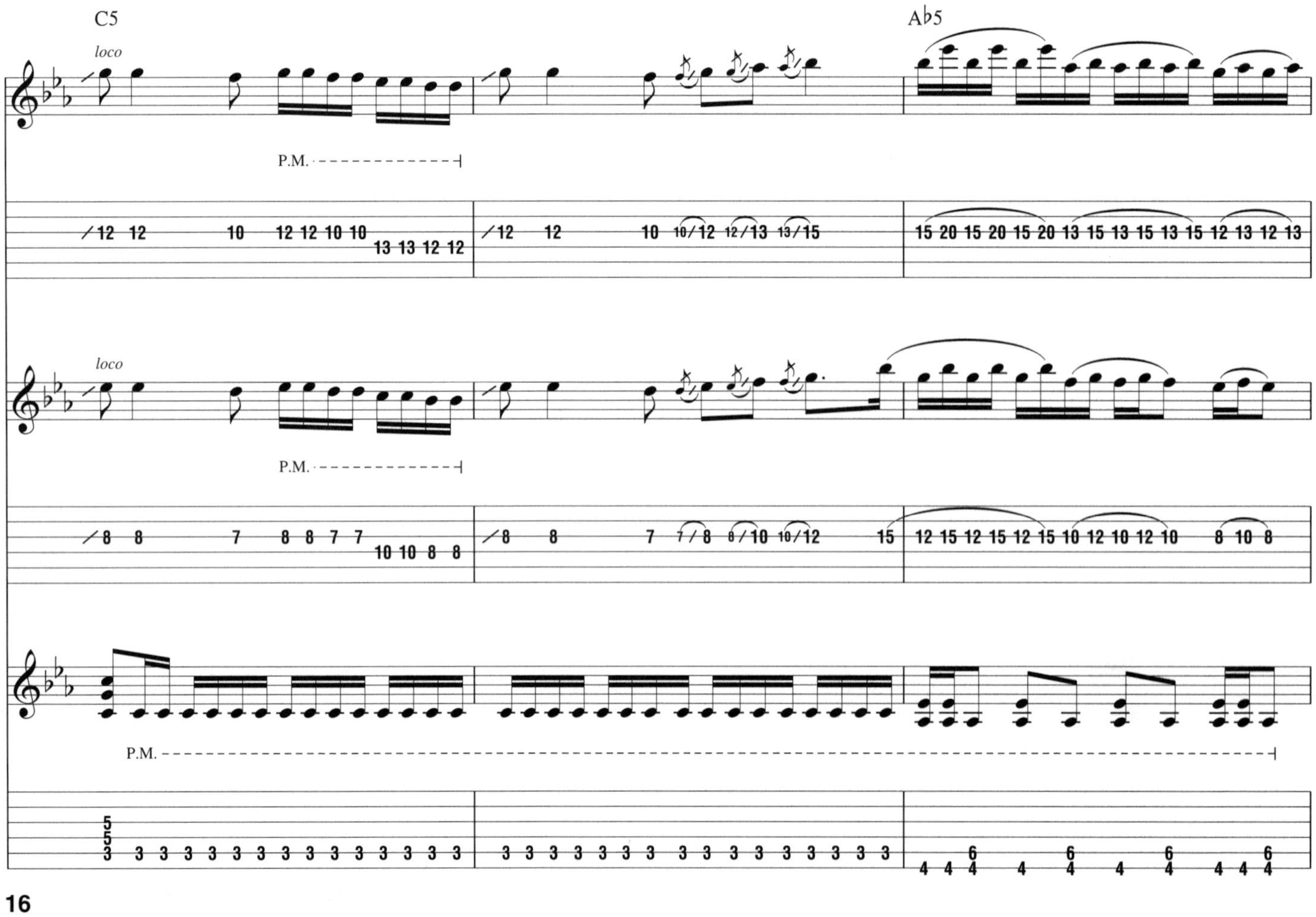

C5 A♭5

loco

P.M.

loco

P.M.

P.M.

B♭5 C5

semi-P.H.

semi-P.H.

Rhy. Fig. 8

P.M.

End double-time feel

A♭5 B♭5 A♭5 G5 F5 C5 N.C.

8va 15ma

P.H.

Pitch: B

8va 15ma

P.H.

Pitch: G

End Rhy. Fig. 8

P.M.

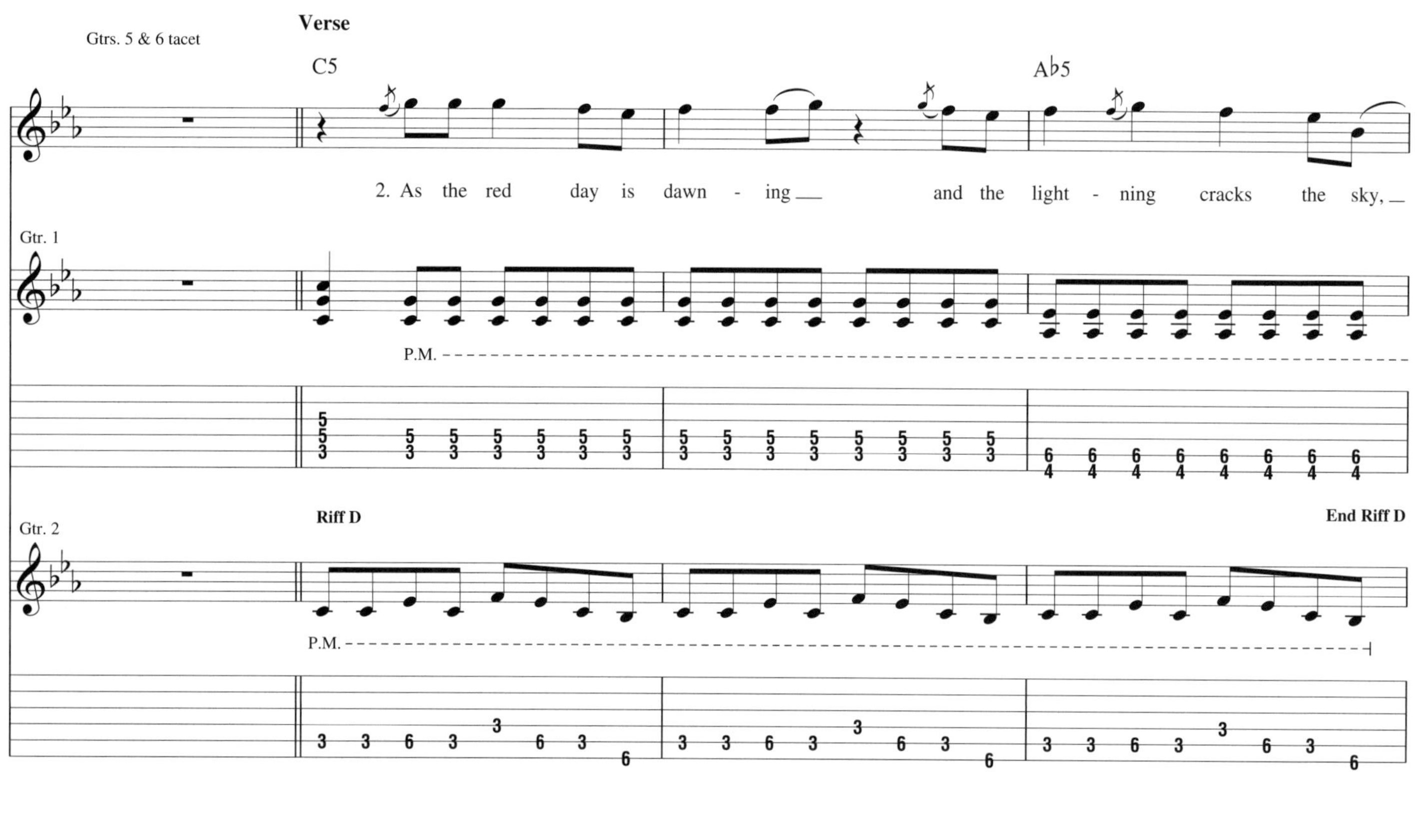
Gtrs. 5 & 6 tacet
Verse
C5
A♭5
2. As the red day is dawn - ing and the light - ning cracks the sky,
Gtr. 1
P.M.
Gtr. 2
Riff D
End Riff D
P.M.

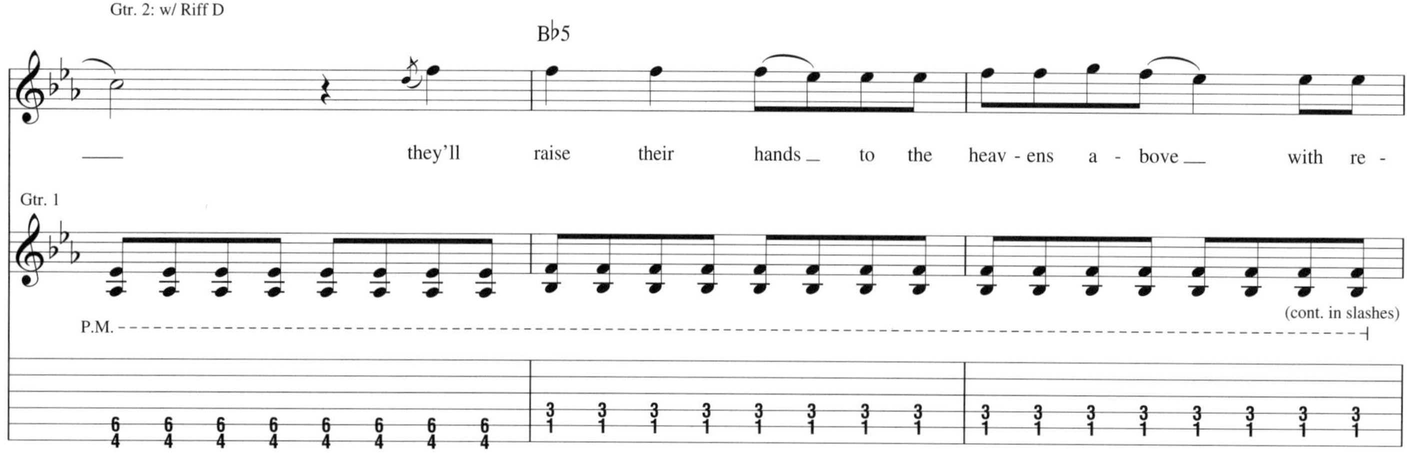
Gtr. 2: w/ Riff D
B♭5
they'll raise their hands to the heav - ens a - bove with re -
Gtr. 1
(cont. in slashes)
P.M.

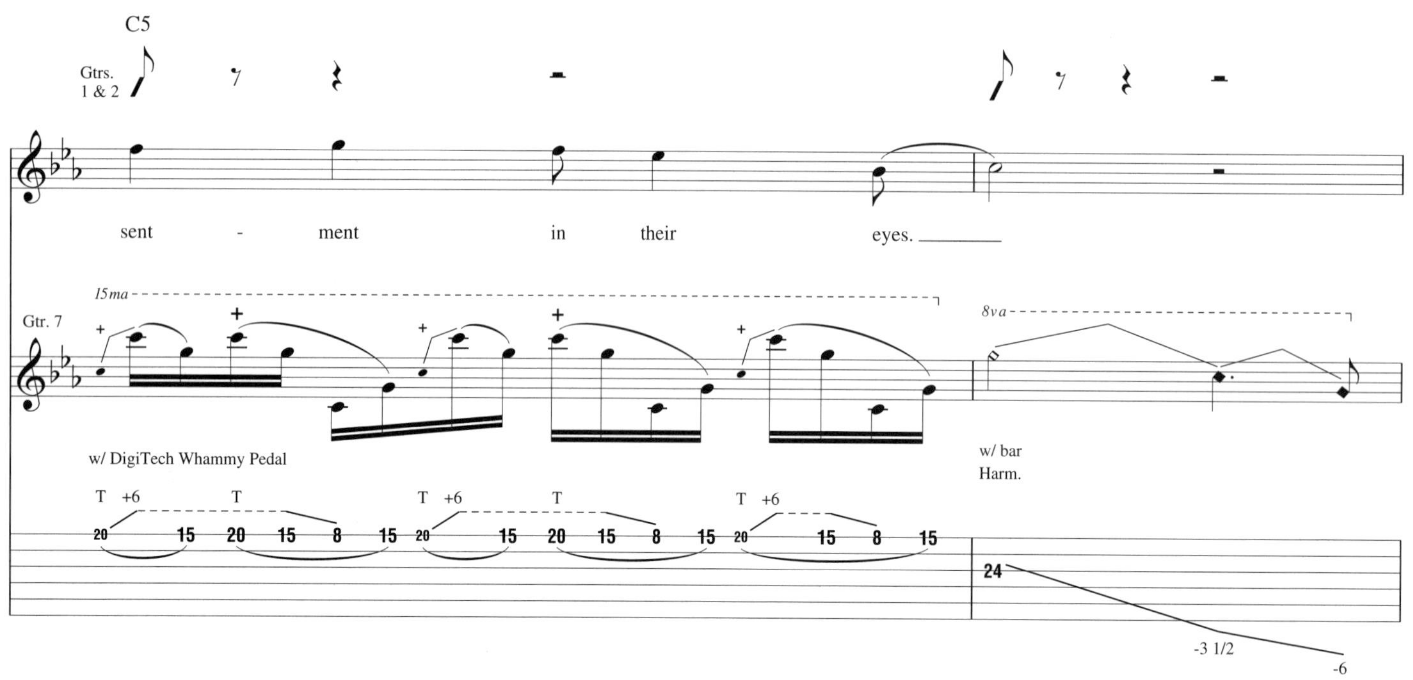
C5
Gtrs. 1 & 2
sent - ment in their eyes.
15ma
8va
Gtr. 7
w/ DigiTech Whammy Pedal
w/ bar
Harm.

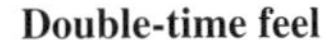
Double-time feel

Gtrs. 1 & 2: w/ Rhy. Fig. 2
Gtr. 7 tacet
C5
Bb5
Ab5
Run-ning back from the mid-morn-ing light there's a bur-den in my heart. We're

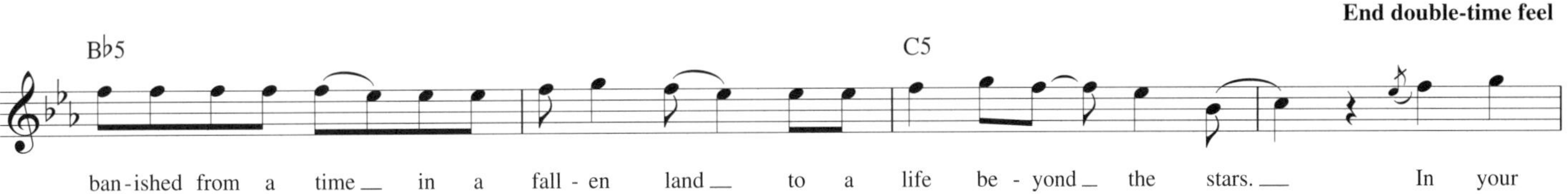
End double-time feel
Bb5
C5
ban-ished from a time in a fall-en land to a life be-yond the stars. In your

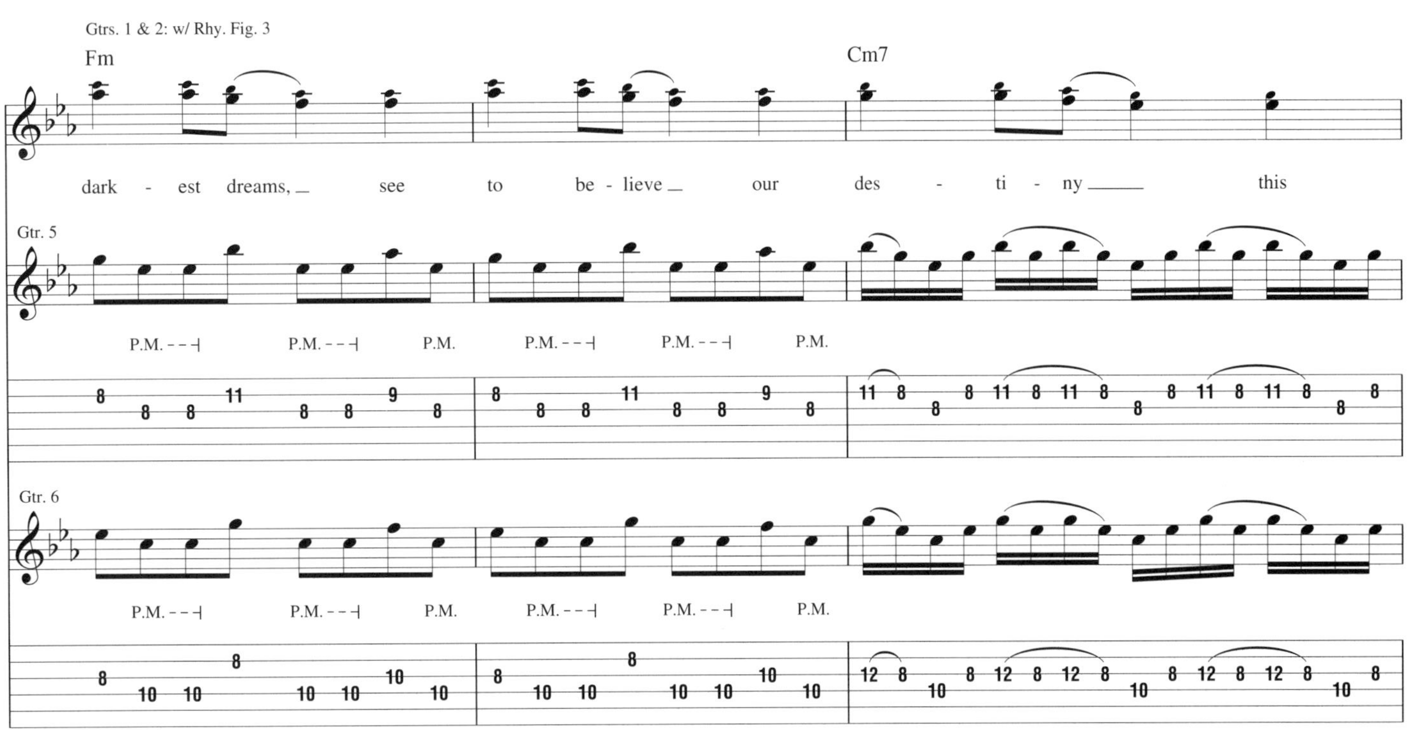
Gtrs. 1 & 2: w/ Rhy. Fig. 3
Fm
Cm7
dark-est dreams, see to be-lieve our des-ti-ny this
Gtr. 5
P.M.
Gtr. 6
P.M.

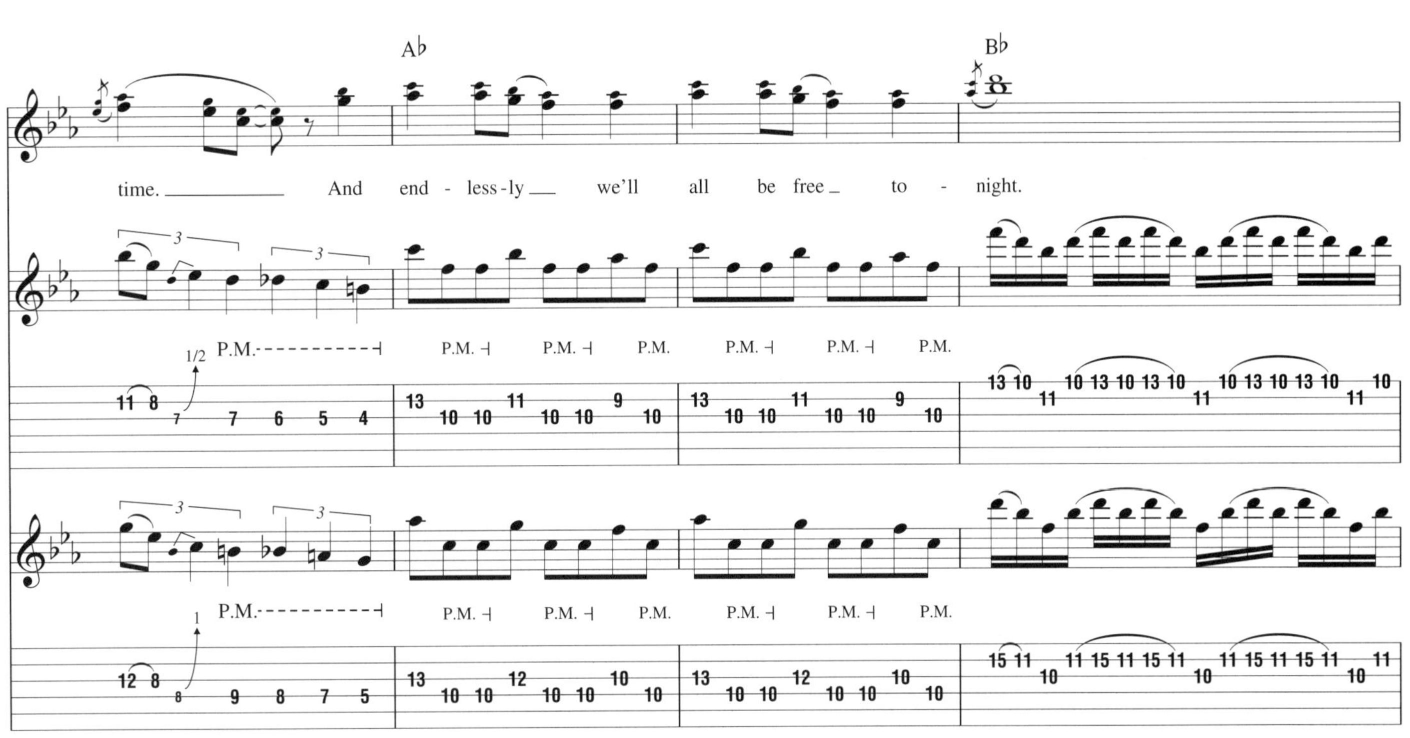
Ab
Bb
time. And end-less-ly we'll all be free to-night.
P.M.

*Composite arrangement

**Tap pick edge against strings while sliding down.

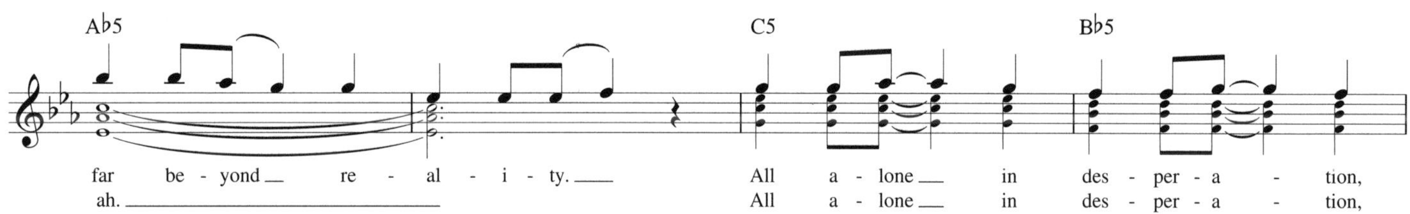

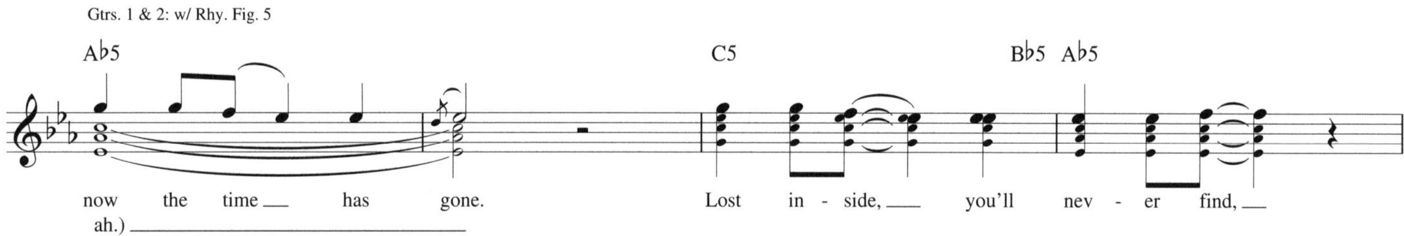

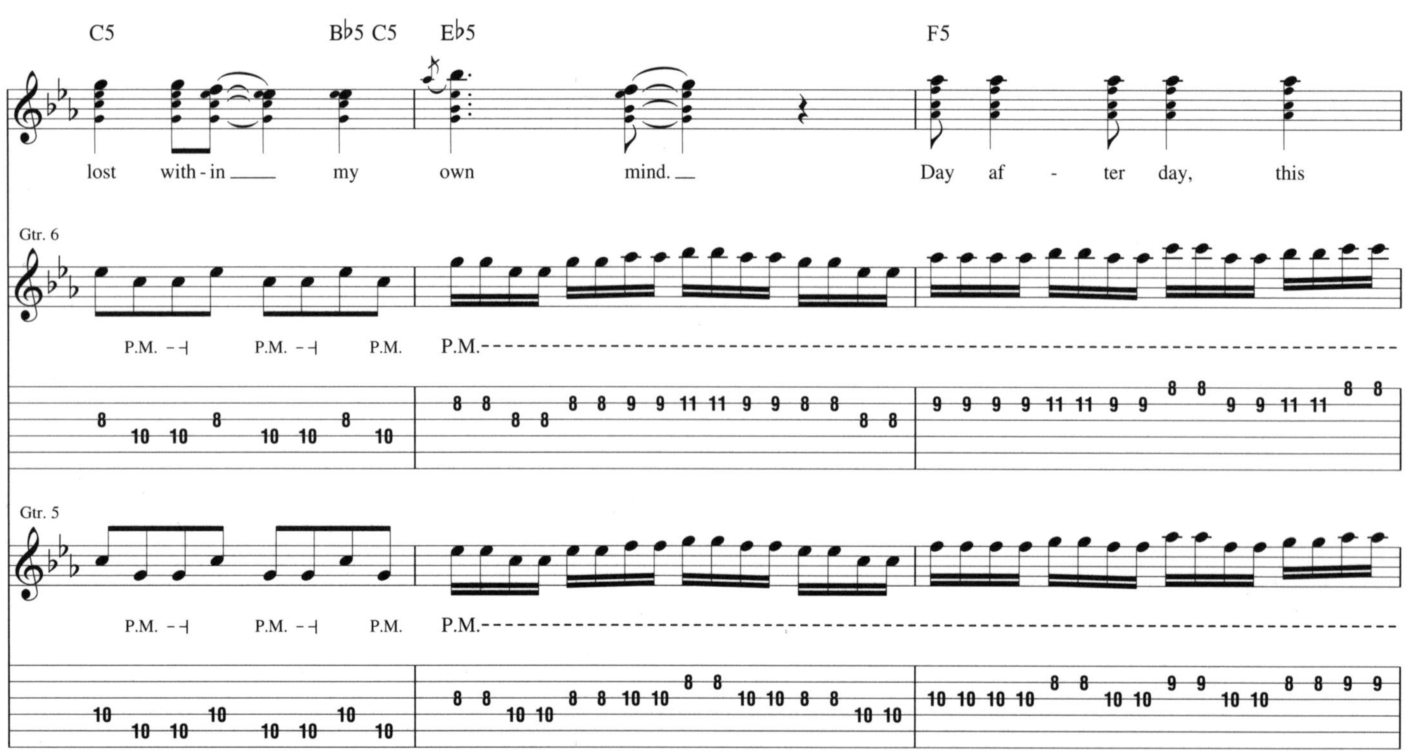

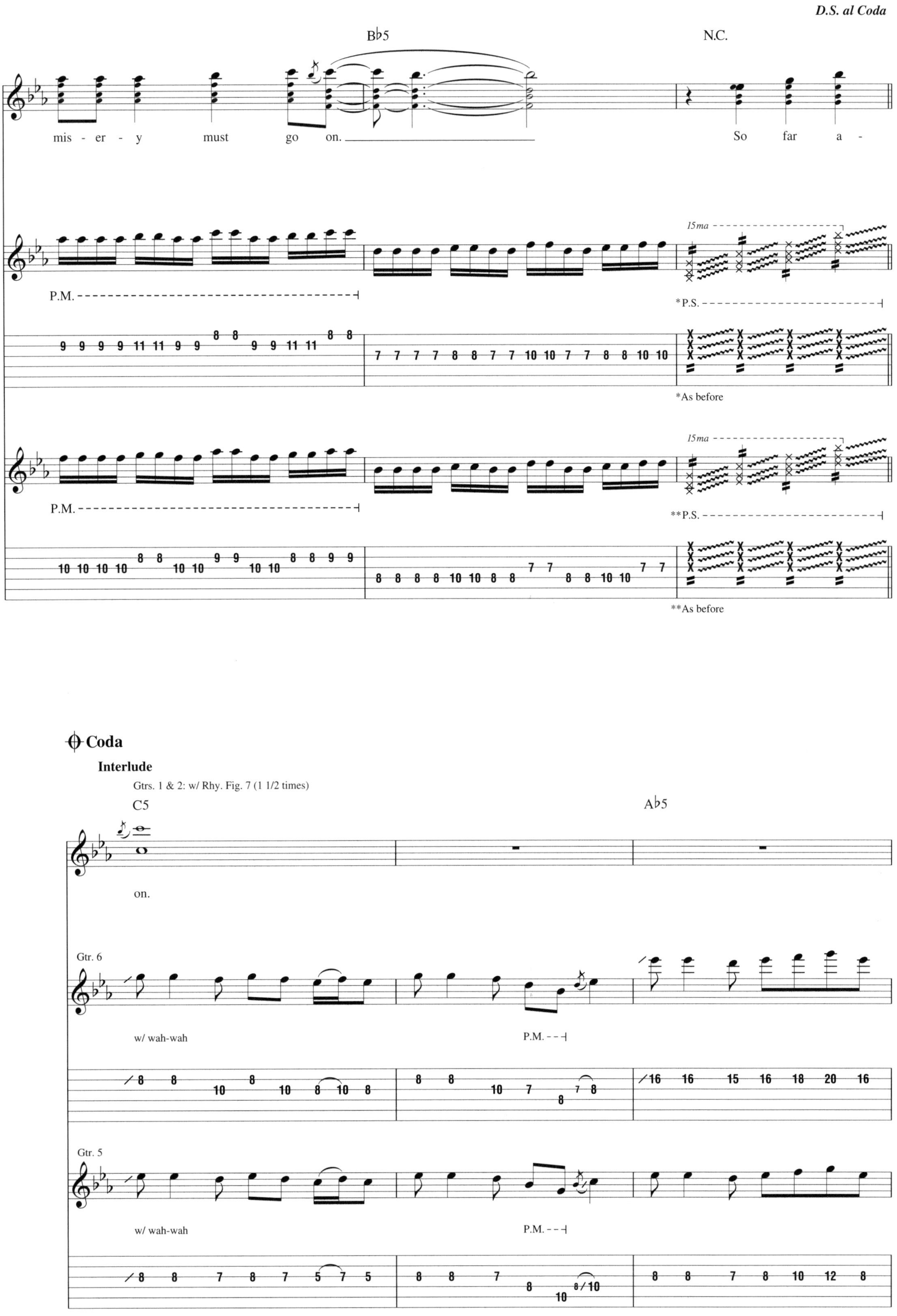

D.S. al Coda

B♭5 N.C.

mis - er - y must go on. So far a -

P.M.

15ma

*P.S.

*As before

P.M.

15ma

**P.S.

**As before

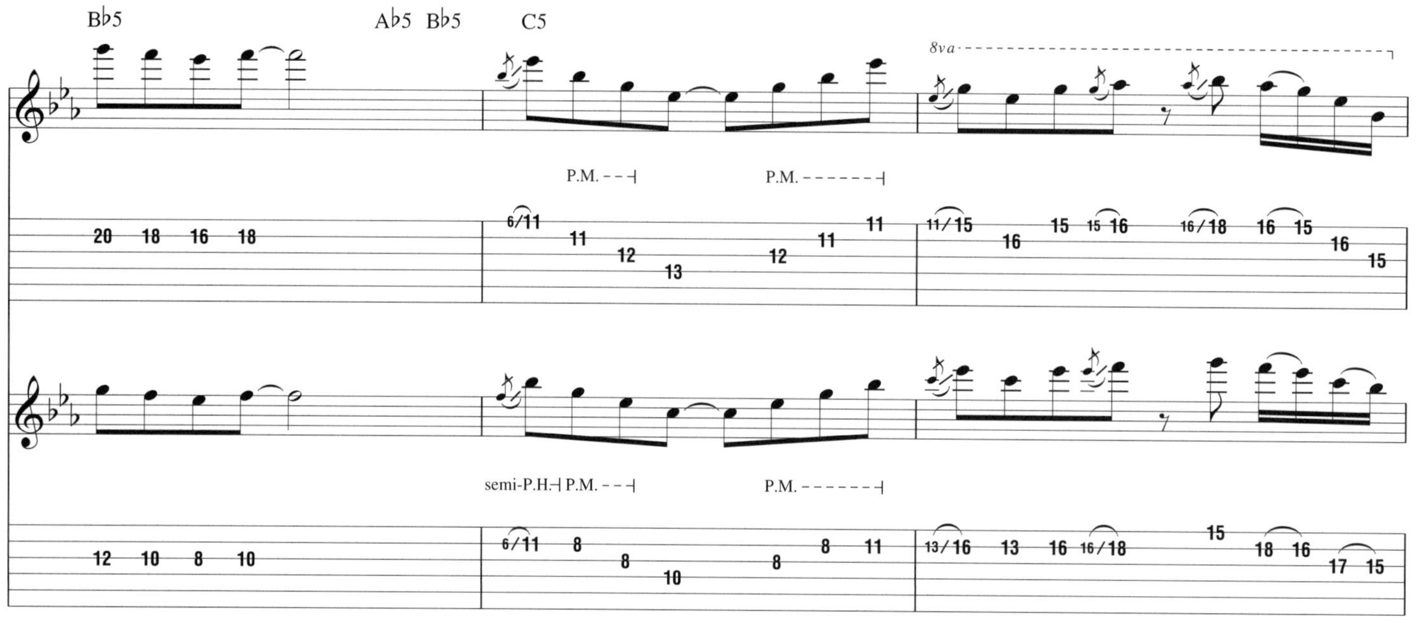
B♭5
A♭5 B♭5
C5
8va
P.M.
P.M.
semi-P.H.
P.M.
P.M.

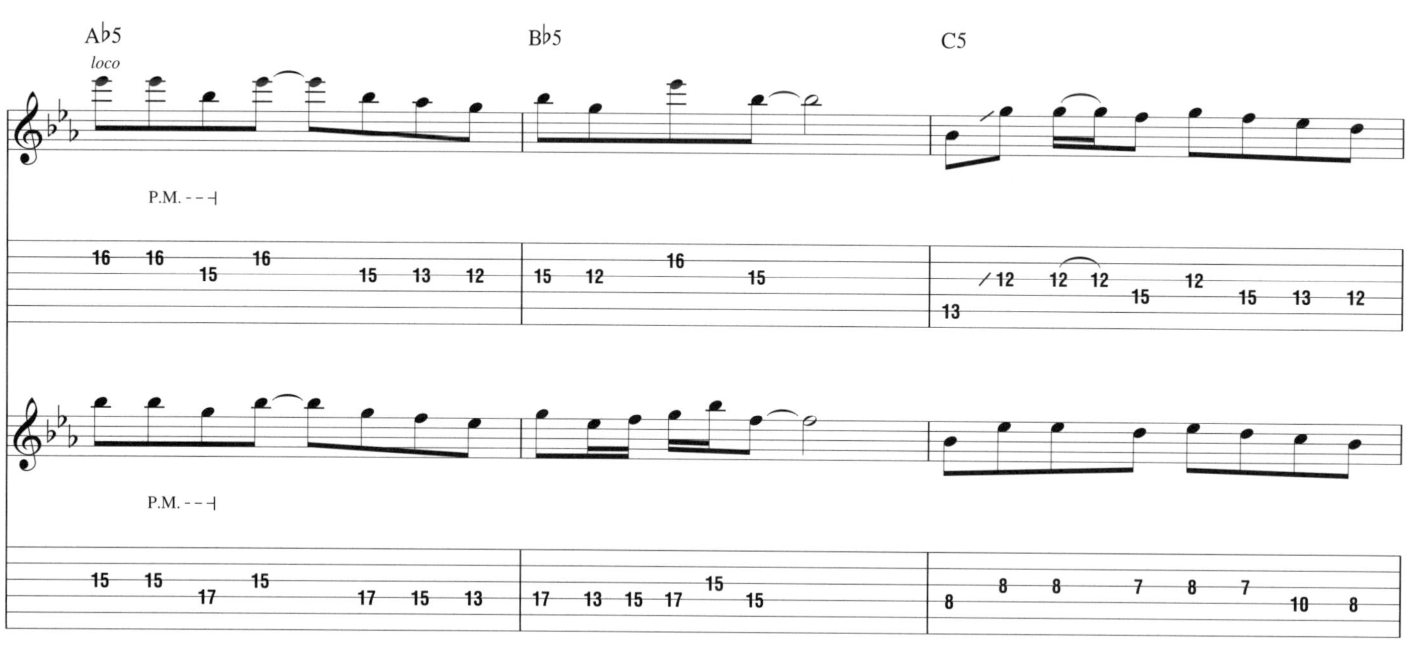
A♭5
loco
B♭5
C5
P.M.
P.M.

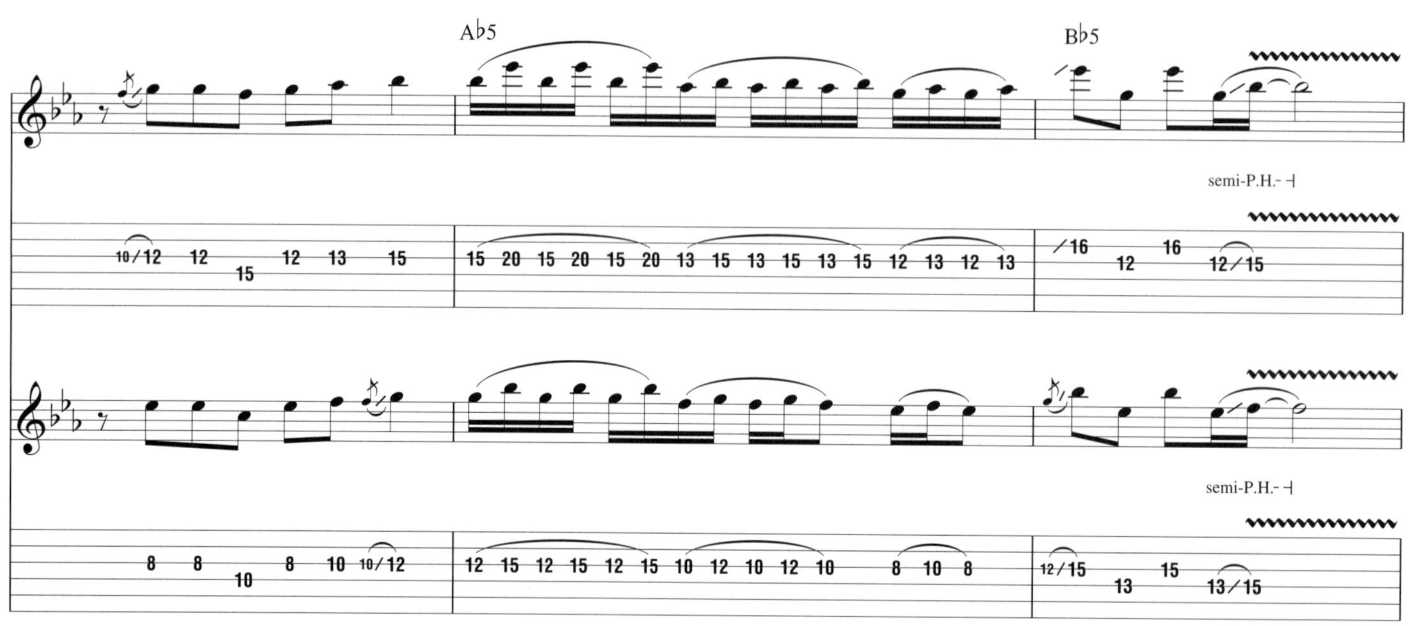
A♭5
B♭5
semi-P.H.
semi-P.H.

Gtrs. 1 & 2: w/ Rhy. Fig. 8
C5
Ab5
8va

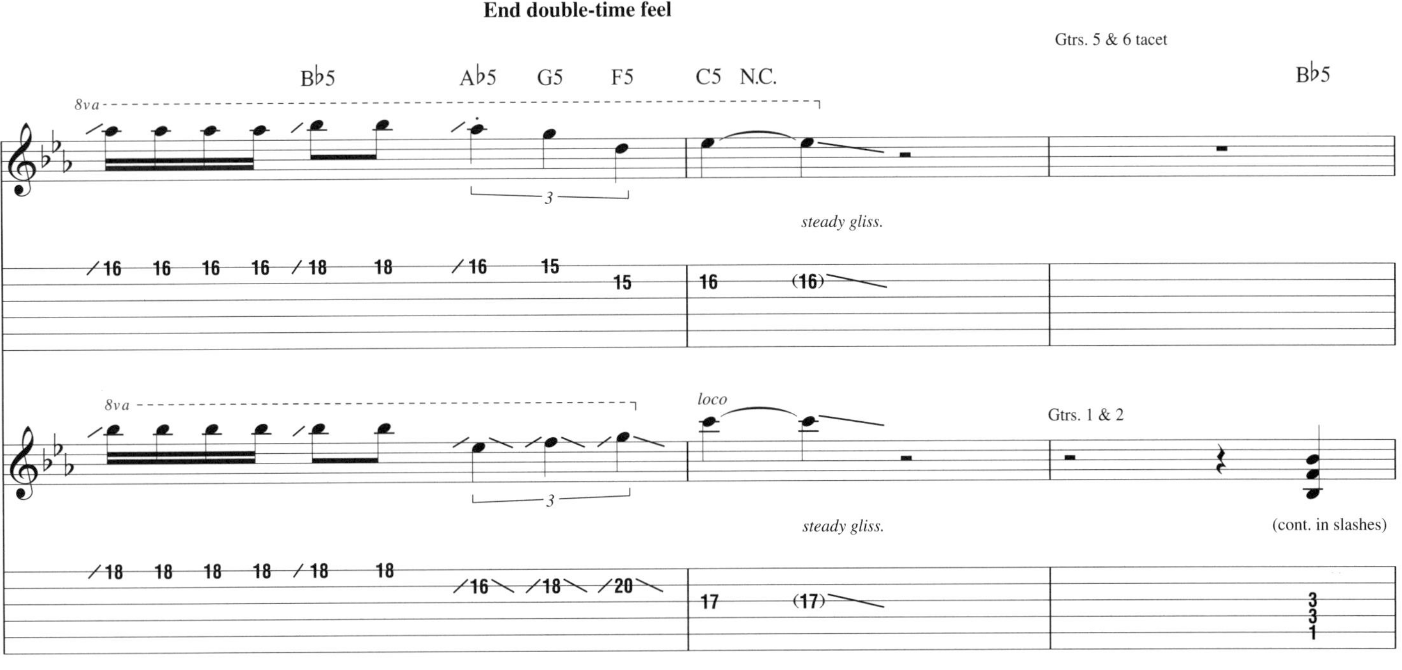
End double-time feel
Gtrs. 5 & 6 tacet
Bb5
Ab5
G5
F5
C5
N.C.
Bb5
8va
steady gliss.
loco
Gtrs. 1 & 2
(cont. in slashes)

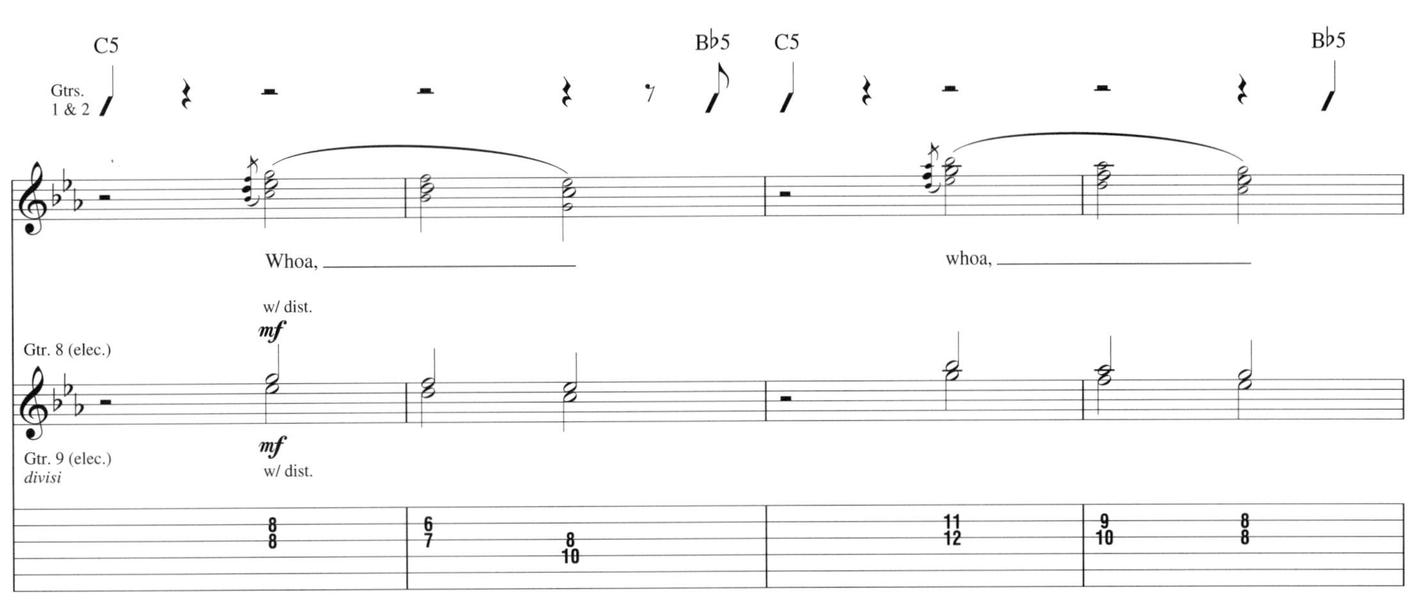
C5
Bb5
C5
Bb5
Gtrs. 1 & 2
Whoa,
whoa,
w/ dist.
mf
Gtr. 8 (elec.)
Gtr. 9 (elec.)
divisi

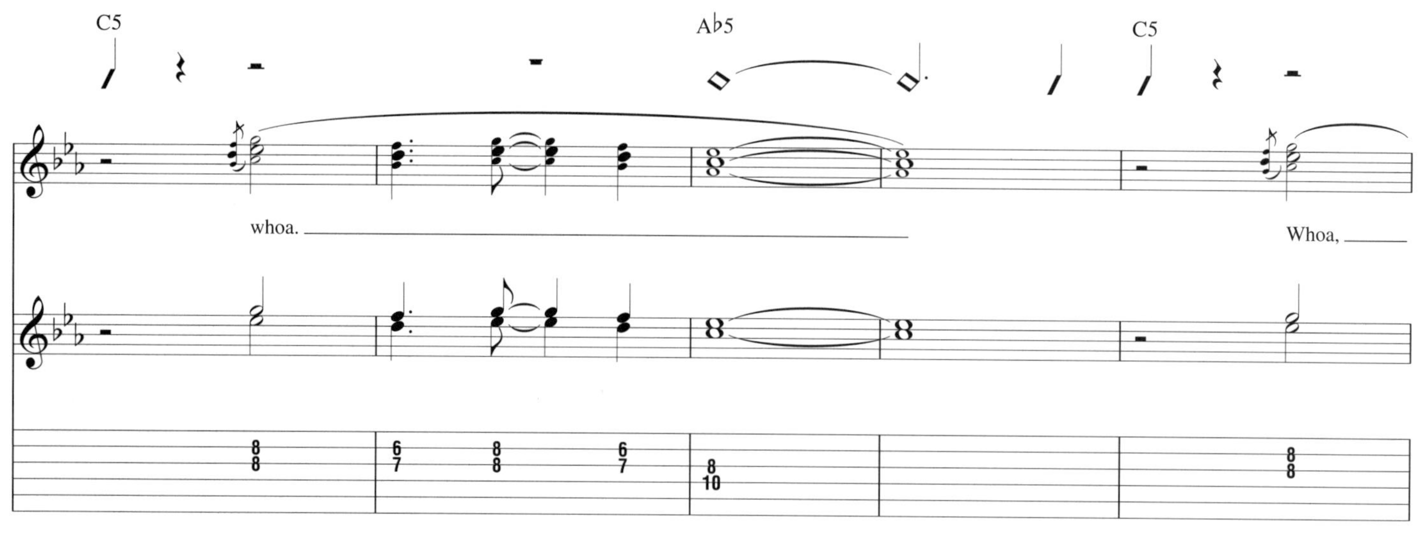

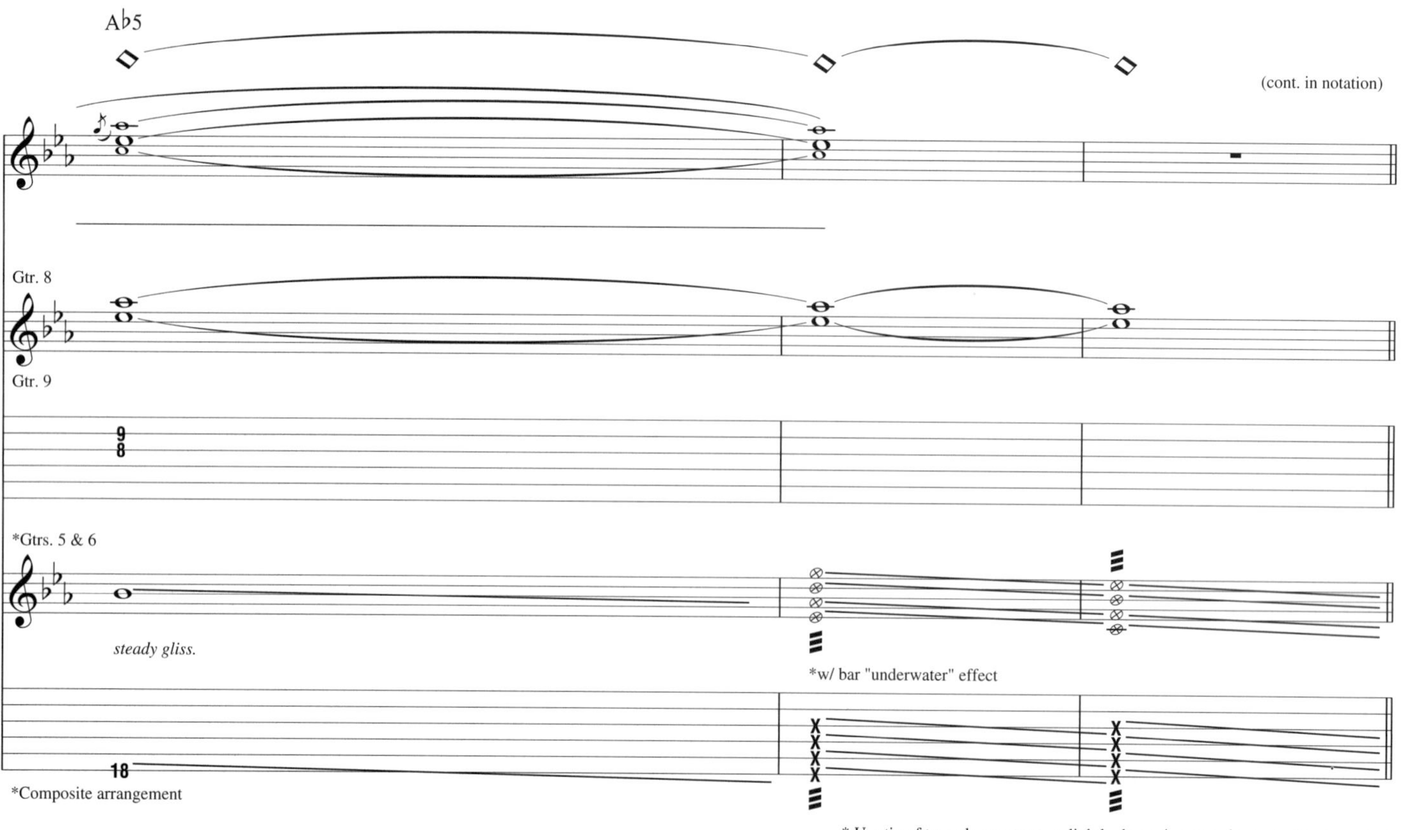

*Composite arrangement

* Use tip of tremolo arm to stum lightly, bouncing on strings, moving down neck

Guitar Solo
Slower, double-time feel ♩ = 170
Gtrs. 8 & 9 tacet
C5
Riff E
End Riff E
Gtr. 5
P.M.
Riff E1
End Riff E1
Gtr. 6
Rhy. Fig. 9
Gtrs. 1 & 2
Gtrs. 5 & 6: w/ Riffs E & E1
G5
A♭5
B♭5
End Rhy. Fig. 9
C5
Gtr. 7 tacet
Gtr. 7
Rhy. Fig. 10

Bb5
C5
Ab5
Bb5
C5
semi-P.H.
P.M.
8va
15ma
P.H.
P.M.
Gtrs. 5 & 6 tacet
G5
Gtr. 7
Ab5
Bb5
P.M.
w/ bar
Gtrs. 1 & 2
End Rhy. Fig. 10
P.M.
P.M.
P.M.
Gtrs. 1 & 2: w/ Rhy. Fig. 9
Gtrs. 5 & 6: w/ Riffs E & E1 (2 times)
C5
Gtr. 7
P.M.
G5
Ab5
Bb5
P.M.

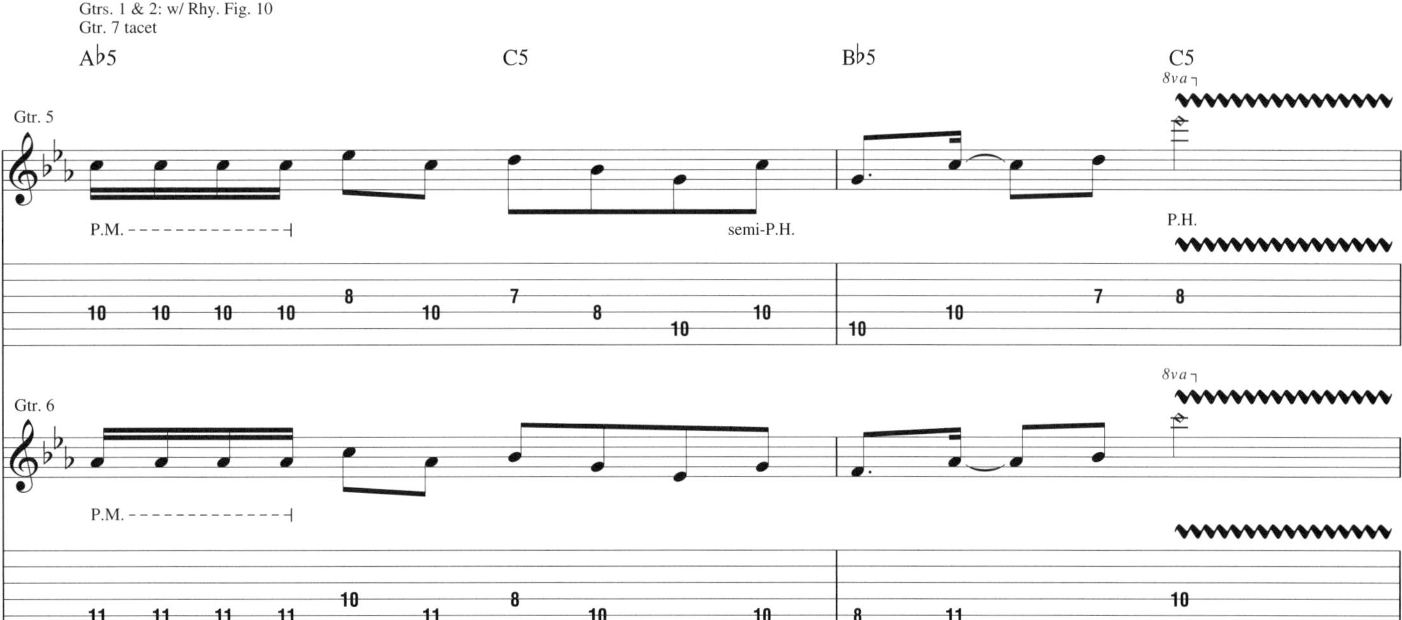
Gtrs. 1 & 2: w/ Rhy. Fig. 10
Gtr. 7 tacet
A♭5
C5
B♭5
C5
8va
Gtr. 5
P.M.
semi-P.H.
P.H.
Gtr. 6
P.M.

Gtrs. 5 & 6 tacet
A♭5
B♭5
15ma
Gtr. 7
P.H.

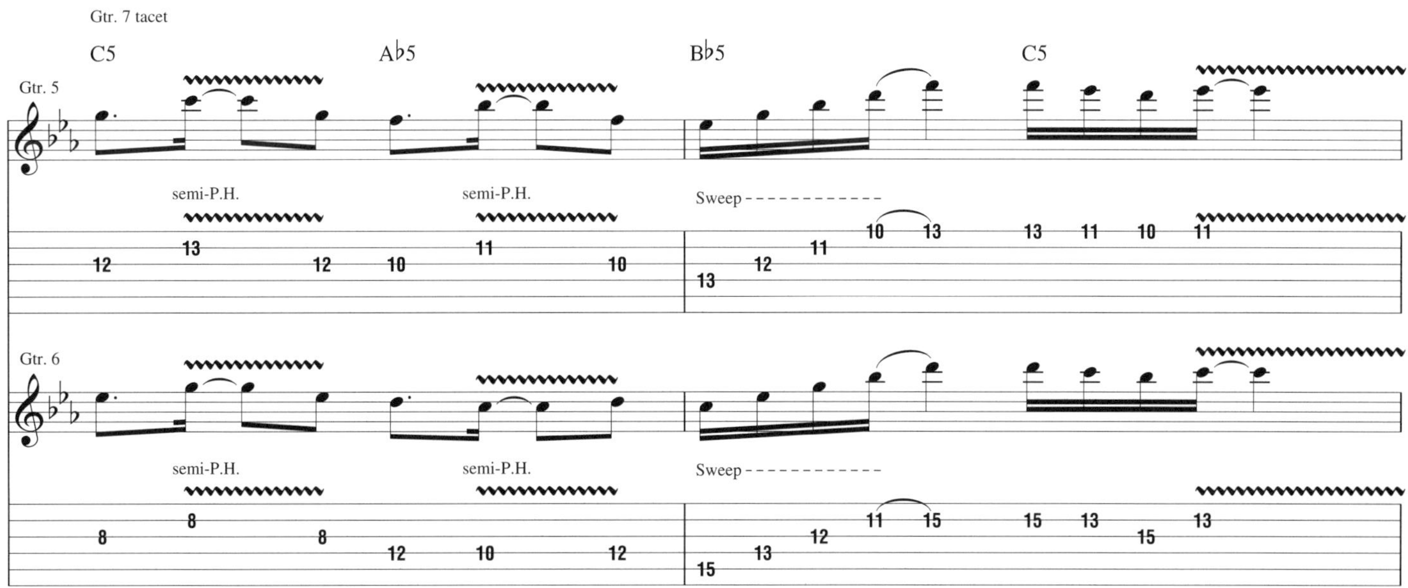
Gtr. 7 tacet
C5
A♭5
B♭5
C5
Gtr. 5
semi-P.H.
semi-P.H.
Sweep
Gtr. 6
semi-P.H.
semi-P.H.
Sweep

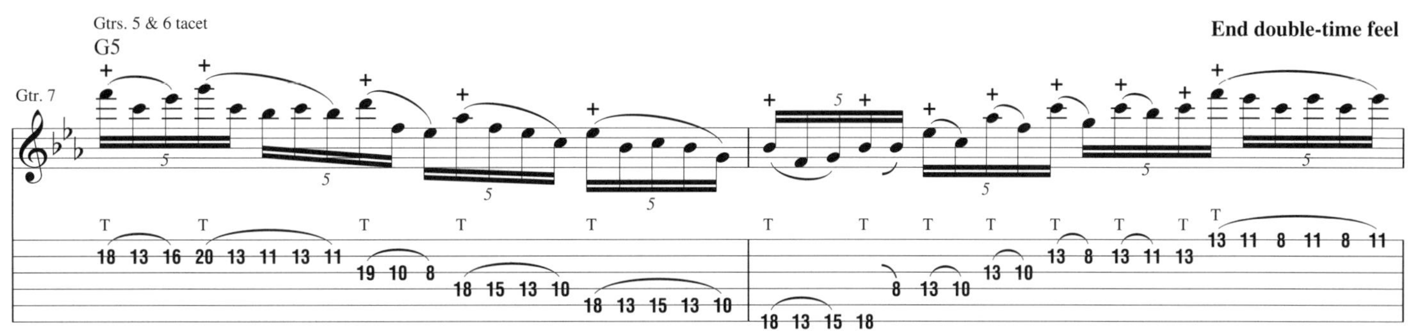
Gtrs. 5 & 6 tacet
G5
End double-time feel
Gtr. 7

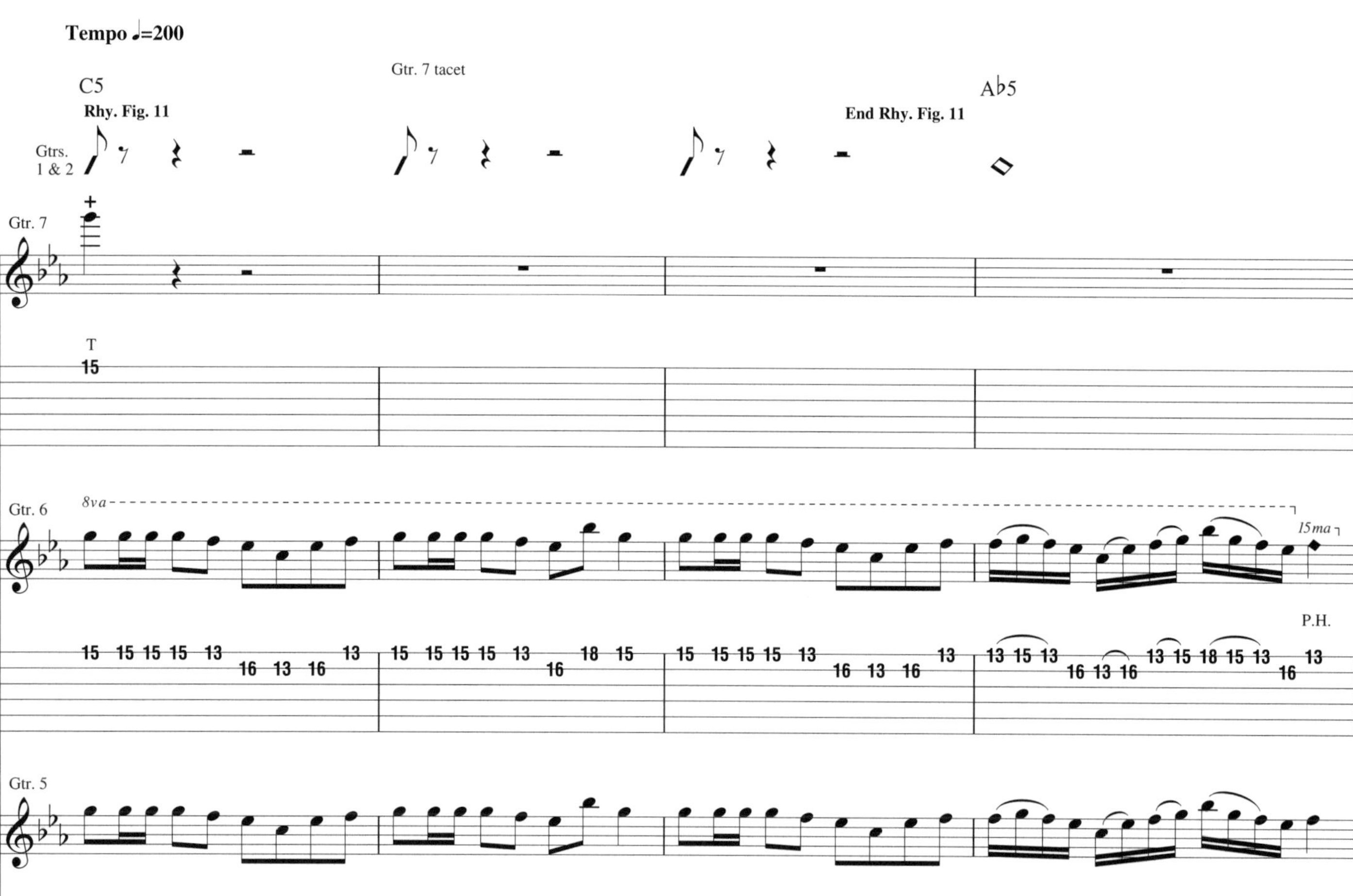
Tempo ♩=200
C5
Rhy. Fig. 11
Gtrs. 1 & 2
Gtr. 7 tacet
End Rhy. Fig. 11
A♭5
Gtr. 7
Gtr. 6
8va
15ma
P.H.
Gtr. 5

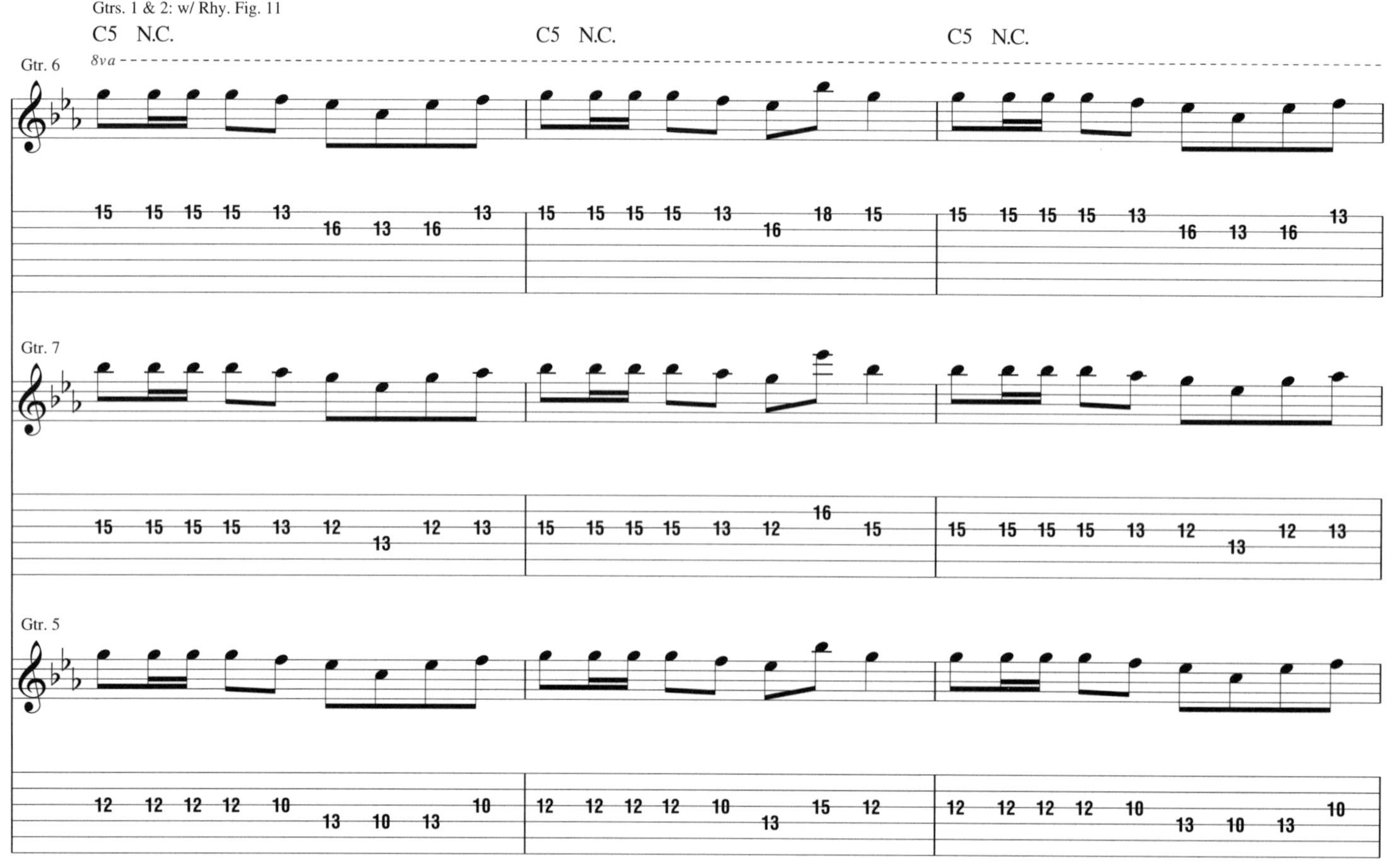
Gtrs. 1 & 2: w/ Rhy. Fig. 11
C5 N.C.
C5 N.C.
C5 N.C.
Gtr. 6
8va
Gtr. 7
Gtr. 5

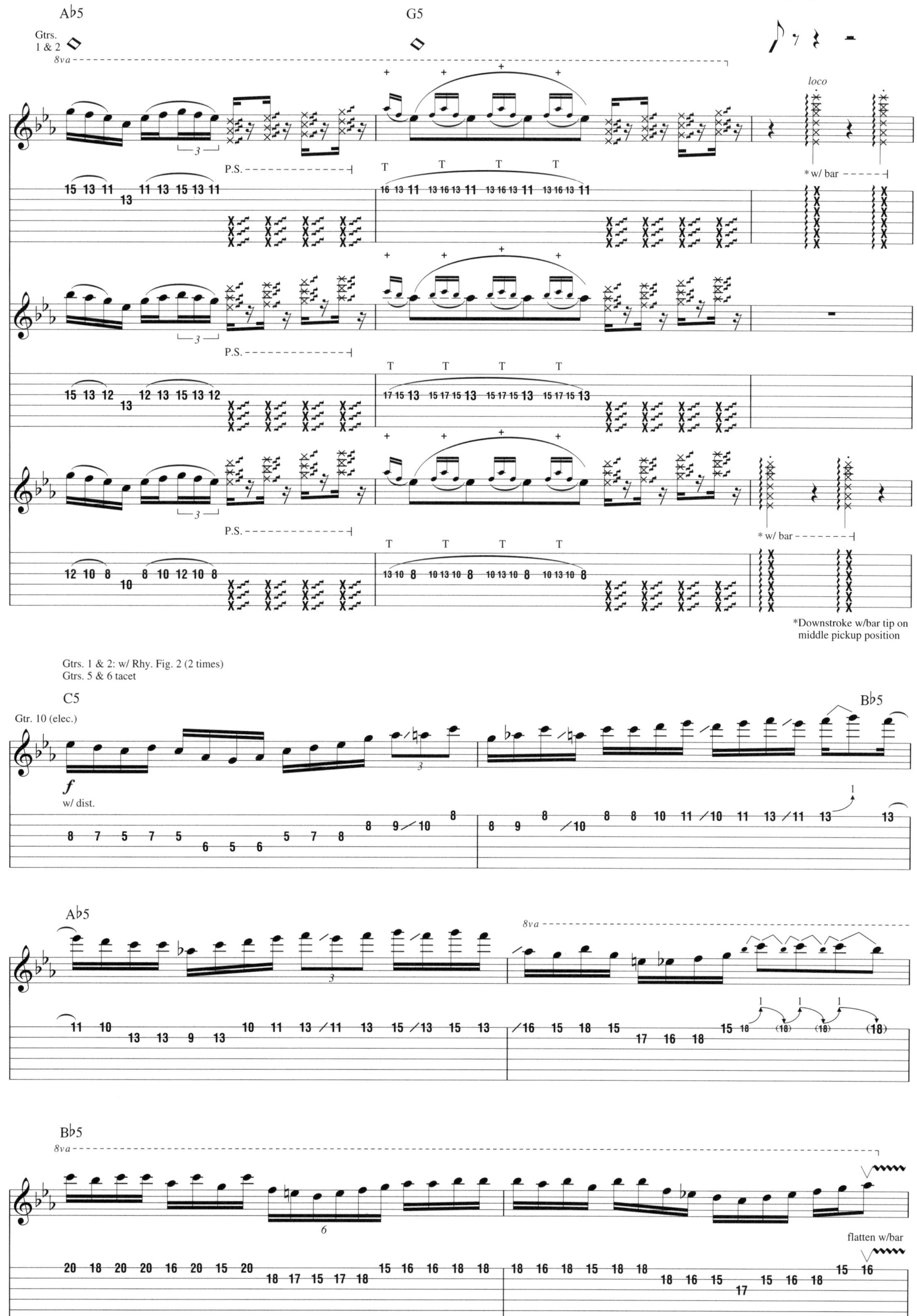

Ab5
G5
Gtr. 7 tacet
Gtrs. 1 & 2
8va
loco
P.S.
* w/ bar
*Downstroke w/bar tip on middle pickup position
Gtrs. 1 & 2: w/ Rhy. Fig. 2 (2 times)
Gtrs. 5 & 6 tacet
C5
Gtr. 10 (elec.)
w/ dist.
Bb5
Ab5
Bb5
flatten w/bar

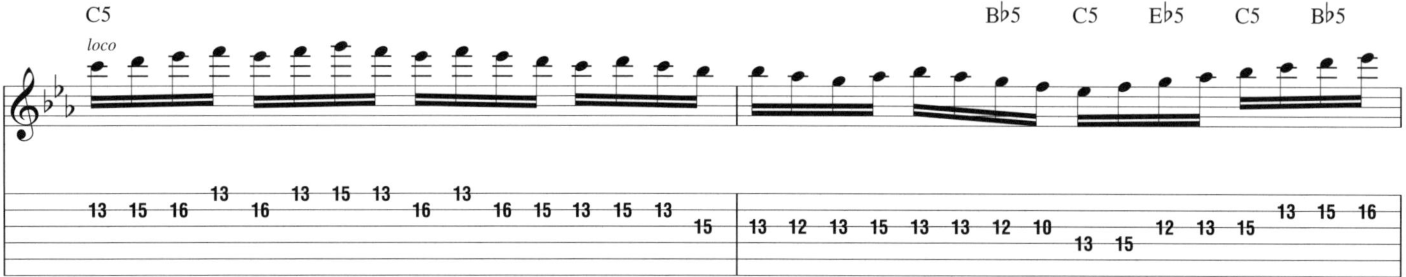

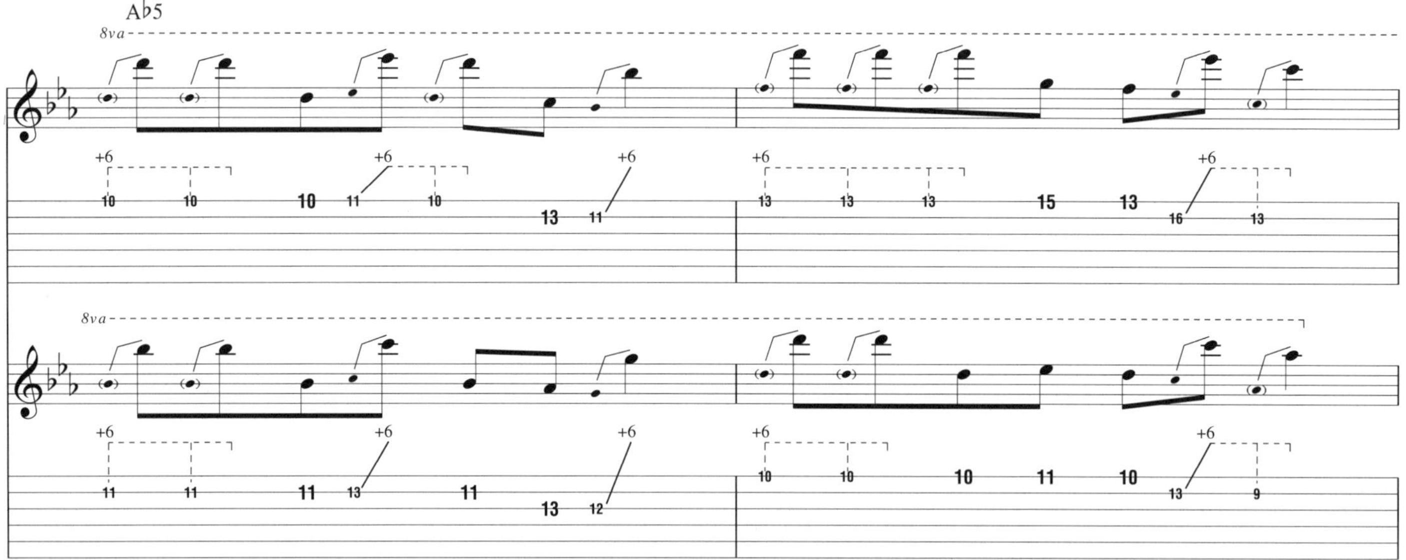

Gtr. 11 tacet

B♭5

8va

Gtr. 10

15ma

C5
Gtr. 10
15ma
loco
Gtr. 11
8va
Gtr. 11 tacet
F5
C5
N.C.
B♭5
Gtr. 5
P.M.
Gtr. 6
Gtrs. 1 & 2

Gtr. 10 tacet

C5 N.C. A♭5

8va

Gtr. 6

Gtr. 5

8va

Gtrs. 1 & 2

P.M. P.M. P.M.

B♭5 N.C. B♭5 A♭5 B♭5

8va

8va

loco

Harm.
w/ bar

P.H.
w/ bar

-3 1/2

8va

15ma

loco

Harm.
w/ bar

P.H.
w/ bar

-3 1/2

P.M.

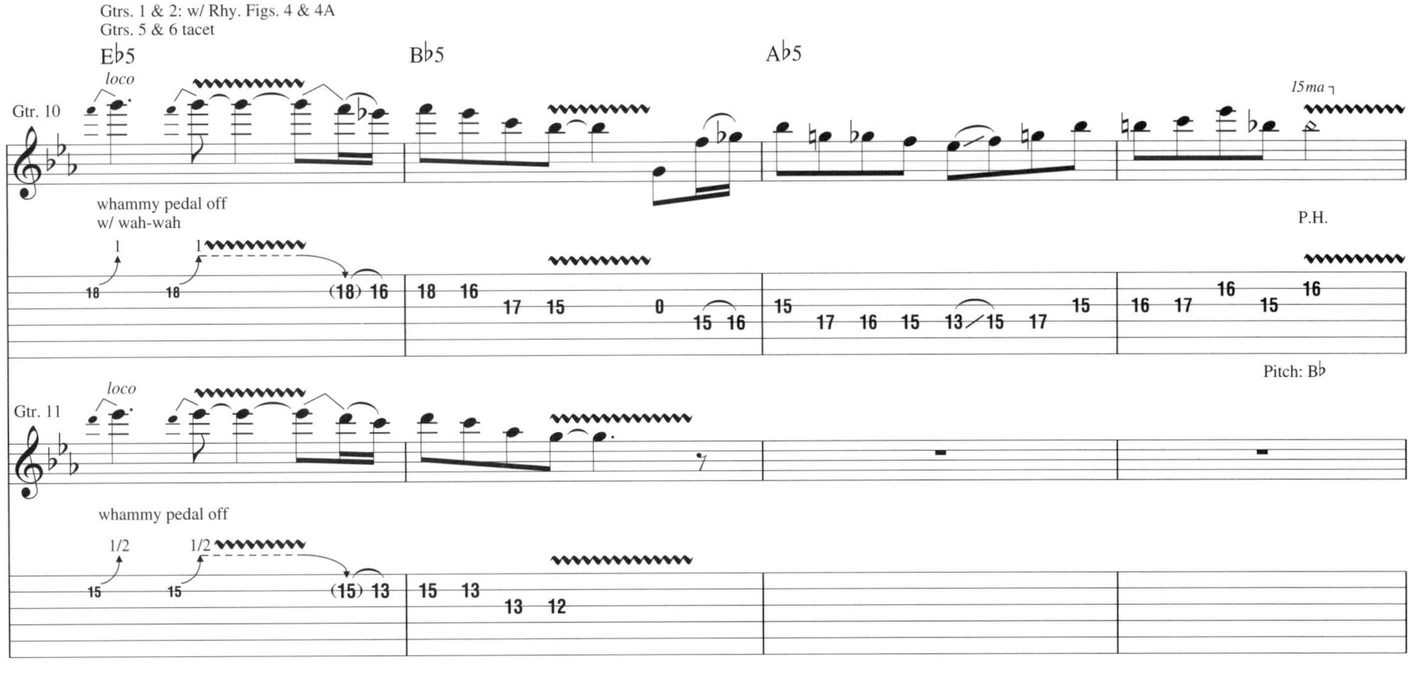
Gtrs. 1 & 2: w/ Rhy. Figs. 4 & 4A
Gtrs. 5 & 6 tacet
E♭5
B♭5
A♭5
loco
15ma
Gtr. 10
whammy pedal off
w/ wah-wah
P.H.
Pitch: B♭
Gtr. 11
whammy pedal off

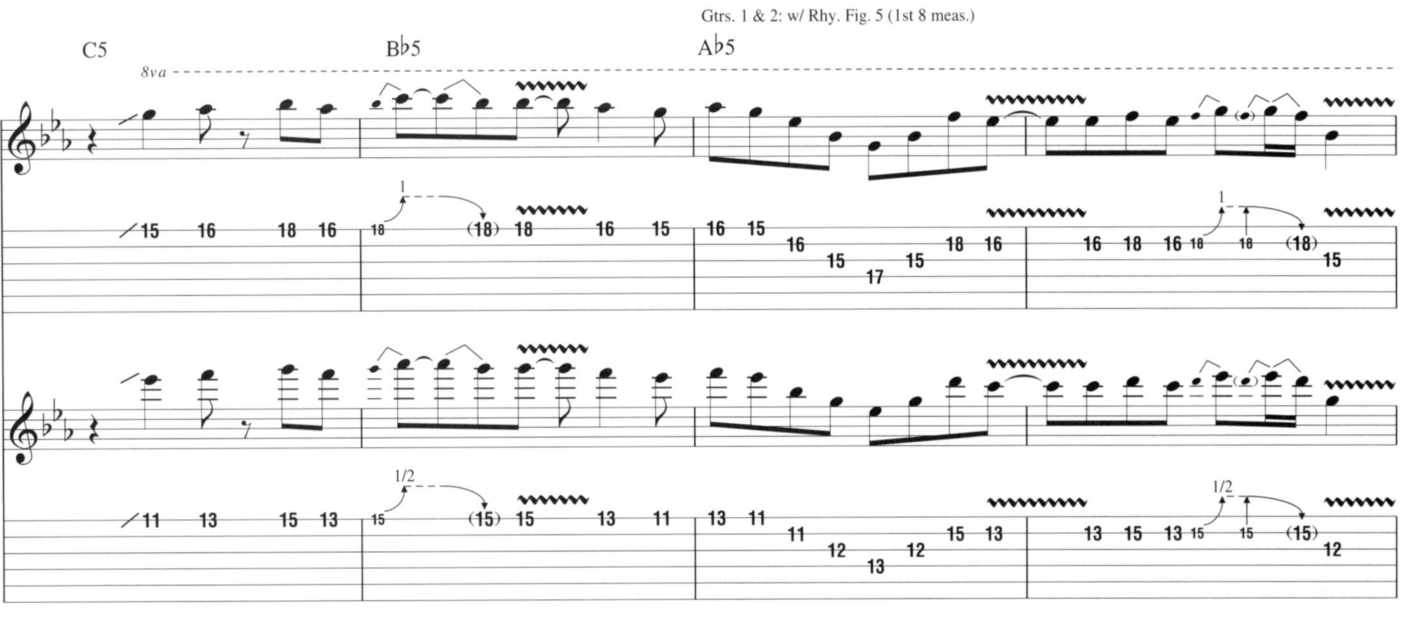
Gtrs. 1 & 2: w/ Rhy. Fig. 5 (1st 8 meas.)
C5
B♭5
A♭5
8va

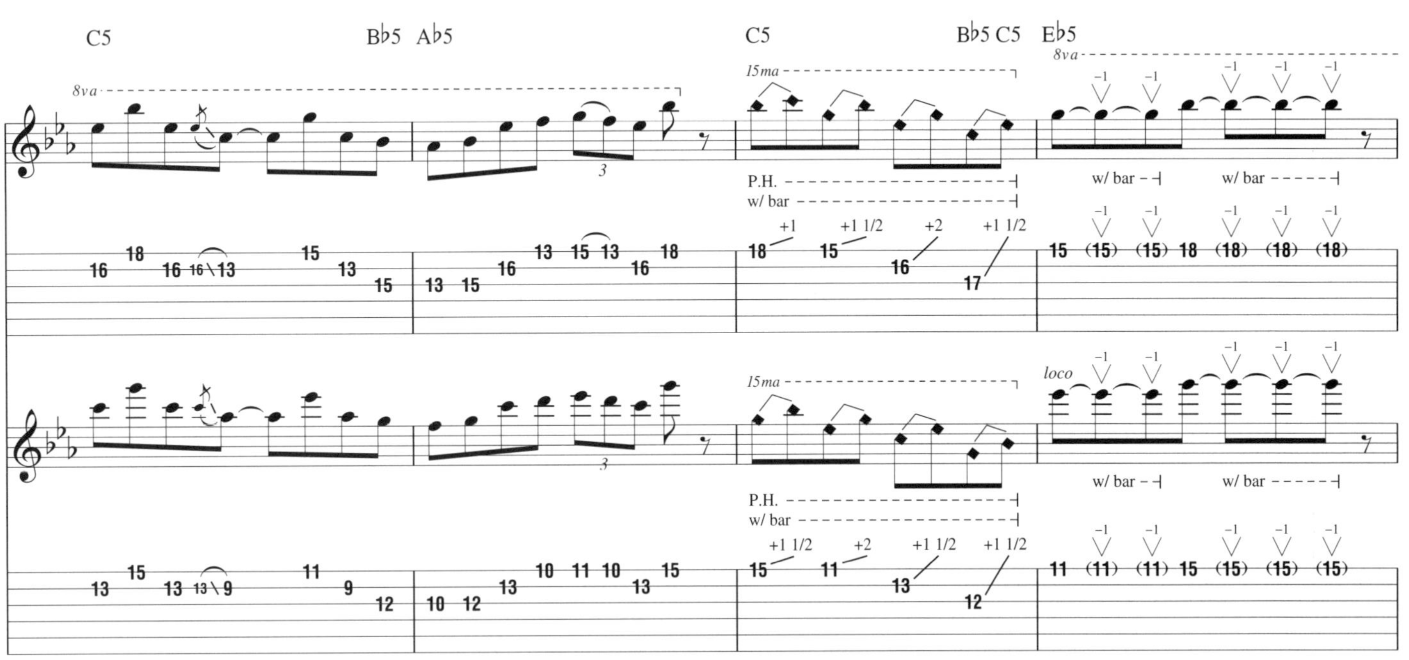
C5
B♭5 A♭5
C5
B♭5 C5
E♭5
8va
15ma
P.H.
w/ bar
loco

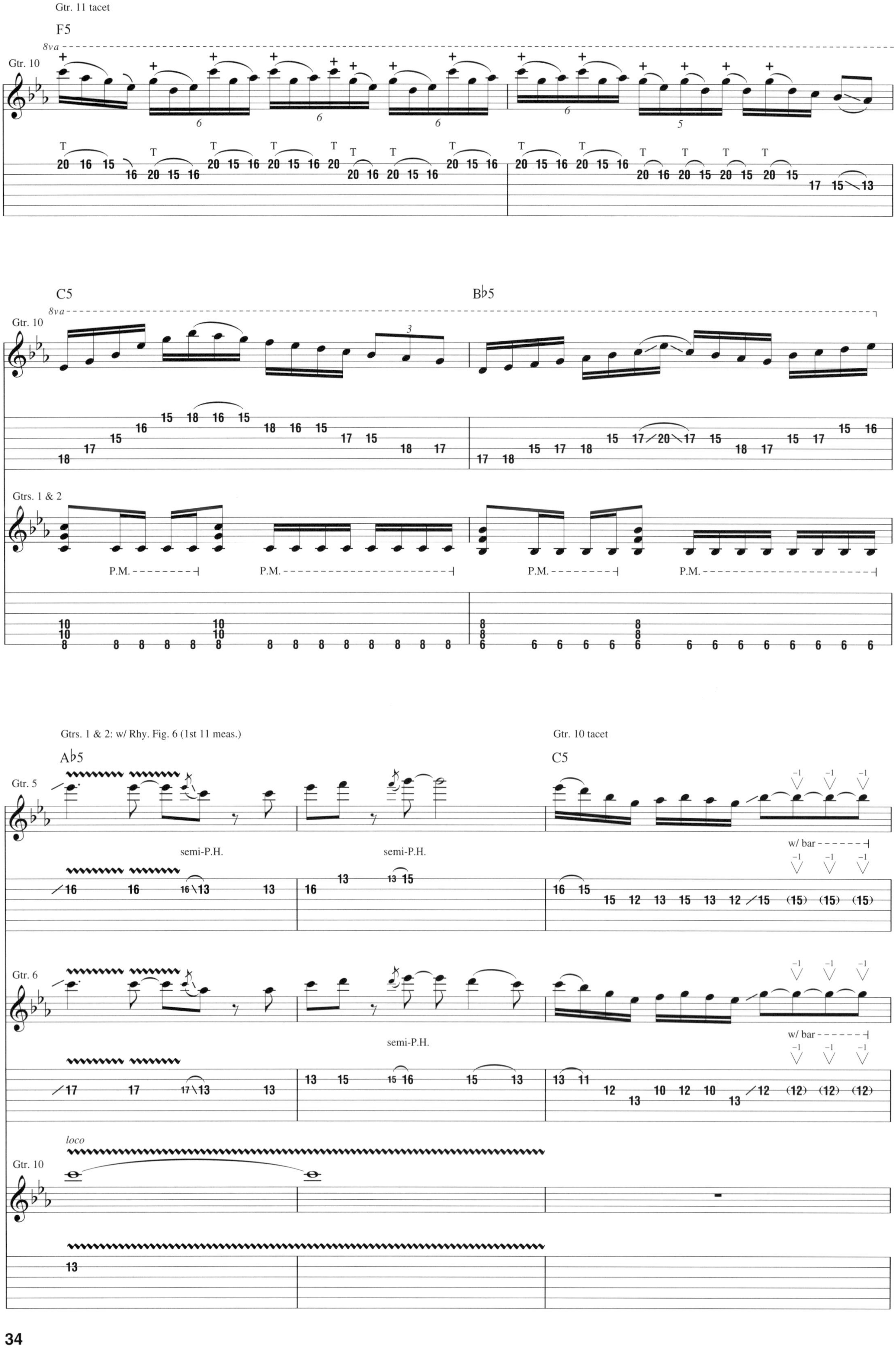

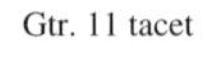

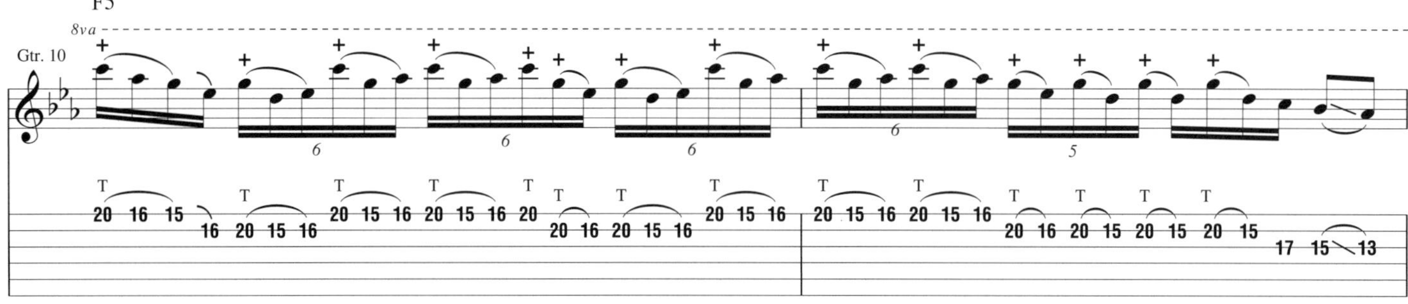

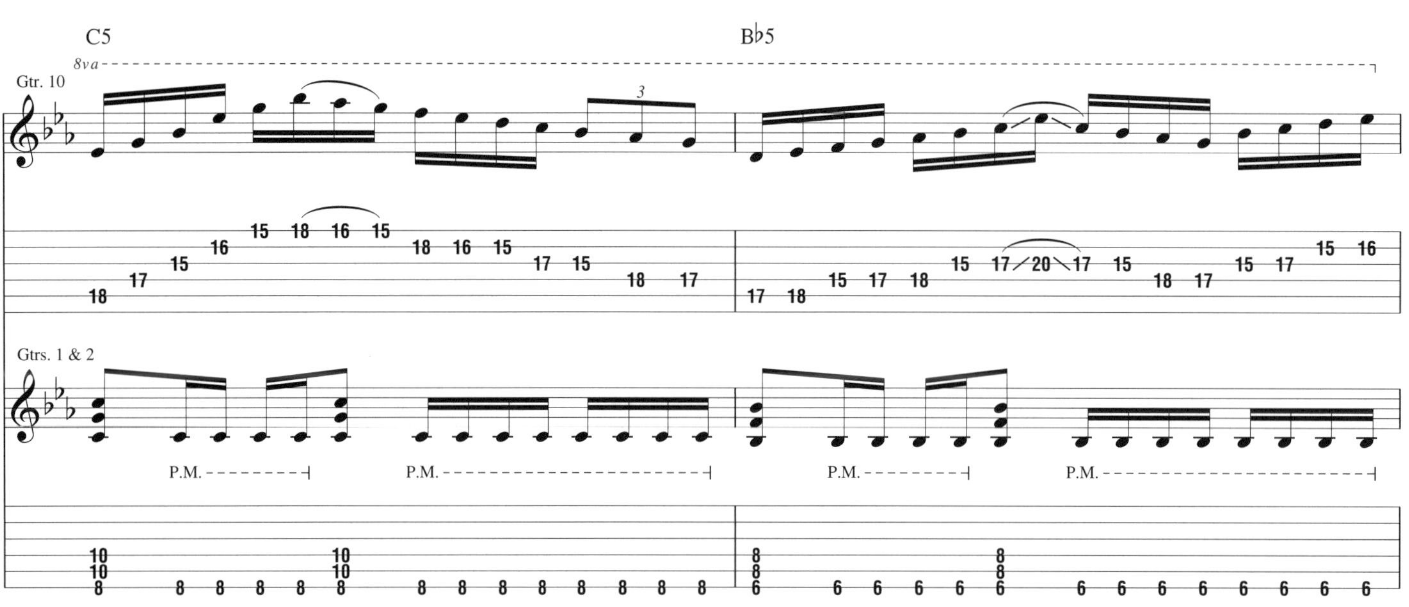

Gtrs. 1 & 2: w/ Rhy. Fig. 6 (1st 11 meas.)

Gtr. 10 tacet

A♭5

C5

Gtr. 5

semi-P.H.

w/ bar

Gtr. 6

semi-P.H.

w/ bar

loco

Gtr. 10

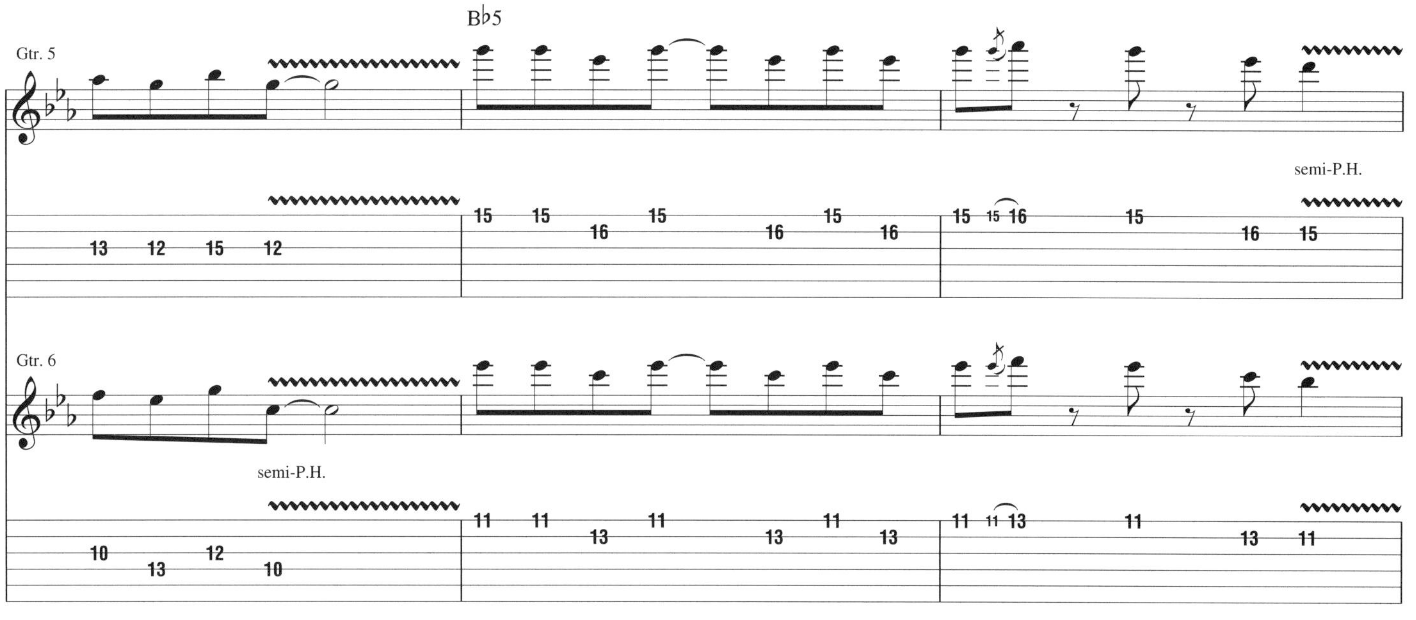
Gtr. 5
B♭5
semi-P.H.
Gtr. 6
semi-P.H.

G5
A♭5
P.M.
loco
P.M.

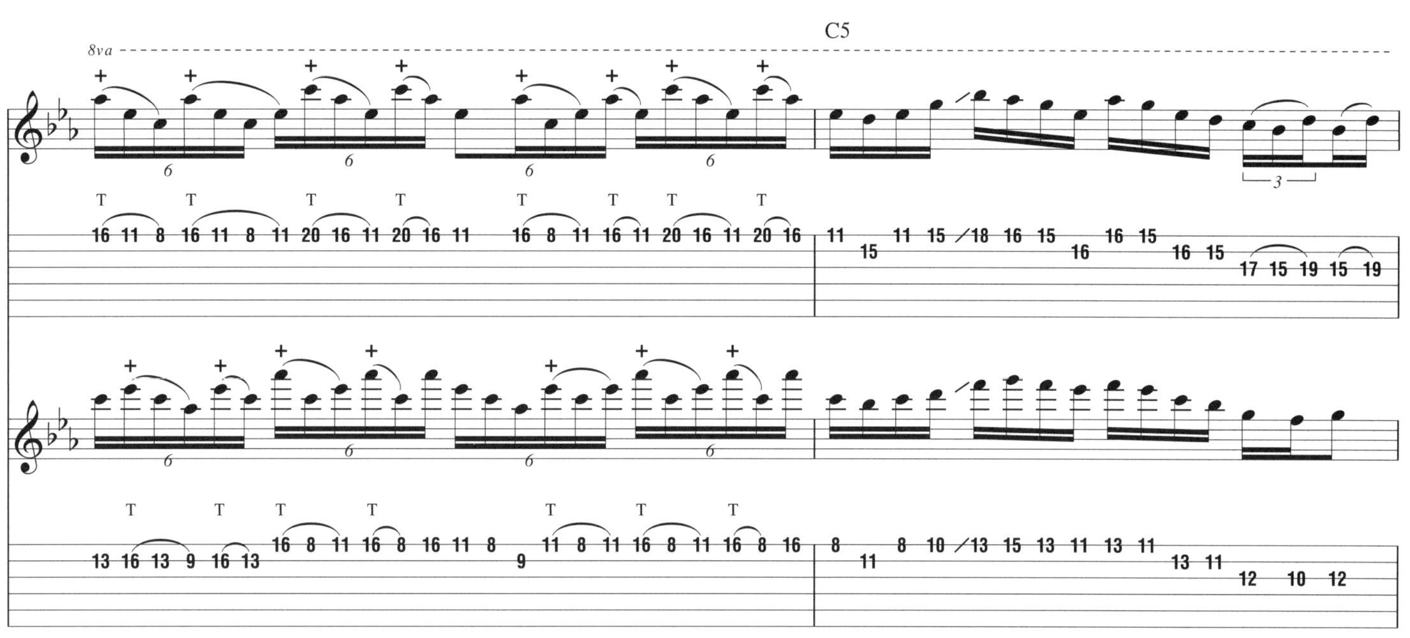
8va
C5

B♭5

8va

w/ bar

P.H.

loco

semi-P.H.

Gtrs. 1 & 2

P.M.

C5

End double-time feel

Now here we

Bridge
Gtrs. 5 & 6 tacet
C5
A♭5
B♭5
are with their blood on our hands. We fought so hard, now can
(Ah, blood on our hands. Ah,
Gtrs. 1 & 2
E♭5
C5
we un - der - stand? I'll break the seal of this curse if I
we un - der - stand. Ah.)
A♭5
B♭5
pos - si - bly can, for free - dom of ev - er - y
(cont. in slashes)

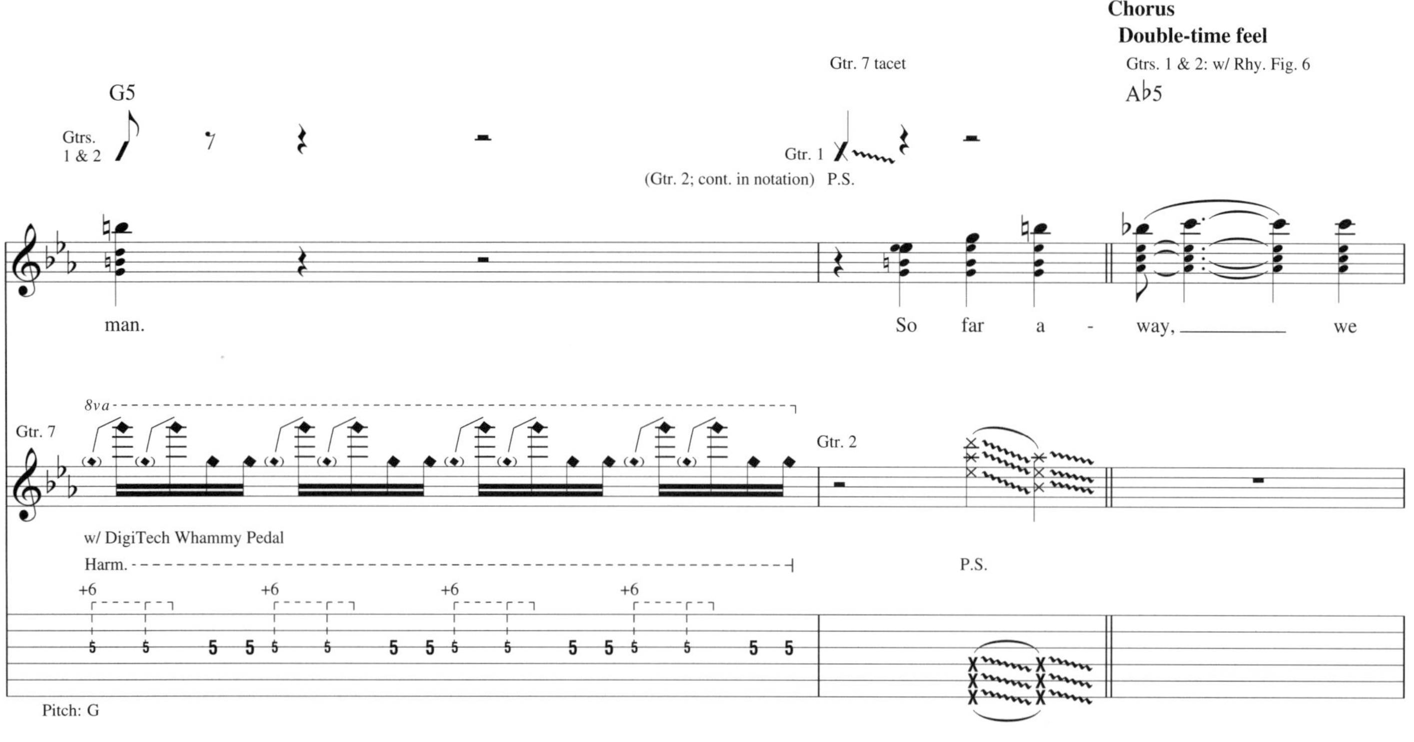
Chorus
Double-time feel
Gtr. 7 tacet
Gtrs. 1 & 2: w/ Rhy. Fig. 6
G5
A♭5
Gtrs. 1 & 2
Gtr. 1
(Gtr. 2; cont. in notation) P.S.
man.
So far a - way, we
Gtr. 7
8va
Gtr. 2
w/ DigiTech Whammy Pedal
Harm.
P.S.
Pitch: G

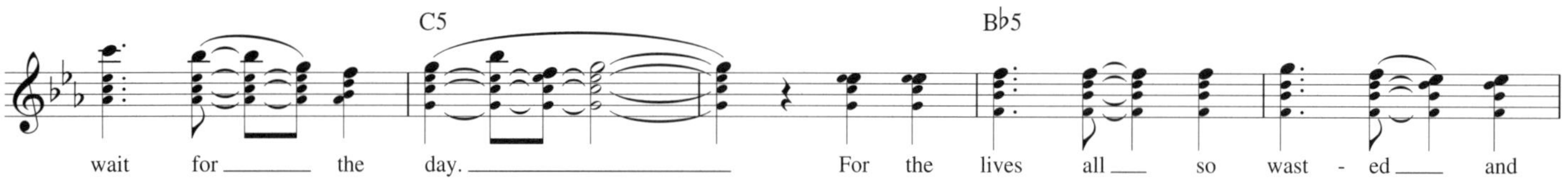
C5
B♭5
wait for the day.
For the lives all so wast - ed and

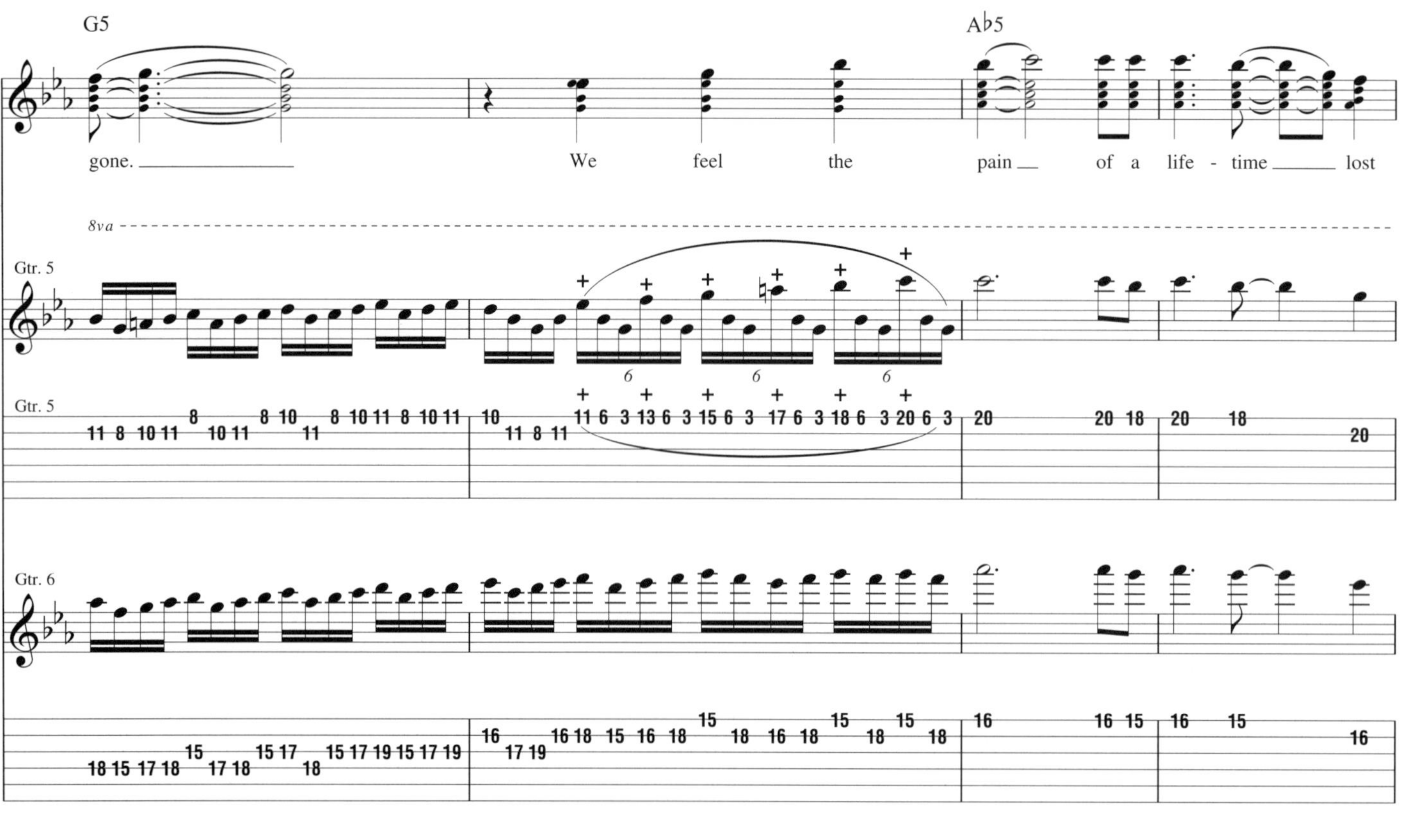
G5
A♭5
gone.
We feel the pain of a life - time lost
8va
Gtr. 5
Gtr. 6

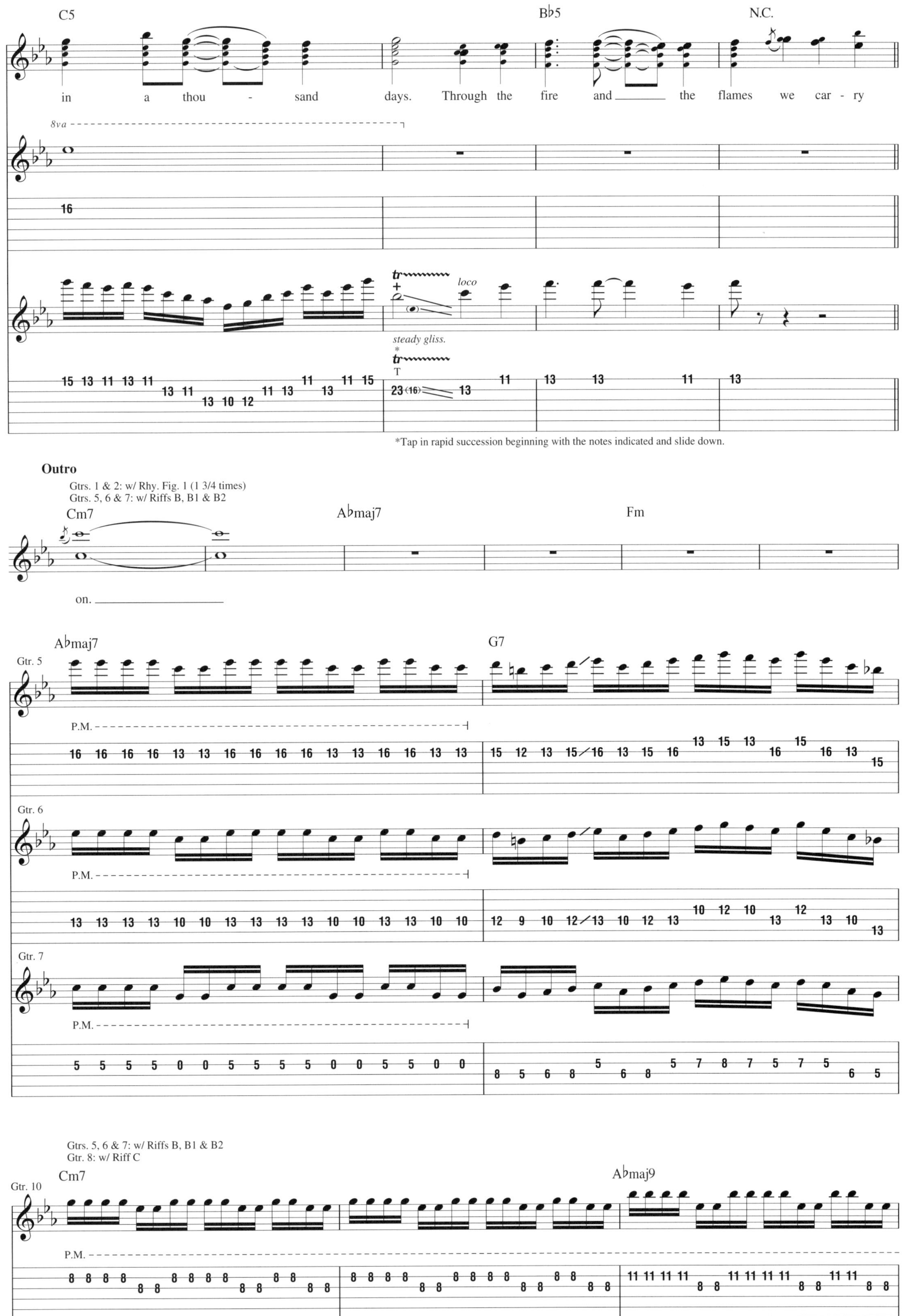

C5
Bb5
N.C.
in a thou - sand days. Through the fire and the flames we car - ry
8va
steady gliss.
loco
*Tap in rapid succession beginning with the notes indicated and slide down.
Outro
Gtrs. 1 & 2: w/ Rhy. Fig. 1 (1 3/4 times)
Gtrs. 5, 6 & 7: w/ Riffs B, B1 & B2
Cm7
Abmaj7
Fm
on.
Abmaj7
G7
Gtr. 5
Gtr. 6
Gtr. 7
P.M.
Gtrs. 5, 6 & 7: w/ Riffs B, B1 & B2
Gtr. 8: w/ Riff C
Cm7
Abmaj9
Gtr. 10
P.M.

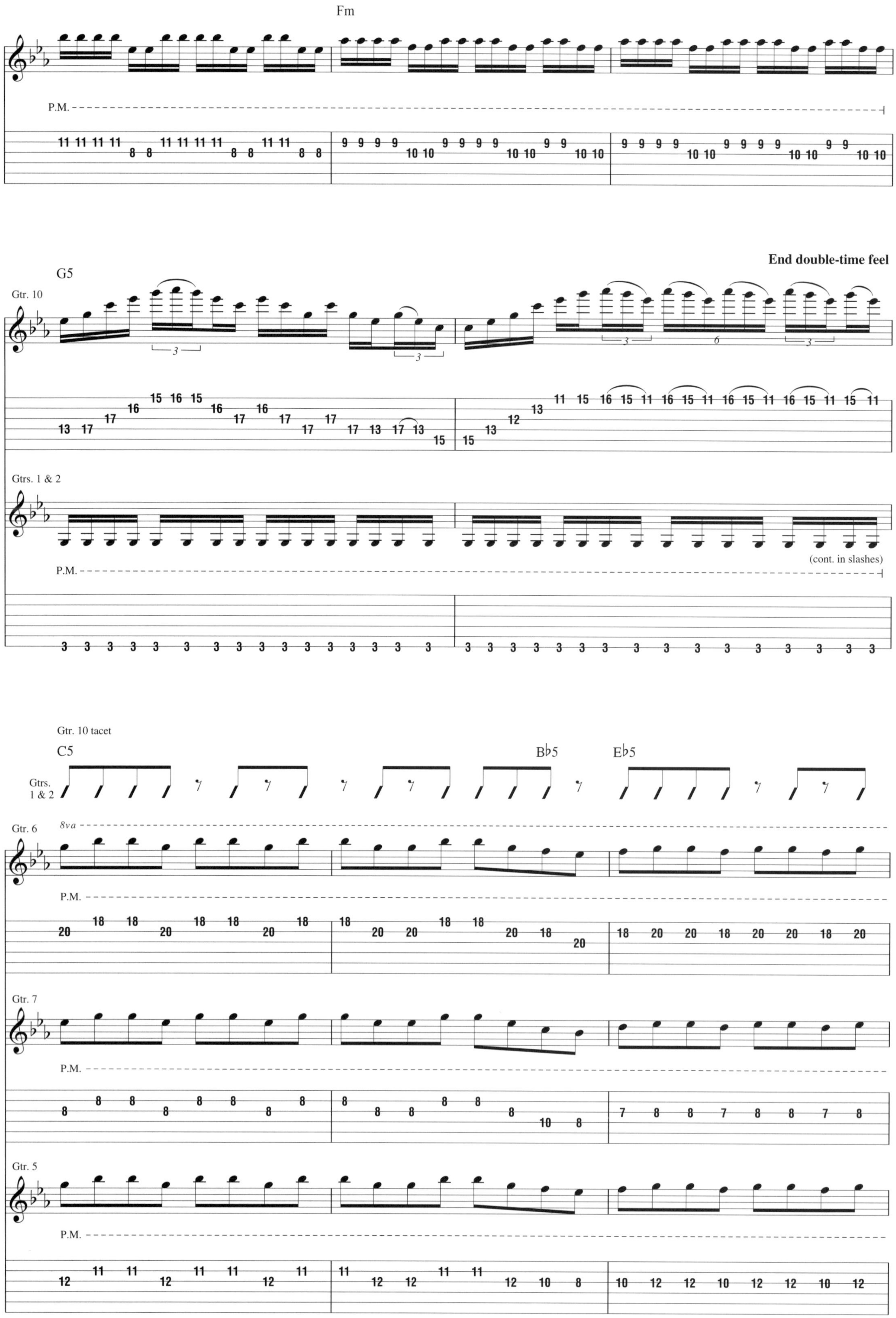

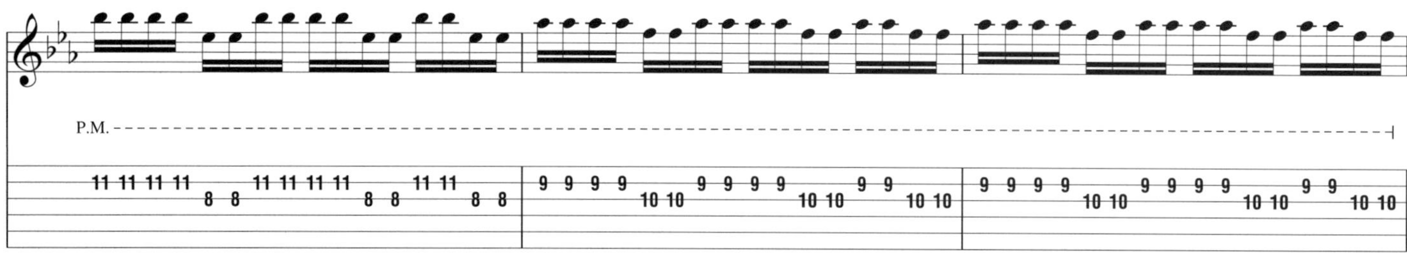

Gtr. 10 tacet

C5 B♭5 E♭5

Gtrs. 1 & 2

Gtr. 6

8va

P.M.

Gtr. 7

P.M.

Gtr. 5

P.M.

Gtr. 7 tacet

F5 E♭5 F5

P.M. P.S.

20 18 18 20 21 20 18 20

P.M.

8 7 7 8 10 8 7 10

P.M. P.S.

12 10 10 12 13 12 10 8

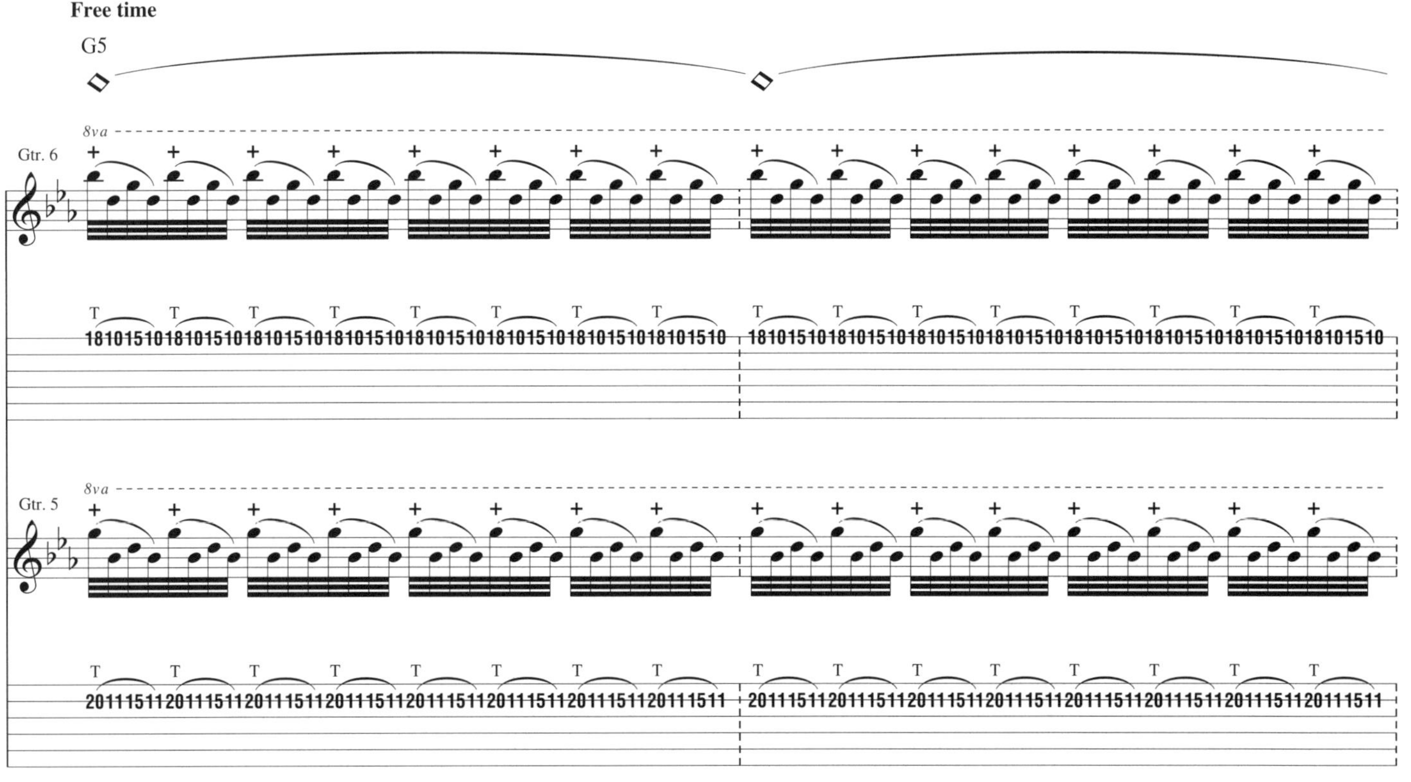

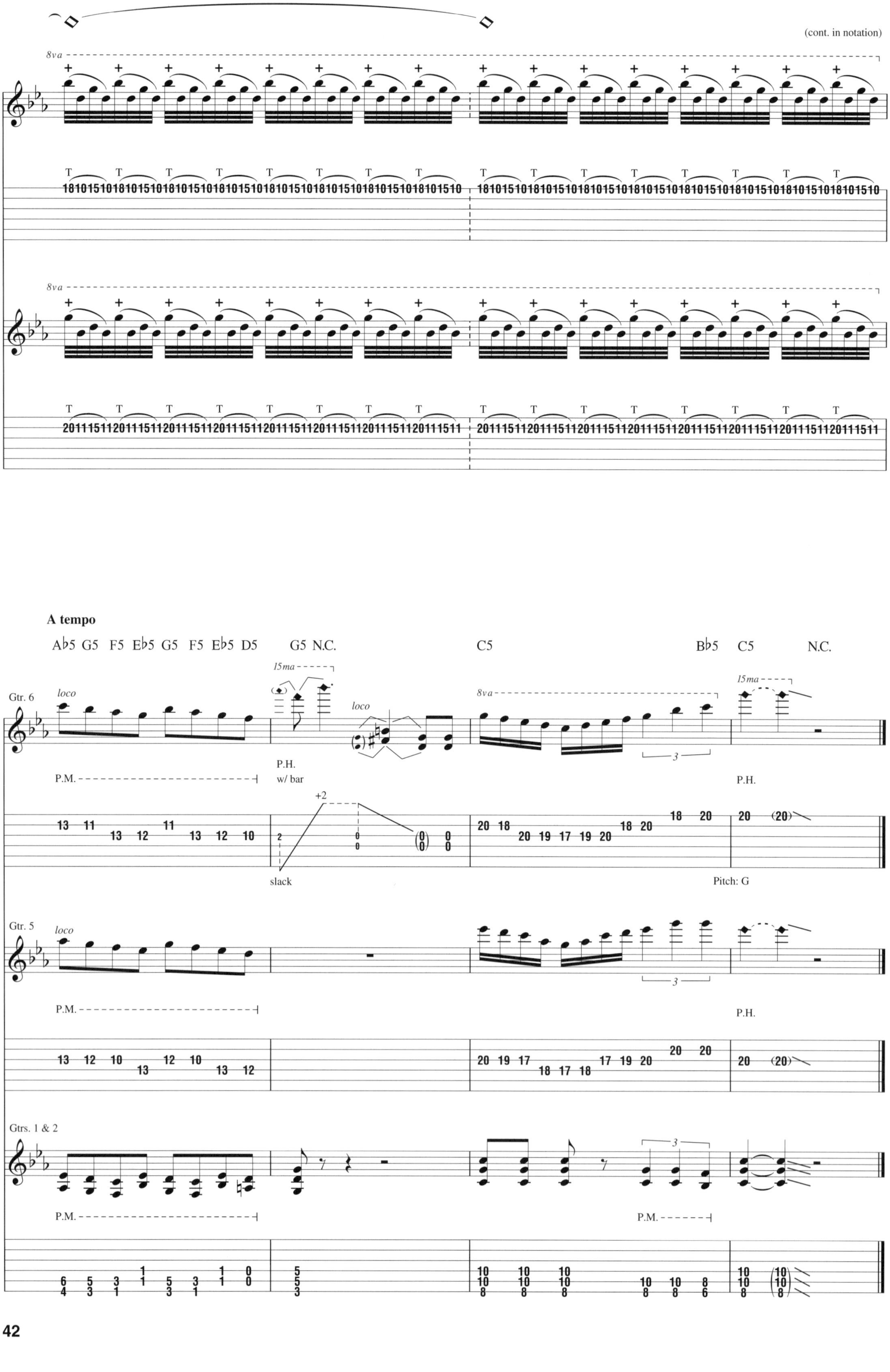

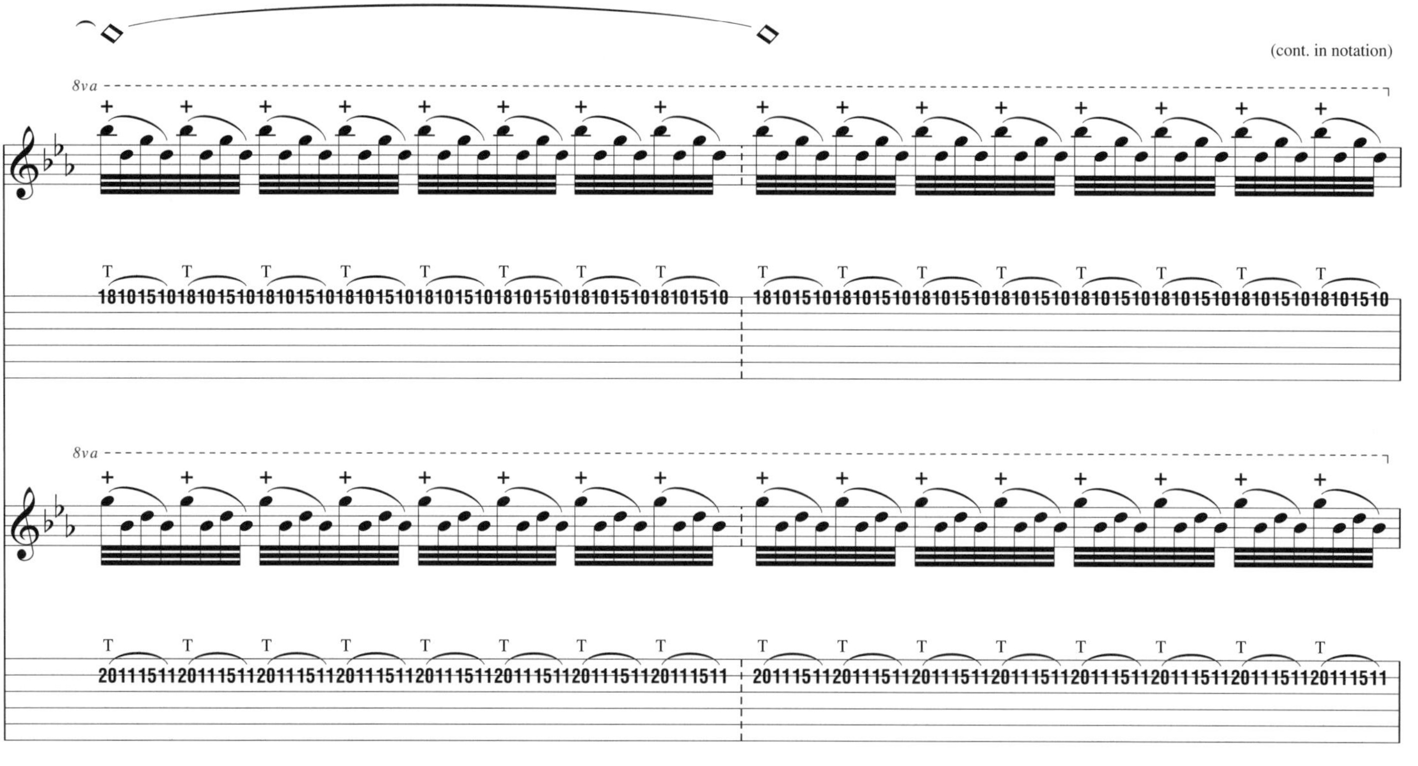

A tempo

A♭5 G5 F5 E♭5 G5 F5 E♭5 D5 G5 N.C. C5 B♭5 C5 N.C.

Gtr. 6

loco

15ma

loco

8va

15ma

P.M.

P.H.
w/ bar

+2

slack

P.H.

Pitch: G

Gtr. 5

loco

P.M.

P.H.

Gtrs. 1 & 2

P.M.

P.M.

Revolution Deathsquad

Words and Music by Herman Li, ZP Theart, Sam Totman and Vadim Pruzhanov

D5
5fr
134
B♭5
6fr
134
C5
134
F5
8fr
134
C5VIII
8fr
134
A5
11

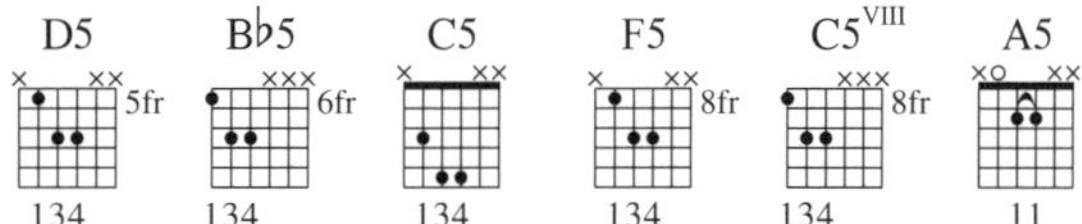

Gtr. 6: 7-string tuning:
(low to high) B-E-A-D-G-B-E

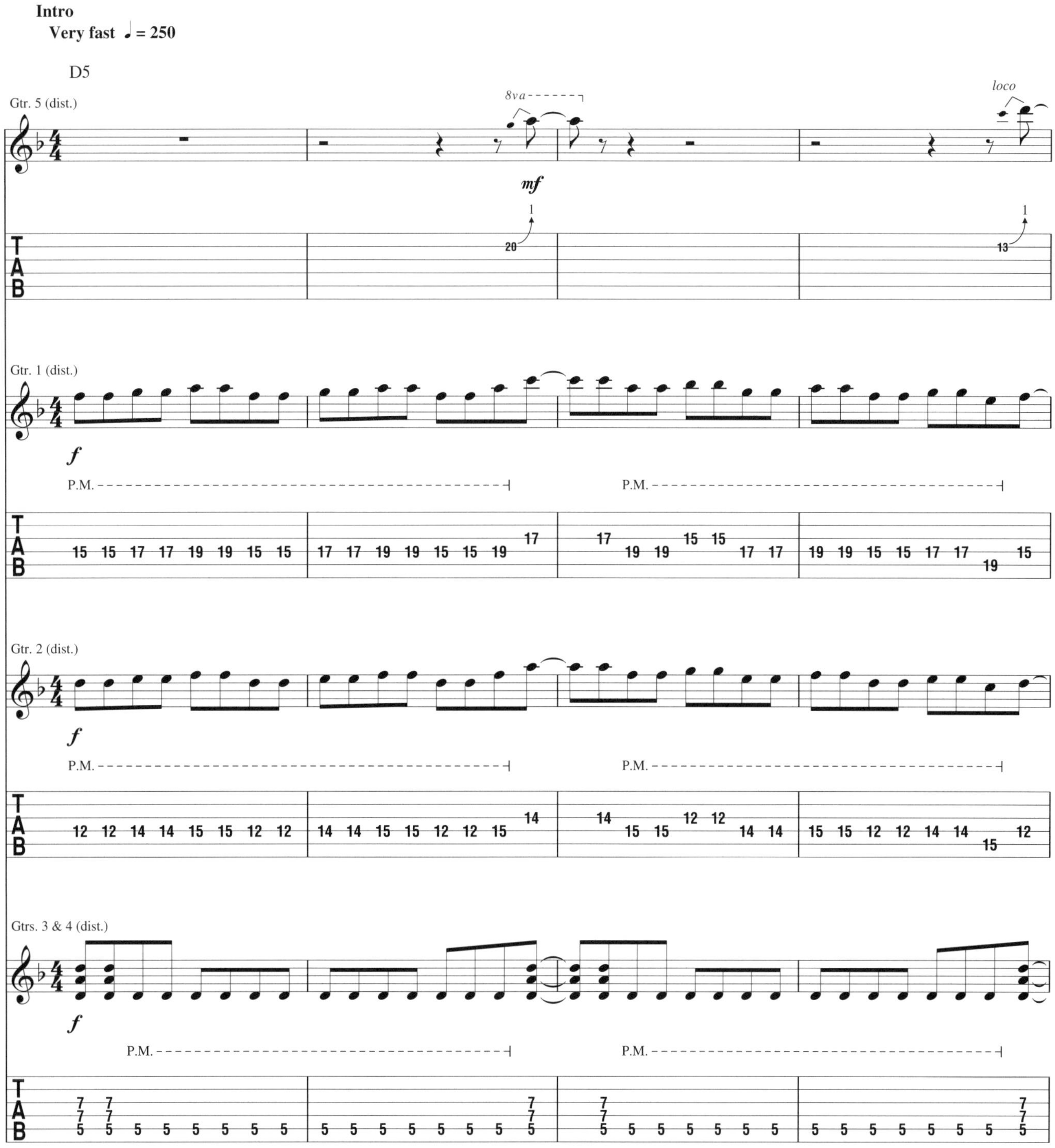

Intro
Very fast ♩ = 250
D5
Gtr. 5 (dist.)
8va
loco
mf
Gtr. 1 (dist.)
f
P.M.
Gtr. 2 (dist.)
f
P.M.
Gtrs. 3 & 4 (dist.)
f
P.M.

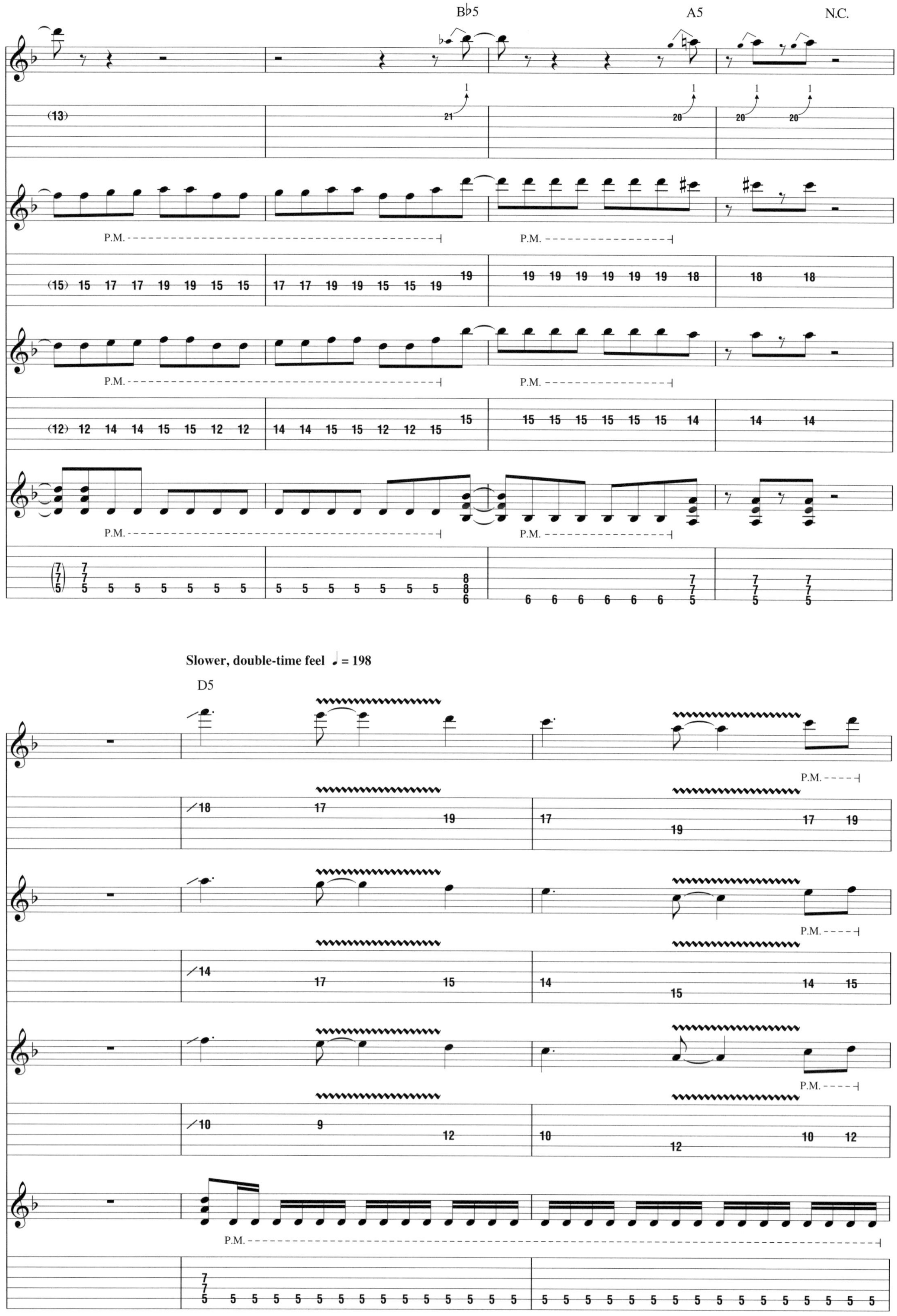

B♭5 A5 N.C.

P.M. P.M.

P.M. P.M.

P.M. P.M.

Slower, double-time feel ♩ = 198

D5

P.M.

P.M.

P.M.

P.M.

B♭5
D5
8va
B♭5
D5
C5
15ma
P.M.
P.H.

D5
A5
B♭5
F5
C5
8va
w/ bar
P.M.
loco
D5
A5

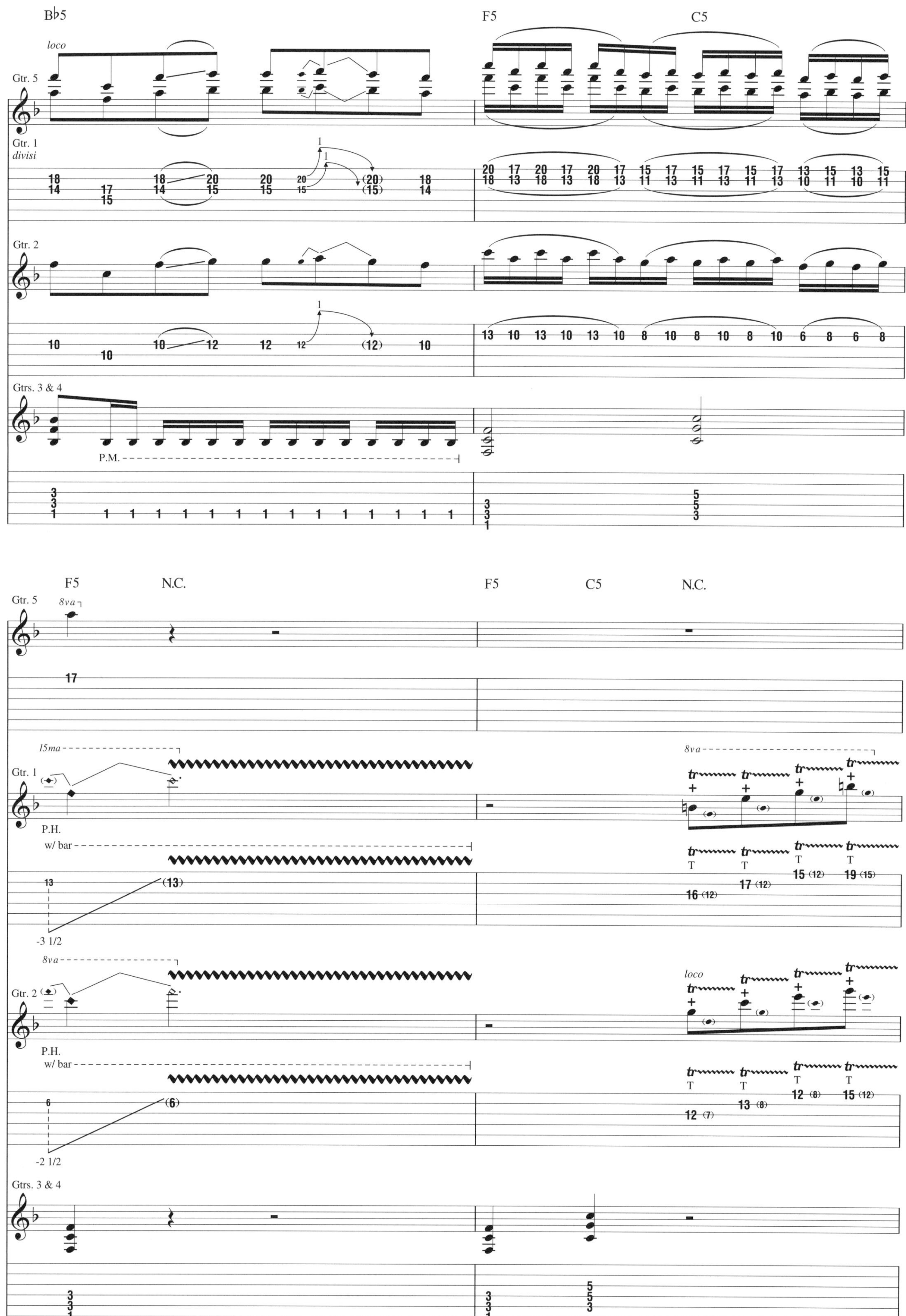
B♭5
F5
C5
loco
Gtr. 5
Gtr. 1
divisi
Gtr. 2
Gtrs. 3 & 4
P.M.
F5
N.C.
F5
C5
N.C.
8va
15ma
P.H.
w/ bar
-3 1/2
-2 1/2
tr
T

Gtr. 5 tacet

B♭5 N.C. B♭5 N.C. A5 N.C.

8va

P.H. P.H.

w/ bar

-3 1/2 -3 1/2

Pitch: F

loco 8va loco 15ma

P.H.

w/ bar

15ma

P.H.

w/ bar

P.M. P.M.

𝄋 Verse
Gtrs. 1 & 2 tacet
*D5
1. Fly - ing o - ver dark - ened skies the bat - tle will call. Dis - tant an - gels cry - ing in the
2. Search - ing through the mem - o - ries to o - pen the door. Liv - ing on the edge of life like
Rhy. Fig. 1
Gtrs. 3 & 4
w/ variation on repeats
P.M.
P.M.
P.M.

*Chord symbols reflect basic harmony

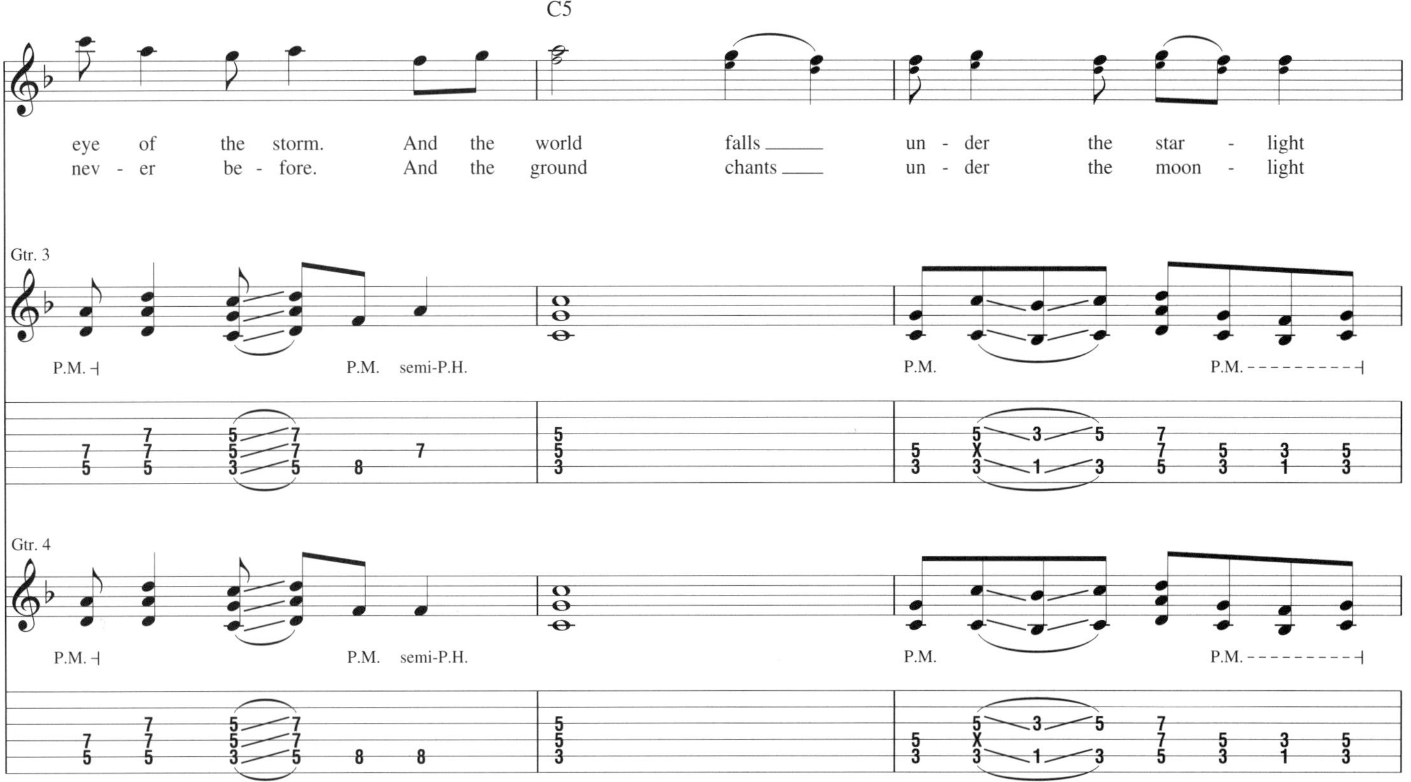
C5
eye of the storm. And the world falls un - der the star - light
nev - er be - fore. And the ground chants un - der the moon - light
Gtr. 3
P.M. semi-P.H.
P.M.
Gtr. 4
P.M. semi-P.H.
P.M.

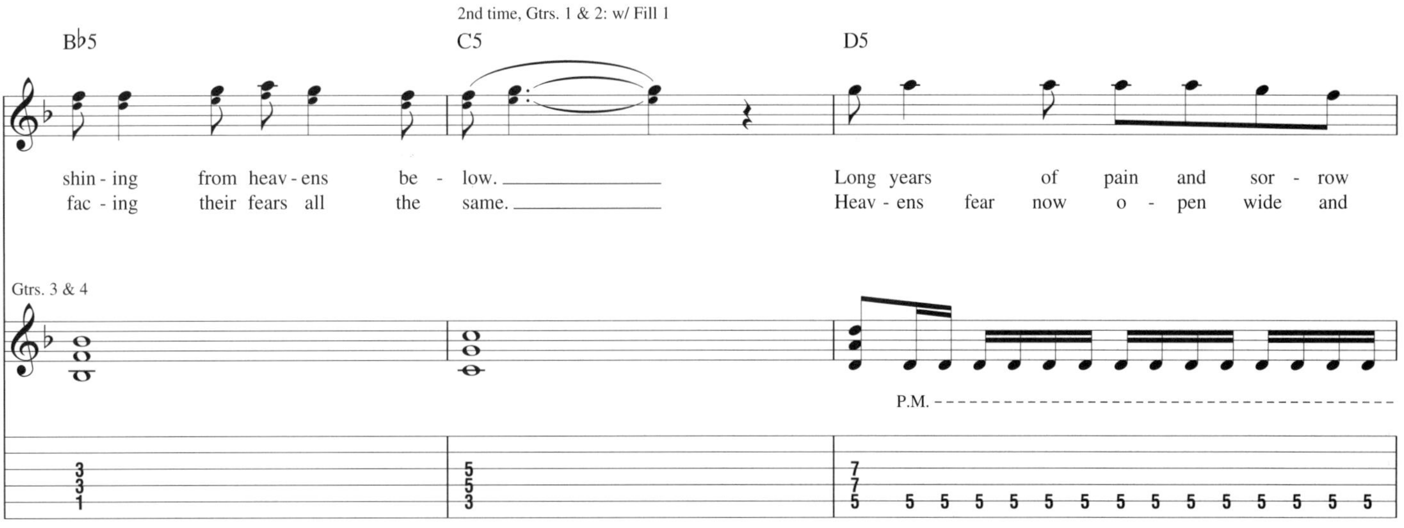
2nd time, Gtrs. 1 & 2: w/ Fill 1
B♭5
C5
D5
shin - ing from heav - ens be - low.
fac - ing their fears all the same.
Long years of pain and sor - row
Heav - ens fear now o - pen wide and
Gtrs. 3 & 4
P.M.

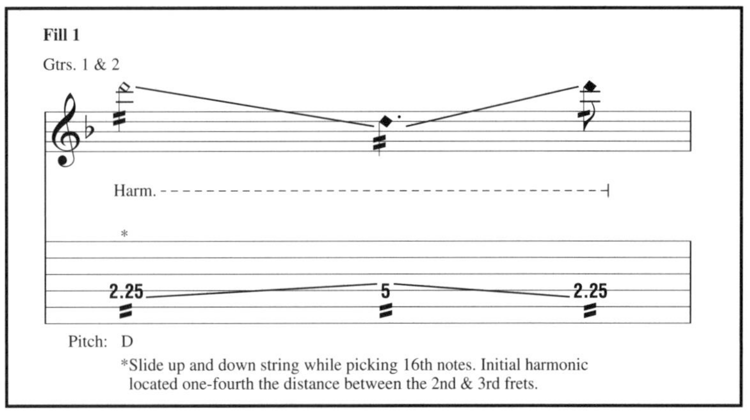
Fill 1
Gtrs. 1 & 2
Harm.
Pitch: D
*Slide up and down string while picking 16th notes. Initial harmonic located one-fourth the distance between the 2nd & 3rd frets.

search - ing for more. Cry for the touch of an - gels nev - er be - fore. And the
up for the call. All in stark re - al - i - ty the an - gels will fall. And the
Gtr. 3
P.M.
semi-P.H.
Gtr. 4

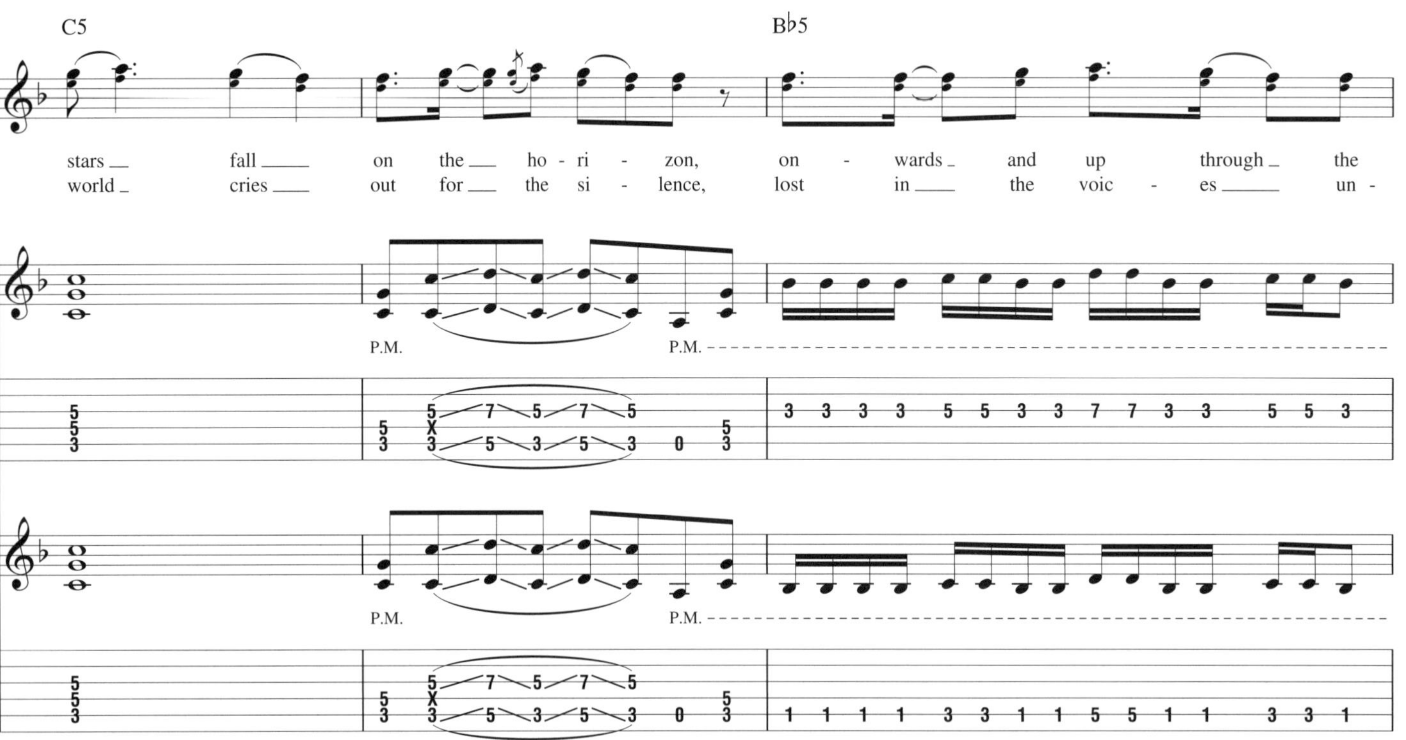
C5
B♭5
stars fall on the ho - ri - zon, on - wards and up through the
world cries out for the si - lence, lost in the voic - es un -
P.M.

C
B♭5
C5
pain. Ride the wind and fight the de - mon
known. Blind - ed by the force of e - vil
End Rhy. Fig. 1
Rhy. Fig. 2
*Gtrs. 3 & 4
P.M.
P.H.
w/ variation on repeats

*Composite arrangement

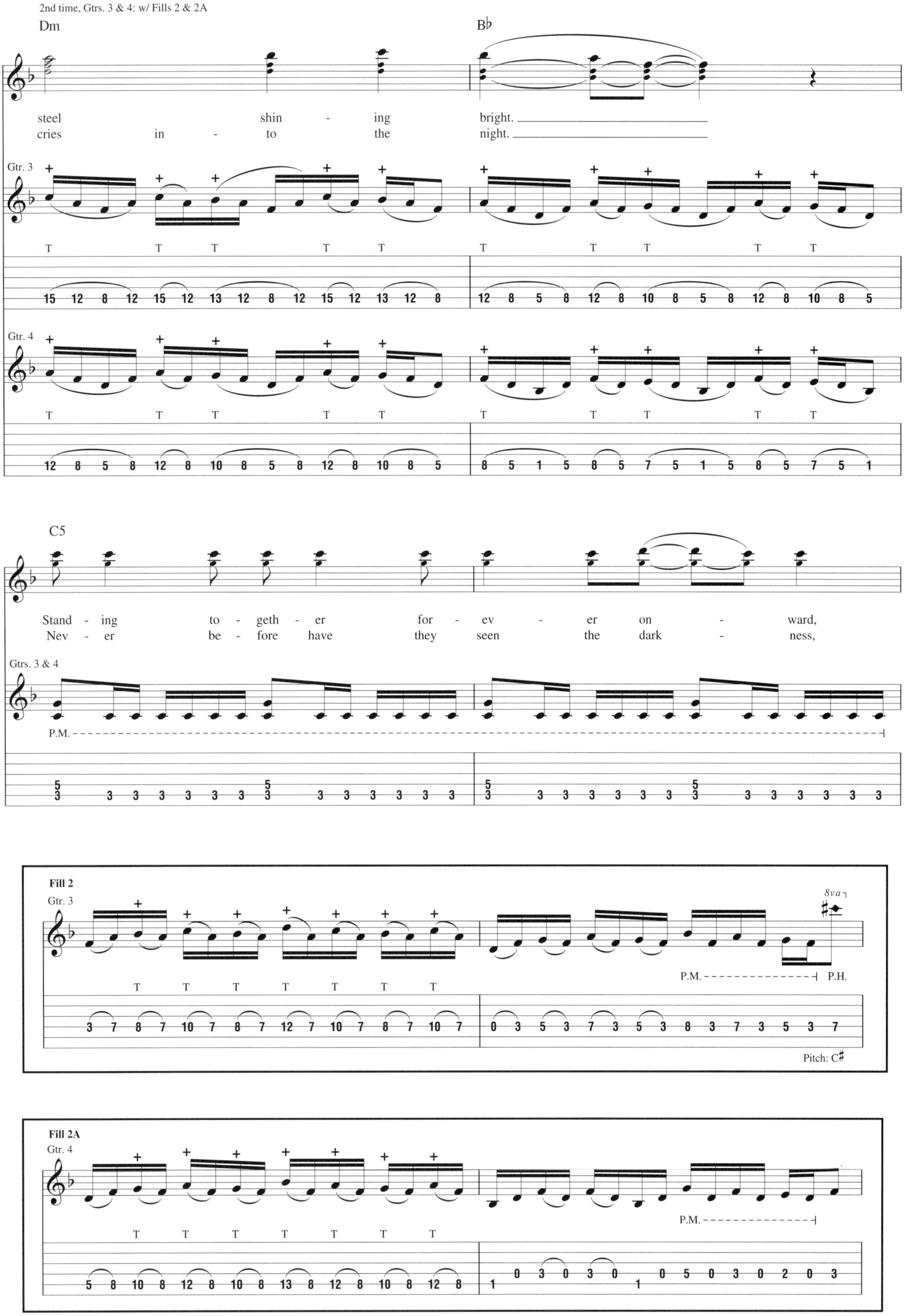

2nd time, Gtrs. 3 & 4: w/ Fills 2 & 2A

Dm B♭

steel shin - ing bright.
cries in - to the night.

Gtr. 3

T T T T T T T T T T

15 12 8 12 15 12 13 12 8 12 15 12 13 12 8 | 12 8 5 8 12 8 10 8 5 8 12 8 10 8 5

Gtr. 4

T T T T T T T T T T

12 8 5 8 12 8 10 8 5 8 12 8 10 8 5 | 8 5 1 5 8 5 7 5 1 5 8 5 7 5 1

C5

Stand - ing to - geth - er for - ev - er on - ward,
Nev - er be - fore have they seen the dark - ness,

Gtrs. 3 & 4

P.M.

5 5 | 5 5
3 3 3 3 3 3 3 3 3 3 3 3 3 3 | 3 3 3 3 3 3 3 3 3 3 3 3 3 3

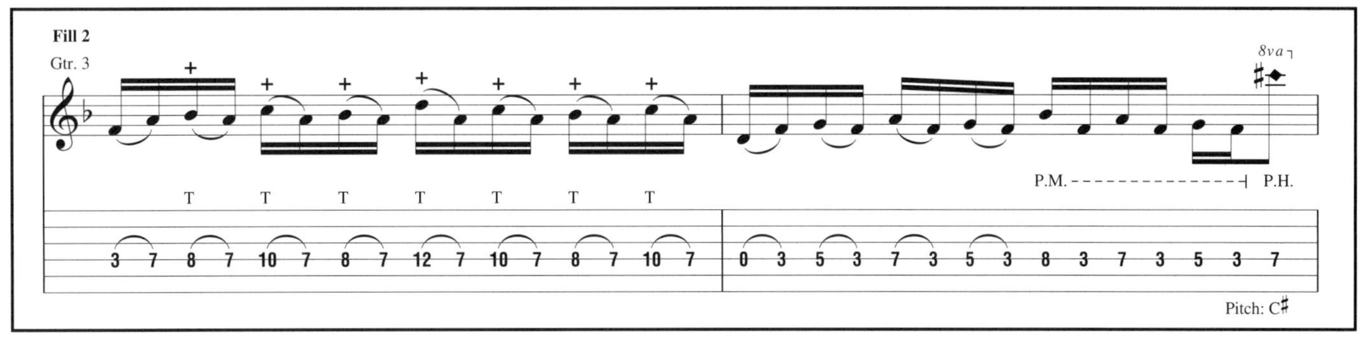

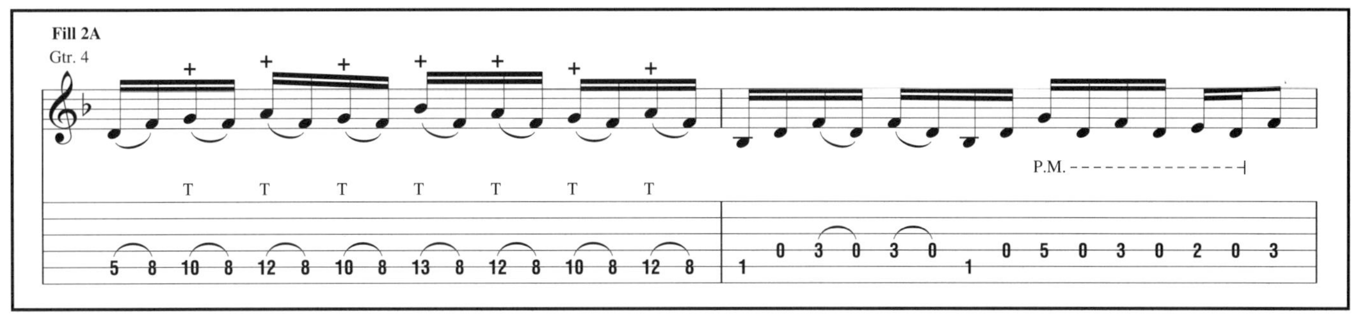

F5
B♭5
C5
flames burn - ing strong.
now they're all gone.
Hot wind in hell of pain and sor - row
Out from the shad - ows, storm - ing on the
P.M.
P.M.
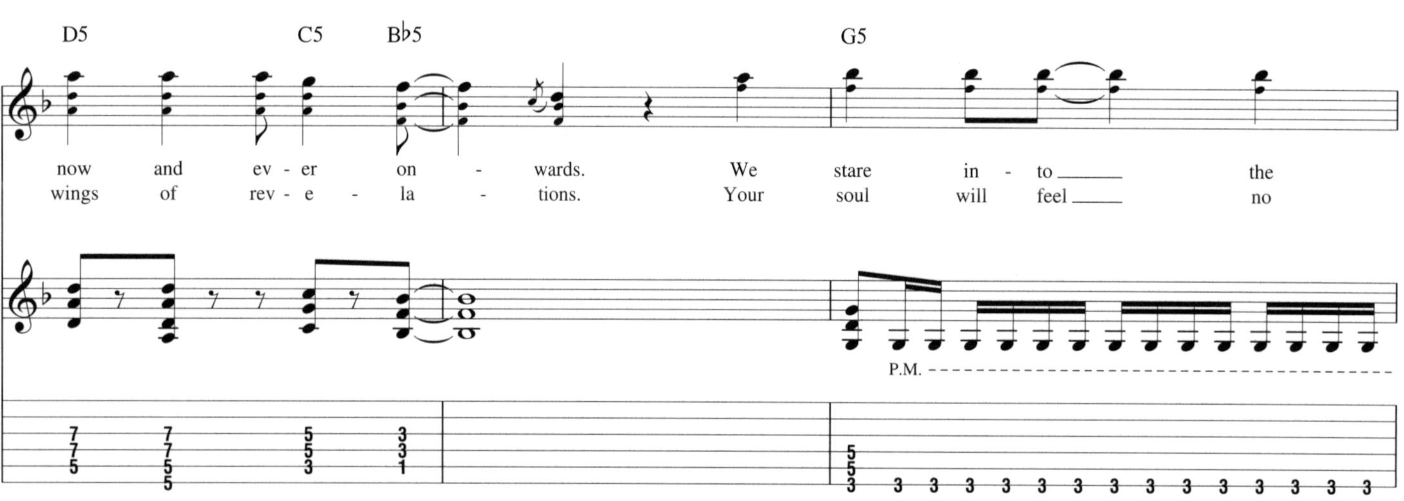
D5
C5
B♭5
G5
now and ev - er on - wards. We stare in - to the
wings of rev - e - la - tions. Your soul will feel no
P.M.
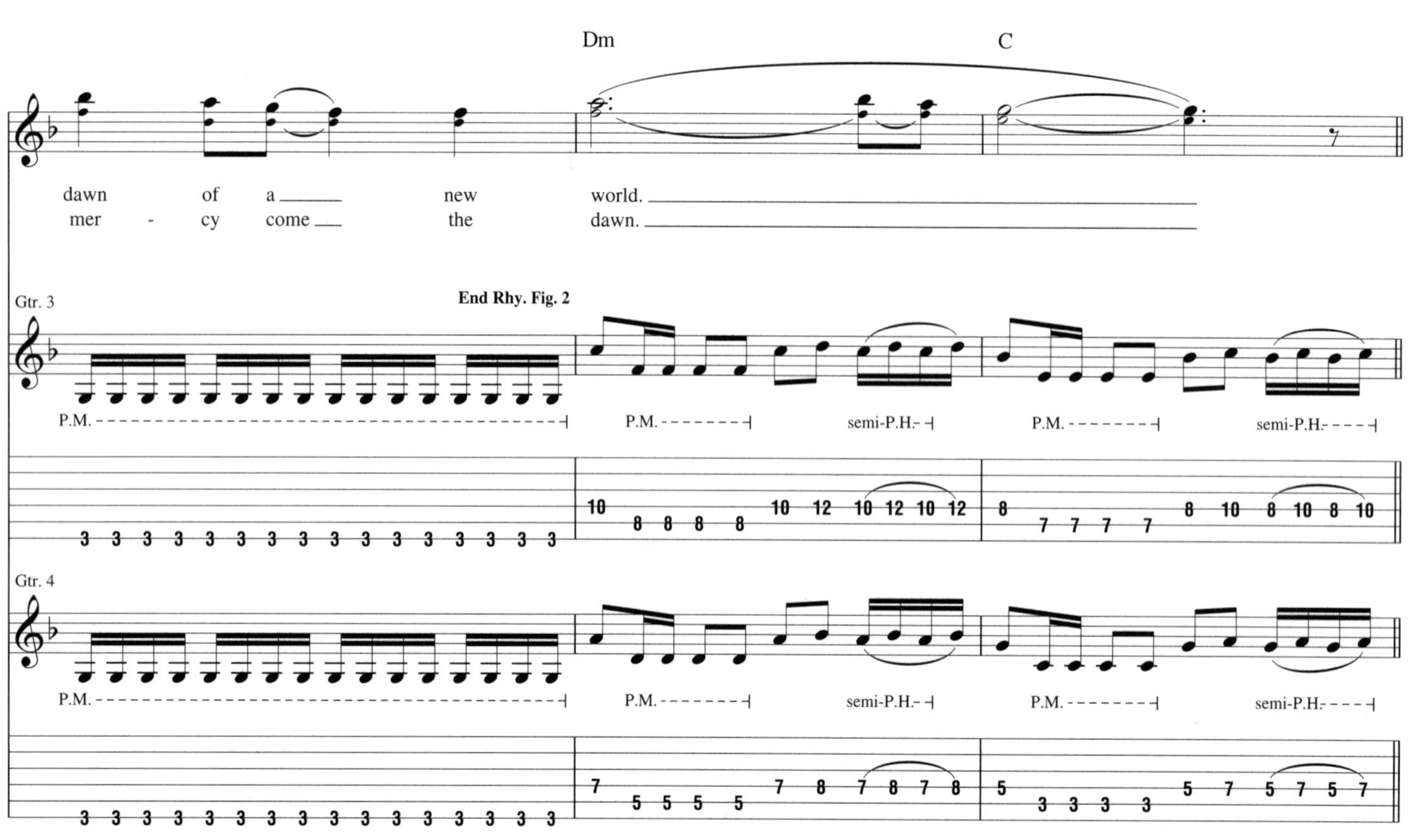
Dm
C
dawn of a new world.
mer - cy come the dawn.
Gtr. 3
End Rhy. Fig. 2
P.M.
semi-P.H.
Gtr. 4

Pre-Chorus
A5 N.C.
B♭5
D5
Cry out for the fall - en he - roes lost in time a - go.
Hold on for the morn - ing af - ter, nev - er to let go.
Riff A
Gtr. 5
w/ bar
Gtrs. 3 & 4
P.M.
P.M.
P.M.

C5
B♭5
A5
In our minds they still be - long when the
In the fires burn - ing strong, when the
w/ bar
w/ bar
w/ bar
P.M.
P.M.
P.M.

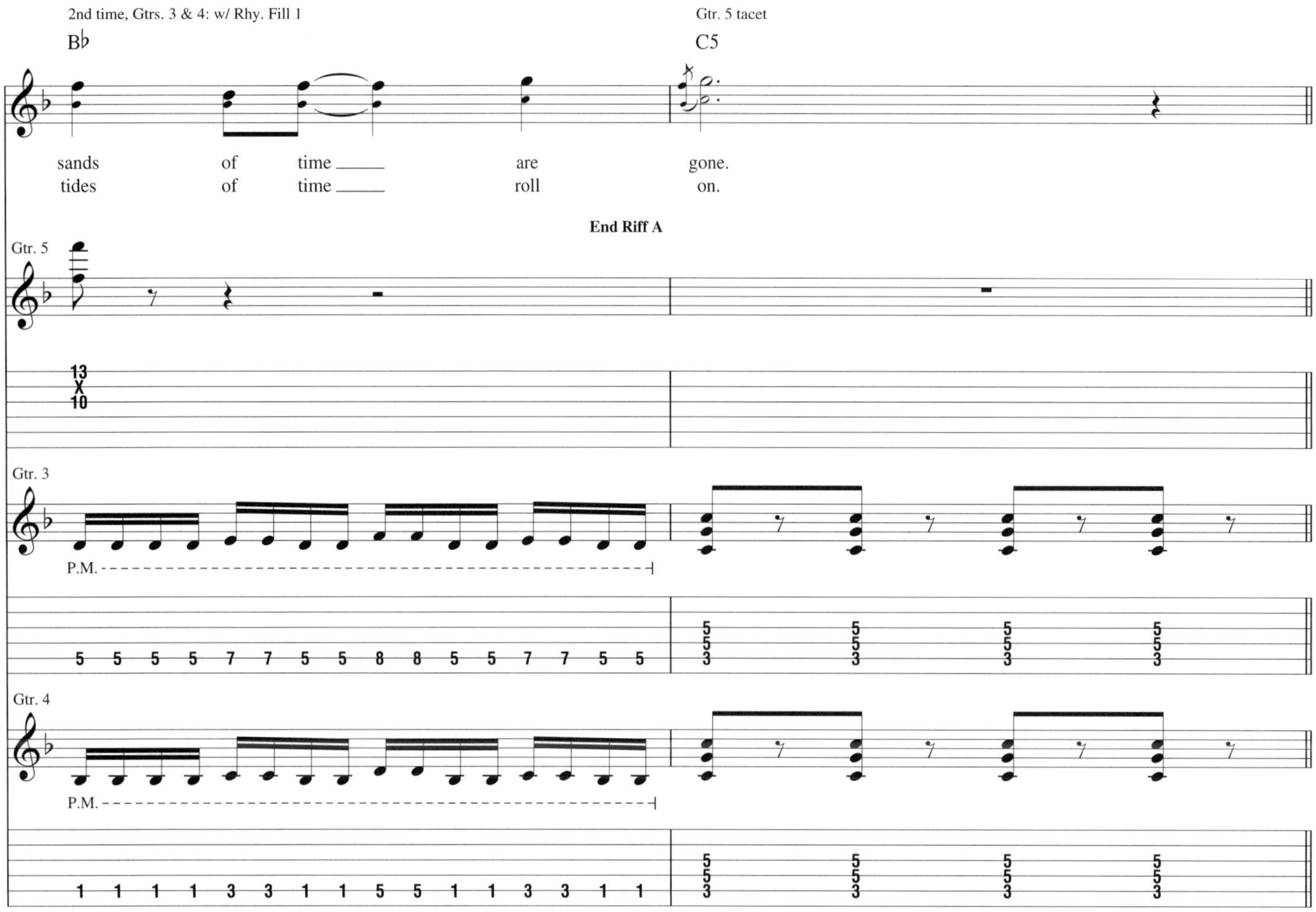

2nd time, Gtrs. 3 & 4: w/ Rhy. Fill 1
Gtr. 5 tacet
B♭
C5
sands of time are gone.
tides of time roll on.
End Riff A
Gtr. 5
Gtr. 3
P.M.
Gtr. 4
P.M.

Chorus

D5
B♭5
Rise o - ver shad - ow moun - tains, blaz - ing with
(Ah, blaz - ing with
Rhy. Fig. 3
Gtrs. 3 & 4
w/ variation on repeats
P.M.
P.M.

Rhy. Fill 1
Gtrs. 3 & 4

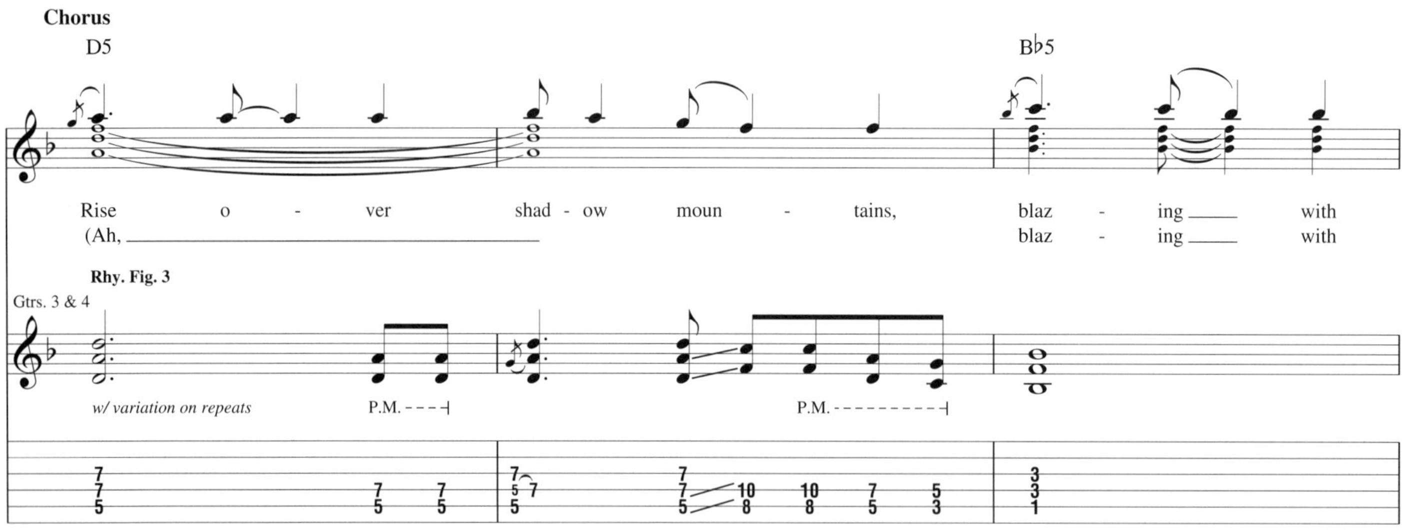

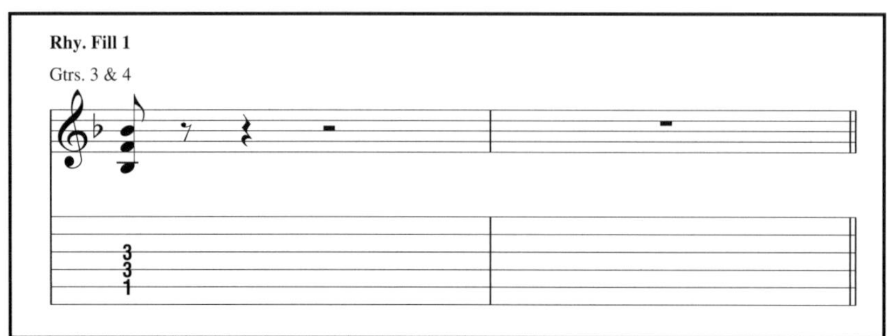

C5
D5
pow - er. Crossing val - leys, end - less tears, in
pow - er. Ah, in
P.M.
semi-P.H.
P.M.
A5
B♭5
C5
F5
u - ni - ty we stand. Far and wide a -
u - ni - ty we stand. Ah,
P.M.
P.M.
cross the land, the vic - to - ry is ours.
vic - to - ry is ours.)
B♭5
C5
P.M.
P.M.
To Coda 1
A5
B♭5
C5 N.C.
On to - wards the gates of rea - son, fight for the truth and the free - dom, Glo - ri -
End Rhy. Fig. 3
P.M.
P.M.
(1st time, cont. in slashes)

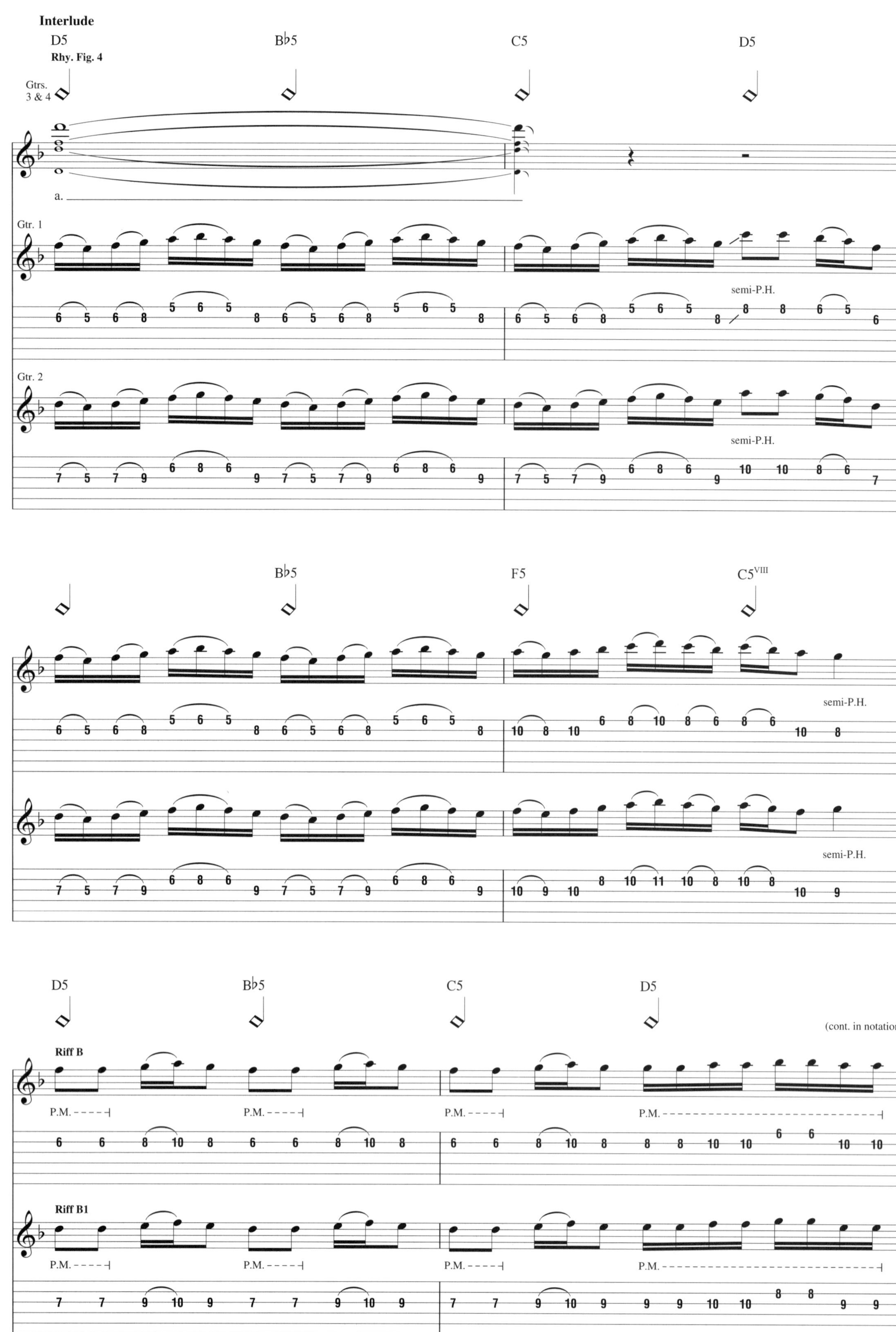
Interlude
D5
B♭5
C5
D5
Rhy. Fig. 4
Gtrs. 3 & 4
a.
Gtr. 1
semi-P.H.
Gtr. 2
semi-P.H.
B♭5
F5
C5VIII
semi-P.H.
semi-P.H.
D5
B♭5
C5
D5
(cont. in notation)
Riff B
P.M.
Riff B1
P.M.

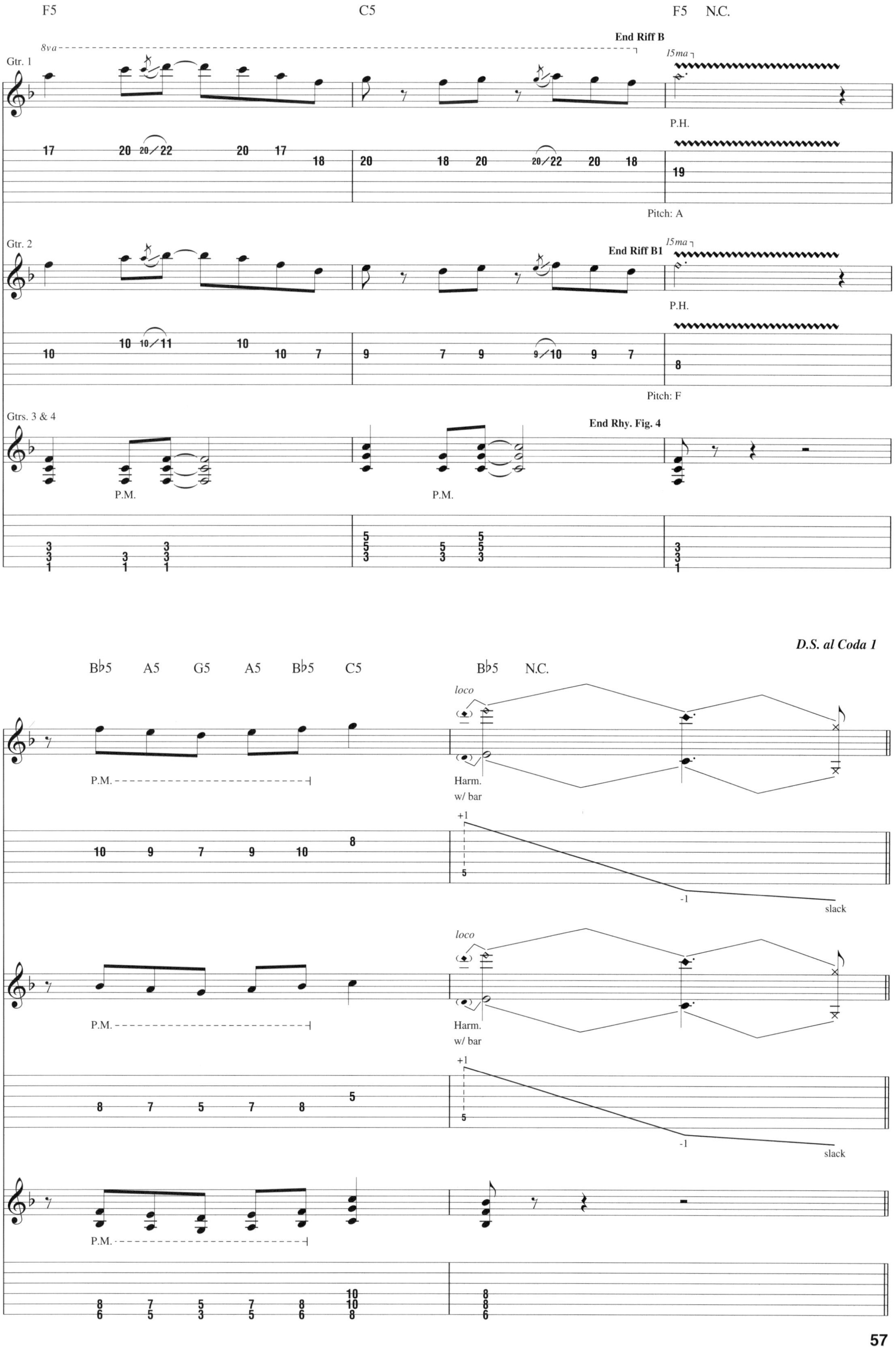

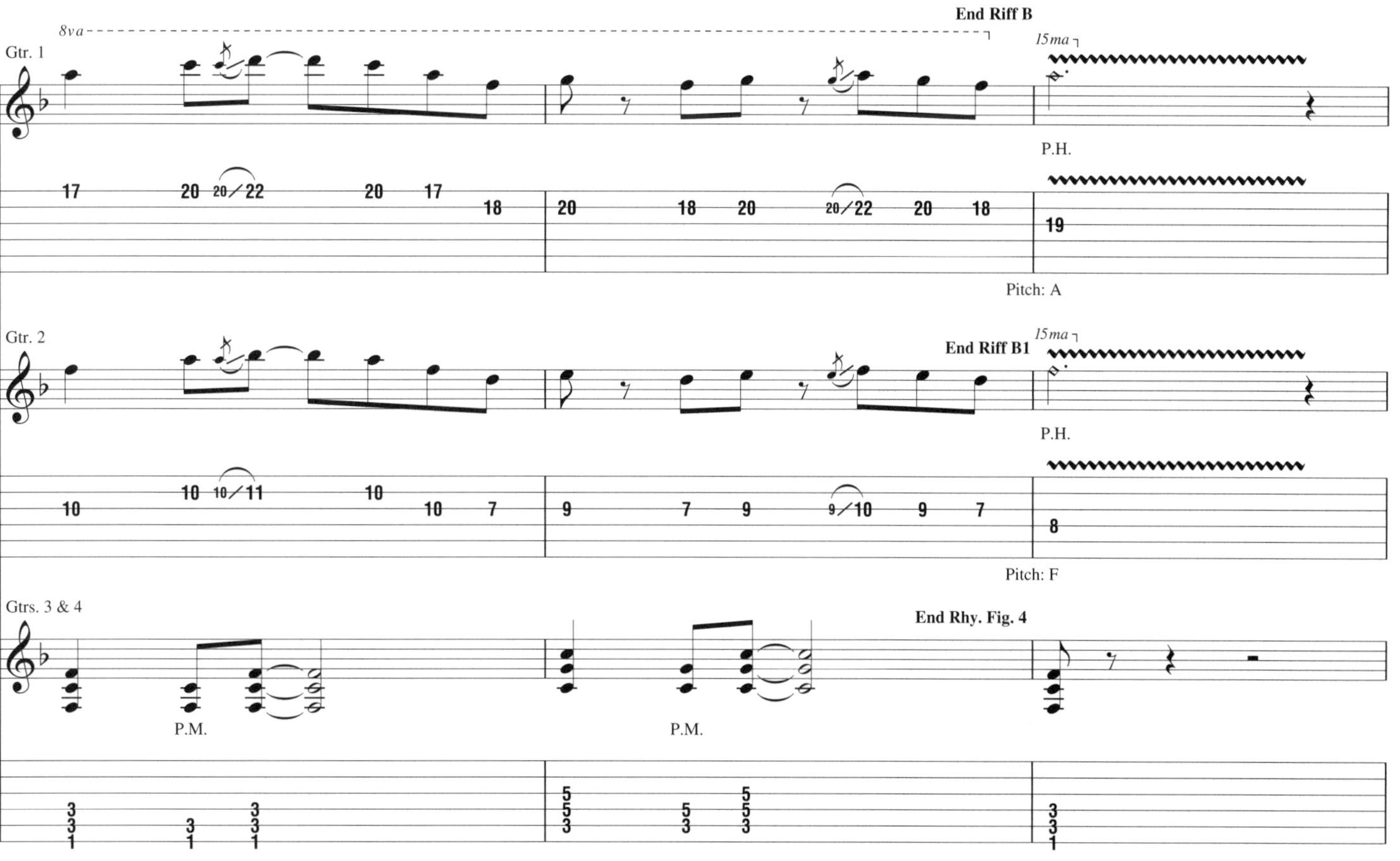

F5
C5
F5 N.C.
8va
End Riff B
15ma
Gtr. 1
P.H.
Pitch: A
Gtr. 2
End Riff B1
15ma
P.H.
Pitch: F
Gtrs. 3 & 4
End Rhy. Fig. 4
P.M.
P.M.
D.S. al Coda 1
B♭5
A5
G5
A5
B♭5
C5
B♭5
N.C.
loco
P.M.
Harm.
w/ bar
+1
-1
slack
loco
P.M.
Harm.
w/ bar
+1
-1
slack
P.M.

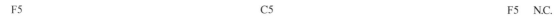

Coda 1

Interlude

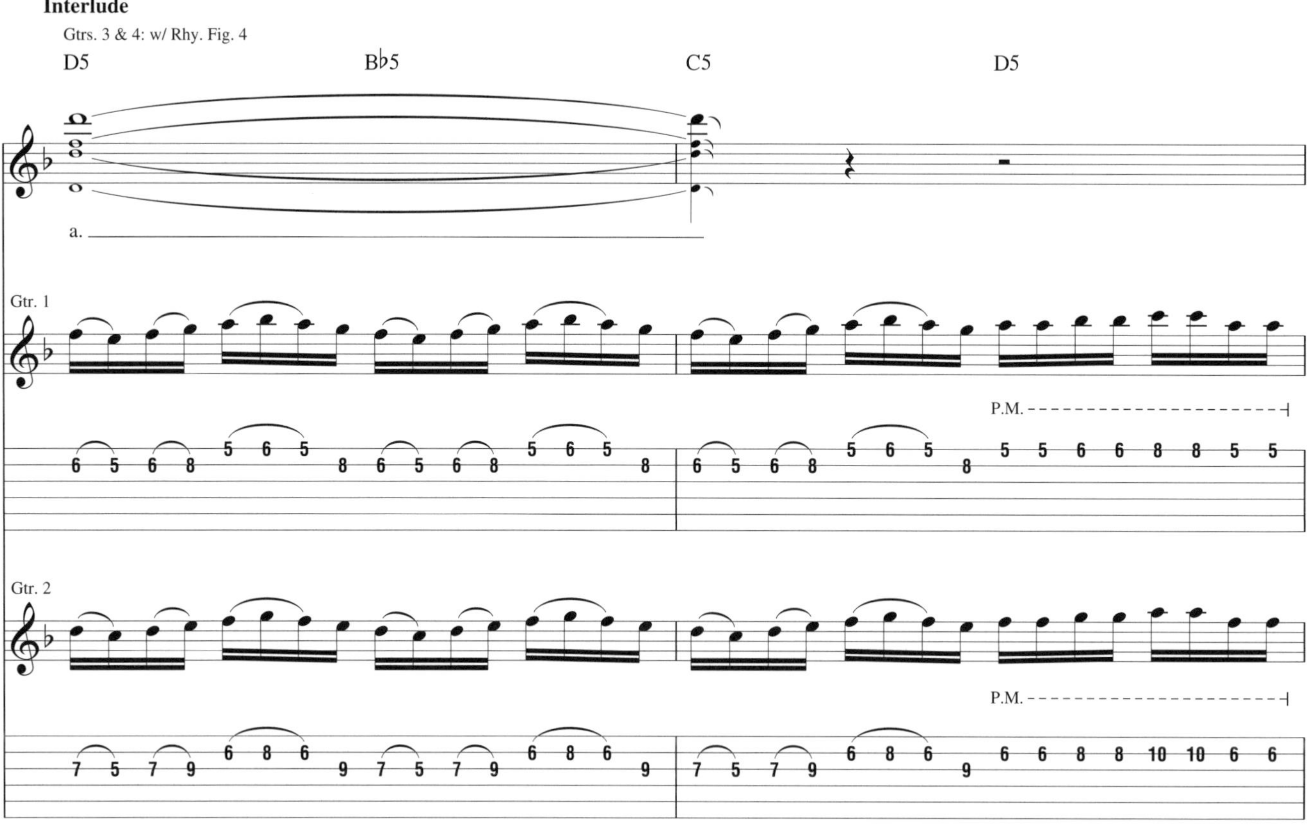

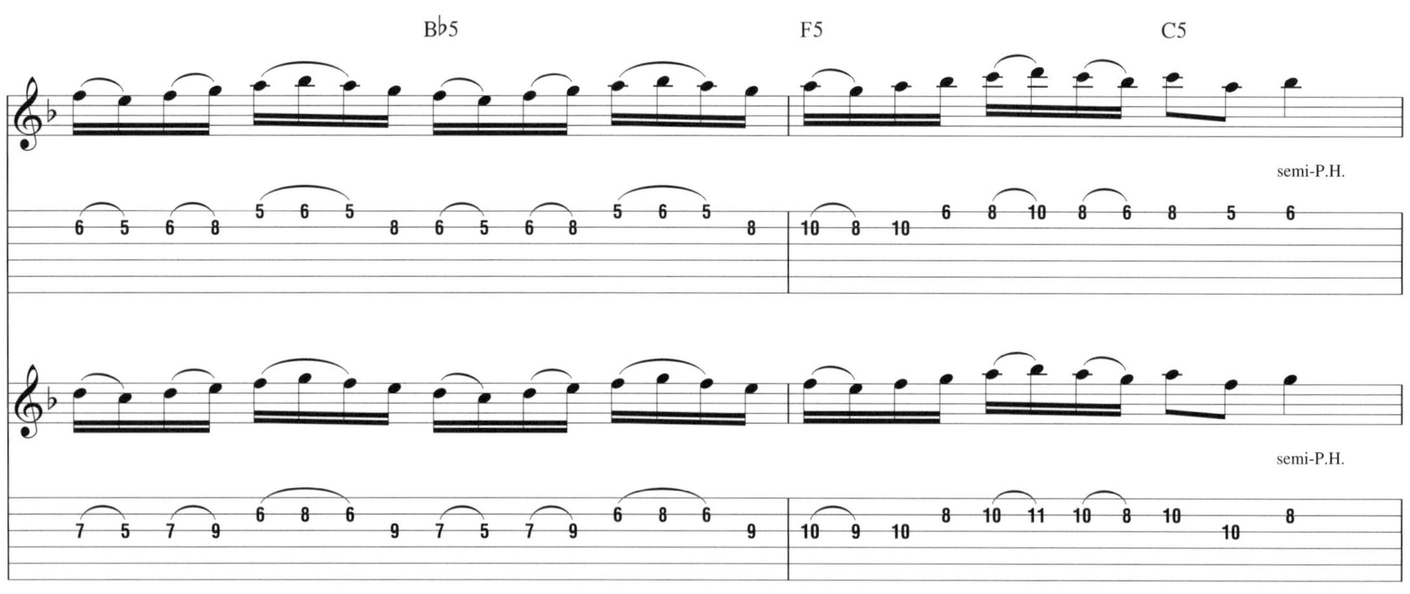

End double-time feel

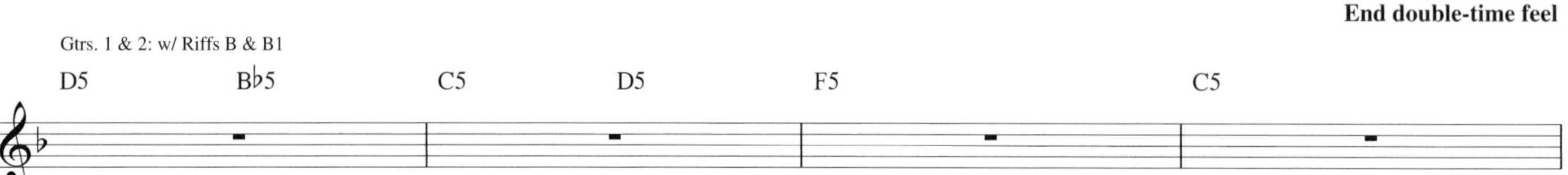

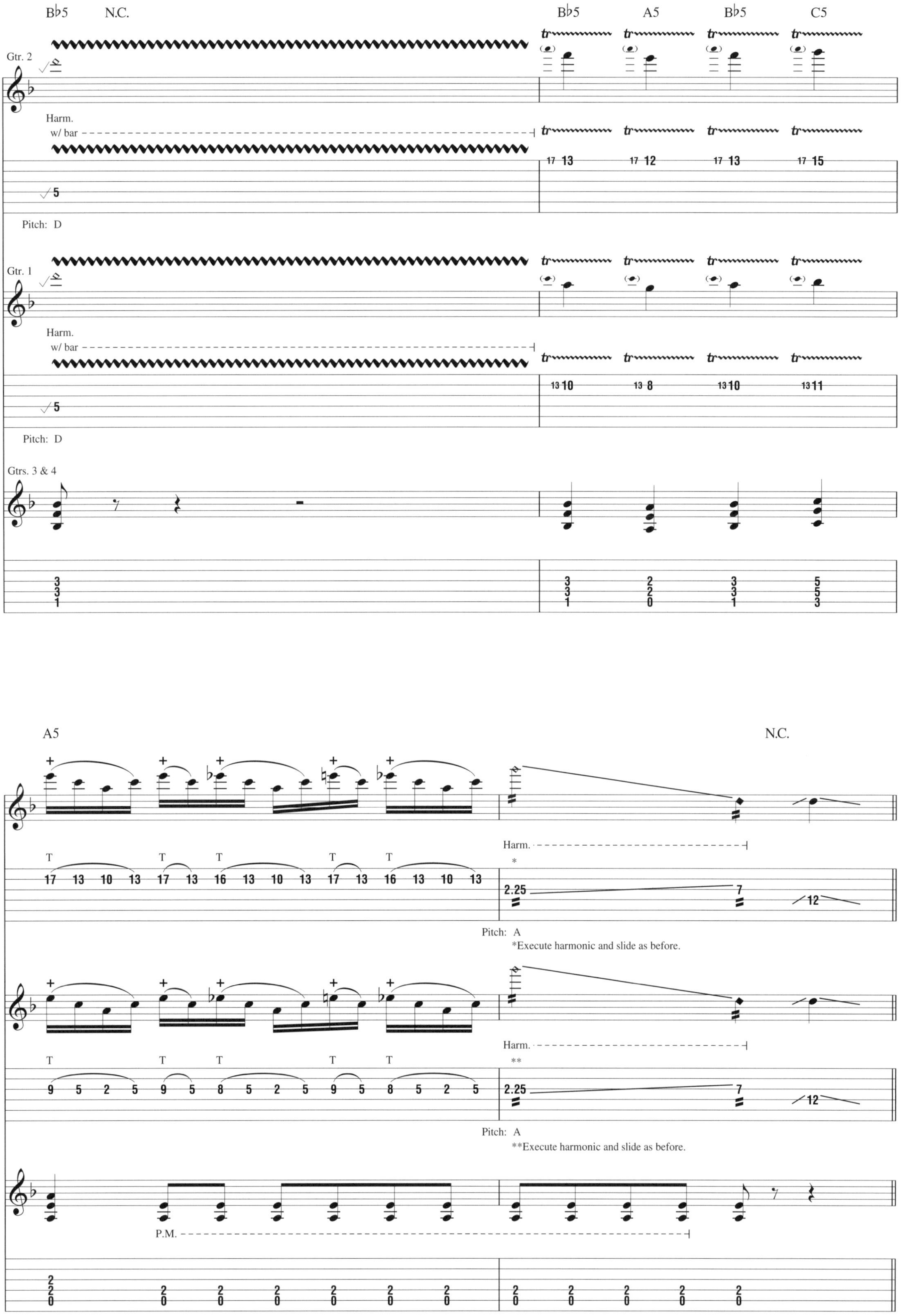

B♭5 N.C. B♭5 A5 B♭5 C5

Gtr. 2

Harm.
w/ bar

Pitch: D

Gtr. 1

Harm.
w/ bar

Pitch: D

Gtrs. 3 & 4

A5 N.C.

Harm.

Pitch: A

*Execute harmonic and slide as before.

Harm.

Pitch: A

**Execute harmonic and slide as before.

P.M.

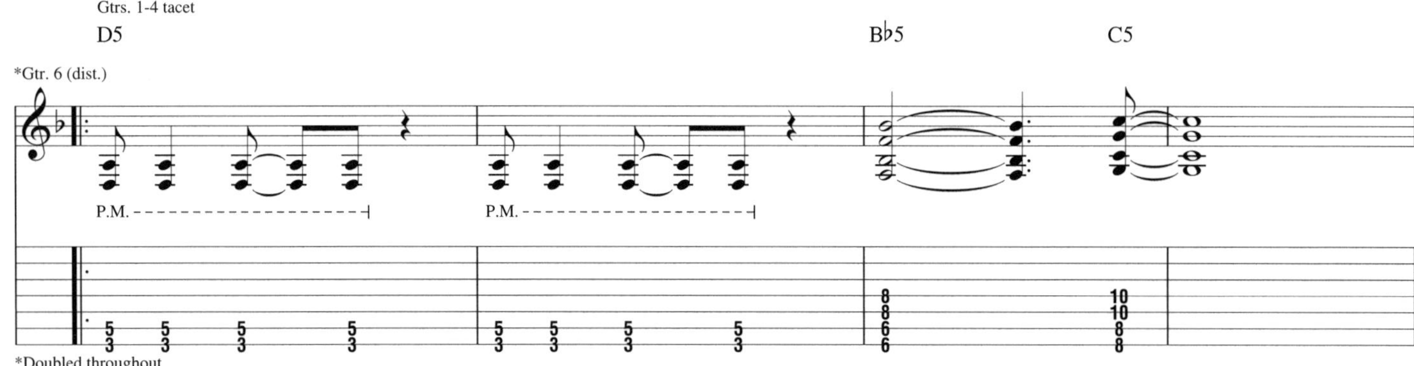
Gtrs. 1-4 tacet
D5
B♭5
C5
*Gtr. 6 (dist.)
P.M.
P.M.
*Doubled throughout

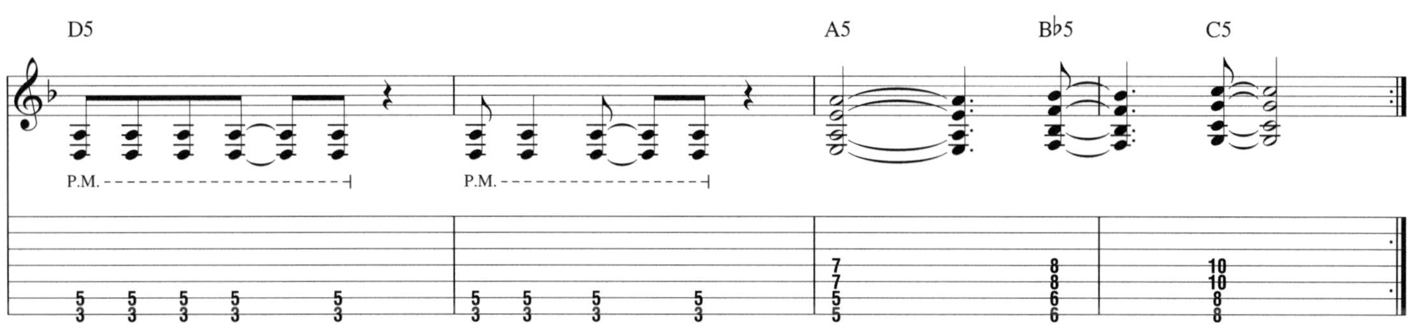
D5
A5
B♭5
C5
P.M.
P.M.

Guitar Solo

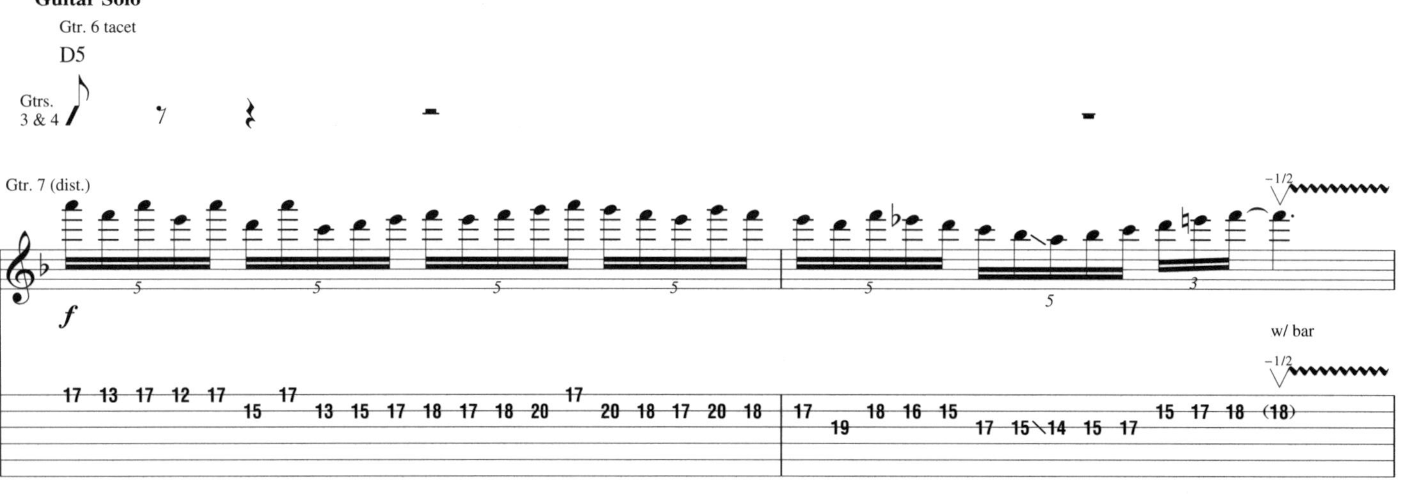
Gtr. 6 tacet
D5
Gtrs. 3 & 4
Gtr. 7 (dist.)
f
w/ bar
−1/2

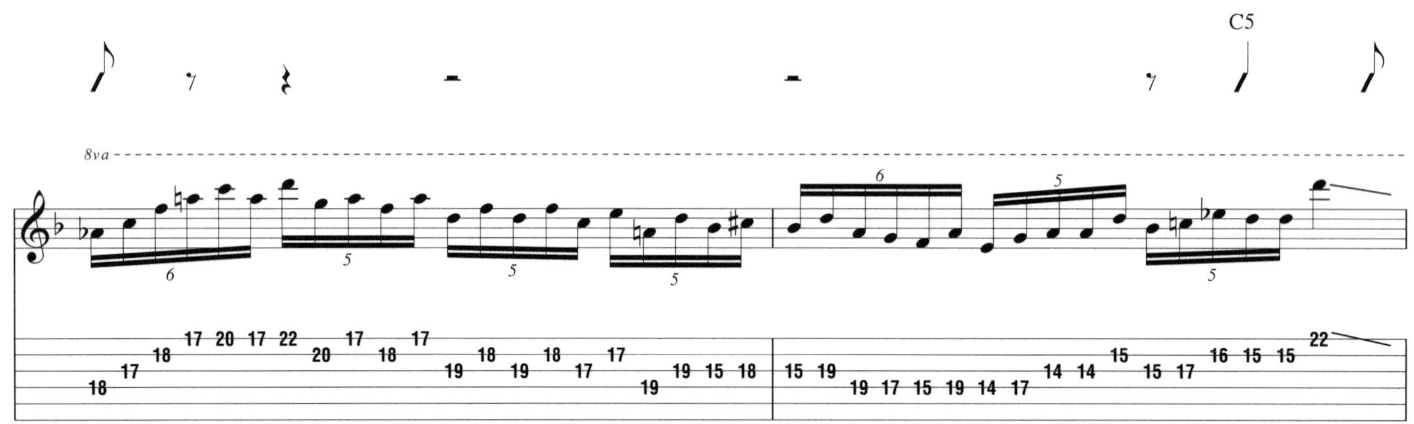
C5
8va

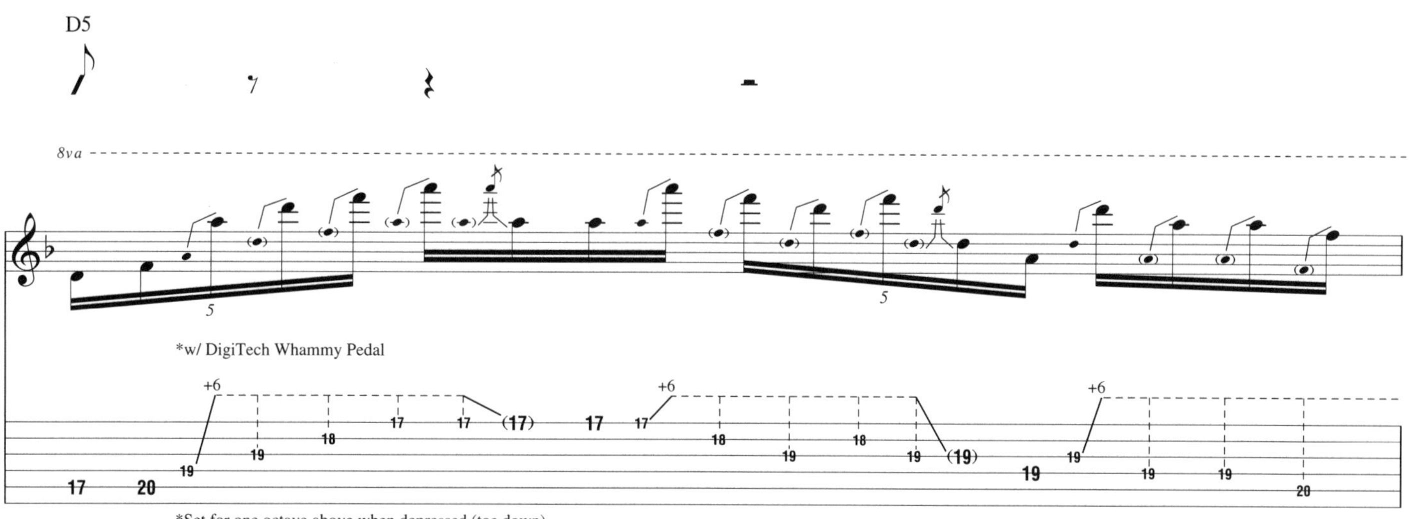

*Set for one octave above when depressed (toe down).

B♭5

P.M. (cont. in notation)

8va

Gtr. 7

15ma

Gtr. 1

8va

**w/ slide
***w/ octaver

**Detach vibrato bar and use as a slide.
***Set for one octave above.

Gtr. 2

8va

†w/ slide
††w/ octaver

†Detach vibrato bar and use as a slide.
††Set for one octave above.

Gtr. 7 tacet
C5
Dm
C
B♭
8va
Gtr. 1
loco
Gtr. 2
Gtr. 5
Gtrs. 3 & 4
P.M.
1/2
1

C
A5
C5
Dm
C
B♭
8va
P.M.
C
Csus4
Dm
C
B♭
8va
Gtr. 5
P.M.

To Coda 2
C5
8va
1/2
P.M.
Gtrs. 1 & 2 tacet
Am
G
F5
G
Gsus4
Am
Gtr. 9 (dist.)
f
w/ wah-wah
Gtr. 8 (dist.)
f
w/ wah-wah
P.M.
Gtrs. 3 & 4
P.M.

G5 F5

8va

loco

P.H.

Pitch: C♯

P.M.

G5

8va

P.M.

P.M.

P.M. P.M. P.M. P.M. P.M. P.M.

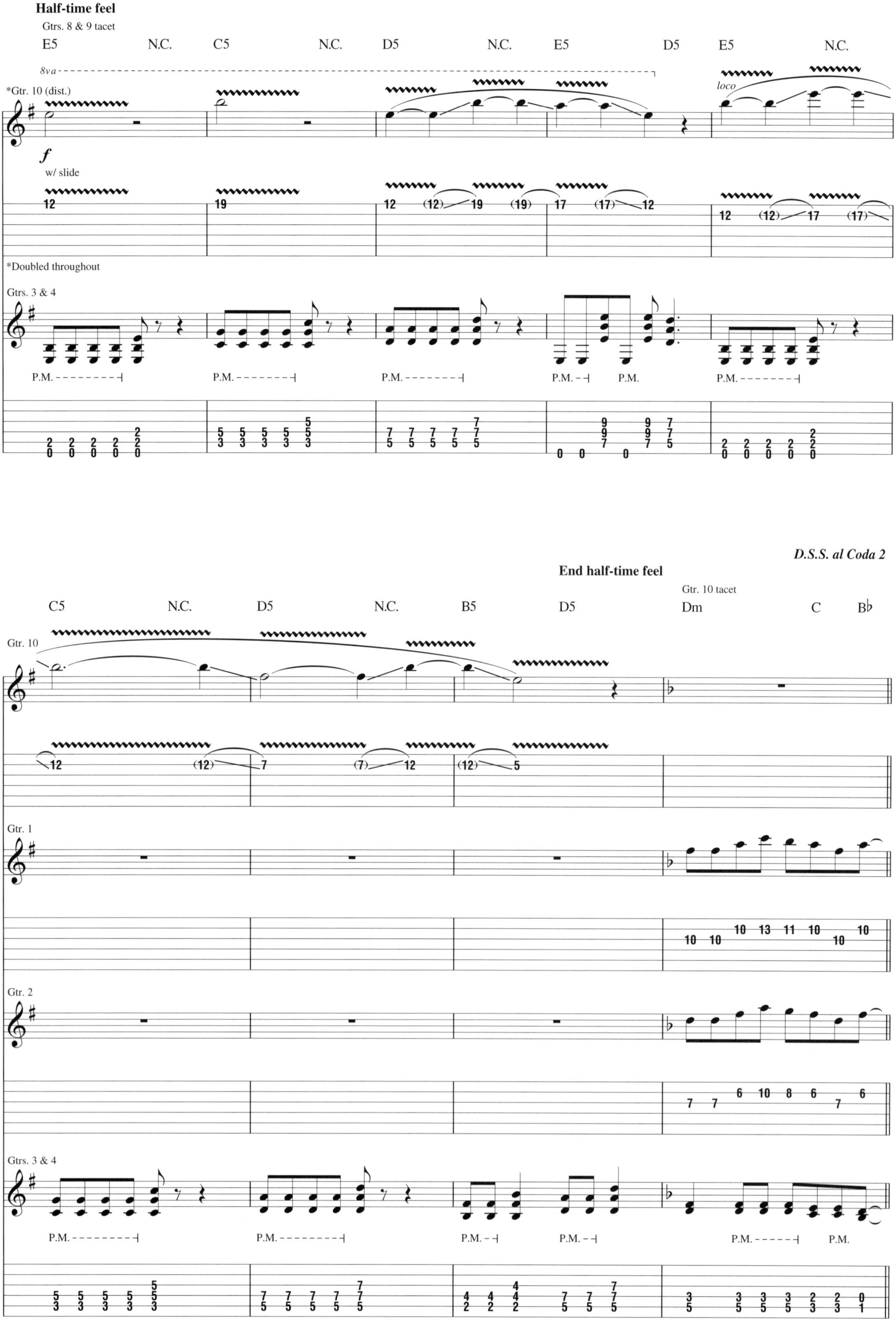

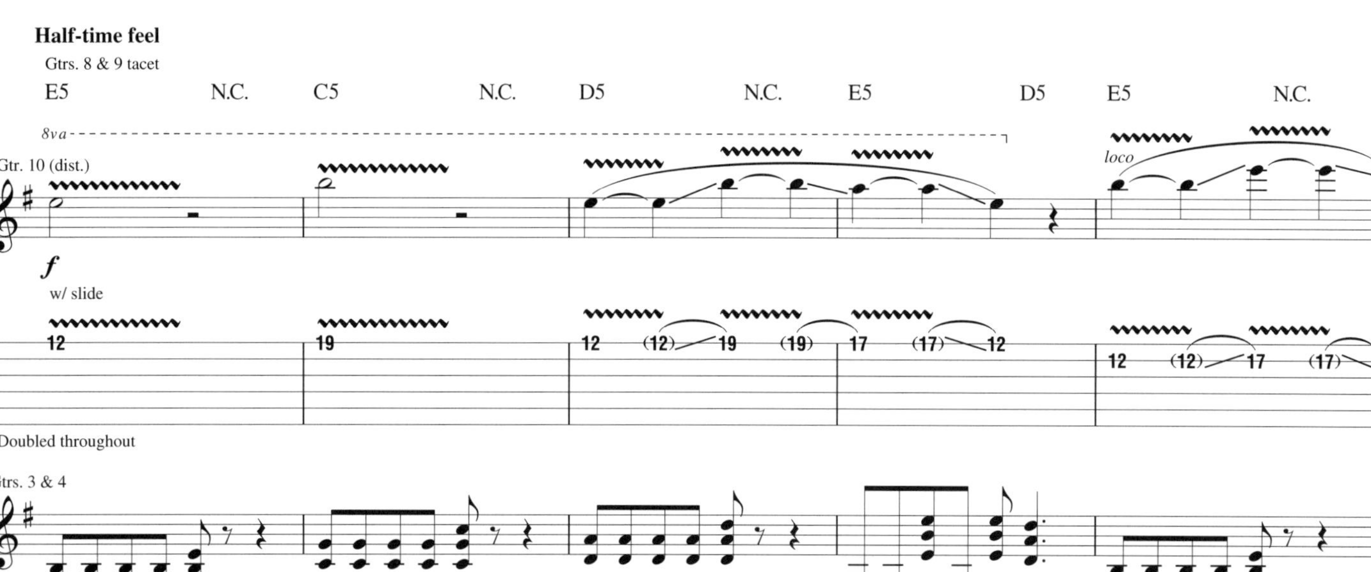

Half-time feel
Gtrs. 8 & 9 tacet
E5 N.C. C5 N.C. D5 N.C. E5 D5 E5 N.C.
8va
loco
*Gtr. 10 (dist.)
f
w/ slide
*Doubled throughout
Gtrs. 3 & 4
P.M.
D.S.S. al Coda 2
End half-time feel
Gtr. 10 tacet
C5 N.C. D5 N.C. B5 D5 Dm C B♭
Gtr. 10
Gtr. 1
Gtr. 2
Gtrs. 3 & 4
P.M.

Coda 2

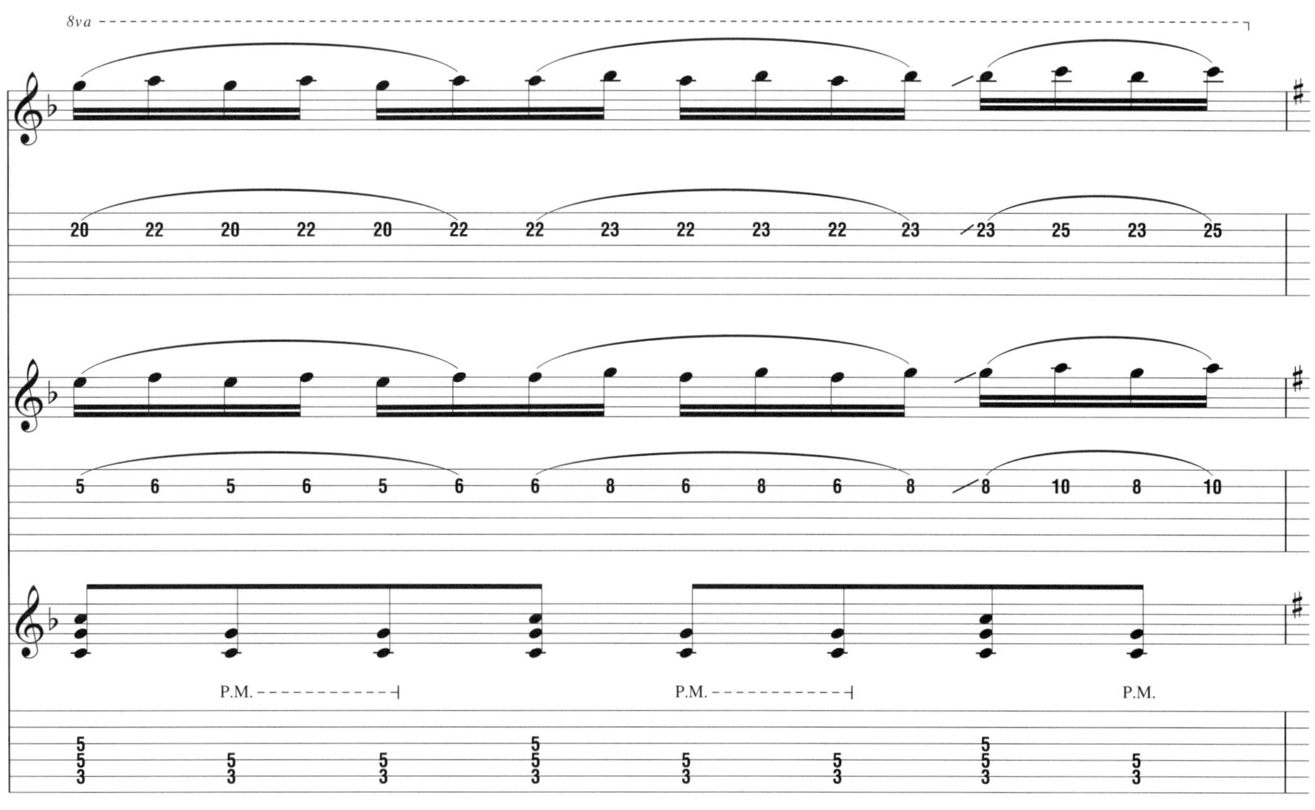

Gtrs. 1 & 2 tacet

E5

Gtr. 3

Gtr. 4

P.M.

B5 B♭5 A5 E5

8va

Gtr. 5

P.H.

Pitch: D♯ D C♯

Gtrs. 3 & 4

P.M.

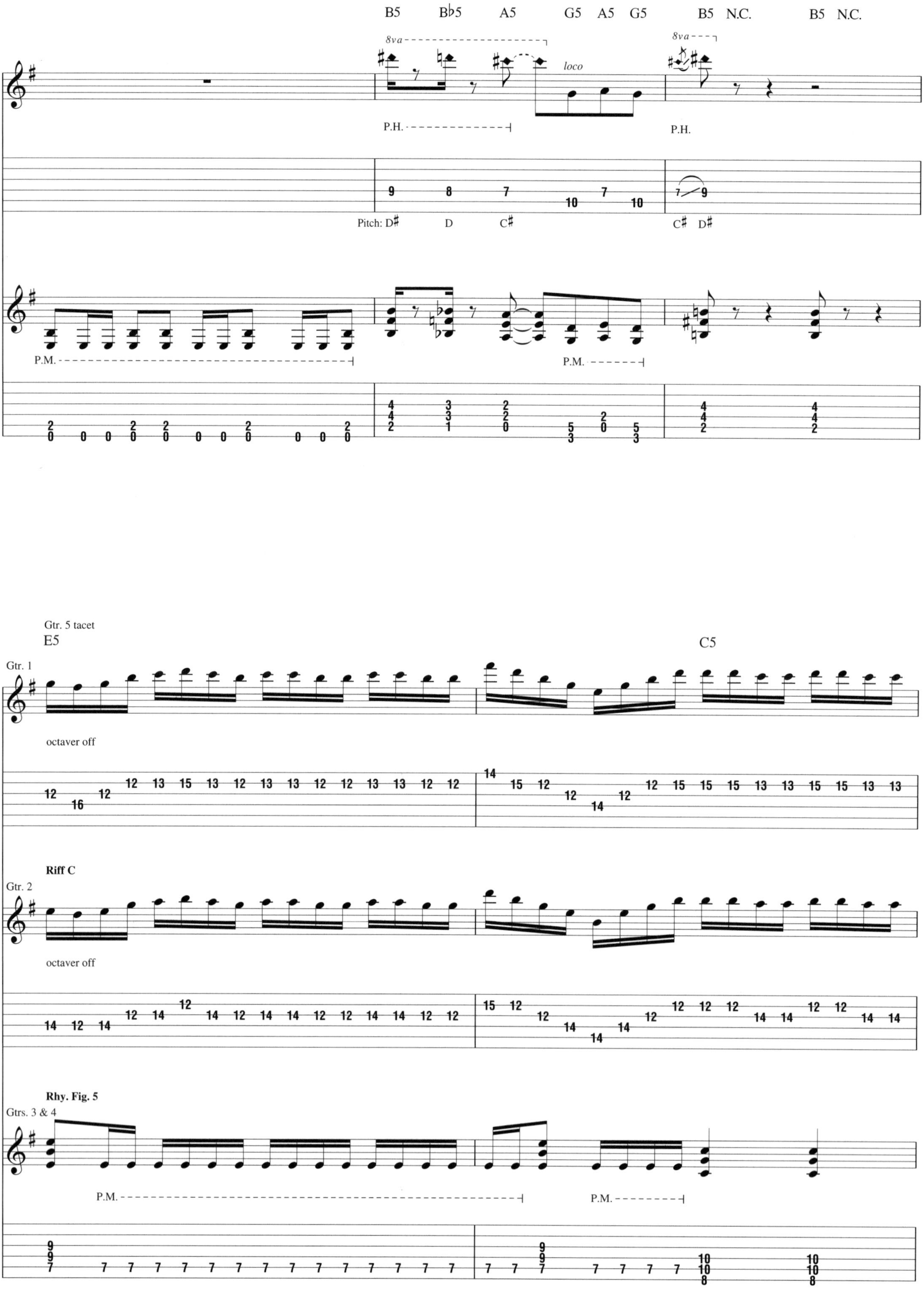

Gtr. 5 tacet
E5 C5

Gtr. 1
octaver off

Riff C
Gtr. 2
octaver off

Rhy. Fig. 5
Gtrs. 3 & 4
P.M.

E5
C5
P.M.
P.M.
P.M.
End Rhy. Fig. 5
Gtrs. 3 & 4: w/ Rhy. Fig. 5
E5
C5
8va
Gtr. 1
Gtr. 2
End Riff C
E5
C5
8va

D5
B♭5
Gtr. 1
loco
Gtr. 2
Rhy. Fig. 6
Gtrs. 3 & 4
P.M.
8va
End Rhy. Fig. 6

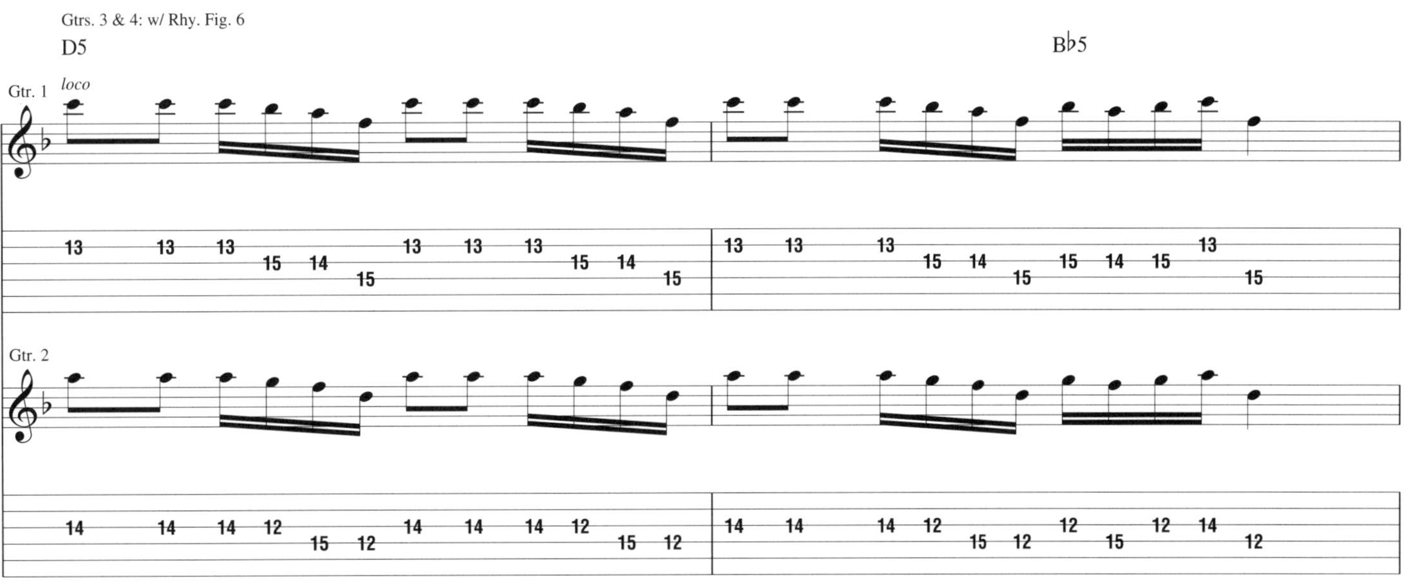
Gtrs. 3 & 4: w/ Rhy. Fig. 6
D5
B♭5
Gtr. 1
loco
13 13 13 15 14 15 13 13 13 15 14 15
13 13 13 15 14 15 15 14 15 13 15
Gtr. 2
14 14 14 12 15 12 14 14 14 12 15 12
14 14 14 12 15 12 12 15 12 14 12

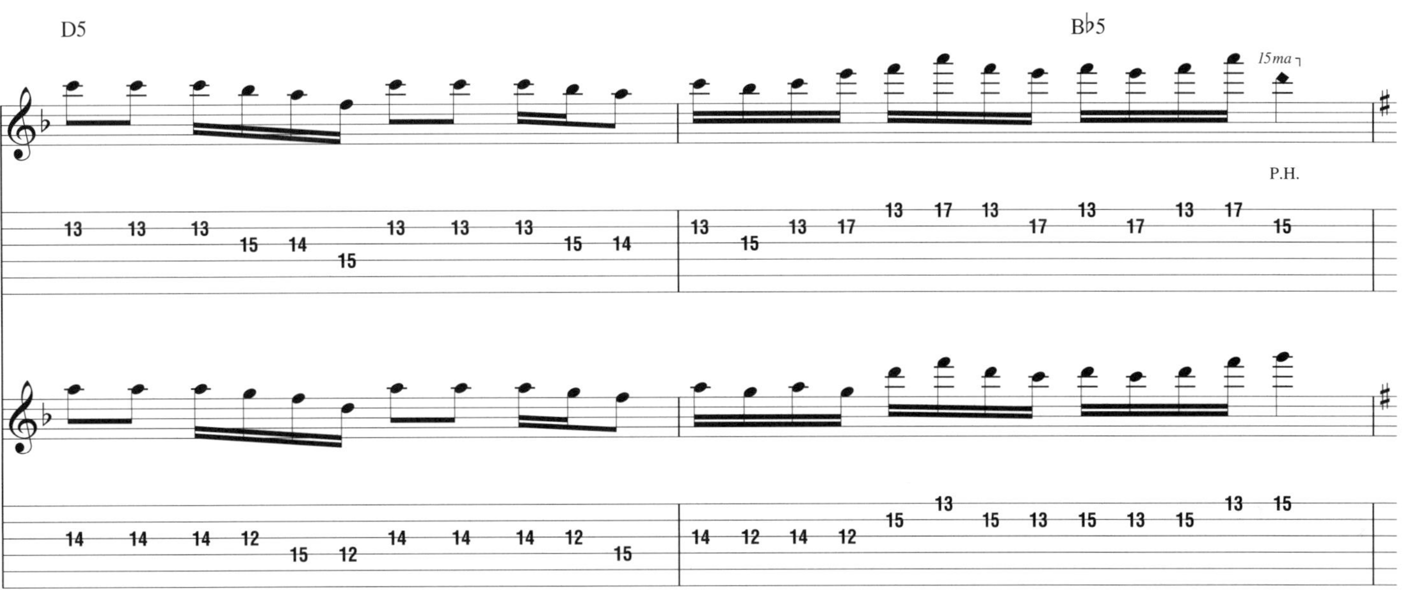
D5
B♭5
15ma
P.H.
13 13 13 15 14 15 13 13 13 15 14
13 15 13 17 13 17 13 17 13 17 13 17 15
14 14 14 12 15 12 14 14 14 12 15
14 12 14 12 15 13 15 13 15 13 15 13 15

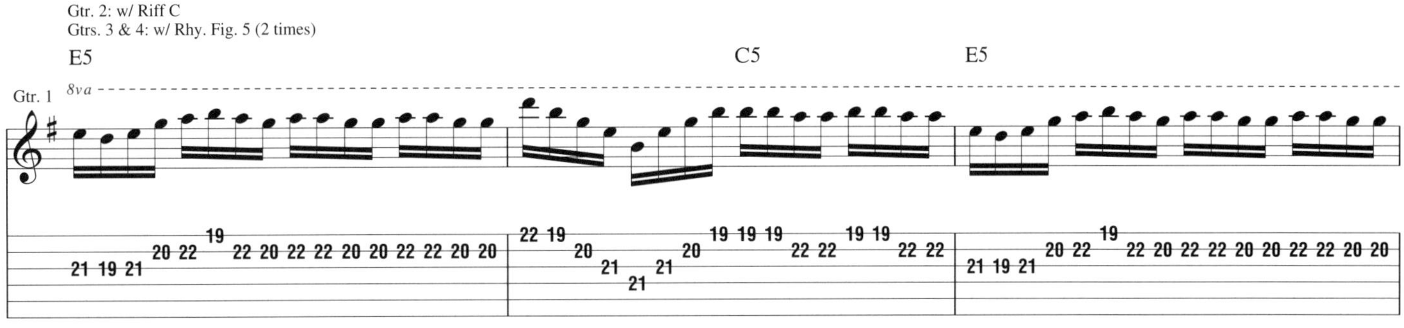
Gtr. 2: w/ Riff C
Gtrs. 3 & 4: w/ Rhy. Fig. 5 (2 times)
E5
C5
E5
Gtr. 1
8va
21 19 21 20 22 19 22 20 22 22 20 20 22 22 20 20
22 19 20 21 21 21 20 19 19 19 22 22 19 19 22 22
21 19 21 20 22 19 22 20 22 22 20 20 22 22 20 20

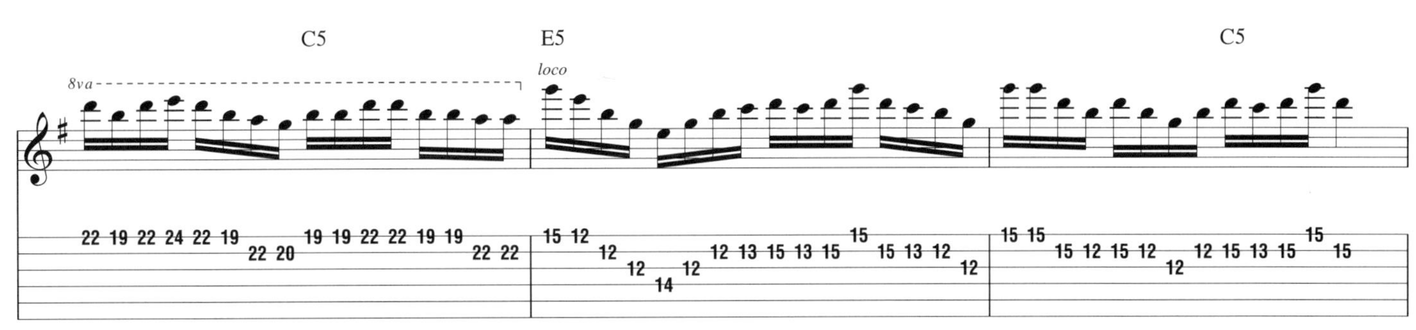
C5
E5
C5
8va
loco
22 19 22 24 22 19 22 20 19 19 22 22 19 19 22 22
15 12 12 12 14 12 12 13 15 13 15 15 15 13 12 12
15 15 15 12 15 12 12 12 15 13 15 15 15

End double-time feel
E5
C5
Gtr. 1
Gtr. 2

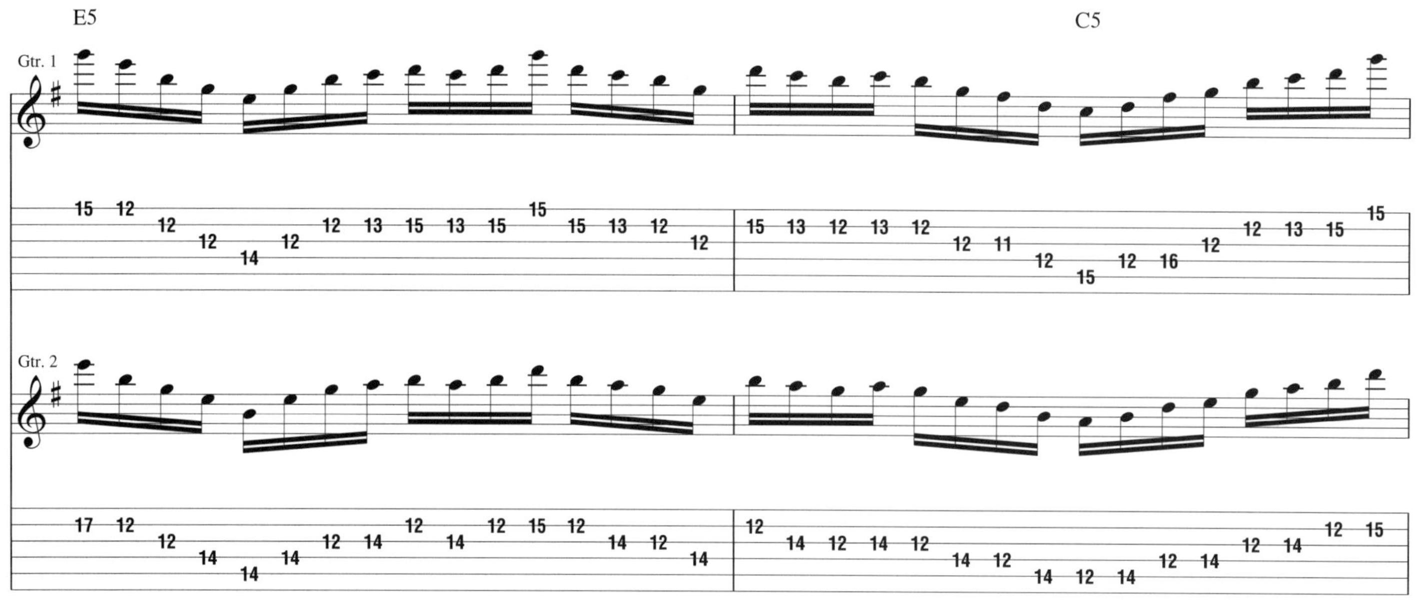

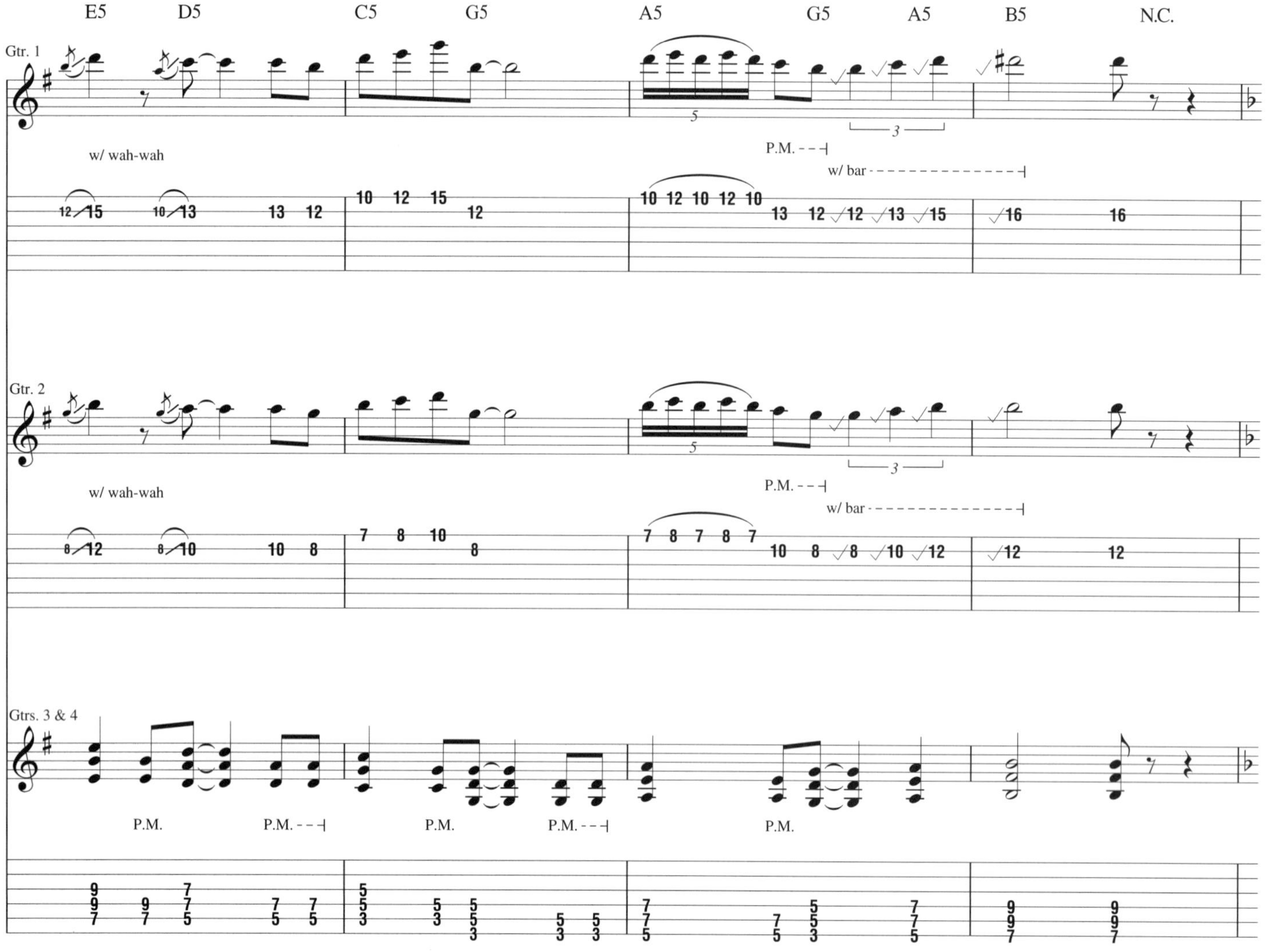

E5
D5
C5
G5
A5
G5
A5
B5
N.C.
Gtr. 1
w/ wah-wah
P.M.
w/ bar
Gtr. 2
w/ wah-wah
P.M.
w/ bar
Gtrs. 3 & 4
P.M.
P.M.
P.M.
P.M.
P.M.

Gtrs. 3 & 4: w/ Rhy. Fig. 1
D5
Gtr. 1
8va
loco
15ma
P.H.
w/ bar
-1 1/2
Gtr. 2
Pitch: G A G
-2

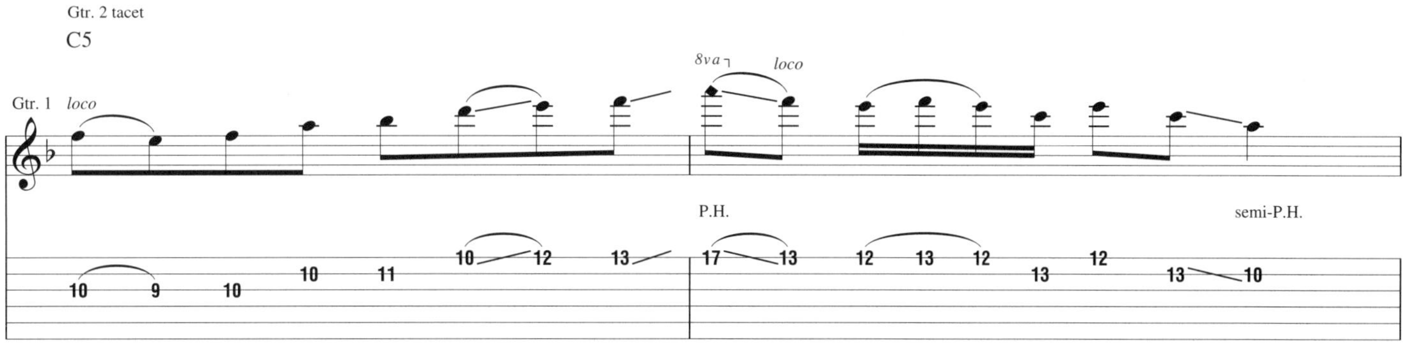
Gtr. 2 tacet
C5
Gtr. 1
loco
8va
P.H.
semi-P.H.

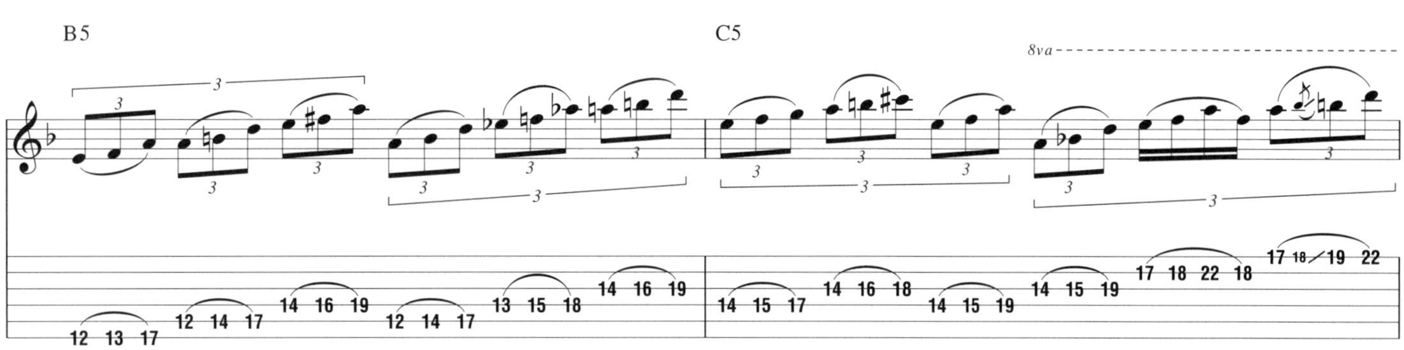
B5
C5
8va

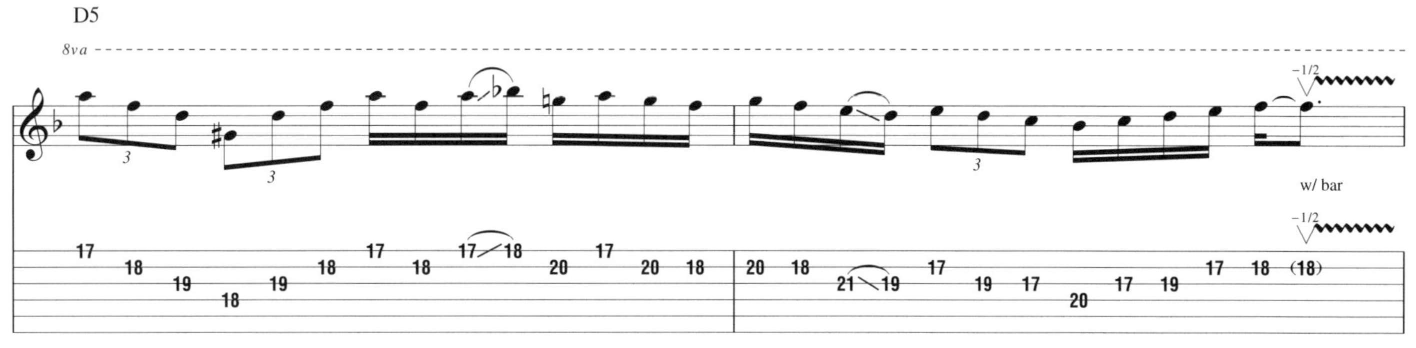
D5
8va
-1/2
w/ bar

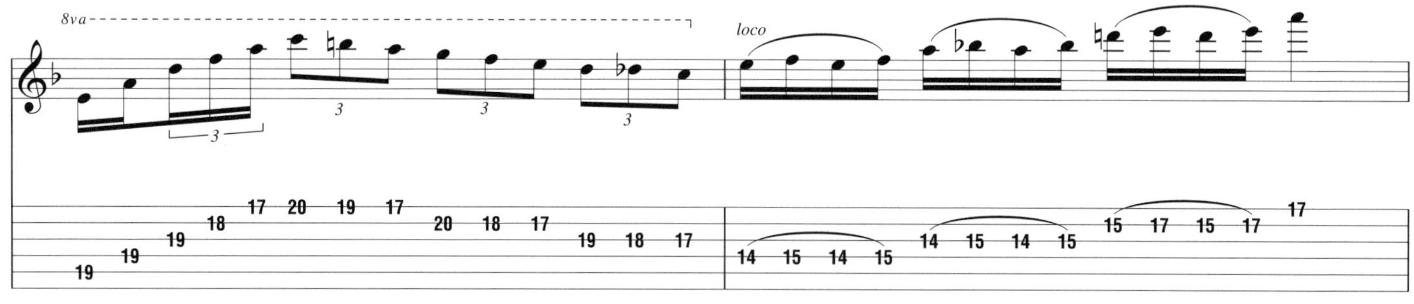
8va
loco
17 20 19 17
18
19
19
19
20 18 17
19 18 17
14 15 14 15
14 15 14 15
15 17 15 17
17

C5
8va
Gtr. 1
Tap with edge of pick
Slide with edge of pick to achieve
DigiTech Whammy Pedal effect.
22 18 17 22 18 17 22 18 17 22 18 17 X 18 17 X 18 17
17 13 17 13 17 13 17 12 17 12 17 12 X 13 12 X 13
Gtr. 2
loco
Tap with edge of pick
Slide with edge of pick to achieve
DigiTech Whammy Pedal effect.
18 15 13 18 15 13 18 15 13 18 15 13 X 15 13 X 15
13 10 8 13 10 8 13 10 8 13 10 8 X 10 8 X 10

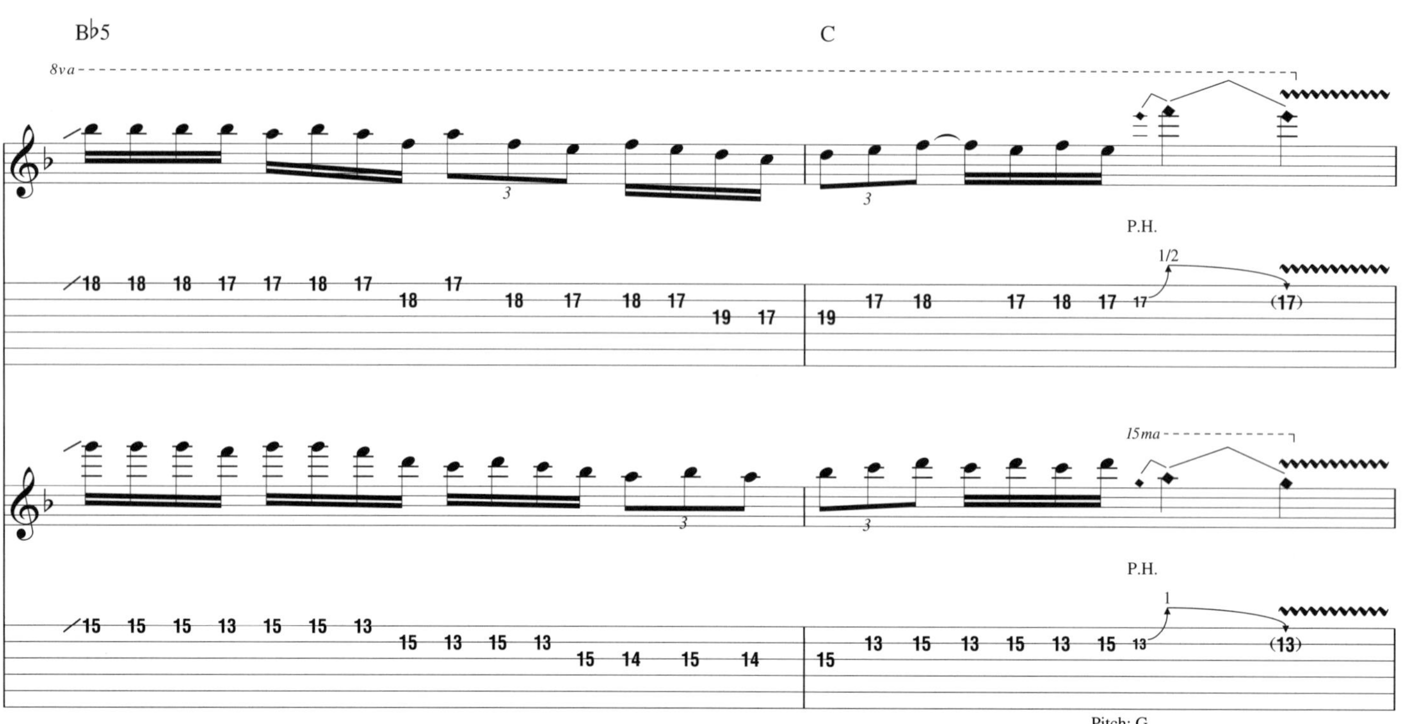
B♭5
C
8va
P.H.
1/2
18 18 18 17 17 18 17 18 17 18 17 18 17 19 17
19 17 18 17 18 17 17 (17)
15ma
P.H.
1
15 15 15 13 15 15 13 15 13 15 13 15 14 15 14
15 13 15 13 15 13 15 13 (13)
Pitch: G

Gtrs. 3 & 4: w/ Rhy. Fig. 2

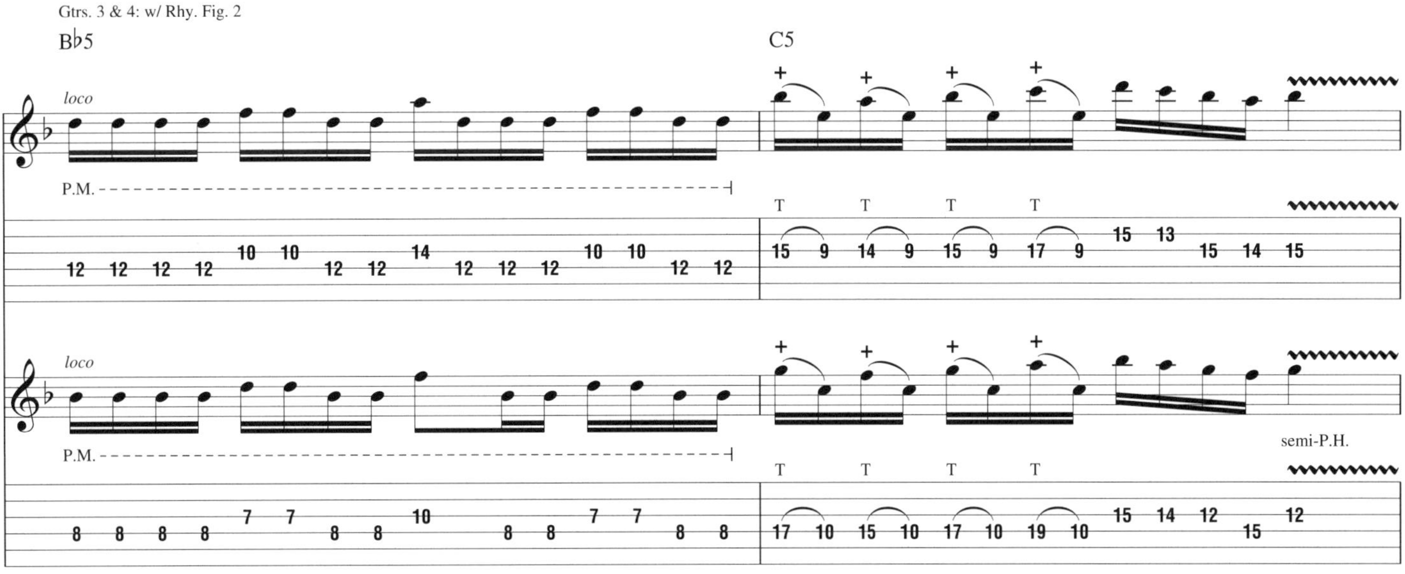

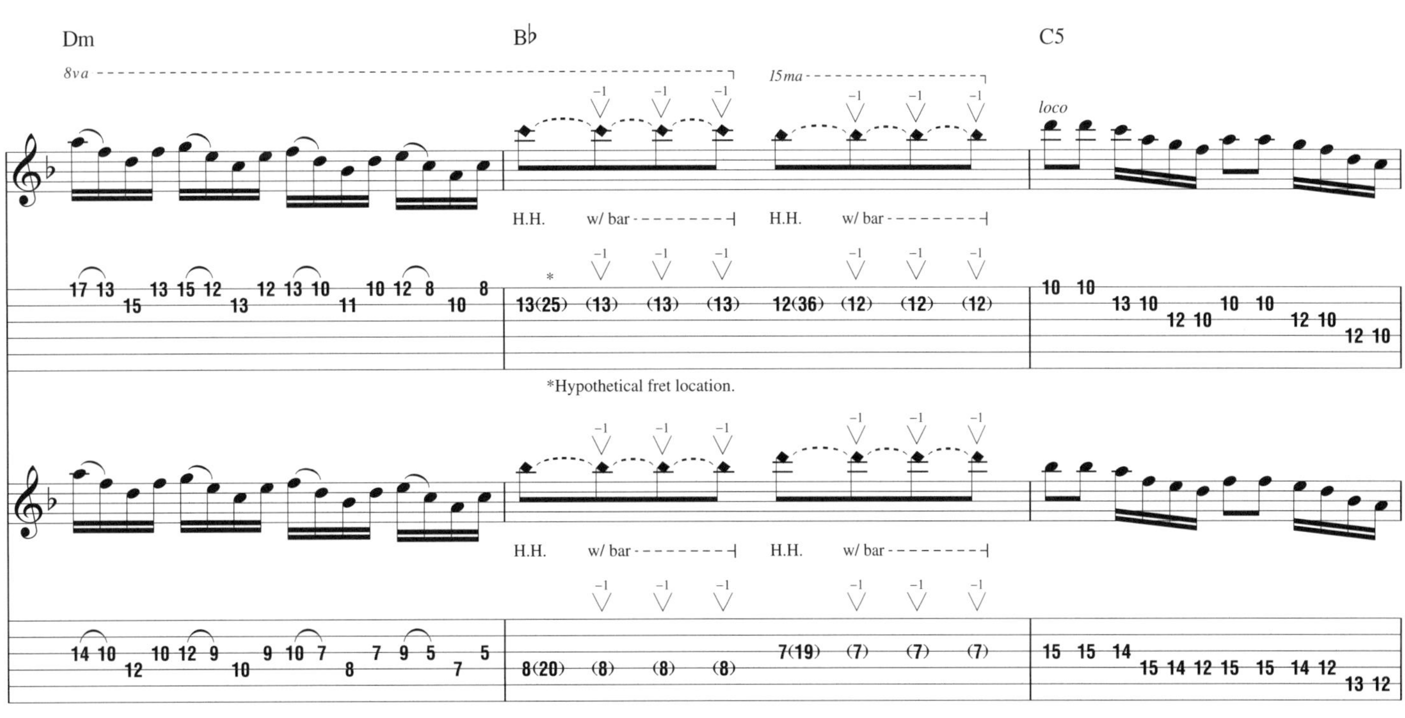

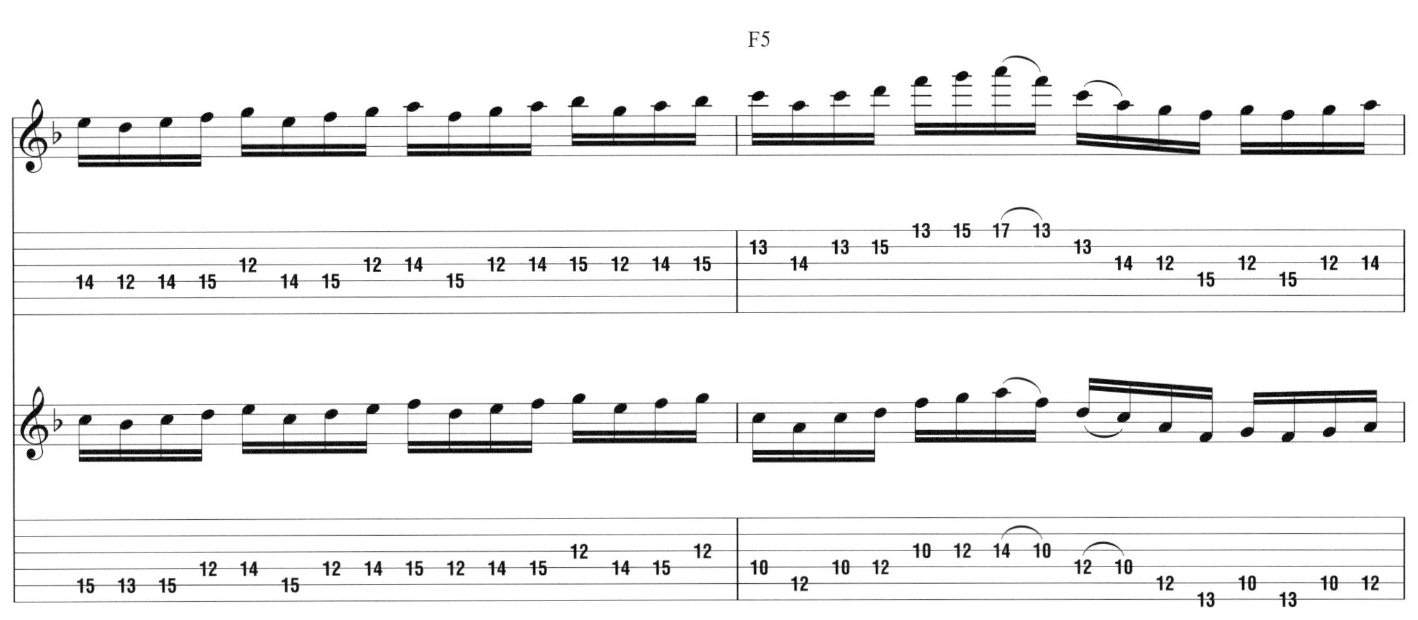

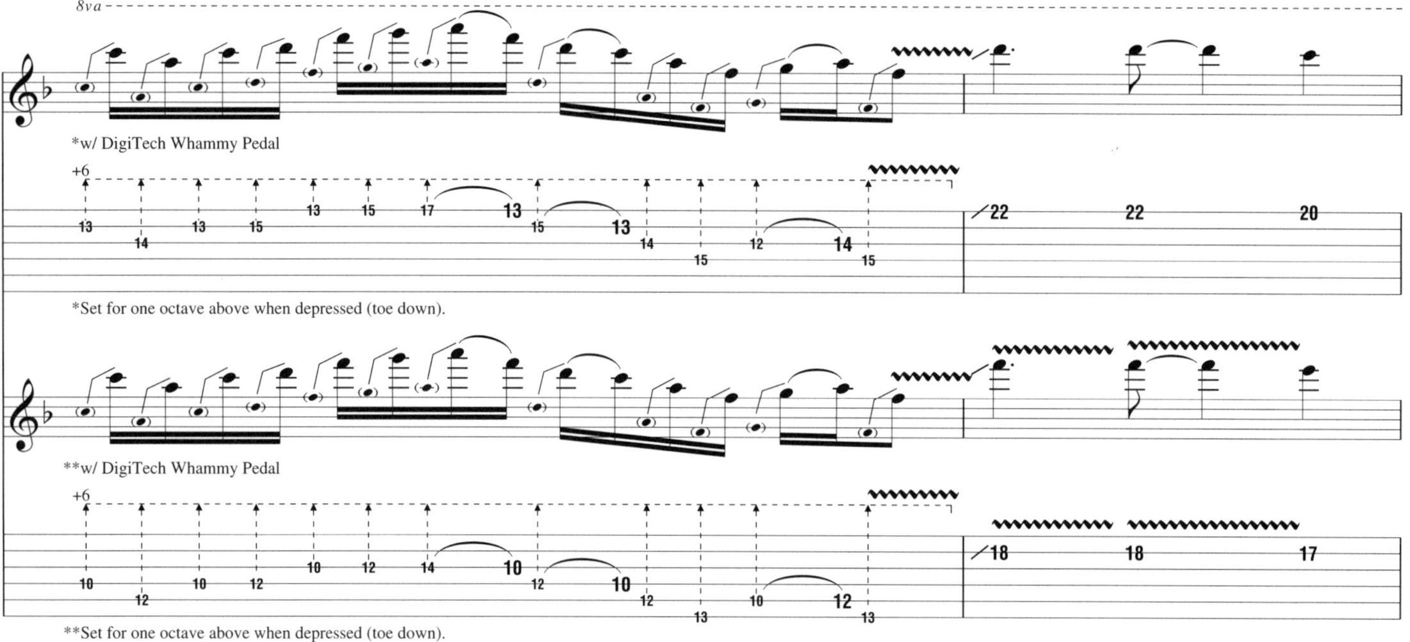
B♭5
8va
*w/ DigiTech Whammy Pedal
*Set for one octave above when depressed (toe down).
**w/ DigiTech Whammy Pedal
**Set for one octave above when depressed (toe down).

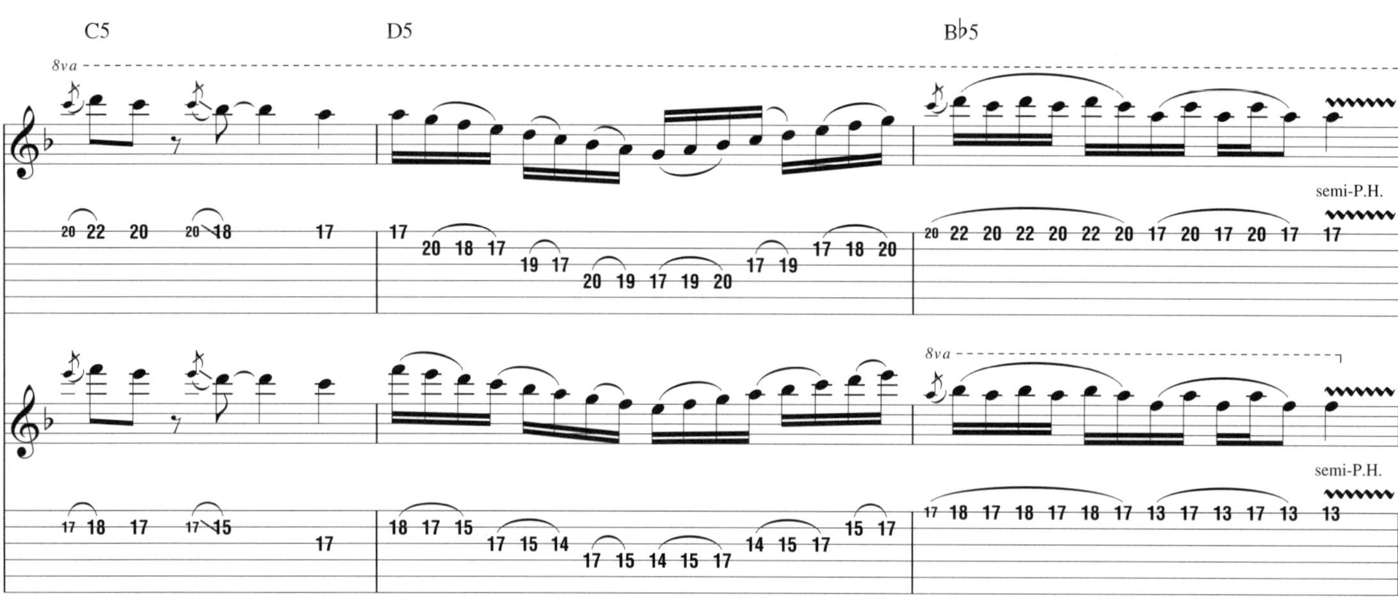
C5
D5
B♭5
8va
semi-P.H.
8va
semi-P.H.

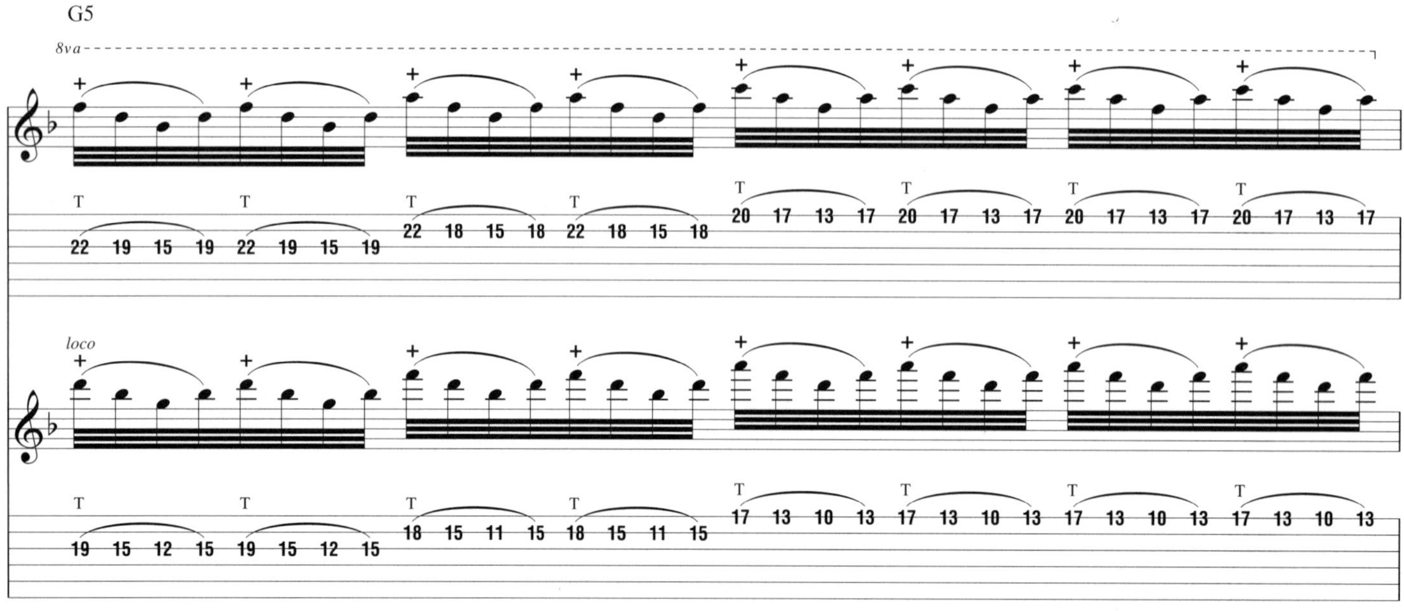
G5
8va
loco

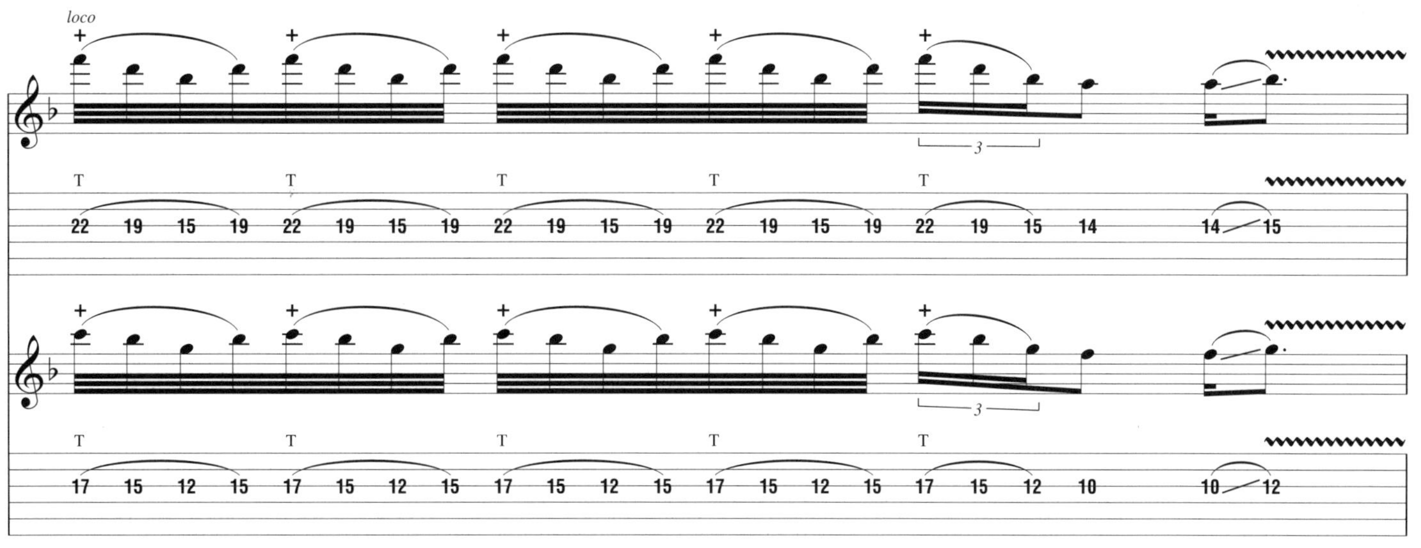

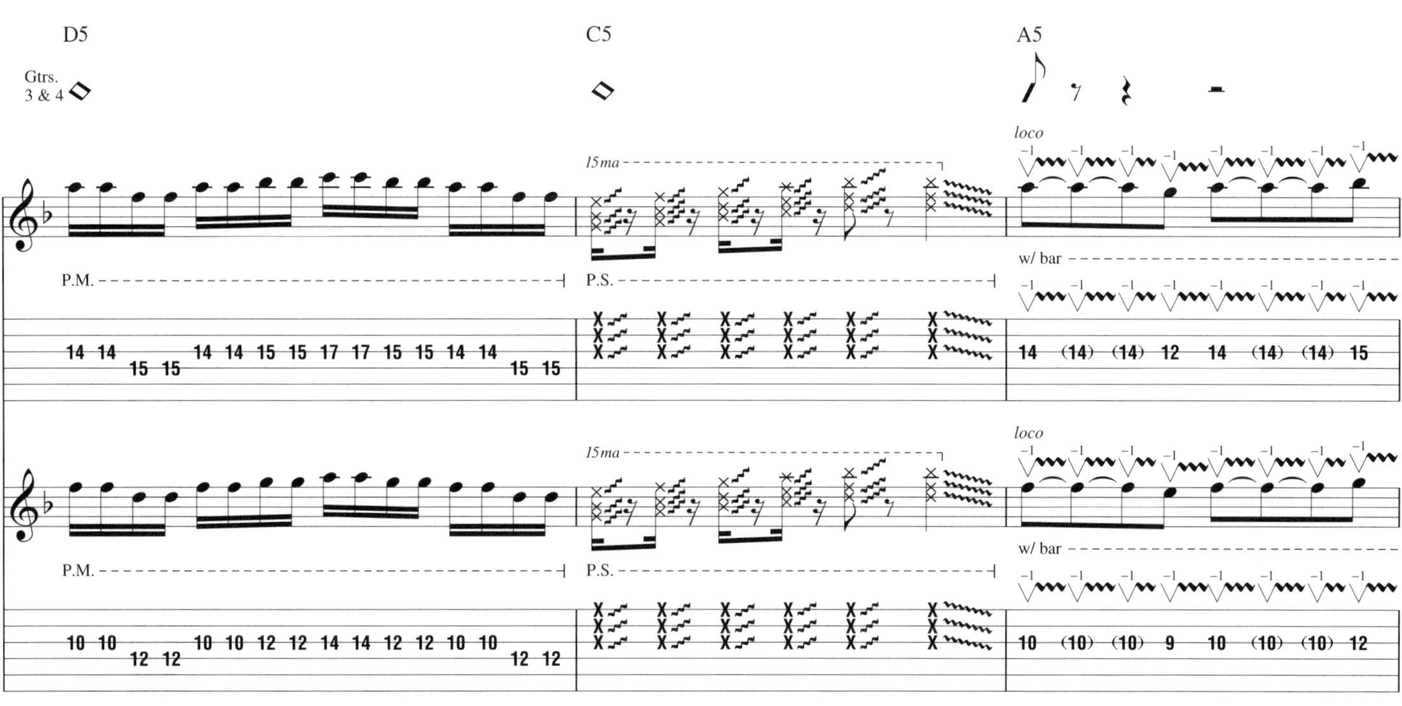

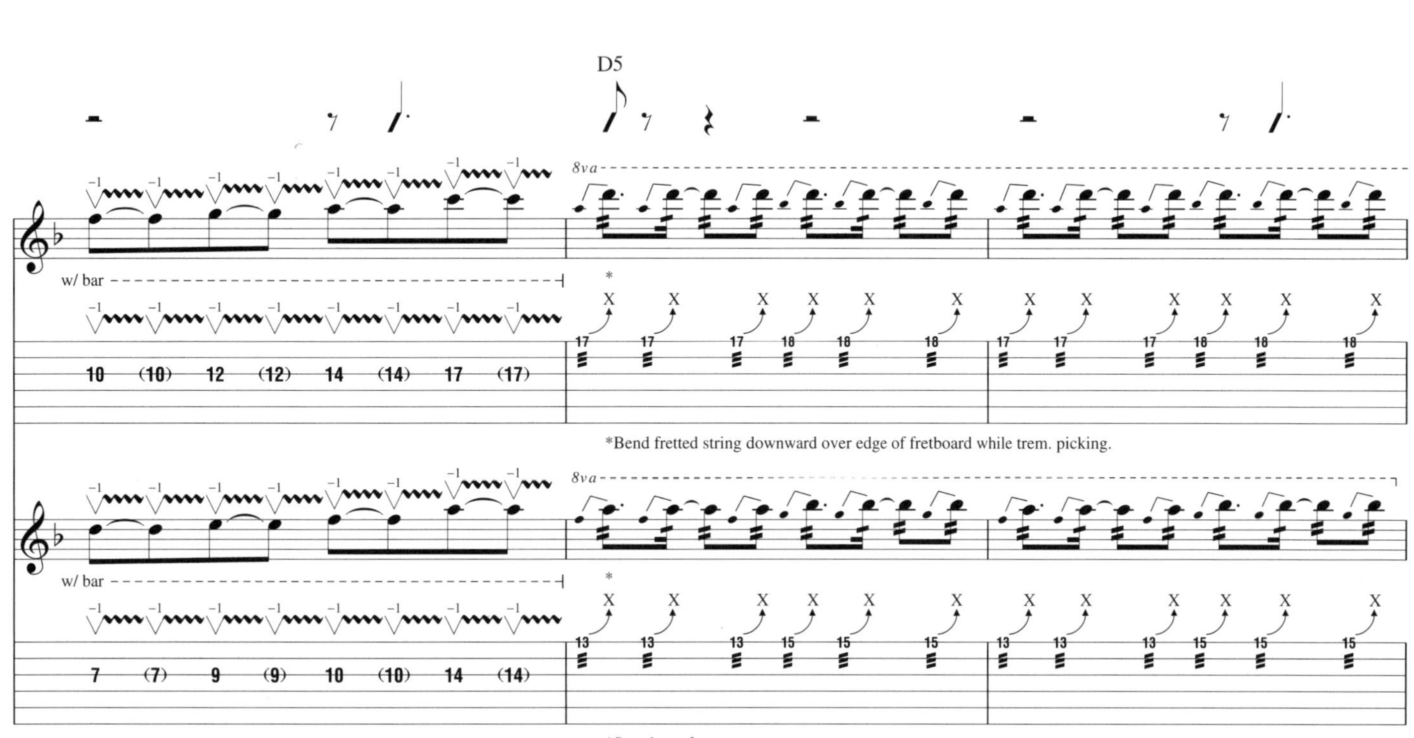

*Bend fretted string downward over edge of fretboard while trem. picking.

*See above footnote.

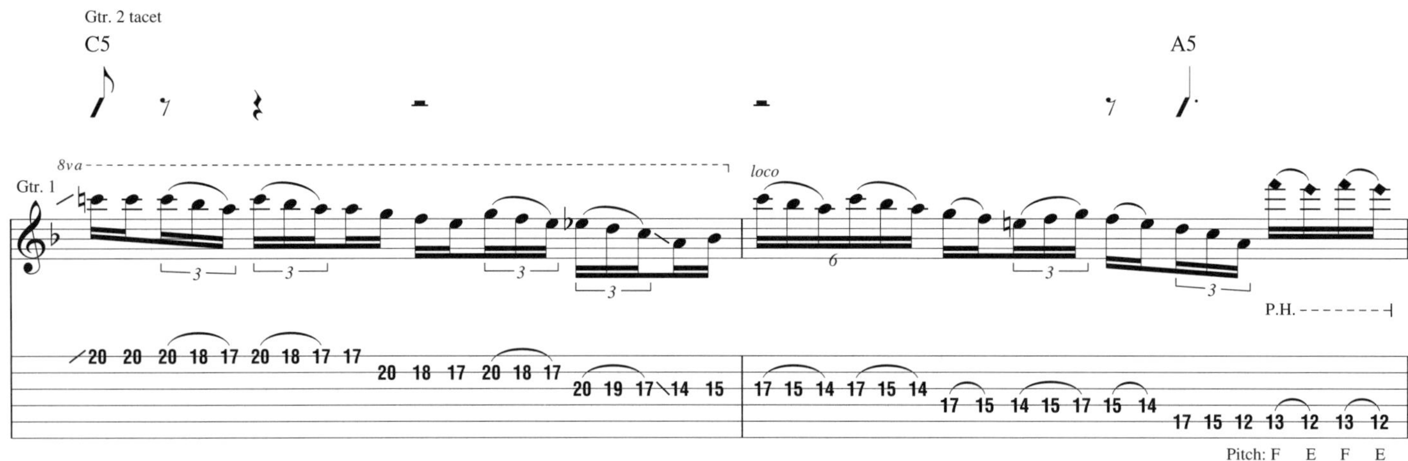
Gtr. 2 tacet
C5
A5
8va
loco
Gtr. 1
P.H.
Pitch: F E F E

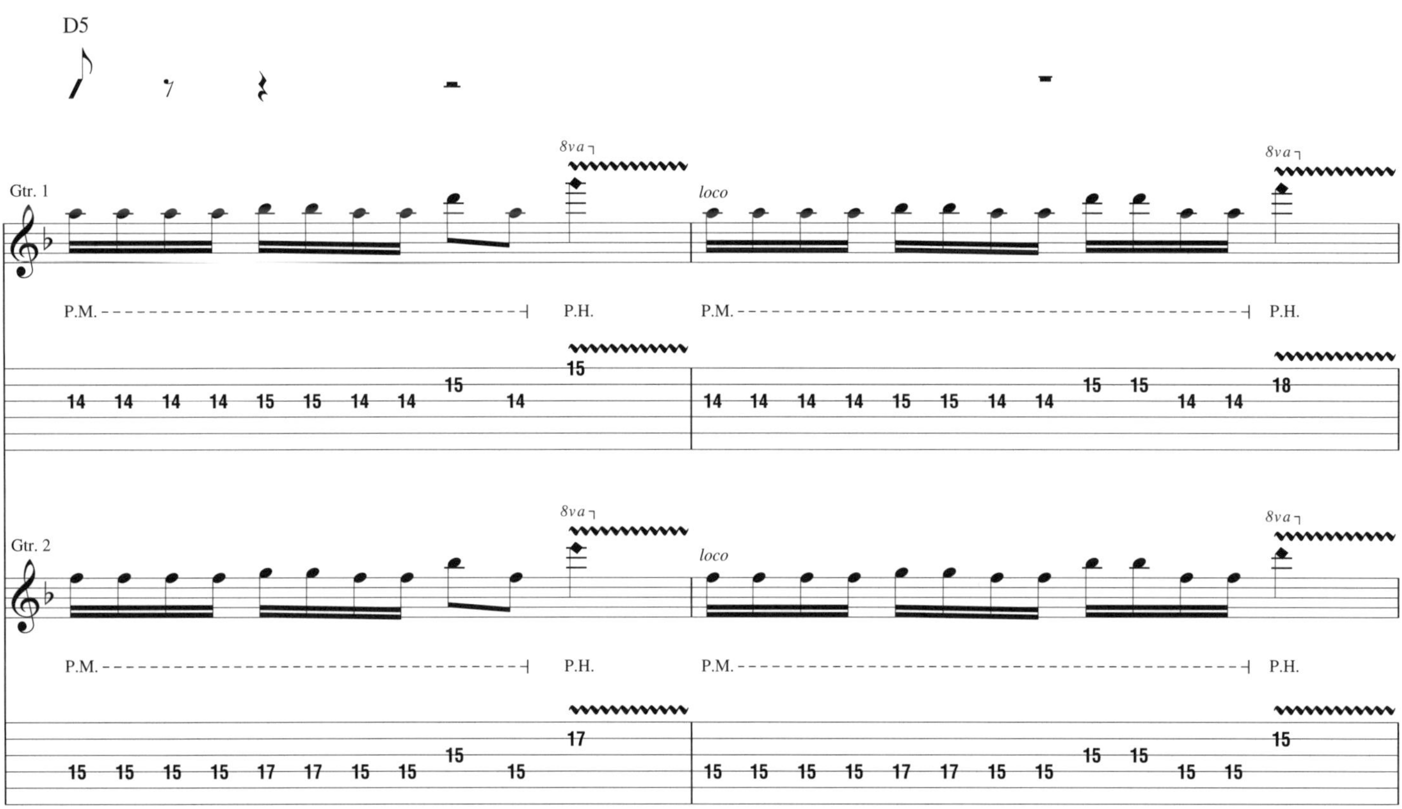
D5
8va
loco
Gtr. 1
P.M.
P.H.
Gtr. 2
P.M.
P.H.

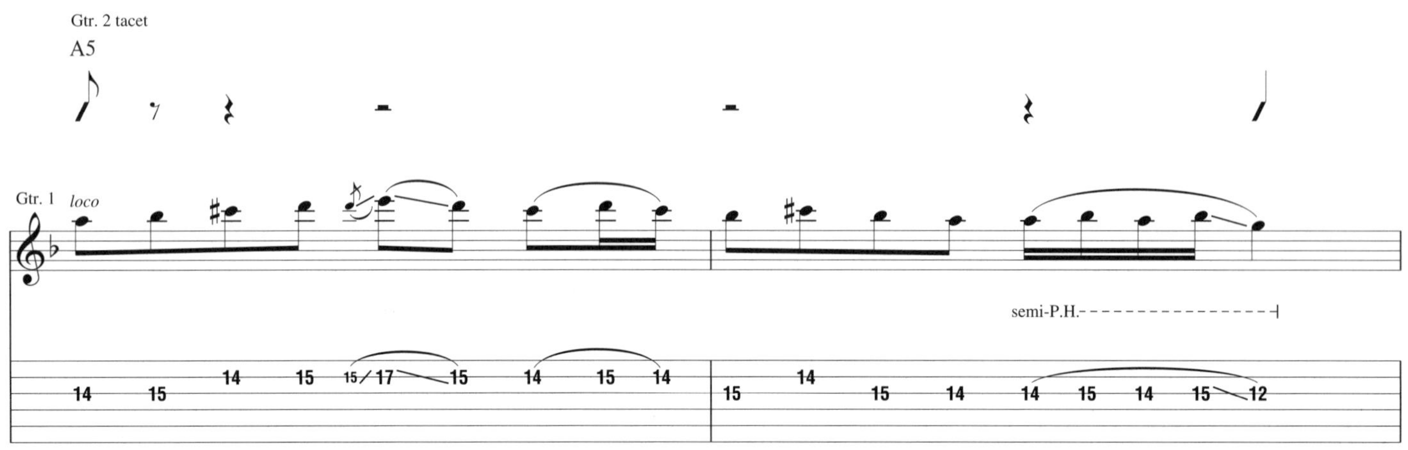
Gtr. 2 tacet
A5
Gtr. 1
loco
semi-P.H.

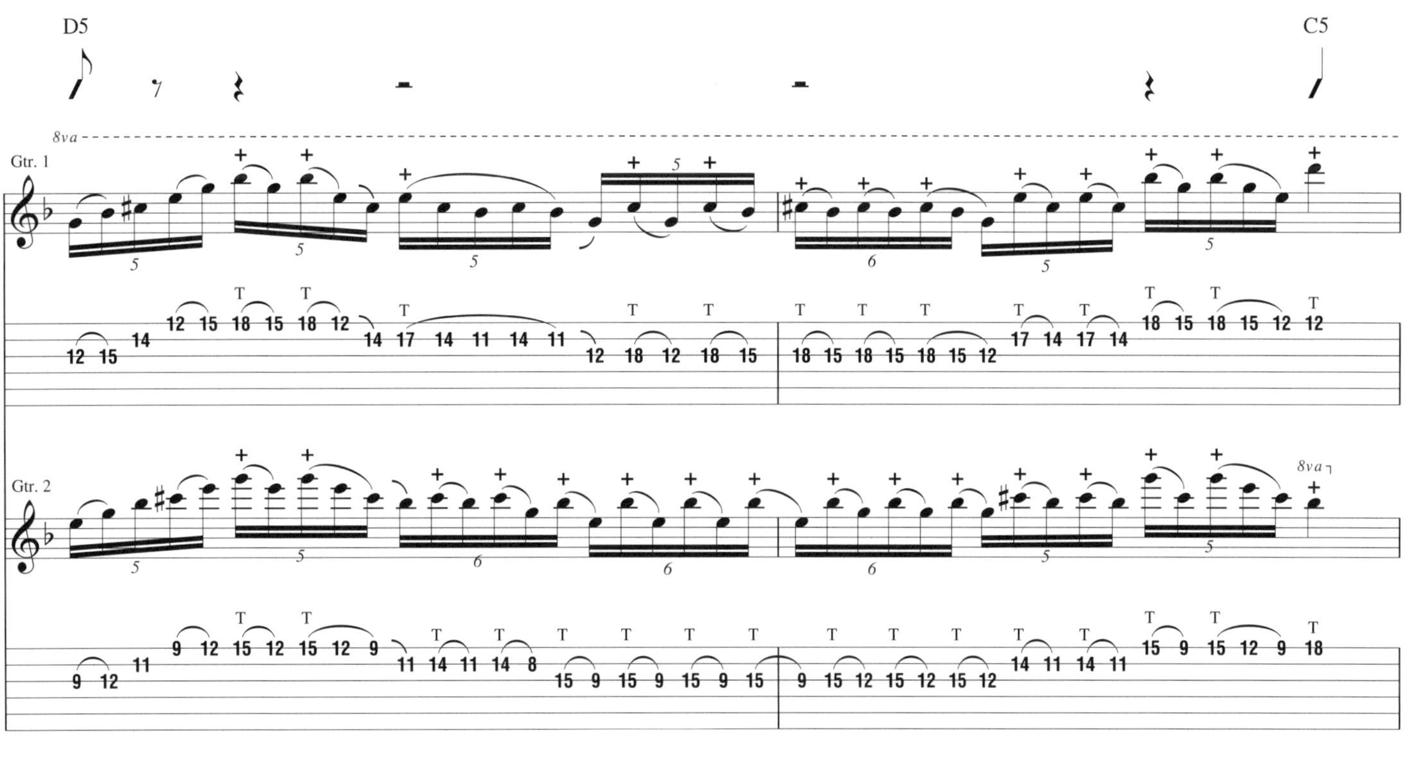
D5
C5
8va
Gtr. 1
Gtr. 2
T
+

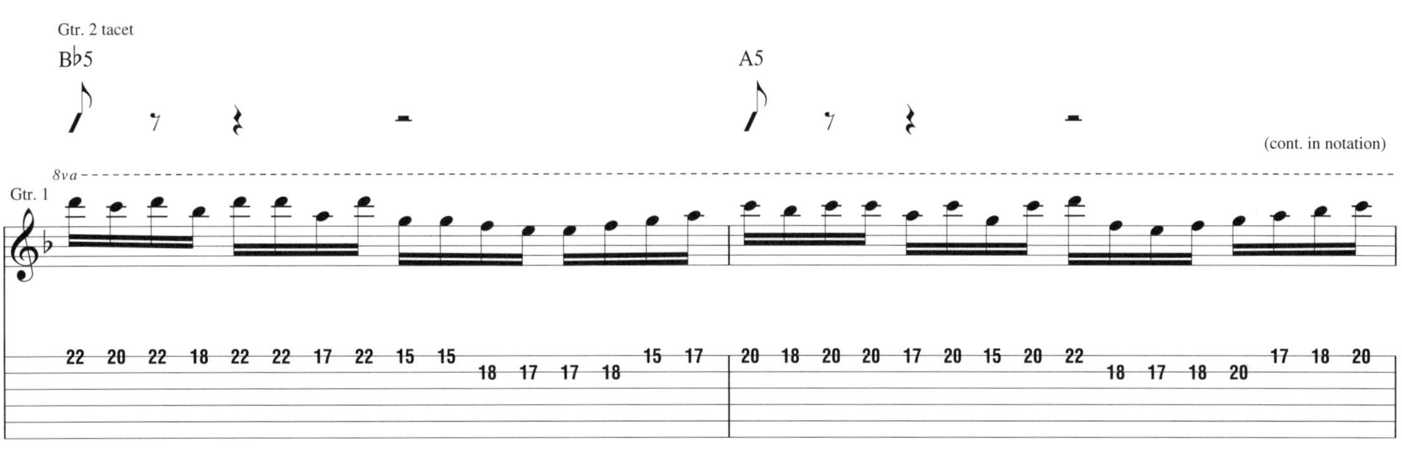
Gtr. 2 tacet
B♭5
A5
(cont. in notation)
8va
Gtr. 1

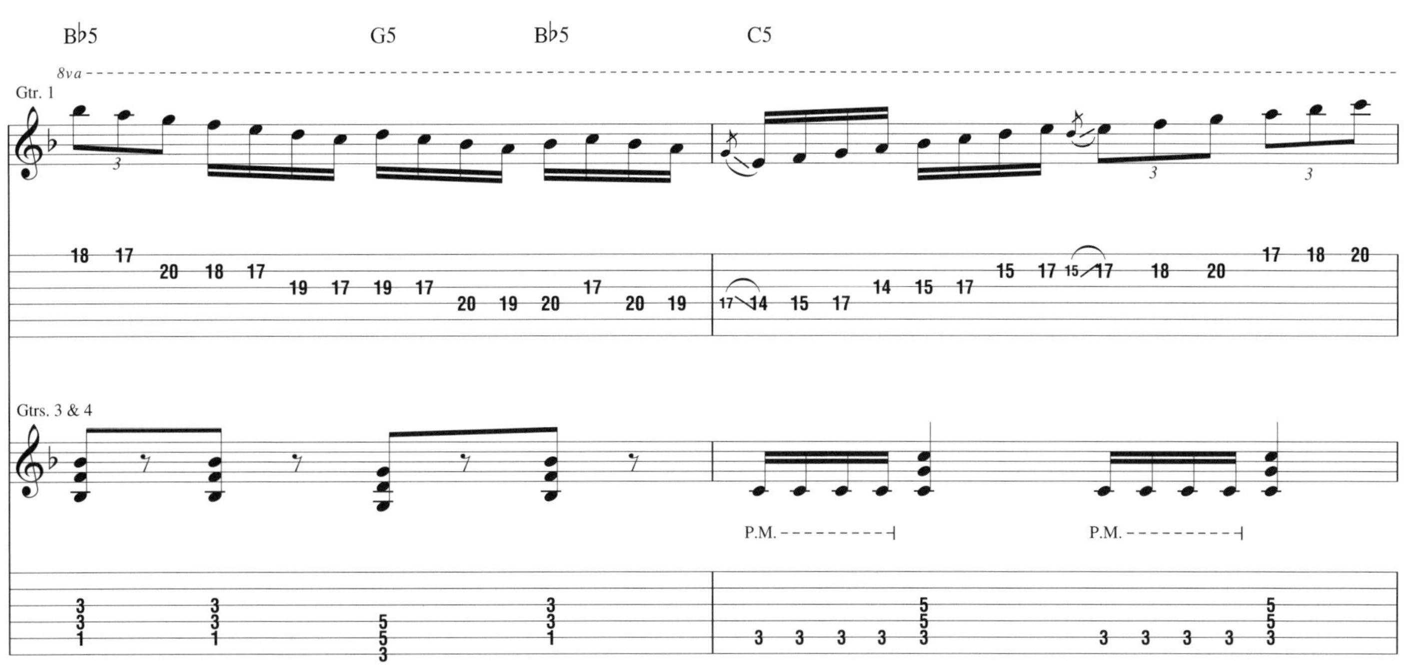
B♭5
G5
B♭5
C5
8va
Gtr. 1
Gtrs. 3 & 4
P.M.

Gtrs. 3 & 4: w/ Rhy. Fig. 3

D5

8va

Gtr. 1

Gtr. 8

Gtr. 9
divisi

wah-wah off

15ma

P.H.

Pitch: C

Gtr. 1 tacet

B♭5

C5

8va

Gtr. 8

loco

Gtr. 9

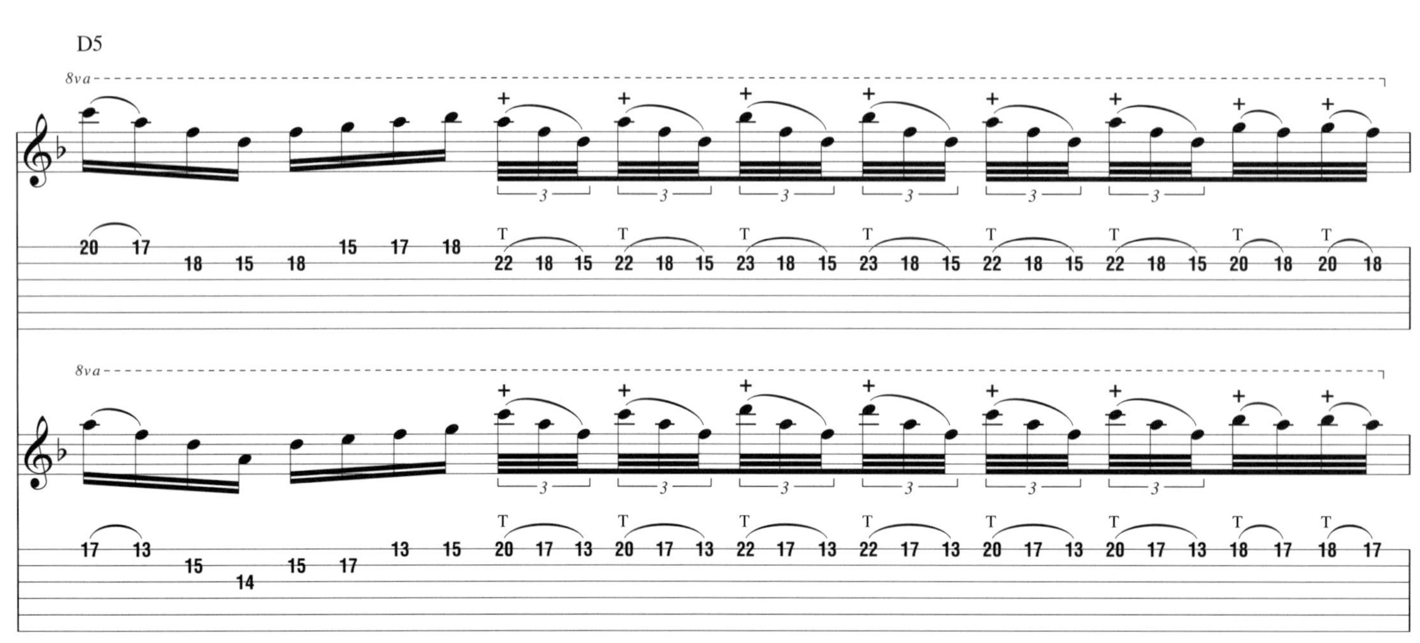

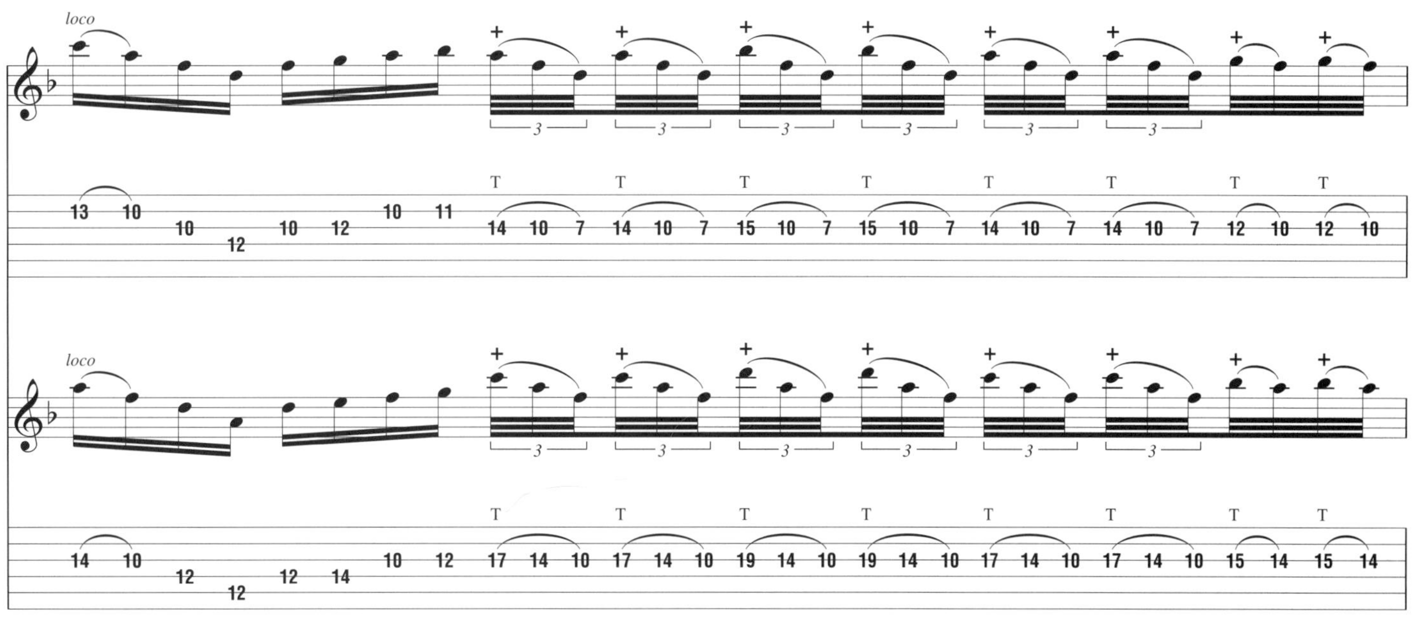
loco
T
13 10 10 12 10 12 10 11
14 10 7 14 10 7 15 10 7 15 10 7 14 10 7 14 10 7 12 10 12 10
loco
14 10 12 12 12 14 10 12
17 14 10 17 14 10 19 14 10 19 14 10 17 14 10 17 14 10 15 14 15 14

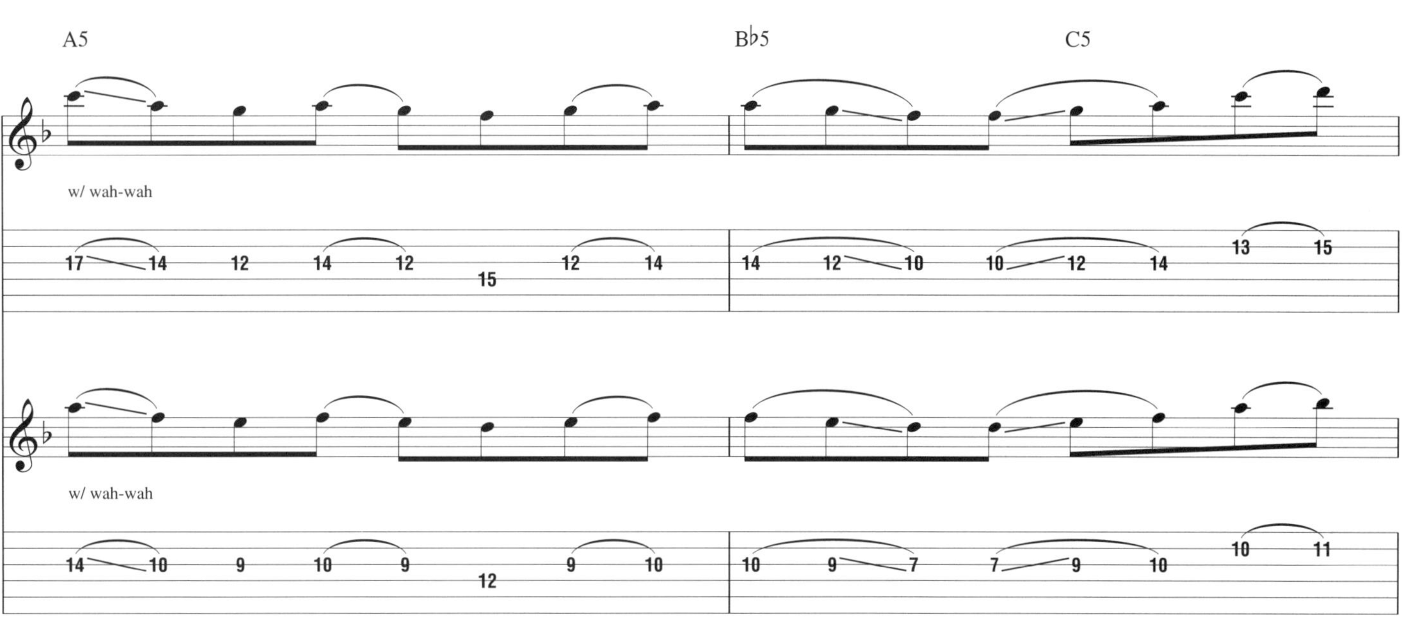
A5
B♭5
C5
w/ wah-wah
17 14 12 14 12 15 12 14
14 12 10 10 12 14 13 15
w/ wah-wah
14 10 9 10 9 12 9 10
10 9 7 7 9 10 10 11

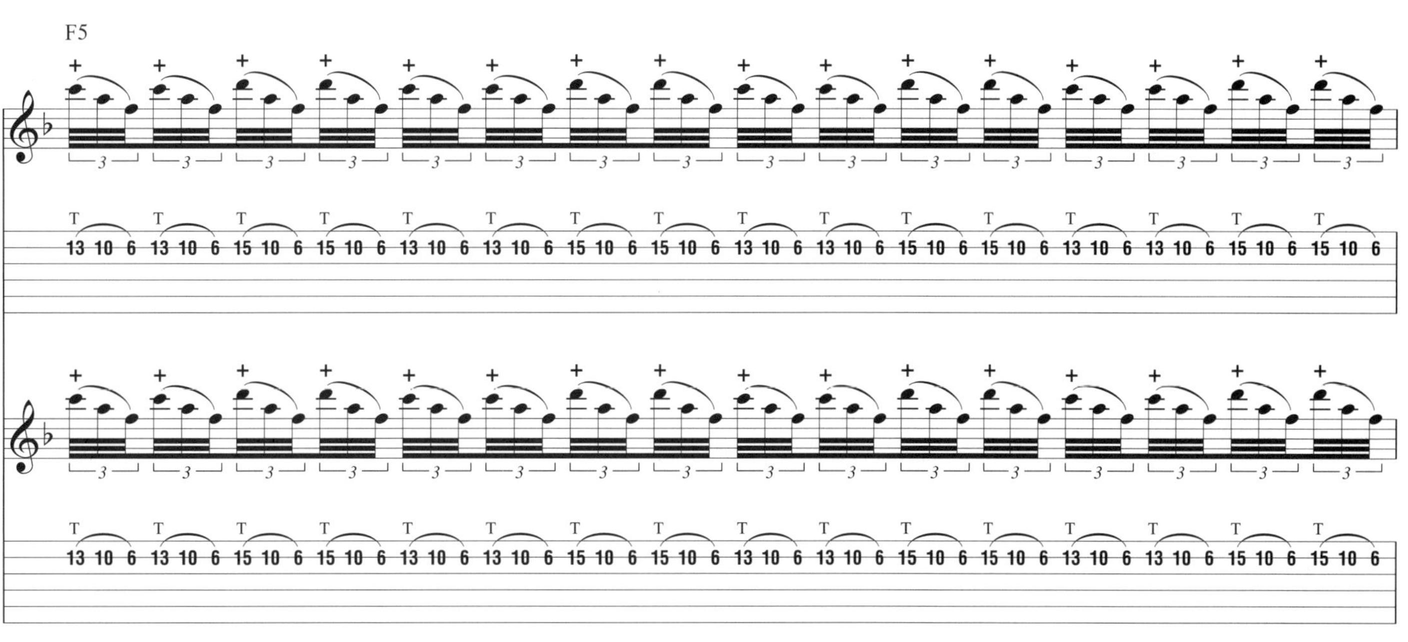
F5
T
13 10 6 13 10 6 15 10 6 15 10 6 13 10 6 13 10 6 15 10 6 15 10 6 13 10 6 13 10 6 15 10 6 15 10 6 13 10 6 13 10 6 15 10 6 15 10 6

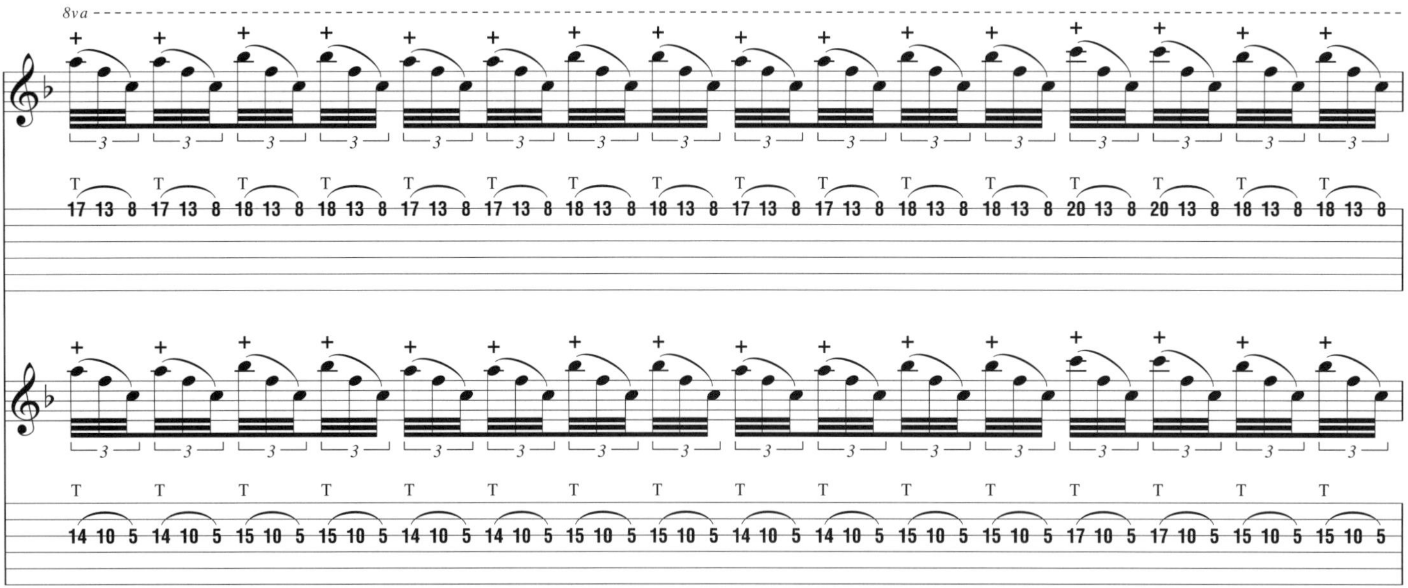

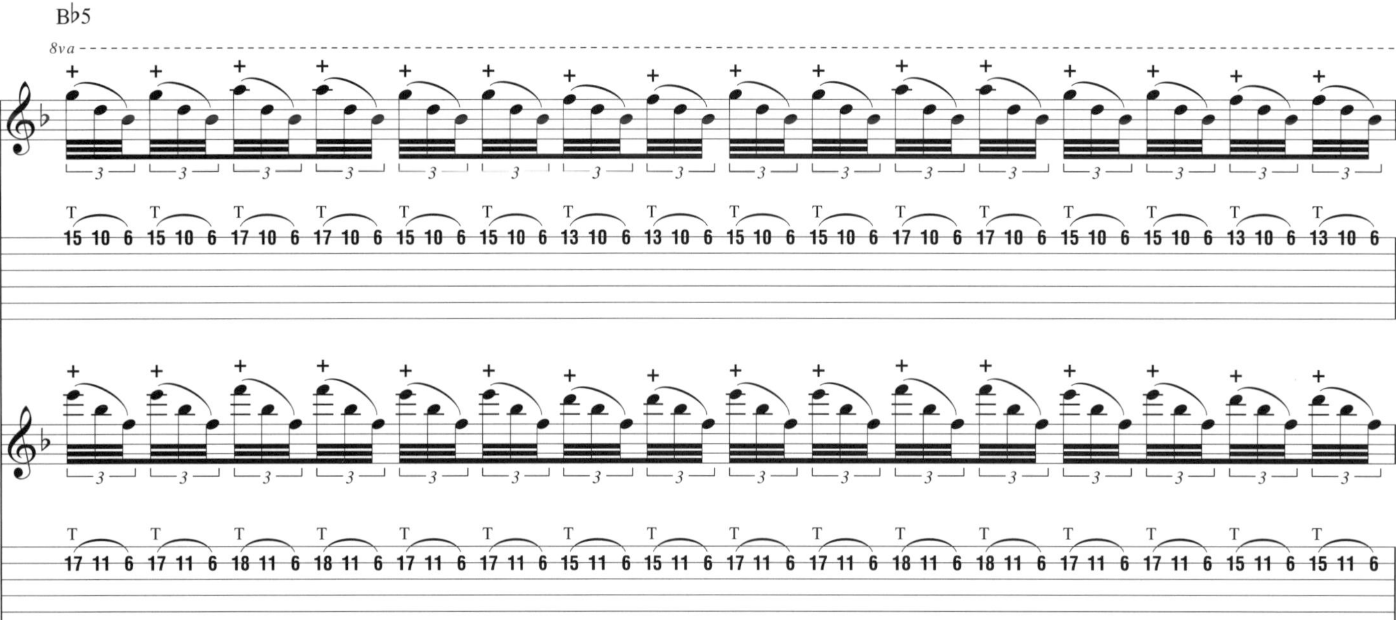

C5

8va

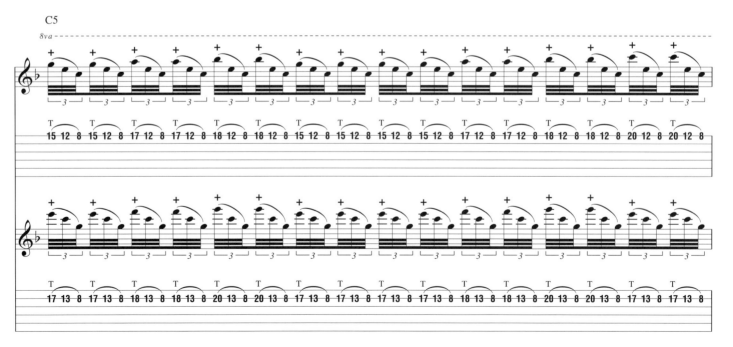

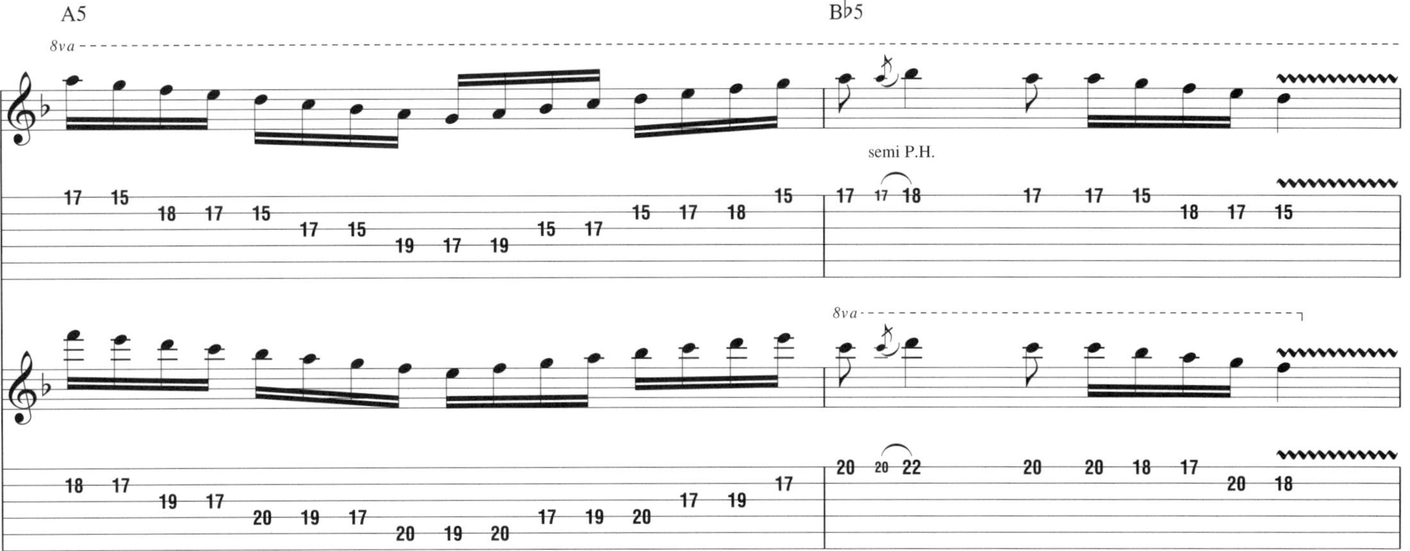
A5
B♭5
8va
semi P.H.

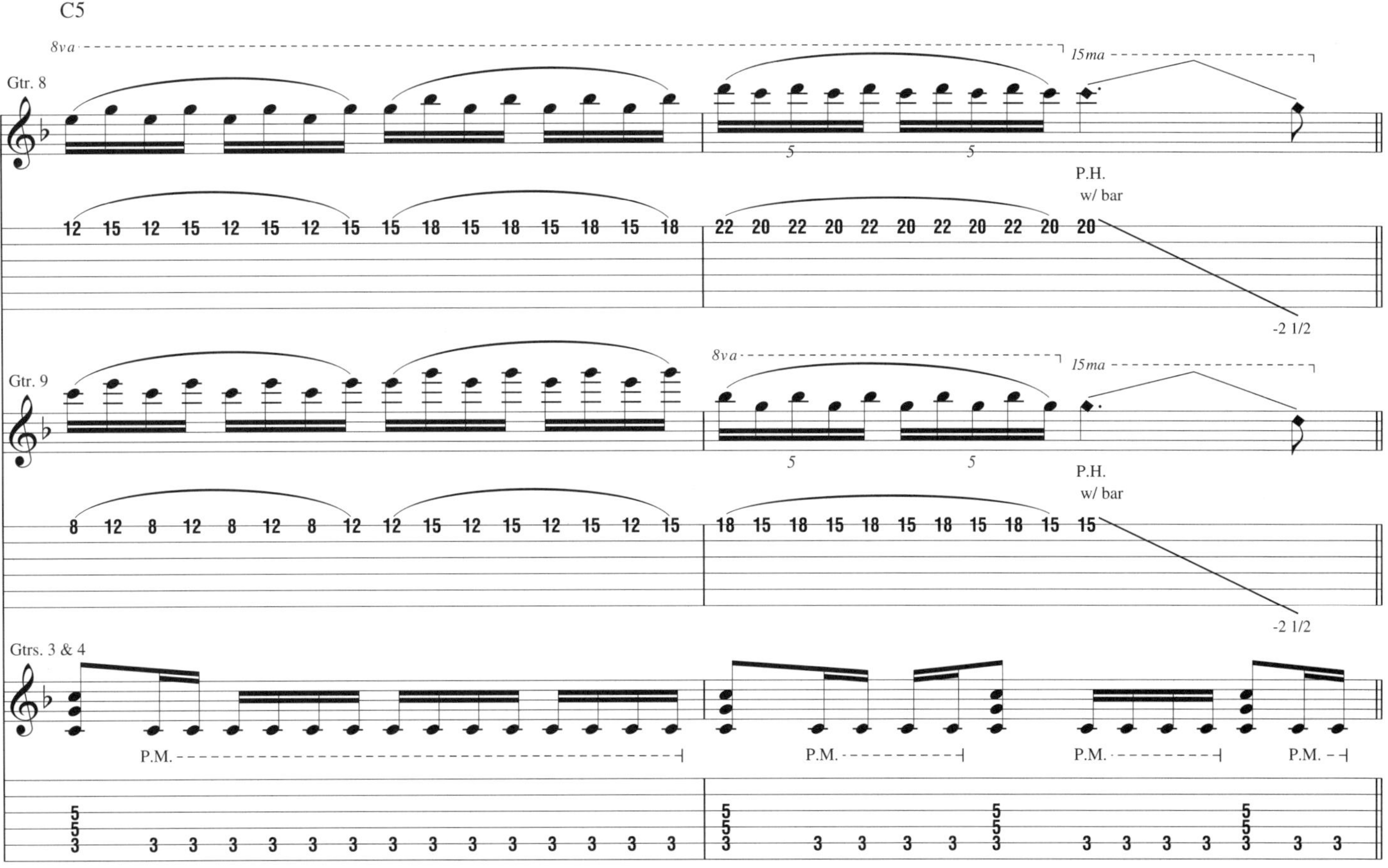
C5
8va
15ma
Gtr. 8
P.H.
w/ bar
-2 1/2
Gtr. 9
P.H.
w/ bar
-2 1/2
Gtrs. 3 & 4
P.M.

Interlude

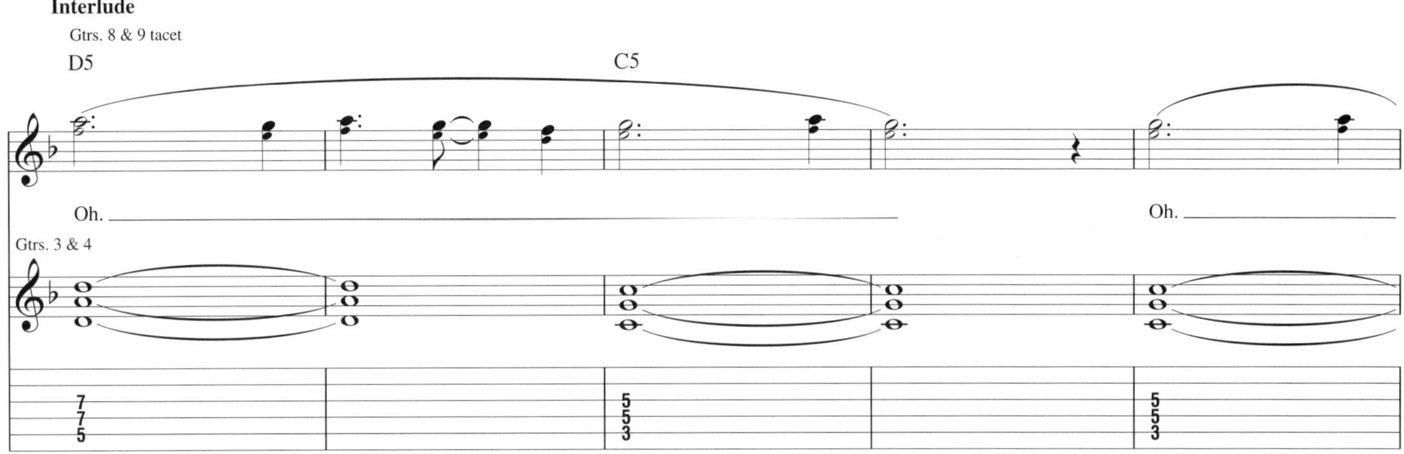
Gtrs. 8 & 9 tacet
D5
C5
Oh.
Oh.
Gtrs. 3 & 4

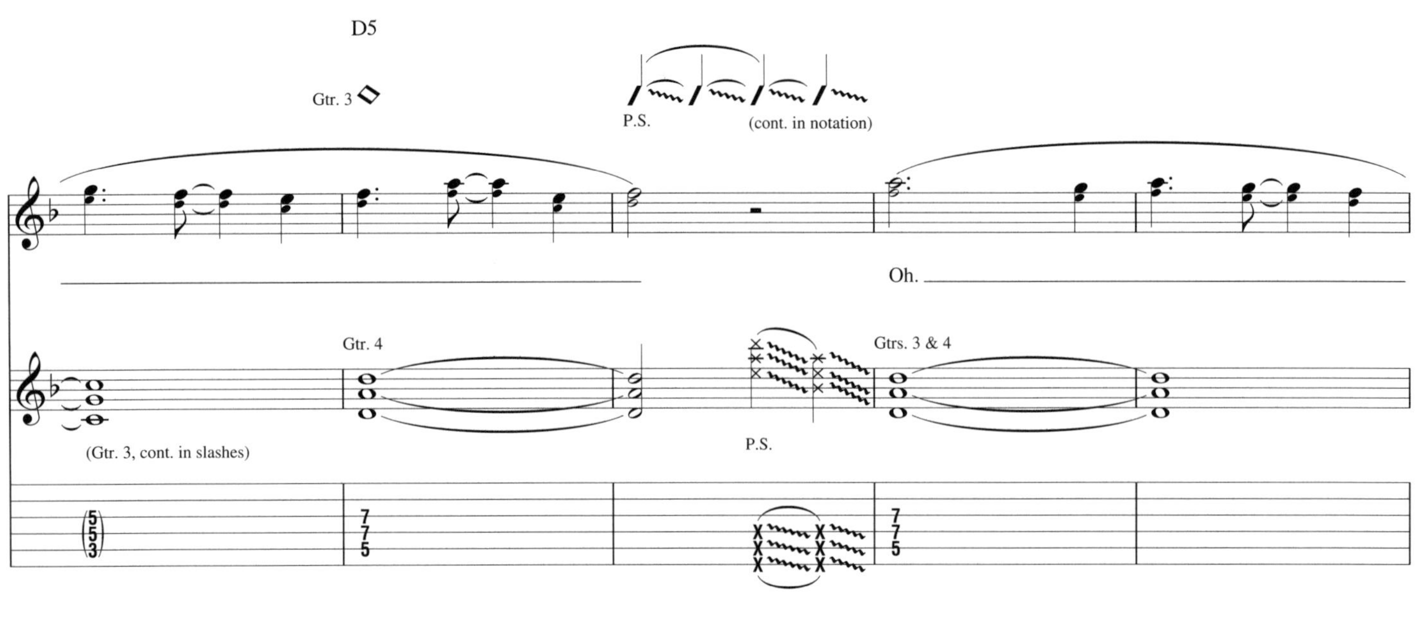
D5
Gtr. 3
P.S.
(cont. in notation)
Oh.
Gtr. 4
P.S.
Gtrs. 3 & 4
(Gtr. 3, cont. in slashes)

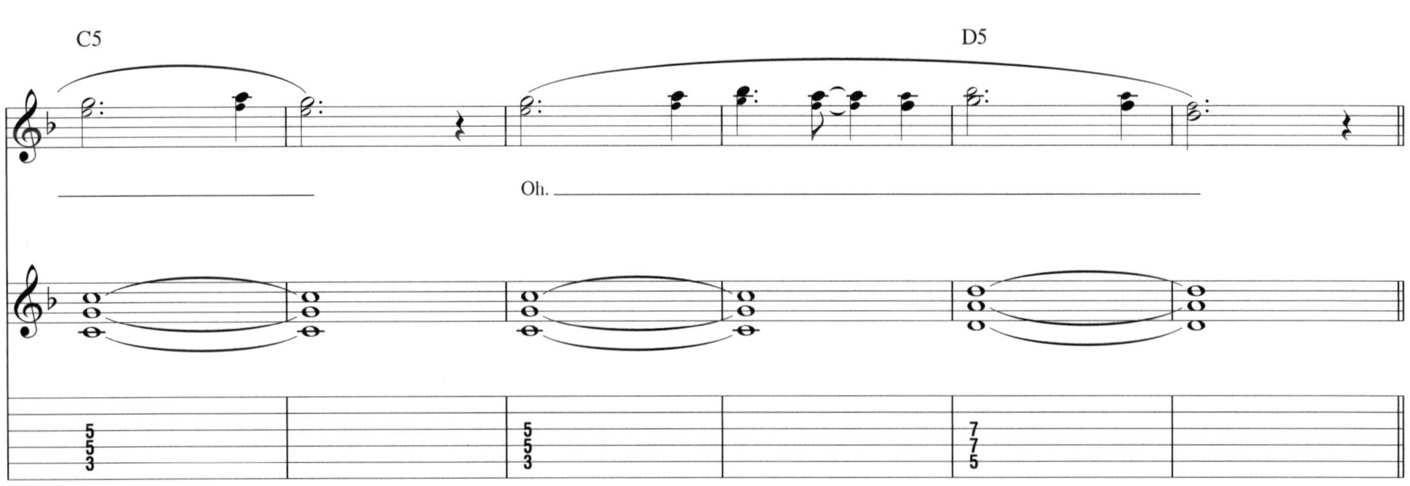
C5
D5
Oh.

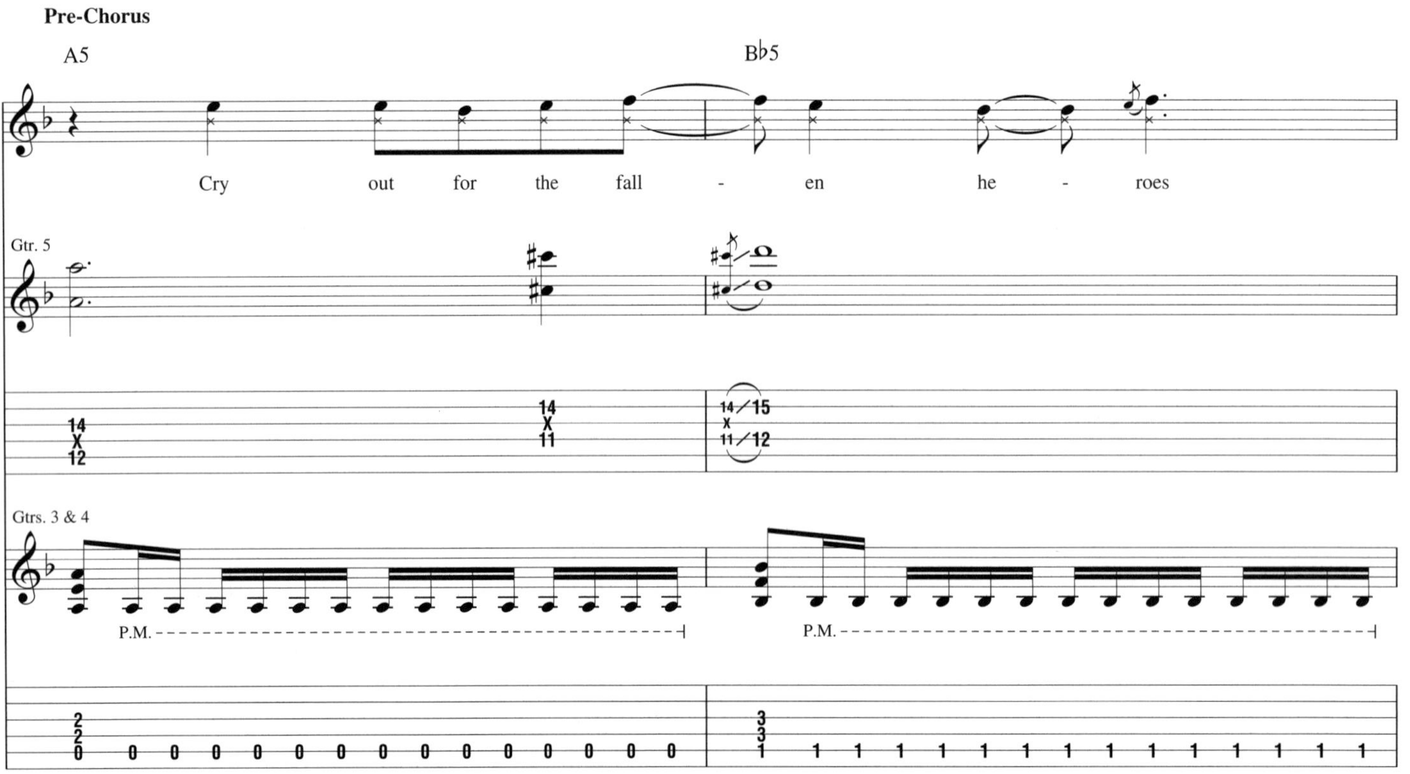
Pre-Chorus
A5
B♭5
Cry out for the fall - en he - roes
Gtr. 5
Gtrs. 3 & 4
P.M.
P.M.

Gtr. 5: w/ Riff A
D5
C5
lost in time a - go. In our
Gtr. 4
P.M.
Gtr. 3
P.M.
B♭5
A5
B♭5 N.C.
minds they still be - long when the sands of time are gone.
Gtrs. 3 & 4
Chorus
Gtrs. 3 & 4: w/ Rhy. Fig. 3
D5
B♭5
Rise o - ver shad - ow moun - tains, blaz - ing with
(Ah, blaz - ing with
C5
D5
A5
pow - er. Cross - ing val - leys, end - less tears, in u - ni - ty we
pow - er. Ah, in u - ni - ty we
B♭5
C5
F5
stand. Far and wide a - cross the land, the
stand. Ah,

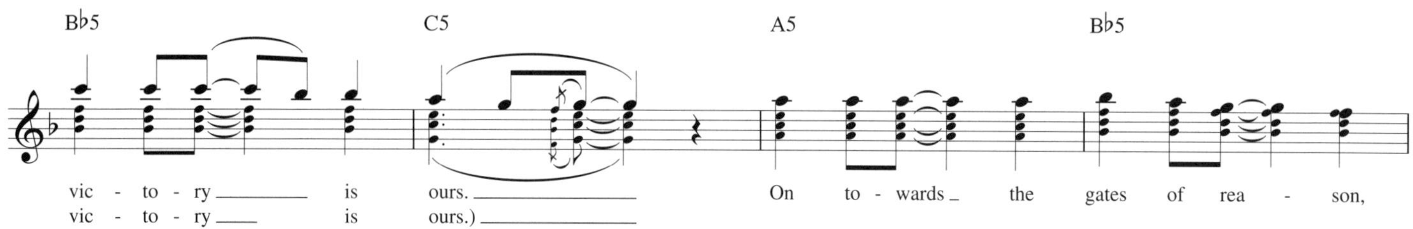

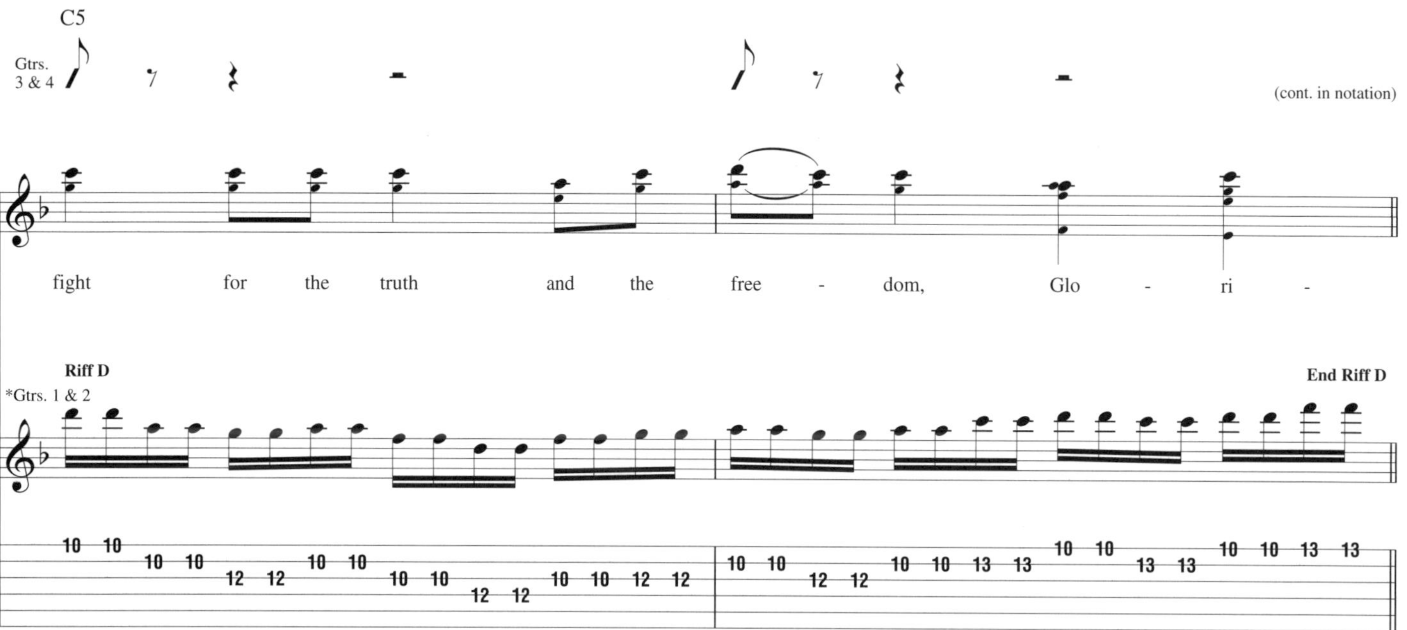

*Gtr. 1 w/ DigiTech Whammy Pedal, toe down.

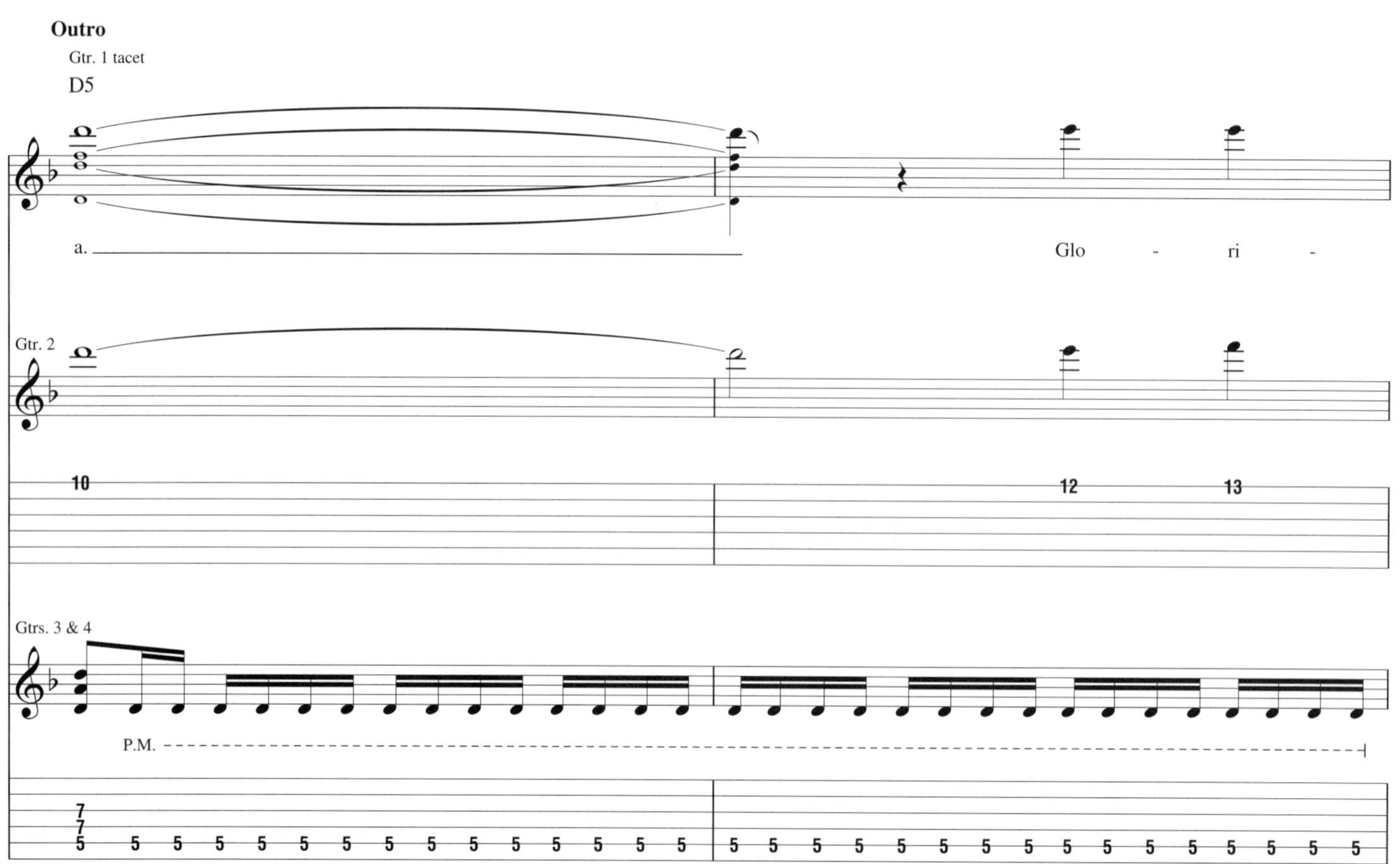

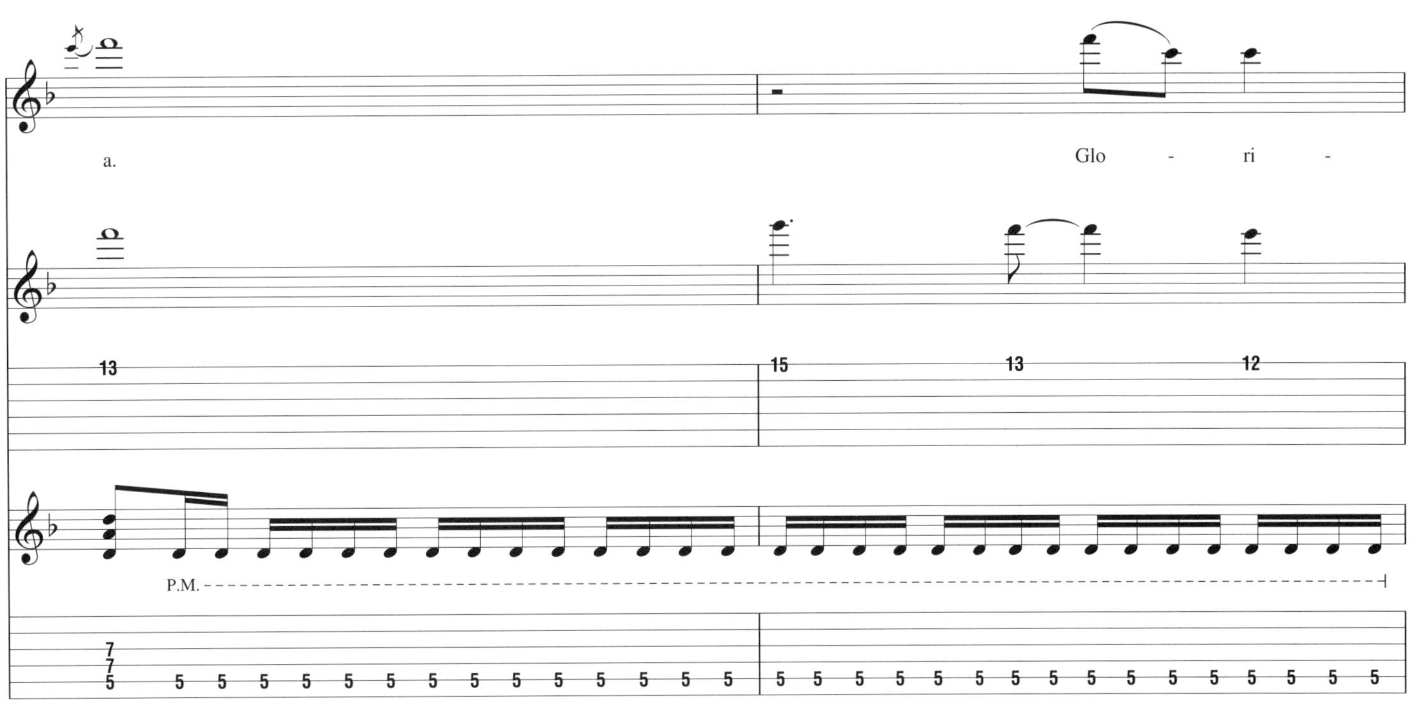
a.
Glo - ri -
P.M.

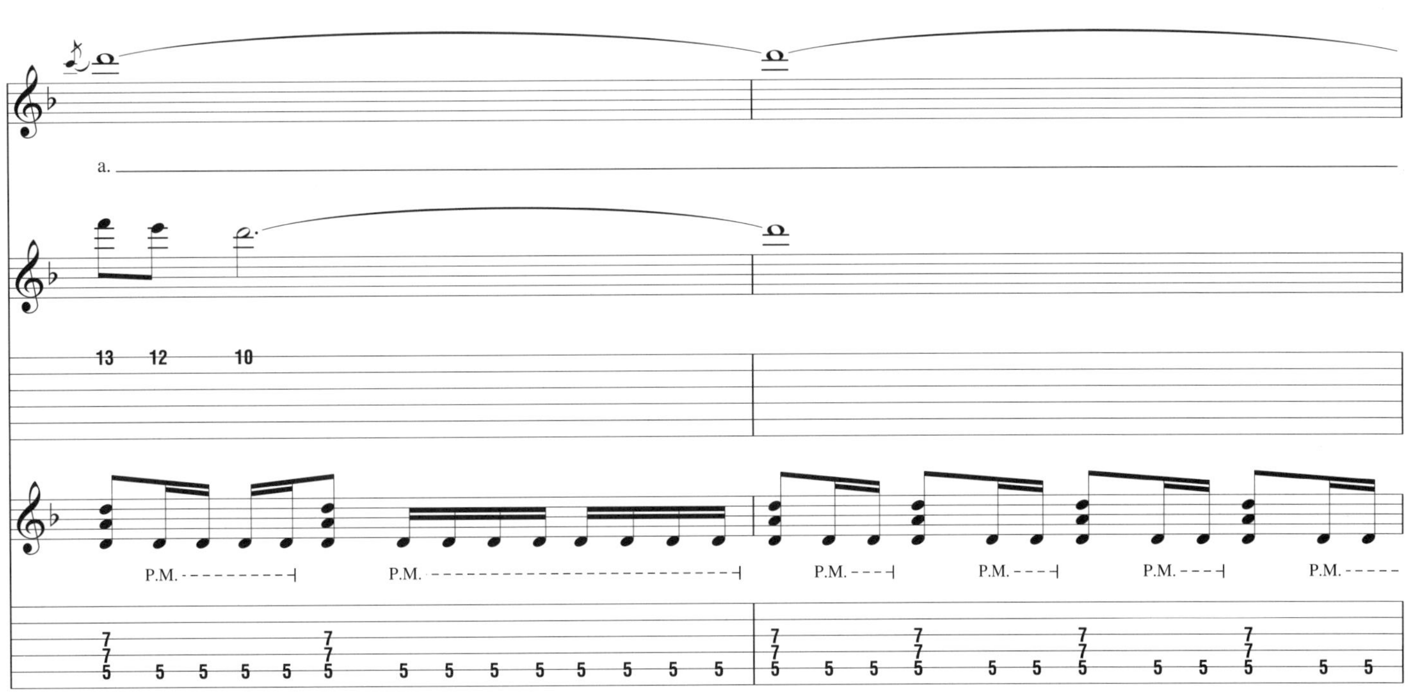
a.
P.M.
P.M.
P.M.
P.M.
P.M.
P.M.

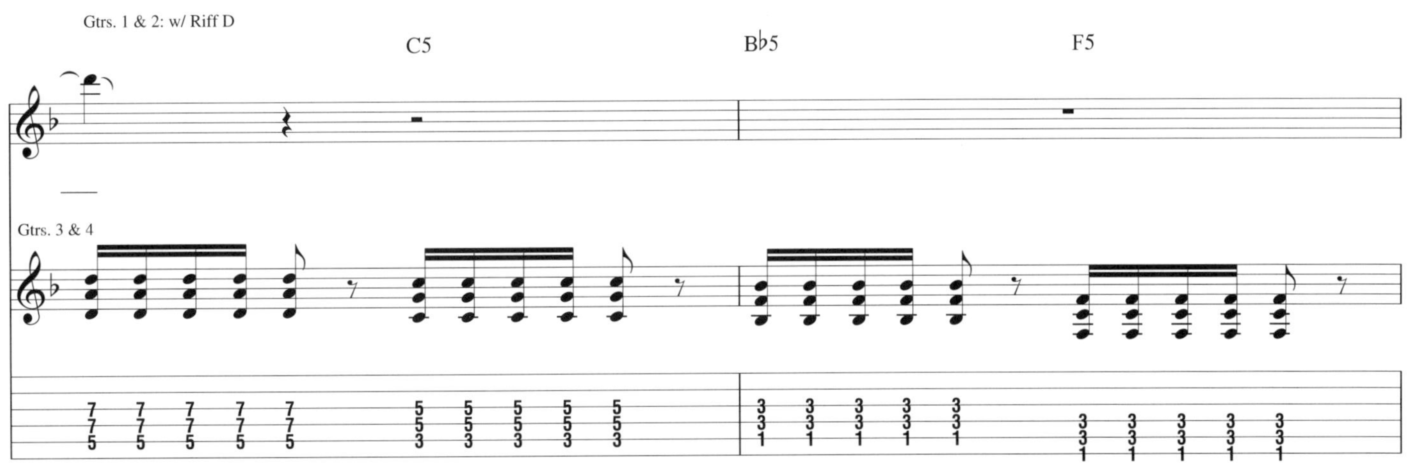
Gtrs. 1 & 2: w/ Riff D
C5
B♭5
F5
Gtrs. 3 & 4

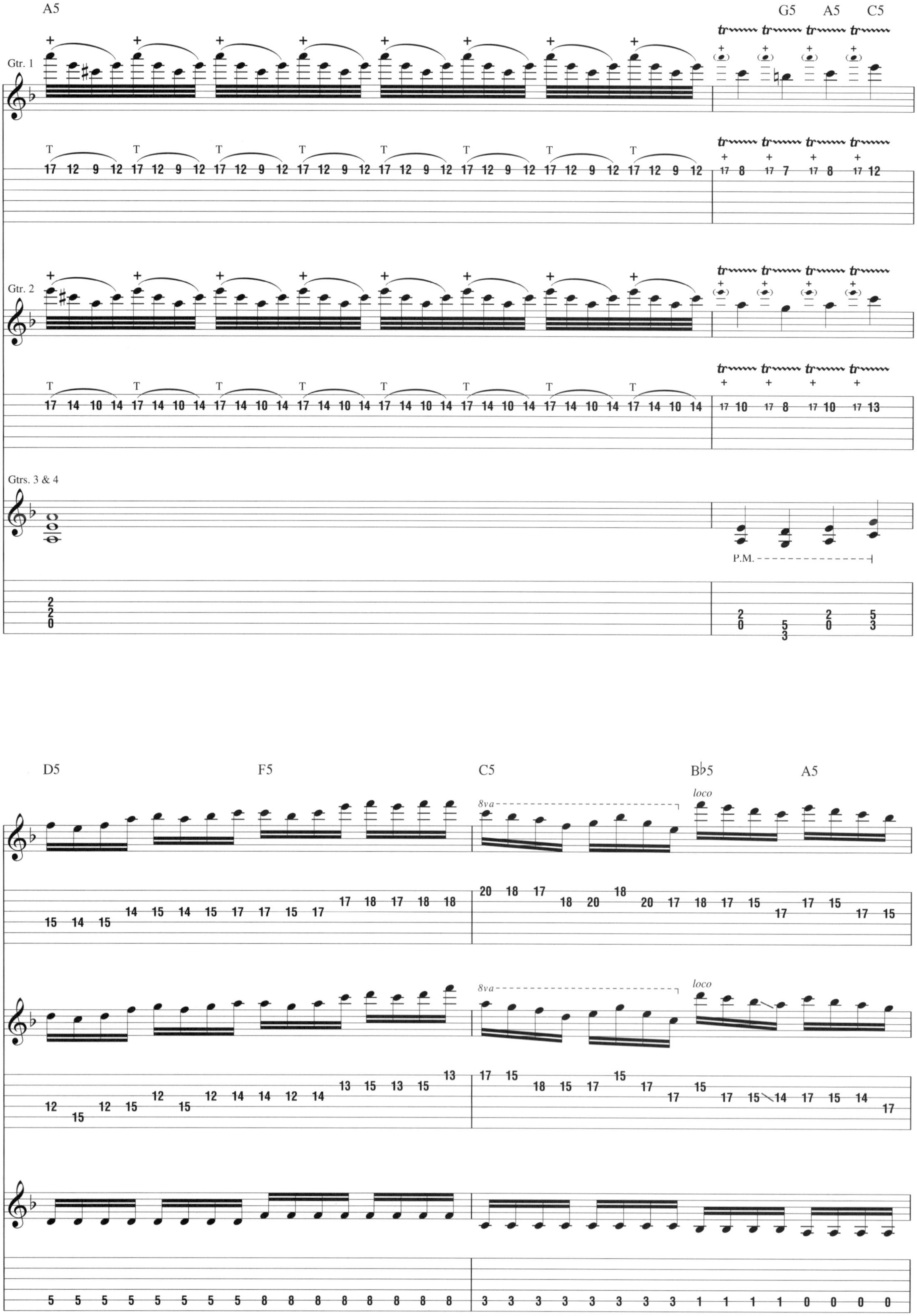

A5 G5 A5 C5

Gtr. 1

Gtr. 2

Gtrs. 3 & 4

P.M.

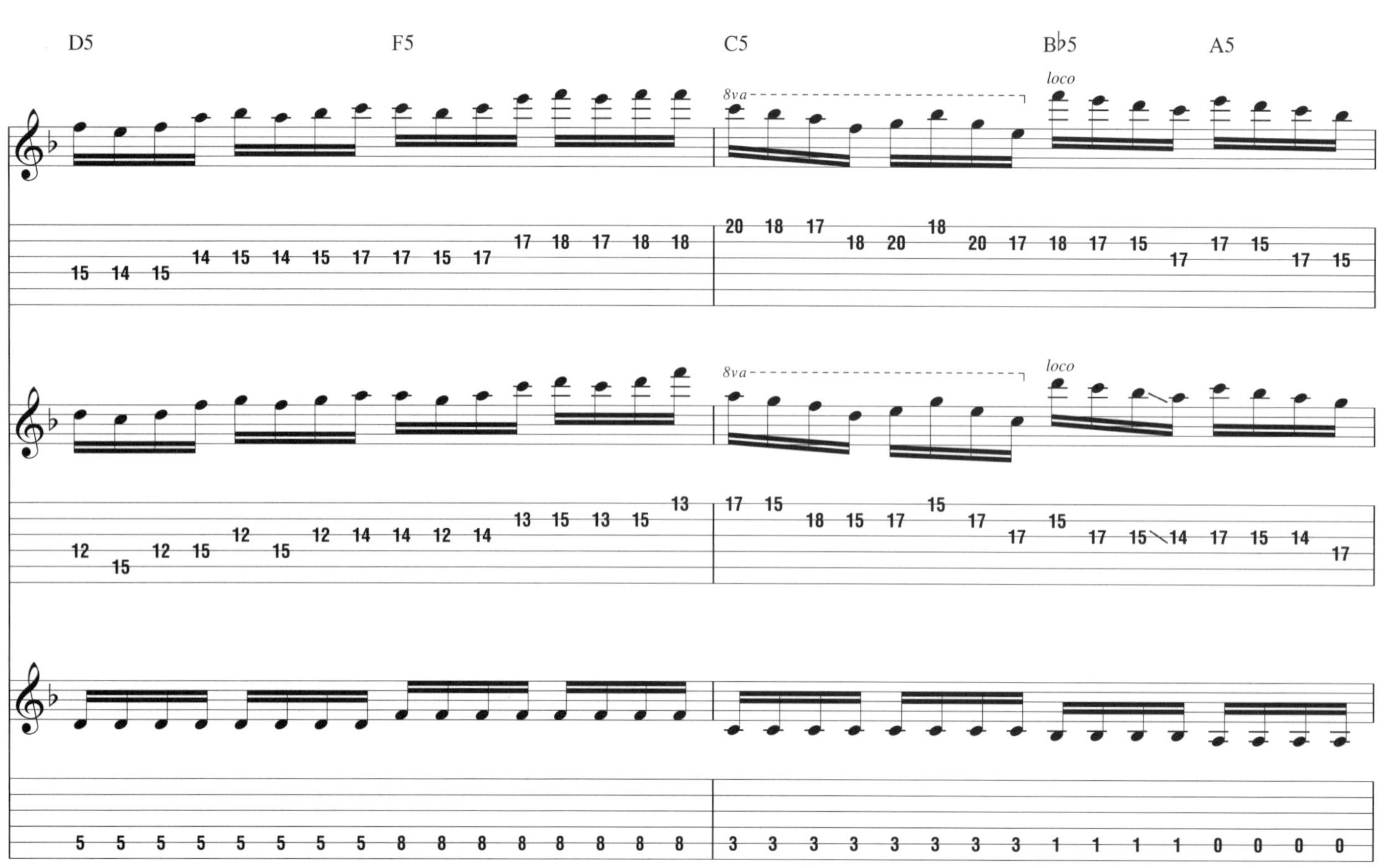

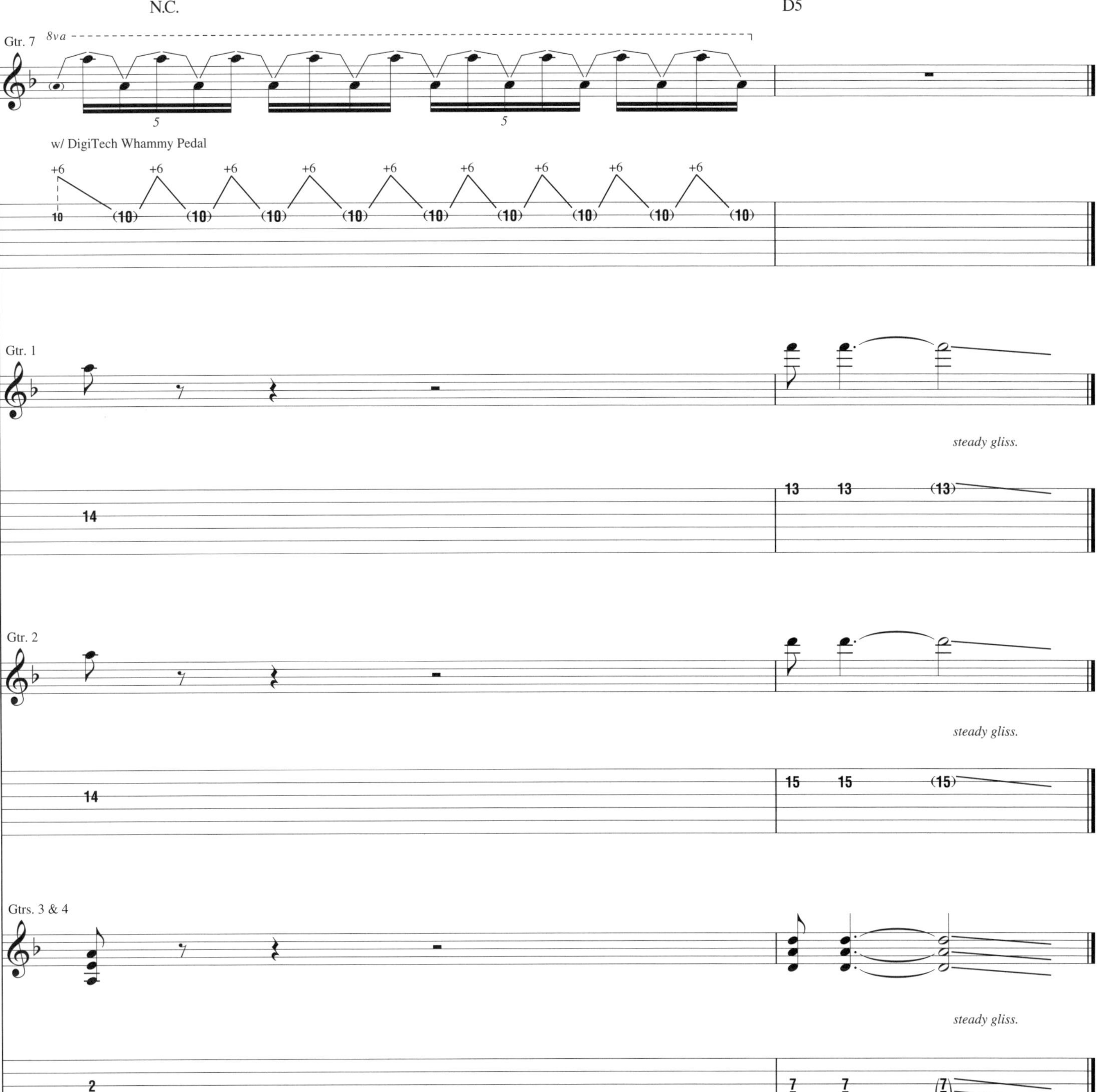
N.C.
D5
Gtr. 7
8va
5
5
w/ DigiTech Whammy Pedal
+6
10
(10)
Gtr. 1
steady gliss.
14
13
13
(13)
Gtr. 2
steady gliss.
14
15
15
(15)
Gtrs. 3 & 4
steady gliss.
2
2
0
7
7
5

Storming the Burning Fields

Words and Music by Herman Li, ZP Theart, Sam Totman and Vadim Pruzhanov

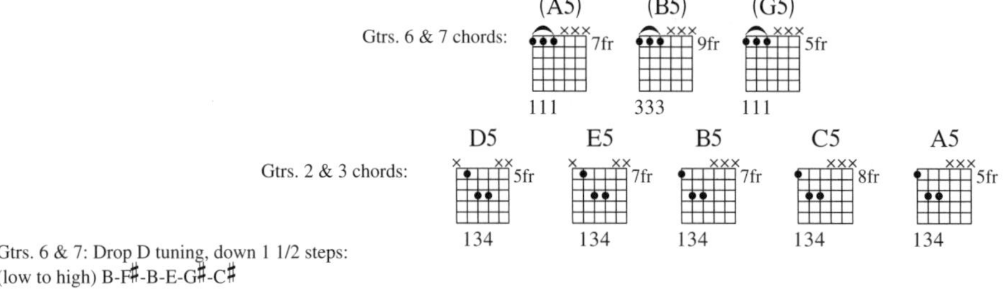

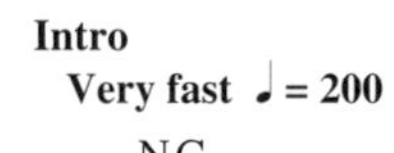

Intro

Very fast ♩ = 200

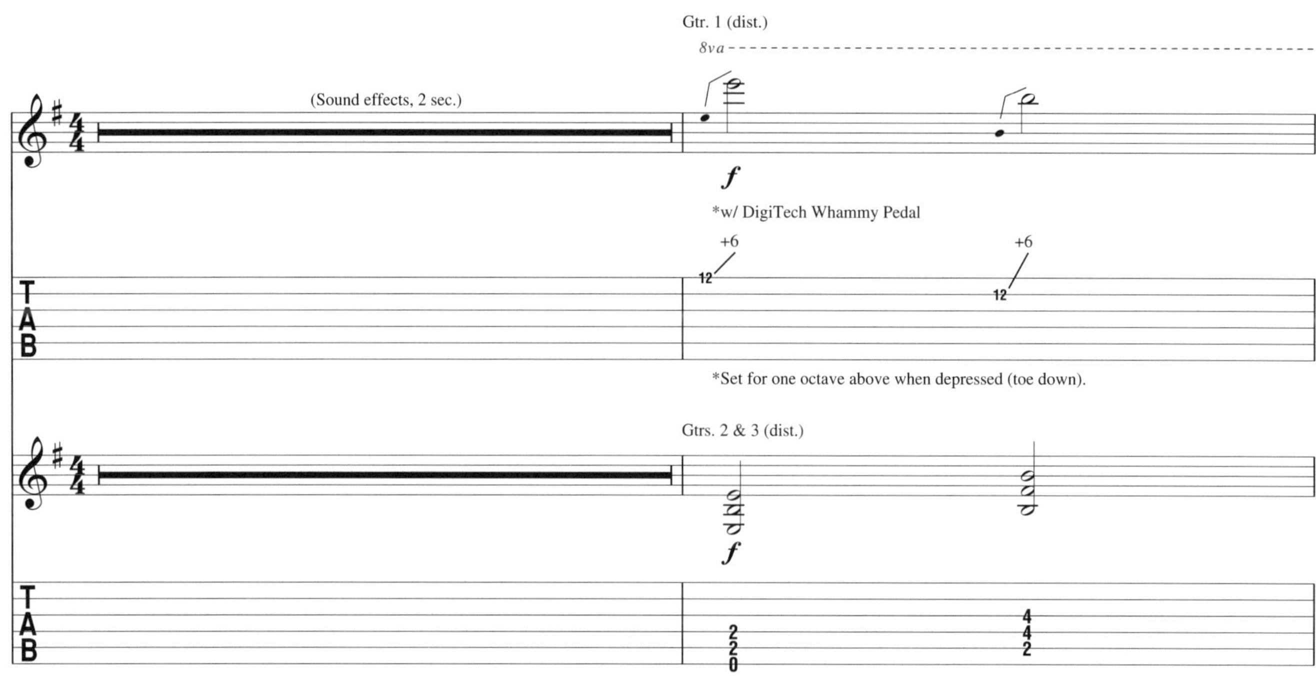

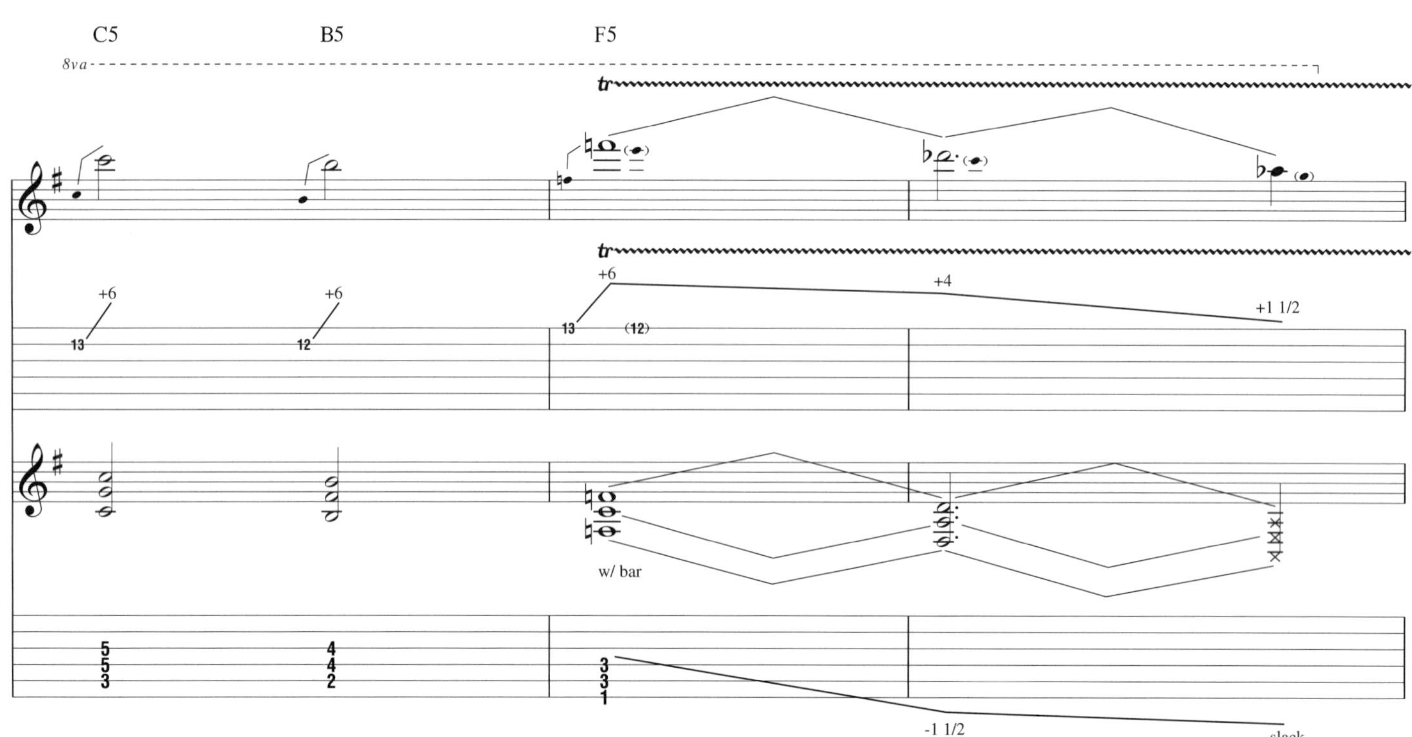

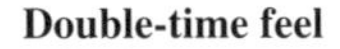
Double-time feel

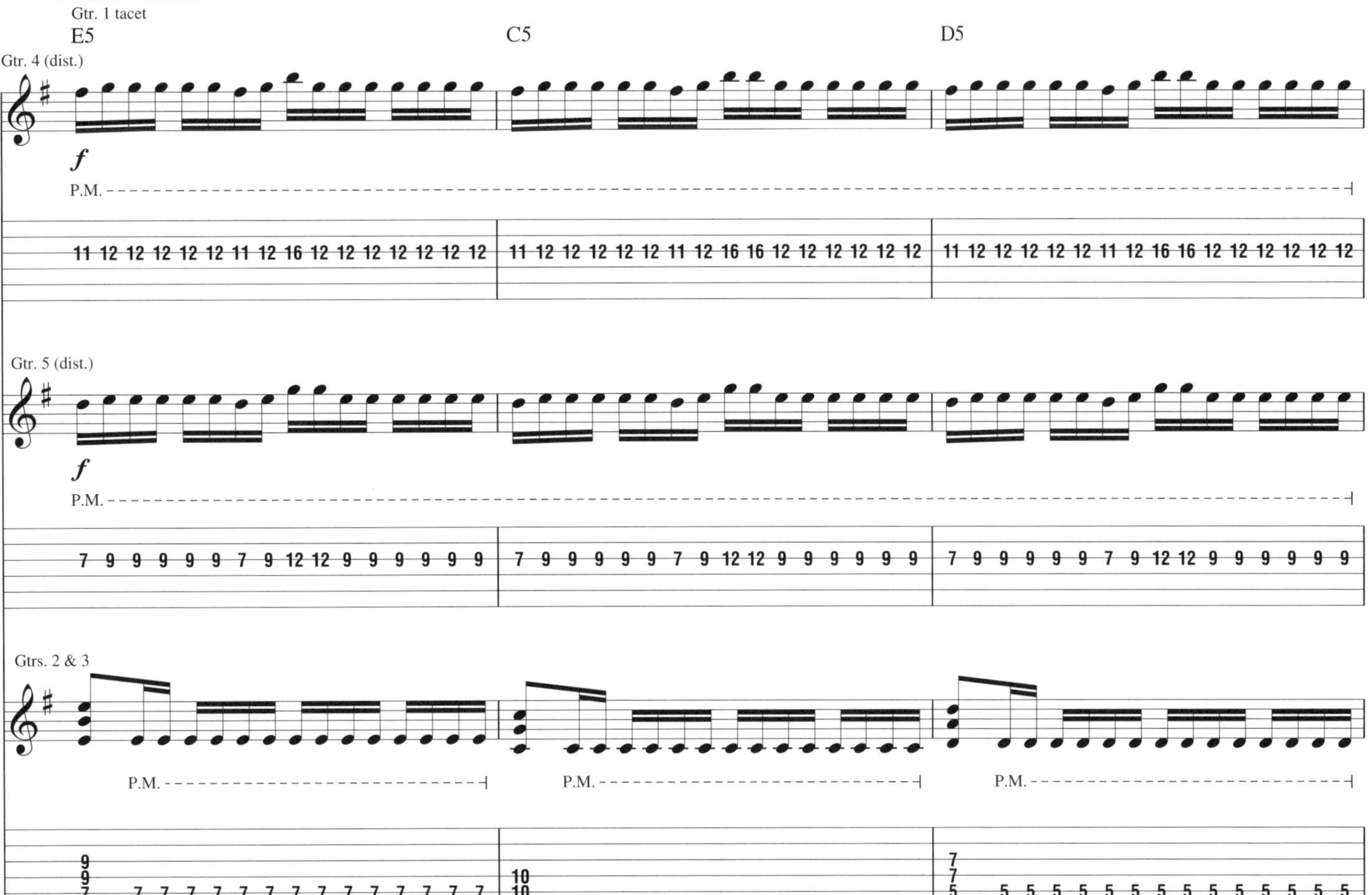
Gtr. 1 tacet
E5
C5
D5
Gtr. 4 (dist.)
f
P.M.
Gtr. 5 (dist.)
f
P.M.
Gtrs. 2 & 3
P.M.
P.M.
P.M.

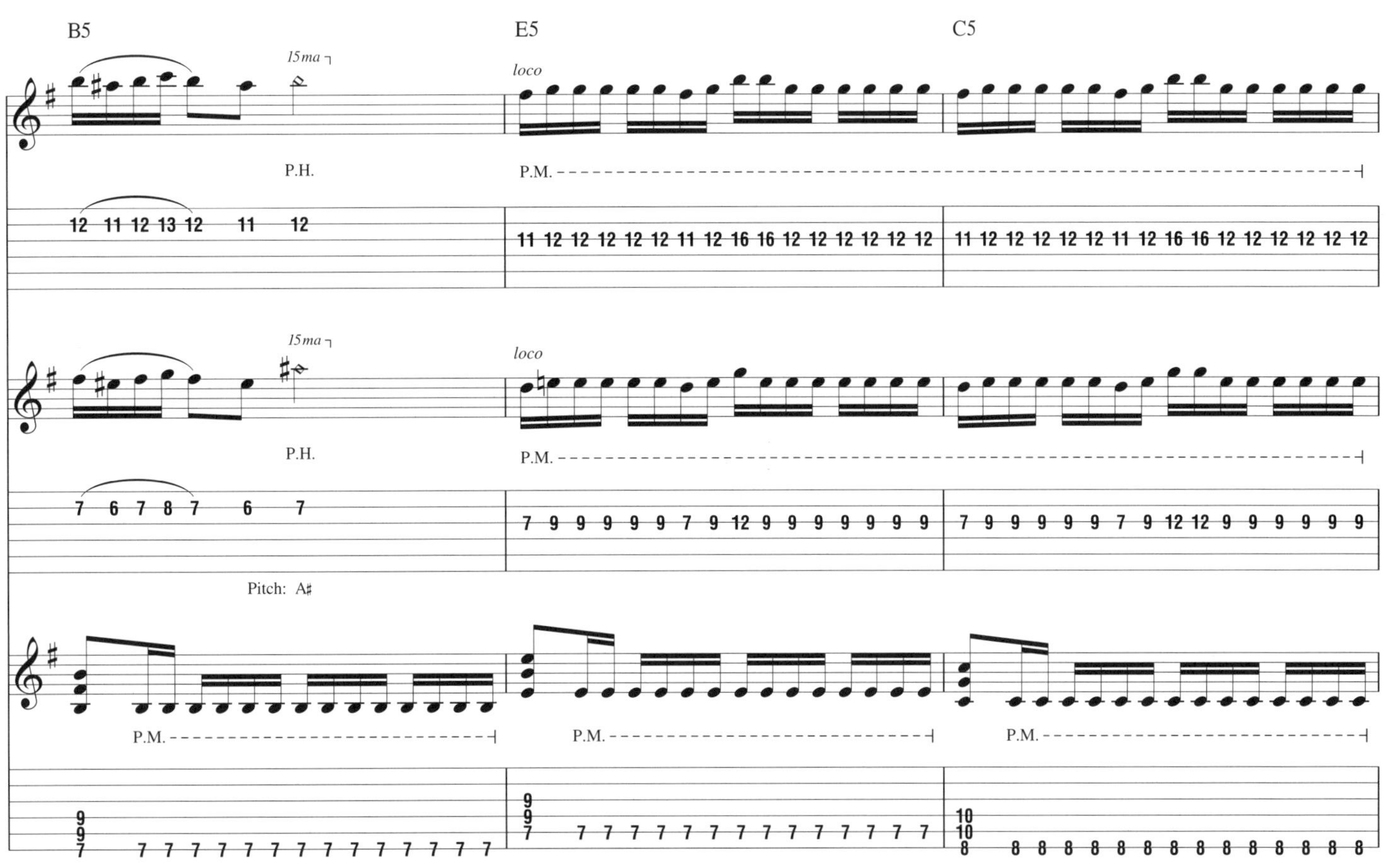
B5
E5
C5
15ma
loco
P.H.
P.M.
15ma
loco
P.H.
P.M.
Pitch: A♯
P.M.
P.M.
P.M.

F5
B5
E5
15ma
loco
Harm.
w/ bar
Pitch: B
Pitch: F♯
semi-P.H.
P.M.
C5
D5
B5
tr

E5 C5

P.M. w/ bar semi-P.H.

11 12 12 12 12 12 11 12 16 12 12 12 12 12 12 12 | 11 12 12 12 12 12 11 12 16 16 12 12 12 12 12 12 | 16 16 12 12 14 14 16 16 15 17 19

P.M. w/ bar semi-P.H.

7 9 9 9 9 9 7 9 12 12 9 9 9 9 9 9 | 7 9 9 9 9 9 7 9 12 12 9 9 9 9 9 9 | 12 12 9 9 11 11 12 12 12 13 15

P.M. P.M.

9 9 7 7 7 7 7 7 7 7 7 7 7 7 7 7 7 7 | 10 10 8 8 8 8 8 8 8 8 8 8 8 8 8 8 8 8 | 10 10 8

B5 C5 N.C. B5 N.C.

tr 15ma 8va

P.S. w/ bar Harm. P.S.

tr 15 (17) +1 1/2 5

tr 15ma 8va

P.S. w/ bar Harm. P.S.

tr 12 (13) +1 1/2 5

9 9 7 | 10 10 8 | | 9 9 7 9 9 7 9 9 7 |

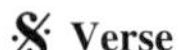

Verse

Gtrs. 4 & 5 tacet

*Em
1. Burst - ing through the fi - res a - veng - ing. Fa - tal warn - ing bat -
2. Blind - ed by the hate and de - si - re burn - ing in your heart
Gtr. 2
w/ variation on repeat
P.M.
P.M.
Gtr. 3
w/ variation on repeat
P.M.
P.M.

*Chord symbols reflect overall harmony.

- tles are rag - ing. Pow - er of dark - ness rise for the fight. We'll be
like a fi - re. Chal - leng - ing all the suf - fer and fear. Our ho -
15ma
loco
P.M.
P.H.
P.M.
Pitch: G
P.M.
P.M.

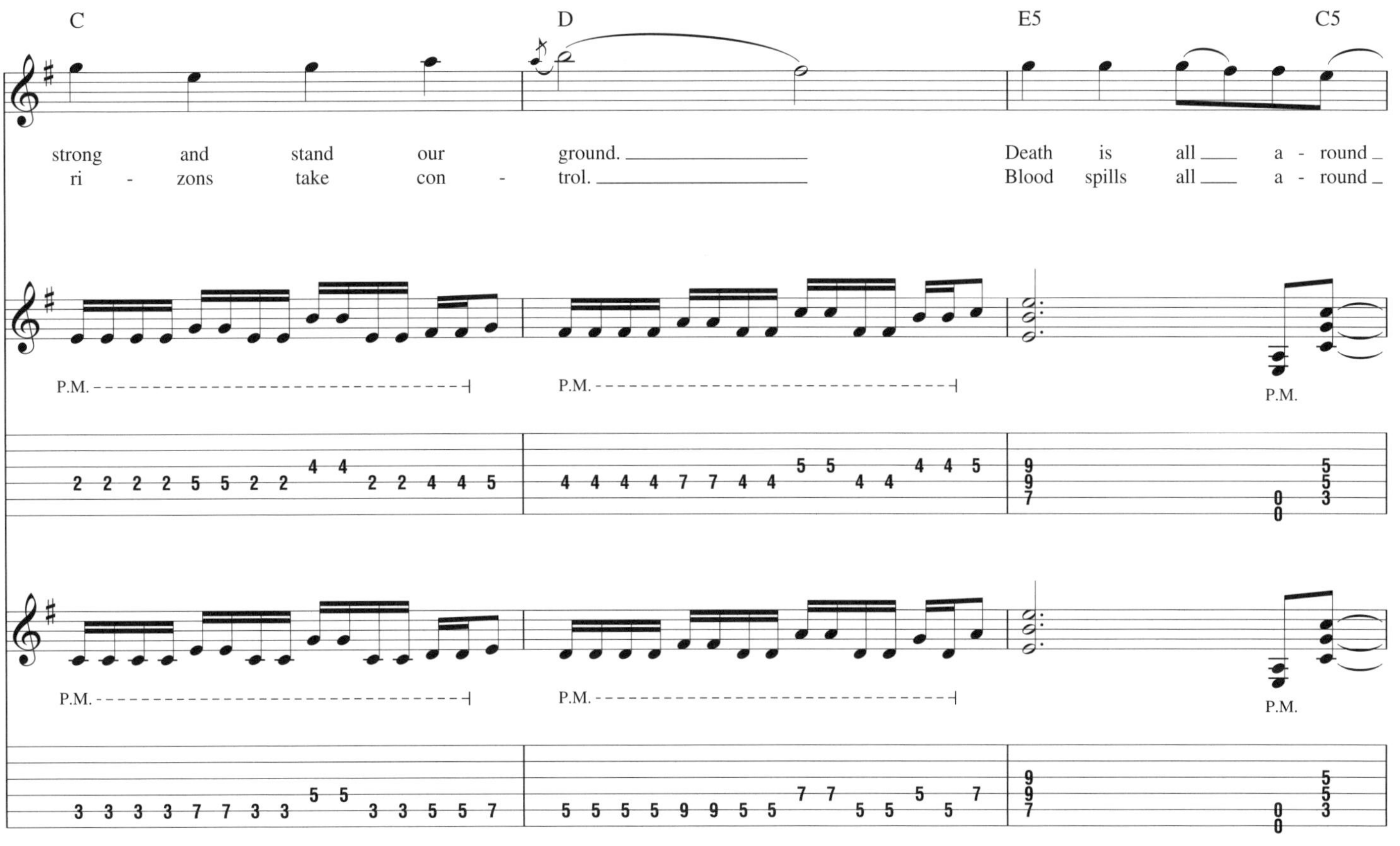
C D E5 C5
strong and stand our ground. Death is all a - round
ri - zons take con - trol. Blood spills all a - round
P.M.
P.M.

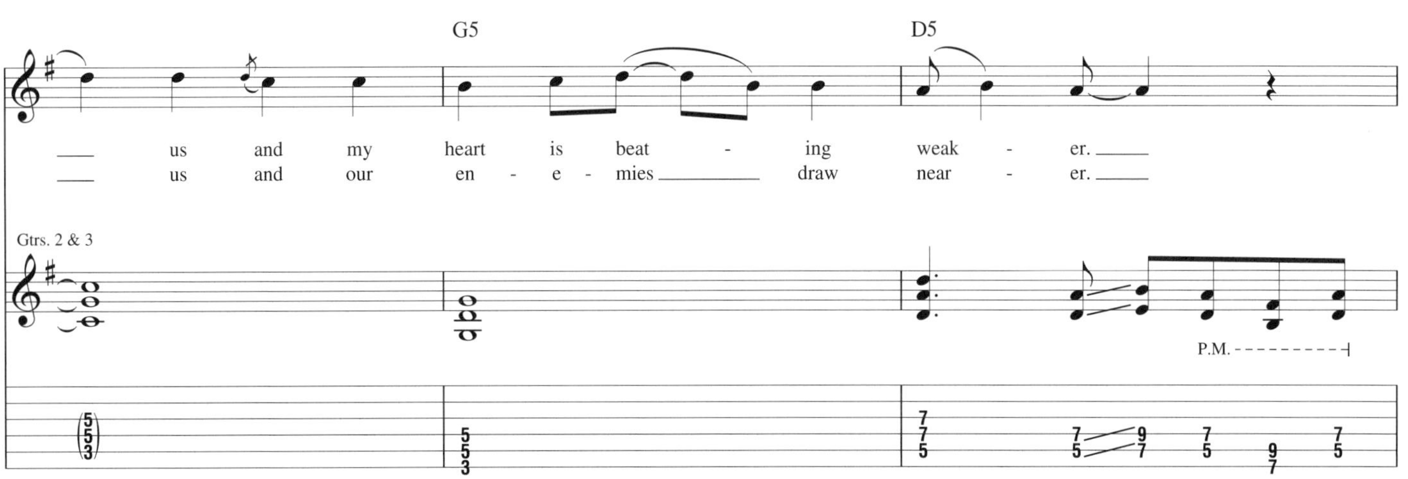
G5 D5
us and my heart is beat - ing weak - er.
us and our en - e - mies draw near - er.
Gtrs. 2 & 3
P.M.

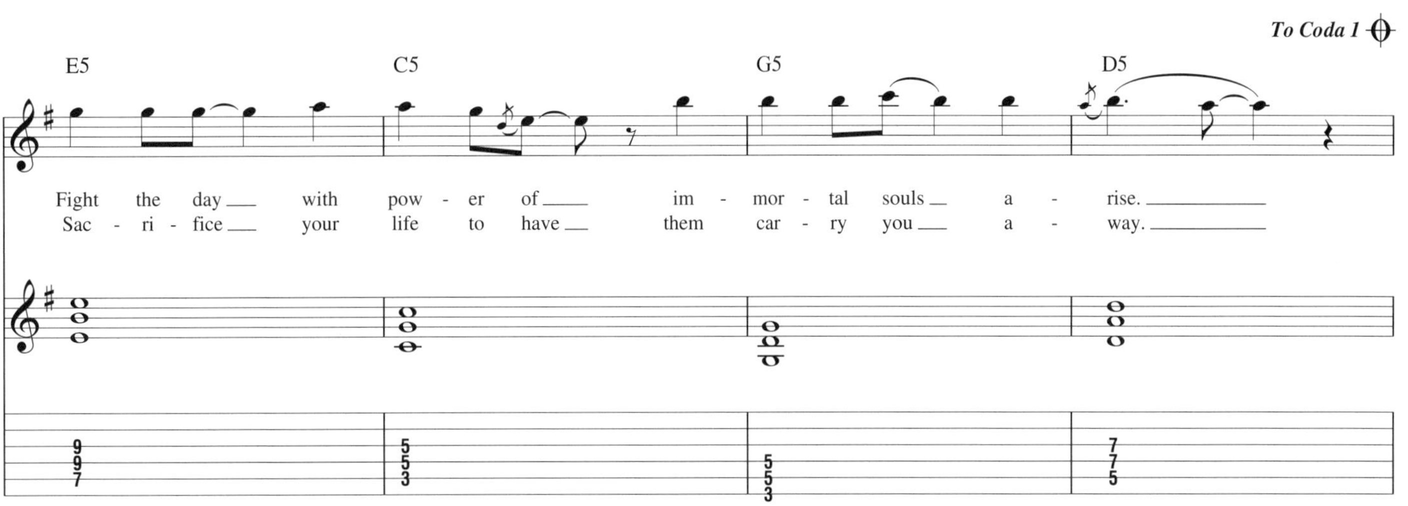
To Coda 1
E5 C5 G5 D5
Fight the day with pow - er of im - mor - tal souls a - rise.
Sac - ri - fice your life to have them car - ry you a - way.

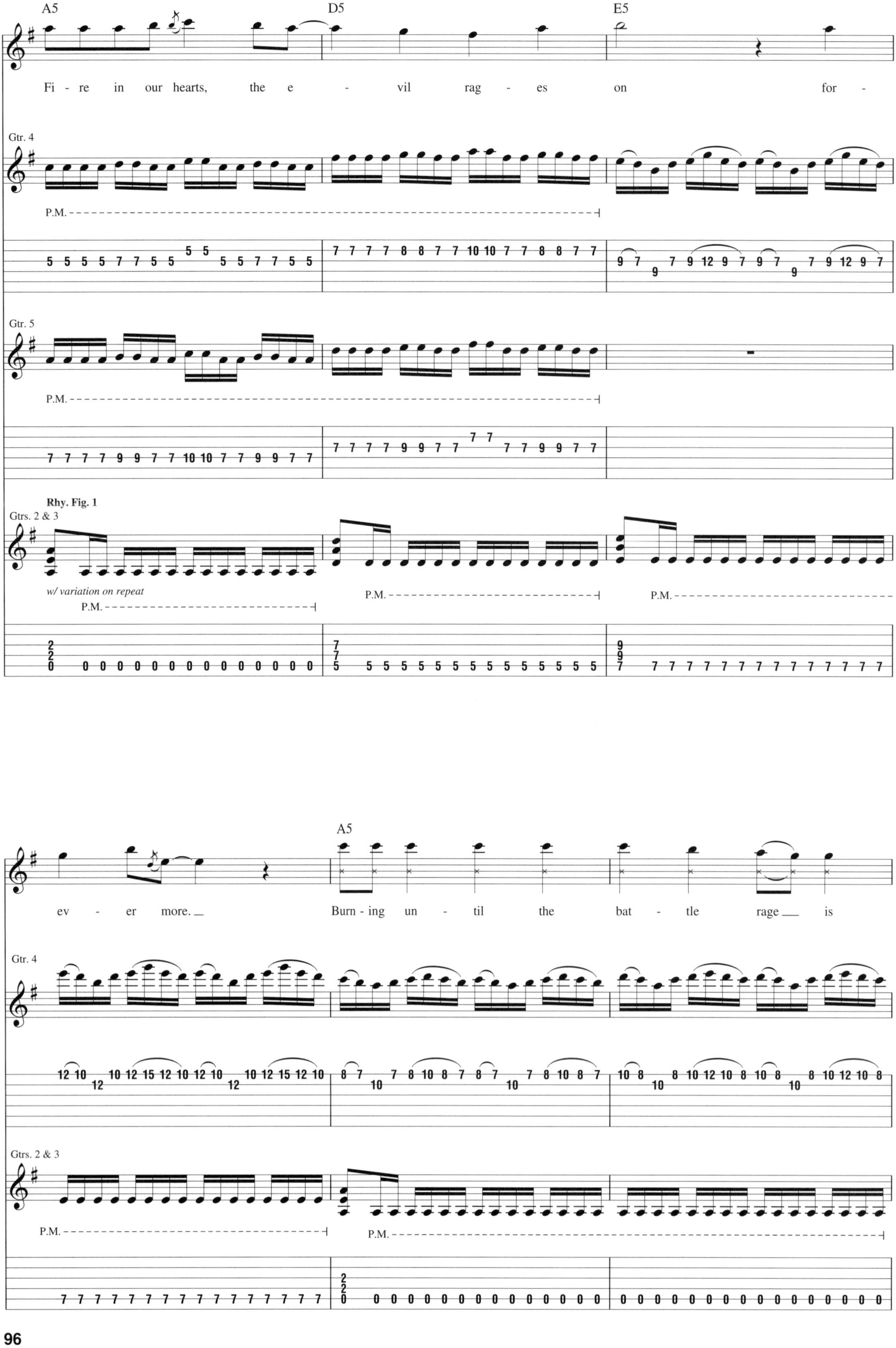

A5 D5 E5

Fi - re in our hearts, the e - vil rag - es on for -

Gtr. 4

P.M.

Gtr. 5

P.M.

Rhy. Fig. 1

Gtrs. 2 & 3

w/ variation on repeat

P.M. P.M. P.M.

A5
ev - er more. Burn - ing un - til the bat - tle rage is
Gtr. 4
Gtrs. 2 & 3
P.M.
P.M.

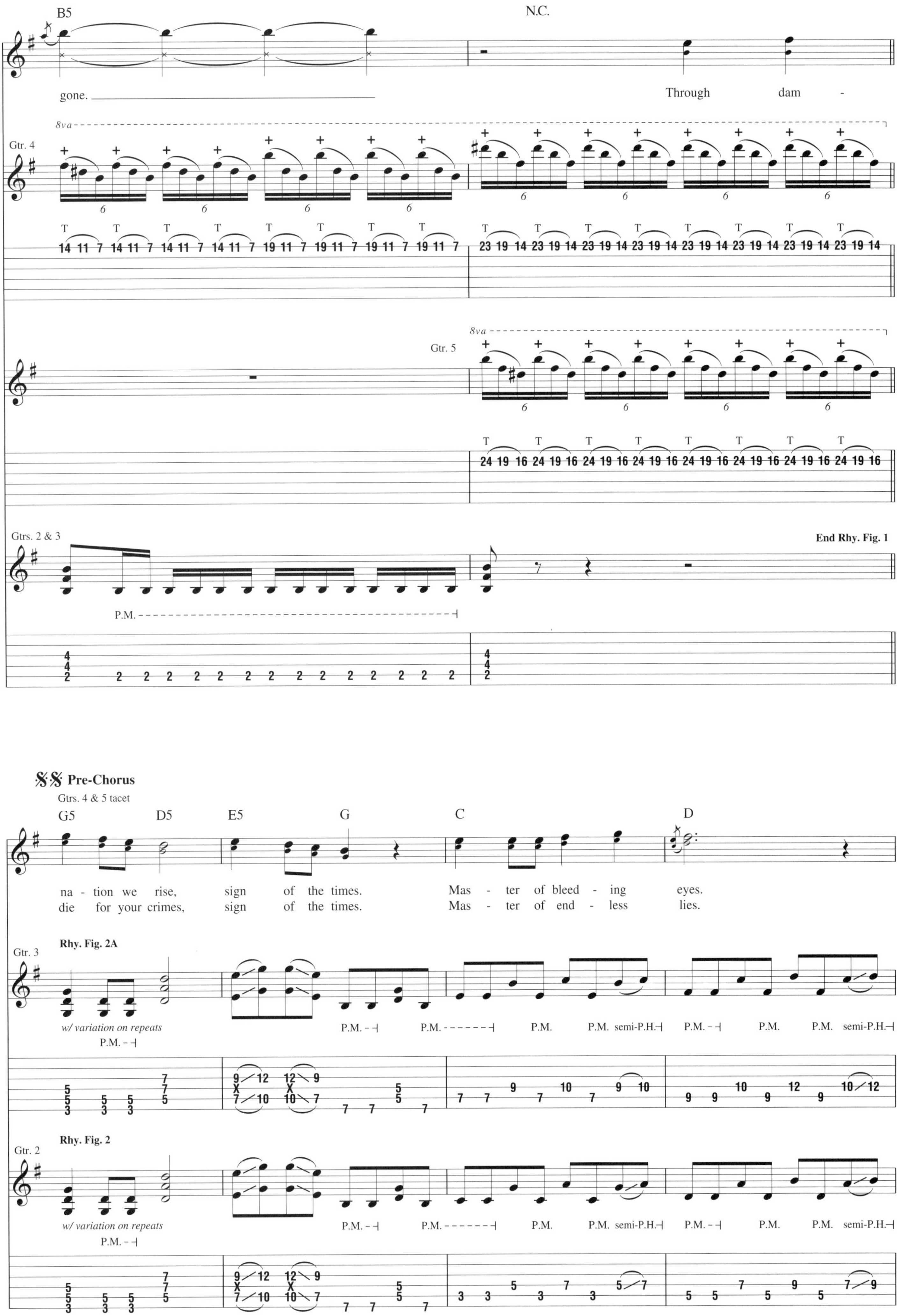

B5
N.C.
gone.
Through dam -
8va
Gtr. 4
T
14 11 7 14 11 7 14 11 7 14 11 7 19 11 7 19 11 7 19 11 7 19 11 7
23 19 14 23 19 14 23 19 14 23 19 14 23 19 14 23 19 14 23 19 14 23 19 14
Gtr. 5
24 19 16 24 19 16 24 19 16 24 19 16 24 19 16 24 19 16 24 19 16 24 19 16
Gtrs. 2 & 3
End Rhy. Fig. 1
P.M.
Pre-Chorus
Gtrs. 4 & 5 tacet
G5 D5 E5 G C D
na - tion we rise, sign of the times. Mas - ter of bleed - ing eyes.
die for your crimes, sign of the times. Mas - ter of end - less lies.
Rhy. Fig. 2A
Gtr. 3
w/ variation on repeats
P.M.
semi-P.H.
Rhy. Fig. 2
Gtr. 2
w/ variation on repeats
P.M.
semi-P.H.

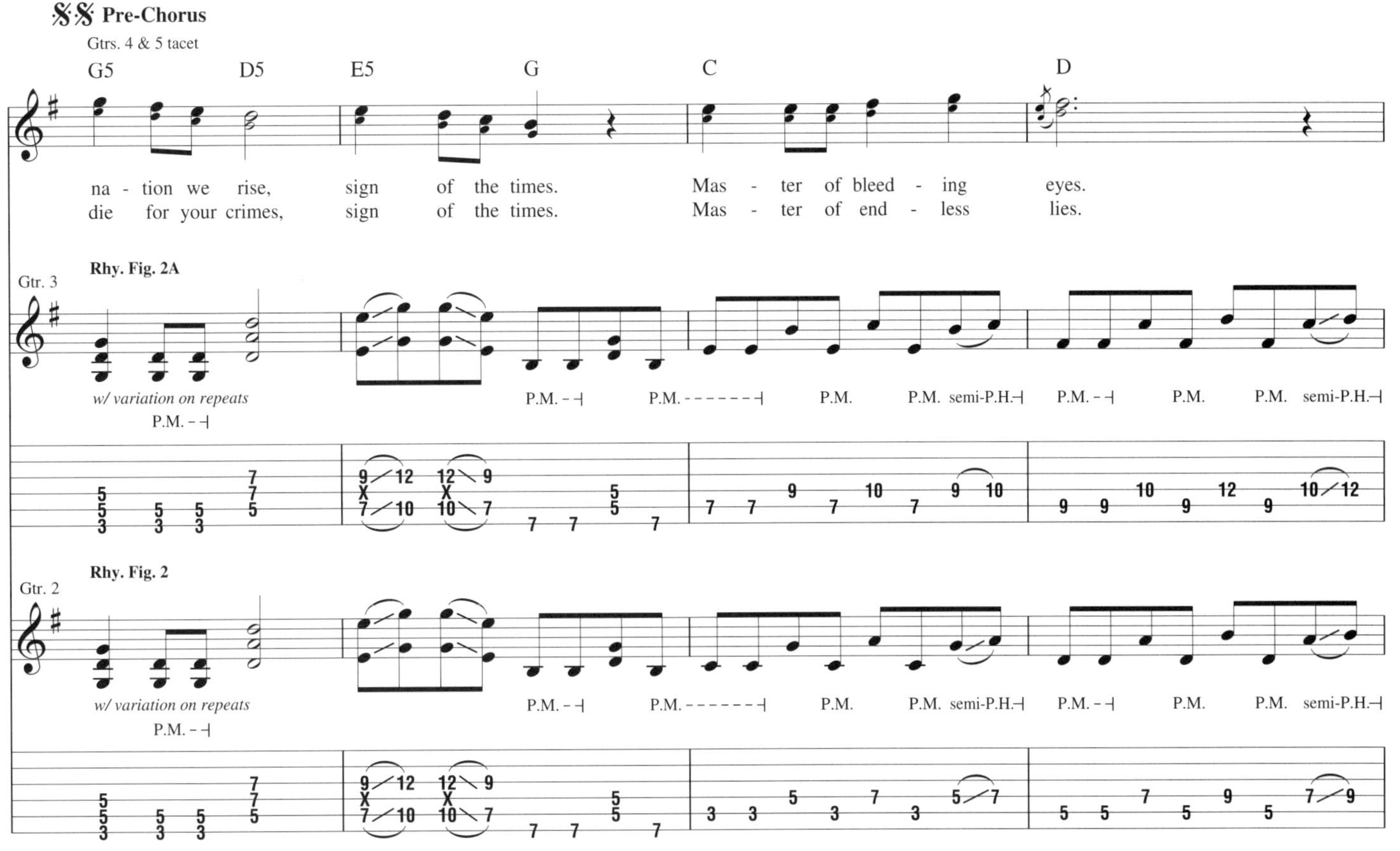

G5
D5
E5
G5
A5
Thun - der on high, look to the sky. You're nev - er gon - na take us
Fight to the end, now we as - cend. To - geth - er we will take them
End Rhy. Fig. 2A
P.M.
End Rhy. Fig. 2

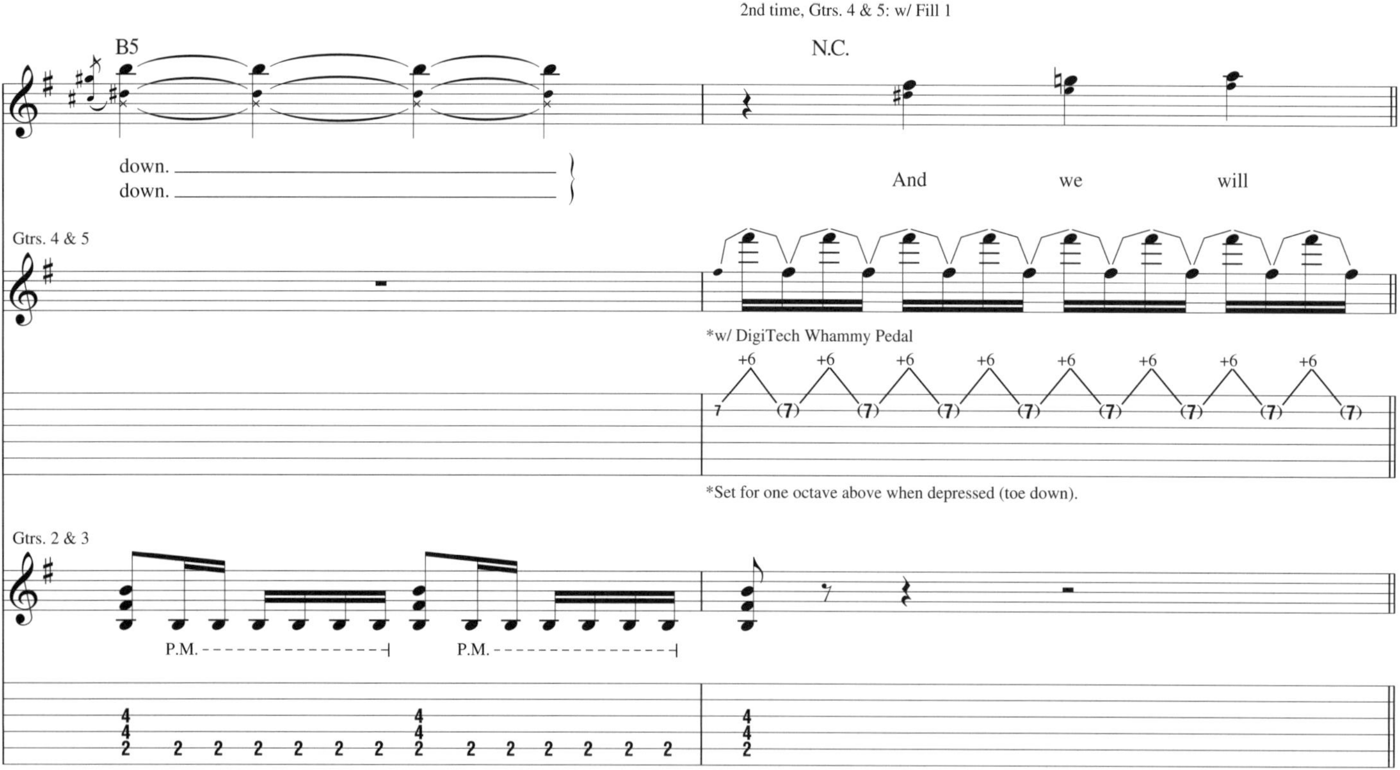
2nd time, Gtrs. 4 & 5: w/ Fill 1
B5
N.C.
down.
down.
And we will
Gtrs. 4 & 5
*w/ DigiTech Whammy Pedal
*Set for one octave above when depressed (toe down).
Gtrs. 2 & 3
P.M.

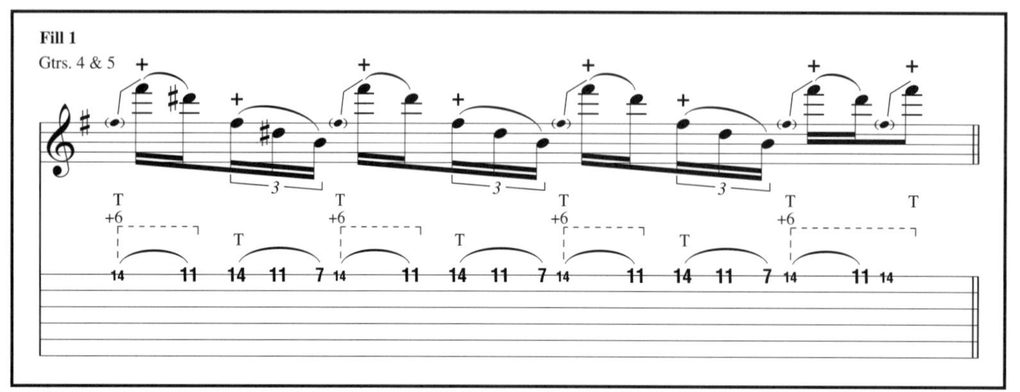
Fill 1
Gtrs. 4 & 5

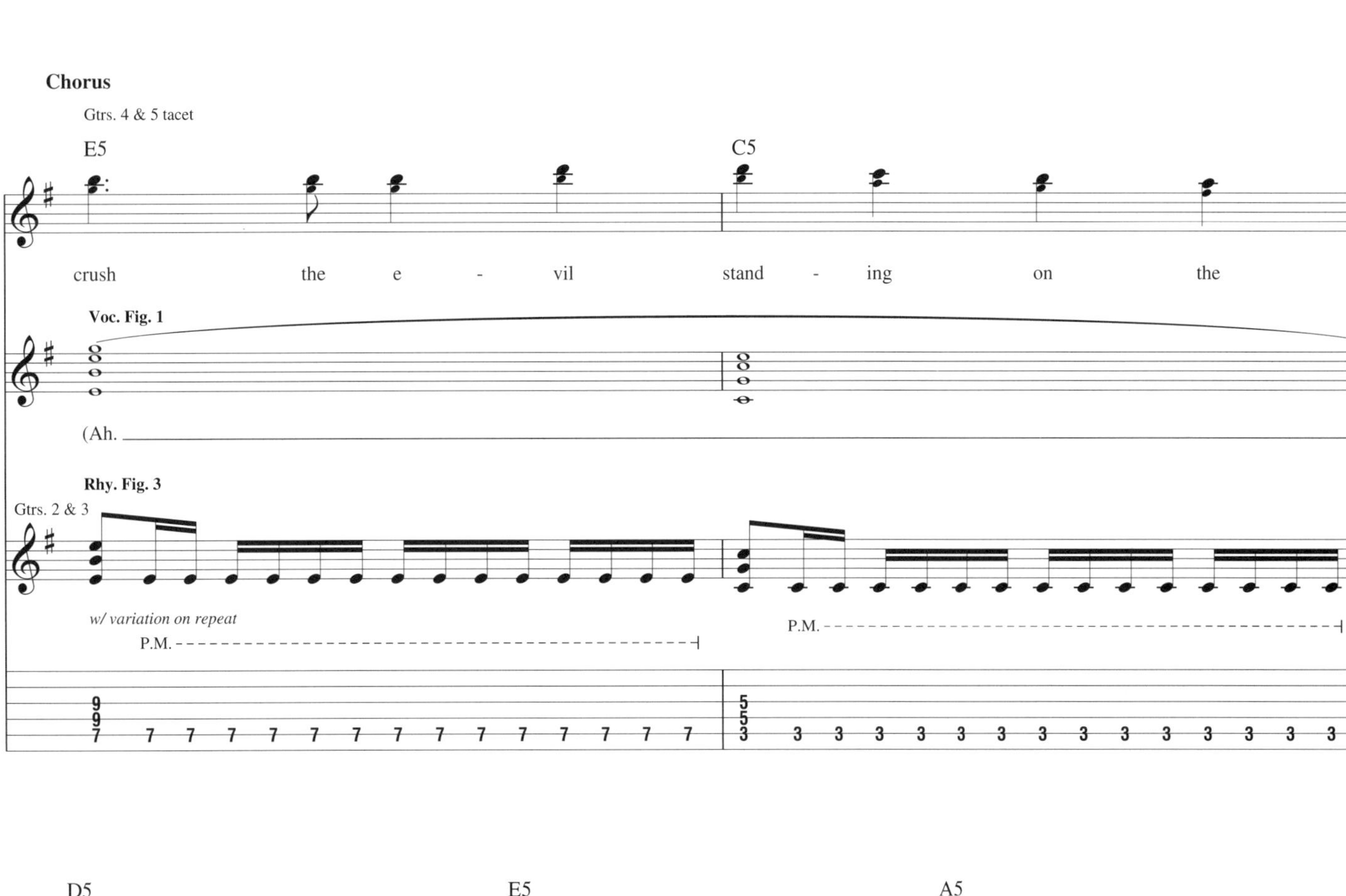
Chorus
Gtrs. 4 & 5 tacet
E5
C5
crush the e - vil stand - ing on the
Voc. Fig. 1
(Ah.
Rhy. Fig. 3
Gtrs. 2 & 3
w/ variation on repeat
P.M.
P.M.
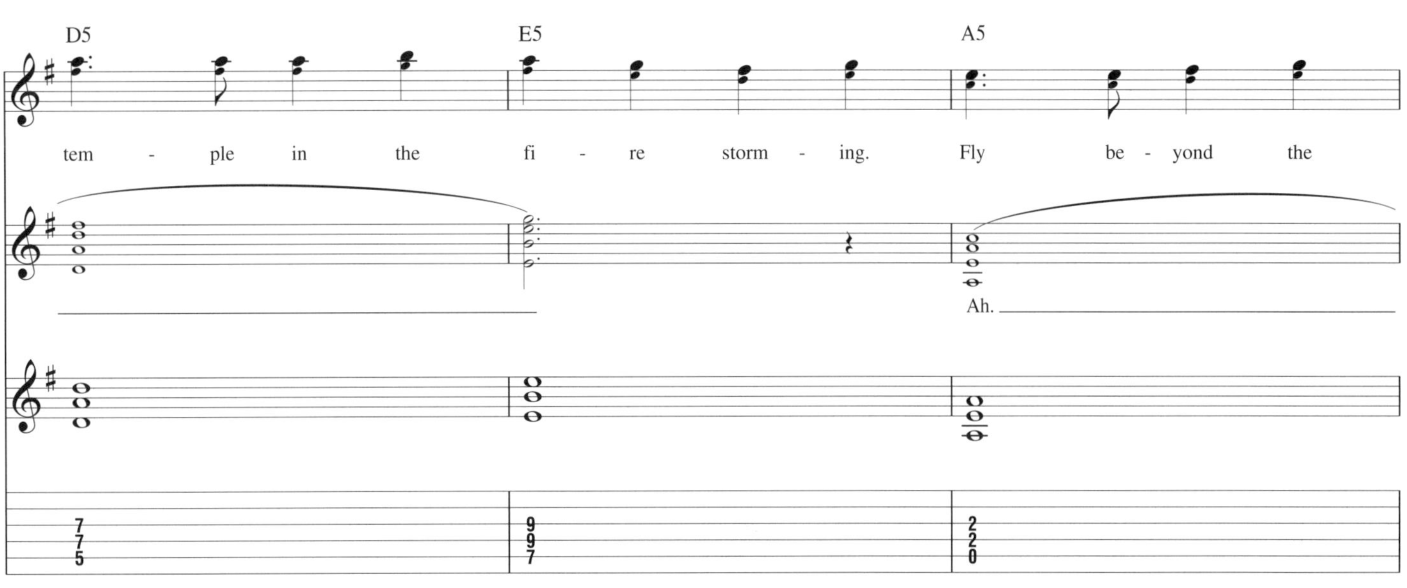
D5
E5
A5
tem - ple in the fi - re storm - ing. Fly be - yond the
Ah.
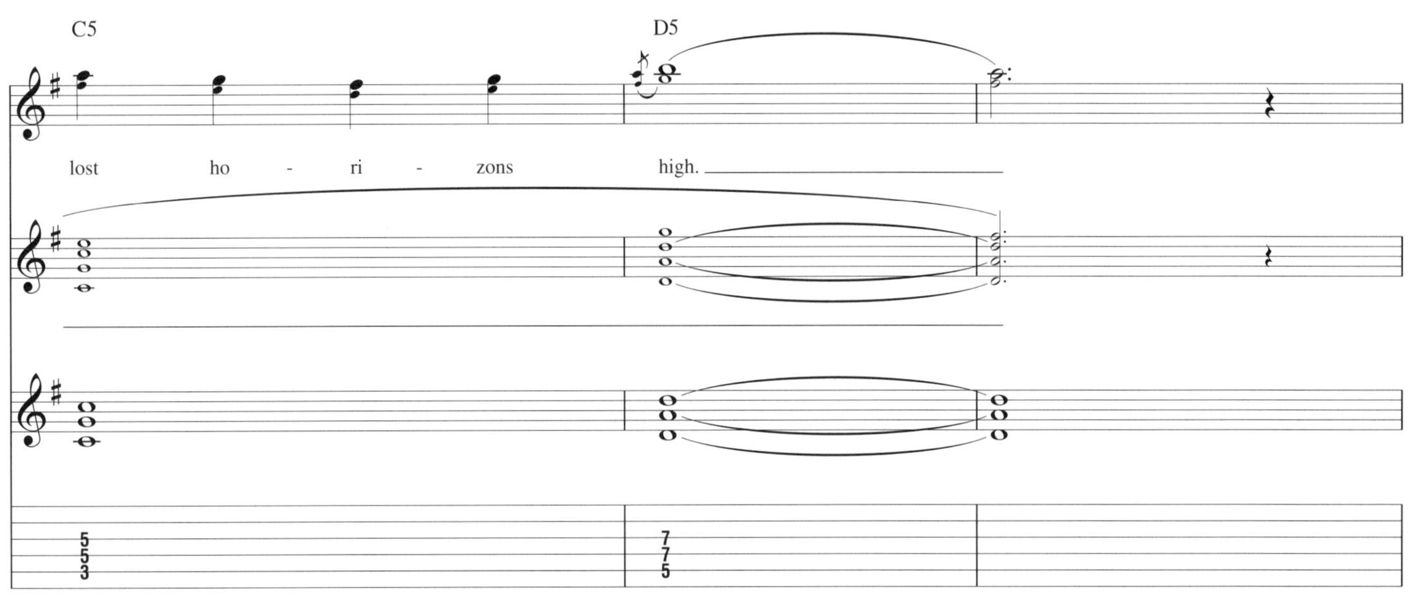
C5
D5
lost ho - ri - zons high.

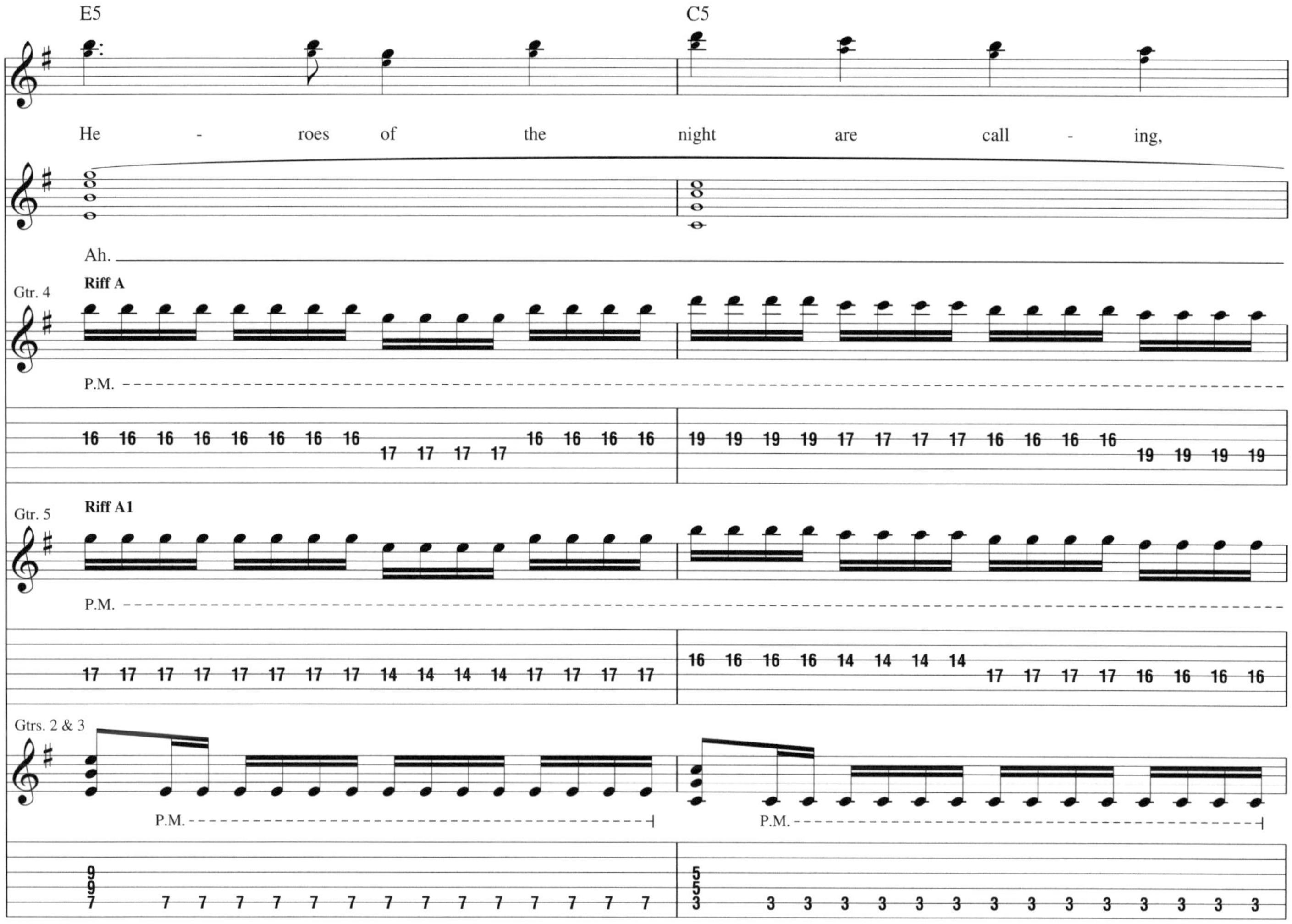

E5 C5

He - roes of the night are call - ing,

Ah.

Gtr. 4 Riff A

P.M.

16 16 16 16 16 16 16 16 17 17 17 17 16 16 16 16 | 19 19 19 19 17 17 17 17 16 16 16 16 19 19 19 19

Gtr. 5 Riff A1

P.M.

17 17 17 17 17 17 17 17 14 14 14 14 17 17 17 17 | 16 16 16 16 14 14 14 14 17 17 17 17 16 16 16 16

Gtrs. 2 & 3

P.M. P.M.

9 9 7 7 7 7 7 7 7 7 7 7 7 7 7 7 7 | 5 5 3 3 3 3 3 3 3 3 3 3 3 3 3 3 3

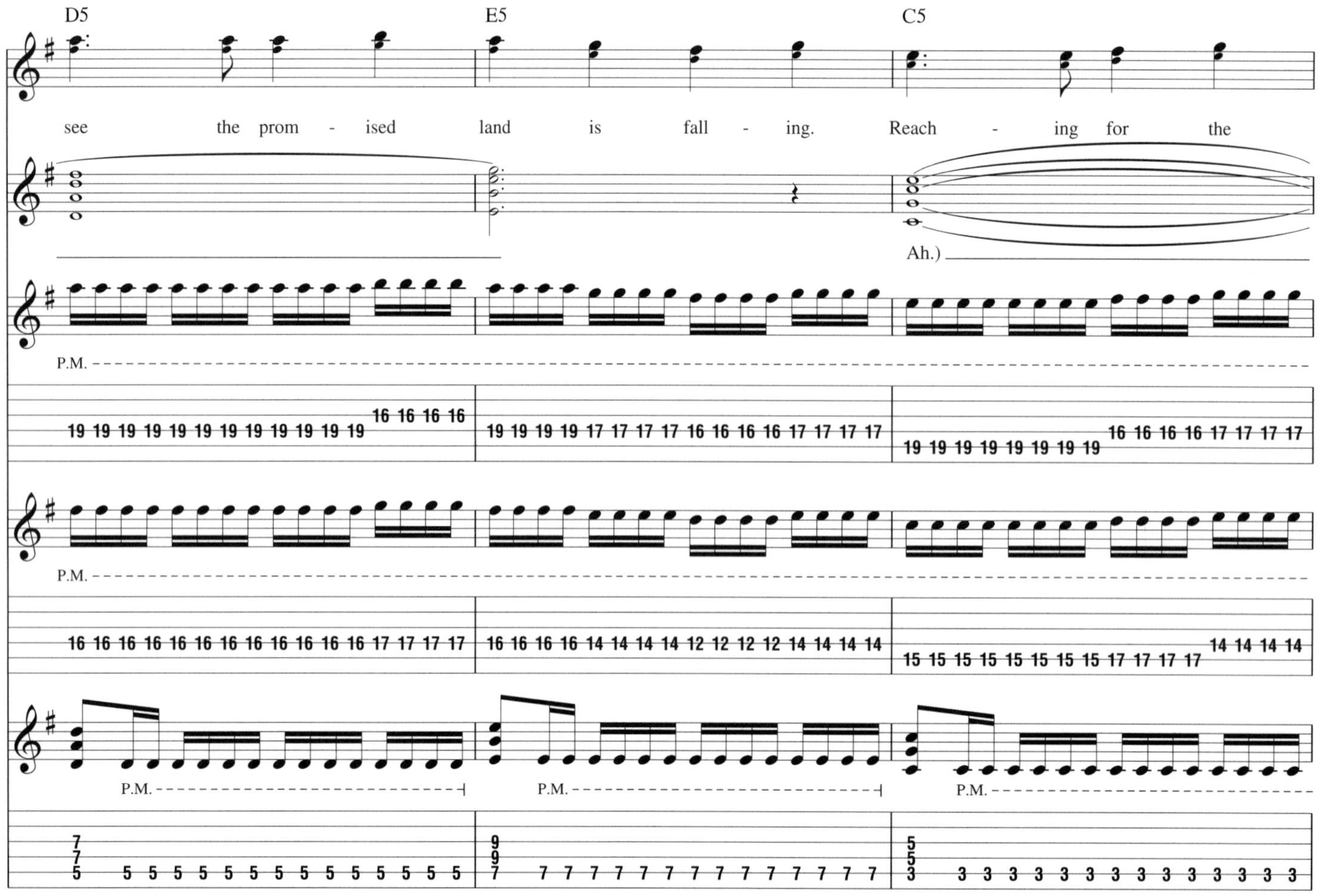

D5 E5 C5

see the prom - ised land is fall - ing. Reach - ing for the

Ah.)

P.M.

19 19 19 19 19 19 19 19 19 19 19 19 16 16 16 16 | 19 19 19 19 17 17 17 17 16 16 16 16 17 17 17 17 | 19 19 19 19 19 19 19 19 16 16 16 16 17 17 17 17

P.M.

16 16 16 16 16 16 16 16 16 16 16 16 17 17 17 17 | 16 16 16 16 14 14 14 14 12 12 12 12 14 14 14 14 | 15 15 15 15 15 15 15 15 17 17 17 17 14 14 14 14

P.M. P.M. P.M.

7 7 5 5 5 5 5 5 5 5 5 5 5 5 5 5 5 | 9 9 7 7 7 7 7 7 7 7 7 7 7 7 7 7 7 | 5 5 3 3 3 3 3 3 3 3 3 3 3 3 3 3 3

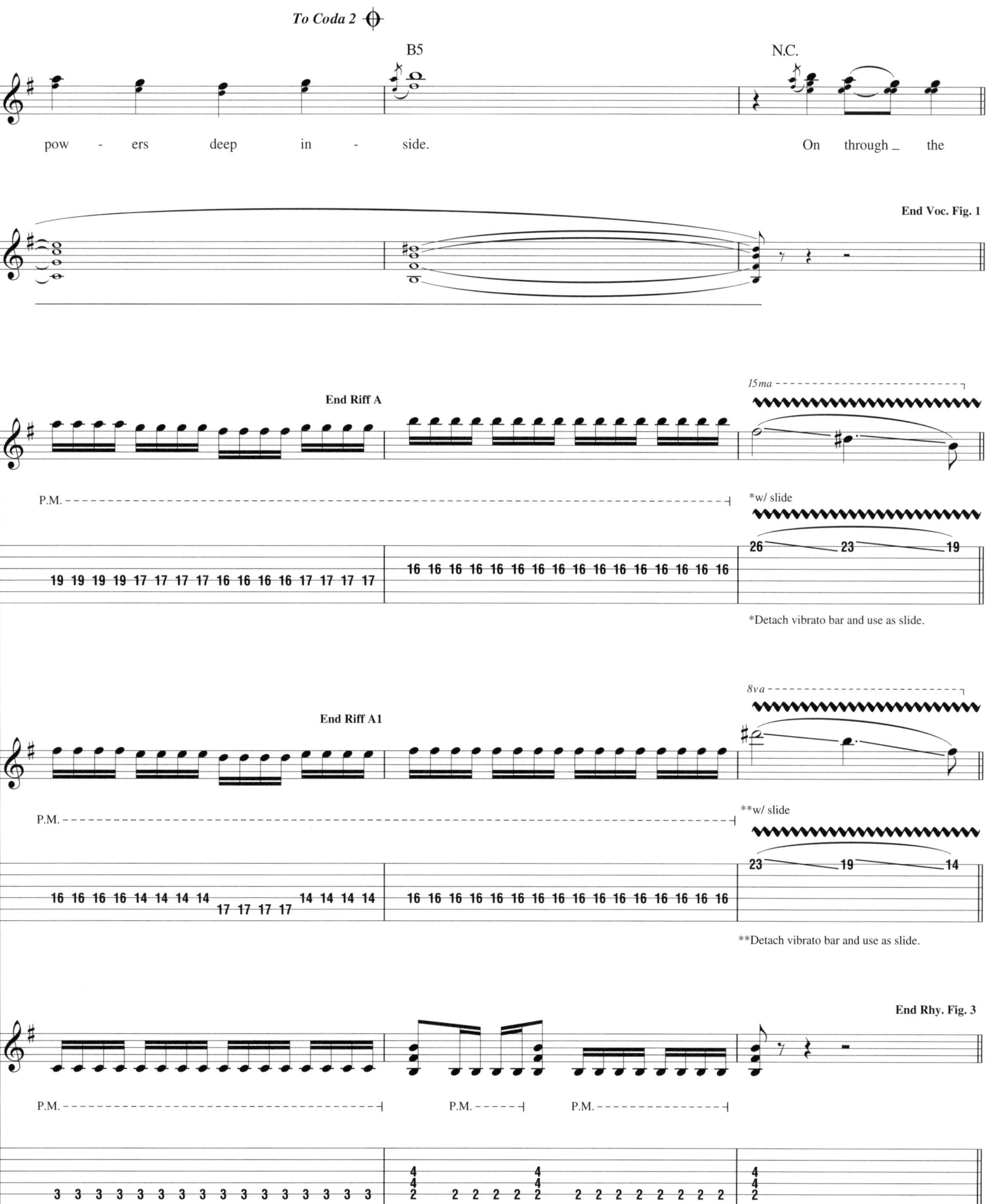
To Coda 2
B5
N.C.
pow - ers deep in - side.
On through the
End Voc. Fig. 1
End Riff A
15ma
P.M.
*w/ slide
19 19 19 19 17 17 17 17 16 16 16 16 17 17 17 17
16 16 16 16 16 16 16 16 16 16 16 16 16 16 16 16
26 23 19
*Detach vibrato bar and use as slide.
8va
End Riff A1
P.M.
**w/ slide
16 16 16 16 14 14 14 14 17 17 17 17 14 14 14 14
16 16 16 16 16 16 16 16 16 16 16 16 16 16 16 16
23 19 14
**Detach vibrato bar and use as slide.
End Rhy. Fig. 3
P.M.
P.M.
P.M.
3 3 3 3 3 3 3 3 3 3 3 3 3 3 3 3
4 4 2 2 2 2 2 2 4 4 2 2 2 2 2 2 2 2 2
4 4 2

Interlude
E5
C5
night.
Gtr. 5
15ma
P.M.
P.H.
Pitch: B
Gtr. 4
8va
P.M.
P.H.
Pitch: G
Gtrs. 2 & 3
P.M.
F5
B5
A5
loco
15ma
loco
P.M.
P.H.
loco
15ma
loco
P.M.
P.H.
P.M.
P.M.

C5 D5

8va loco 15ma

P.H.

Pitch: G

8va loco 15ma

P.H.

P.M.

E5 C5 D5 E5

loco 8va

loco

semi-P.H.

P.M. P.M.

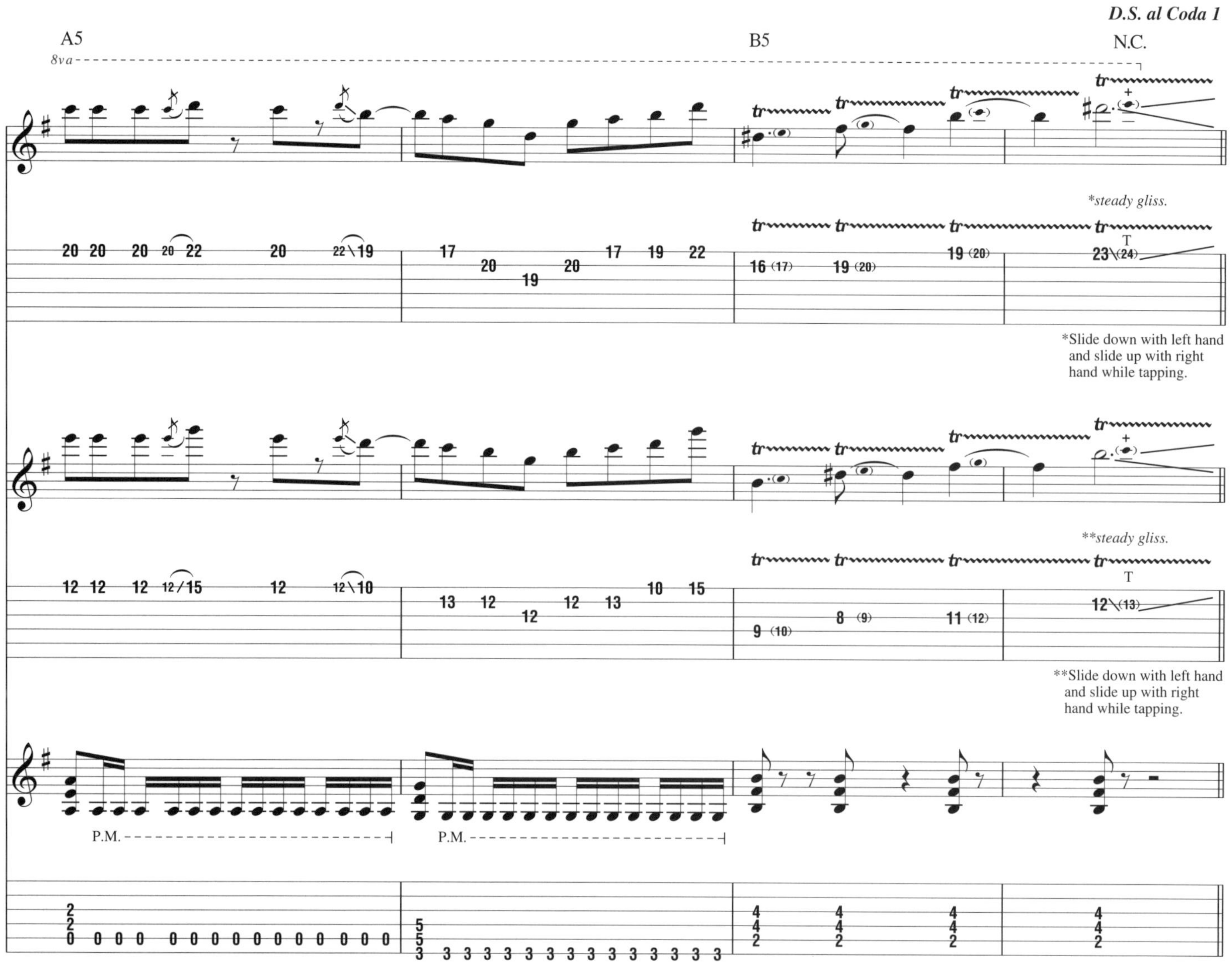

D.S. al Coda 1
A5
B5
N.C.
8va
*steady gliss.
*Slide down with left hand and slide up with right hand while tapping.
**steady gliss.
**Slide down with left hand and slide up with right hand while tapping.
P.M.
P.M.

Coda 1
Gtrs. 2 & 3: w/ Rhy. Fig. 1
A5
D5
E5
Take us to the place of death and car - ry on for -
Gtr. 4
P.M.
Gtr. 5
P.M.

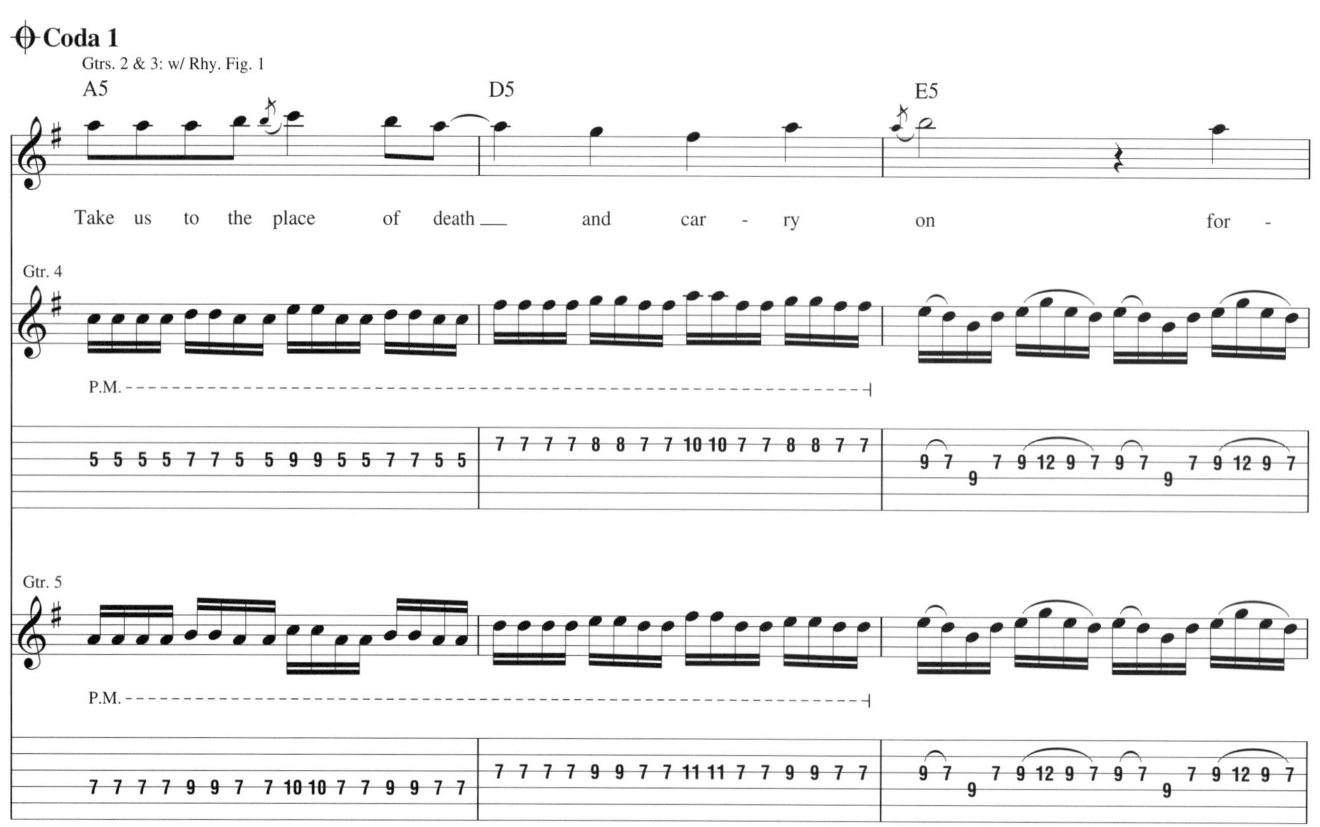

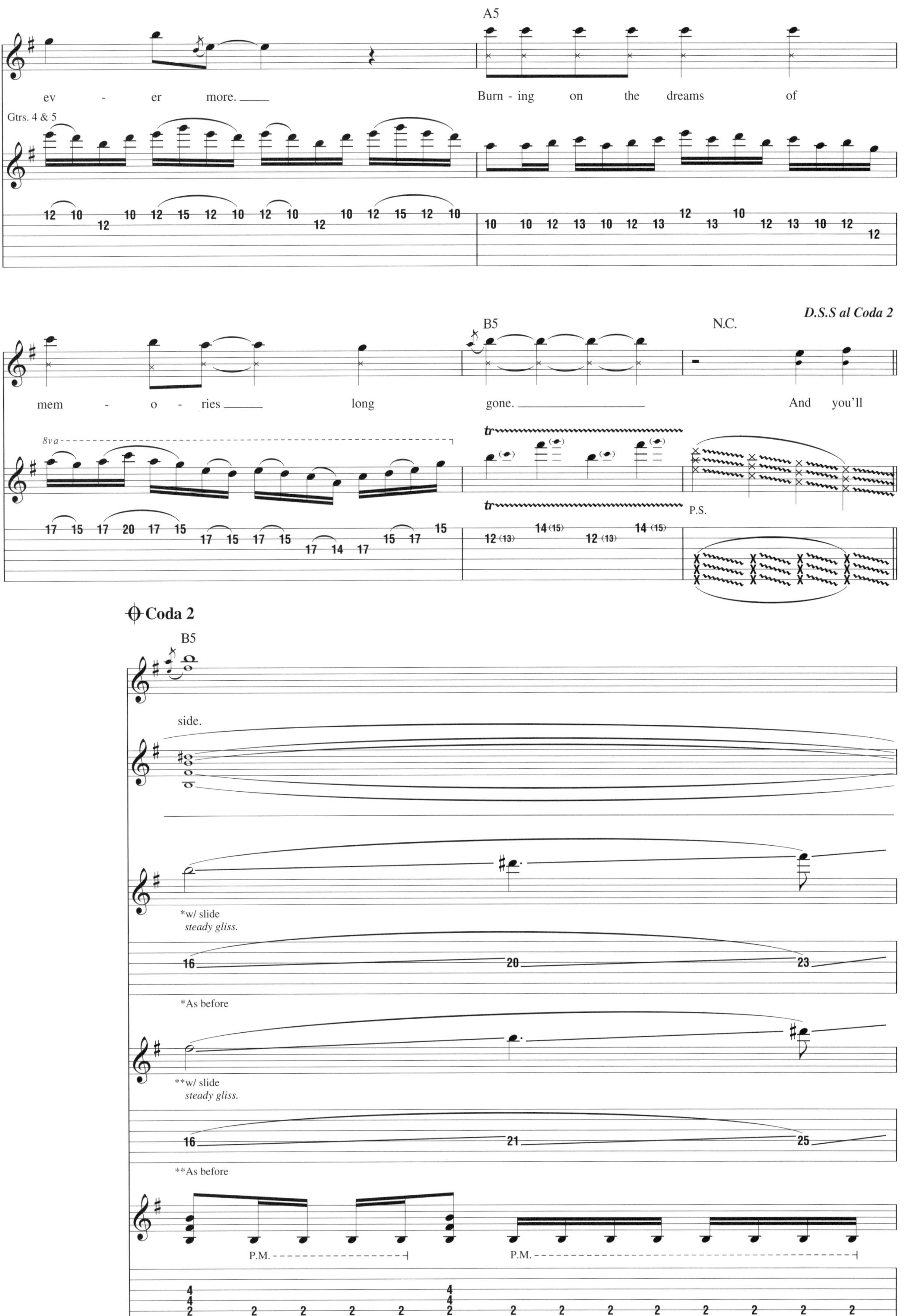
A5
ev - er more.
Burn - ing on the dreams of
Gtrs. 4 & 5
B5
N.C.
D.S.S al Coda 2
mem - o - ries long
gone.
And you'll
8va
tr
P.S.
Coda 2
B5
side.
*w/ slide
steady gliss.
*As before
**w/ slide
steady gliss.
**As before
P.M.
P.M.

*Symbols in parentheses represent chord names respective to de-tuned guitar. Symbols above represent actual sounding chords.

Gtr. 1 tacet

G♯m (Bm) N.C. B (D) N.C. G♯m (Bm) N.C.

8va

Gtr. 4

Gtr. 5

Gtr. 6

Gtr. 7 *divisi*

*P.M. P.M. P.M.

*Applies to both gtrs.

B (D) N.C. F♯5 (A5) G♯5 (B5)

8va

w/ DigiTech Whammy Pedal

w/ bar w/ bar

w/ DigiTech Whammy Pedal

w/ bar w/ bar

Gtrs. 6 & 7

P.M.

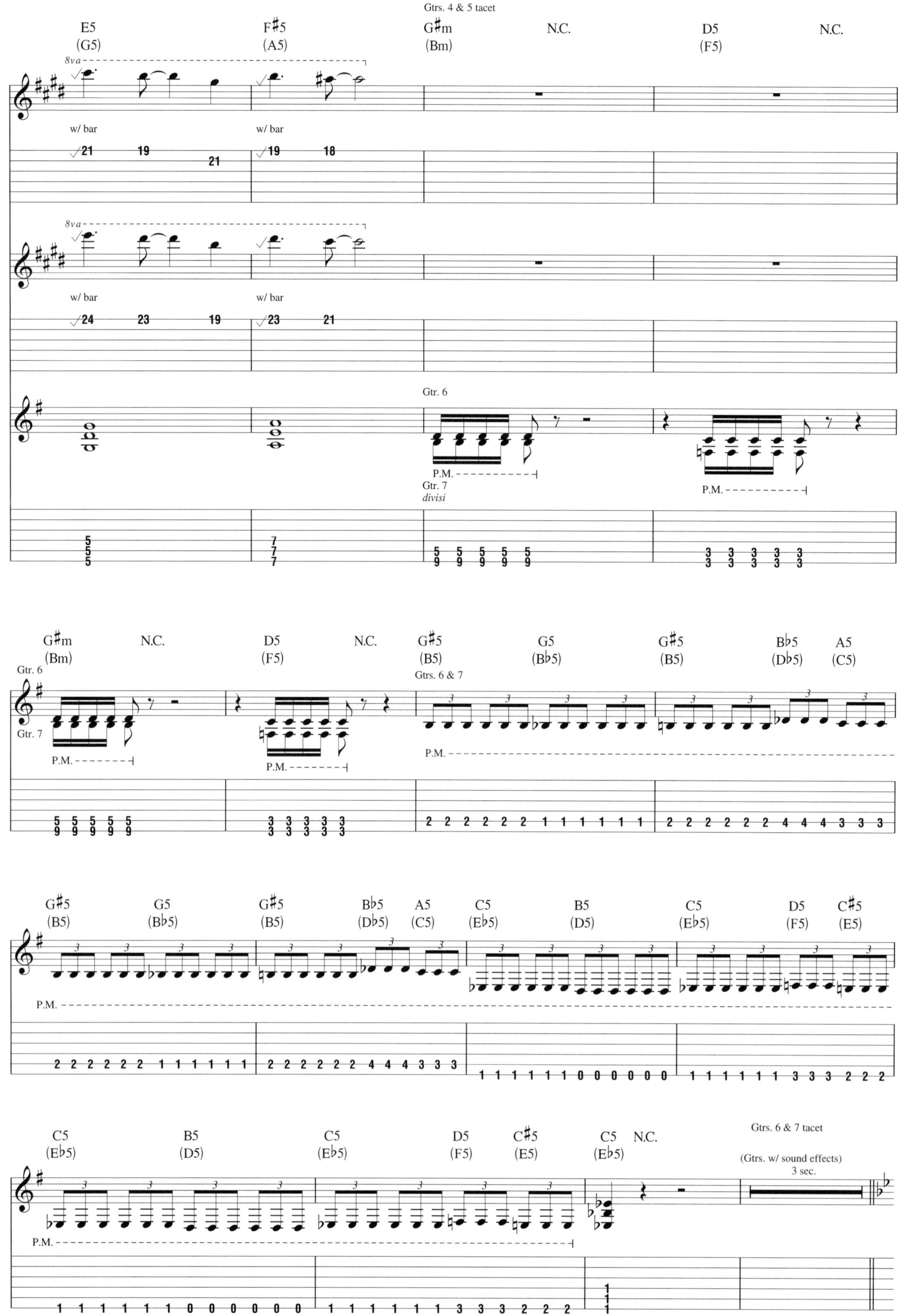

Gtrs. 4 & 5 tacet
E5 (G5)
F#5 (A5)
G#m (Bm)
N.C.
D5 (F5)
8va
w/ bar
Gtr. 6
Gtr. 7
divisi
P.M.
G#5 (B5)
G5 (Bb5)
Bb5 (Db5)
A5 (C5)
Gtrs. 6 & 7
C5 (Eb5)
B5 (D5)
C#5 (E5)
Gtrs. 6 & 7 tacet
(Gtrs. w/ sound effects)
3 sec.

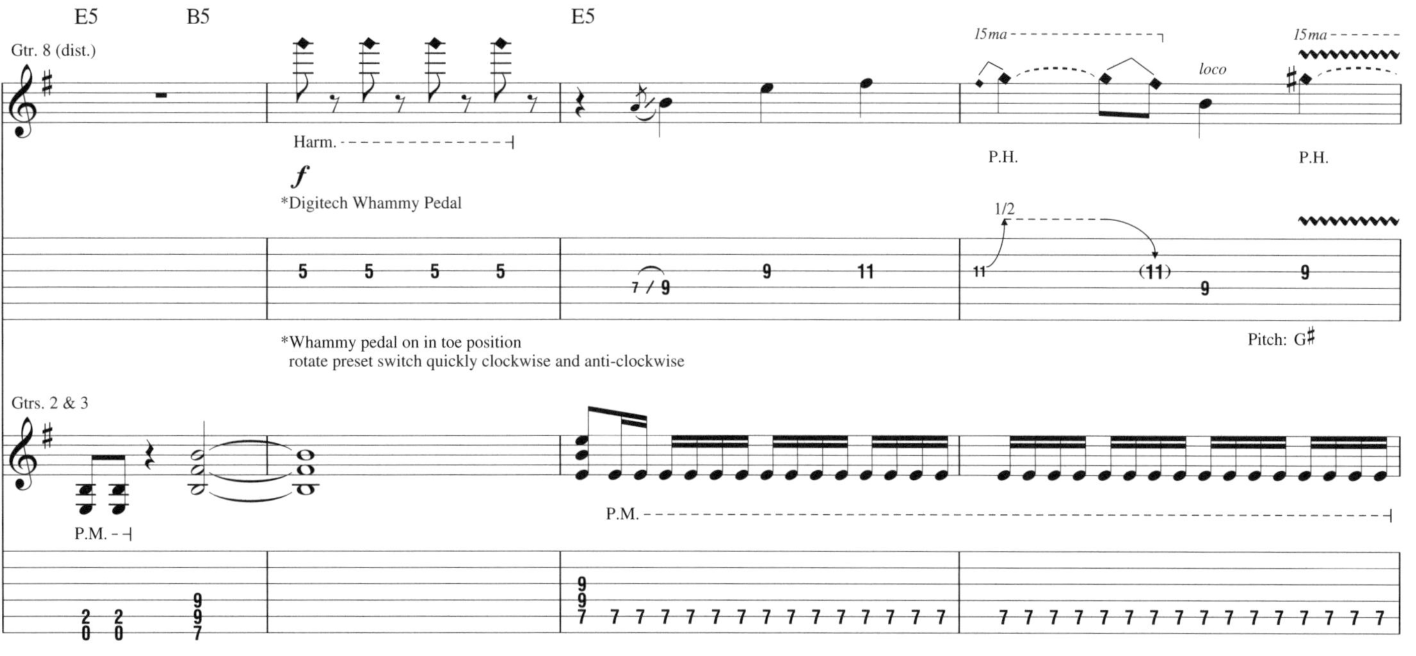
E5
B5
E5
Gtr. 8 (dist.)
15ma
loco
15ma
Harm.
P.H.
P.H.
f
*Digitech Whammy Pedal
1/2
*Whammy pedal on in toe position
rotate preset switch quickly clockwise and anti-clockwise
Pitch: G♯
Gtrs. 2 & 3
P.M.
P.M.

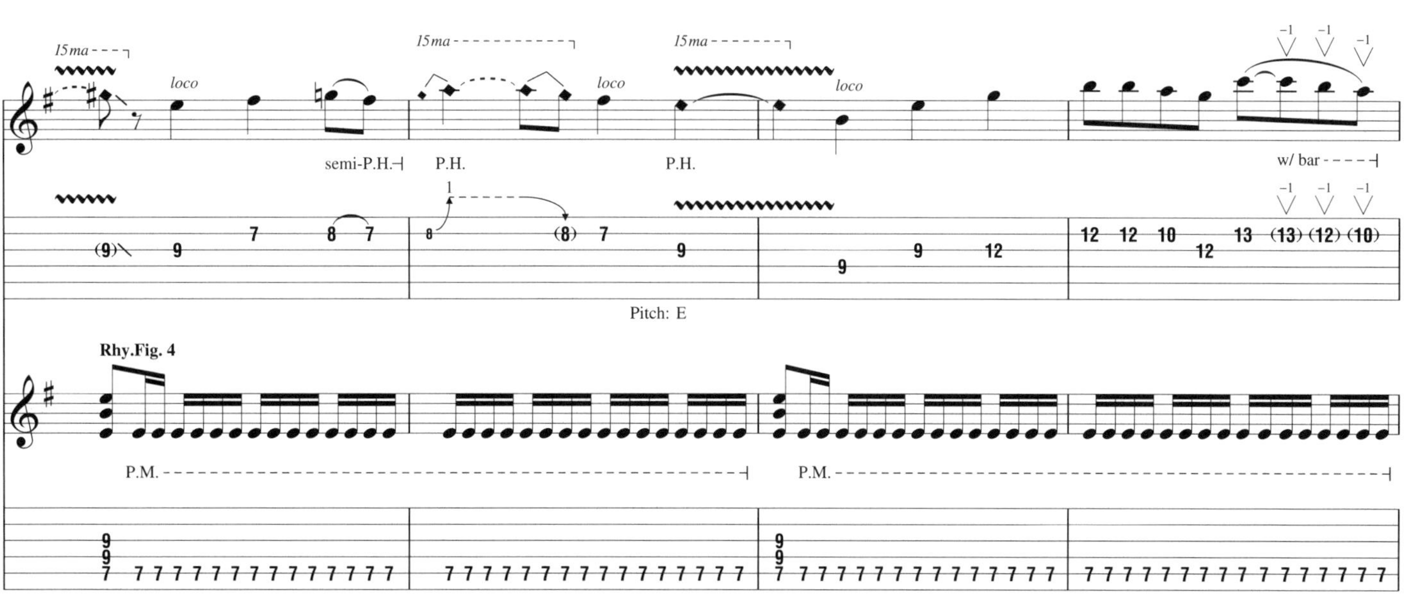
15ma
loco
15ma
loco
15ma
loco
semi-P.H.
P.H.
P.H.
w/ bar
Pitch: E
Rhy.Fig. 4
P.M.
P.M.

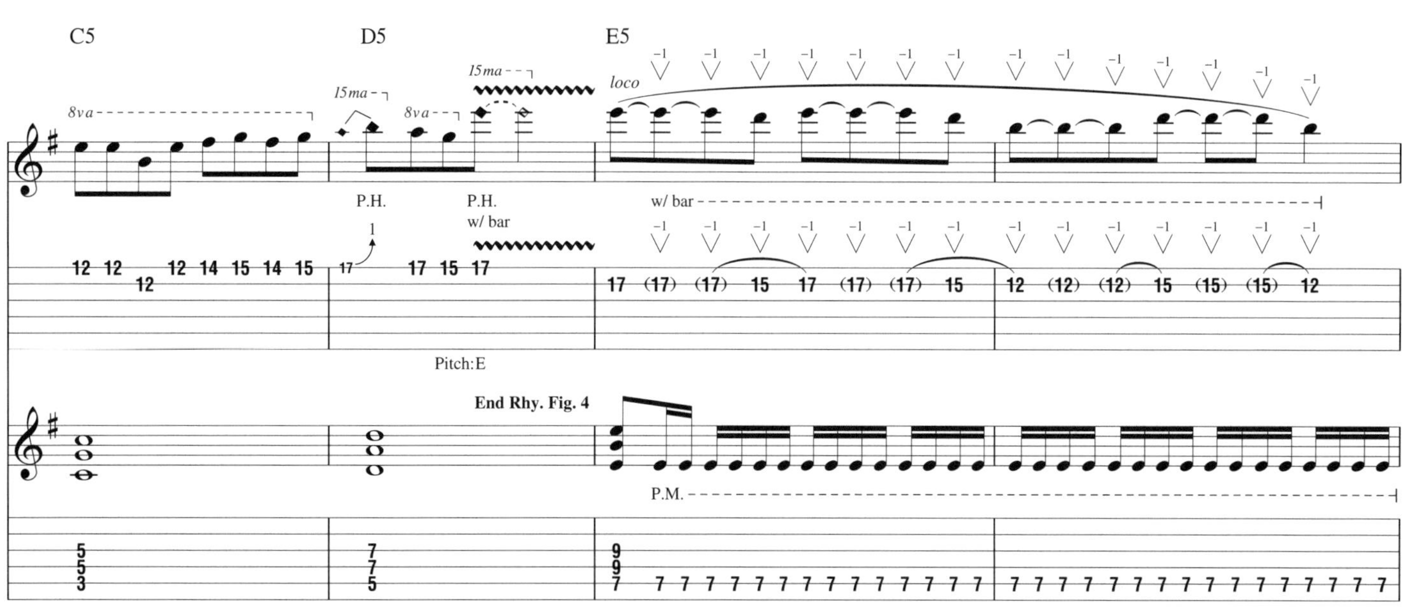
C5
D5
E5
8va
15ma
8va
15ma
loco
P.H.
P.H.
w/ bar
w/ bar
Pitch:E
End Rhy. Fig. 4
P.M.

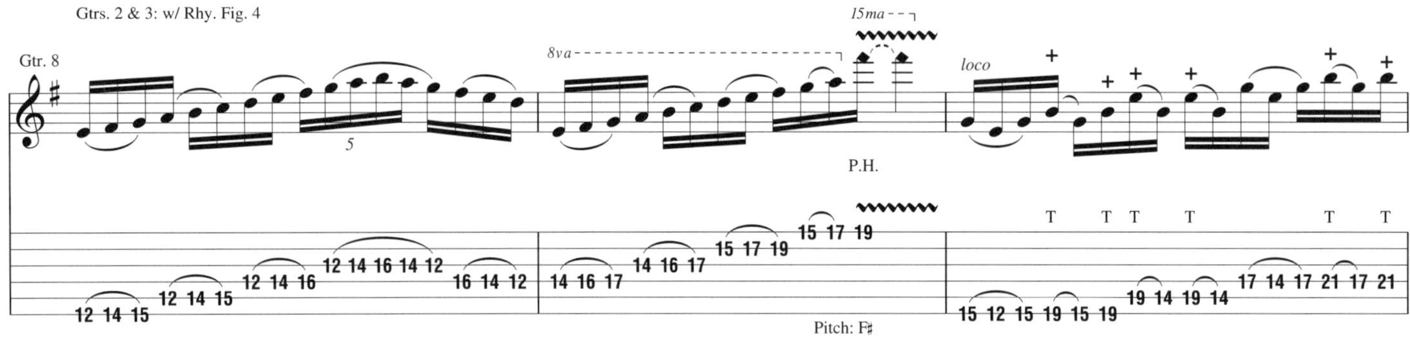

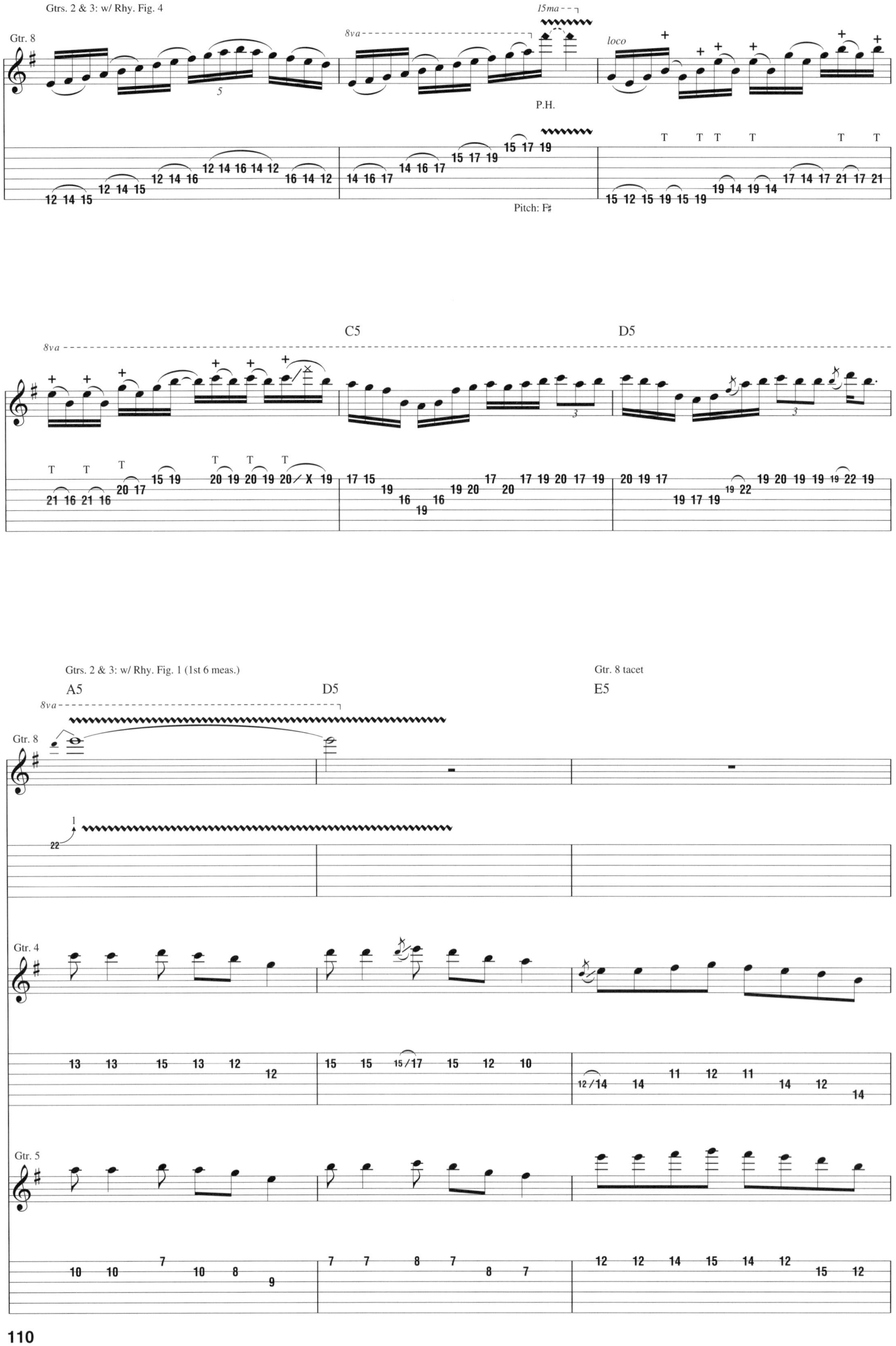

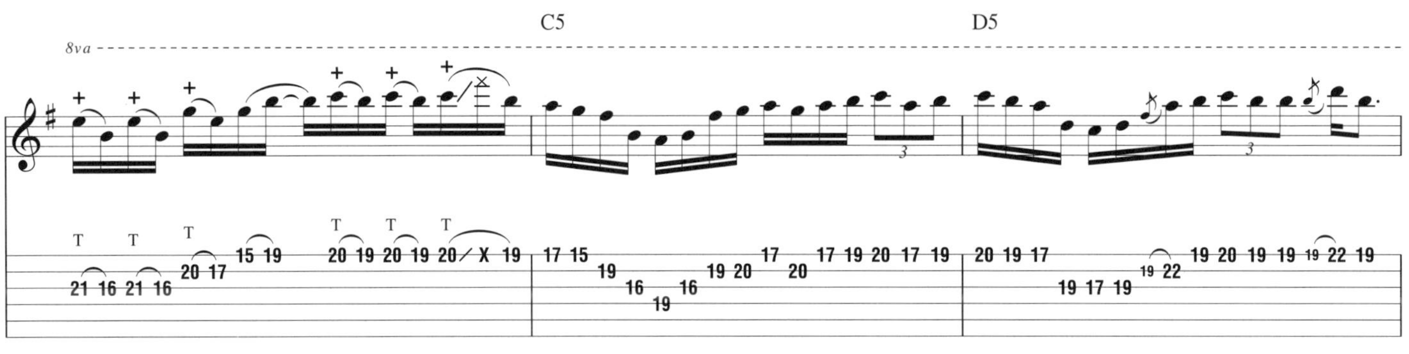

Gtrs. 2 & 3: w/ Rhy. Fig. 1 (1st 6 meas.)

Gtr. 8 tacet

A5 D5 E5

8va

Gtr. 8

Gtr. 4

Gtr. 5

A5
Gtr. 4
w/ bar
8va
Gtr. 5
w/ bar
8va
B5
C5
B5
8va
Gtr. 4
loco
Gtr. 5
loco
8va
Gtrs. 2 & 3
P.M.

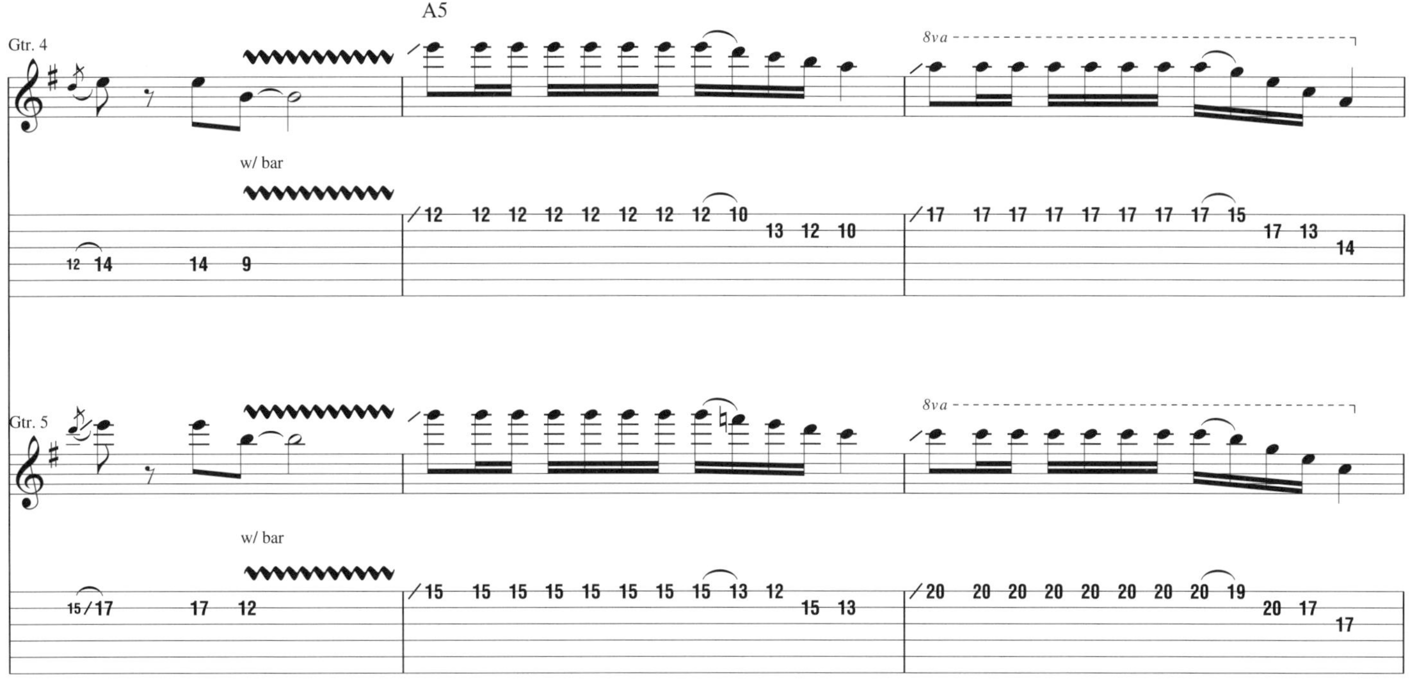

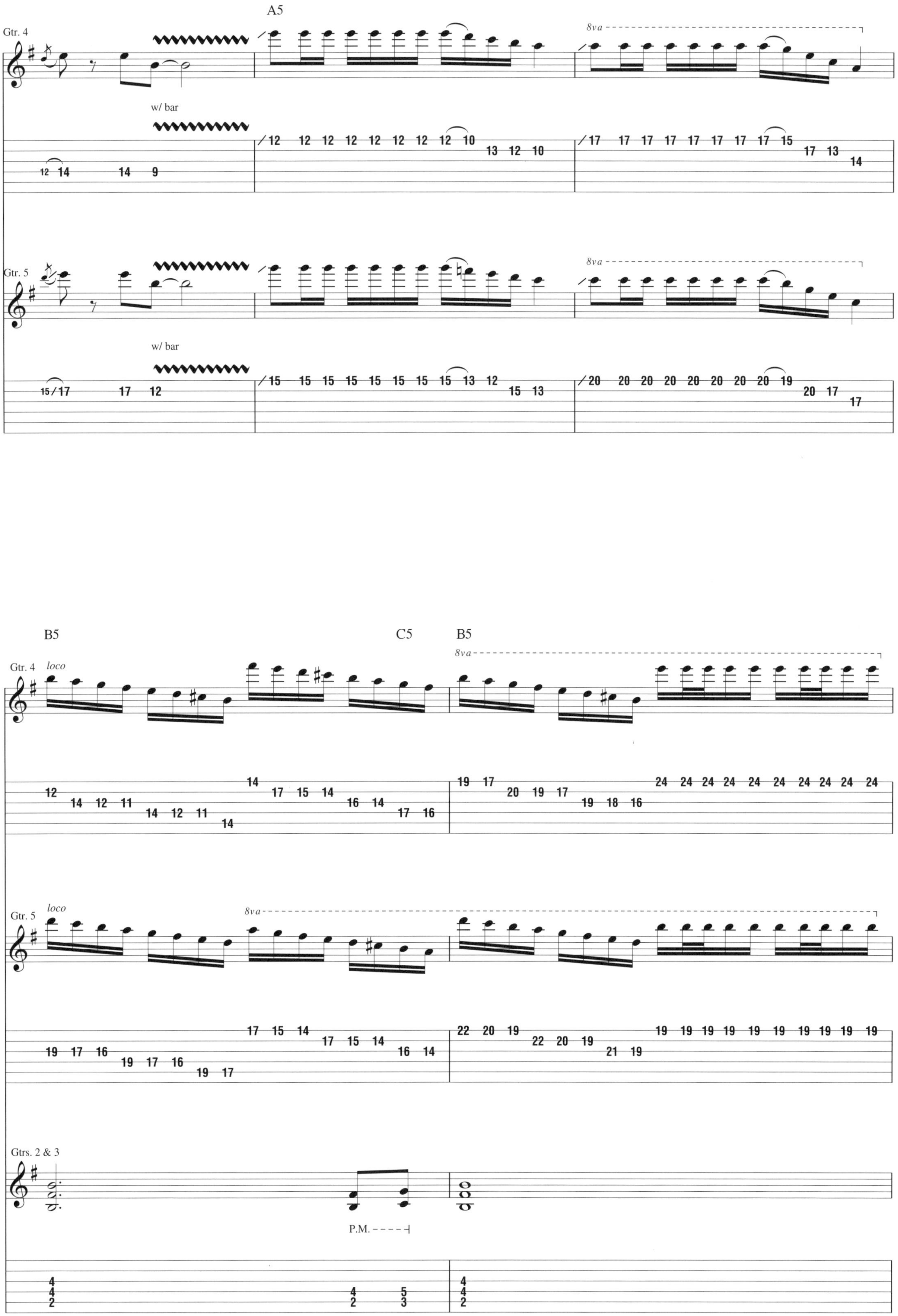

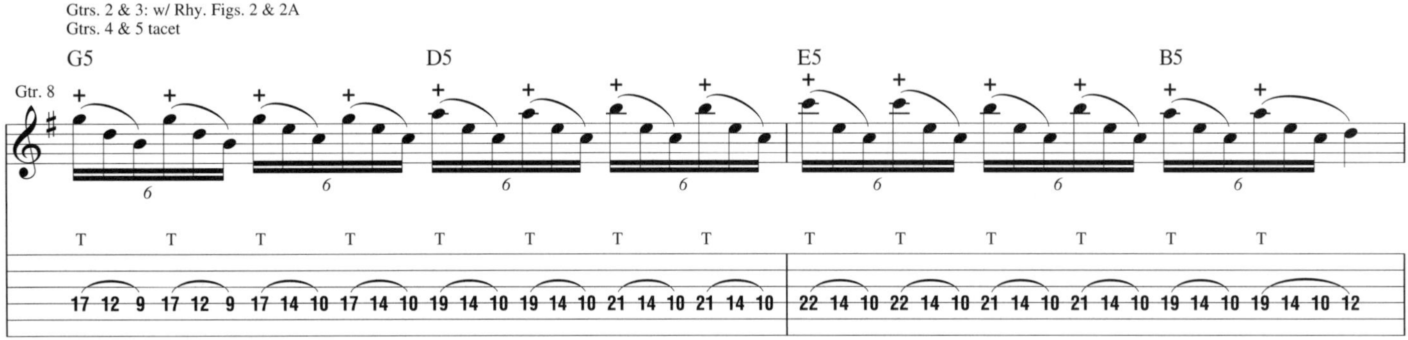
Gtrs. 2 & 3: w/ Rhy. Figs. 2 & 2A
Gtrs. 4 & 5 tacet
G5
D5
E5
B5
Gtr. 8

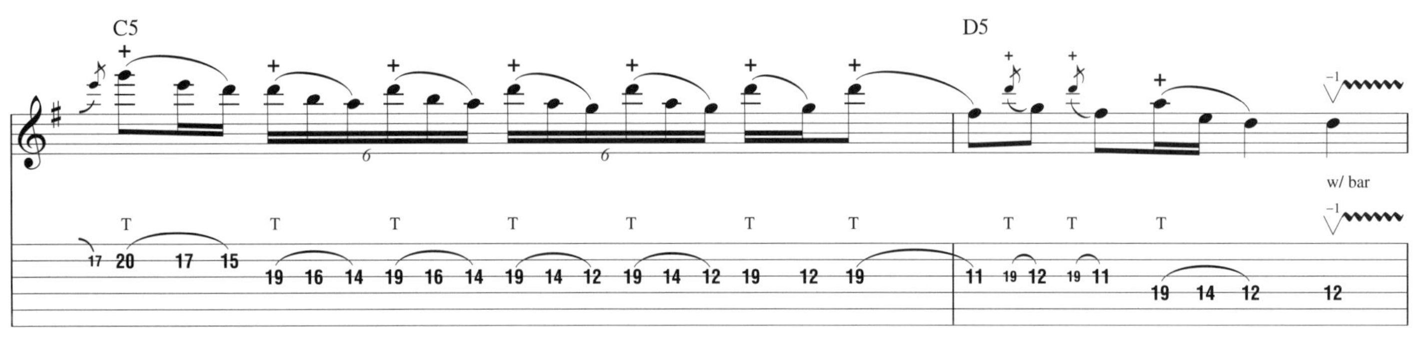
C5
D5
w/ bar

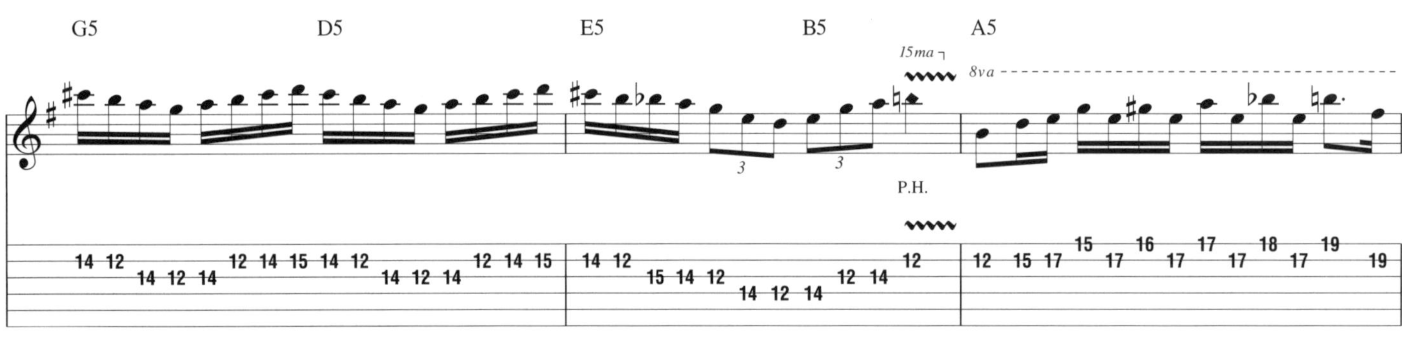
G5
D5
E5
B5
A5
15ma
8va
P.H.

B5
C5
D5
8va
Gtr. 8
Gtrs. 2 & 3
P.M.
P.M.

Gtrs. 2 & 3: w/ Rhy. Fig. 3 (1st 14 meas.)
E5
C5
Gtr. 8 tacet
D5
8va
Gtr. 8
Gtr. 4
Gtr. 5
E5
A5
*w/ octaver
*Set for one octave above.
semi-P.H.
C5
D5
octaver off
loco

8va loco

E5

D5

E5

C5

D5

E5

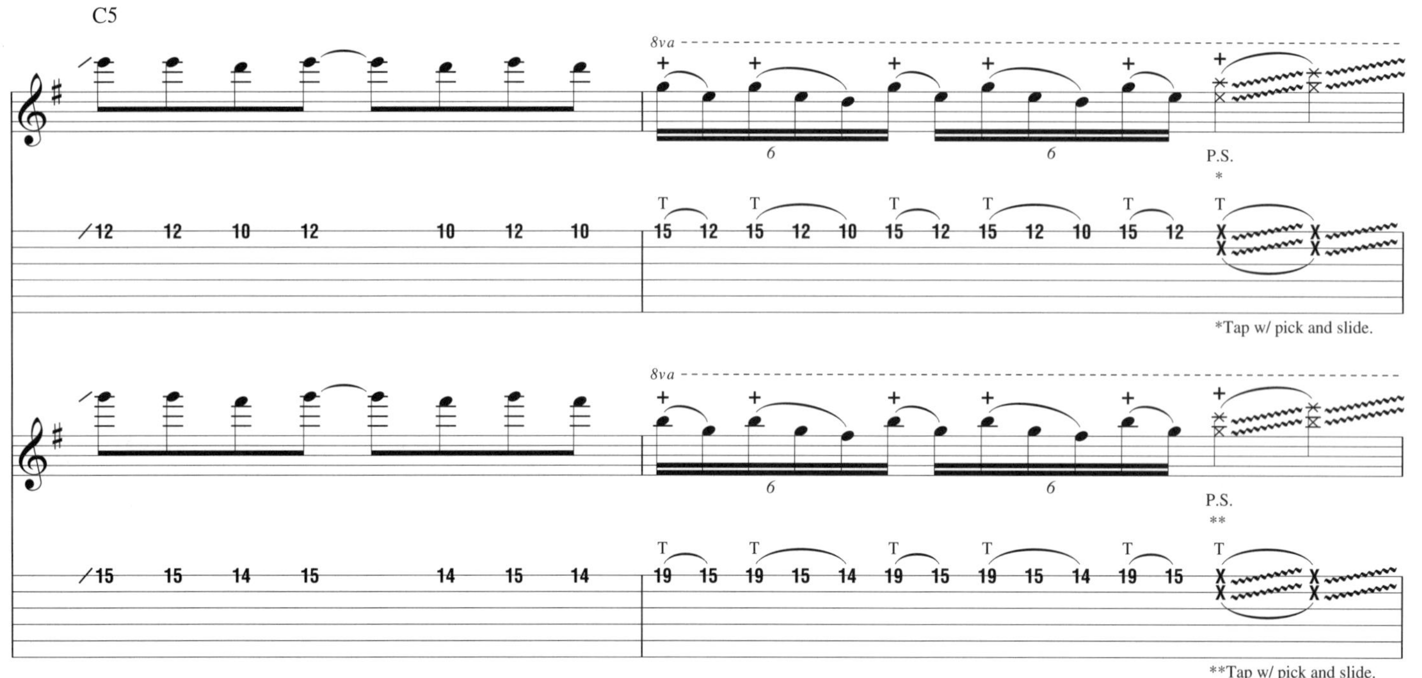

**Tap w/ pick and slide.

B5
End double-time feel
Interlude
G N.C.
Whoa.
Voc. Fig. 2
(Whoa.
Gtr. 4
8va
15ma
P.H.
Gtr. 5
Pitch: B
Gtrs. 2 & 3
P.M.
Gtrs. 2-5 tacet
C
End Voc. Fig. 2
Em
D
Whoa.)

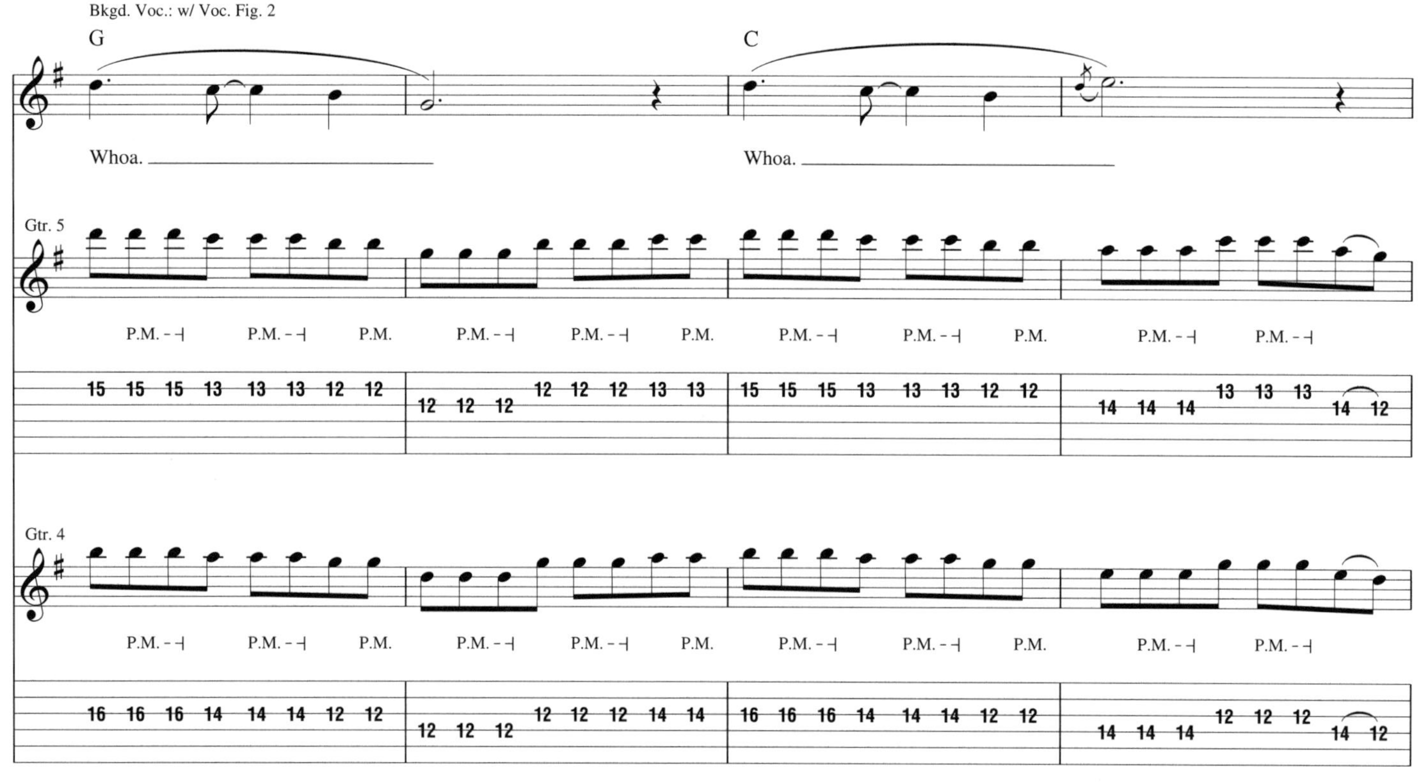

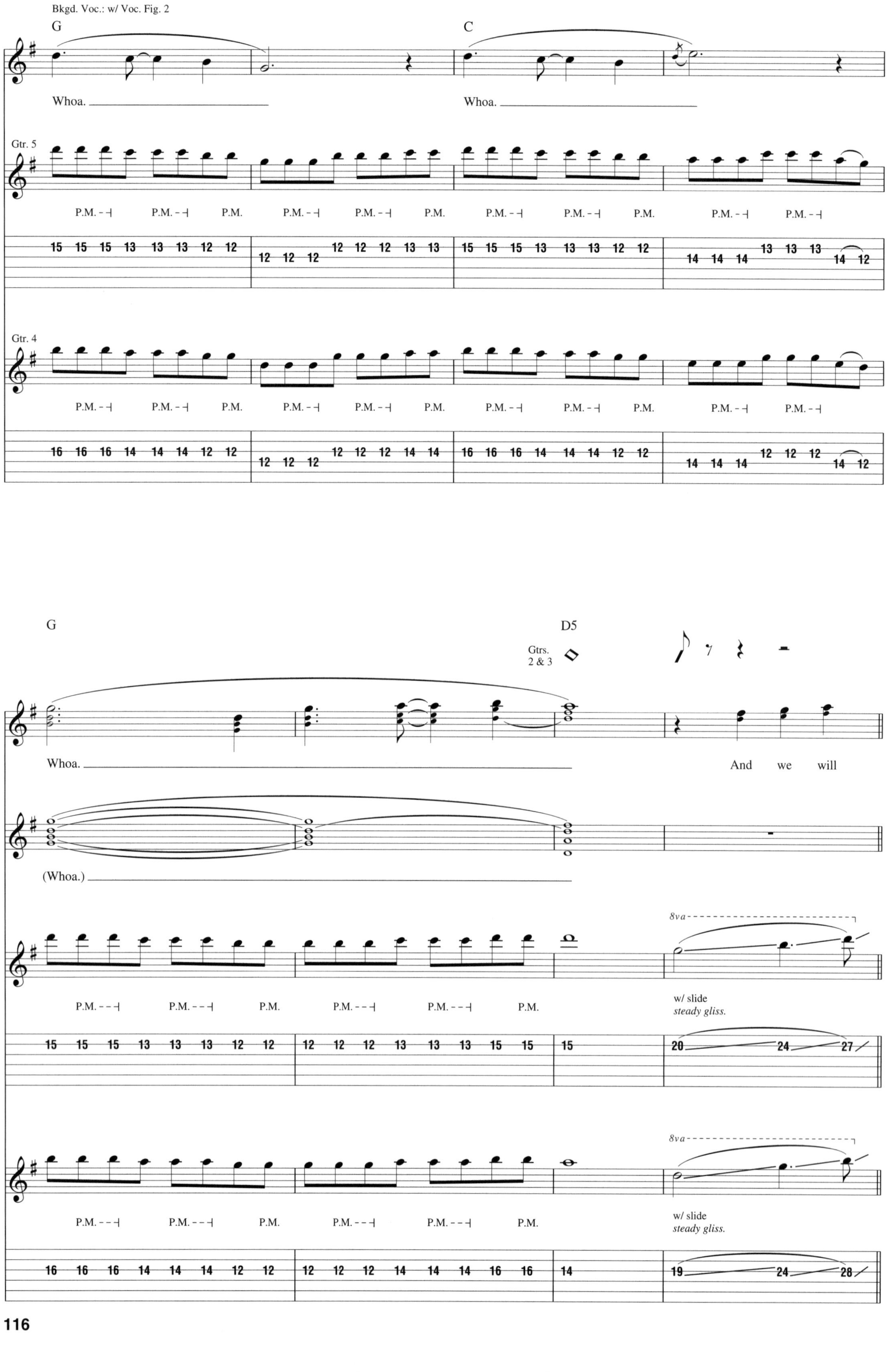

G

D5

Gtrs. 2 & 3

Whoa.

And we will

(Whoa.)

P.M.

8va

w/ slide

steady gliss.

Chorus
Double-time feel

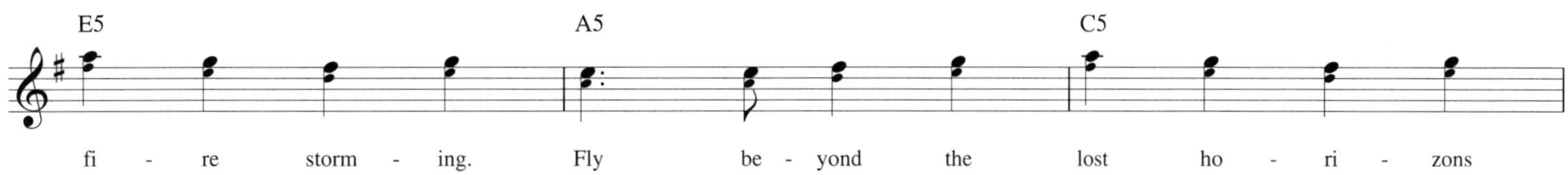

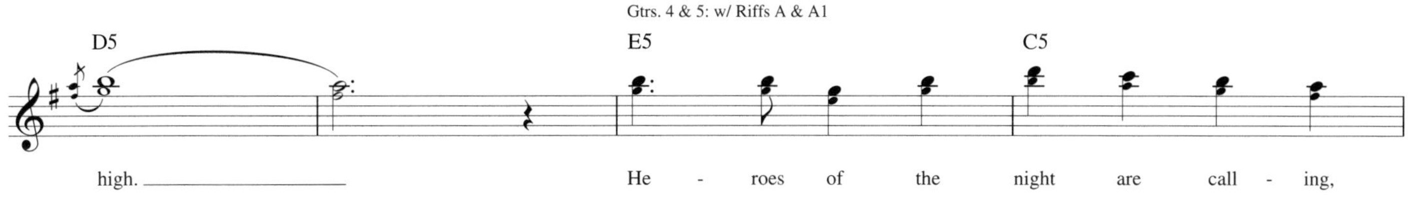

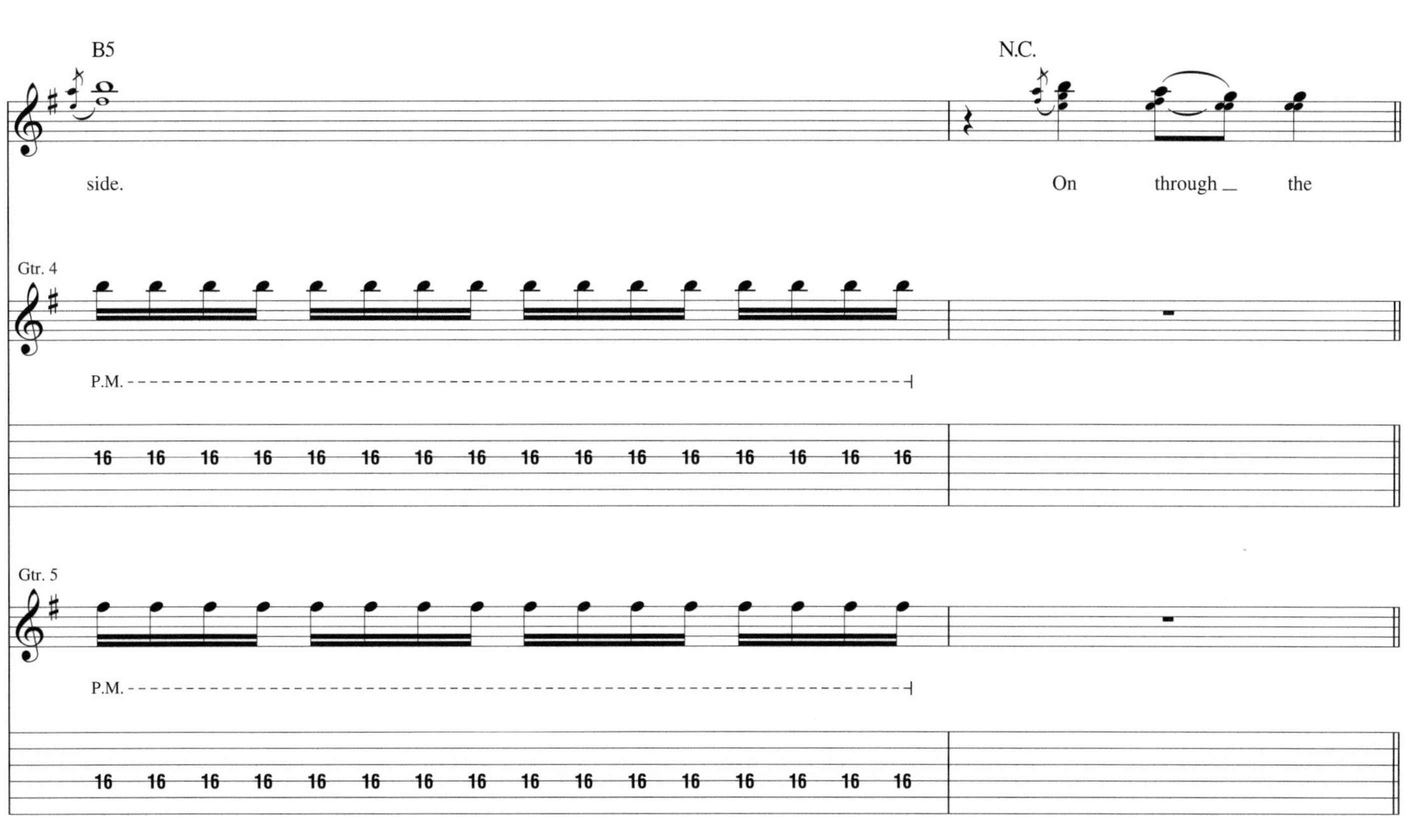

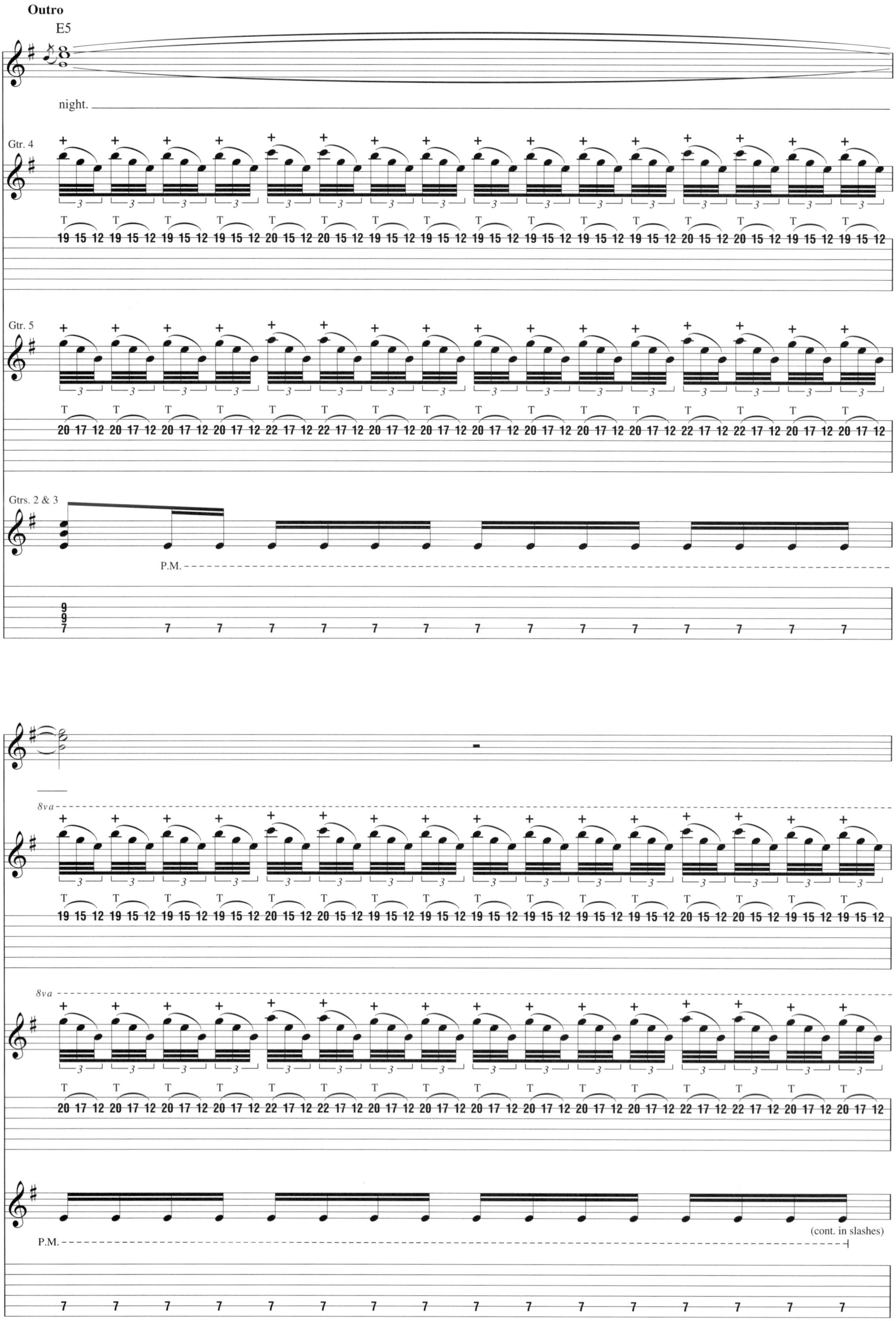

Outro

E5

night.

Gtr. 4

T T T T T T T T T T T T T T T T

19 15 12 19 15 12 19 15 12 19 15 12 20 15 12 20 15 12 19 15 12 19 15 12 19 15 12 19 15 12 19 15 12 19 15 12 20 15 12 20 15 12 19 15 12 19 15 12

Gtr. 5

T T T T T T T T T T T T T T T T

20 17 12 20 17 12 20 17 12 20 17 12 22 17 12 22 17 12 20 17 12 20 17 12 20 17 12 20 17 12 20 17 12 20 17 12 22 17 12 22 17 12 20 17 12 20 17 12

Gtrs. 2 & 3

P.M.

9
9
7 7 7 7 7 7 7 7 7 7 7 7 7 7 7 7

8va

T T T T T T T T T T T T T T T T

19 15 12 19 15 12 19 15 12 19 15 12 20 15 12 20 15 12 19 15 12 19 15 12 19 15 12 19 15 12 19 15 12 19 15 12 20 15 12 20 15 12 19 15 12 19 15 12

8va

T T T T T T T T T T T T T T T T

20 17 12 20 17 12 20 17 12 20 17 12 22 17 12 22 17 12 20 17 12 20 17 12 20 17 12 20 17 12 20 17 12 20 17 12 22 17 12 22 17 12 20 17 12 20 17 12

(cont. in slashes)

P.M.

7 7 7 7 7 7 7 7 7 7 7 7 7 7 7 7

E5 B5 C5 A5 B5

Gtrs. 2 & 3

8va

Gtr. 4

w/ DigiTech Whammy Pedal

+6

| 12 (15) | 12 (13) | 13 (14) 10 (12) | 16 16 16 19 19 19 16 19 16 16 16 19 19 19 16 19 |

8va

Gtr. 5

loco

w/ DigiTech Whammy Pedal

+6

| 12 (15) | 12 (13) | 13 (14) 10 (12) | 11 13 11 12 11 12 11 12 11 13 11 12 11 12 11 12 |

E5

8va

steady gliss.

+6 +4 1/2

| 16 (17) | 15 15 | |

8va

steady gliss.

+6 +3 1/2

| 12 (13) | 12 15 1 | |

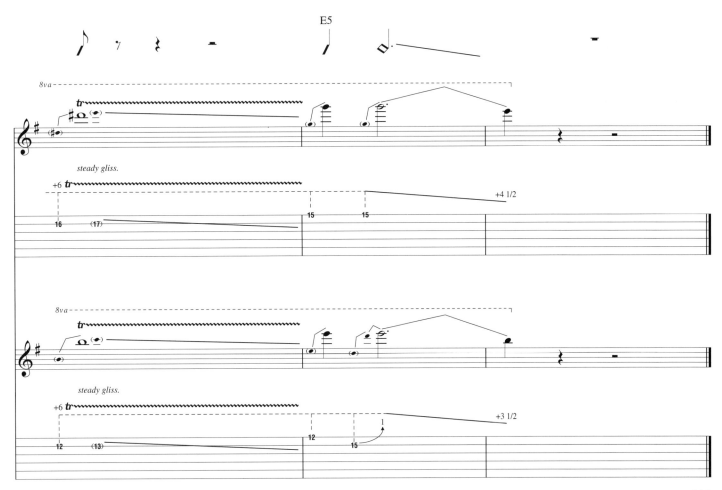

Operation Ground and Pound

Words and Music by Herman Li, ZP Theart, Sam Totman and Vadim Pruzhanov

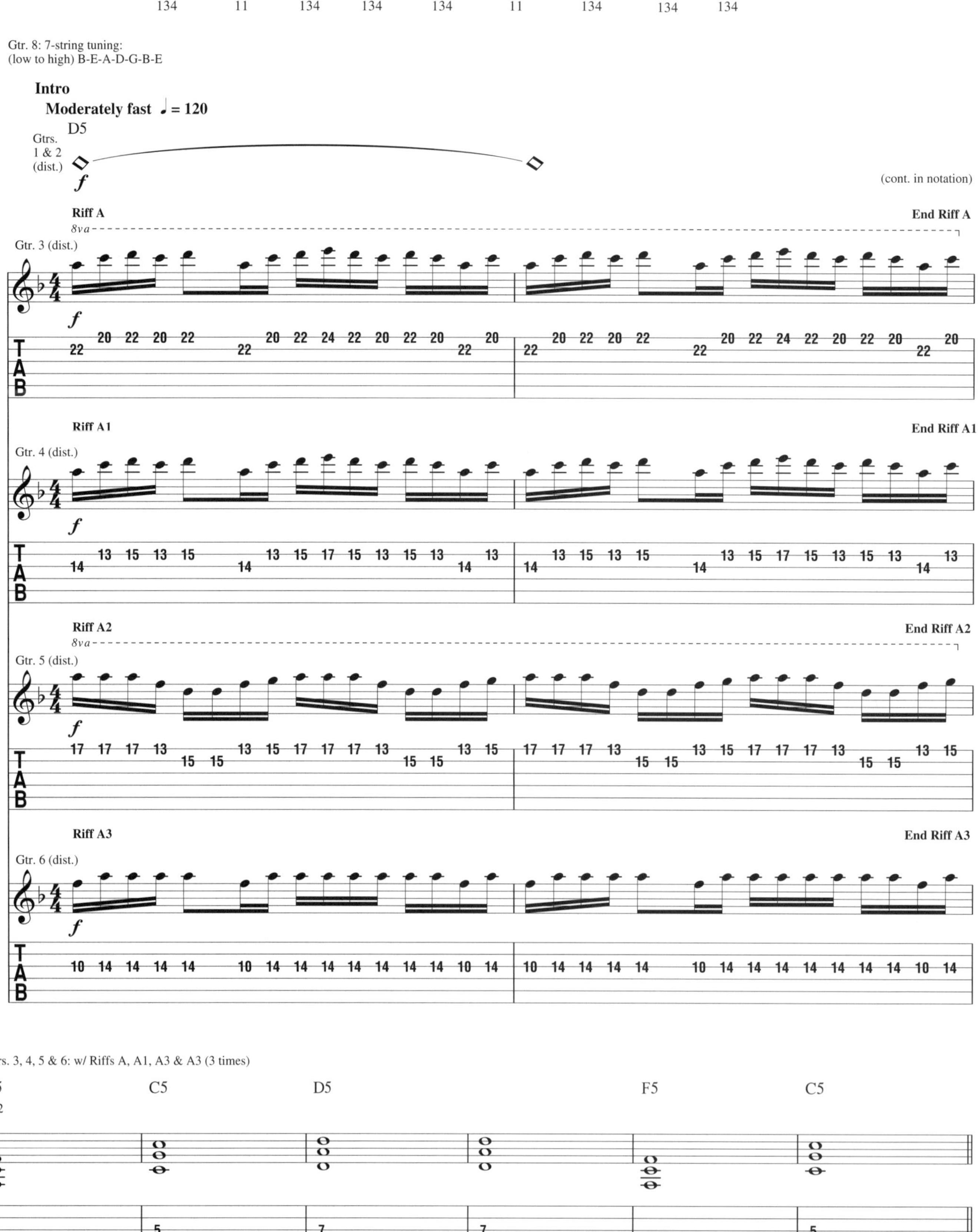

Gtrs. 3, 4, 5 & 6: w/ Riffs A, A1, A3 & A3 (4 times)
Gtrs. 3, 4 & 6: w/ Riffs A, A1 & A3
D5
F5
C5
A5
Faster ♩ = 200
B♭5
loco
8va
Gtr. 3
Gtr. 4
Gtr. 5
Gtr. 6
Gtrs. 1 & 2
semi-P.H.
P.M.
*Vol. swell

D5
semi-P.H.
semi-P.H.
Rhy. Fig. 1
P.M.
P.M.
8va
G5
loco
P.H.
P.M.
P.M.
P.M.

A5
D5
15ma
loco
P.H.
Pitch: B
P.M.
F5

C5
B♭5
P.M.
(cont. in slashes)
A5
D5
C5
D5
Gtrs. 1 & 2
Gtr. 3
8va
Gtr. 4
G5
F5
A5
End Rhy. Fig. 1
(cont. in notation)

Verse
Gtrs. 3 & 4 tacet
*B5
A5
1. Smash - ing through the bound - a - ries,
storm - ing through the burn - ing fields.
die, I watch you die in - side while fear con - trols your
Rhy. Figs. 2 & 2A
Gtrs. 1 & 2
w/ variation on repeat
P.M.
*Chord symbols reflect basic harmony.
G5
Stand be - fore the e - vil one
on to - wards the morn - ing sun.
life. And re - ject this an - i - mos - i - ty that
B5
A5
B5
Fall - ing un - der skies of pain.
Still we're search - ing end - less - ly,
killed so man - y minds. You feel the pow - er
A5
crash - ing o - ver sev - en seas.
deep with - in the fear you hold in - side, just to

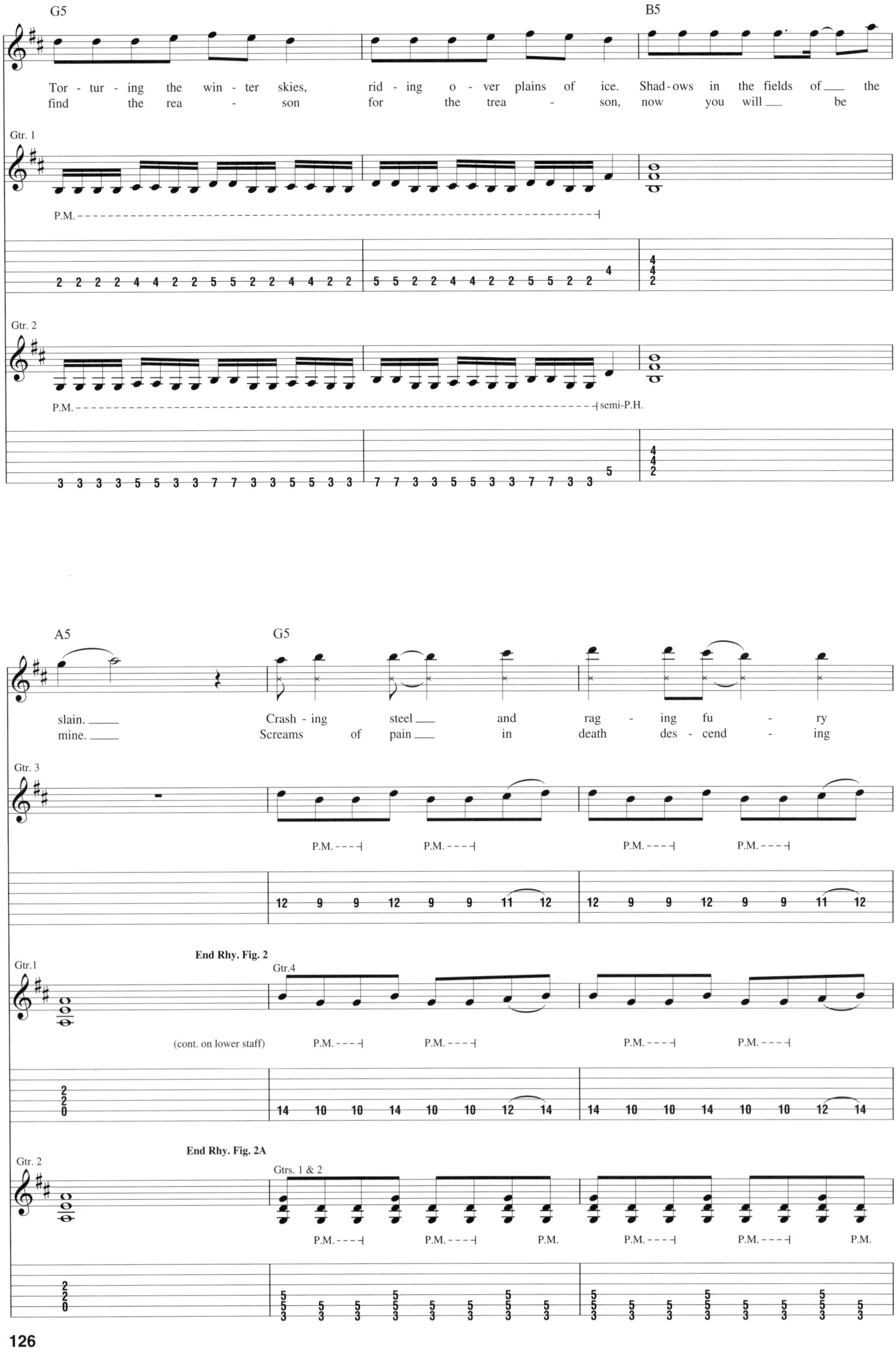

A5 G5

slain. ___ Crash - ing steel ___ and rag - ing fu - ry

mine. ___ Screams of pain ___ in death des - cend - ing

Gtr. 3

P.M. P.M. P.M. P.M.

End Rhy. Fig. 2

Gtr.1

Gtr.4

(cont. on lower staff) P.M. P.M. P.M. P.M.

End Rhy. Fig. 2A

Gtr. 2

Gtrs. 1 & 2

P.M. P.M. P.M. P.M. P.M. P.M.

B5
smash their quest, de - stroy the ar - my.
rise a - gain from hell de - fend - ing.
Gtr. 3
Gtr. 4
divisi
P.M.
Gtr. 1
Gtr. 2
E5
Crash the le - gions of the twi - light,
Burn their hearts with - in the fi - re,
Gtrs. 1 & 2

2nd time, Gtrs. 3 & 4: w/ Fills 1 & 2

B5 A5

tem - plars of steel will burn.
war - ri - ors of light will be slain.

P.M.

14 12 15 14 12 15 14 12 15 14 12 14 14 12 14 11

P.M.

11 9 12 11 9 12 11 9 12 11 9 12 11 9 12 9

P.M.

4 4 2

2 0 2 0 2 0 2 0 2 0 2 0

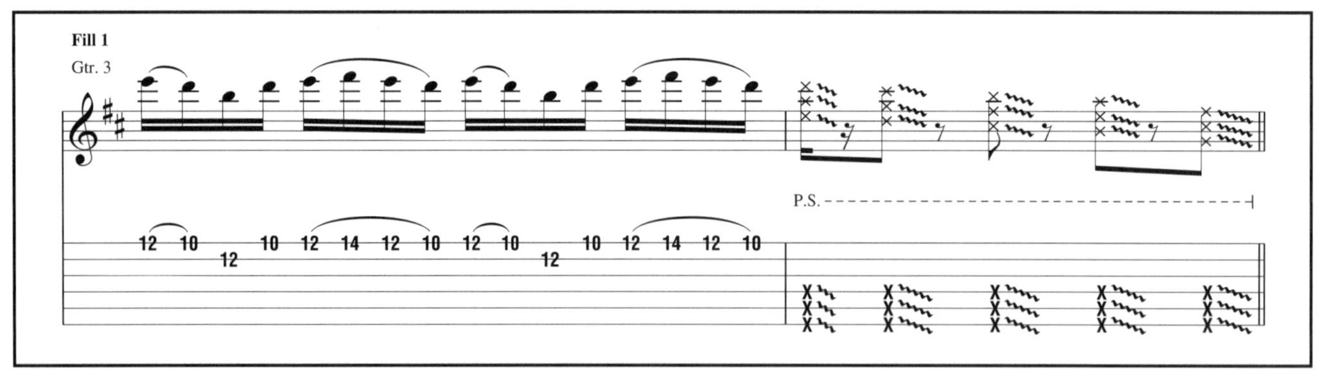

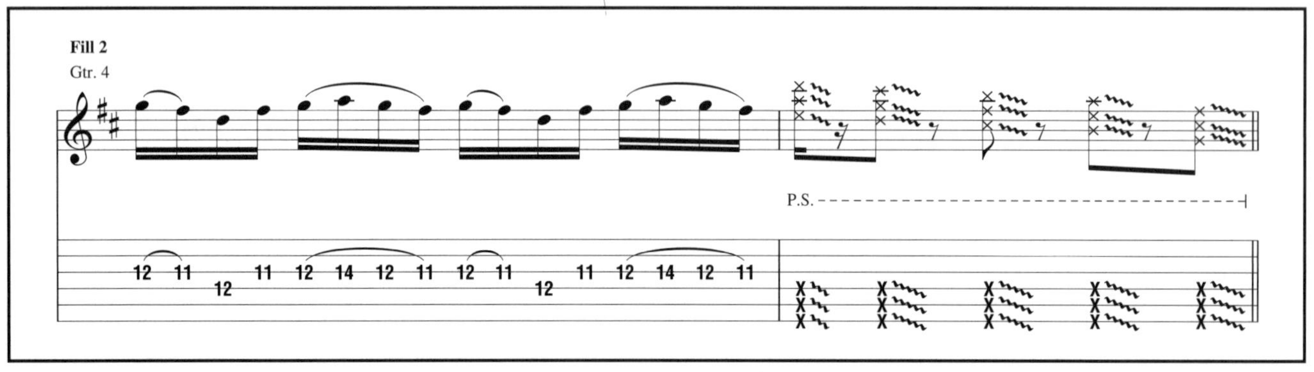

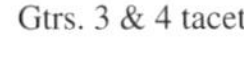
Pre-Chorus

Gtrs. 3 & 4 tacet
D5
A5
B5
G5
Cry far a - way as we reach for the day,
Rise through the pain like the sun will rise a - gain
Rhy. Fig. 3
Gtr. 1
w/ variation on repeat
P.M.
semi-P.H.
Rhy. Fig. 3A
Gtr. 2
w/ variation on repeat
P.M.

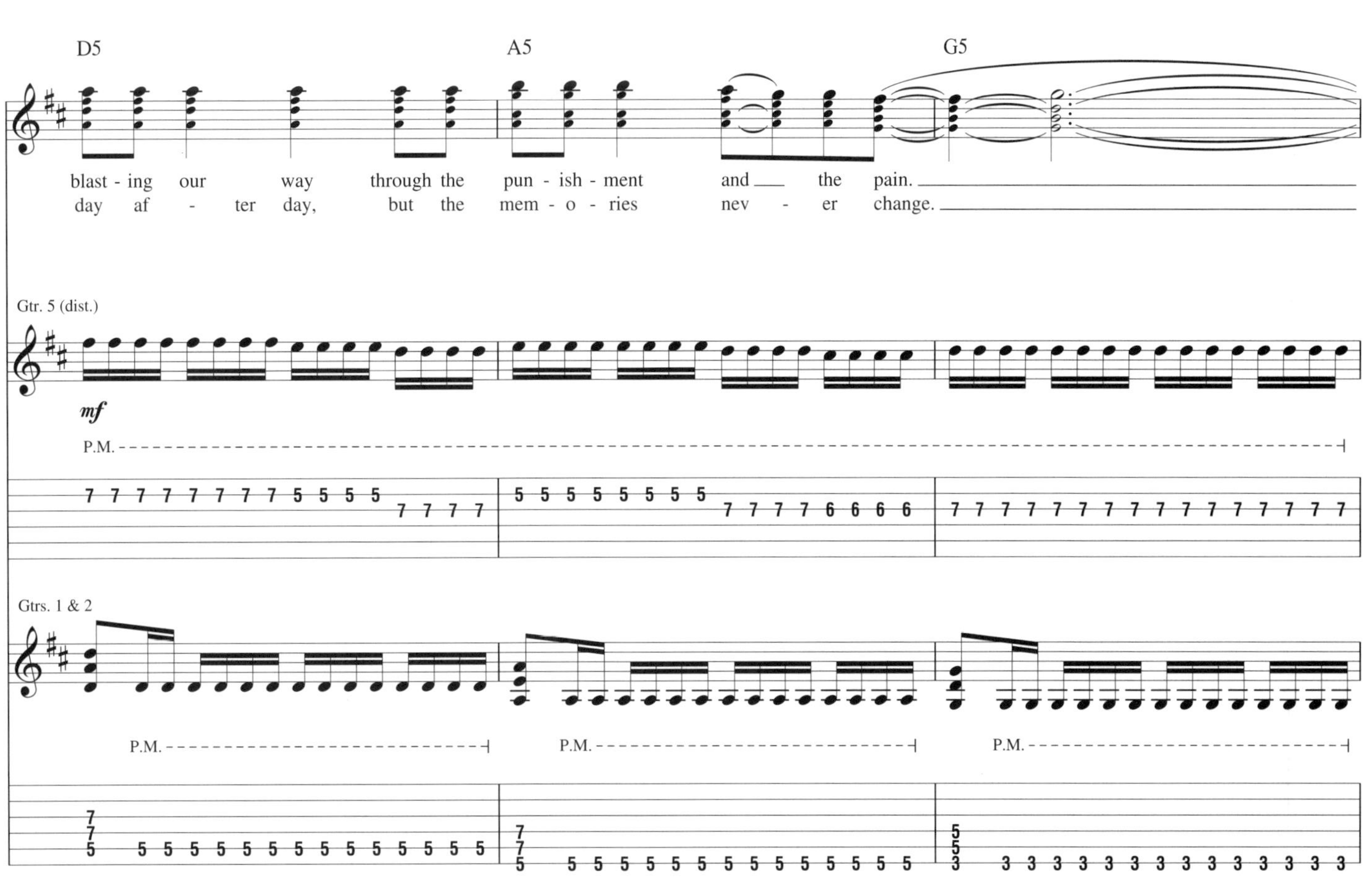
D5
A5
G5
blast - ing our way through the pun - ish - ment and the pain.
day af - ter day, but the mem - o - ries nev - er change.
Gtr. 5 (dist.)
mf
P.M.
Gtrs. 1 & 2
P.M.

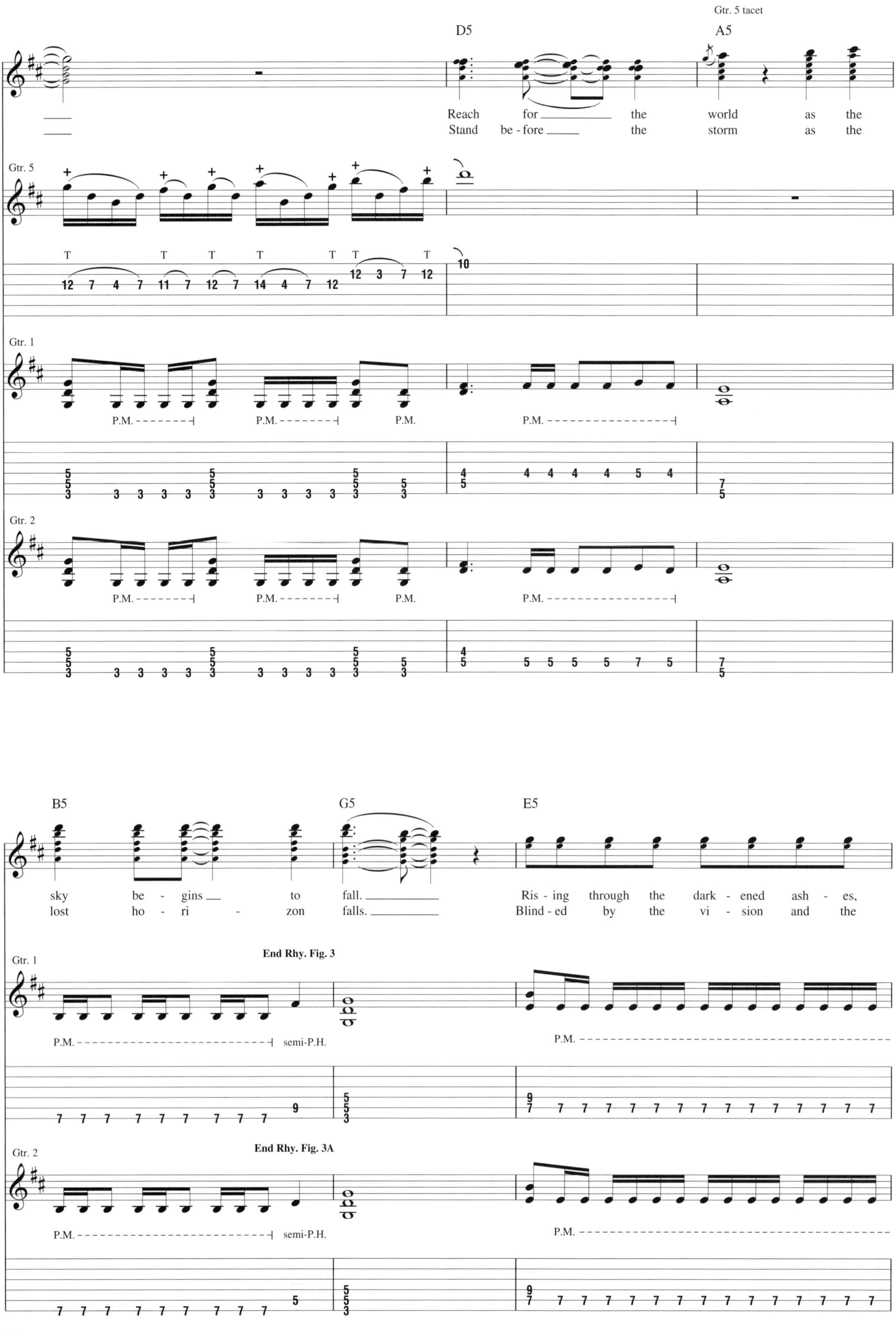

Gtr. 5 tacet

D5 A5

Reach for the world as the
Stand be - fore the storm as the

Gtr. 5

Gtr. 1

P.M. P.M. P.M. P.M.

Gtr. 2

P.M. P.M. P.M. P.M.

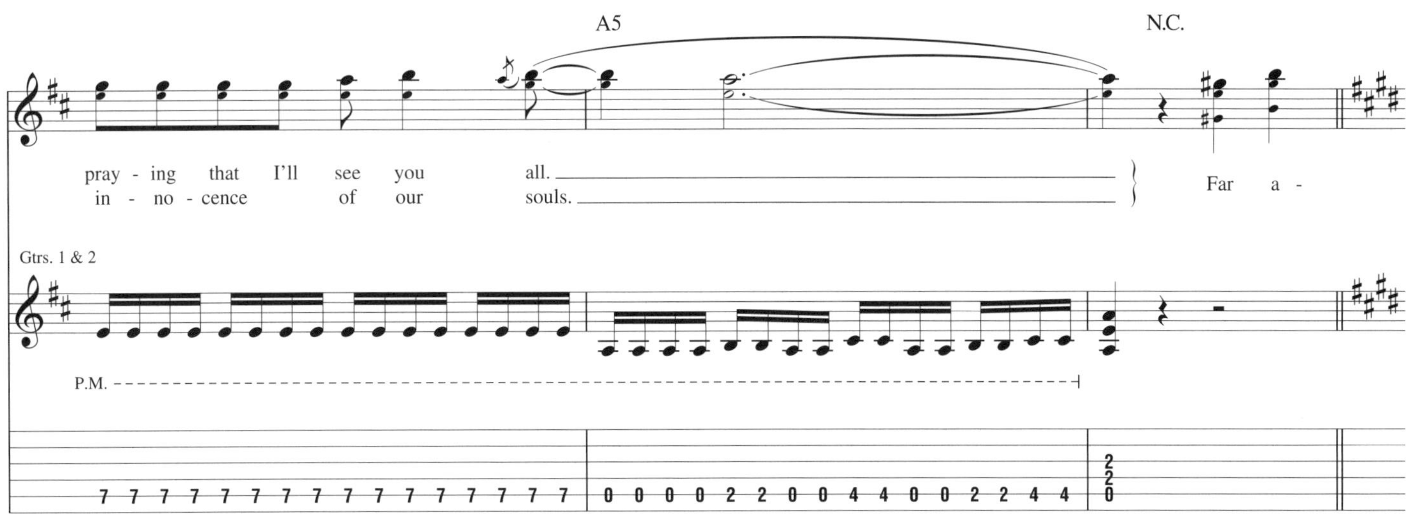
A5
N.C.
pray - ing that I'll see you all.
in - no - cence of our souls.
Far a -
Gtrs. 1 & 2
P.M.
7 7 7 7 7 7 7 7 7 7 7 7 7 7 7 7
0 0 0 0 2 2 0 0 4 4 0 0 2 2 4 4
2
2
0

Chorus

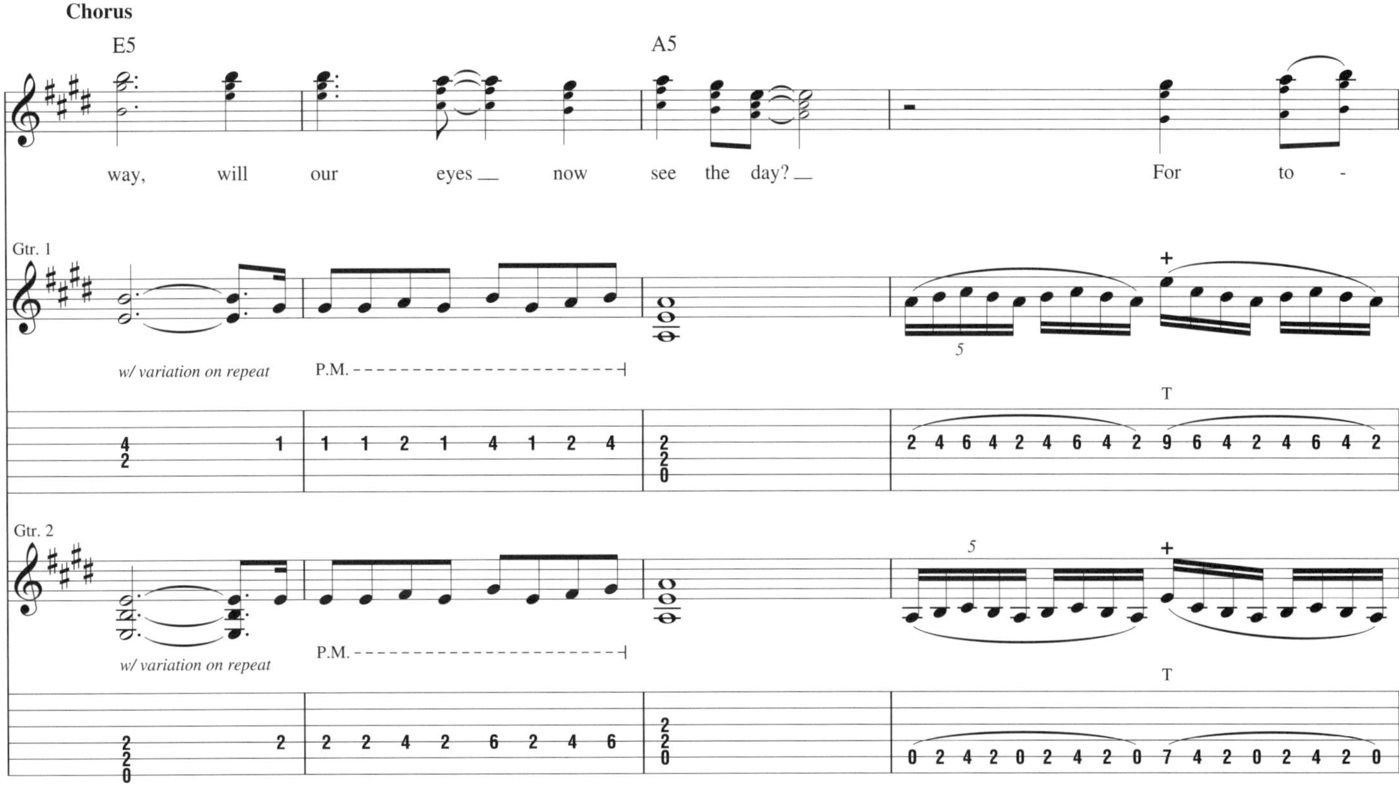
E5
A5
way, will our eyes now see the day? For to -
Gtr. 1
w/ variation on repeat
P.M.
T
Gtr. 2
w/ variation on repeat
P.M.
T

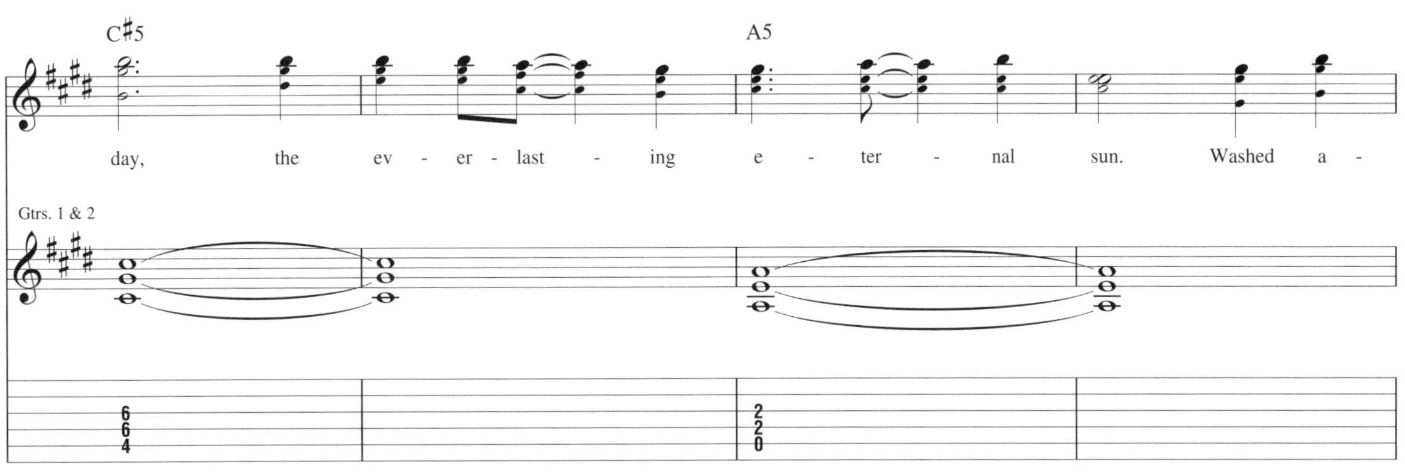
C♯5
A5
day, the ev - er - last - ing e - ter - nal sun. Washed a -
Gtrs. 1 & 2

C#5
A5
way the dreams of a bright - er day.
P.M.
P.M.
B5
For - ev - er hold the dream in - side, the
(Ah.
Gtr. 1
P.M.
P.M.
Gtr. 2
P.M.
P.M.
A5
B5
chance to fight an - oth - er fight. The break - ing hearts that
Ah.)
Gtrs. 1 & 2
P.M.
P.M.

Gtrs. 1 & 2 tacet
A5 N.C.
stand for all our lives live to -
mf
Gtr. 6 (dist.)
P.M.
Gtr. 7 (dist.)
divisi
mf

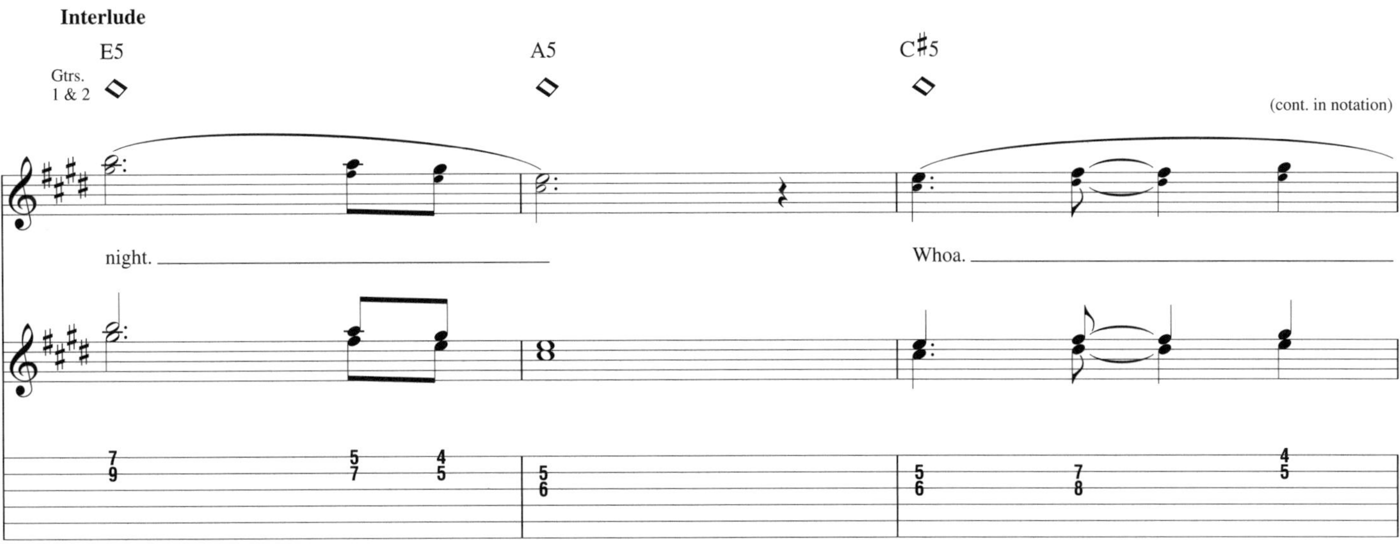
Interlude
E5
A5
C♯5
Gtrs. 1 & 2
(cont. in notation)
night.
Whoa.

To Coda
B5
A5 N.C.
Whoa.
Gtr. 6
Gtr. 7
Gtrs. 1 & 2

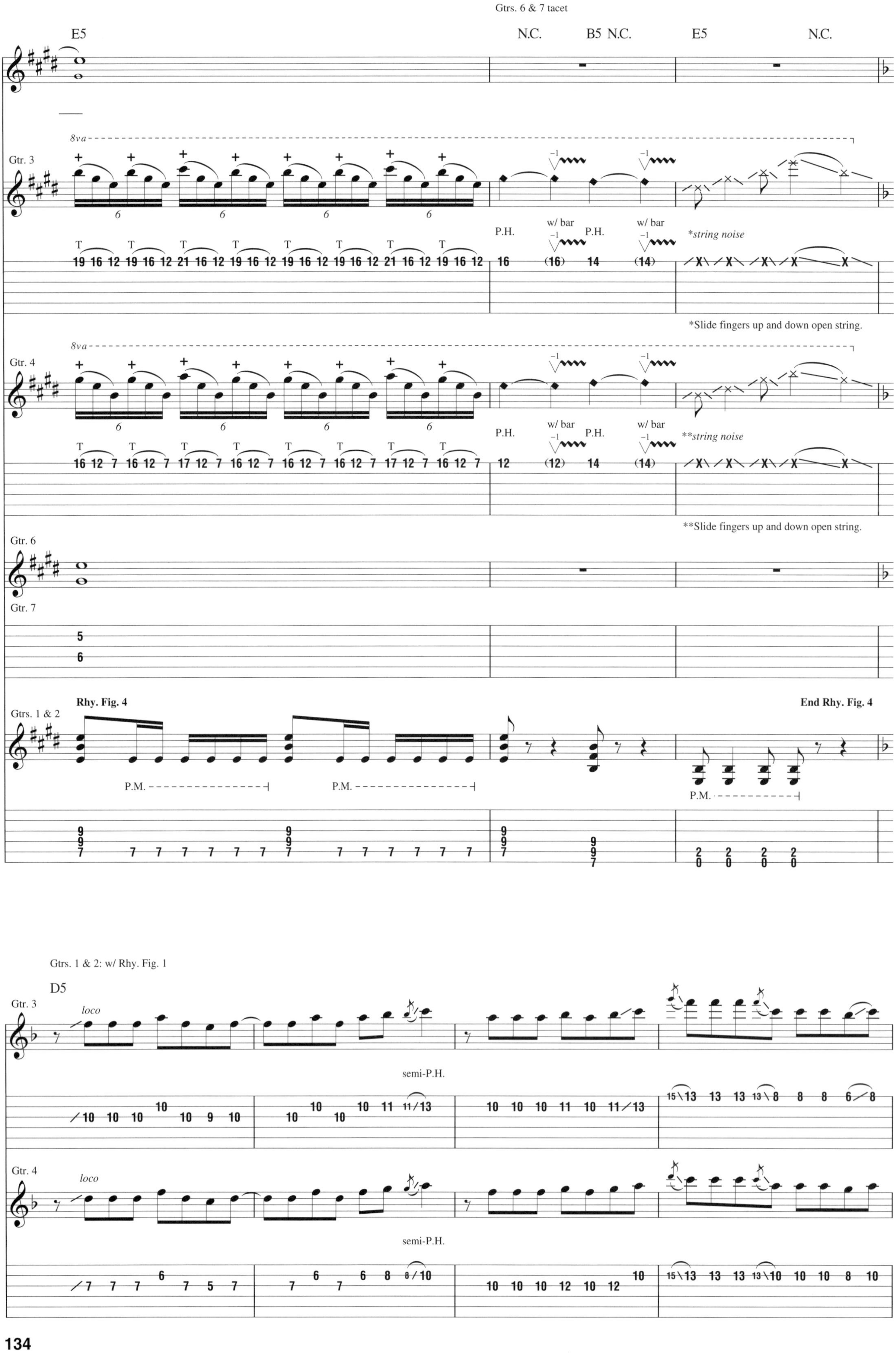

Gtrs. 6 & 7 tacet

E5 N.C. B5 N.C. E5 N.C.

Gtr. 3

8va

P.H. w/ bar P.H. w/ bar *string noise

*Slide fingers up and down open string.

Gtr. 4

8va

P.H. w/ bar P.H. w/ bar **string noise

**Slide fingers up and down open string.

Gtr. 6

Gtr. 7

Gtrs. 1 & 2

Rhy. Fig. 4

End Rhy. Fig. 4

P.M.

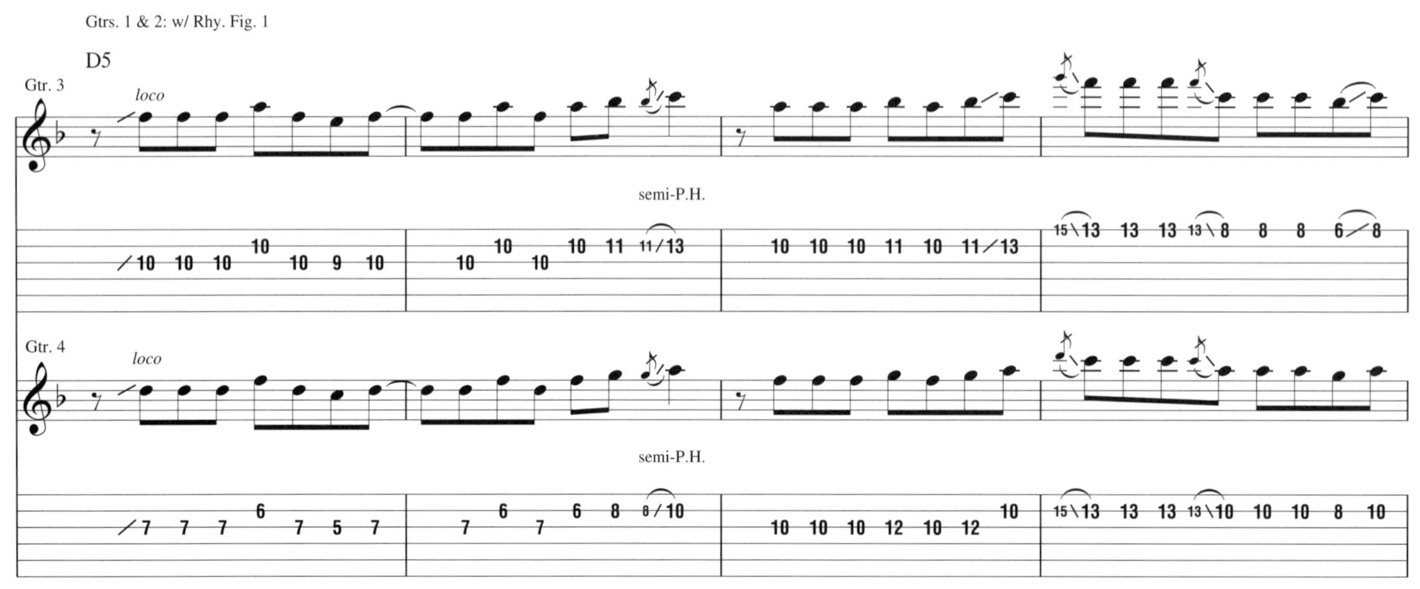

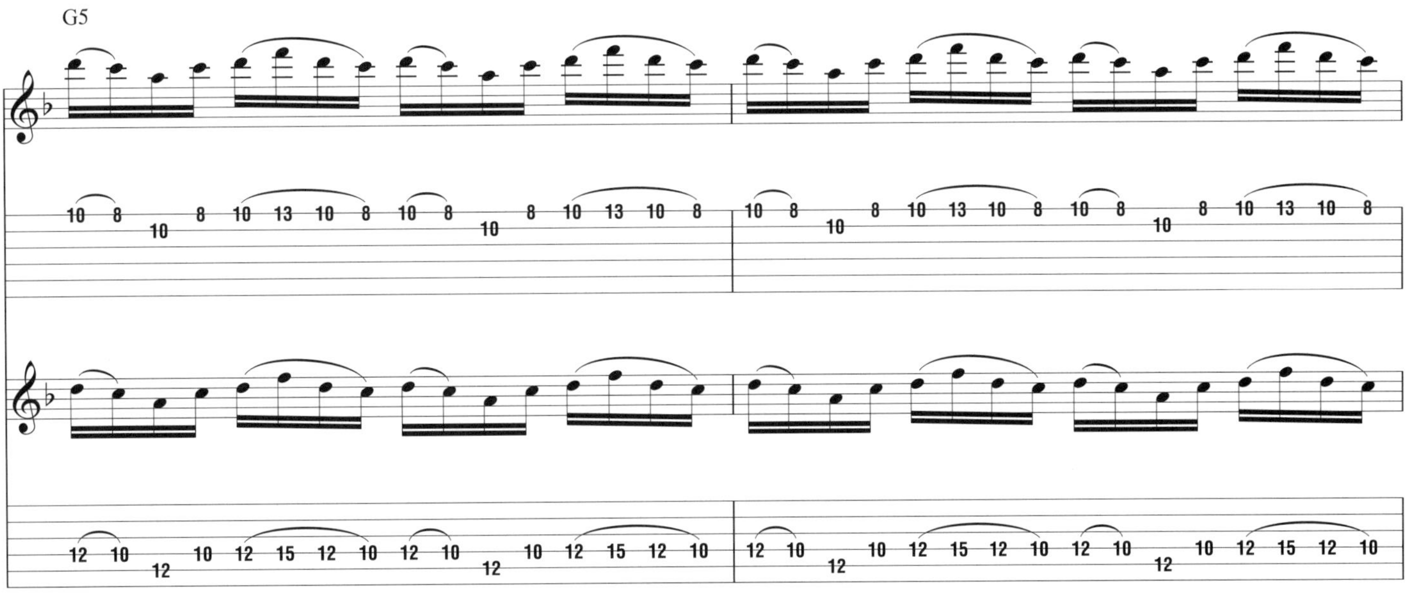
G5

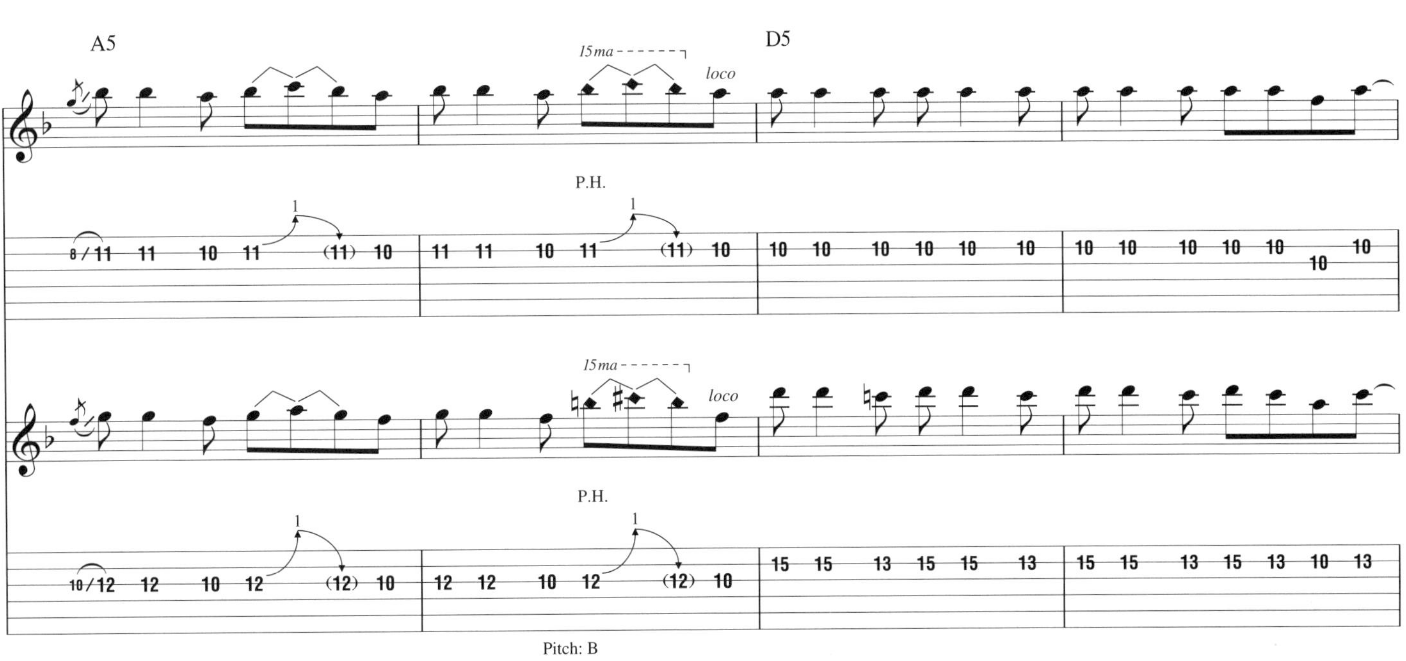
A5
15ma
loco
D5
P.H.
15ma
loco
P.H.
Pitch: B

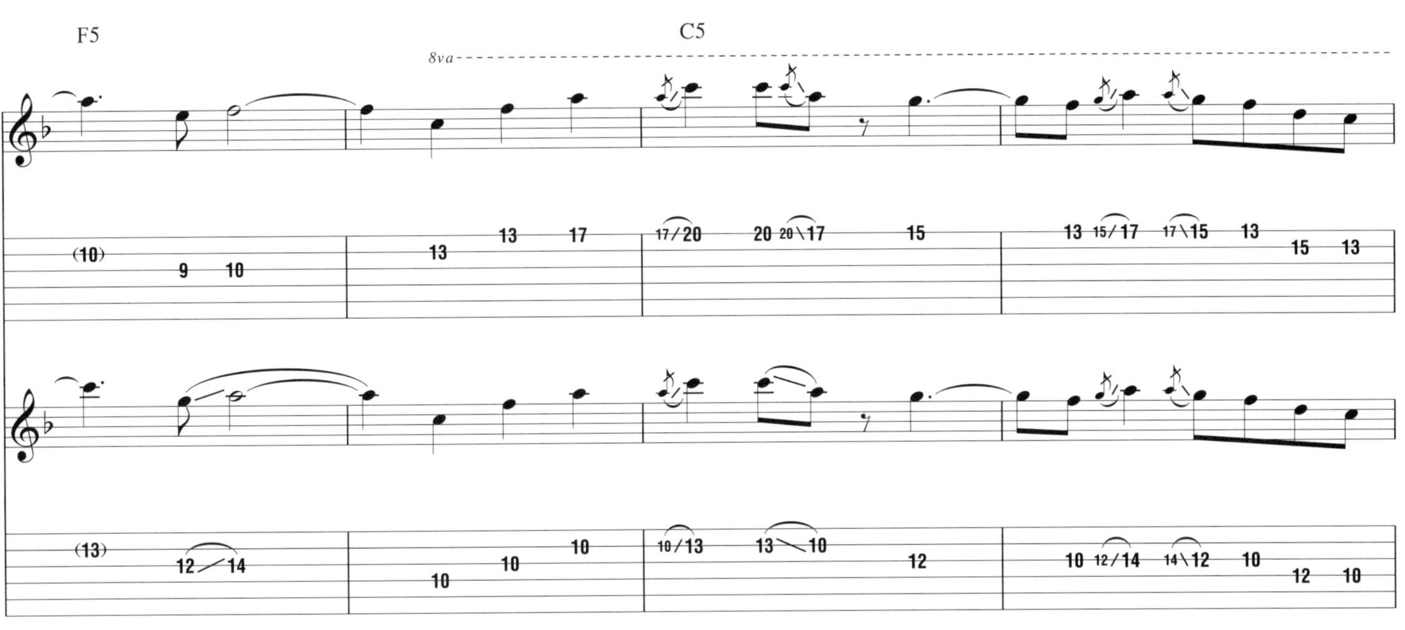
F5
C5
8va

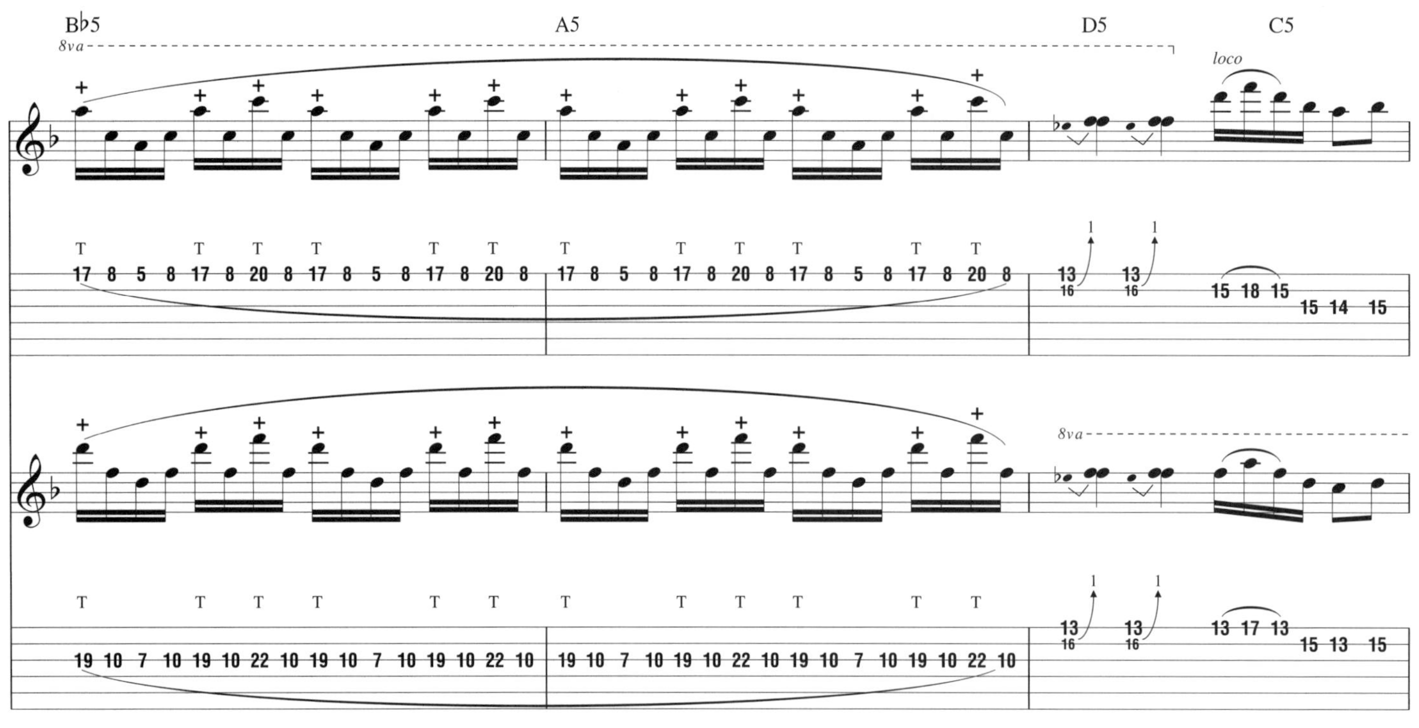

D.S. al Coda

D5 N.C. G5 F5 A5 N.C.

2. Watch you

8va

loco

w/ bar w/ bar

P.H.

-1 1/2

P.H.
w/ bar

-1

-4 1/2

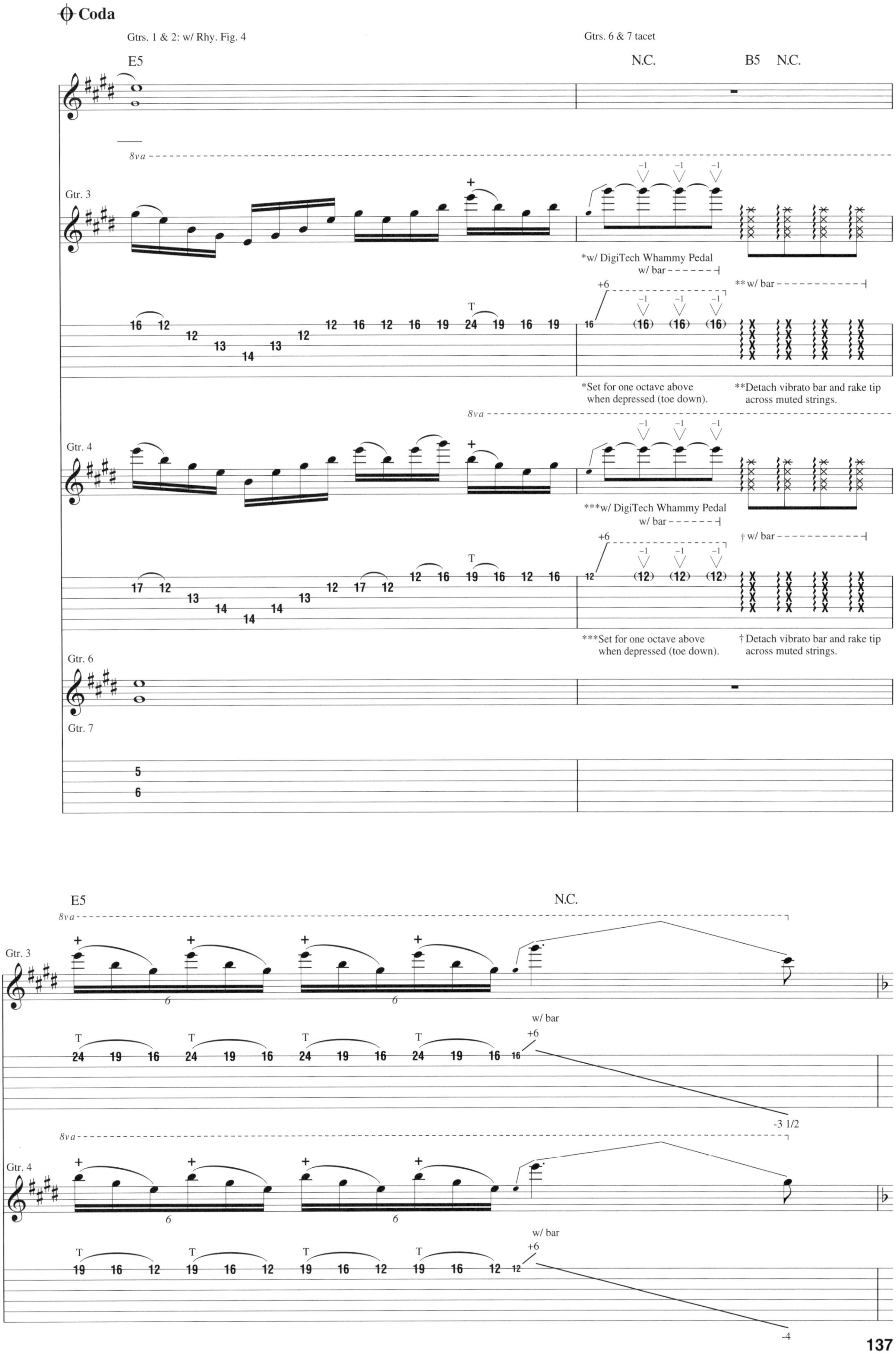

Coda

Gtrs. 1 & 2: w/ Rhy. Fig. 4

Gtrs. 6 & 7 tacet

E5 N.C. B5 N.C.

Gtr. 3

*w/ DigiTech Whammy Pedal
w/ bar

**w/ bar

*Set for one octave above when depressed (toe down).

**Detach vibrato bar and rake tip across muted strings.

Gtr. 4

***w/ DigiTech Whammy Pedal
w/ bar

† w/ bar

***Set for one octave above when depressed (toe down).

† Detach vibrato bar and rake tip across muted strings.

Gtr. 6

Gtr. 7

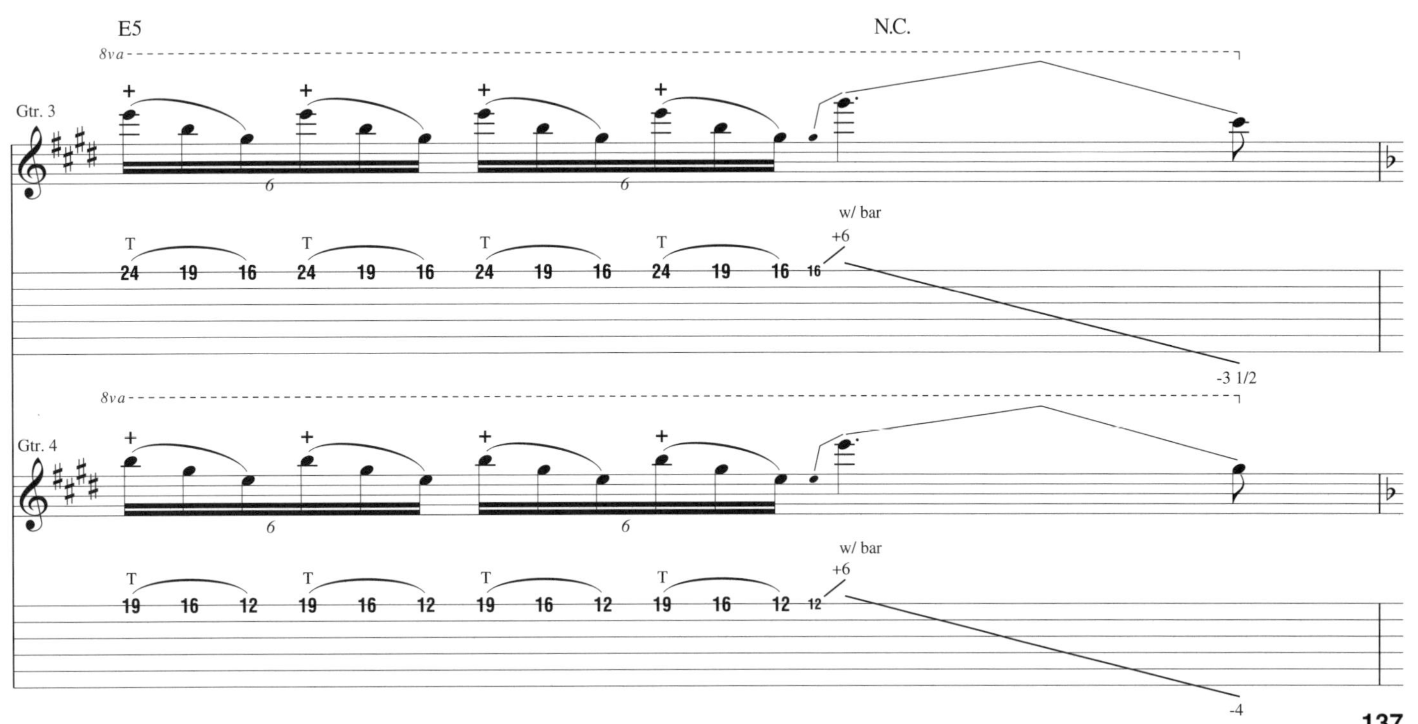

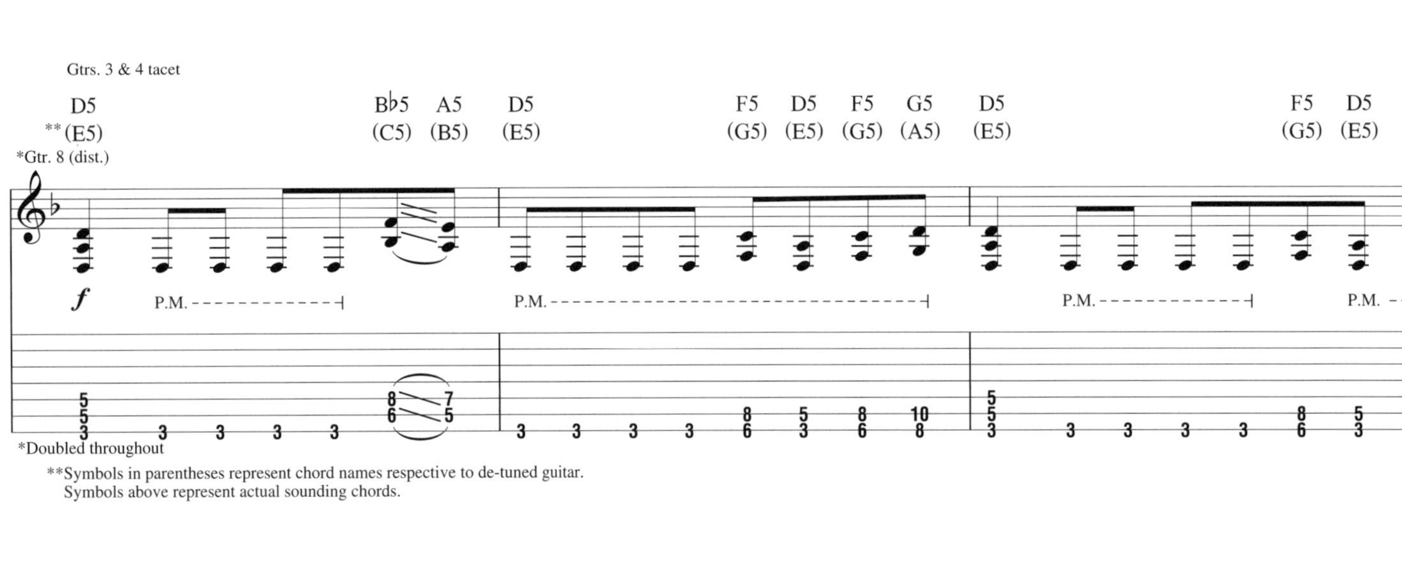

*Doubled throughout

**Symbols in parentheses represent chord names respective to de-tuned guitar. Symbols above represent actual sounding chords.

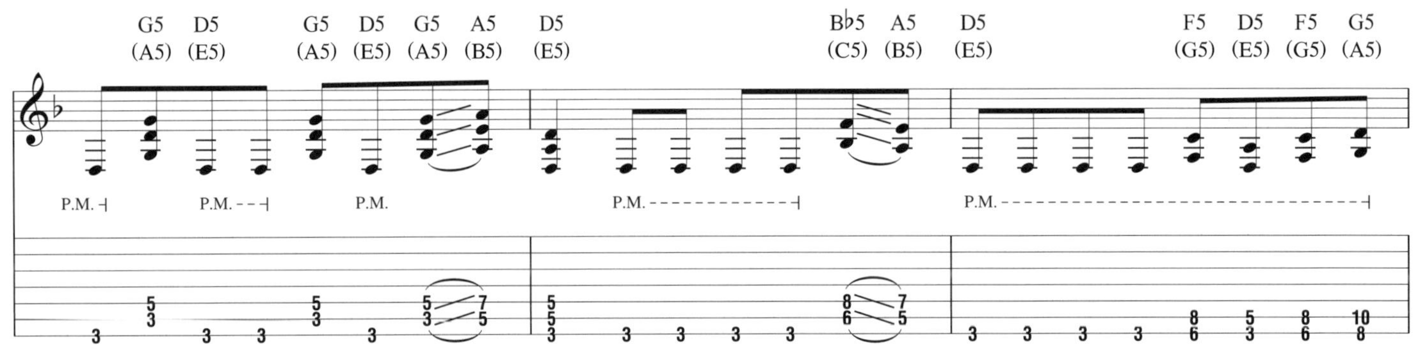

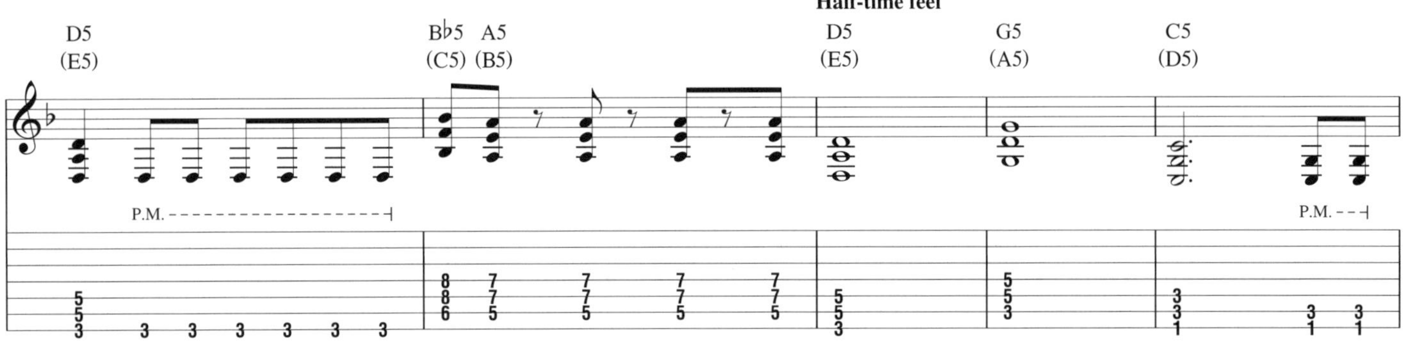

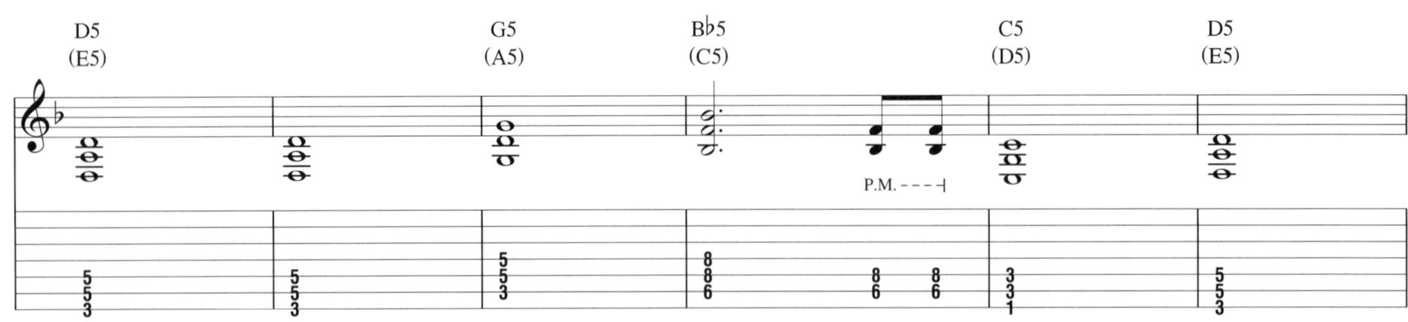

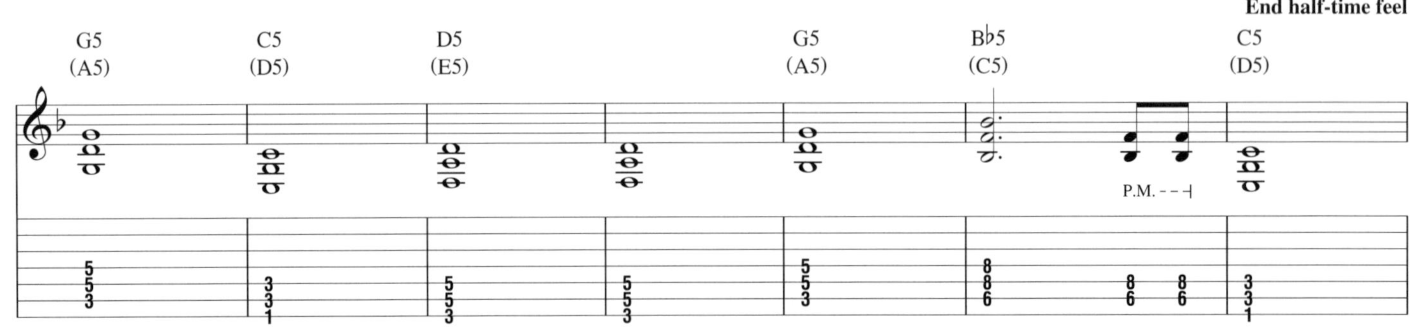

D5 (E5) — Bb5 (C5) A5 (B5) — D5 (E5)

Gtr. 3

P.M.

13 13 11 13 10 10 10 11 | 13 13 11 13 10 10 10 11 | 13 13 11 10 11 11 10 10

Gtr. 4

P.M.

14 14 12 14 10 12 10 12 | 14 14 12 14 10 12 10 12 | 14 14 12 10 12 12 10 12

Rhy. Fig. 5

Gtr. 8

P.M.

P.M.

5/5/3 3 3 3 3 3 3 | 3 3 3 3 3 3 8/6 7/5 | 5/5/3 3 3 3 3 3 3

Bb5 (C5) A5 (B5) Bb5 (C5) C5 (D5) — D5 (E5) — Bb5 (C5) A5 (B5)

P.M.

10 10 9 10 10 10 10 11 | 13 13 11 13 10 10 10 11 | 13 13 11 13 10 10 10 11

P.M.

12 12 10 12 10 12 10 12 | 14 14 12 14 10 12 10 12 | 14 14 12 14 10 12 10 12

P.M.

P.M.

3 3 3 3 8/6 7/5 8/6 10/8 | 5/5/3 3 3 3 3 3 3 | 3 3 3 3 3 3 8/6 7/5

Gtr. 8: w/ Rhy. Fig. 5
D5
(E5)
G5
(A5)
D5
(E5)
G5
(A5)
D5
(E5)
G5
(A5)
A5
(B5)
D5
(E5)
P.M.
P.M.
End Rhy. Fig. 5
P.M.
P.M.
P.M.
B♭5
(C5)
A5
(B5)
D5
(E5)
B♭5
(C5)
A5
(B5)
B♭5
(C5)
C5
(D5)
Gtr. 3
P.M.
Gtr. 4
P.M.
D5
(E5)
B♭5
(C5)
A5
(B5)
D5
(E5)
P.M.
P.M.

G5 (A5) D5 (E5) G5 (A5) D5 (E5) G5 (A5) A5 (B5) C5 (D5) B♭5 (C5) D5 (E5) F5 (G5) D5 (E5) F5 (G5) G5 (A5)
Gtr. 3
P.M.
w/ wah-wah
P.S.
Gtr. 4
Gtr. 8
A5 (B5)
N.C.
8va
wah-wah off
Guitar Solo
Gtrs. 1 & 2: w/ Rhy. Figs. 2 & 2A
Gtrs. 3, 4 & 8 tacet
B5
A5
Gtr. 9 (dist.)
semi-
P.H.

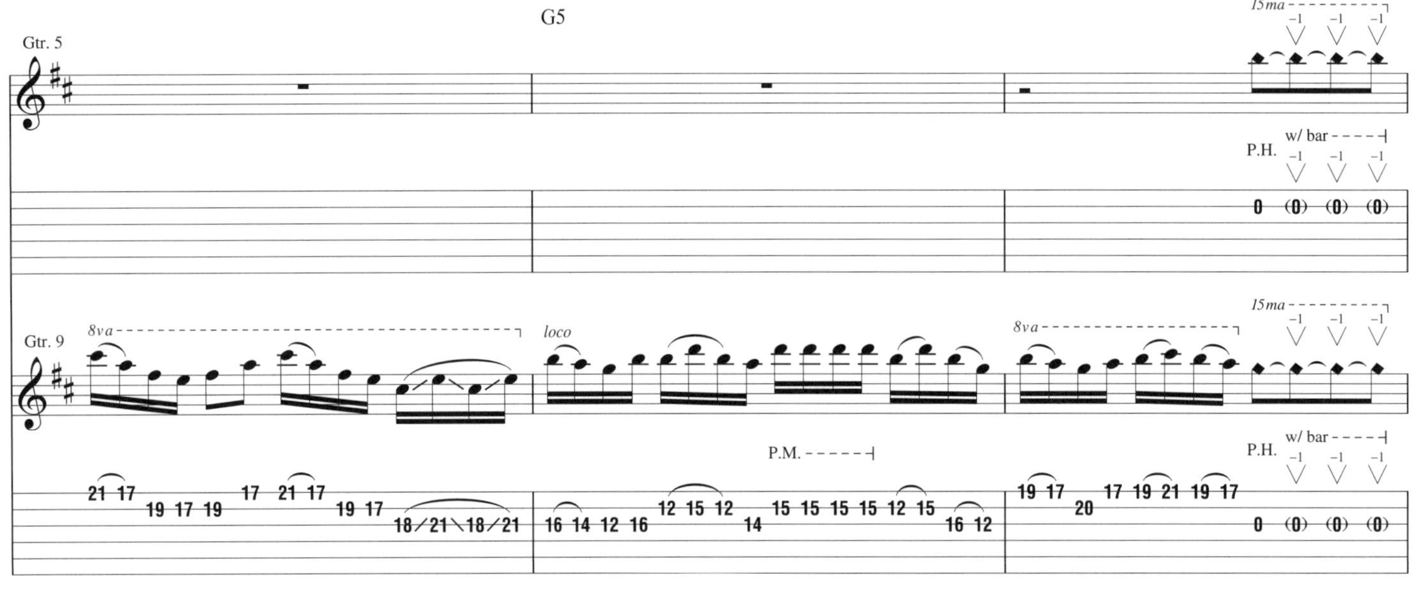
G5
Gtr. 5
15ma
w/ bar
P.H.
Gtr. 9
8va
loco
8va
15ma
P.M.
w/ bar
P.H.

Gtr. 5 tacet
B5
Gtr. 9
8va

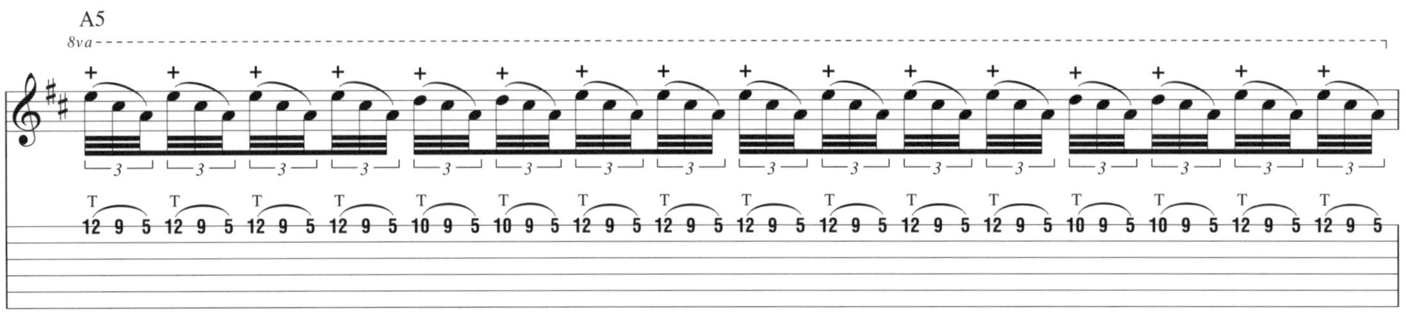
A5
8va

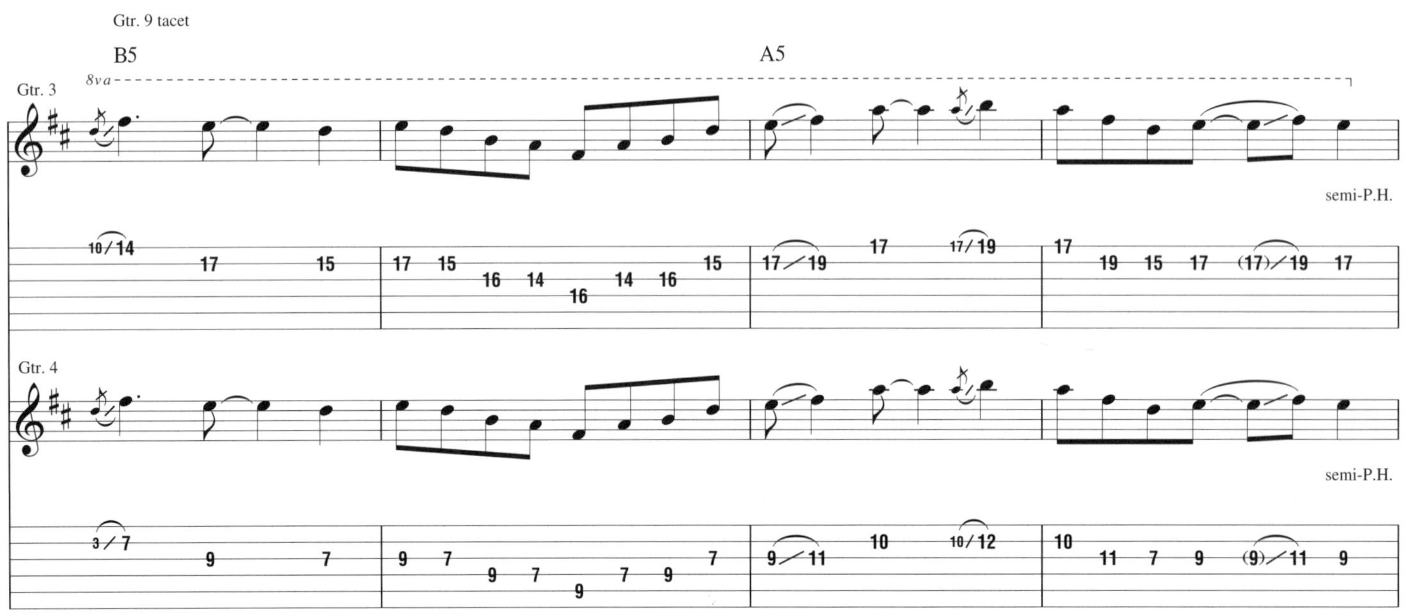
Gtr. 9 tacet
B5
A5
Gtr. 3
8va
semi-P.H.
Gtr. 4
semi-P.H.

Gtrs. 3 & 4 tacet

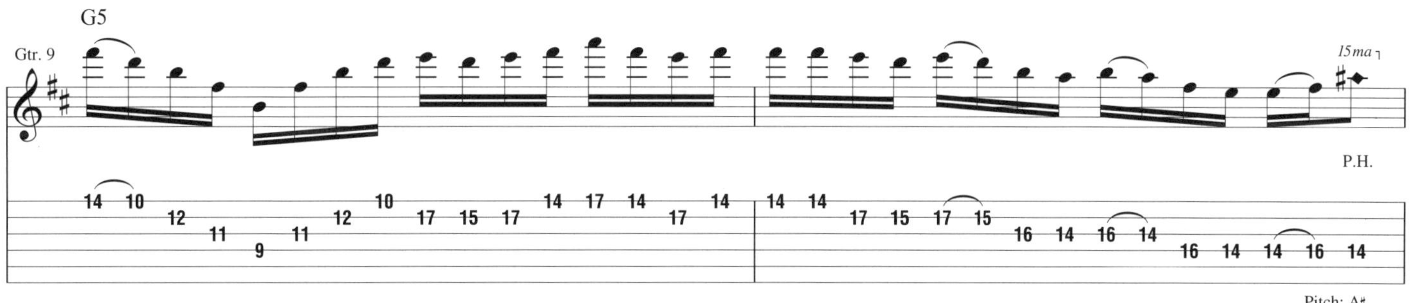
G5
Gtr. 9
15ma
P.H.
Pitch: A♯

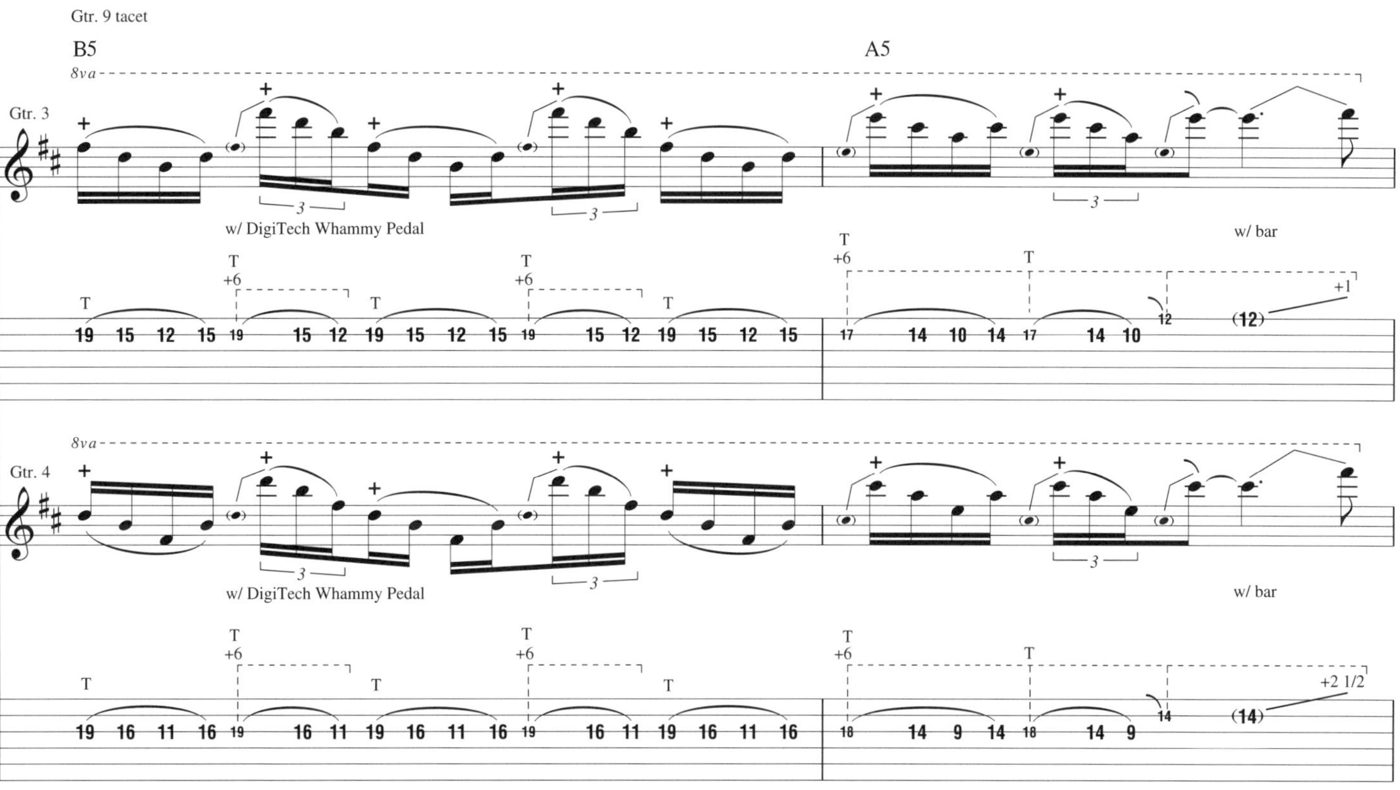
Gtr. 9 tacet
B5
A5
8va
Gtr. 3
w/ DigiTech Whammy Pedal
w/ bar
Gtr. 4
w/ DigiTech Whammy Pedal
w/ bar

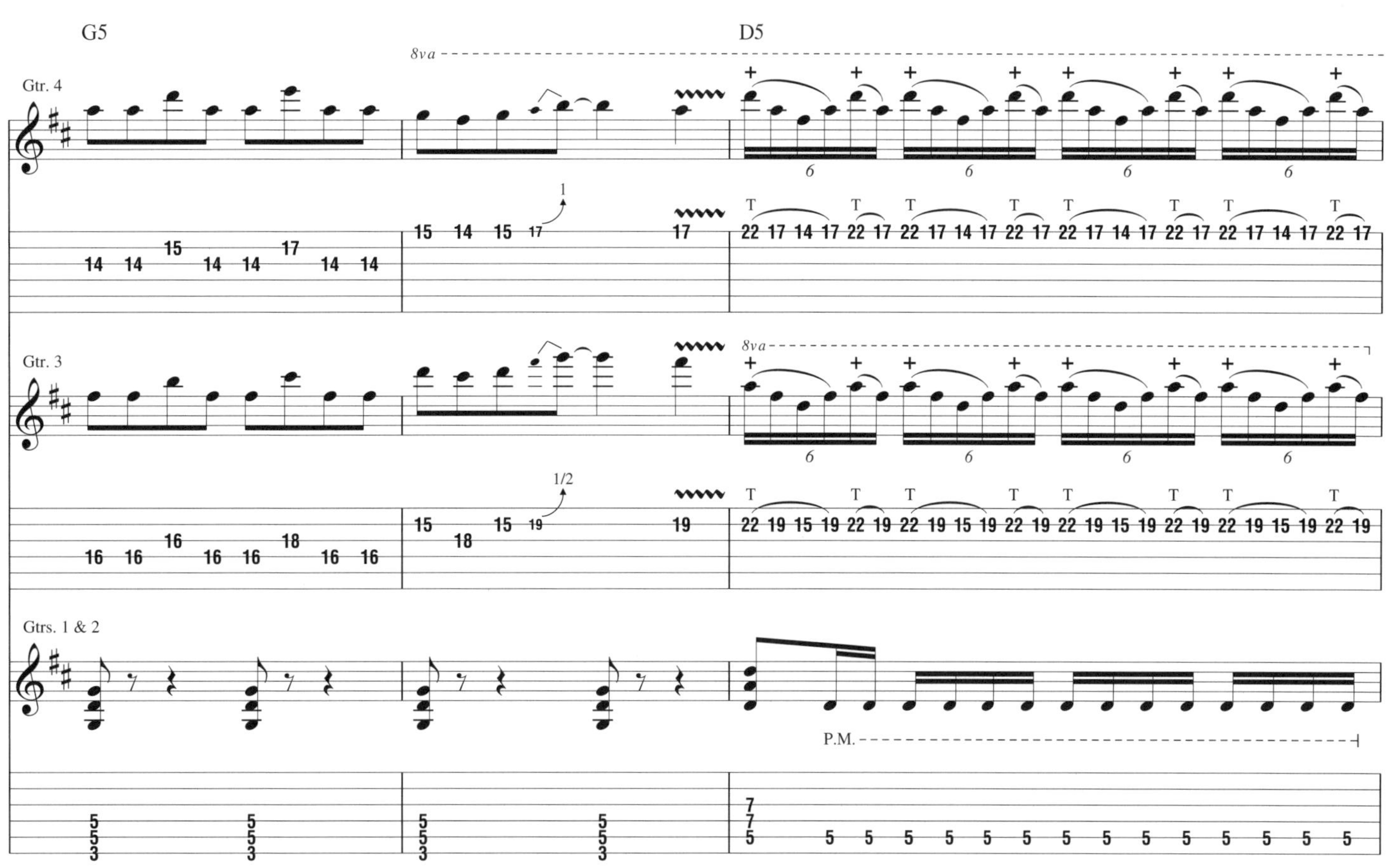
G5
D5
8va
Gtr. 4
Gtr. 3
Gtrs. 1 & 2
P.M.

A5 E5

loco

P.M.

8va

B5 A5

w/ bar

w/ bar

P.M.

P.M.

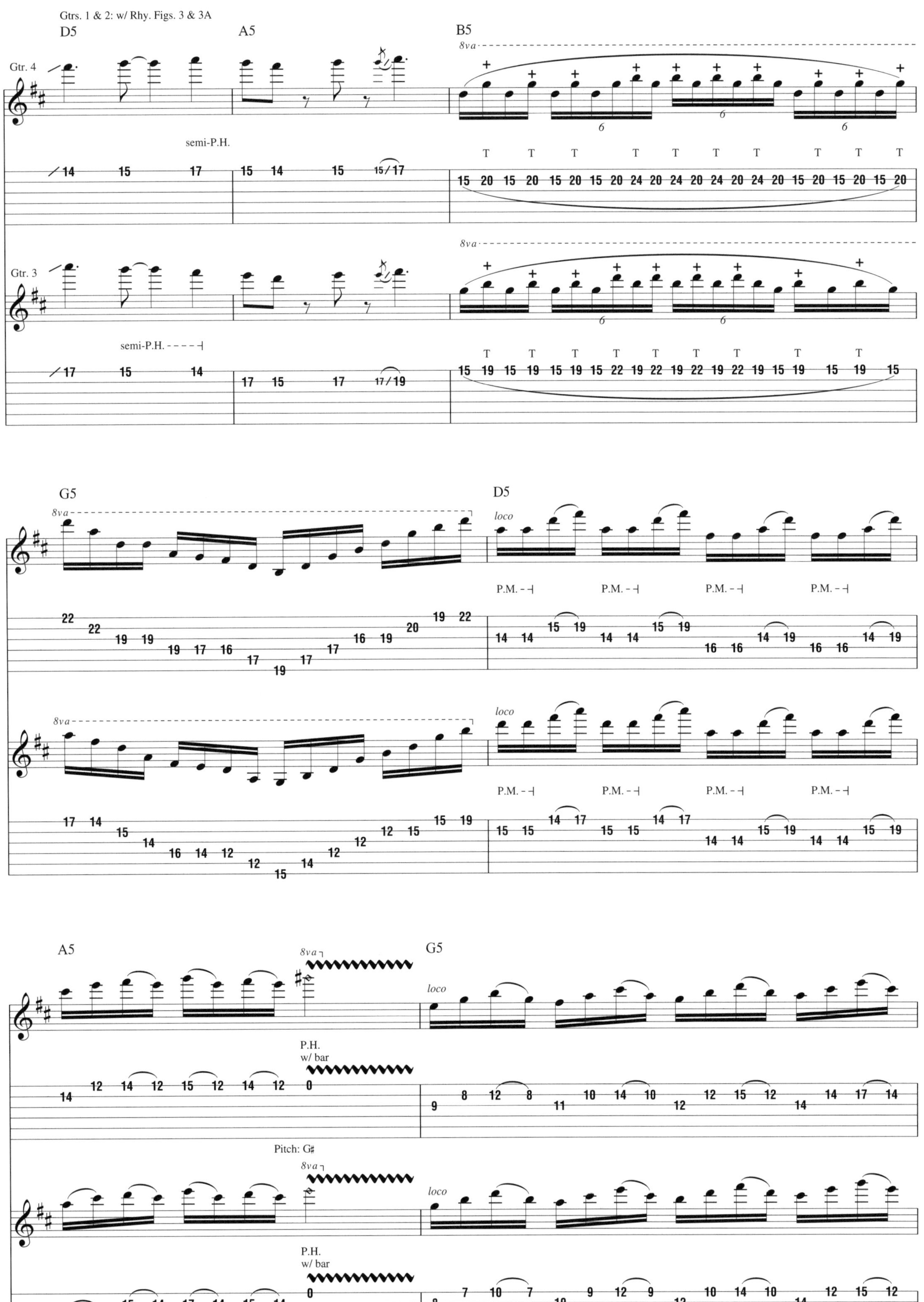
Gtrs. 1 & 2: w/ Rhy. Figs. 3 & 3A
D5
A5
B5
Gtr. 4
Gtr. 3
semi-P.H.
8va
loco
G5
P.M.
P.H.
w/ bar
Pitch: G♯

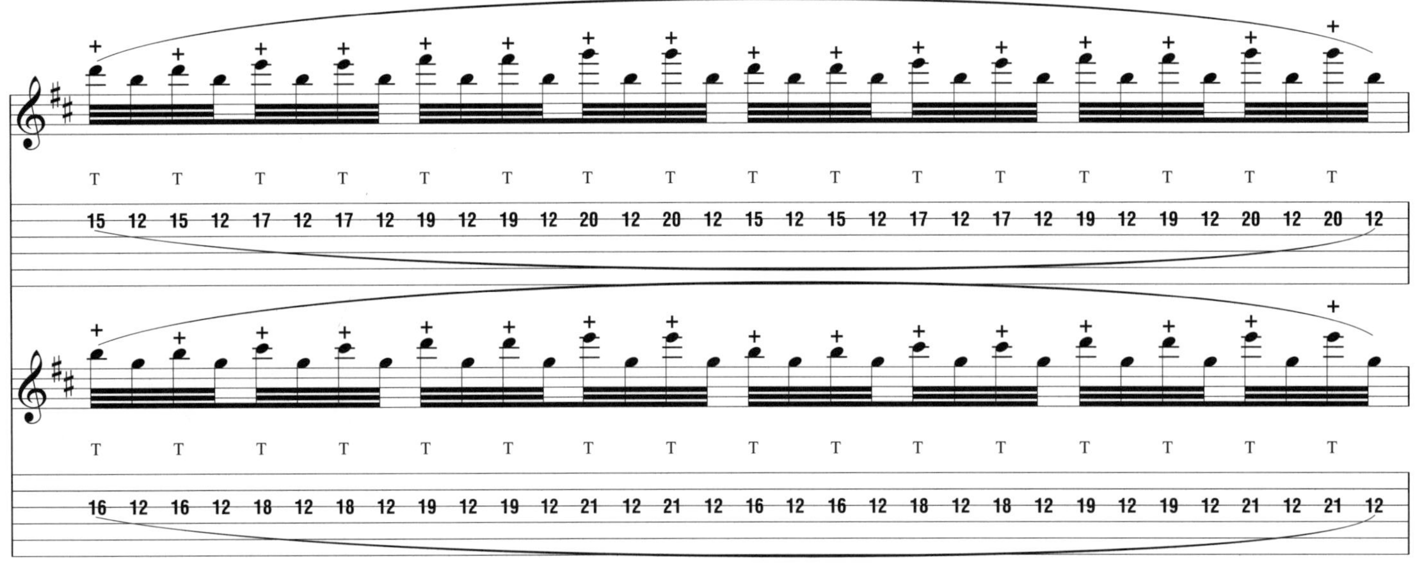
T T T T T T T T T T T T T T T T
15 12 15 12 17 12 17 12 19 12 19 12 20 12 20 12 15 12 15 12 17 12 17 12 19 12 19 12 20 12 20 12
T T T T T T T T T T T T T T T T
16 12 16 12 18 12 18 12 19 12 19 12 21 12 21 12 16 12 16 12 18 12 18 12 19 12 19 12 21 12 21 12

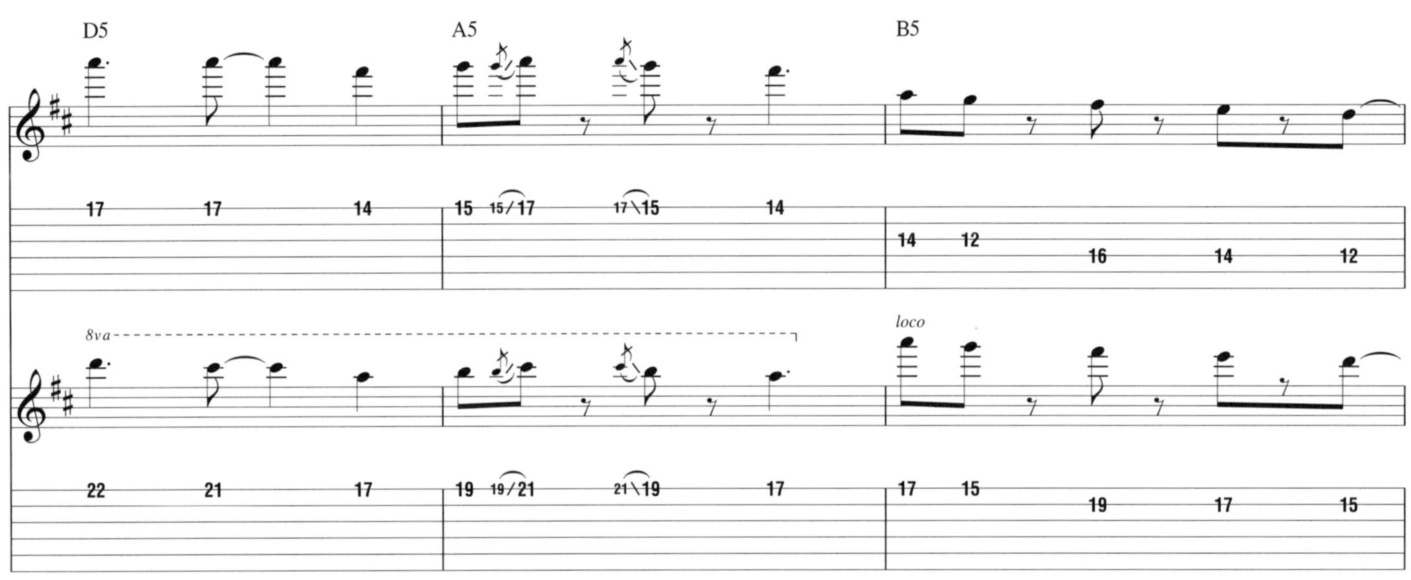
D5
A5
B5
17 17 14
15 15/17 17\15 14
14 12 16 14 12
8va
loco
22 21 17
19 19/21 21\19 17
17 15 19 17 15

Gtr. 4
G5
E5
(12) 14 14/16 14 12
12 12 12 12 14 16 14 16 14 12 12 12 12 14 16 14 16 14
P.M.
P.M.
Gtr. 3
(15) 17 17/19 17 15
9 9 9 9 11 12 11 12 9 9 9 9 11 12 11 12
P.M.
P.M.
Gtrs. 1 & 2
P.M.
5
5
3
9
9
7 7 7 7 7 7 7 7 7 7 7 7 7 7 7 7

8va
P.M.
A5
w/ wah-wah
w/ wah-wah
P.M.
Interlude
Gtrs. 3 & 4 tacet
E5
B5
C♯5
A5
Whoa.
Gtrs. 1 & 2

E5
B5
A5
Whoa.
E5
B5
Whoa.
P.M.
P.M.
C♯5
A5
E5
Whoa.
P.M.
P.M.
B5
A5
P.M.
(cont. in slashes)

Guitar Solo

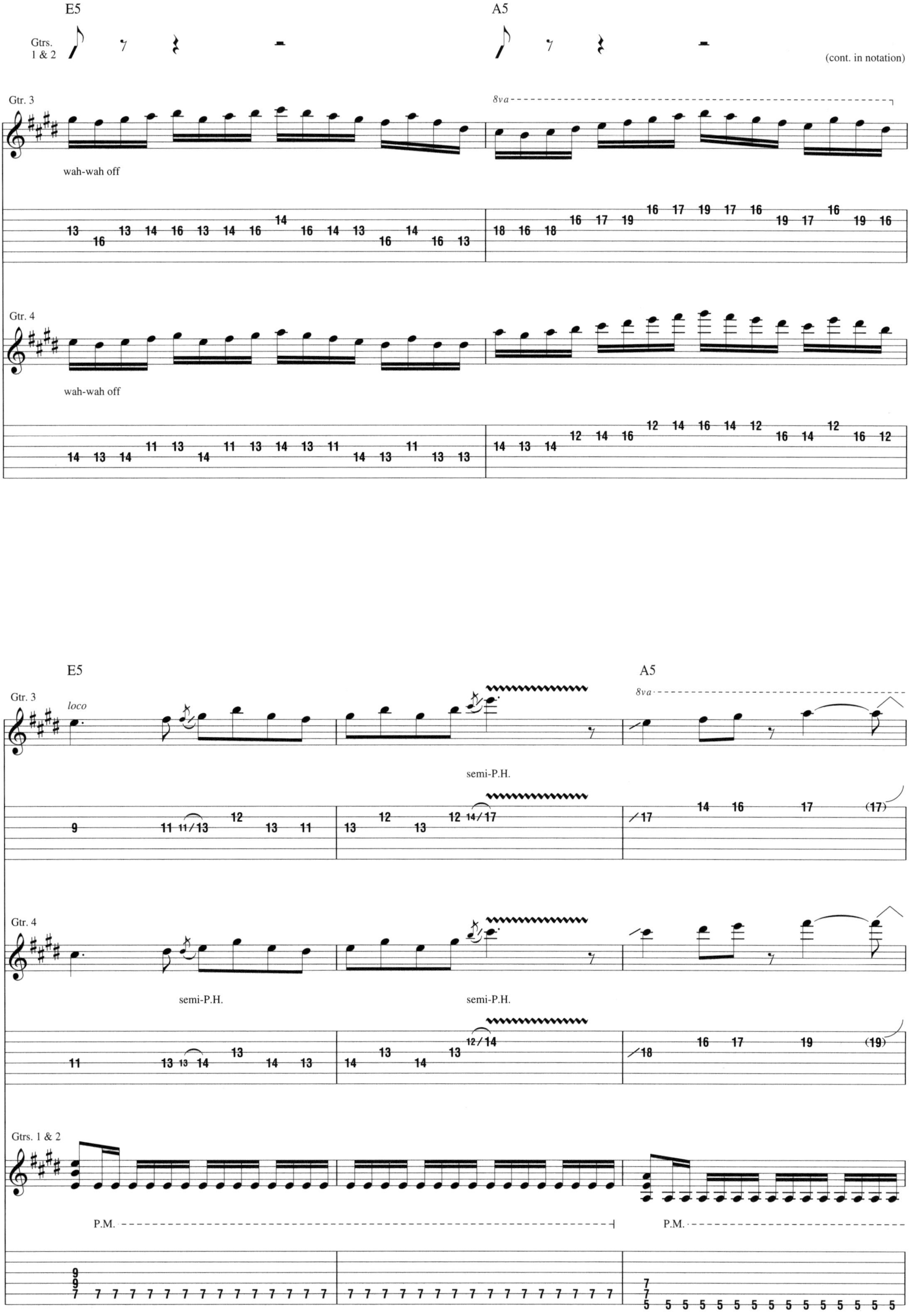

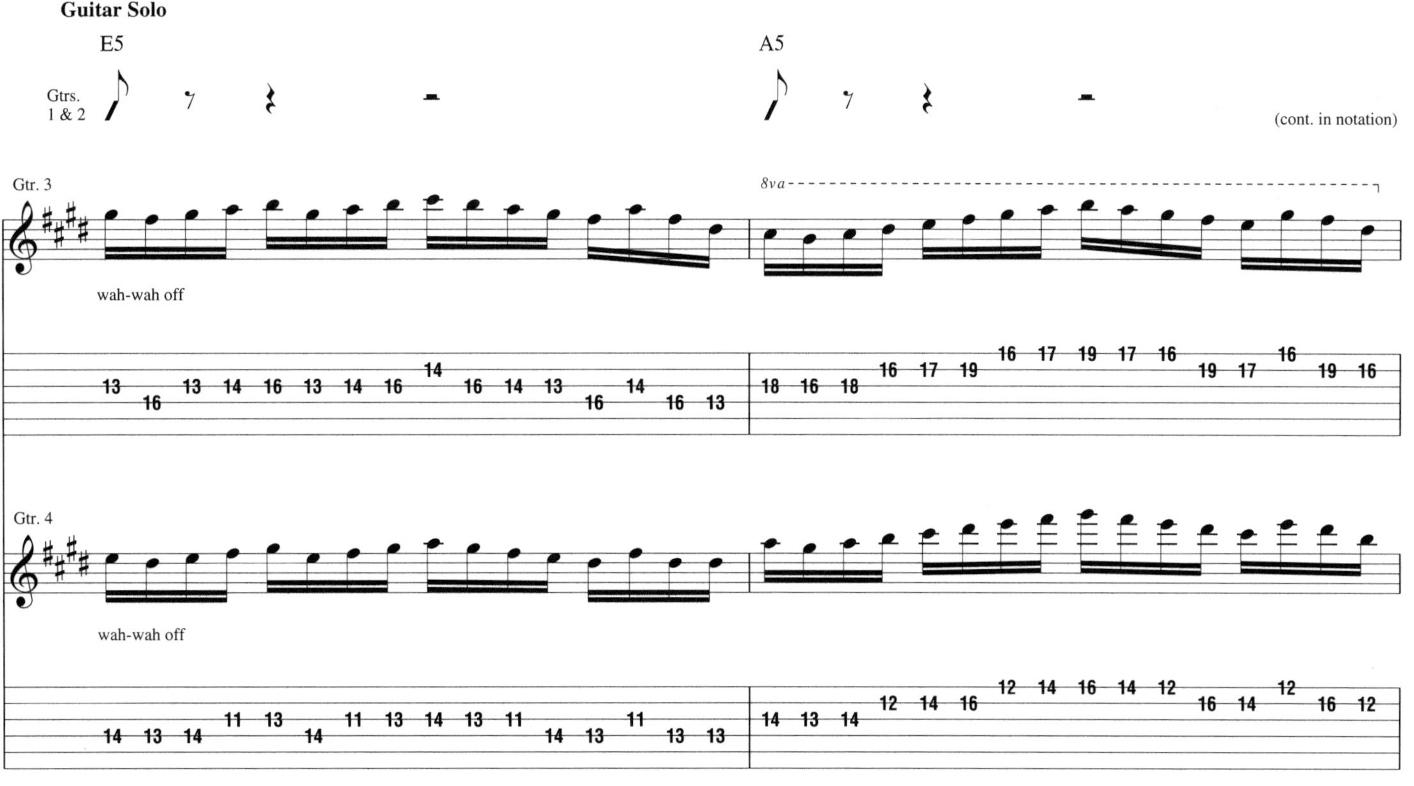

E5

A5

Gtr. 3

loco

8va

semi-P.H.

Gtr. 4

semi-P.H.

semi-P.H.

Gtrs. 1 & 2

P.M.

P.M.

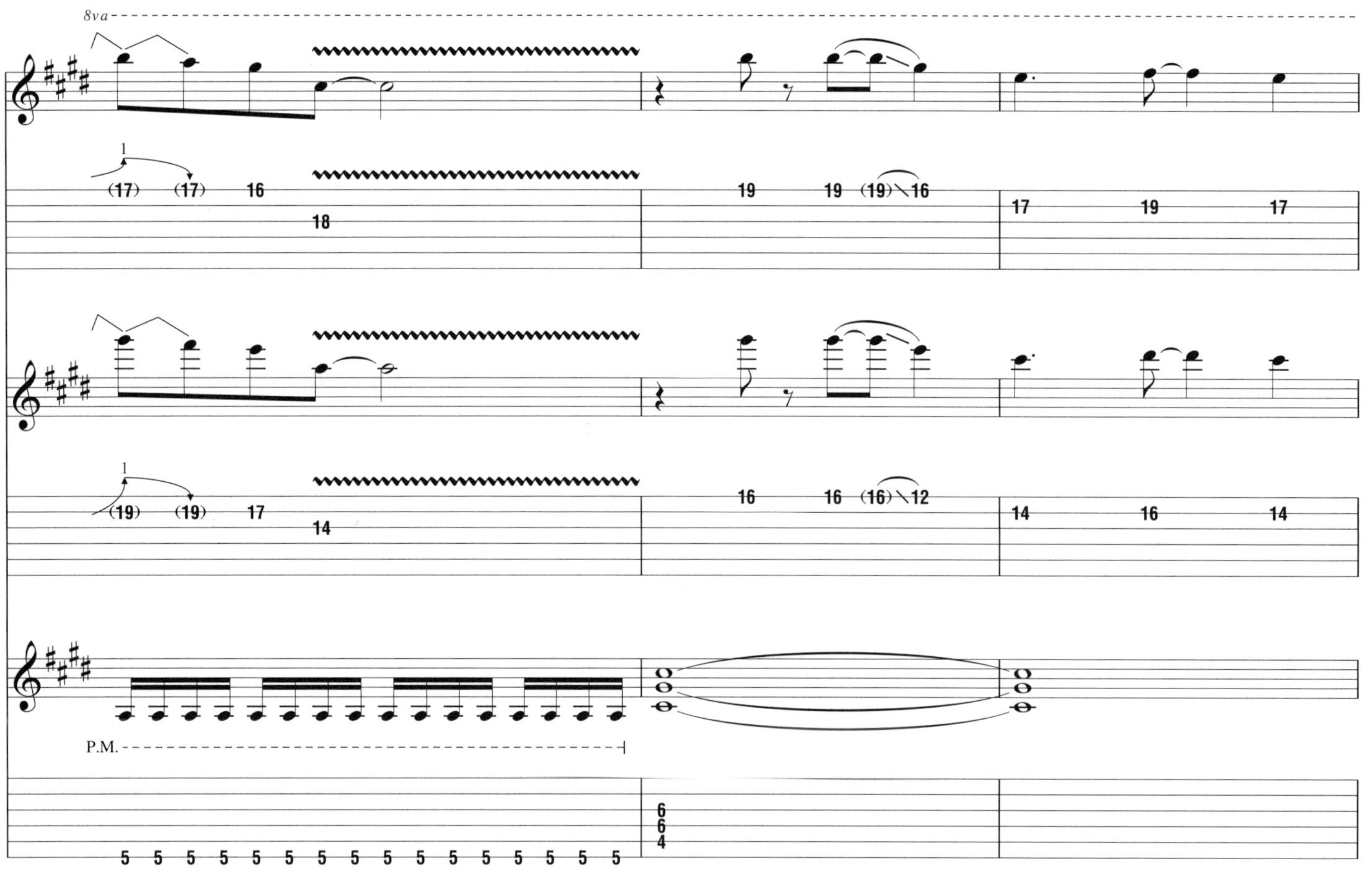

B5

C♯5

8va

15ma

loco

w/ bar

15ma

loco

w/ bar

P.H.

Pitch: A♯

P.M.

A5
8va
loco
P.M.
B5
8va
15ma
w/ bar
P.M.

Gtr. 3 tacet
A5
F♯5
8va
w/ bar
+6
loco
8va
w/ bar
+6
P.M.
B5
Far a -
Gtr. 4
loco
semi-P.H.
Gtrs. 1 & 2
P.M.
P.M.
(cont. in slashes)

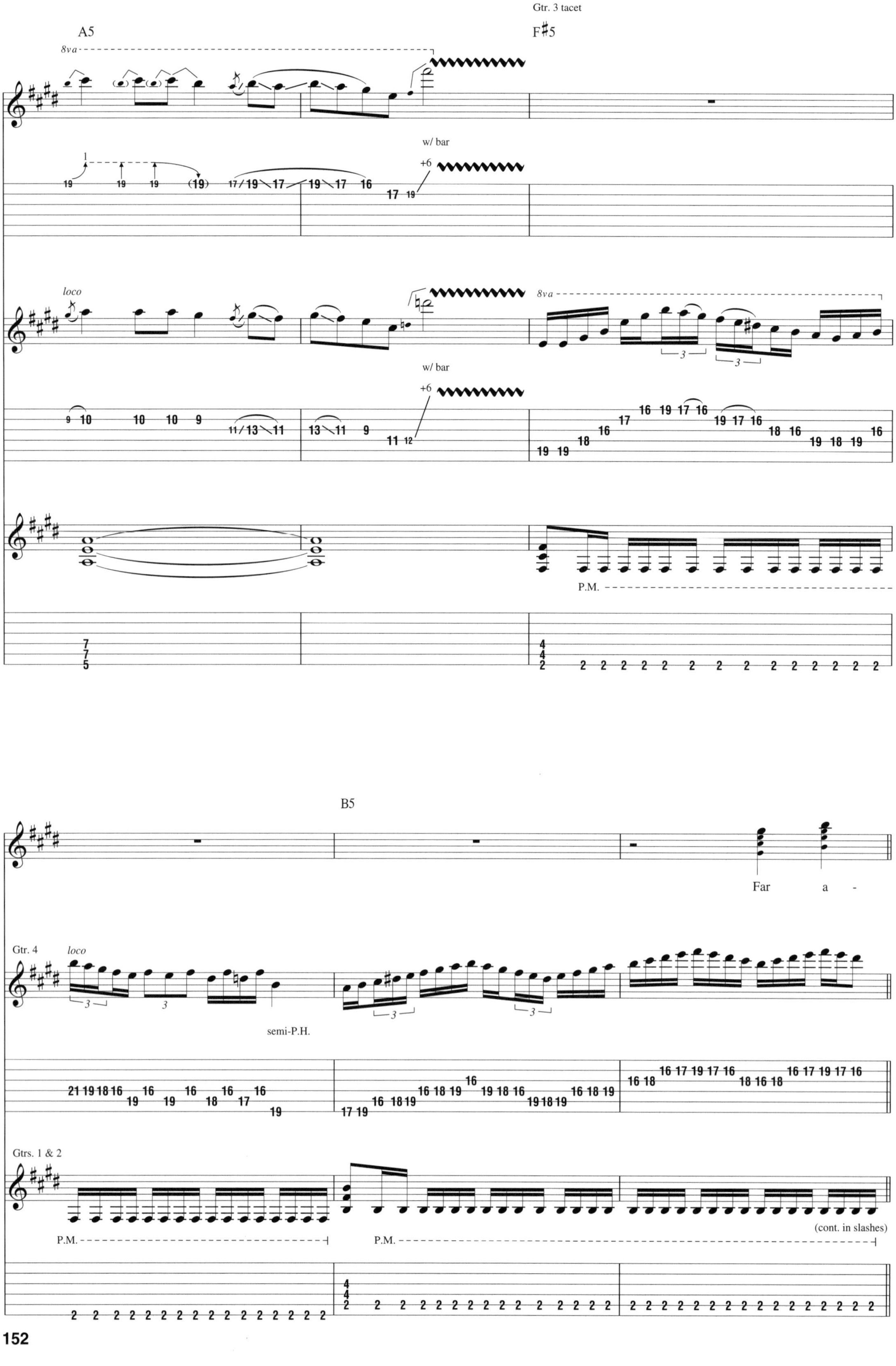

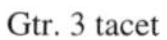

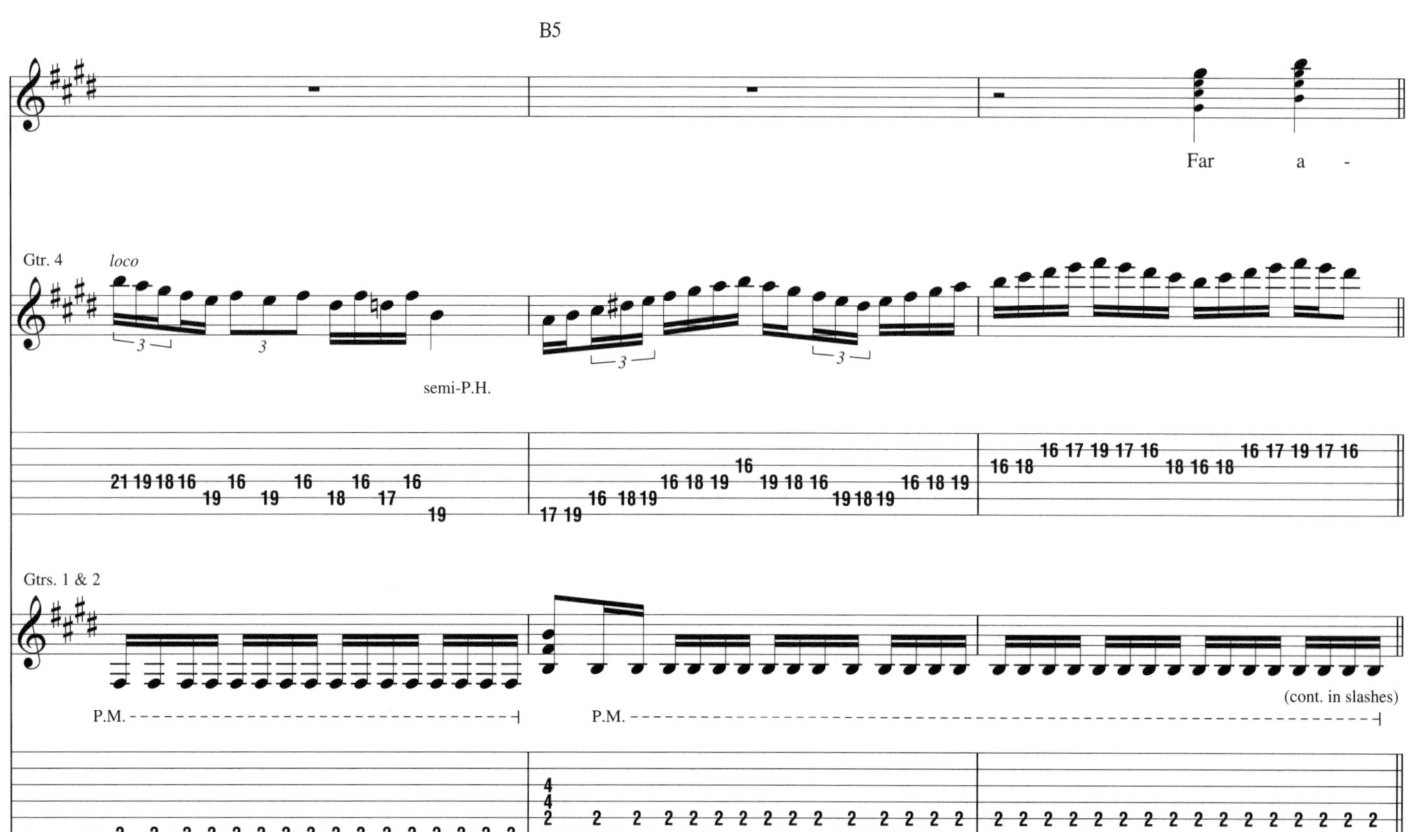

Chorus

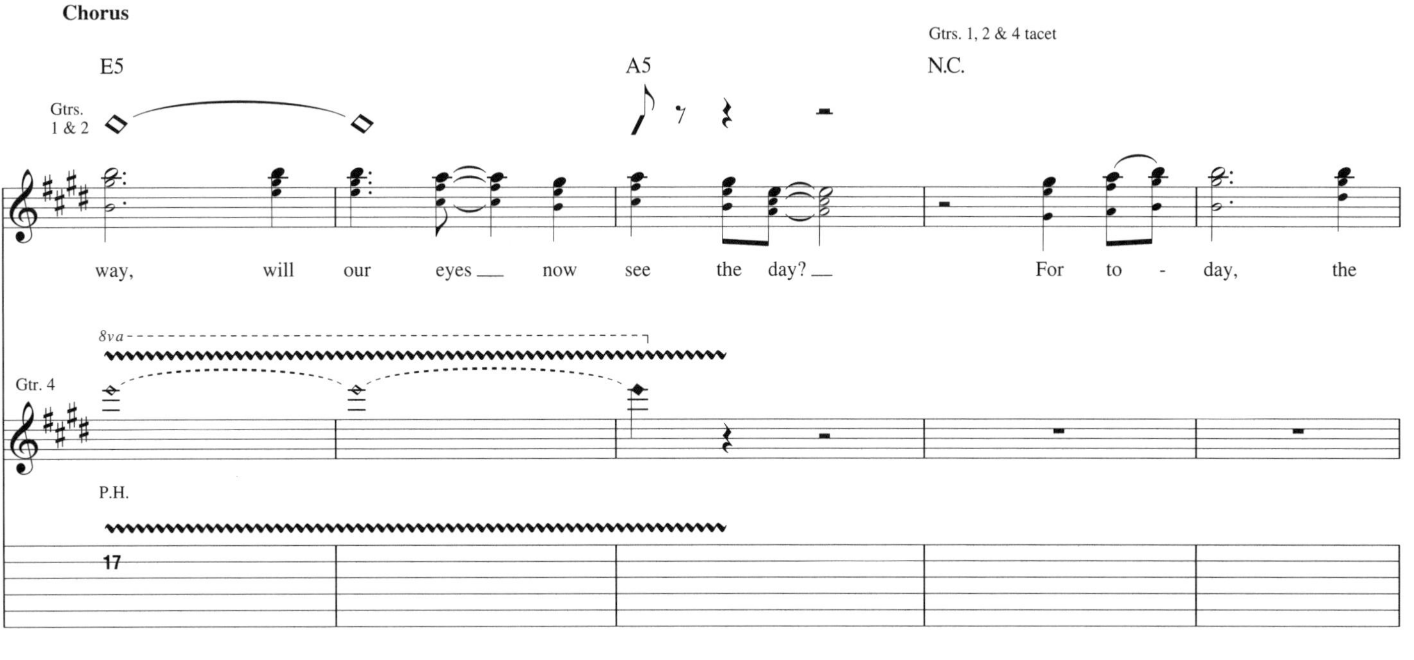
Gtrs. 1, 2 & 4 tacet
E5
A5
N.C.
Gtrs. 1 & 2
way, will our eyes now see the day? For to - day, the
8va
Gtr. 4
P.H.
17

C♯5 B5 G♯5 B5 C♯5 F♯5
ev - er - last - ing e - ter - nal sun. Far a - way, will
Gtrs. 1 & 2
P.M.

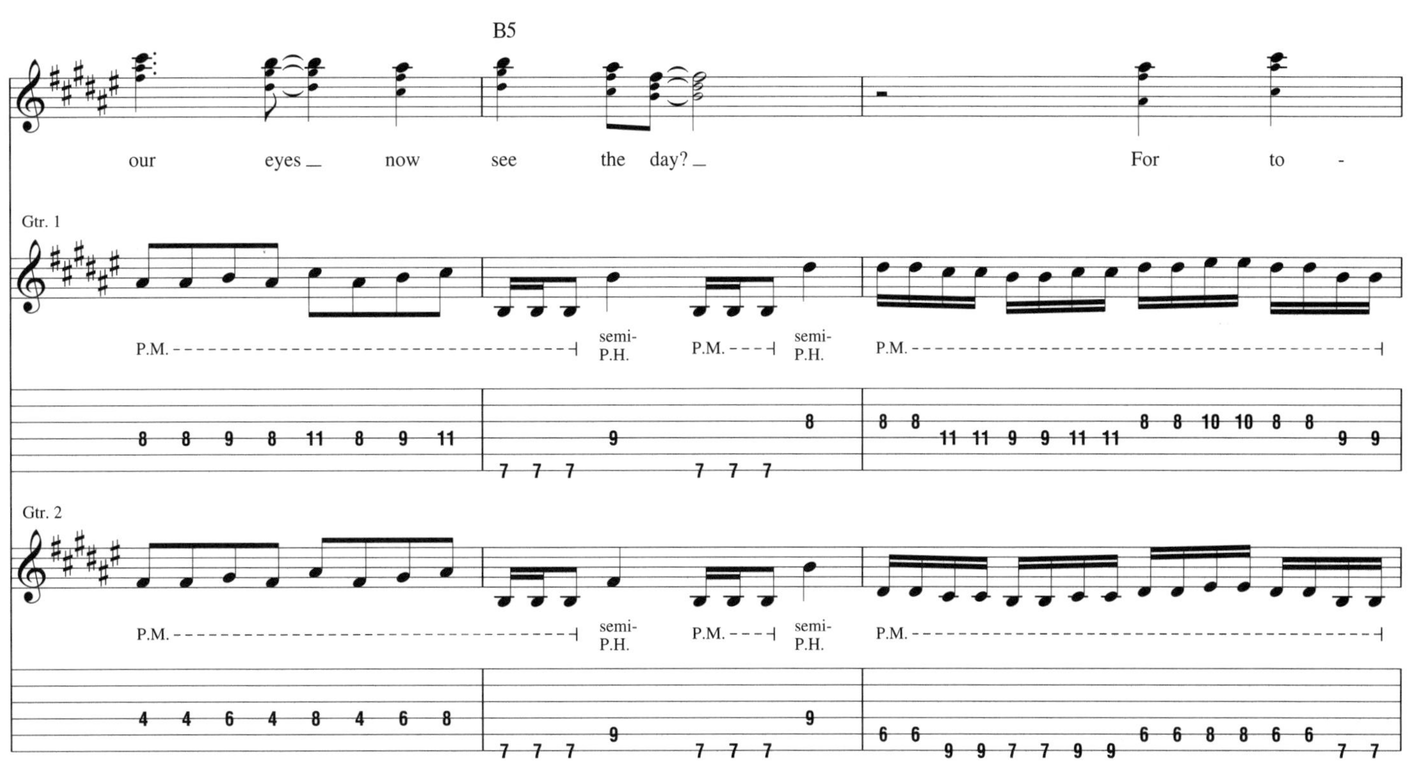
B5
our eyes now see the day? For to -
Gtr. 1
P.M.
semi-P.H.
Gtr. 2

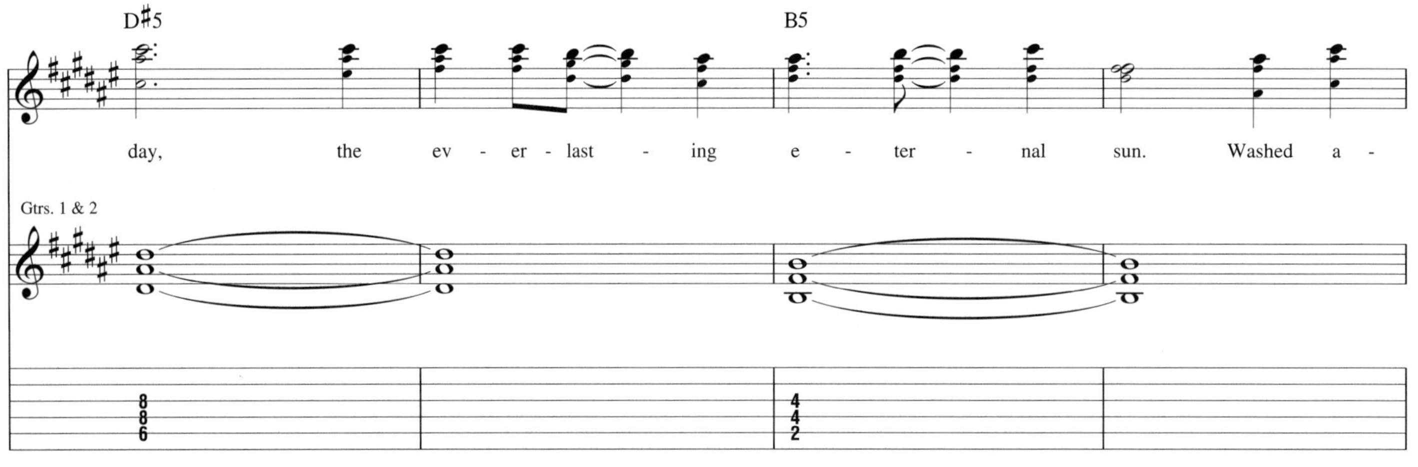
D♯5
B5
day, the ev - er - last - ing e - ter - nal sun. Washed a -
Gtrs. 1 & 2
8
8
6
4
4
2

D♯5
B5
way the dreams of a bright - er day.
P.M.
8
8
6 6 6 6 6 6 6 6 6 6 6 6 6 6 6 6
6 6 6 6 6 6 6 6 6 6 6 6 6 6 6 6
4
4
2 2 2 2 2 2 2 2 2 2 2 2 2 2 2 2

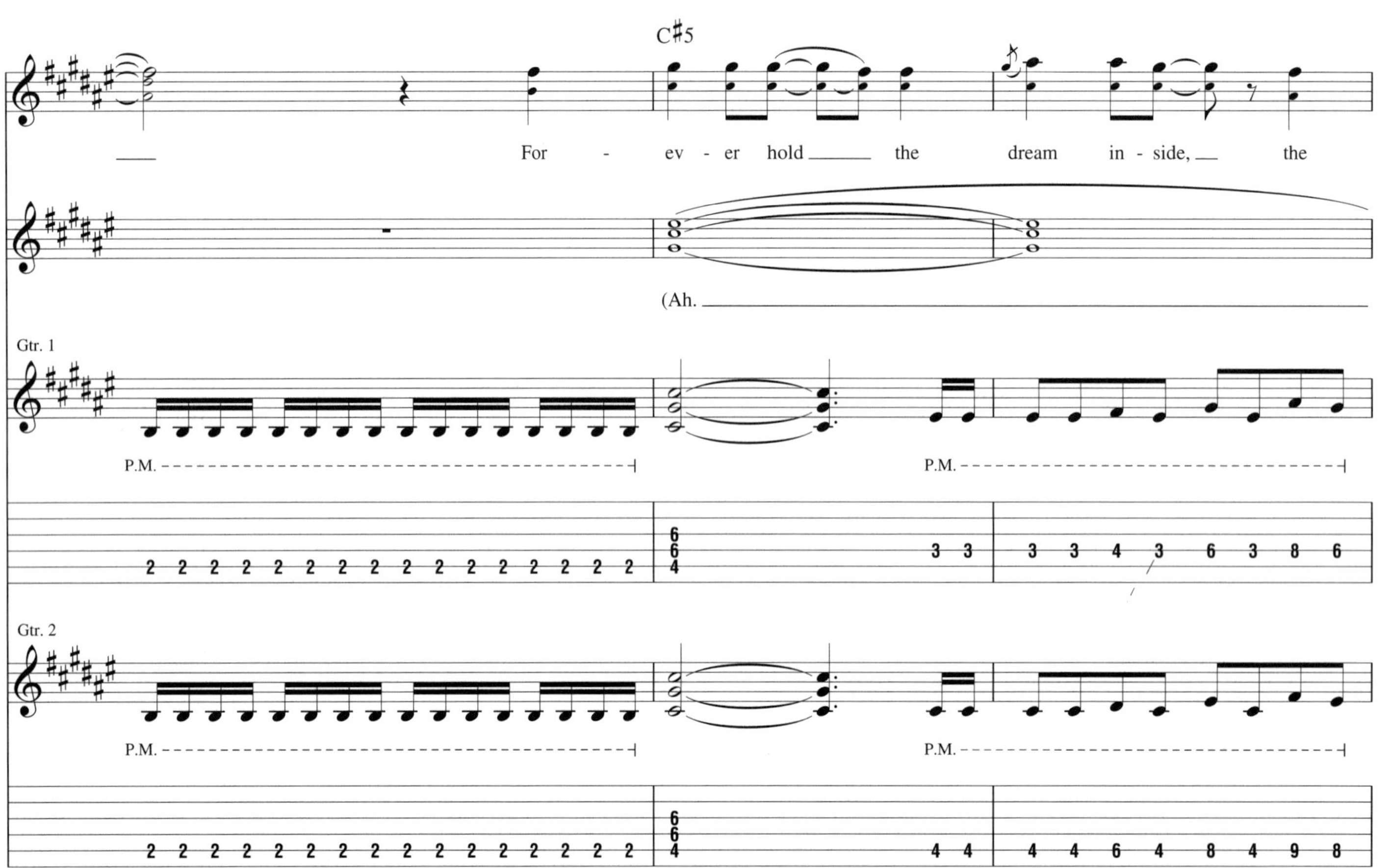
C♯5
For - ev - er hold the dream in - side, the
(Ah.
Gtr. 1
P.M.
2 2 2 2 2 2 2 2 2 2 2 2 2 2 2 2
6
6
4
3 3
3 3 4 3 6 3 8 6
Gtr. 2
P.M.
2 2 2 2 2 2 2 2 2 2 2 2 2 2 2 2
6
6
4
4 4
4 4 6 4 8 4 9 8

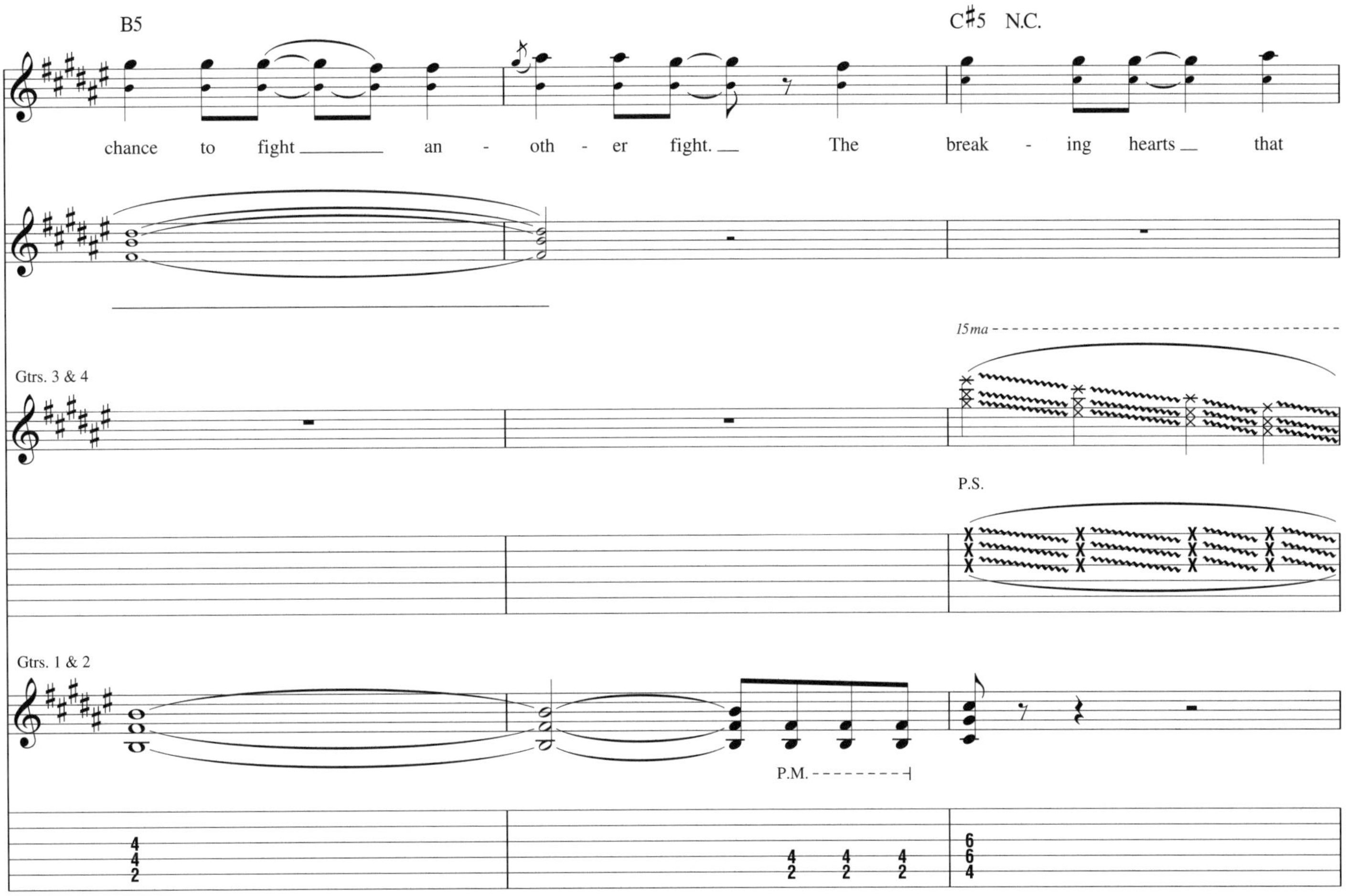

B5 C♯5 N.C.

chance to fight an - oth - er fight. The break - ing hearts that

15ma

Gtrs. 3 & 4

P.S.

Gtrs. 1 & 2

P.M.

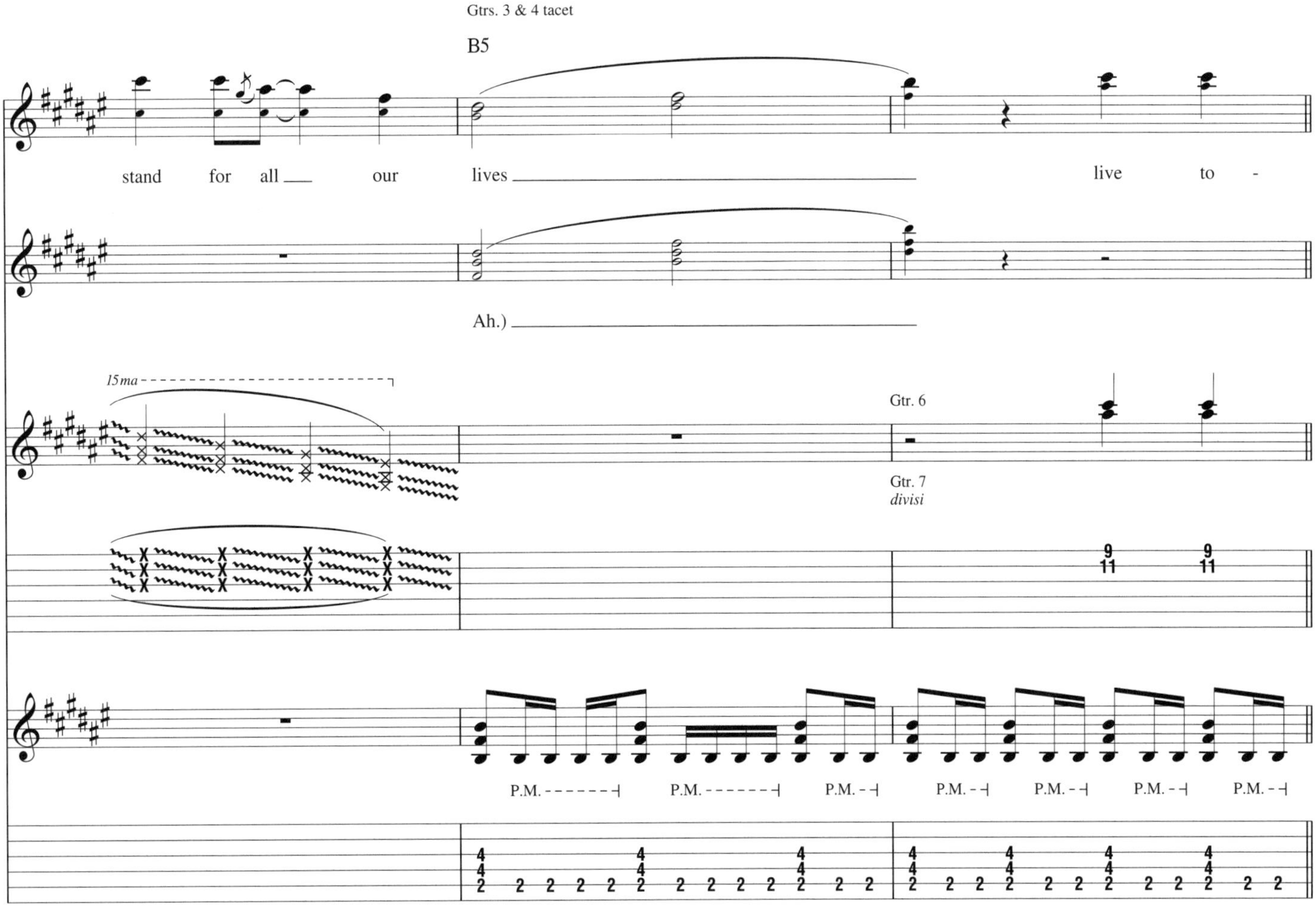

Gtrs. 3 & 4 tacet

B5

stand for all our lives live to -

Ah.)

15ma

Gtr. 6

Gtr. 7
divisi

P.M. P.M. P.M. P.M. P.M. P.M. P.M.

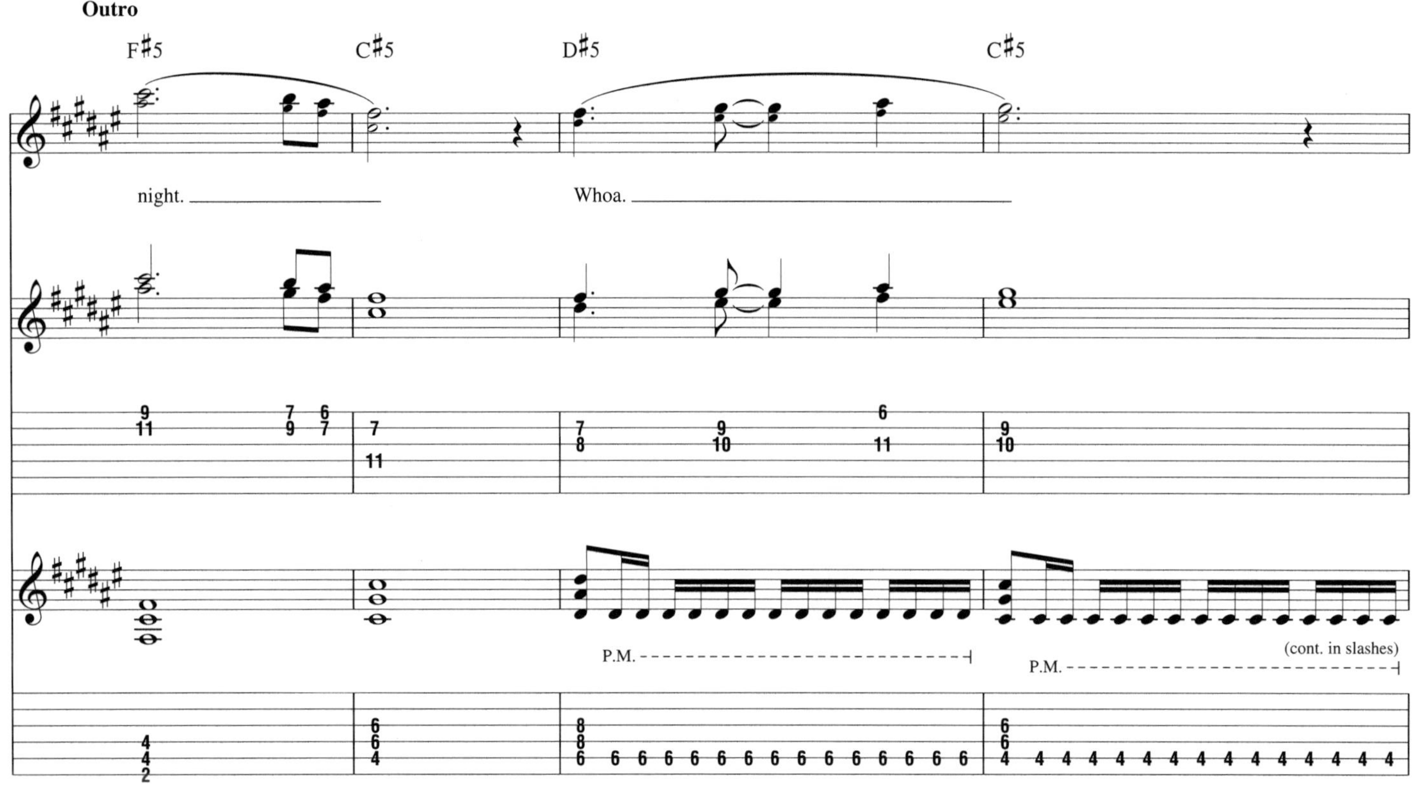

B5 C♯5 B5

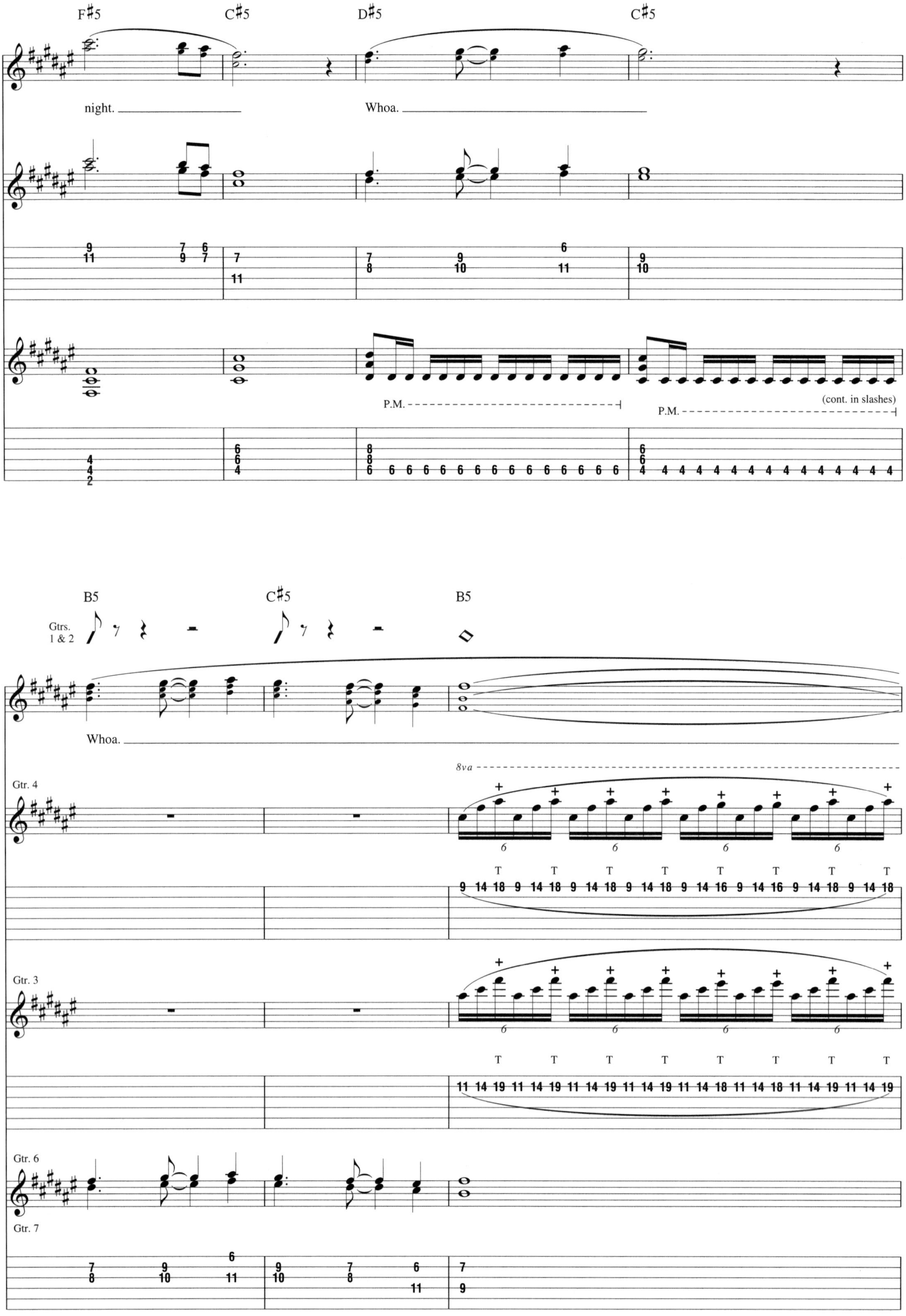

Gtrs. 1 & 2

Whoa.

8va

Gtr. 4

Gtr. 3

Gtr. 6

Gtr. 7

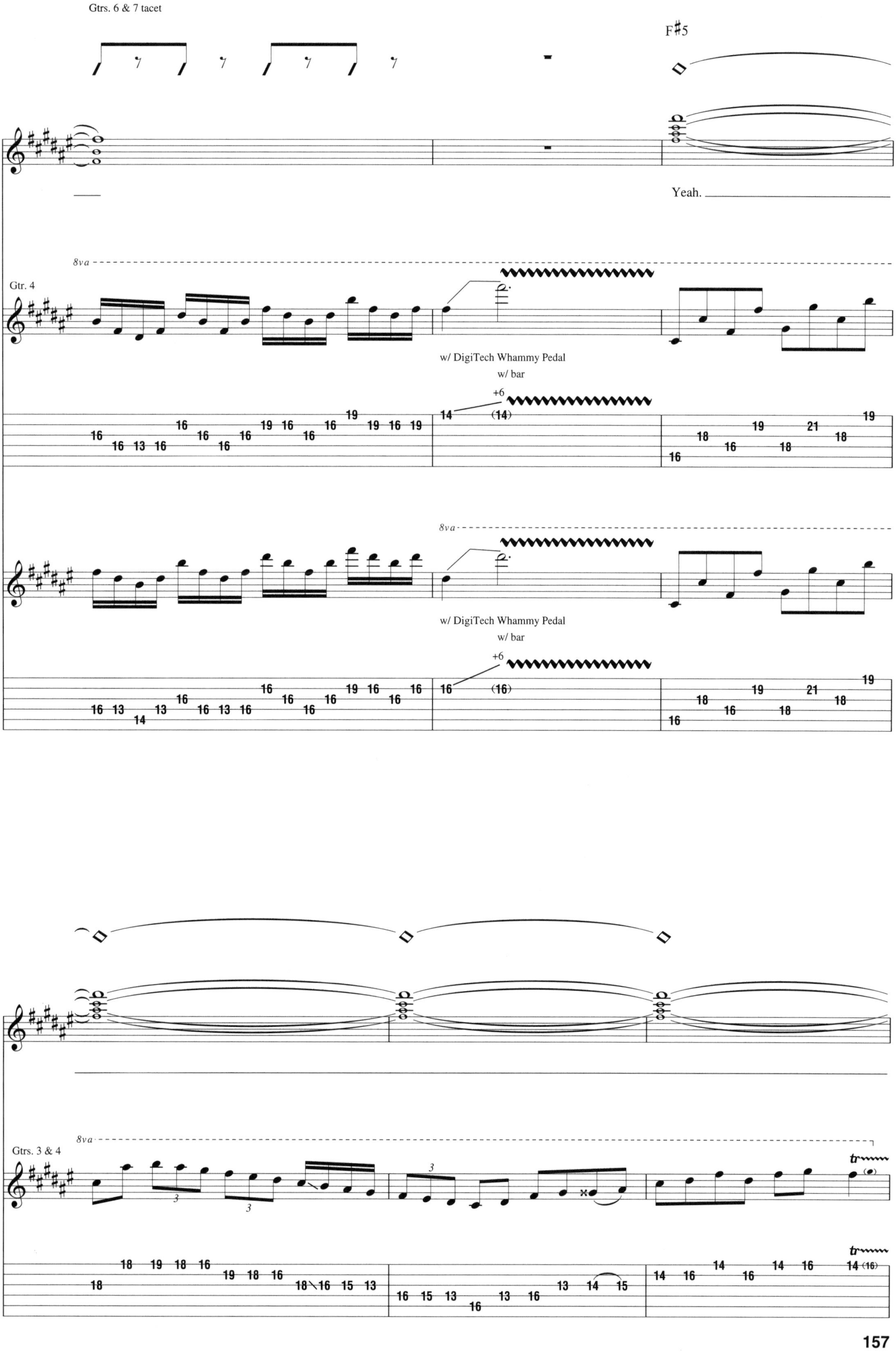

Gtrs. 6 & 7 tacet

F♯5

Yeah.

8va

Gtr. 4

w/ DigiTech Whammy Pedal

w/ bar

+6

8va

w/ DigiTech Whammy Pedal

w/ bar

+6

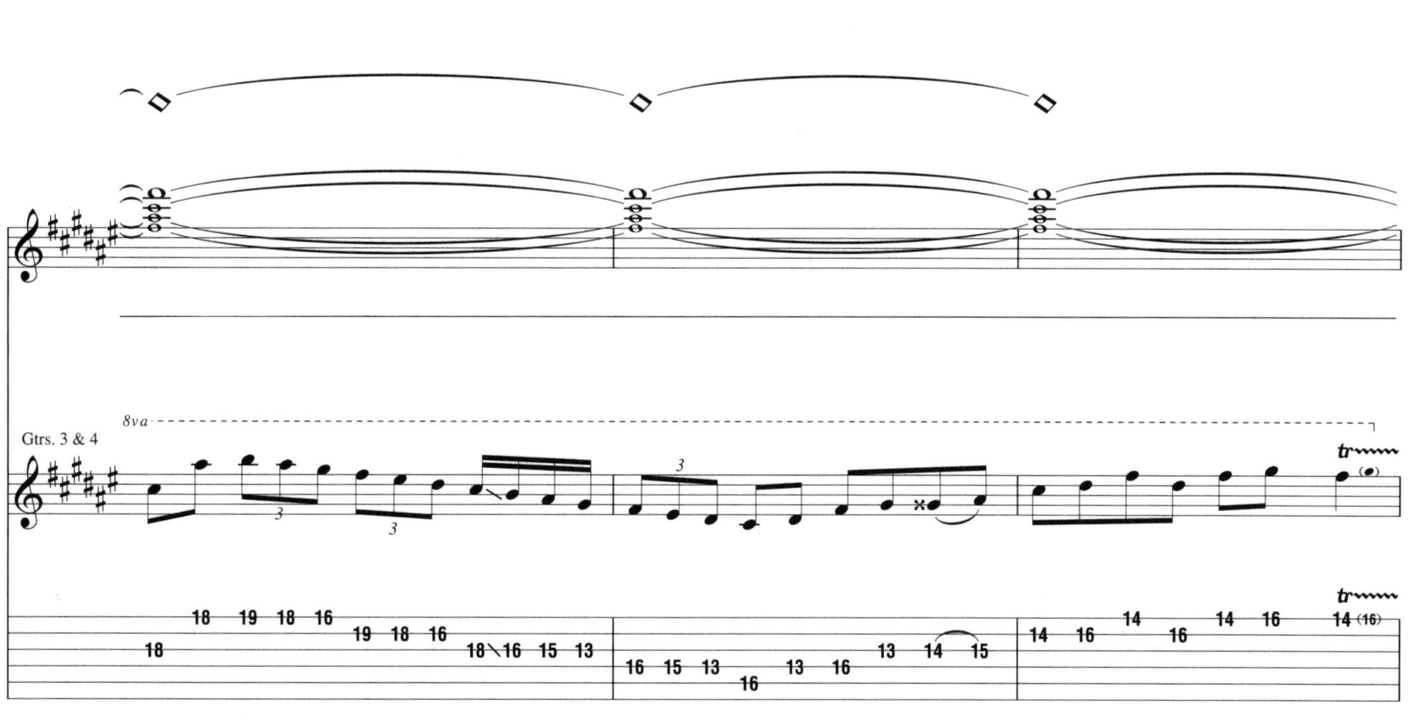

C♯5

(cont. in notation)

loco

Gtr. 4

8va

w/ DigiTech Whammy Pedal

+6 +6

loco

Gtr. 3

w/ DigiTech Whammy Pedal

+6 +6

B5 A♯5 B5 C♯5 F♯5 N.C.

15ma

Gtr. 4

+6

8va

Gtr. 3

+6

Gtrs. 1 & 2

P.M.

Body Breakdown

Words and Music by Herman Li, ZP Theart, Sam Totman and Vadim Pruzhanov

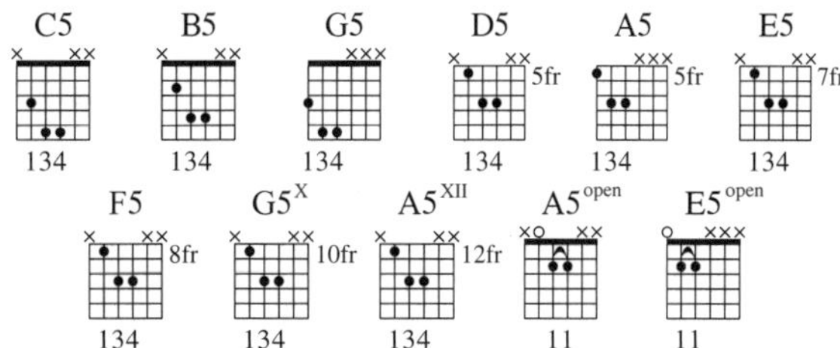

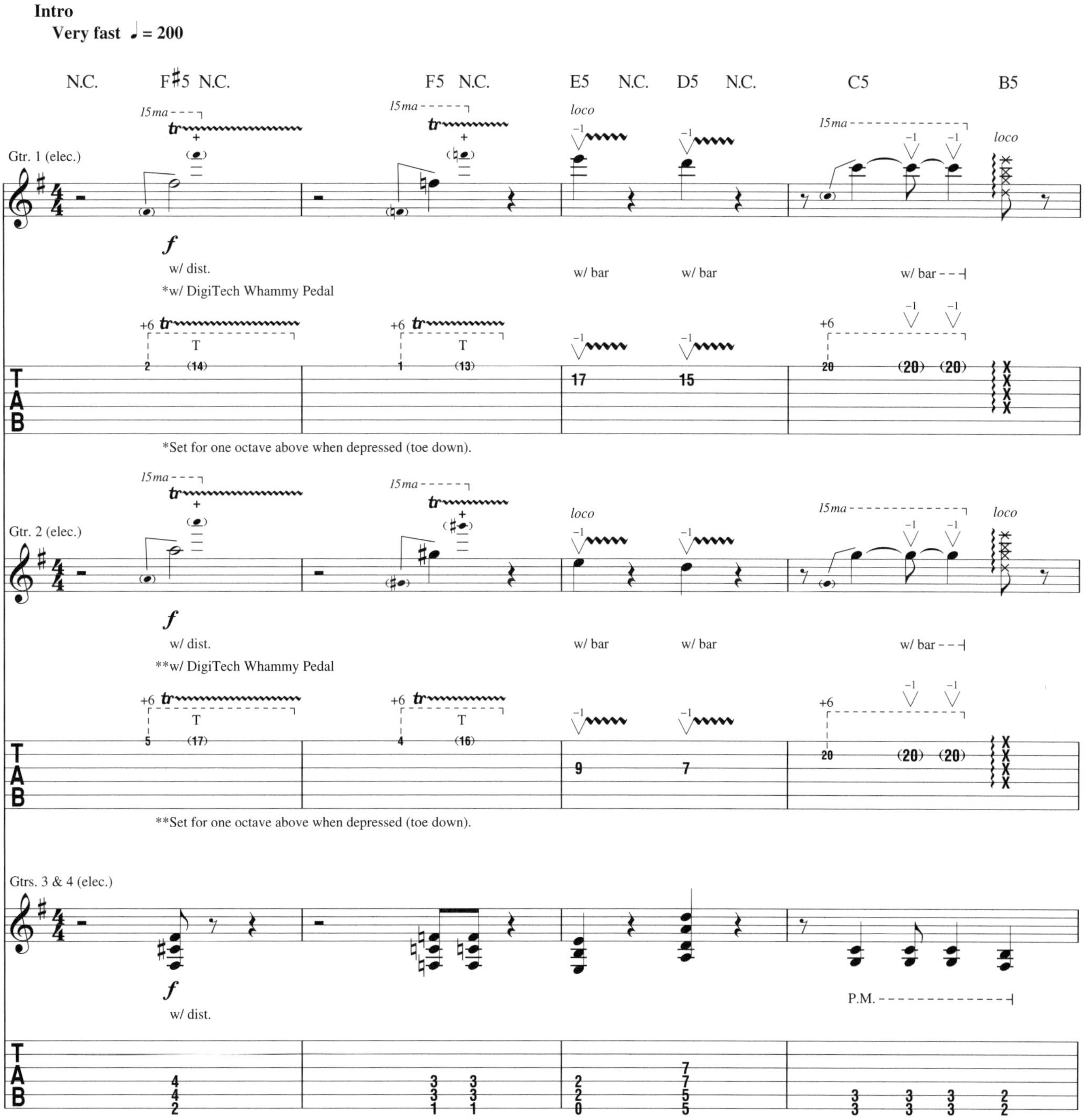

Intro
Very fast ♩ = 200

N.C. F♯5 N.C. F5 N.C. E5 N.C. D5 N.C. C5 B5

15ma loco 15ma loco

Gtr. 1 (elec.)

f

w/ dist.

*w/ DigiTech Whammy Pedal

w/ bar w/ bar w/ bar

*Set for one octave above when depressed (toe down).

Gtr. 2 (elec.)

f

w/ dist.

**w/ DigiTech Whammy Pedal

w/ bar w/ bar w/ bar

**Set for one octave above when depressed (toe down).

Gtrs. 3 & 4 (elec.)

f

w/ dist.

P.M.

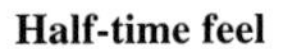

Half-time feel

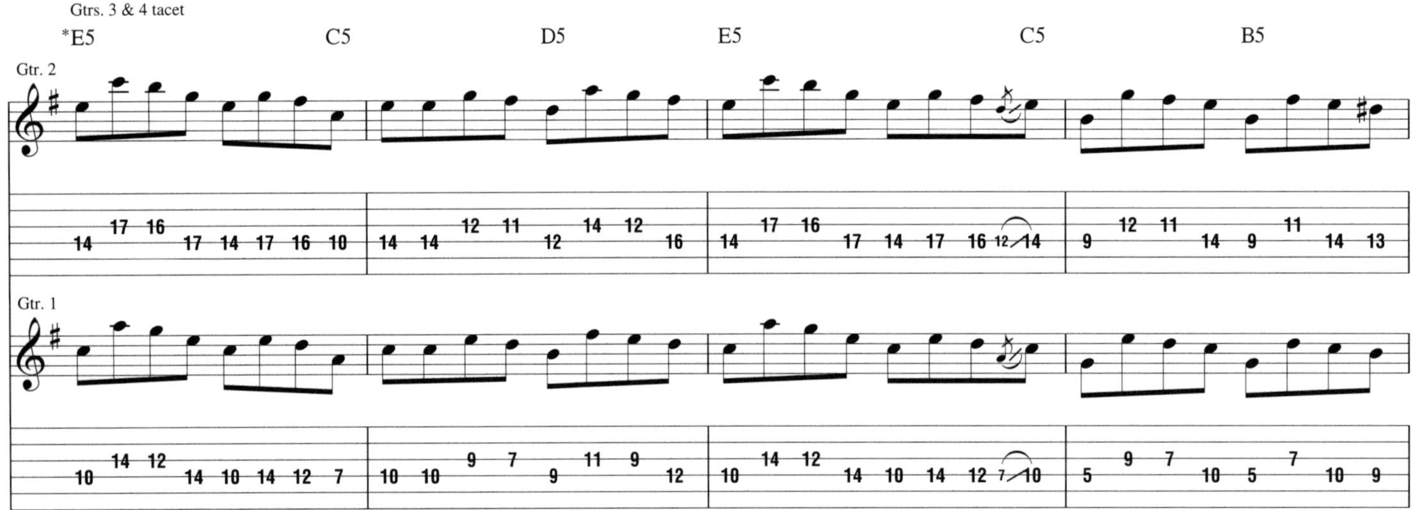

*Chord symbols reflect basic harmony implied by bass, next 7 meas.

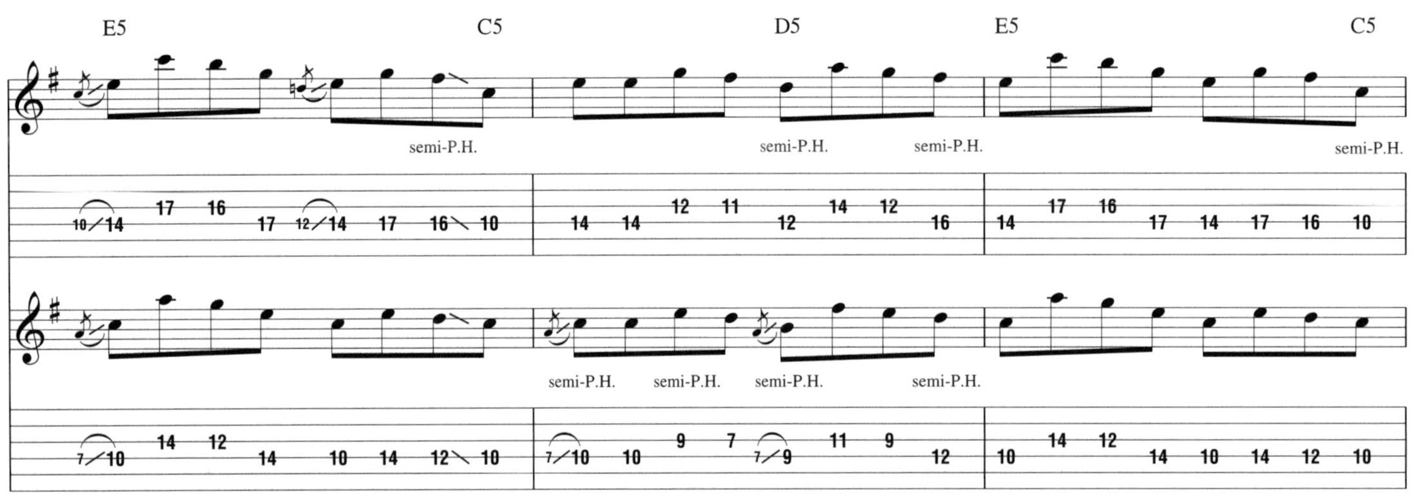

End half-time feel Double-time feel

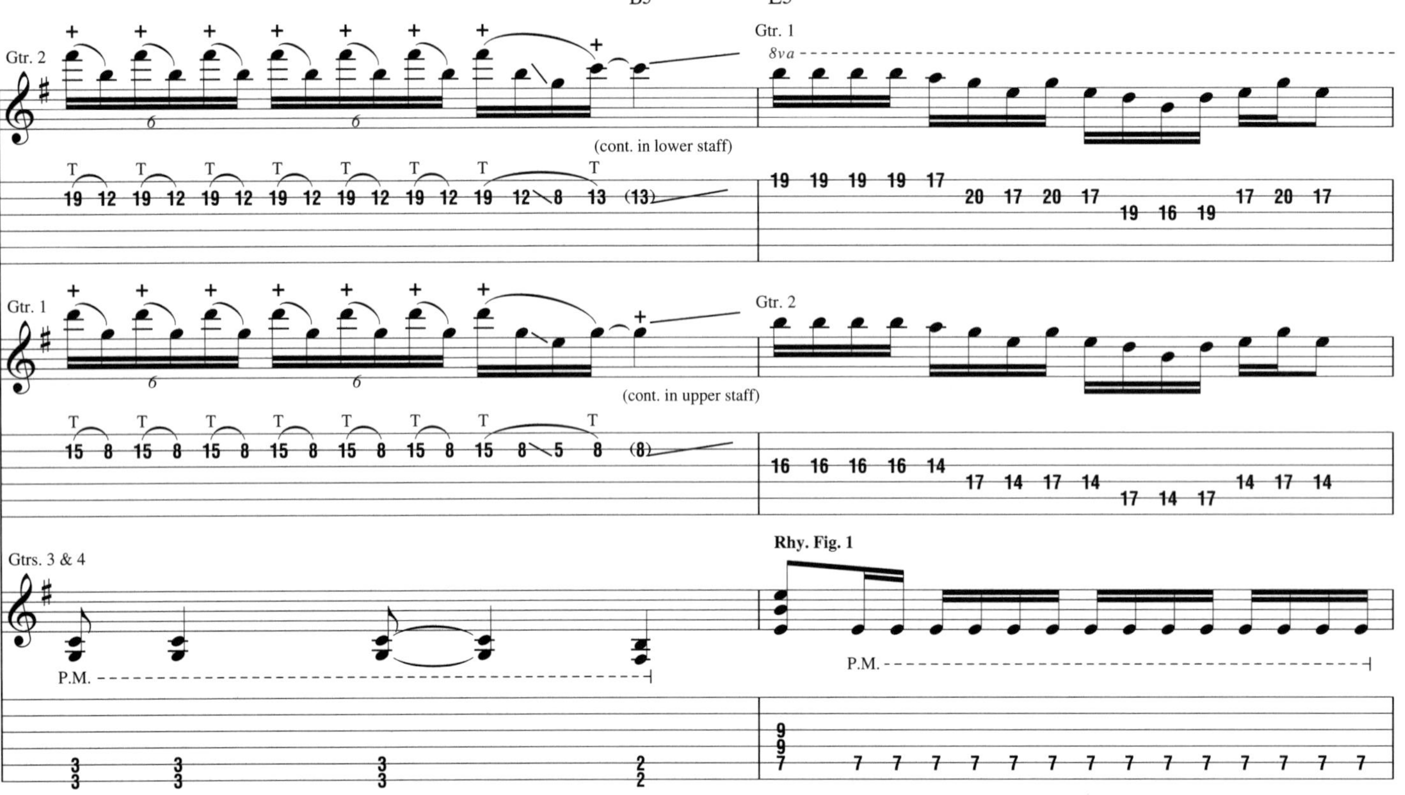

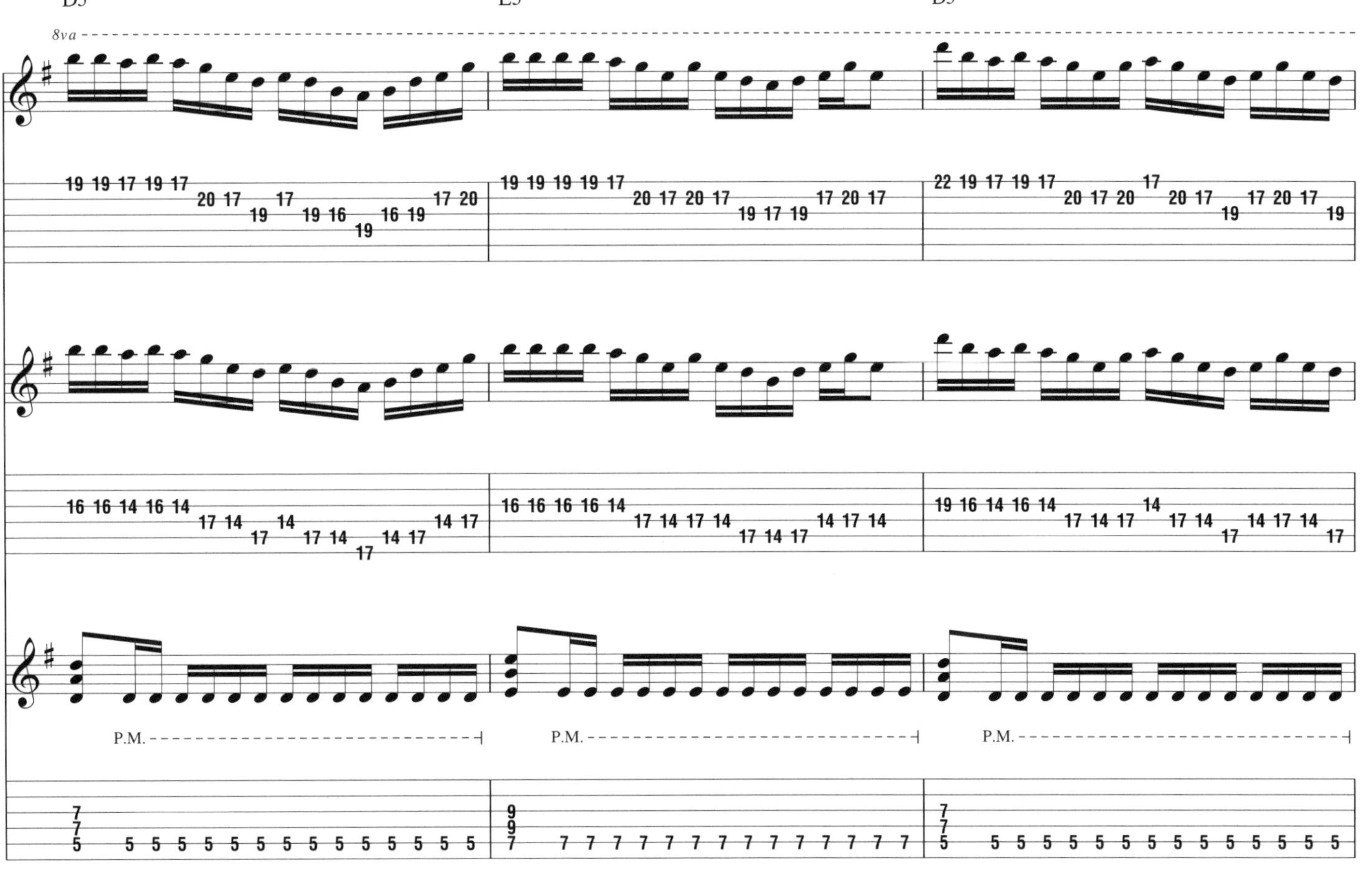

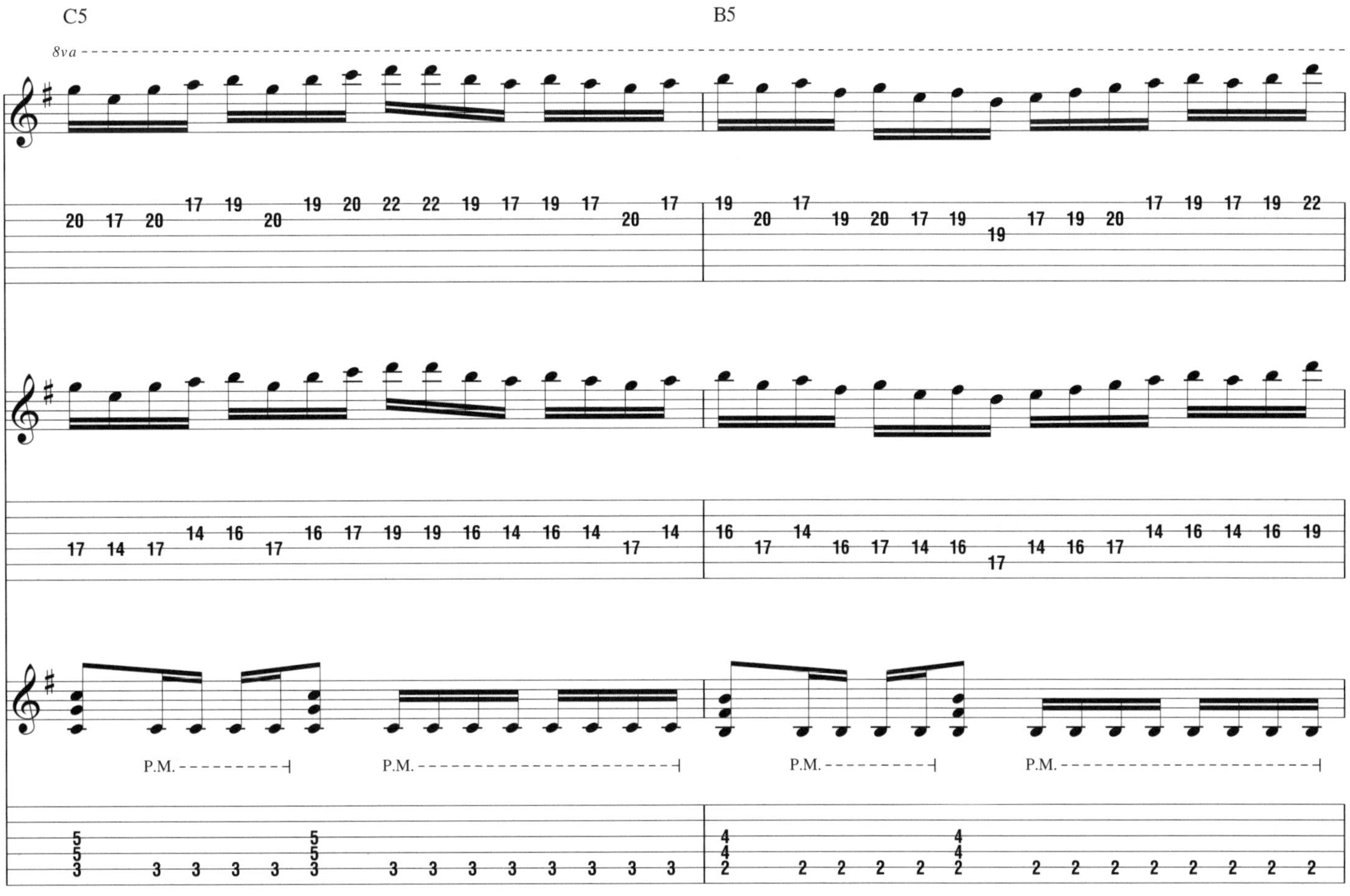

C5
B5
8va
P.M.
P.M.
P.M.
P.M.

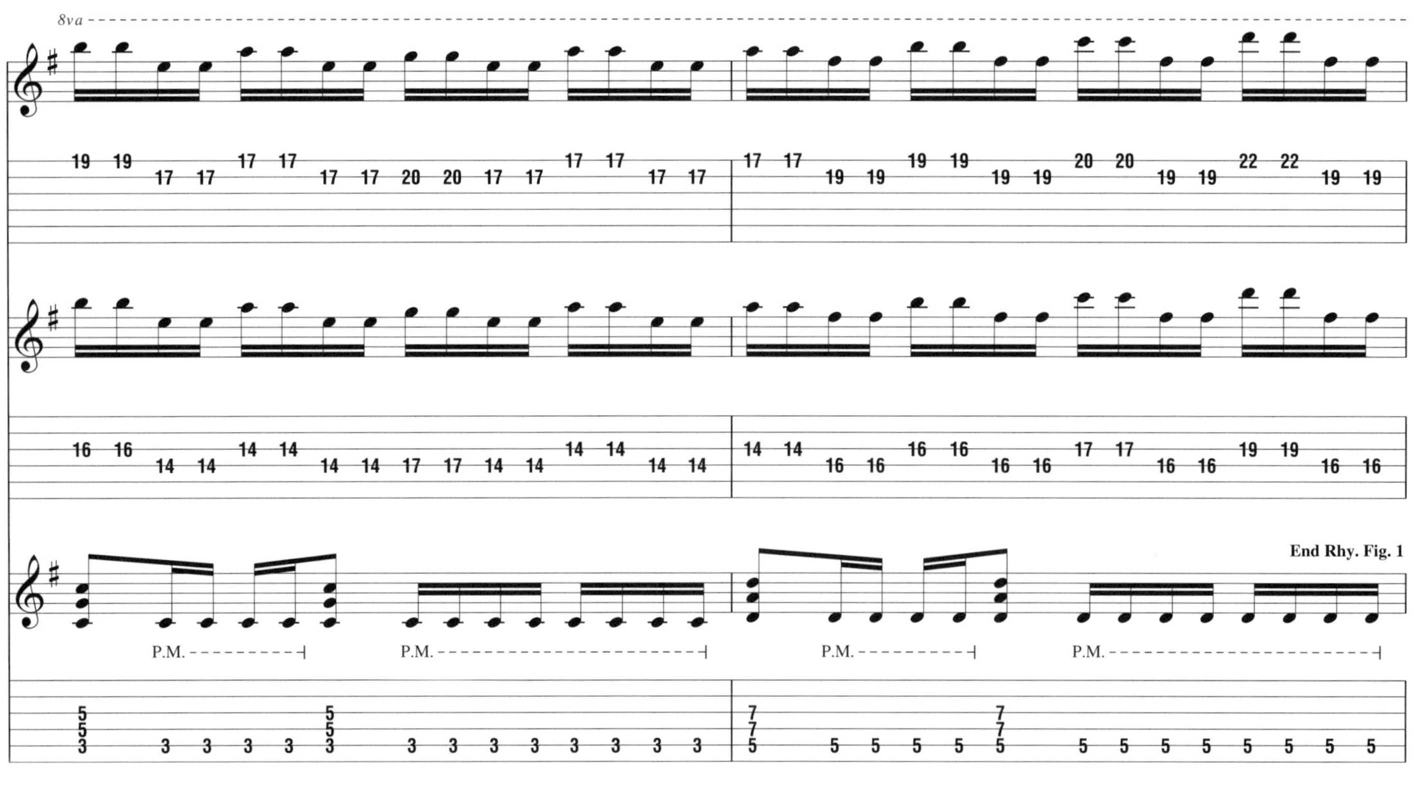
C5
D5
8va
P.M.
P.M.
P.M.
P.M.
End Rhy. Fig. 1

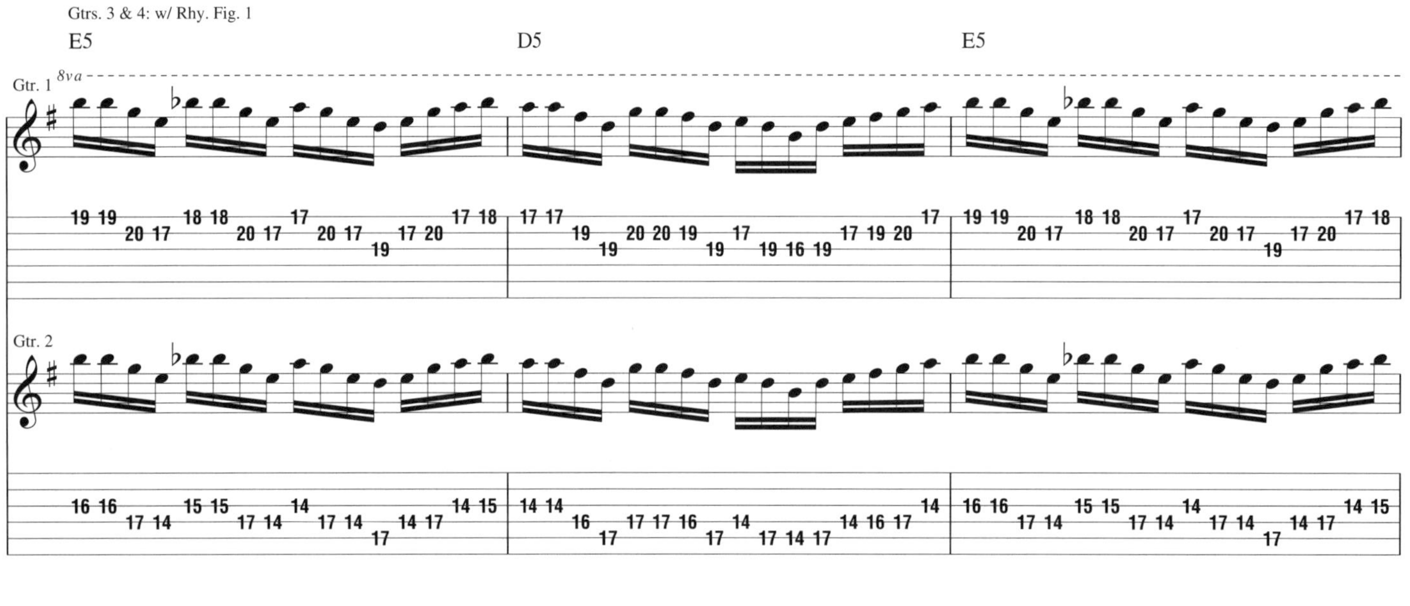
Gtrs. 3 & 4: w/ Rhy. Fig. 1
E5
D5
E5
Gtr. 1
8va
Gtr. 2

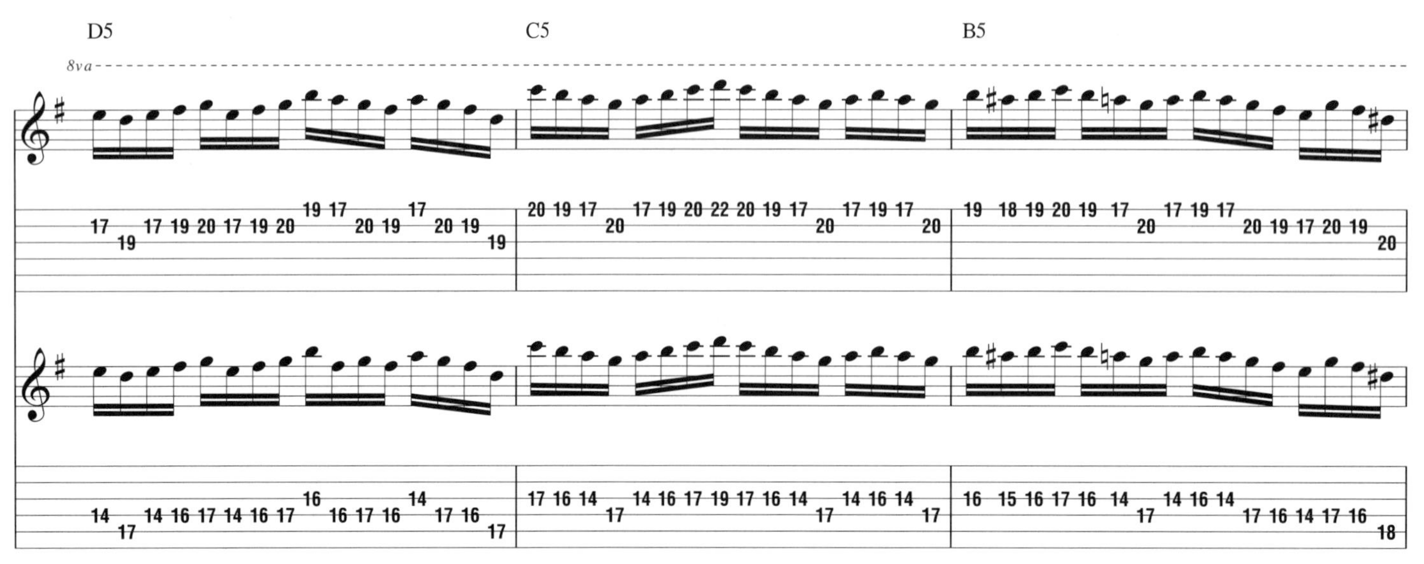
D5
C5
B5
8va

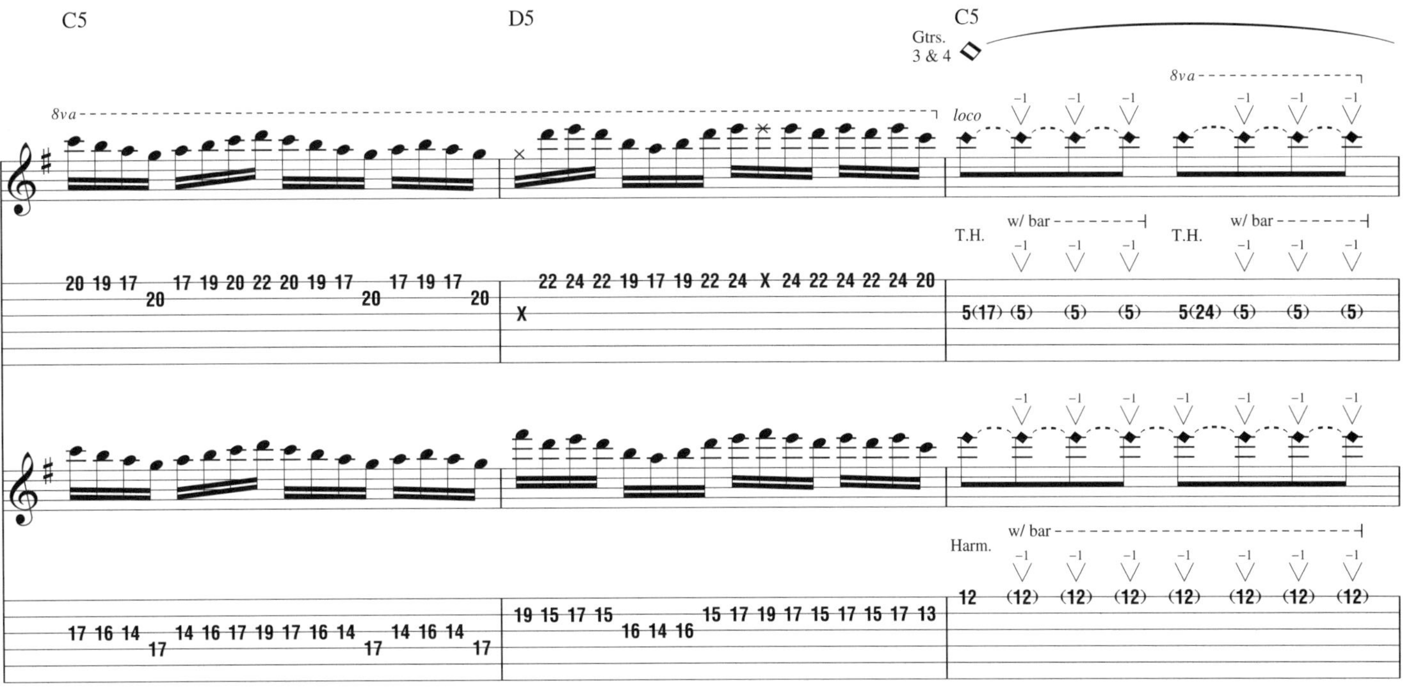
C5
D5
C5
Gtrs. 3 & 4
8va
loco
T.H.
w/ bar
Harm.

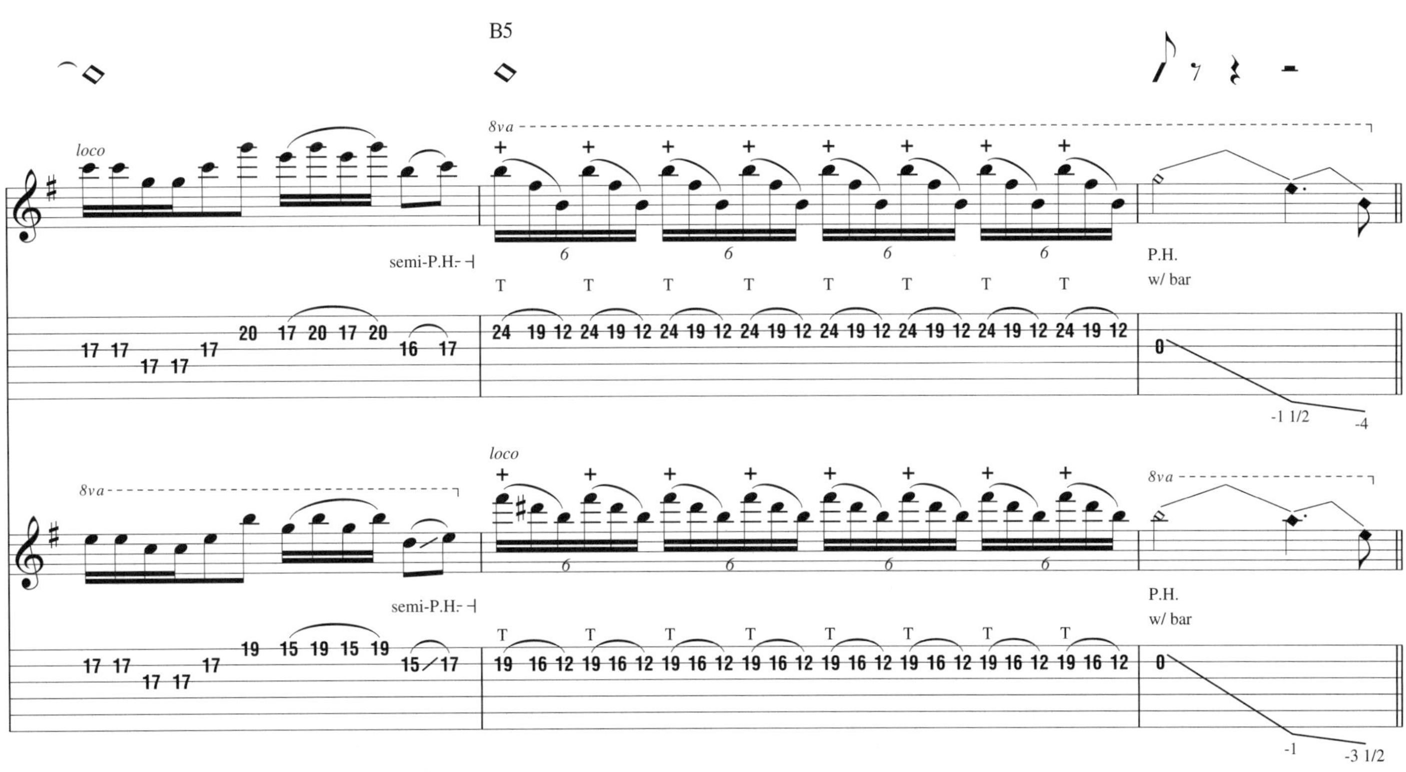
B5
8va
loco
semi-P.H.
P.H.
w/ bar

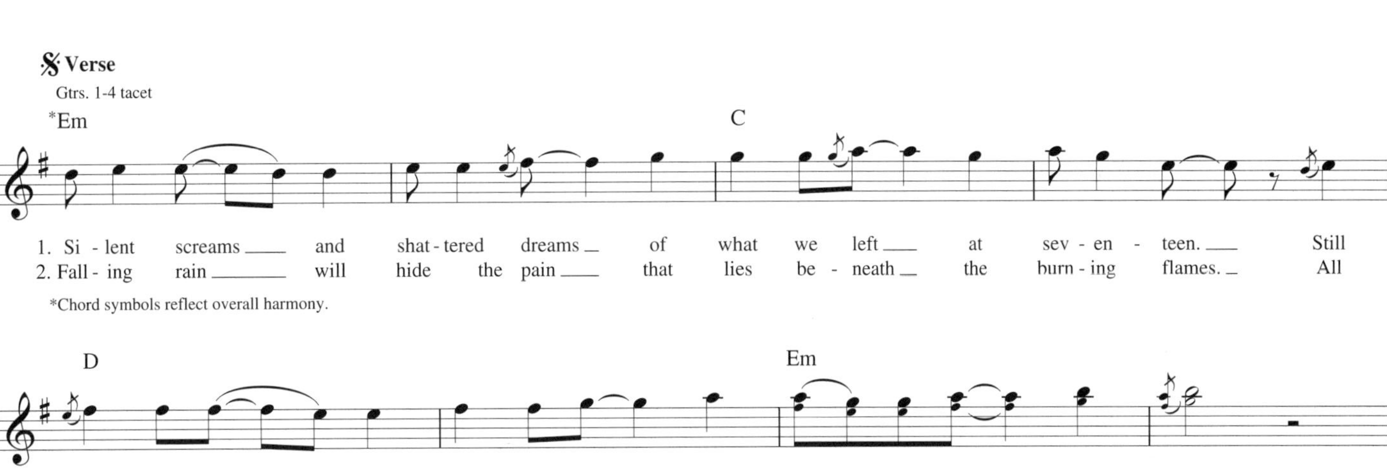
Verse
Gtrs. 1-4 tacet
*Em
C
D
Em
1. Si - lent screams and shat - tered dreams of what we left at sev - en - teen. Still
2. Fall - ing rain will hide the pain that lies be - neath the burn - ing flames. All
lost with - in the mis - er - y and pain that lies in - side.
hope is gone, so car - ry on be - fore the world will fall.

*Chord symbols reflect overall harmony.

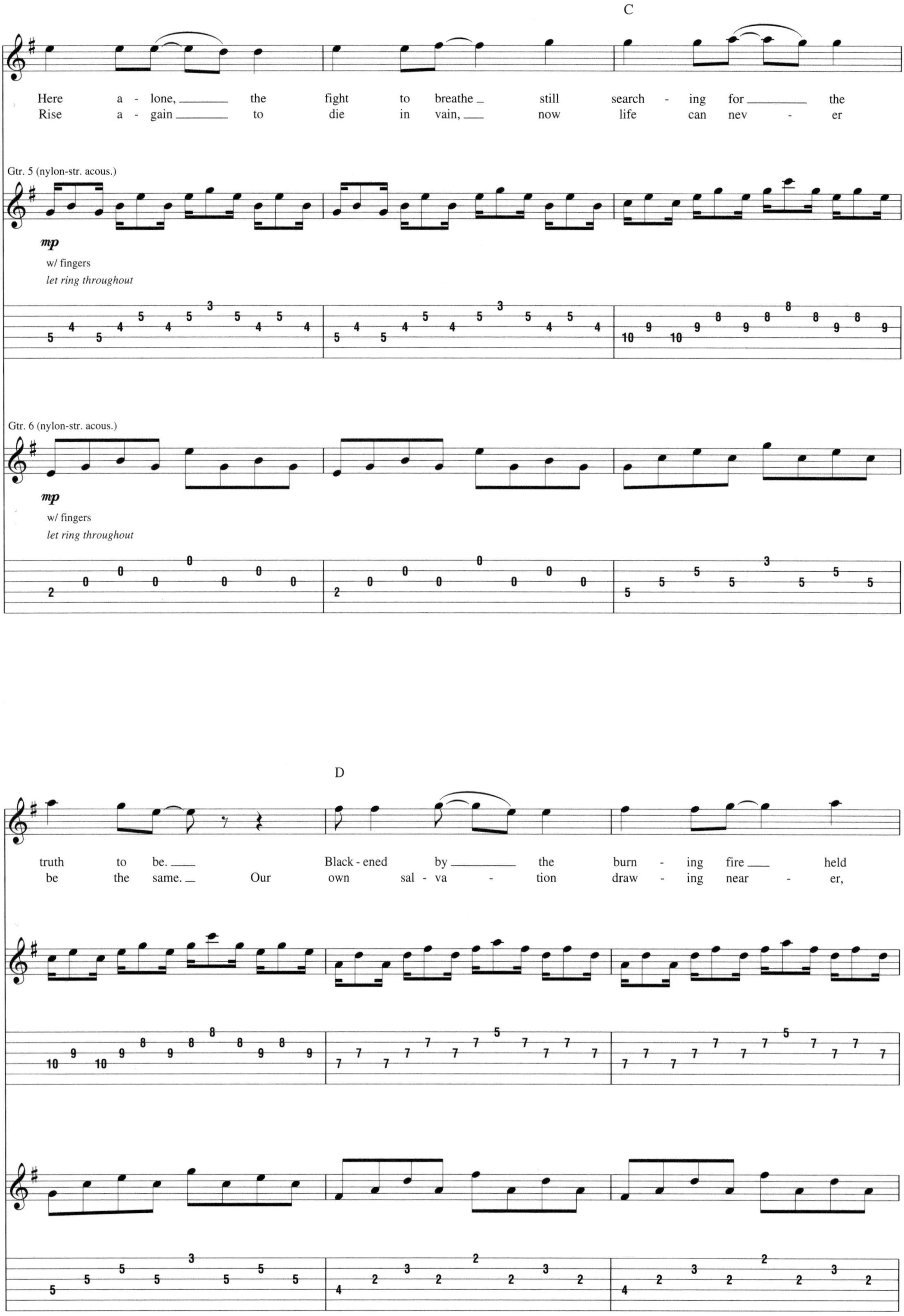

C

Here a - lone, ___ the fight to breathe _ still search - ing for ___ the
Rise a - gain ___ to die in vain, ___ now life can nev - er

Gtr. 5 (nylon-str. acous.)

mp

w/ fingers

let ring throughout

Gtr. 6 (nylon-str. acous.)

mp

w/ fingers

let ring throughout

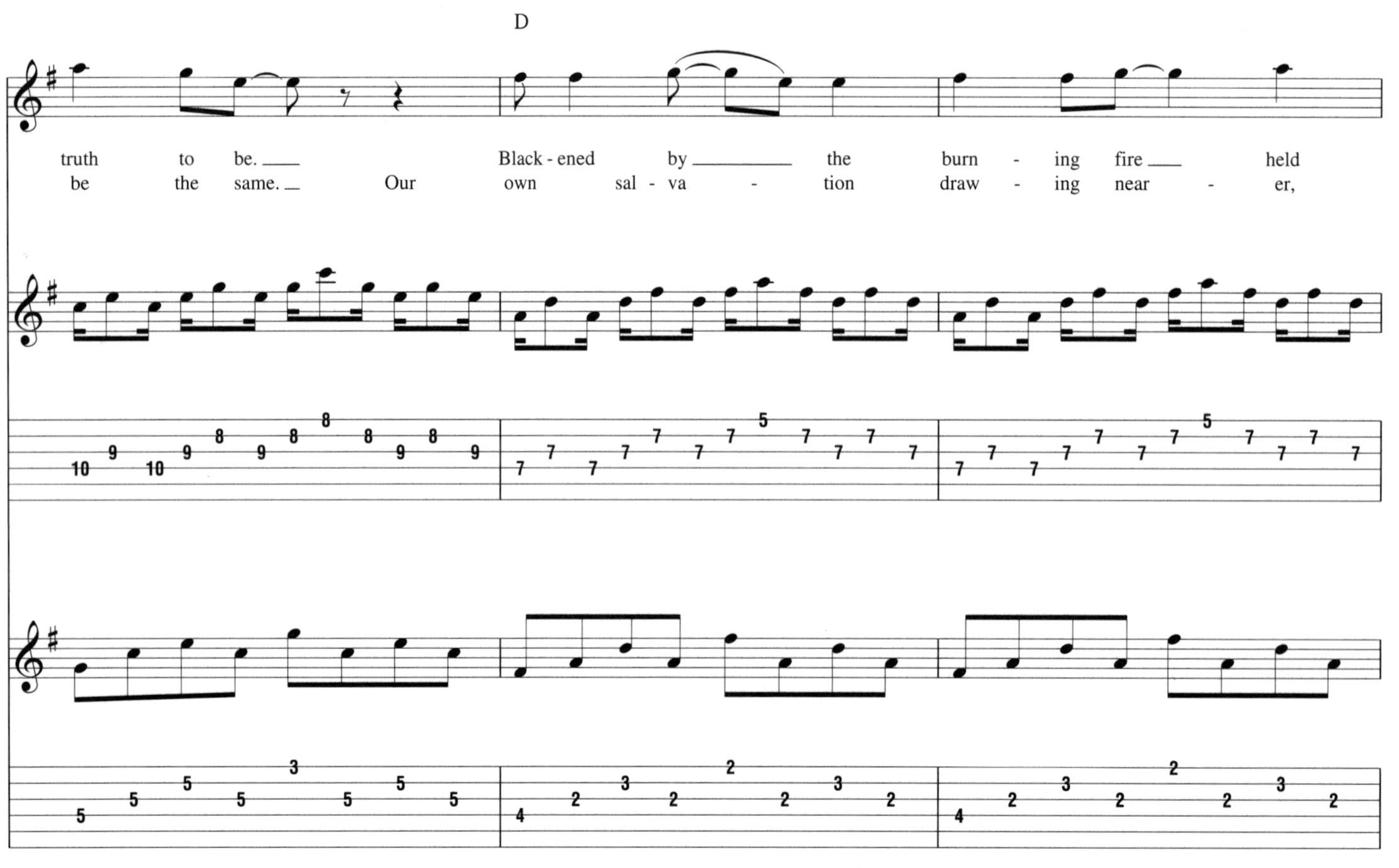
D
truth to be. ___ Black - ened by ___ the burn - ing fire ___ held
be the same. _ Our own sal - va - tion draw - ing near - er,

2nd time, Gtrs. 1 & 2: w/ Fill 1

Gtrs. 5 & 6 tacet

Em | | G5

deep in - side ___ my mind. ___ Far be - yond ___ the
hear the dark - ness call. ___ Skies are fall - ing,

Gtr. 1

8va

loco

w/ DigiTech Whammy Pedal

+6 +5

P.M.

12 (12) | 12 12 12 12 13 13 12 12 15 15 12 12 13 13 12 12

Gtr. 2

8va

loco

w/ DigiTech Whammy Pedal

+6 +5

P.M.

12 (12) | 12 12 12 12 14 14 12 12 16 16 12 12 14 14 12 12

Gtr. 5

Gtrs. 3 & 4

P.M.

5 4 5 4 5 4 5 3 5 4 5 4 | 5 4 5 4 5 4 5 3 5 4 5 4 | 5 5 3 3 3 3 3 3 3 3 3 3 3 3 3 3 3

Gtr. 6

2 0 0 0 0 0 0 0 | 2 0 0 0 0 0 0 0 |

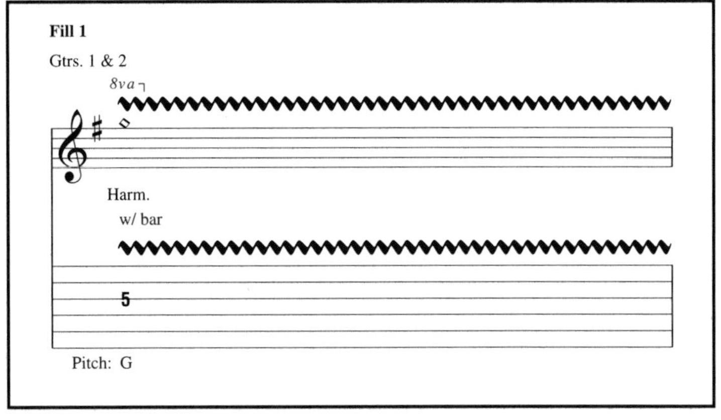

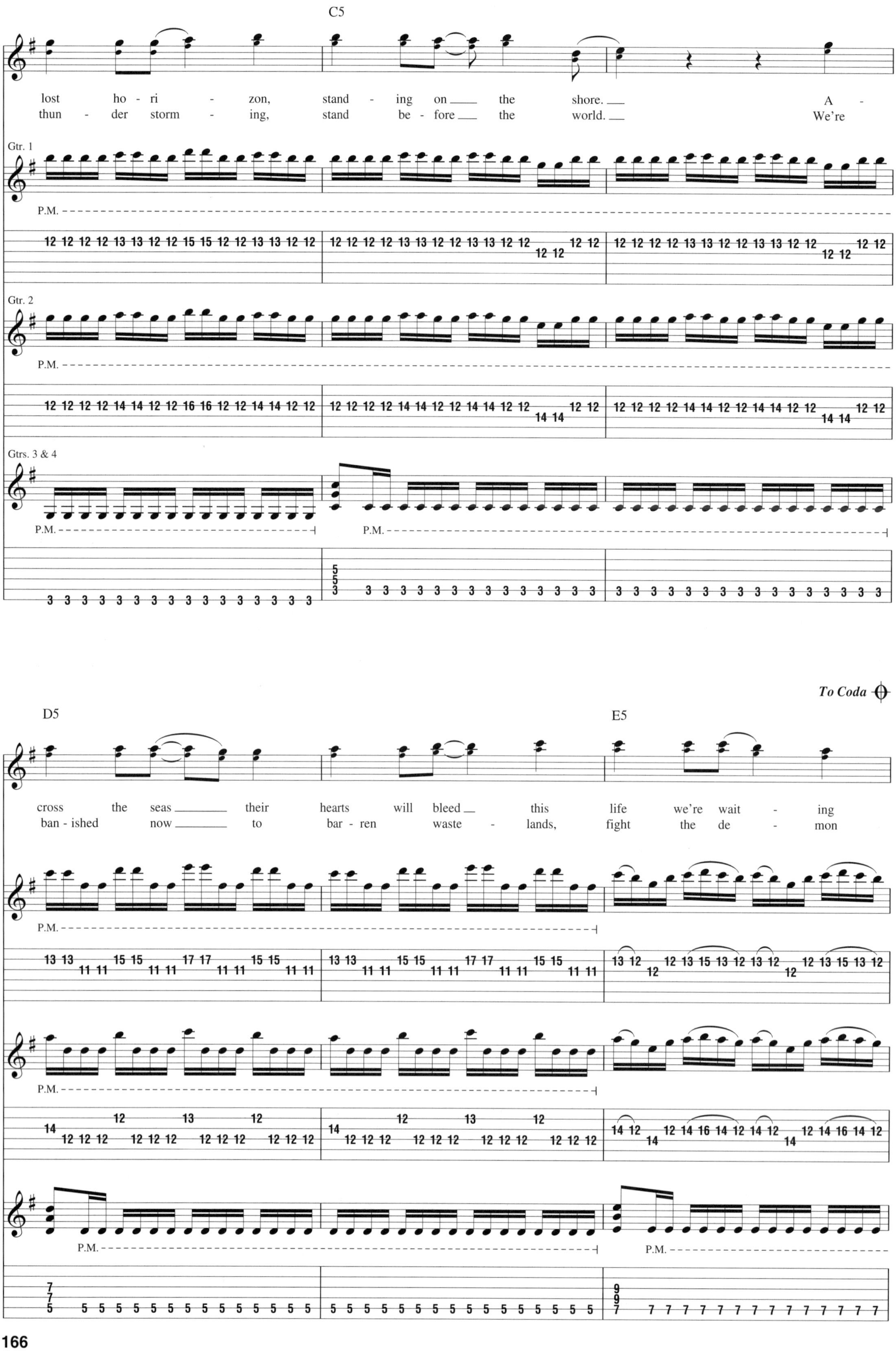

C5

lost ho - ri - zon, stand - ing on___ the shore.___ A -
thun - der storm - ing, stand be - fore___ the world.___ We're

Gtr. 1

P.M.

12 12 12 12 13 13 12 12 15 15 12 12 13 13 12 12 | 12 12 12 12 13 13 12 12 13 13 12 12 12 12 12 12 | 12 12 12 12 13 13 12 12 13 13 12 12 12 12 12 12

Gtr. 2

P.M.

12 12 12 12 14 14 12 12 16 16 12 12 14 14 12 12 | 12 12 12 12 14 14 12 12 14 14 12 12 14 14 12 12 | 12 12 12 12 14 14 12 12 14 14 12 12 14 14 12 12

Gtrs. 3 & 4

P.M.

3 3 3 3 3 3 3 3 3 3 3 3 3 3 3 3 | 5 5 3 3 3 3 3 3 3 3 3 3 3 3 3 3 3 | 3 3 3 3 3 3 3 3 3 3 3 3 3 3 3 3

To Coda

D5 E5

cross the seas___ their hearts will bleed___ this life we're wait - ing
ban - ished now___ to bar - ren waste - lands, fight the de - mon

P.M.

13 13 11 11 15 15 11 11 17 17 11 11 15 15 11 11 | 13 13 11 11 15 15 11 11 17 17 11 11 15 15 11 11 | 13 12 12 12 13 15 13 12 13 12 12 12 13 15 13 12

P.M.

14 12 12 12 12 12 12 12 13 12 12 12 12 12 12 12 | 14 12 12 12 12 12 12 12 13 12 12 12 12 12 12 12 | 14 12 14 12 14 16 14 12 14 12 14 12 14 16 14 12

P.M.

7 7 5 5 5 5 5 5 5 5 5 5 5 5 5 5 5 | 5 5 5 5 5 5 5 5 5 5 5 5 5 5 5 5 | 9 9 7 7 7 7 7 7 7 7 7 7 7 7 7 7 7

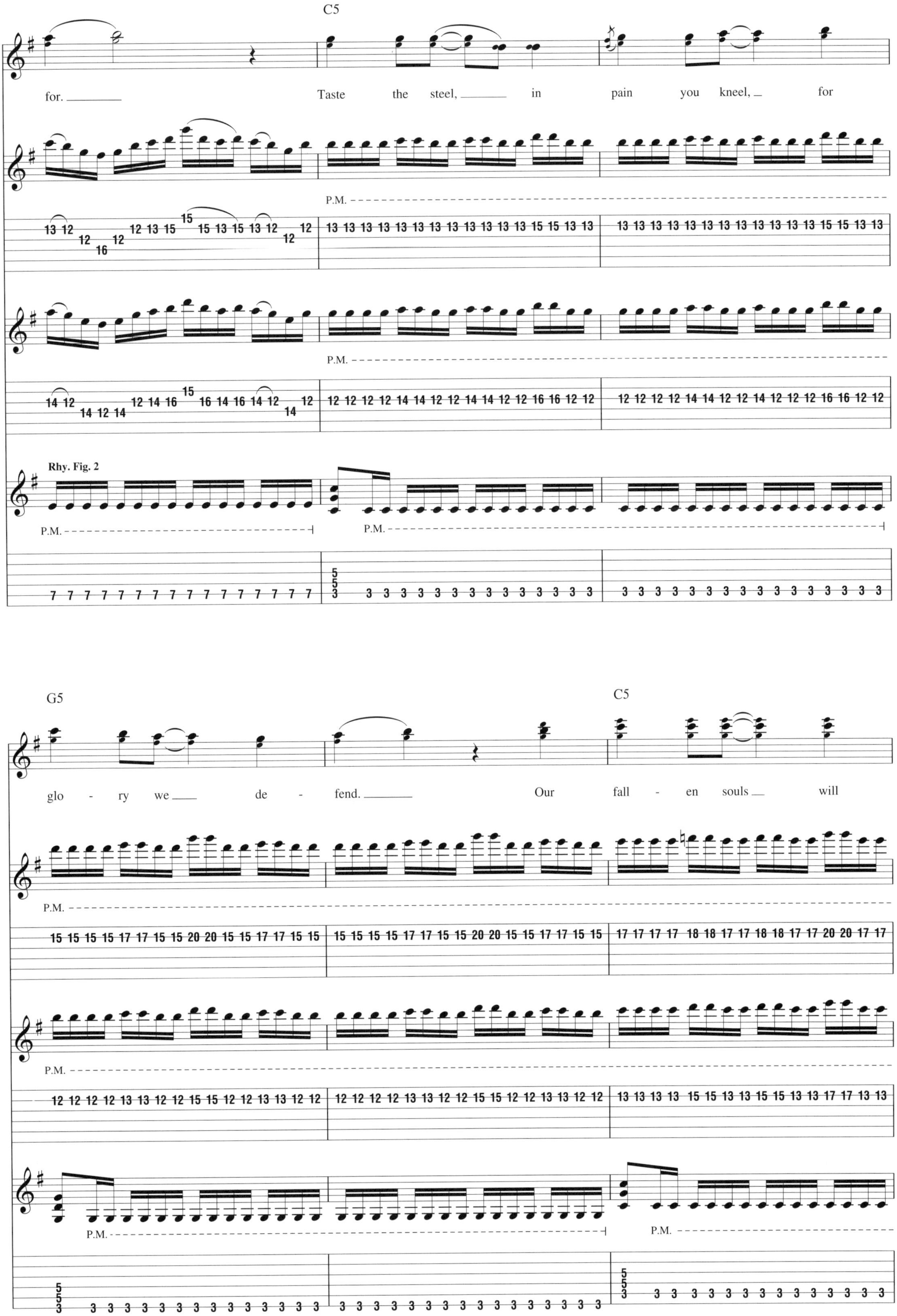

C5

for. ___ Taste the steel, ___ in pain you kneel, _ for

P.M.

13 12 12 16 12 12 13 15 15 15 13 15 13 12 12 12 | 13 13 13 13 13 13 13 13 13 13 13 13 15 15 13 13 | 13 13 13 13 13 13 13 13 13 13 13 13 15 15 13 13

P.M.

14 12 14 12 14 12 14 16 15 16 14 16 14 12 14 12 | 12 12 12 12 14 14 12 12 14 14 12 12 16 16 12 12 | 12 12 12 12 14 14 12 12 14 12 12 12 16 16 12 12

Rhy. Fig. 2

P.M.

P.M.

7 7 7 7 7 7 7 7 7 7 7 7 7 7 7 7 | 5 5 3 3 3 3 3 3 3 3 3 3 3 3 3 3 3 3 | 3 3 3 3 3 3 3 3 3 3 3 3 3 3 3 3

G5 C5

glo - ry we ___ de - fend. ___ Our fall - en souls _ will

P.M.

15 15 15 15 17 17 15 15 20 20 15 15 17 17 15 15 | 15 15 15 15 17 17 15 15 20 20 15 15 17 17 15 15 | 17 17 17 17 18 18 17 17 18 18 17 17 20 20 17 17

P.M.

12 12 12 12 13 13 12 12 15 15 12 12 13 13 12 12 | 12 12 12 12 13 13 12 12 15 15 12 12 13 13 12 12 | 13 13 13 13 15 15 13 13 15 15 13 13 17 17 13 13

P.M.

P.M.

5 5 3 3 3 3 3 3 3 3 3 3 3 3 3 3 3 | 3 3 3 3 3 3 3 3 3 3 3 3 3 3 3 3 | 5 5 5 3 3 3 3 3 3 3 3 3 3 3 3 3 3 3

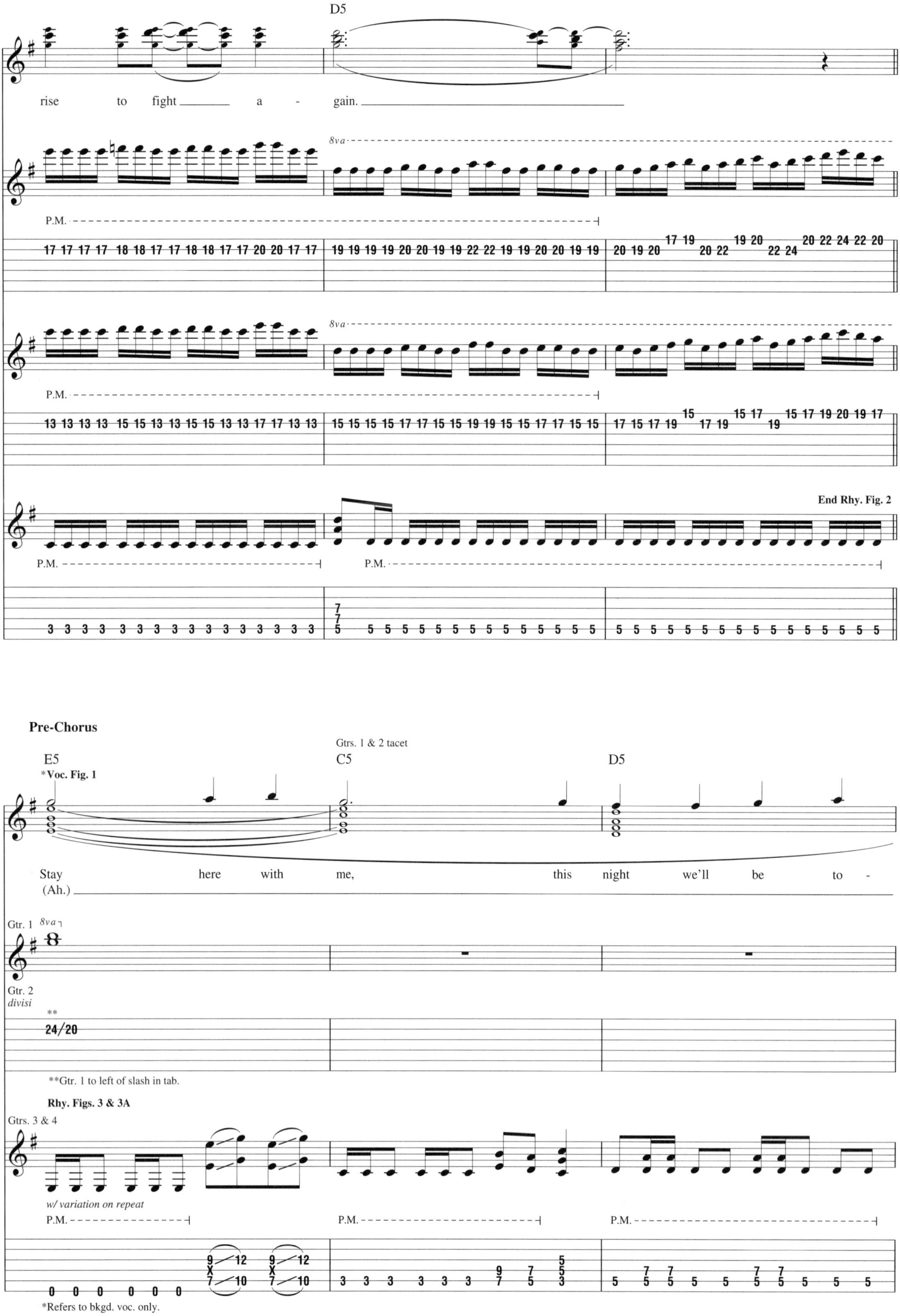

D5

rise to fight a - gain.

P.M.

17 17 17 17 18 18 17 17 18 18 17 17 20 20 17 17 | 19 19 19 19 20 20 19 19 22 22 19 19 20 20 19 19 | 20 19 20 17 19 20 22 19 20 22 24 20 22 24 22 20

P.M.

13 13 13 13 15 15 13 13 15 15 13 13 17 17 13 13 | 15 15 15 15 17 17 15 15 19 19 15 15 17 17 15 15 | 17 15 17 19 15 17 19 15 17 19 15 17 19 20 19 17

End Rhy. Fig. 2

P.M. P.M.

3 3 3 3 3 3 3 3 3 3 3 3 3 3 3 3 | 7 7 5 5 5 5 5 5 5 5 5 5 5 5 5 5 5 5 | 5 5 5 5 5 5 5 5 5 5 5 5 5 5 5 5

Pre-Chorus

Gtrs. 1 & 2 tacet

E5 C5 D5

*Voc. Fig. 1

Stay here with me, this night we'll be to -
(Ah.)

Gtr. 1 8va

Gtr. 2
divisi

** 24/20

**Gtr. 1 to left of slash in tab.

Rhy. Figs. 3 & 3A

Gtrs. 3 & 4

w/ variation on repeat

P.M. P.M. P.M.

0 0 0 0 0 0 9 X 7 12 10 9 X 7 12 10 | 3 3 3 3 3 3 9 7 7 5 5 5 3 | 5 7 5 7 5 5 5 7 5 7 5 5 5 5

*Refers to bkgd. voc. only.

E5 C5 D5

End Voc. Fig. 1

geth - er. Fu - ture in our hands, we'll fight with

Gtr. 3

semi-P.H.

Gtr. 4

P.H.

E5

Bkgd. Voc.: w/ Voc. Fig. 1

free - dom draw - ing near. Stand here with

P.M. semi-P.H.

P.M. semi-P.H.

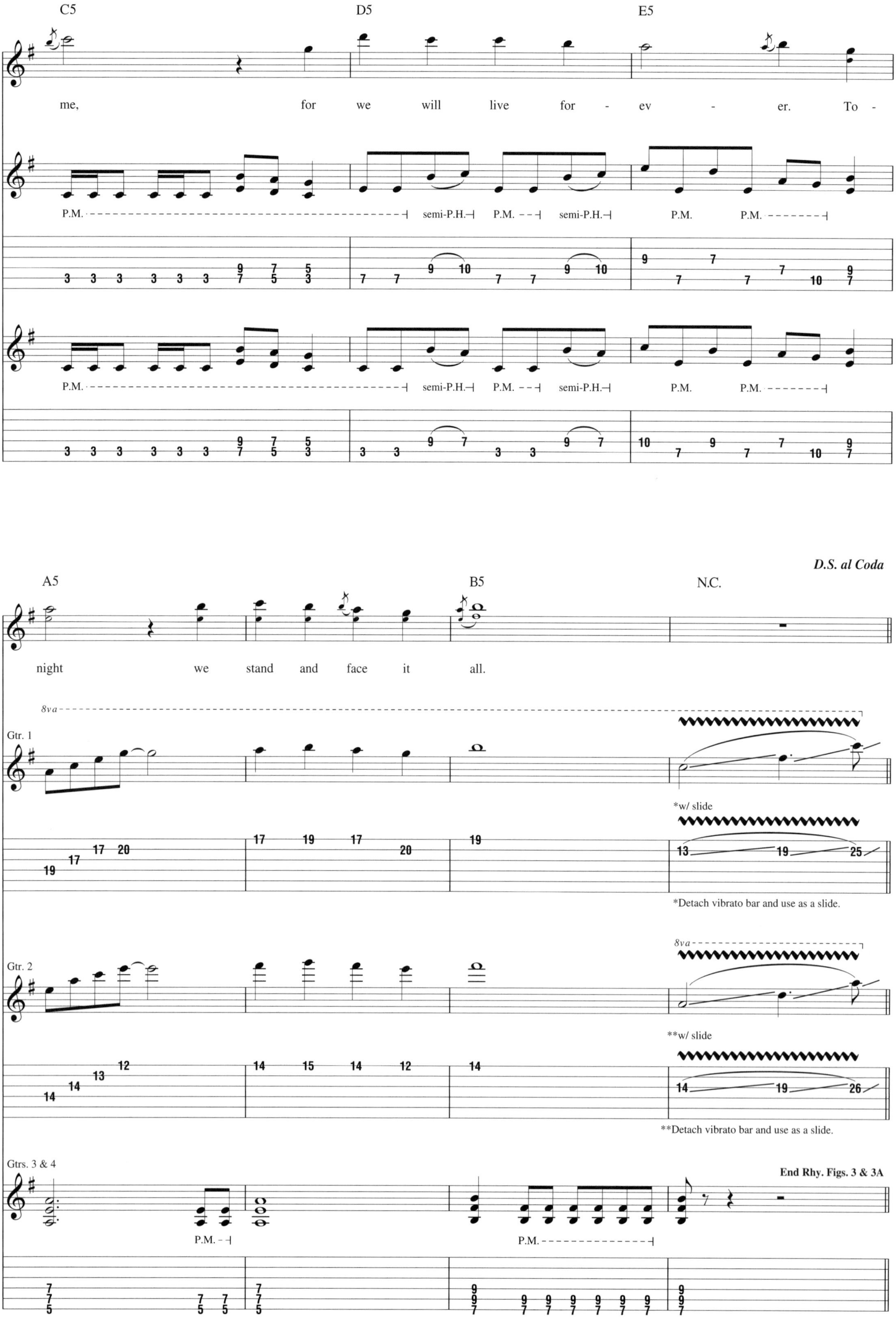

D.S. al Coda

A5 B5 N.C.

night we stand and face it all.

8va

Gtr. 1

*w/ slide

*Detach vibrato bar and use as a slide.

Gtr. 2

8va

**w/ slide

**Detach vibrato bar and use as a slide.

Gtrs. 3 & 4

End Rhy. Figs. 3 & 3A

P.M.

P.M.

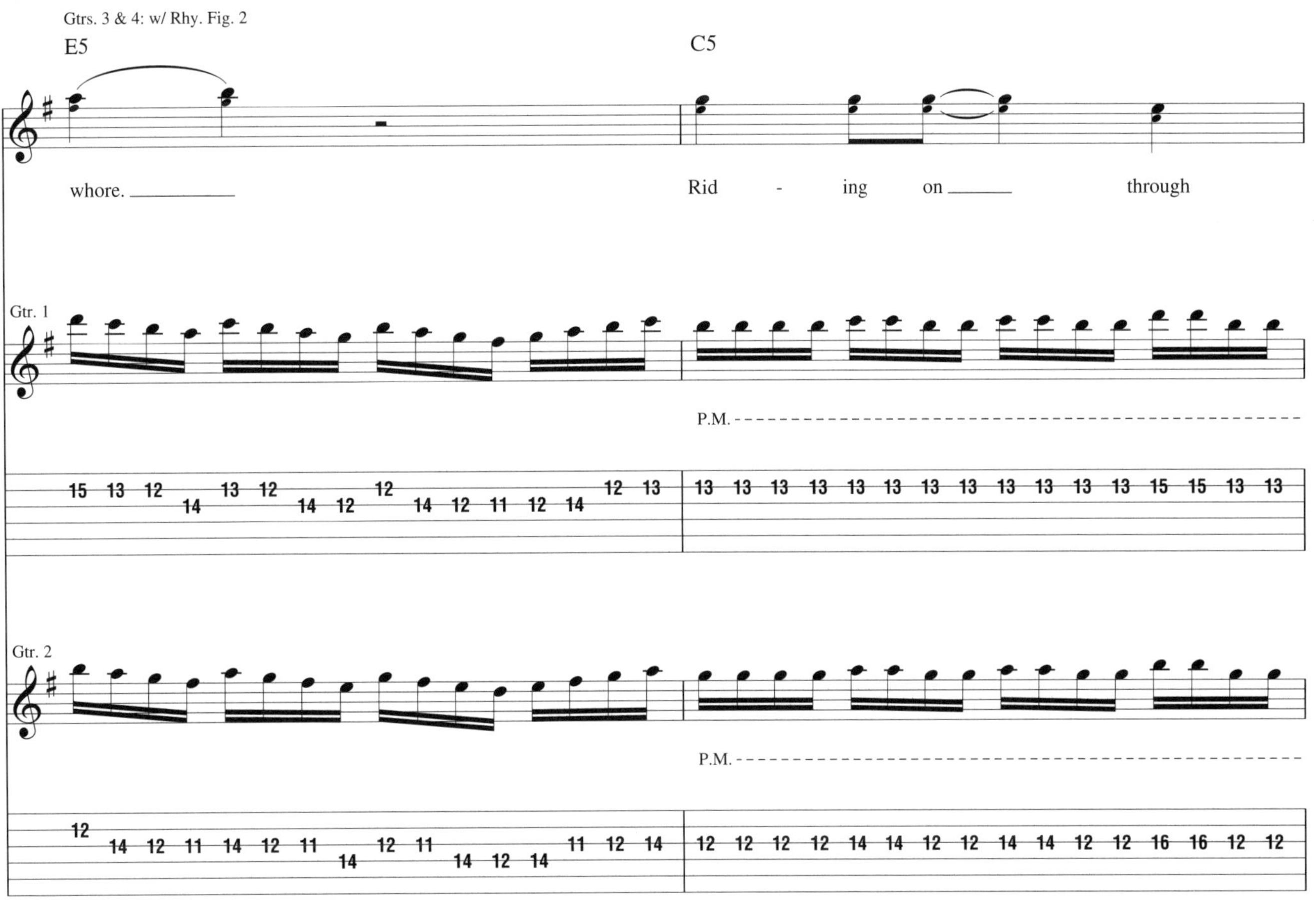
Gtrs. 3 & 4: w/ Rhy. Fig. 2
E5
C5
whore.
Rid - ing on through
Gtr. 1
P.M.
Gtr. 2
P.M.

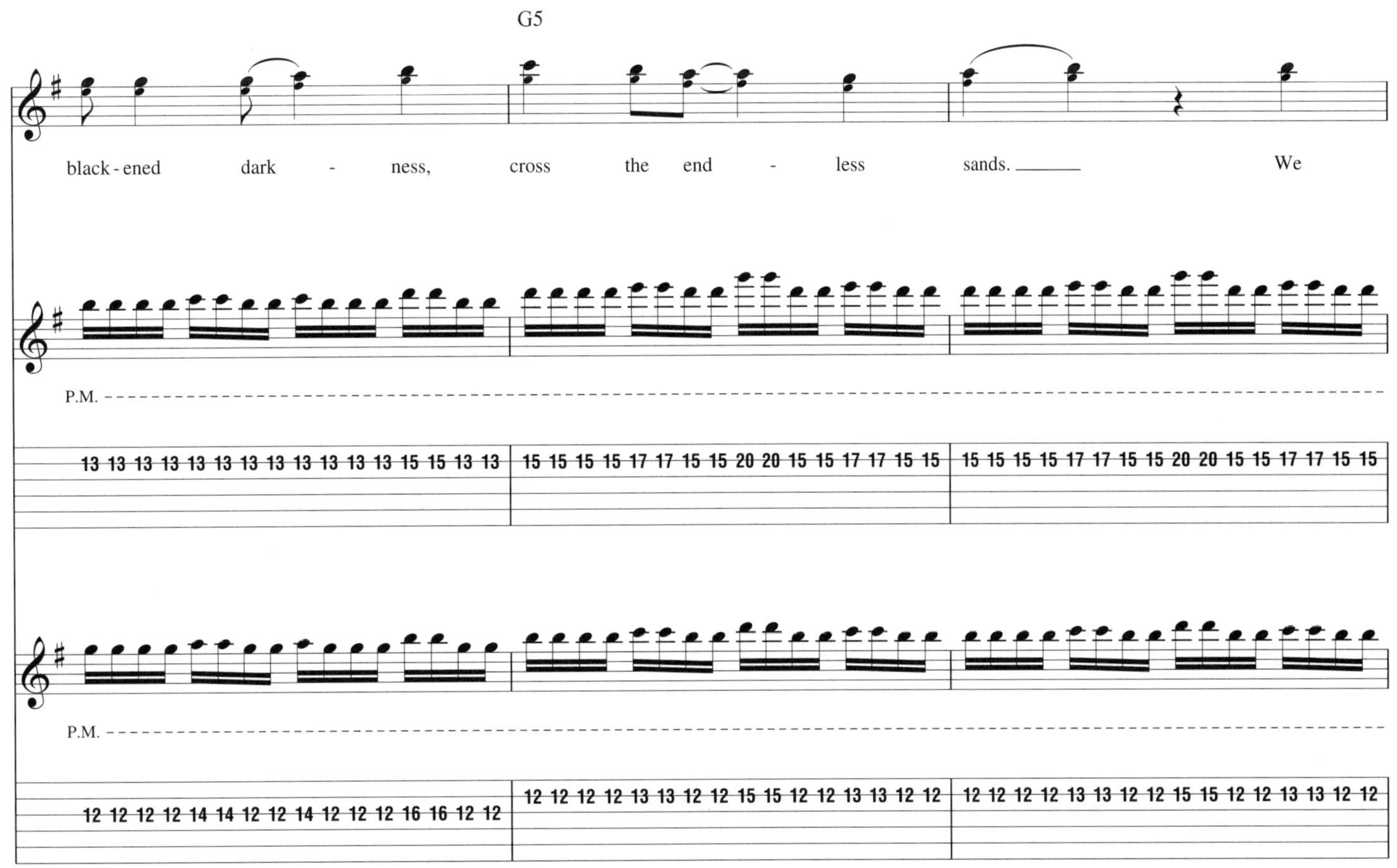
G5
black - ened dark - ness, cross the end - less sands.
We
P.M.
P.M.

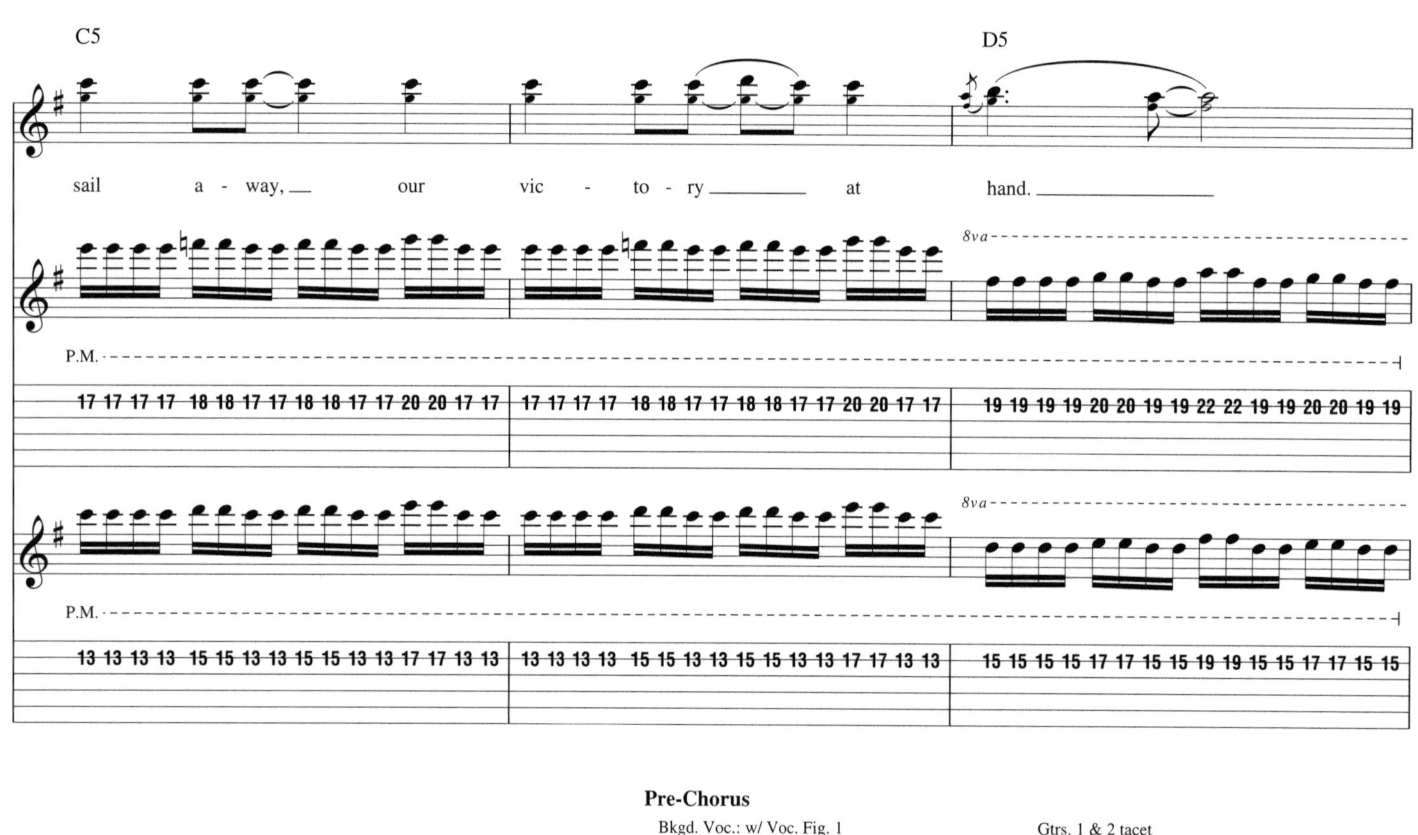
C5
D5
sail a - way, our vic - to - ry at hand.
8va
P.M.
17 17 17 17 18 18 17 17 18 18 17 17 20 20 17 17
17 17 17 17 18 18 17 17 18 18 17 17 20 20 17 17
19 19 19 19 20 20 19 19 22 22 19 19 20 20 19 19
8va
P.M.
13 13 13 13 15 15 13 13 15 15 13 13 17 17 13 13
13 13 13 13 15 15 13 13 15 15 13 13 17 17 13 13
15 15 15 15 17 17 15 15 19 19 15 15 17 17 15 15

Pre-Chorus
Bkgd. Voc.: w/ Voc. Fig. 1
Gtrs. 3 & 4: w/ Rhy. Figs. 3 & 3A
Gtrs. 1 & 2 tacet
E5
C5
Stay here with me, to -
8va
loco
20 19 20 19 20 22 20 19 20 19 20 19 20 19 19 19
20
8va
loco
17 15 17 15 17 19 17 15 17 15 17 15 17 15 16 15
17

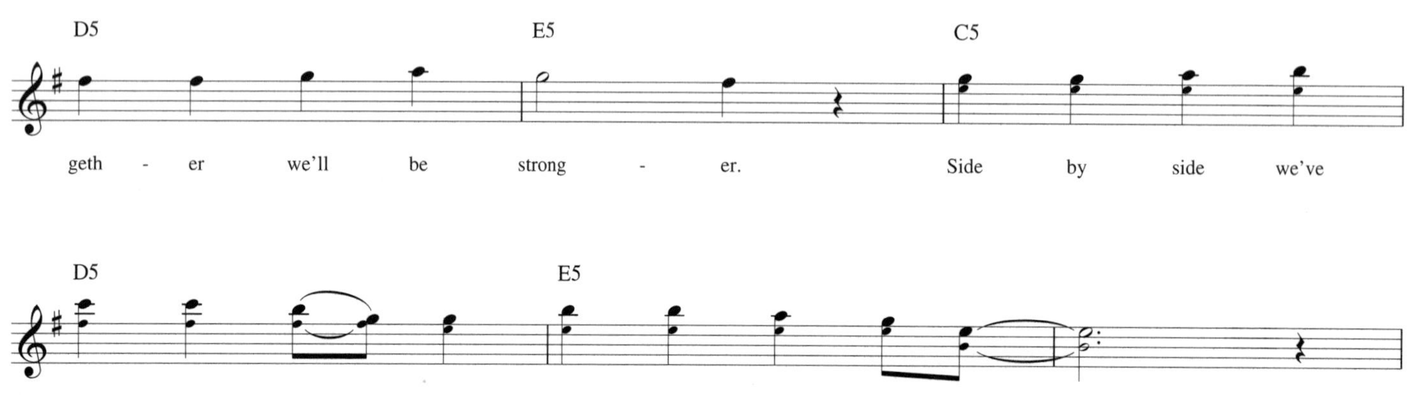
D5
E5
C5
geth - er we'll be strong - er. Side by side we've
D5
E5
con - quered lands and stormed a - cross the seas.

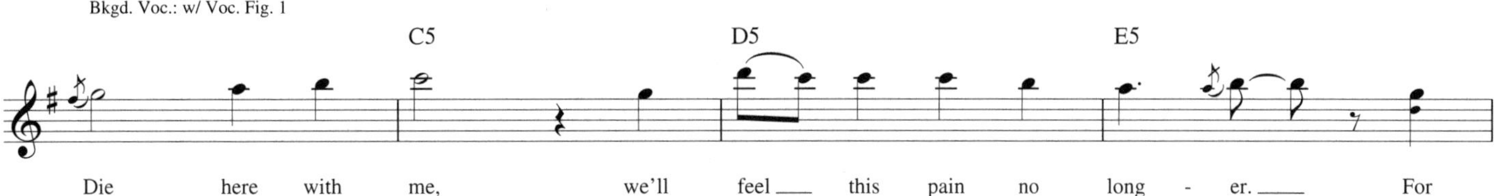
Bkgd. Voc.: w/ Voc. Fig. 1
C5
D5
E5
Die here with me, we'll feel ___ this pain no long - er. ___ For

A5 B5 N.C.

now and ev - er we ___ will be. In my

Gtr. 1 *8va* *15ma*

w/ DigiTech Whammy Pedal

w/ bar

+6

19 17 17 20 | 17 19 17 20 | 19 | 19 (19)

Gtr. 2 *8va*

w/ DigiTech Whammy Pedal

w/ bar

+6

14 14 13 12 | 14 15 14 12 | 14 | 14 (14)

Chorus
Gtrs. 1 & 2 tacet
E5
C5
G5
D5
heart, in ___ my soul I am out of ___ con - trol.
Voc. Fig. 2
(Heart, in ___ my soul, out of ___ con - trol.
Rhy. Figs. 4 & 4A
Gtrs. 3 & 4
w/ variation on repeat
P.M.
P.M.

E5 C5 A5

Fly a - cross the moun - tains and to - wards the dis - tant

Ah.

Gtr. 4

P.M.

P.M.

2 2 0 2 0 5 5 3

3 3 3 3 5 5 3 3 7 7 3 3 5 5 3 3

Gtr. 3

P.M.

P.M.

2 2 0 2 0 5 5 3

5 5 5 5 8 8 5 5 7 7 5 5 8 8 5 5

D5 G5 C5

sun. Tears ev - er - more, we

Tears ev - er - more, we

P.M. P.M. P.M. semi-P.H. P.M. P.M.

4 4 4 7 4 4 4 7 5 5 3 3 3 3 3 3 3 3 3 3 3 3 3 3 3 7 7 7 7 7 9 7 7

P.M. P.M. P.M. semi-P.H. P.M. P.M. semi-P.H.

5 5 5 9 5 5 5 7 5 5 3 3 3 3 3 3 3 3 3 3 3 3 3 3 3 3 3 3 3 3 5 3 4

D5 G5 C5

cry like ___ be - fore. ___ Feel the ___ break -

cry like ___ be - fore. Feel the ___ break -

Gtr. 1

Gtr. 2
divisi

P.M. P.M. P.M.

Gtrs. 3 & 4

P.M. P.M.

D5 N.C.

down of ___ my bod - y. ___ Set me

End Voc. Fig. 2

down of ___ my bod - y.)

Gtrs. 1 & 2

8va

P.M. P.M. P.M.

*

*Tap strings with edge of pick while sliding.

End Rhy. Fis. 4 & 4A

P.M. P.M.

Interlude

E5
D5
G5
free.
Gtr. 2
P.M.
semi-P.H.
Gtr. 1
Gtrs. 3 & 4
B5
C5
w/ bar
P.H.
8va
loco
semi-P.H.

G5 D5 C5

8va

semi-P.H.

semi-P.H.

P.M. P.M. P.M. semi-P.H.

End double-time feel

B5

8va

loco

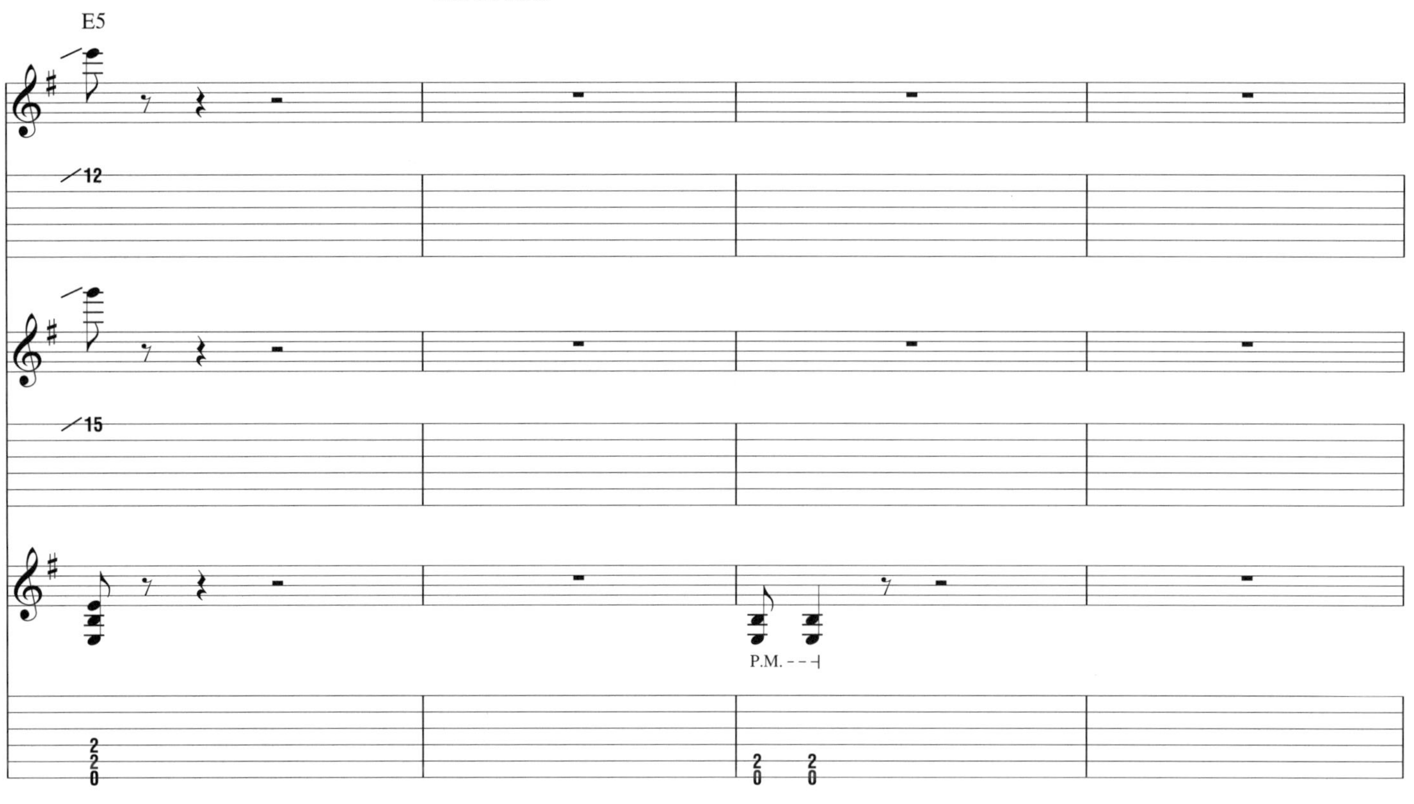

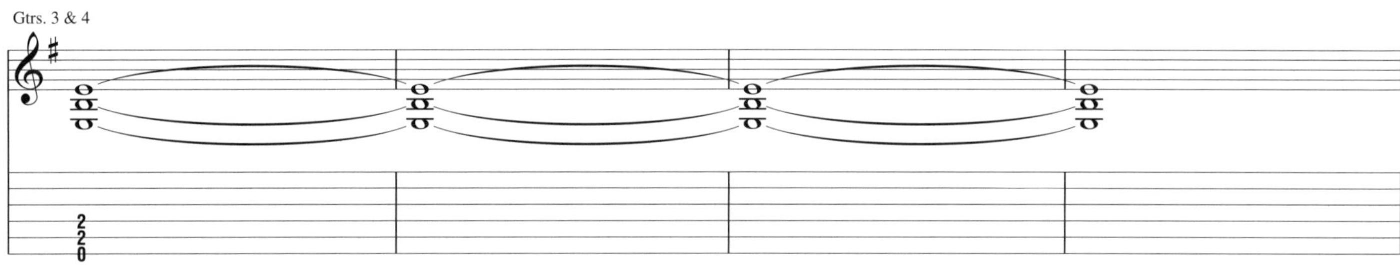

Half-time feel

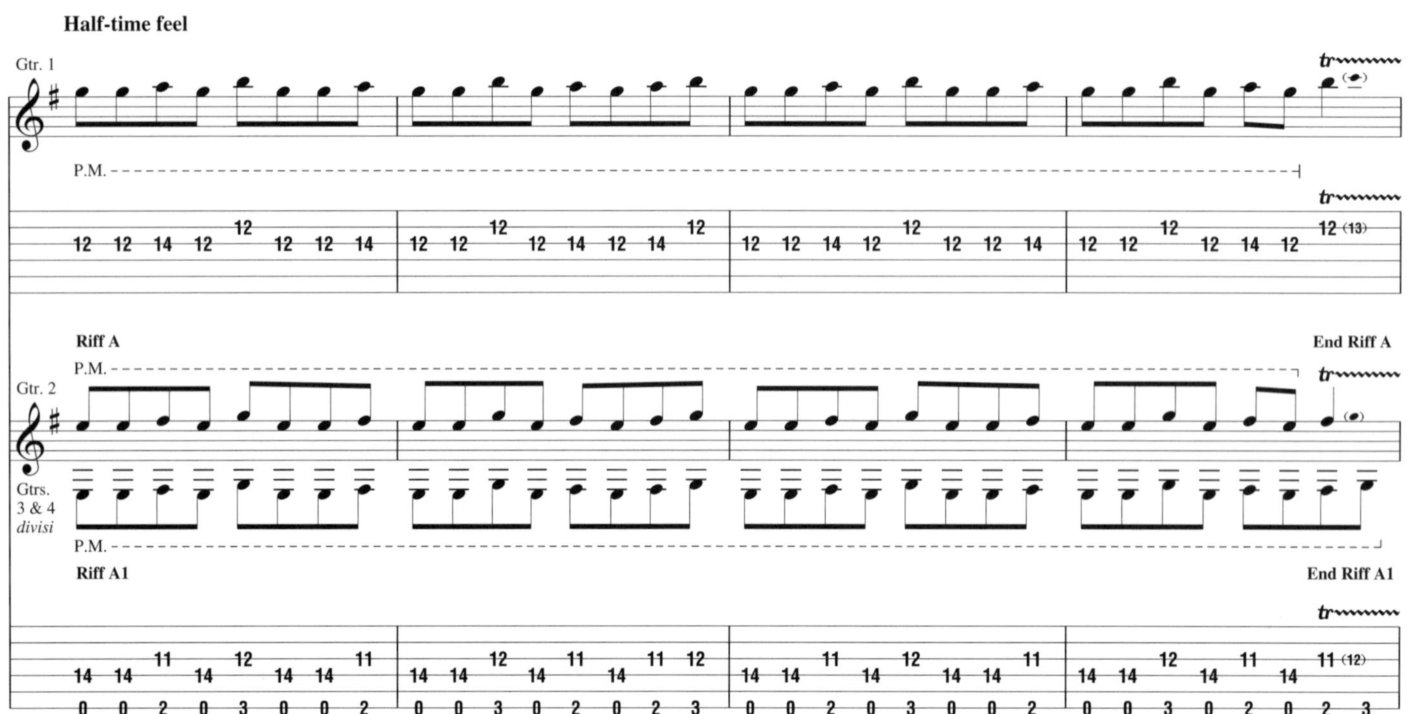

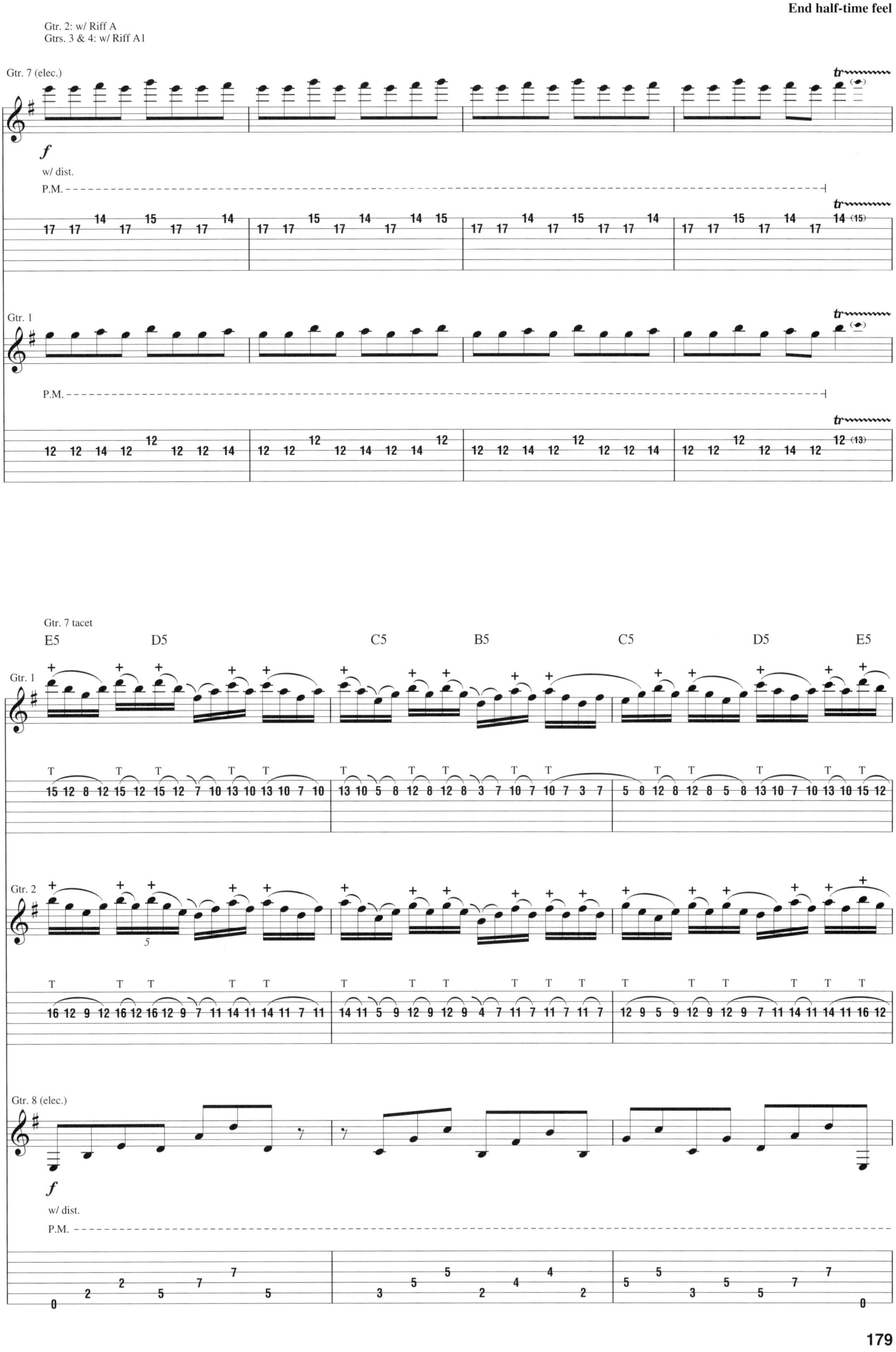

End half-time feel

Gtr. 2: w/ Riff A
Gtrs. 3 & 4: w/ Riff A1

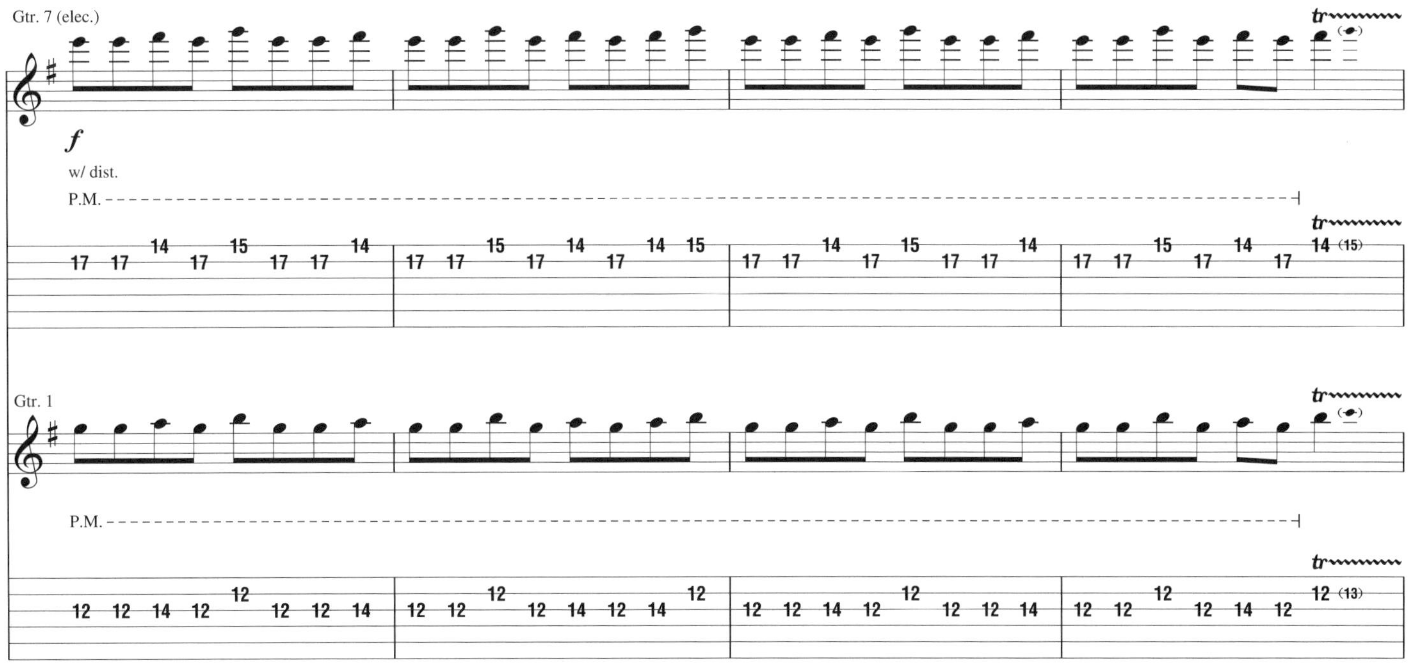

Gtr. 7 tacet

E5 D5 C5 B5 C5 D5 E5

Gtr. 1

Gtr. 2

Gtr. 8 (elec.)

f

w/ dist.

P.M.

D5 C5 D5

8va

T T T T T

8 12 15 12 15 12 8 12 15 12 15 12 8 12 15 12 | 19 15 12 15 19 15 19 15 10 14 17 14 17 14 10 14 | 17 14 8 12 15 12 15 12 10 14 17 14 17 14 10 14

T T T T T

9 12 16 12 16 12 9 12 16 12 9 16 12 9 16 12 | 20 17 12 17 20 17 20 17 10 15 19 15 19 15 10 15 | 19 15 8 13 17 13 17 13 10 15 19 15 19 15 10 15

P.M.

2 2 0 2 2 0 2 0 | 0 2 2 5 7 7 5 | 3 5 5 5 7 7 5

A5 G5 F5 D5

8va

T T T T T

15 12 8 12 15 12 15 12 7 10 15 10 15 10 8 5 8 | 13 8 5 8 13 8 13 8 5 8 13 8 13 8 5 8 | 17 14 10 14 17 14 17 14 10 14 15 14 17 14 10 14

T T T T T T

17 13 10 13 17 13 17 13 8 12 15 12 15 12 8 13 10 | 13 10 6 10 13 10 13 10 6 10 13 10 13 10 6 10 | 19 15 10 15 19 15 19 15 10 15 17 15 19 15 10 15

P.M.

5 7 7 5 3 5 3 1 | 1 3 3 1 3 3 1 3 | 5 7 7 5 7 7 5 7

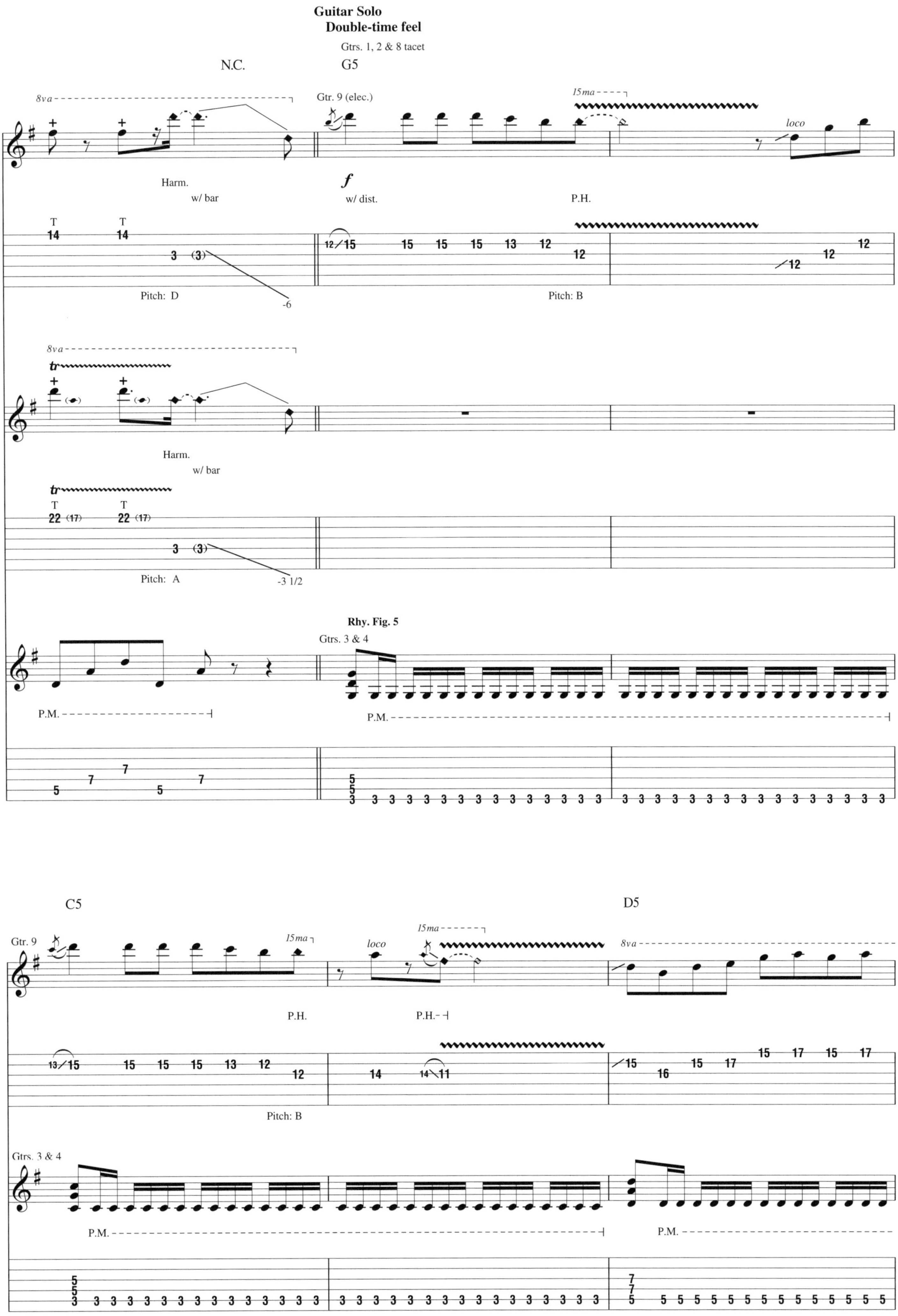

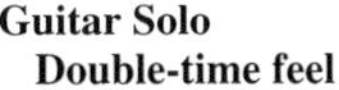

Gtrs. 1, 2 & 8 tacet

N.C.
G5

8va
Gtr. 9 (elec.)
15ma
loco
Harm.
w/ bar
f
w/ dist.
P.H.
Pitch: D
Pitch: B

8va
tr
Harm.
w/ bar
Pitch: A

Rhy. Fig. 5
Gtrs. 3 & 4
P.M.

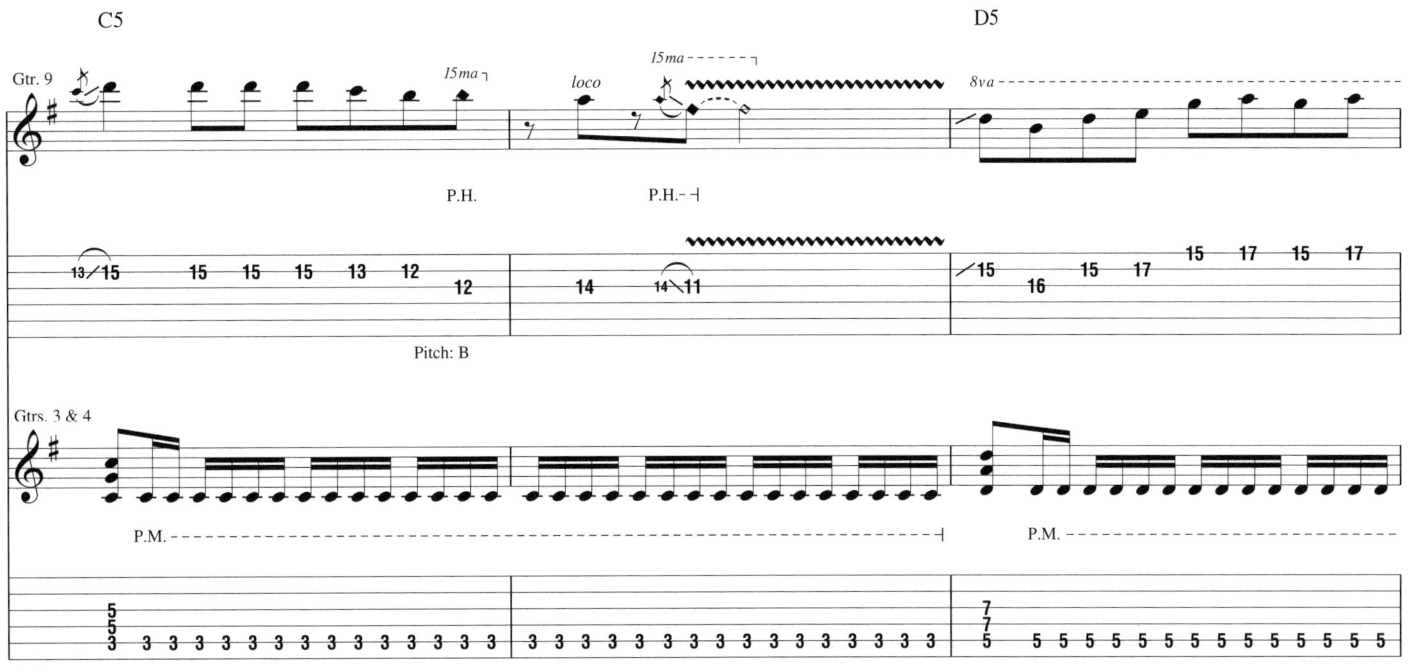

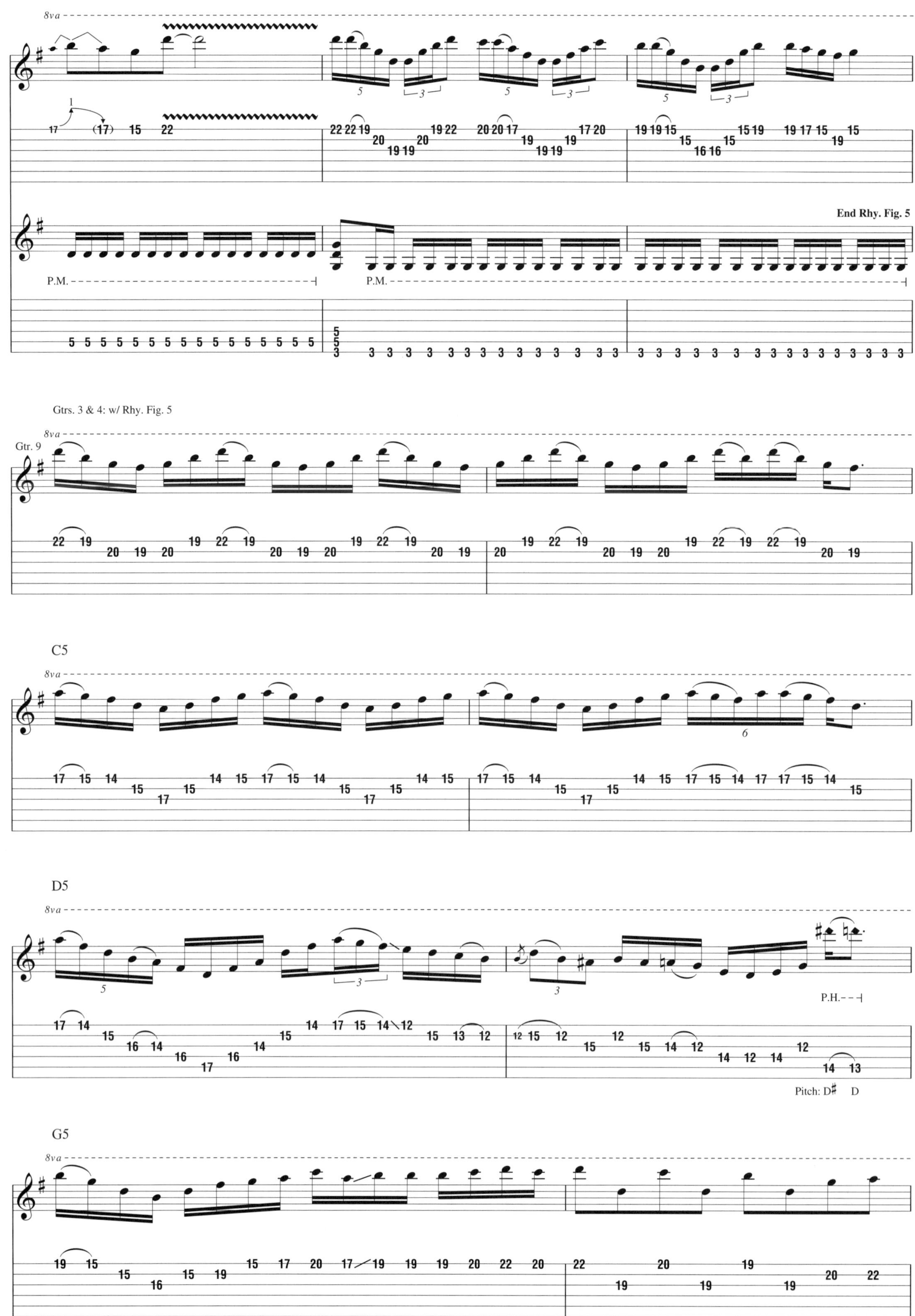
G5
8va
End Rhy. Fig. 5
P.M.
P.M.
Gtrs. 3 & 4: w/ Rhy. Fig. 5
Gtr. 9
C5
D5
P.H.
Pitch: D♯ D
G5

A5
G5
D5
Gtr. 9 tacet
8va
Gtr. 9
Gtr. 2
Gtr. 1
Gtrs. 3 & 4
P.M.
E5
A5
G5
Gtr. 2
semi-P.H.
w/ wah-wah
Gtr. 1
semi-P.H.
w/ wah-wah
Gtrs. 3 & 4
P.M.

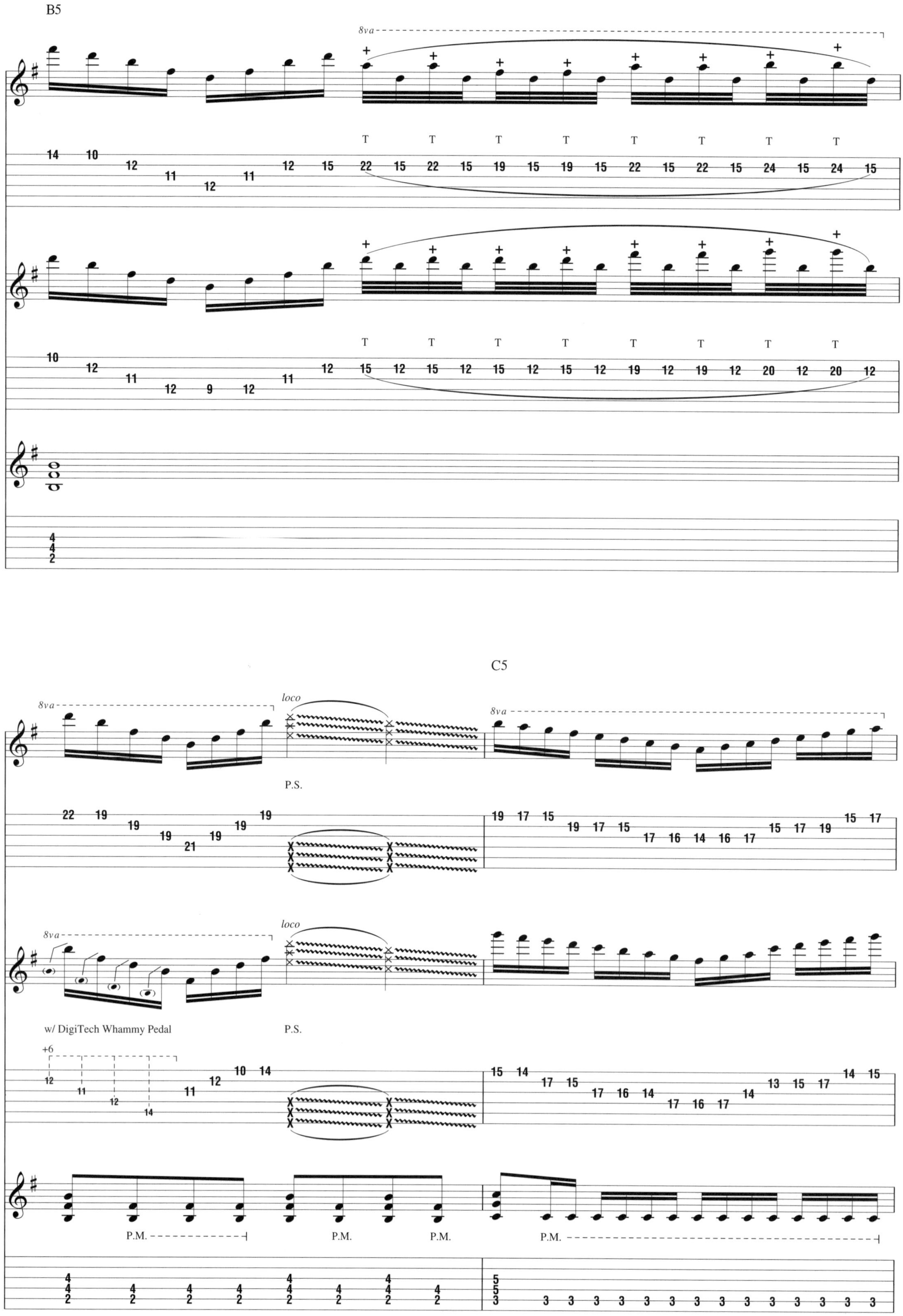

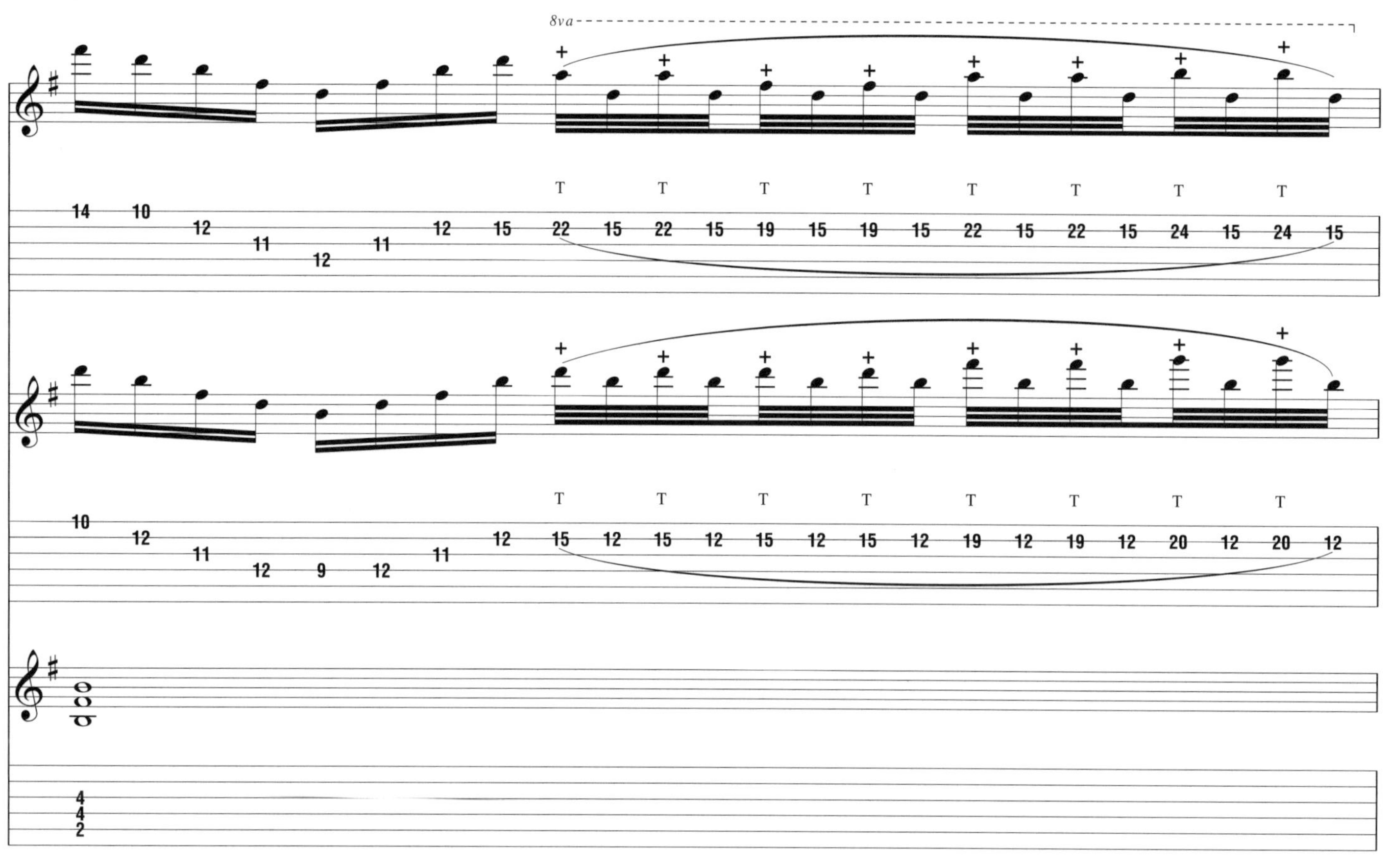

C5

8va

loco

P.S.

8va

loco

w/ DigiTech Whammy Pedal

P.S.

+6

P.M.

P.M.

P.M.

P.M.

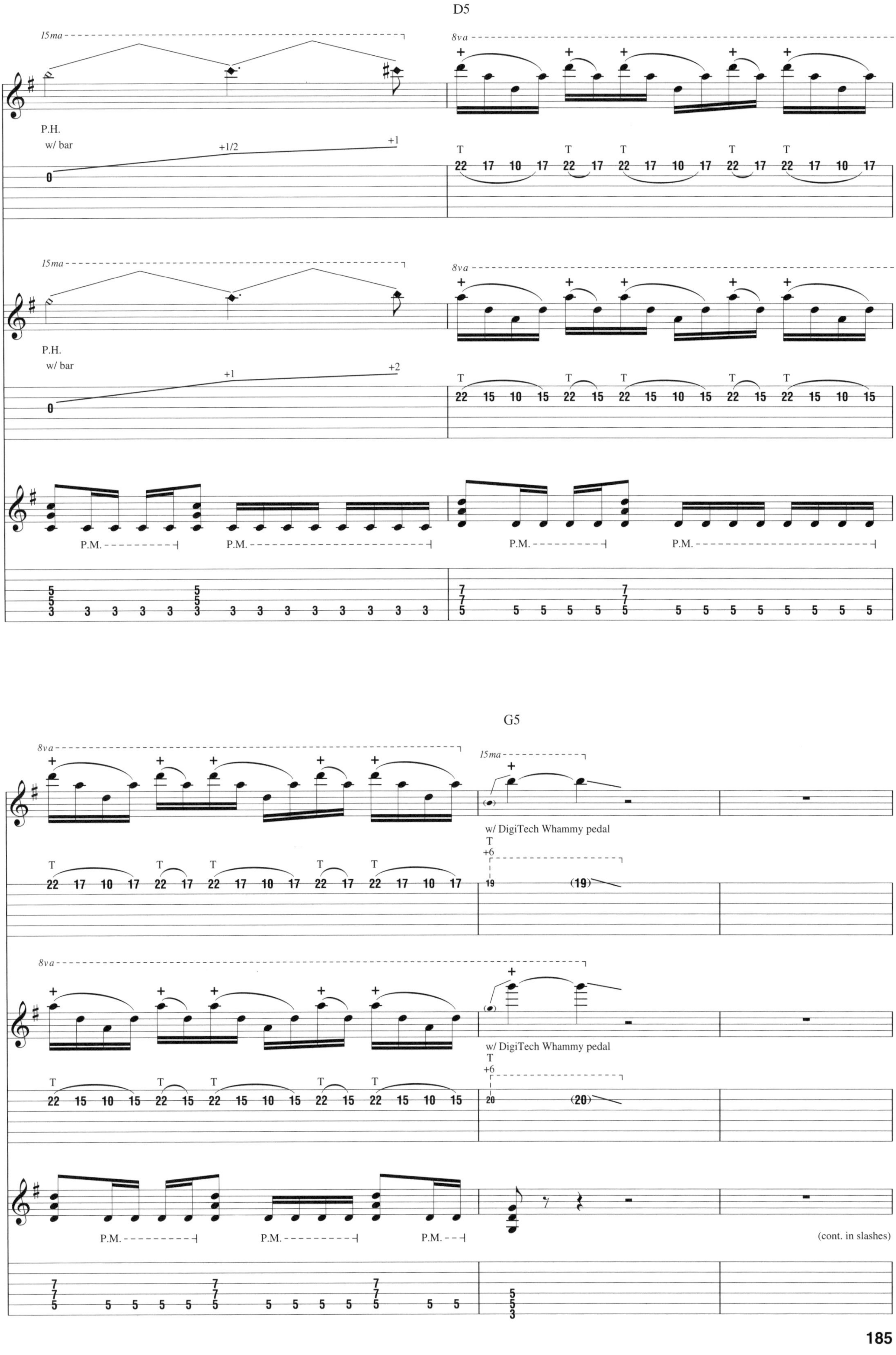

D5

15ma

8va

P.H.

w/ bar

+1/2

+1

T

15ma

8va

P.H.

w/ bar

+1

+2

T

P.M.

P.M.

P.M.

P.M.

G5

8va

15ma

w/ DigiTech Whammy pedal

T

+6

8va

w/ DigiTech Whammy pedal

T

+6

P.M.

P.M.

P.M.

(cont. in slashes)

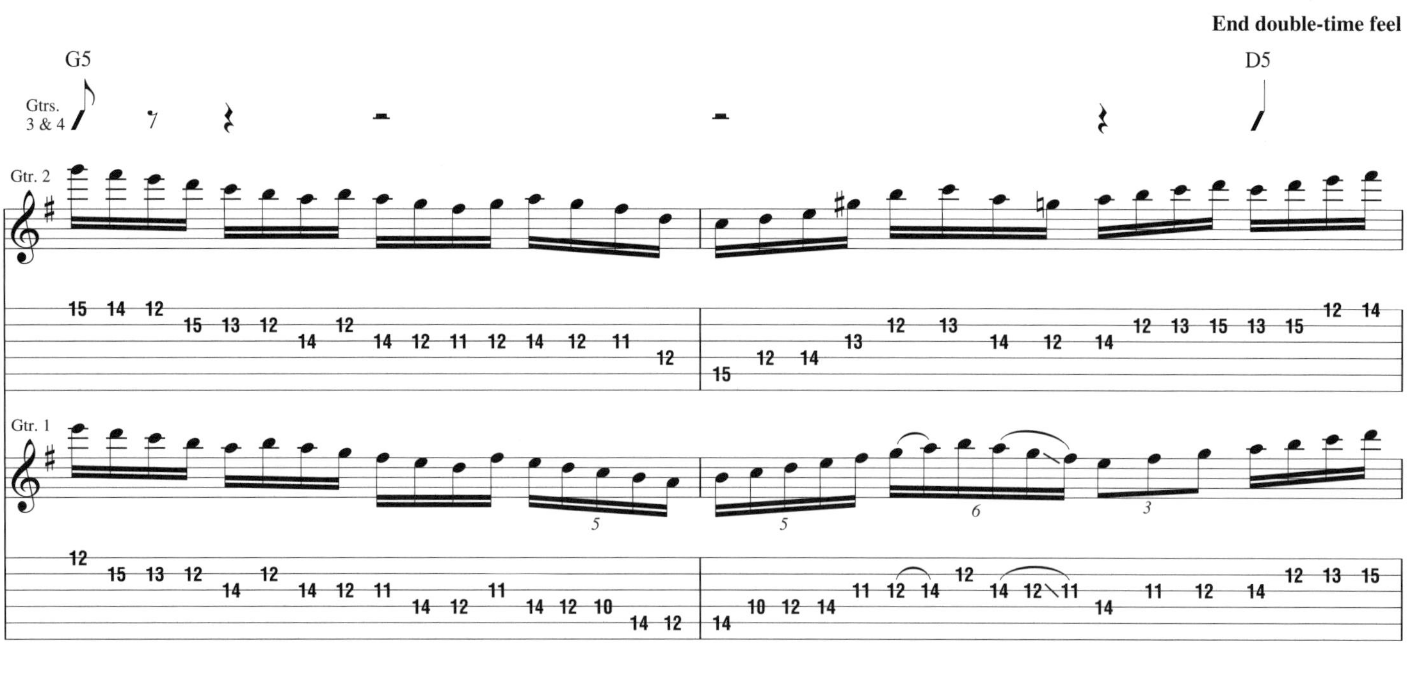
End double-time feel
G5
D5
Gtrs. 3 & 4
Gtr. 2
Gtr. 1

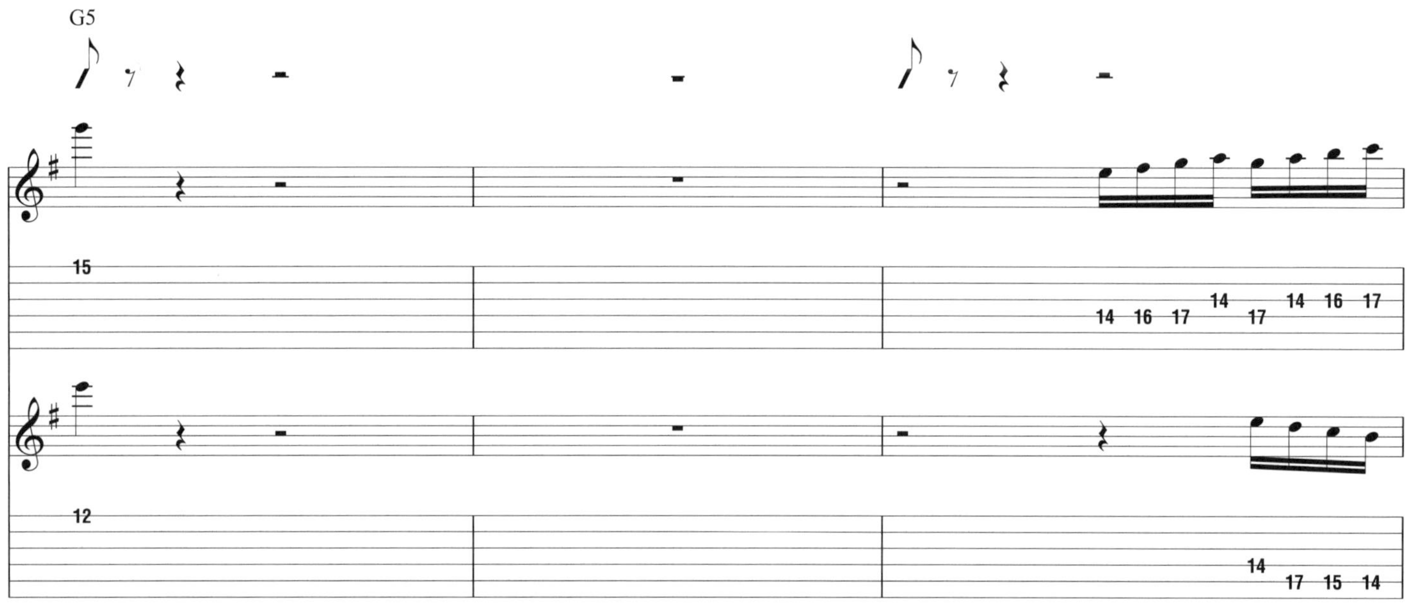
G5

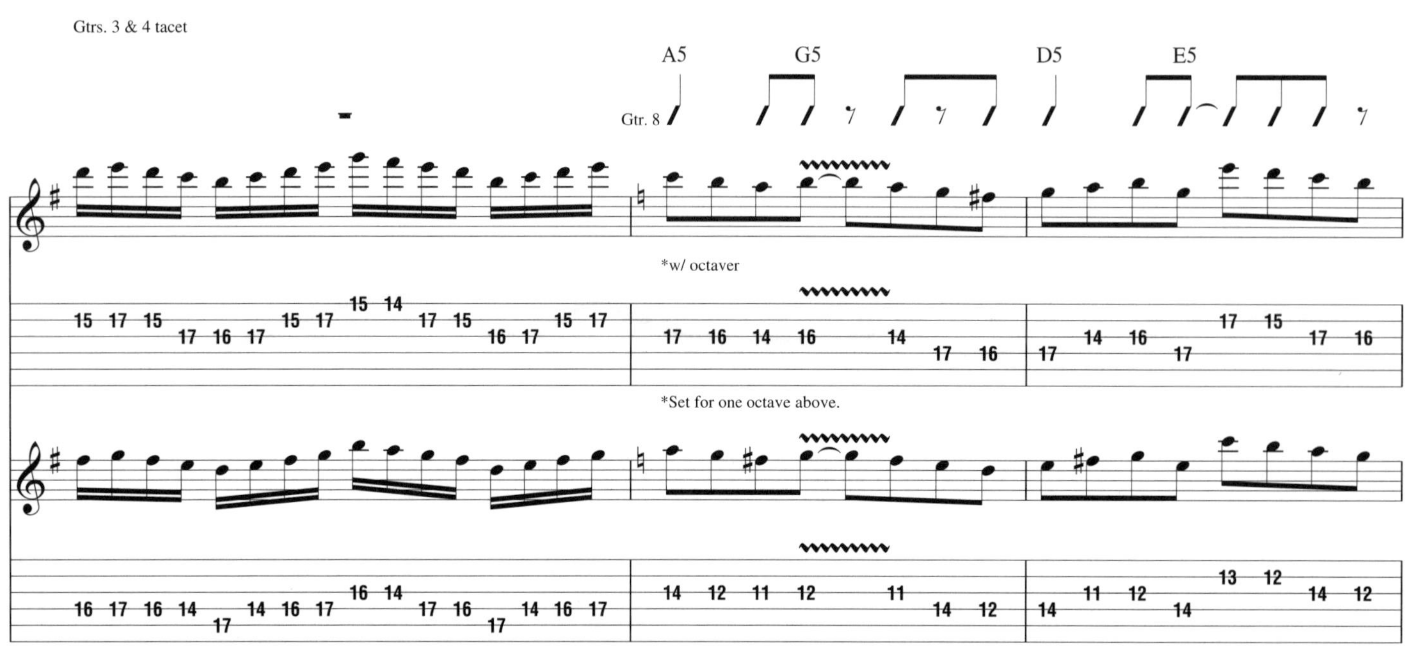
Gtrs. 3 & 4 tacet
A5
G5
D5
E5
Gtr. 8
*w/ octaver
*Set for one octave above.

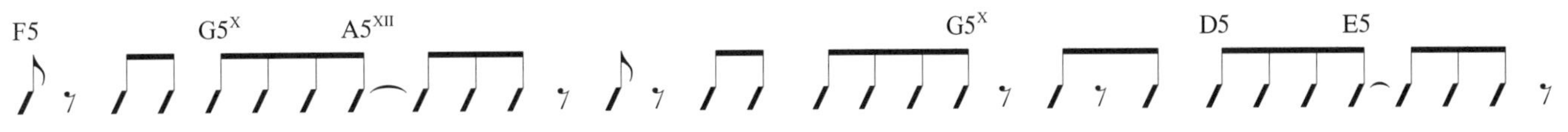

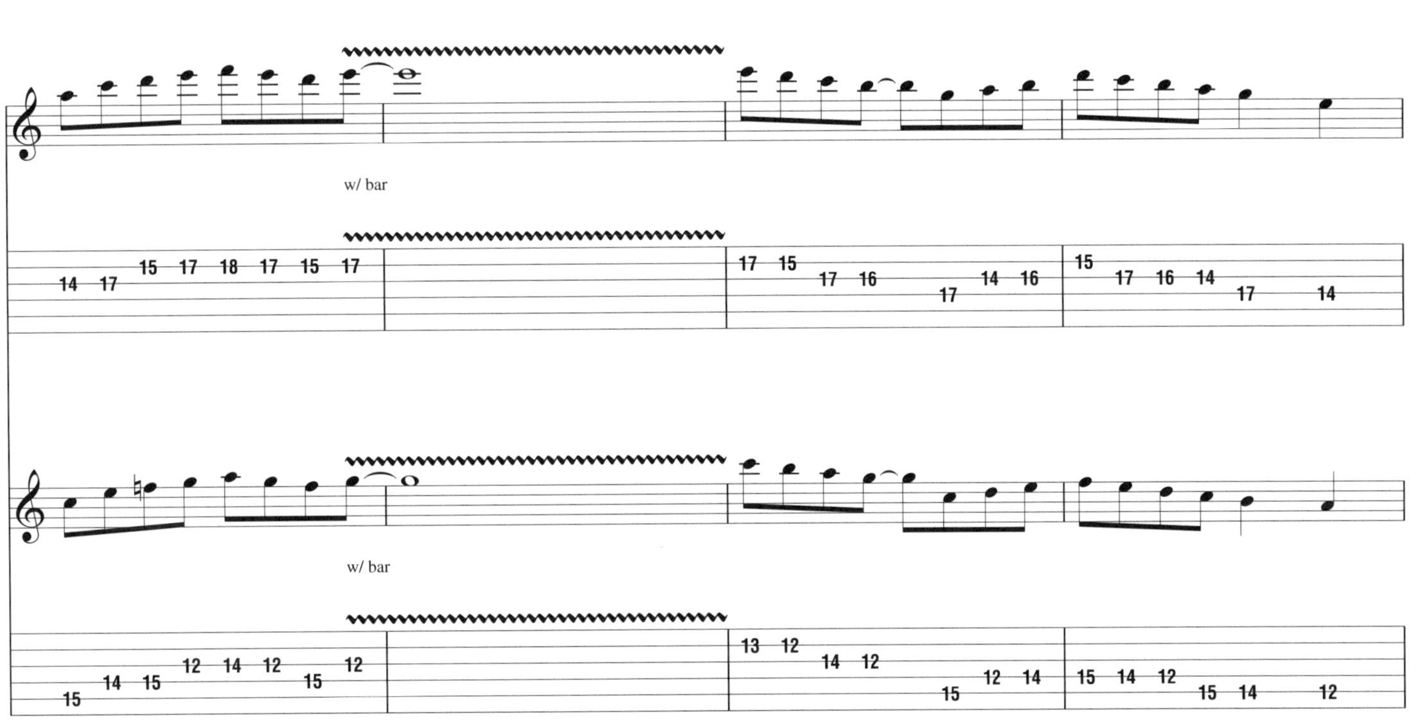

F5 E5 F5 E5

Gtr. 8 tacet
N.C.

Double-time feel
A5
C5
Gtr. 2
Gtr. 1
Rhy. Fig. 6
Gtrs. 3 & 4
P.M.
G5
A5
semi-P.H.
semi-P.H.
P.M.
P.M.
End Rhy. Fig. 6

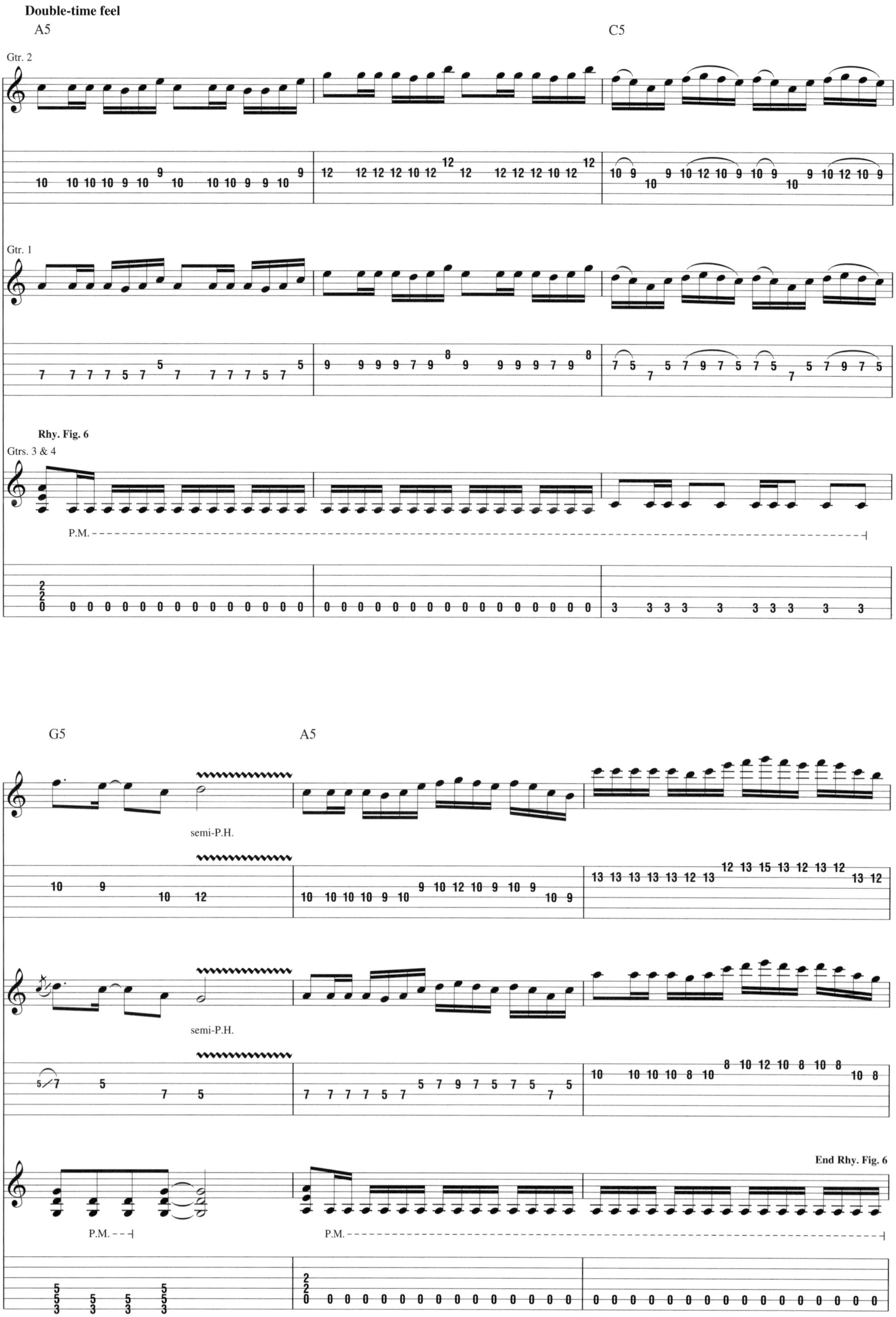

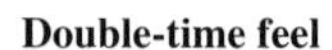

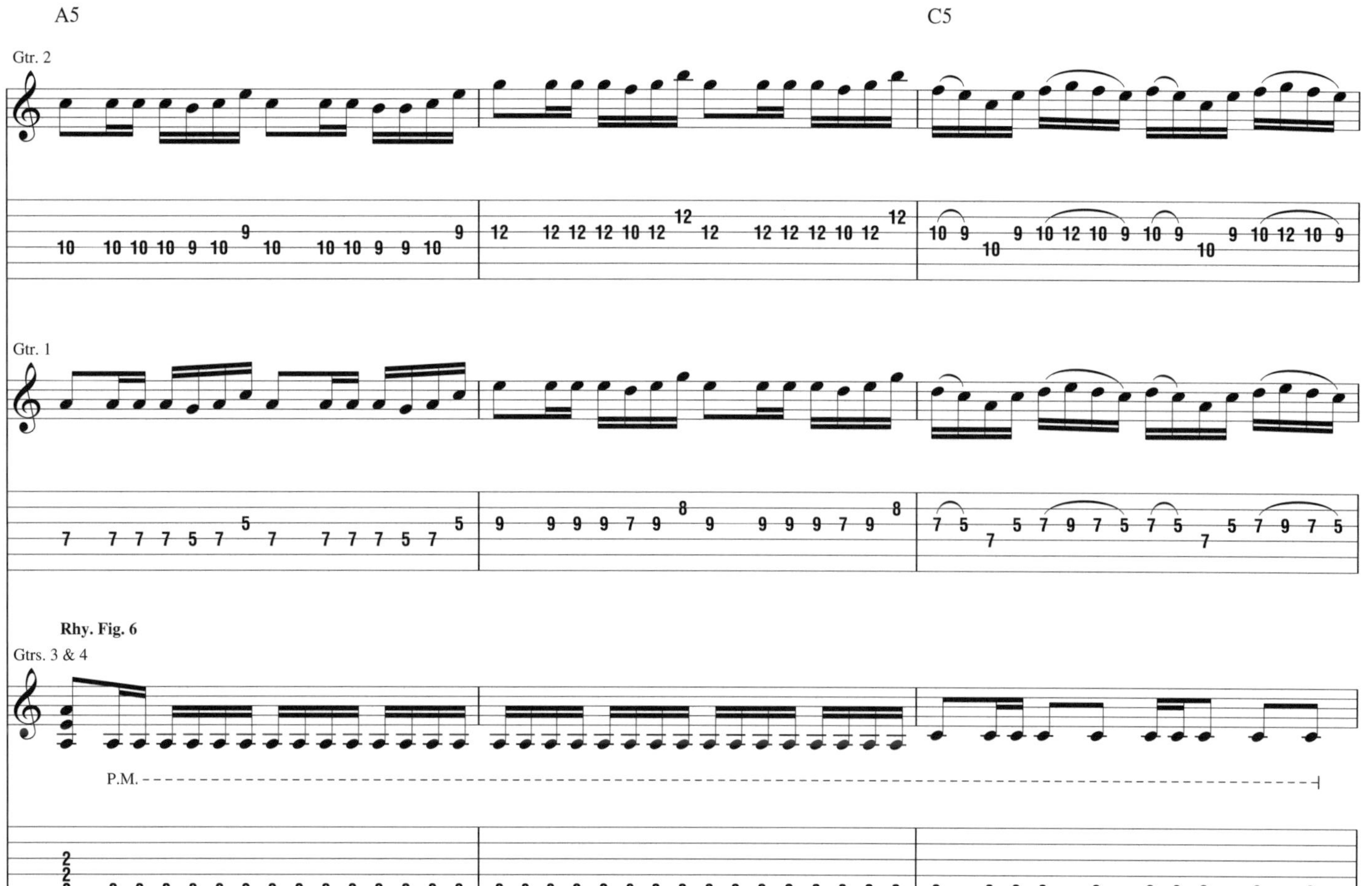

F5
G5
8va
P.M.
Gtrs. 3 & 4: w/ Rhy. Fig. 6
A5
C5
Gtr. 2
8va
semi-P.H.
Gtr. 1
semi-P.H.
G5
A5
8va
semi-P.H.
semi-P.H.

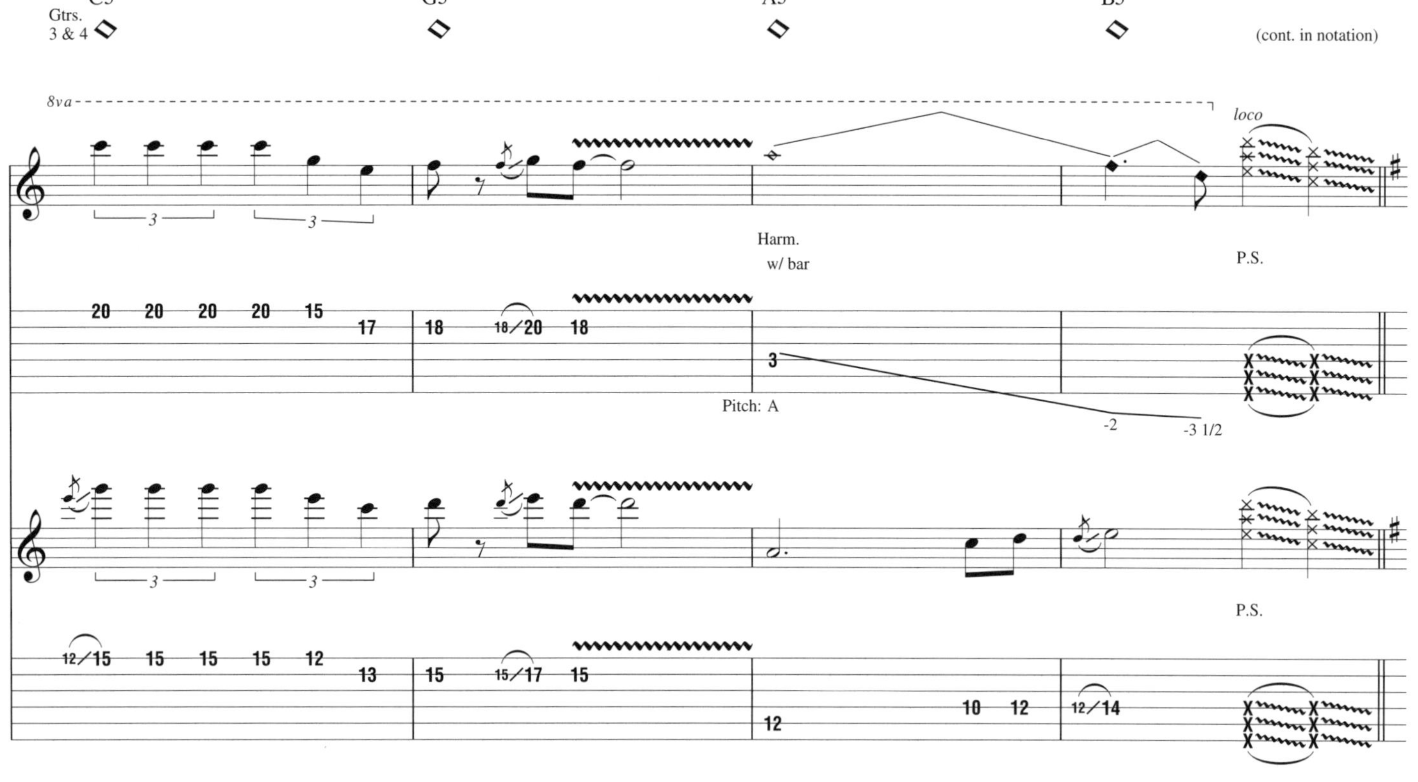

Keyboard Solo

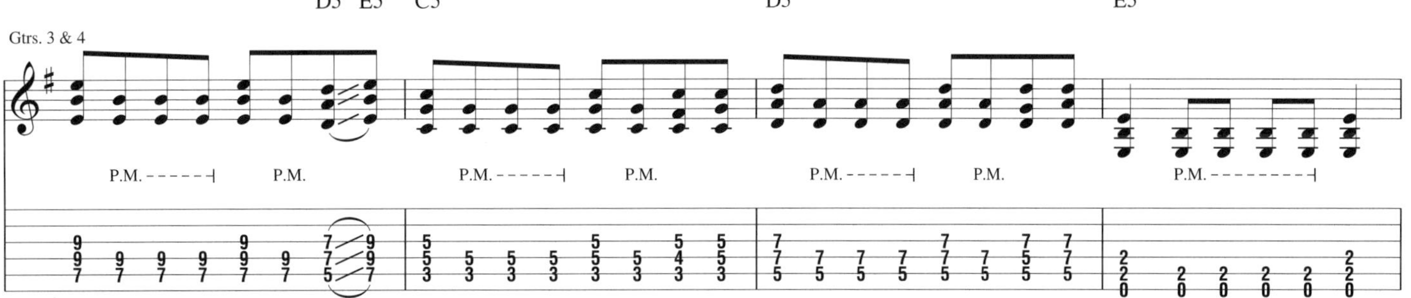
D5 E5 C5
D5
E5
Gtrs. 3 & 4
P.M.
P.M.
P.M.
P.M.
P.M.
P.M.
P.M.

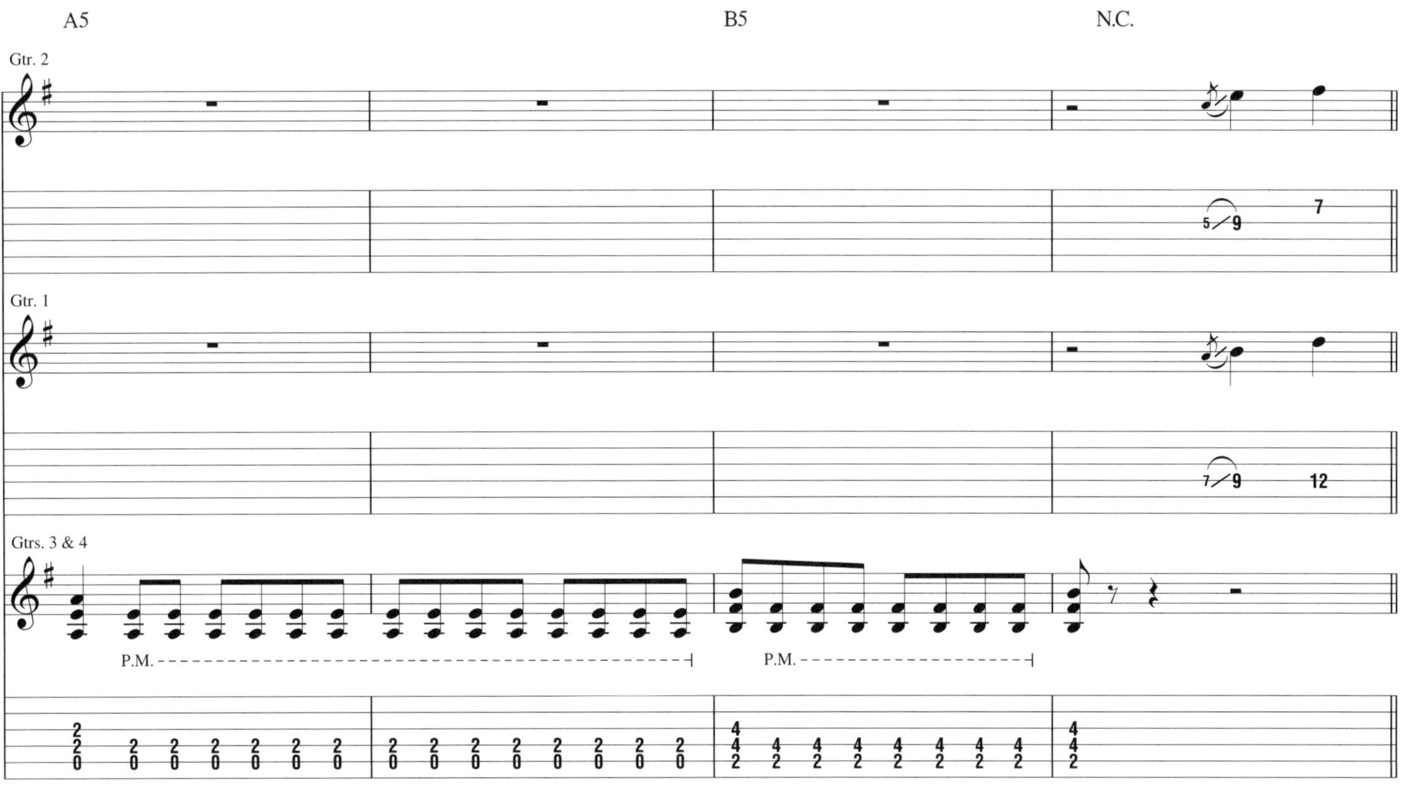
A5
B5
N.C.
Gtr. 2
Gtr. 1
Gtrs. 3 & 4
P.M.
P.M.

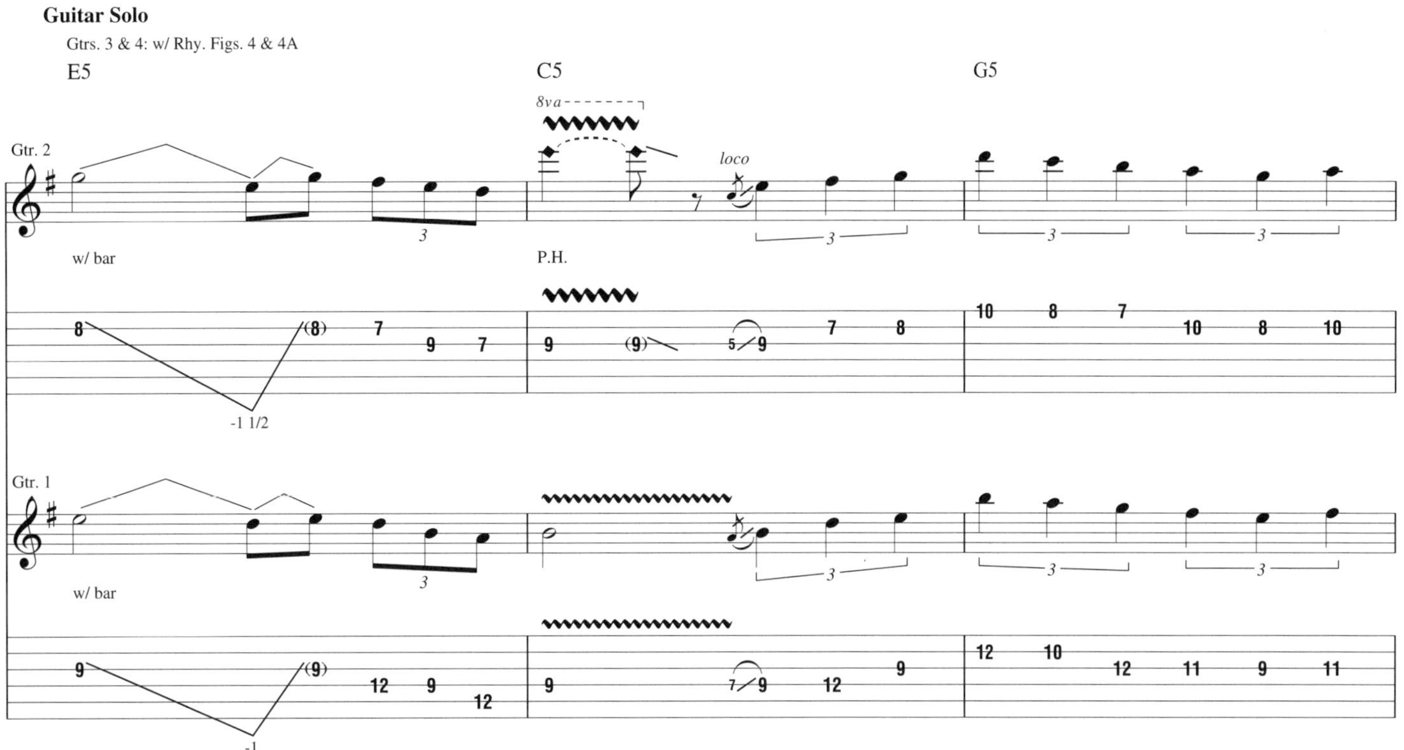
Guitar Solo
Gtrs. 3 & 4: w/ Rhy. Figs. 4 & 4A
E5
C5
G5
Gtr. 2
8va
loco
w/ bar
P.H.
-1 1/2
Gtr. 1
w/ bar
-1

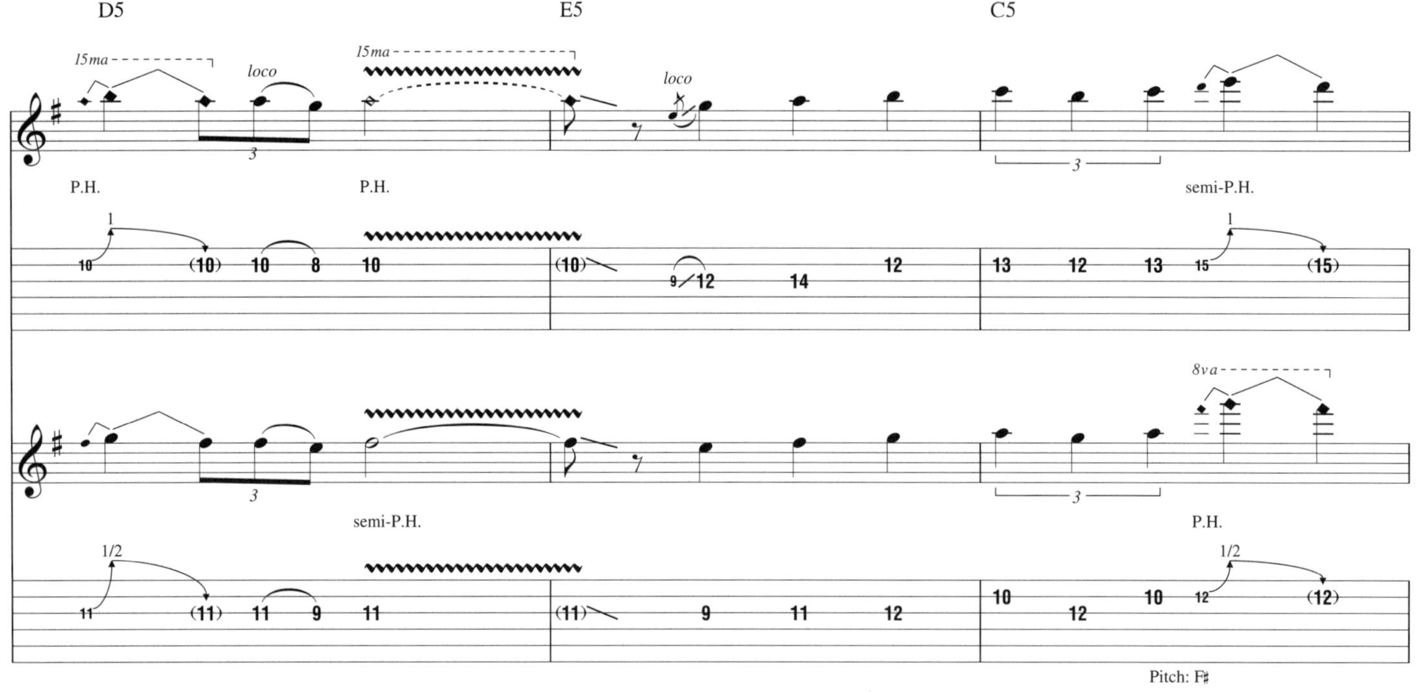
D5
E5
C5
15ma
loco
P.H.
semi-P.H.
8va
Pitch: F♯

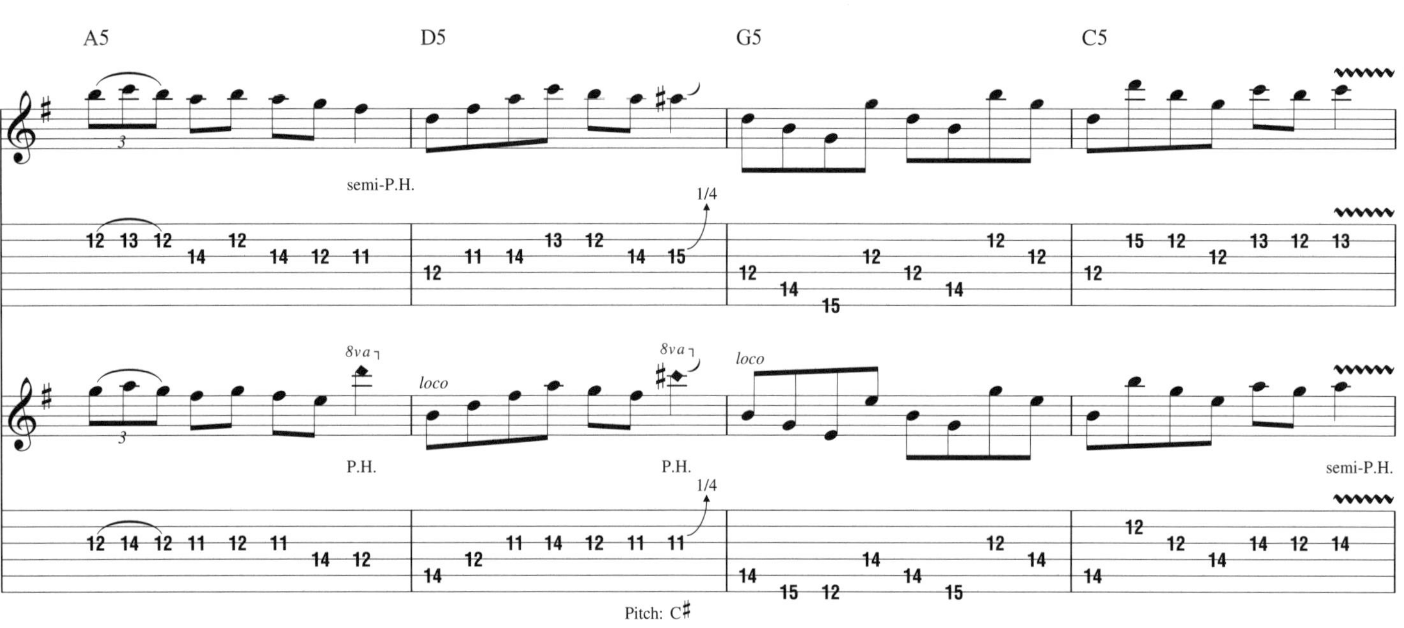
A5
D5
G5
C5
semi-P.H.
8va
loco
P.H.
Pitch: C♯

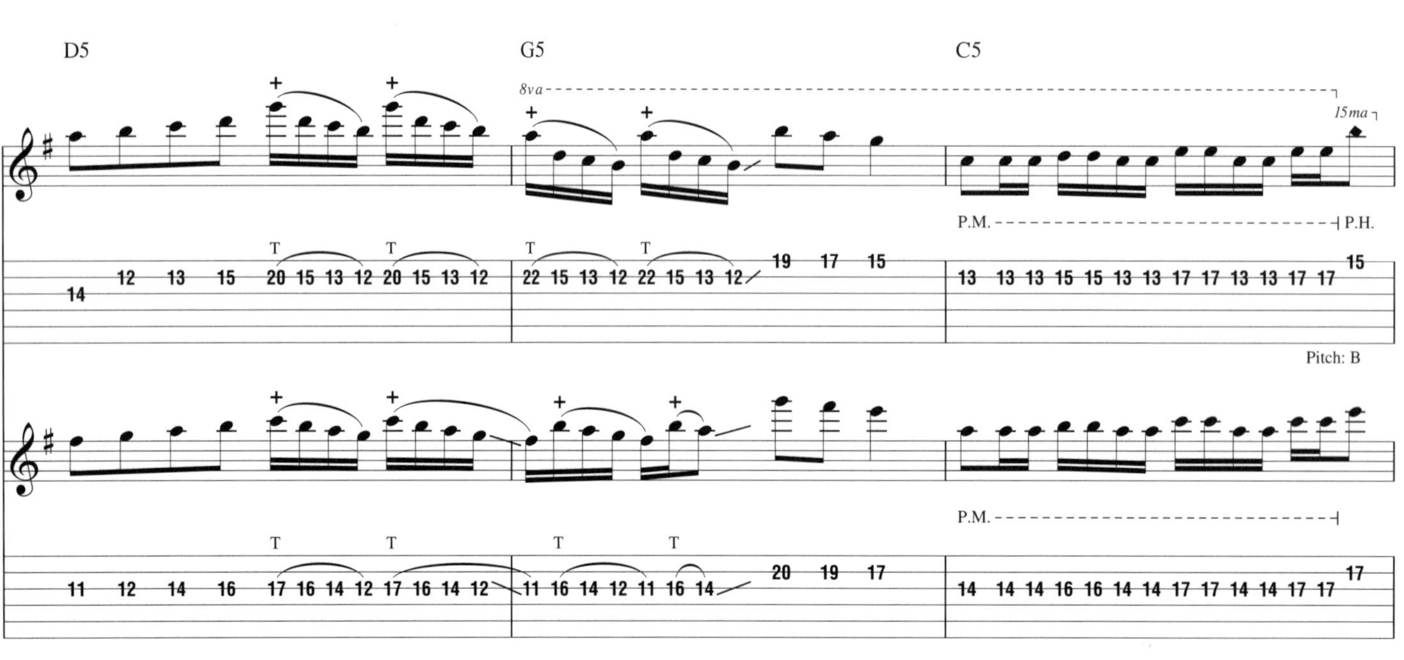
D5
G5
C5
8va
15ma
P.M.
P.H.
Pitch: B

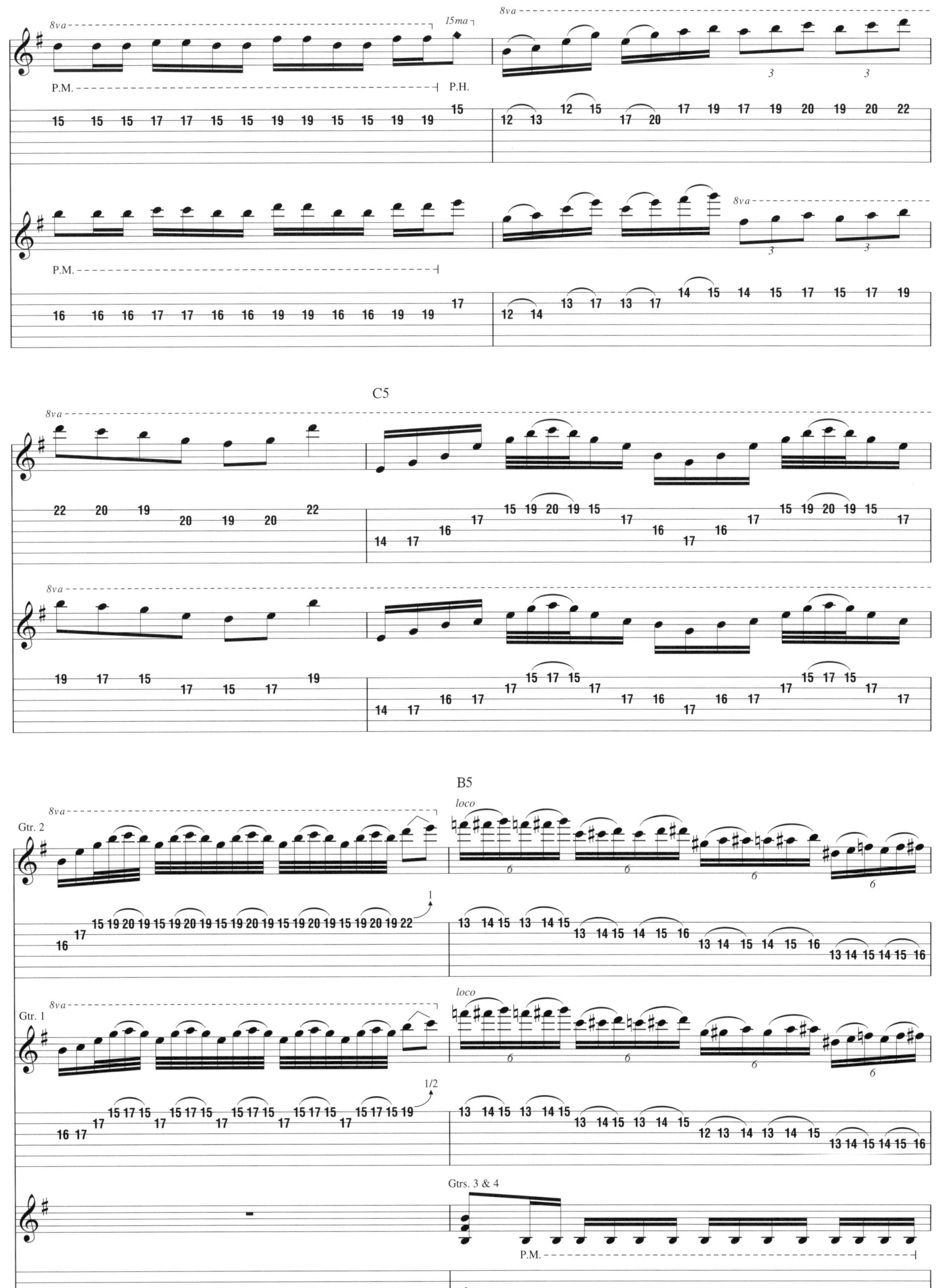

Gtrs. 3 & 4: w/ Rhy. Figs. 4 & 4A (last 4 meas.)
D5
8va
15ma
P.M.
P.H.
C5
B5
loco
Gtr. 2
Gtr. 1
Gtrs. 3 & 4

Chorus

Bkgd. Voc.: w/ Voc. Fig. 2
Gtrs. 1 & 2 tacet

Gtrs. 3 & 4 tacet

*Em C G

In my heart, in ___ my soul I am out of ___ con -

8va

P.H.
w/ bar

0

Pitch: F

-1/2 -2 1/2

8va

P.H.
w/ bar

0

-1 -2 1/2

P.M. P.M. P.M. P.M.

4 4 4 4
4 4 4 4
2 2 2 2 2 2 2 2 2 2 2 2

2
2
0

*Chord symbols reflect harmony played by kybds., next 16 meas.

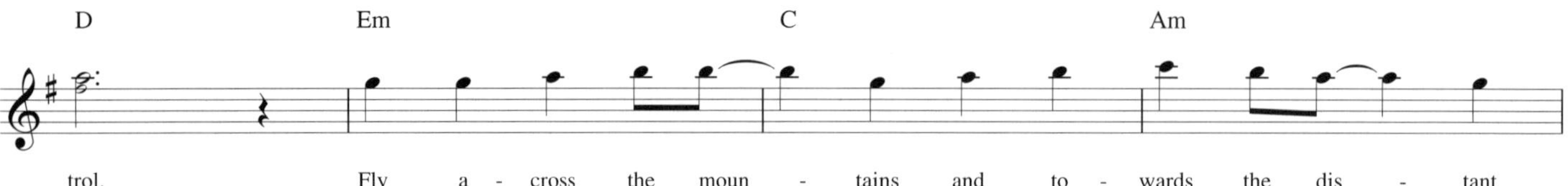

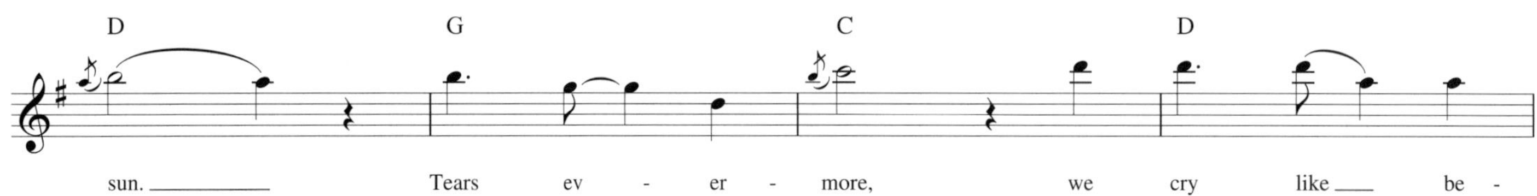

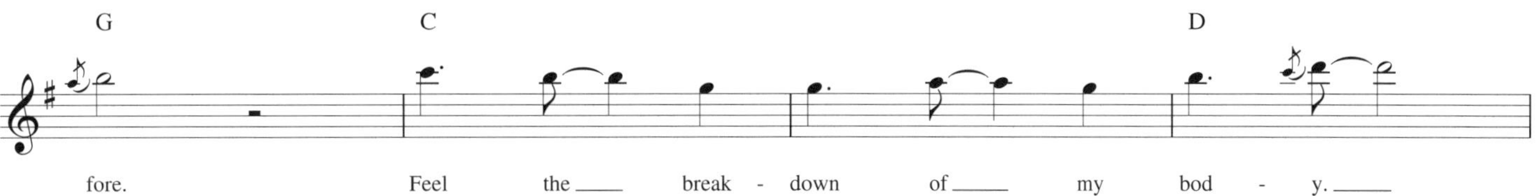
G
C
D
fore.
Feel the break - down of my bod - y.

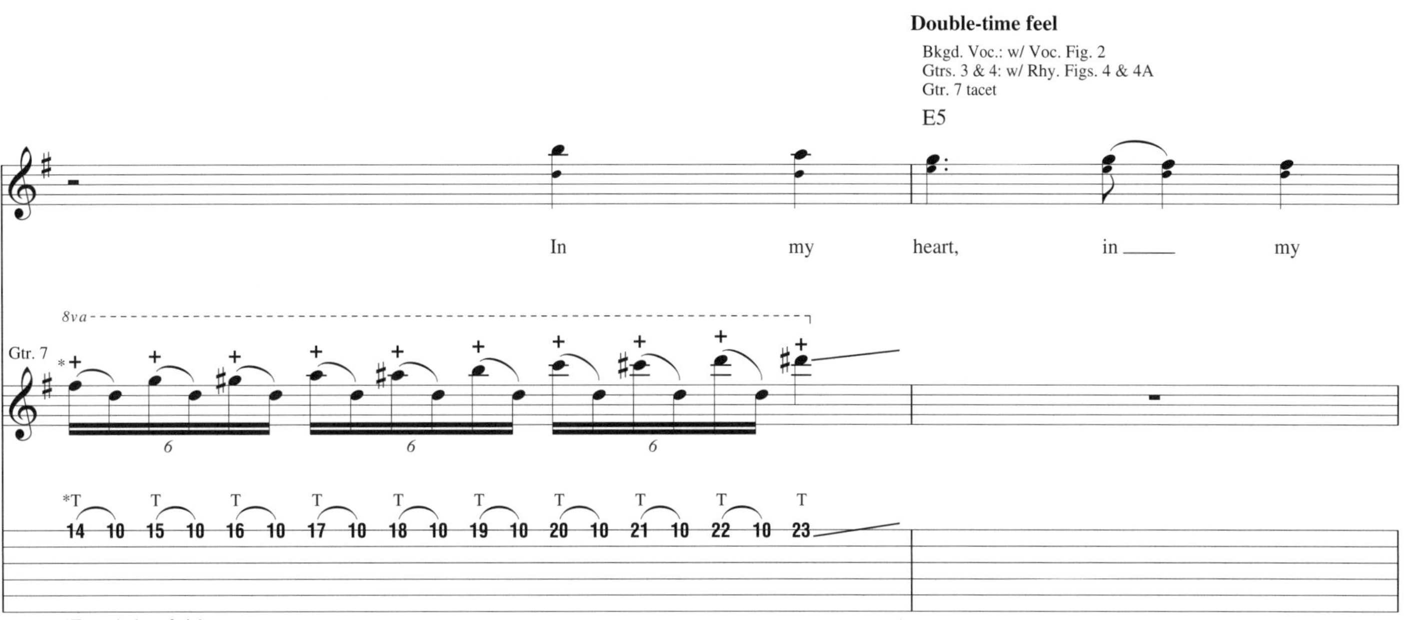
Double-time feel
Bkgd. Voc.: w/ Voc. Fig. 2
Gtrs. 3 & 4: w/ Rhy. Figs. 4 & 4A
Gtr. 7 tacet
E5
In my heart, in my
8va
Gtr. 7
*T T T T T T T T T T
14 10 15 10 16 10 17 10 18 10 19 10 20 10 21 10 22 10 23
*Tap w/ edge of pick.

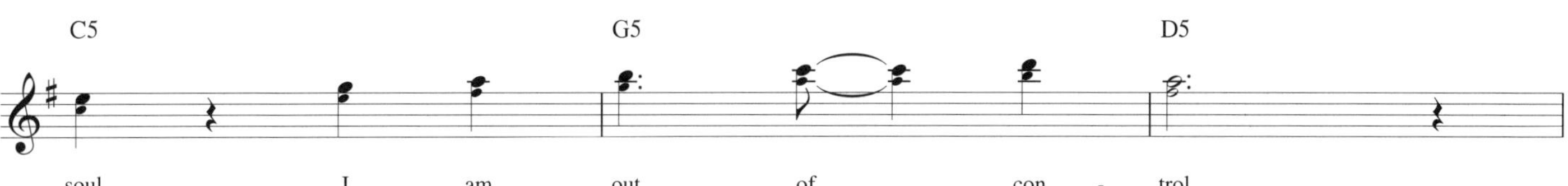
C5
G5
D5
soul I am out of con - trol.

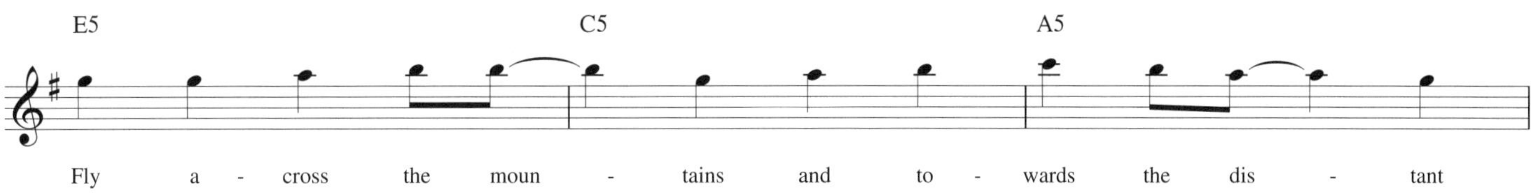
E5
C5
A5
Fly a - cross the moun - tains and to - wards the dis - tant

D5
G5
C5
sun. Tears ev - er - more, we

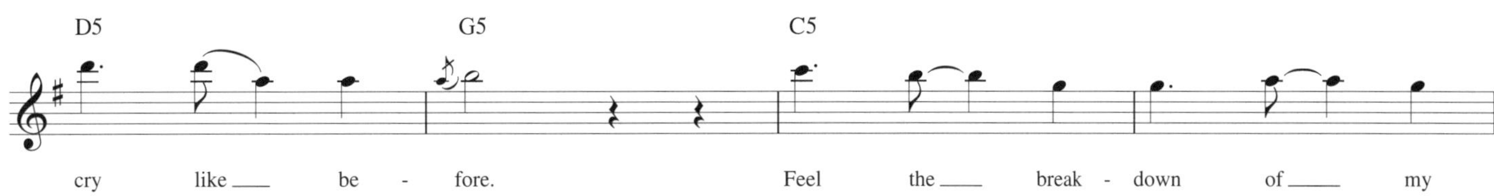
D5
G5
C5
cry like be - fore. Feel the break - down of my

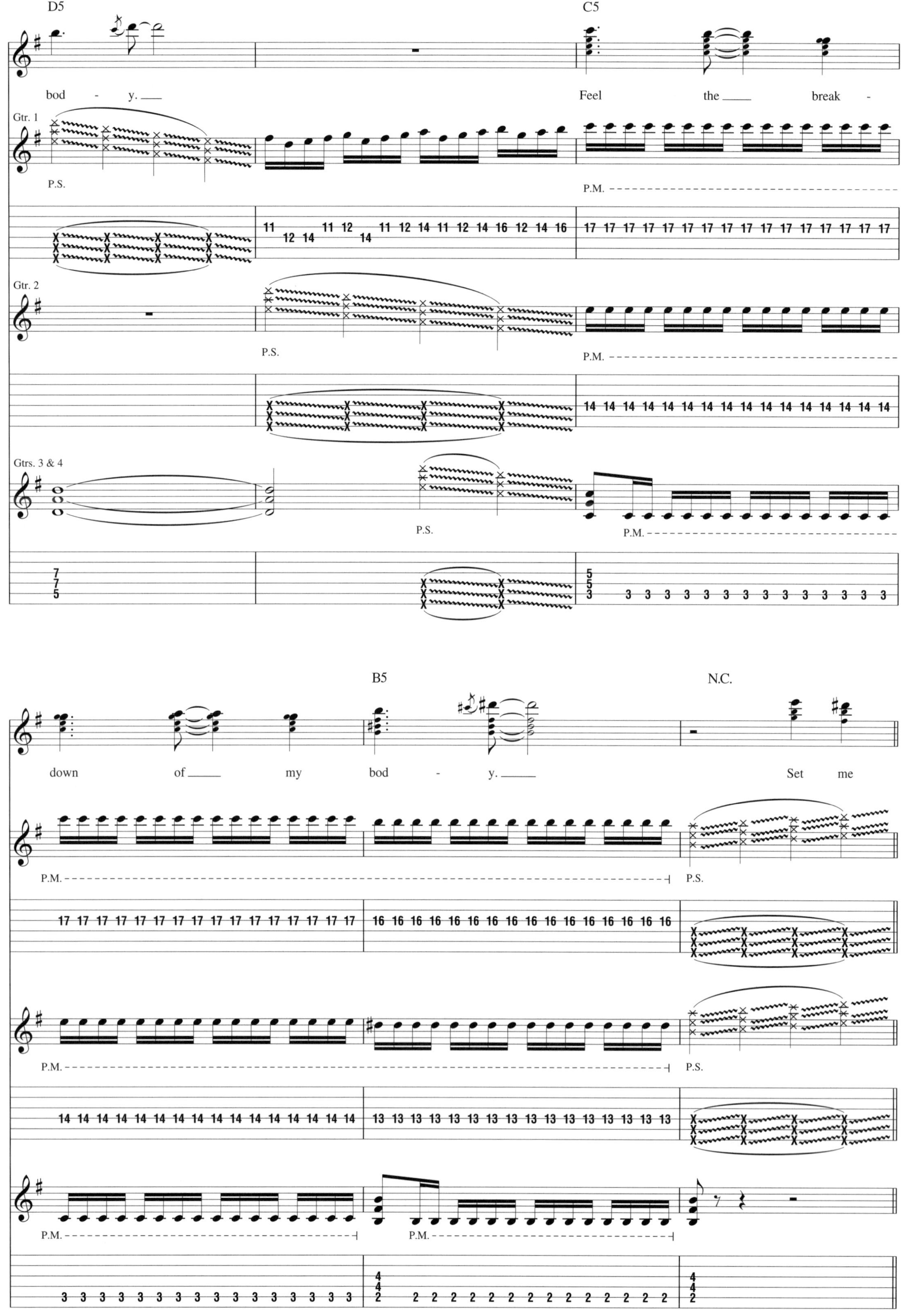
D5
C5
bod - y.
Feel the break -
Gtr. 1
P.S.
P.M.
11 12 14 11 12 14 11 12 14 11 12 14 16 12 14 16
17 17 17 17 17 17 17 17 17 17 17 17 17 17 17 17
Gtr. 2
P.S.
P.M.
14 14 14 14 14 14 14 14 14 14 14 14 14 14 14 14
Gtrs. 3 & 4
P.S.
P.M.
7 7 5
5 5 3 3 3 3 3 3 3 3 3 3 3 3 3 3 3 3
B5
N.C.
down of my bod - y.
Set me
P.M.
P.S.
17 17 17 17 17 17 17 17 17 17 17 17 17 17 17 17
16 16 16 16 16 16 16 16 16 16 16 16 16 16 16 16
14 14 14 14 14 14 14 14 14 14 14 14 14 14 14 14
13 13 13 13 13 13 13 13 13 13 13 13 13 13 13 13
3 3 3 3 3 3 3 3 3 3 3 3 3 3 3 3
4 4 2 2 2 2 2 2 2 2 2 2 2 2 2 2 2 2
4 4 2

Outro

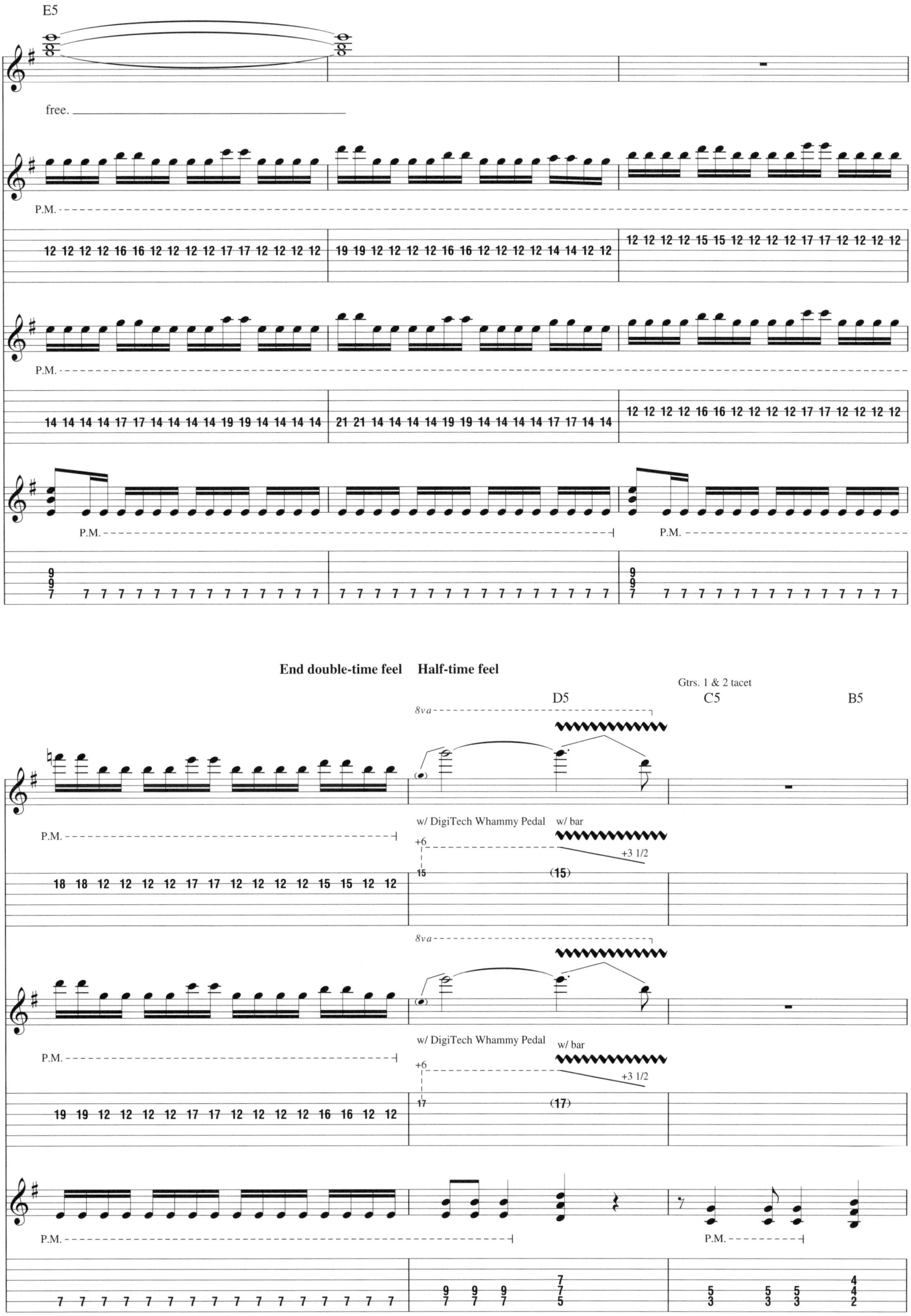

E5

free.

P.M.

12 12 12 12 16 16 12 12 12 12 17 17 12 12 12 12 | 19 19 12 12 12 12 16 16 12 12 12 12 14 14 12 12 | 12 12 12 12 15 15 12 12 12 12 17 17 12 12 12 12

P.M.

14 14 14 14 17 17 14 14 14 14 19 19 14 14 14 14 | 21 21 14 14 14 14 19 19 14 14 14 14 17 17 14 14 | 12 12 12 12 16 16 12 12 12 12 17 17 12 12 12 12

P.M. P.M.

9 9 7 7 7 7 7 7 7 7 7 7 7 7 7 7 7 | 7 7 7 7 7 7 7 7 7 7 7 7 7 7 7 7 | 9 9 7 7 7 7 7 7 7 7 7 7 7 7 7 7 7

End double-time feel **Half-time feel**

Gtrs. 1 & 2 tacet

D5 C5 B5

8va

P.M.

w/ DigiTech Whammy Pedal w/ bar

+6 +3 1/2

18 18 12 12 12 12 17 17 12 12 12 12 15 15 12 12 | 15 (15)

8va

P.M.

w/ DigiTech Whammy Pedal w/ bar

+6 +3 1/2

19 19 12 12 12 12 17 17 12 12 12 12 16 16 12 12 | 17 (17)

P.M. P.M.

7 7 7 7 7 7 7 7 7 7 7 7 7 7 7 7 | 9 7 9 7 9 7 7 7 5 | 5 3 5 3 5 3 4 4 2

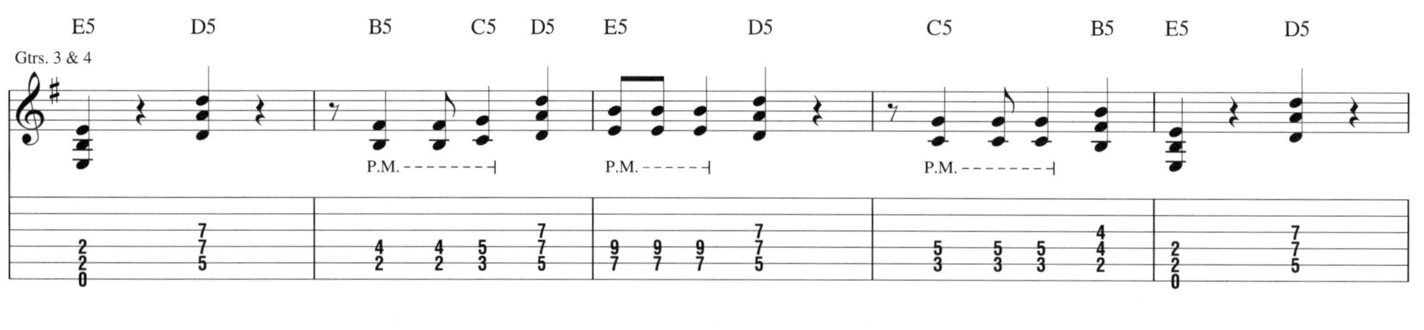
E5
D5
B5
C5
D5
E5
D5
C5
B5
E5
D5
Gtrs. 3 & 4
P.M.
P.M.
P.M.

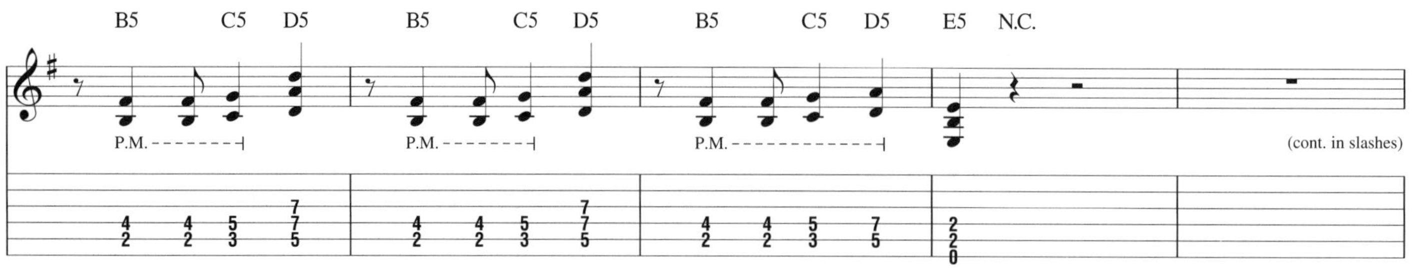
B5
C5
D5
B5
C5
D5
B5
C5
D5
E5
N.C.
P.M.
P.M.
P.M.
(cont. in slashes)

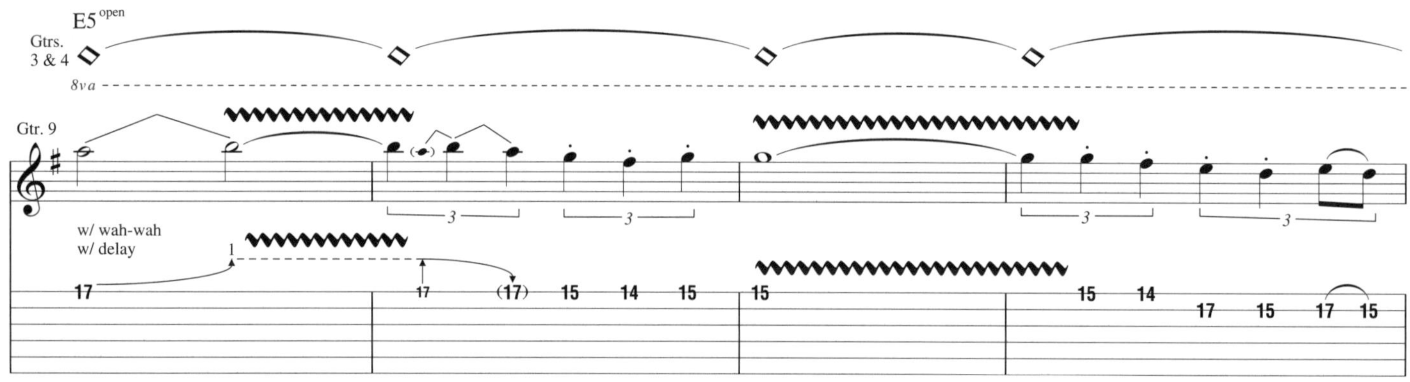
E5 open
Gtrs. 3 & 4
8va
Gtr. 9
w/ wah-wah
w/ delay

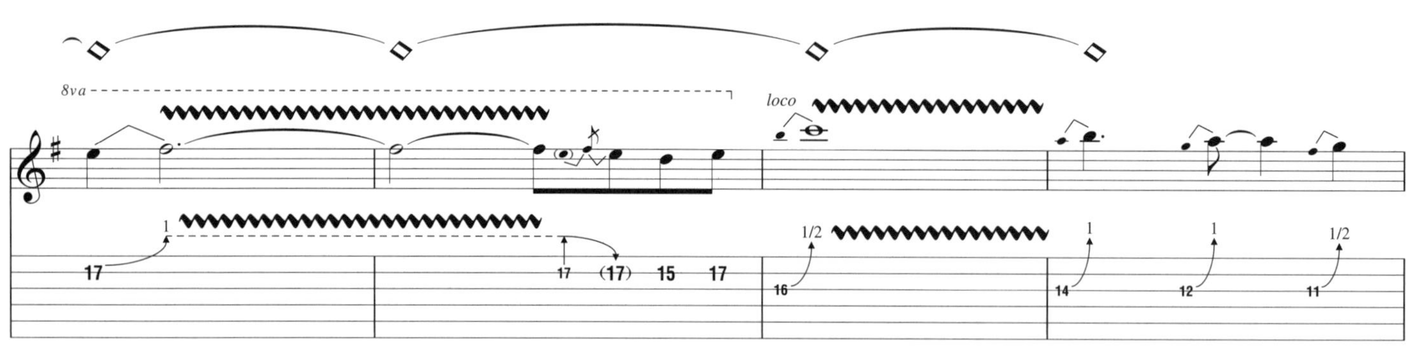
8va
loco

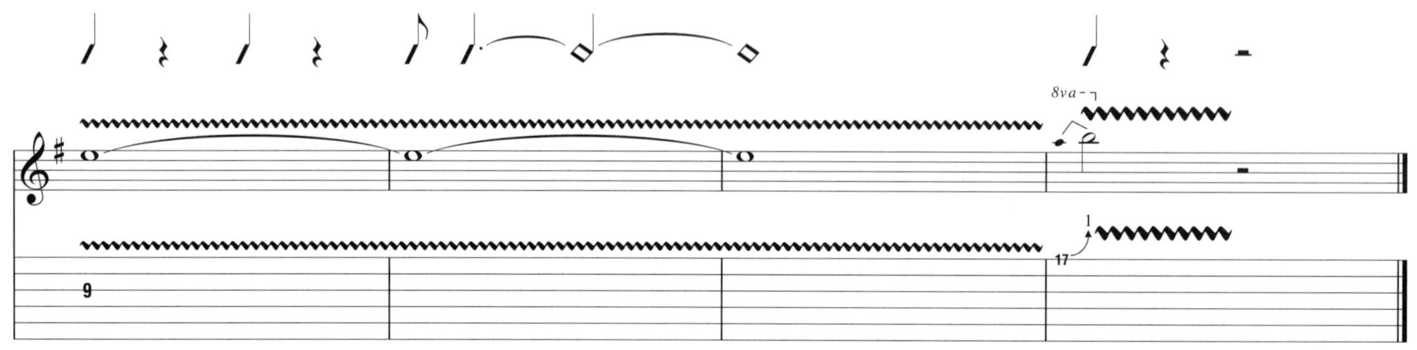
8va

Cry for Eternity

Words and Music by Herman Li, ZP Theart, Sam Totman and Vadim Pruzhanov

A5
G5
C5
F5
F5 VIII
E5
8fr
11
134
134
134
134
11

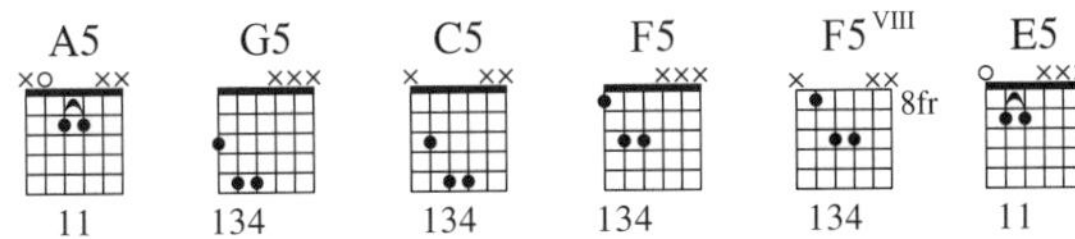

Intro
Fast ♩ = 140

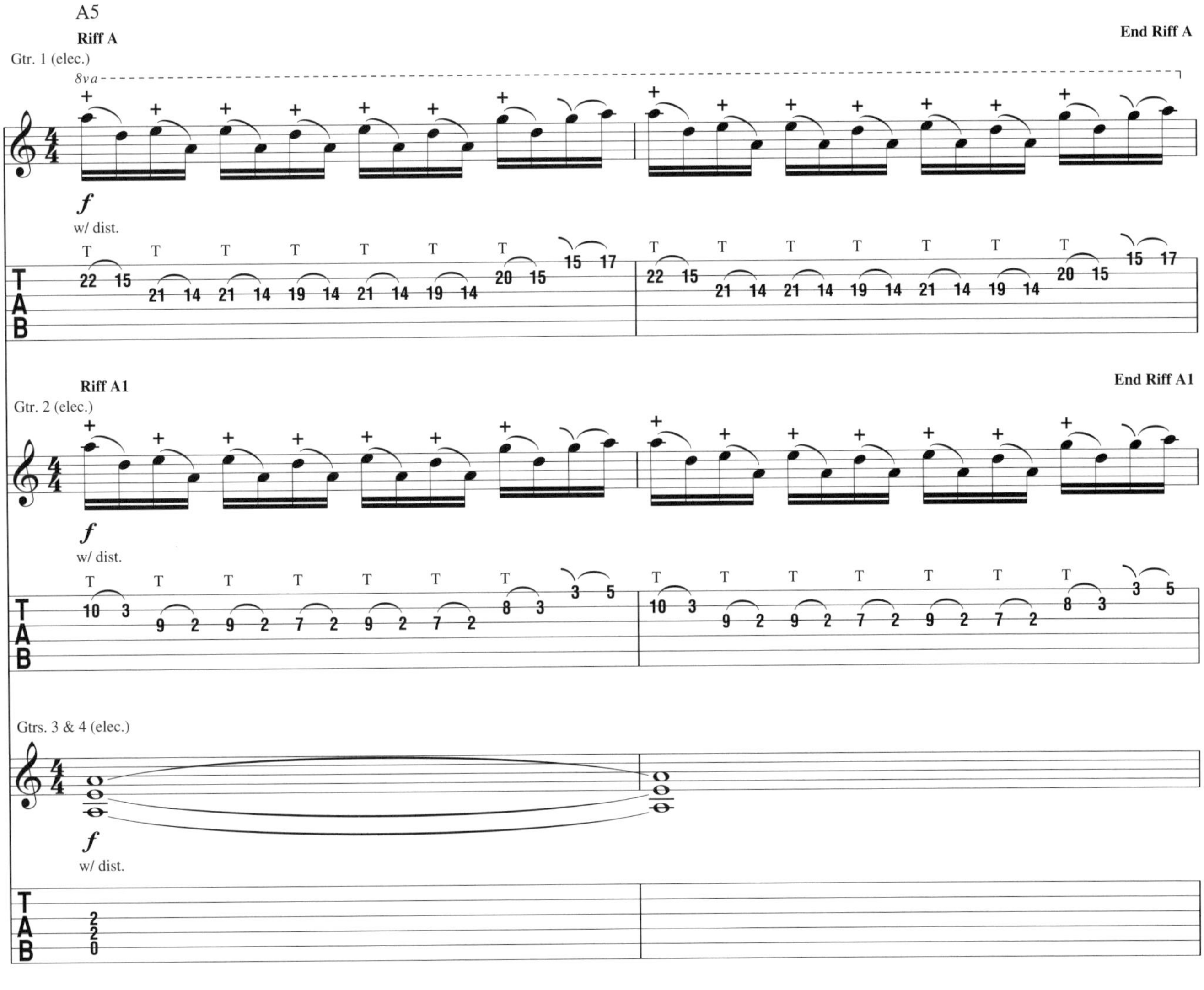

A5
Riff A
End Riff A
Gtr. 1 (elec.)
8va
f
w/ dist.
Riff A1
End Riff A1
Gtr. 2 (elec.)
f
w/ dist.
Gtrs. 3 & 4 (elec.)
f
w/ dist.

Gtrs. 1 & 2: w/ Riffs A & A1 (3 times)
Gtrs. 3 & 4
G5
A5
P.M.
(Gtr. 3, cont. in slashes)

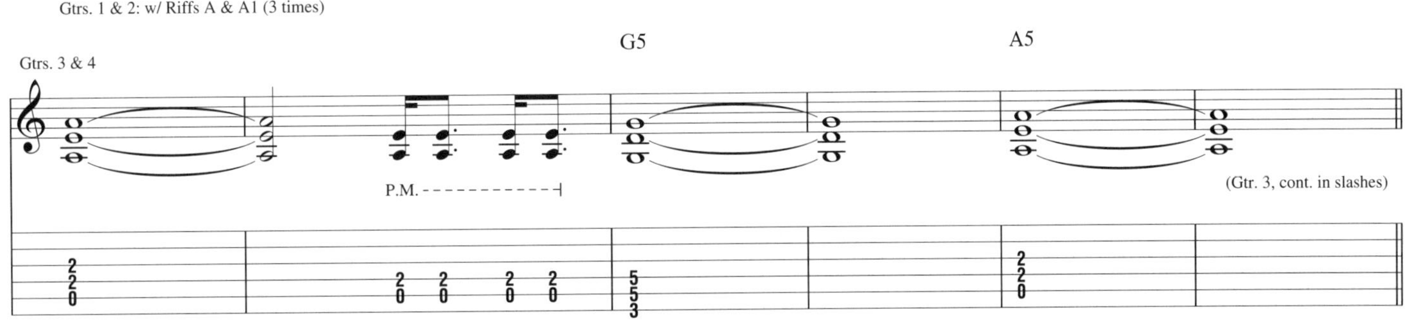

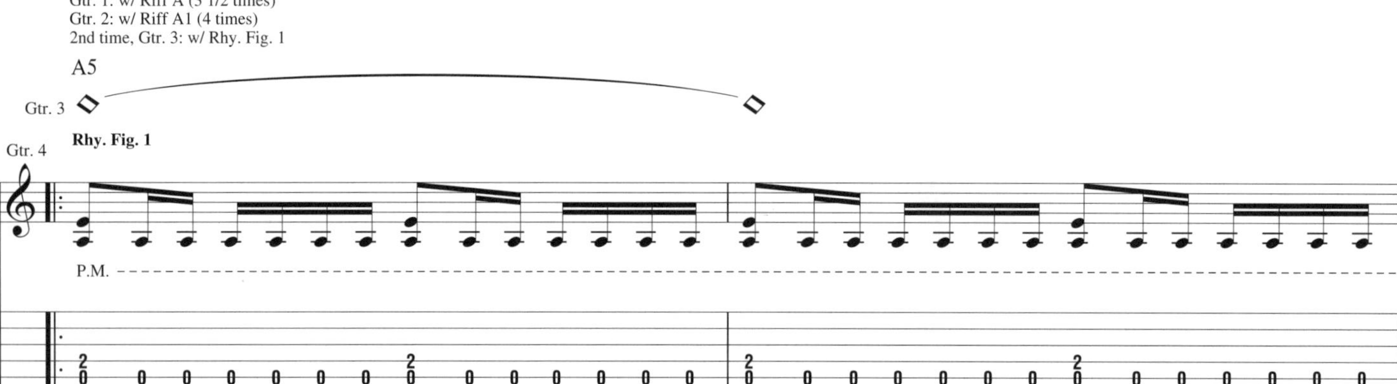
Gtr. 1: w/ Riff A (3 1/2 times)
Gtr. 2: w/ Riff A1 (4 times)
2nd time, Gtr. 3: w/ Rhy. Fig. 1
A5
Gtr. 3
Rhy. Fig. 1
Gtr. 4
P.M.

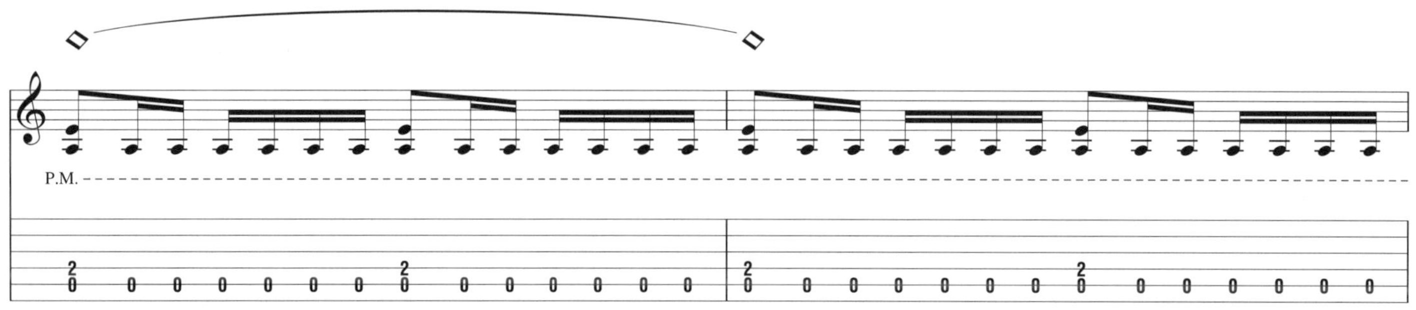
P.M.

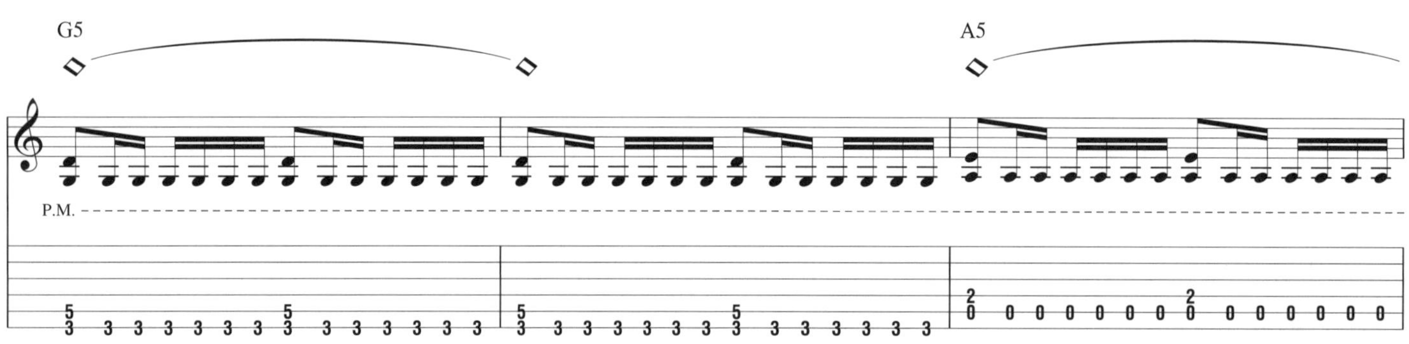
G5
A5
P.M.

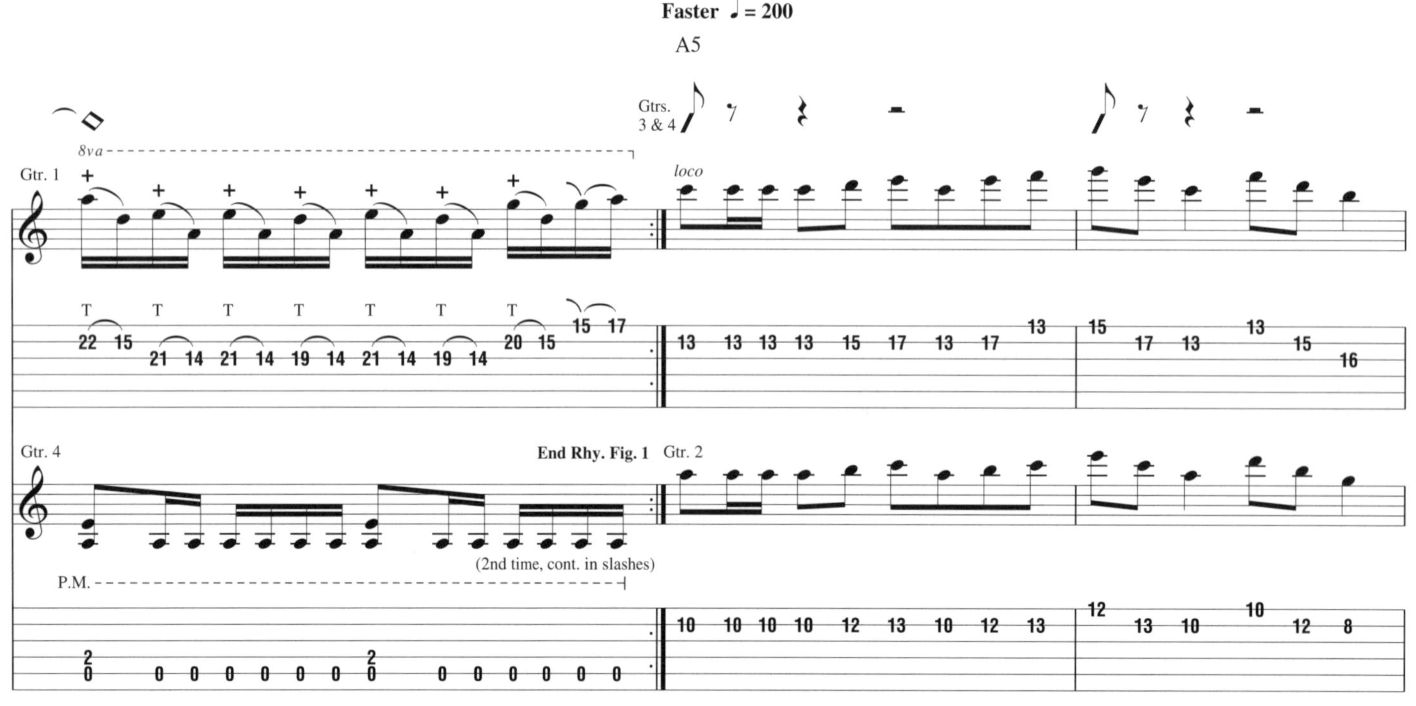
Faster ♩ = 200
A5
Gtrs. 3 & 4
8va
Gtr. 1
loco
Gtr. 4
End Rhy. Fig. 1
Gtr. 2
(2nd time, cont. in slashes)
P.M.

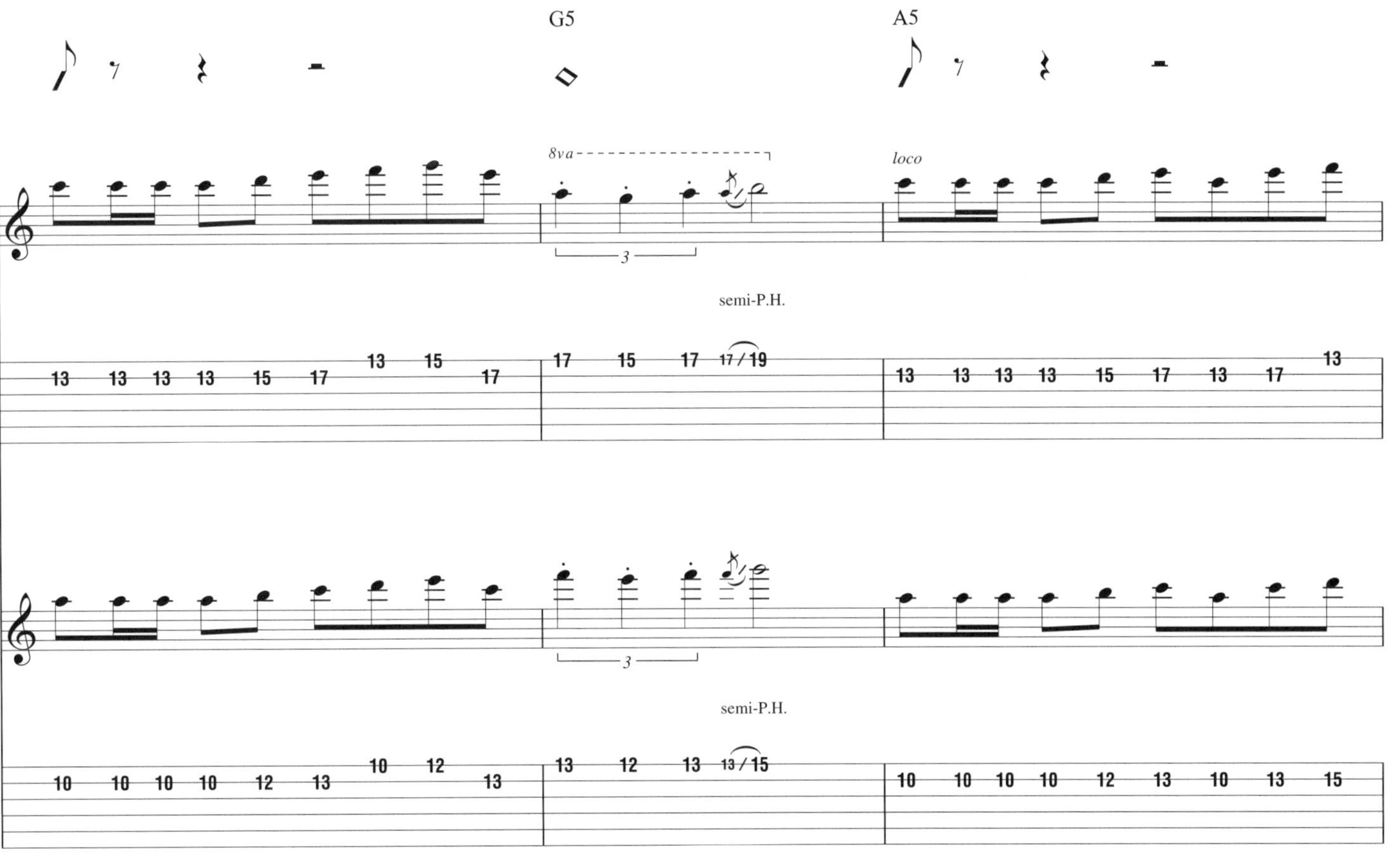
G5
A5
8va
loco
semi-P.H.
semi-P.H.

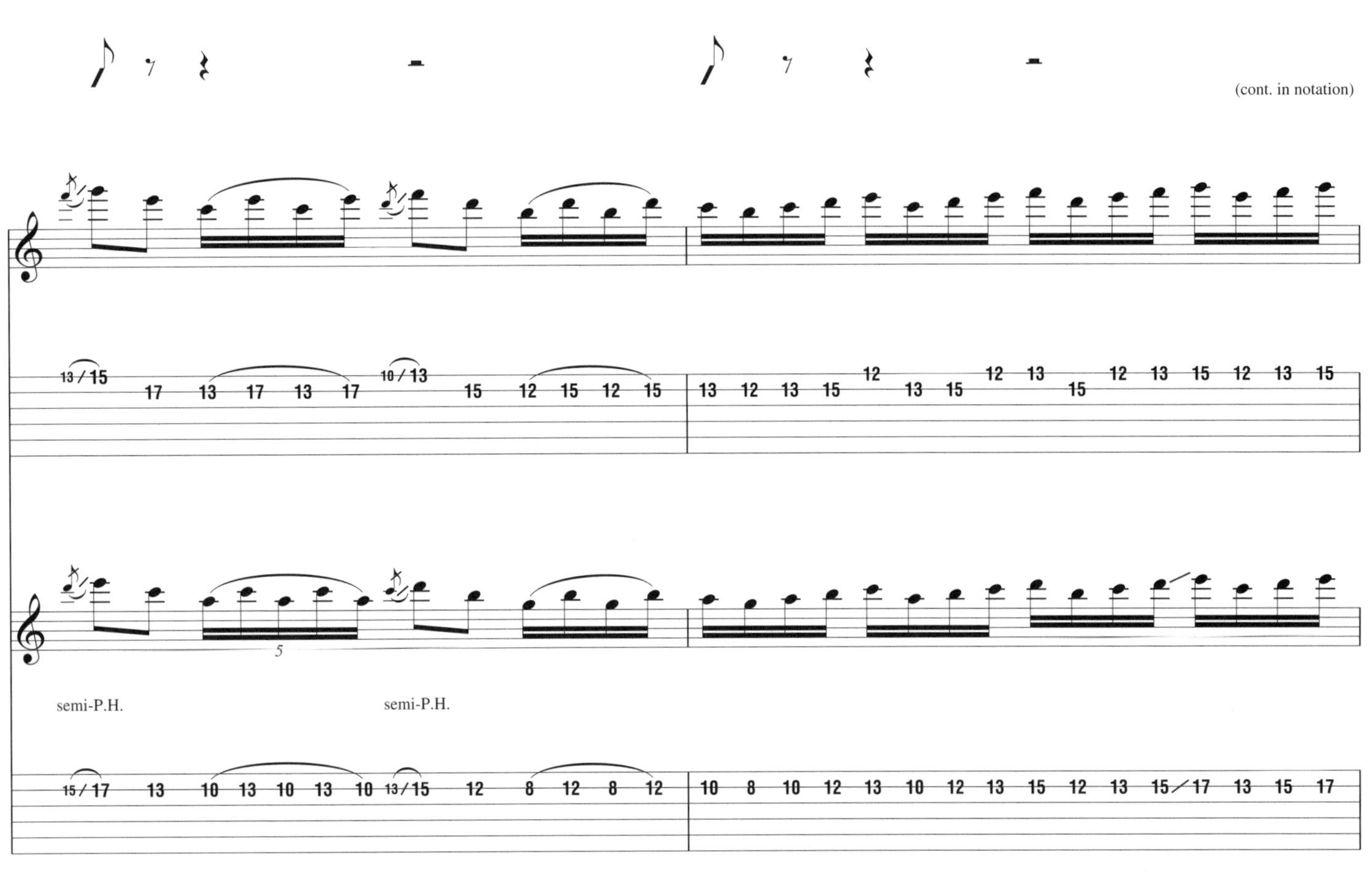
(cont. in notation)
semi-P.H.
semi-P.H.

*Chord symbols reflect basic harmony.

semi-P.H.
semi-P.H.
8va
semi-P.H.
P.H.
End Rhy. Fig. 2
P.M.
P.M.
P.M.
Gtrs. 3 & 4: w/ Rhy. Fig. 2
A5
8va
Gtr. 1
Gtr. 2
loco
Gtr. 5

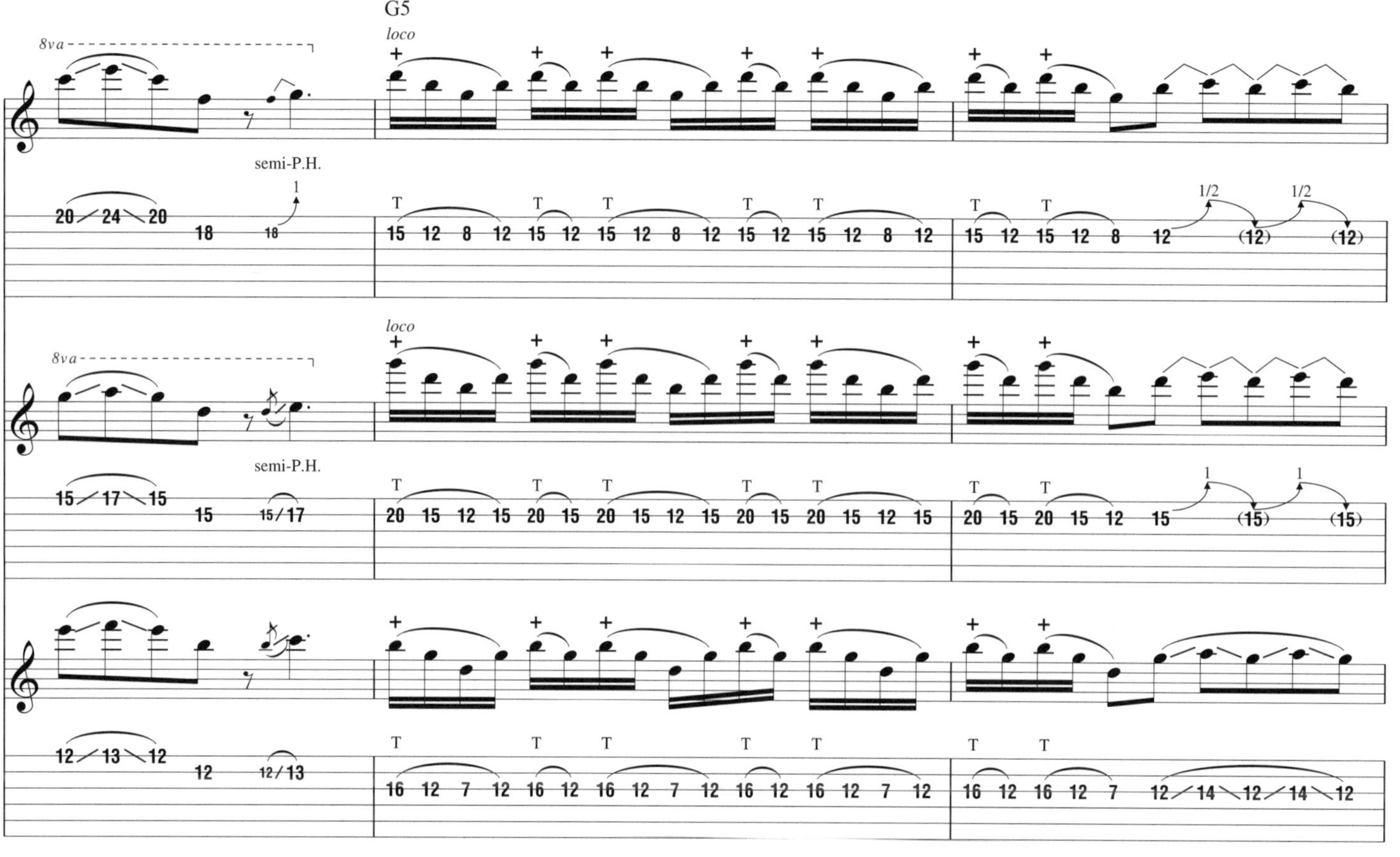

E5

N.C.

Gtrs. 1, 2 & 5 tacet

1. Fall - ing from the

Gtr. 1

8va

Gtr. 2

Gtr. 5

Gtrs. 3 & 4

P.M.

Verse
2nd time, Gtr. 5 tacet
A5
sky, now, the sign of the burn - ing sun.
2. So now the fall - en will live a - gain.
Gtrs. 3 & 4
P.M.
F5
In - to the face of the e - vil one.
They feel the pain burn in - side of them.
P.M.
A5
No - where to hide, now, we're on the run
Re - mem - ber now what you feel a - gain
(Gtr. 3, cont. in slashes)
P.M.
C5
Gtr. 3
G5
(cont. in notation)
right be - fore your eyes. We're
deep down in - side. Still
Gtr. 4

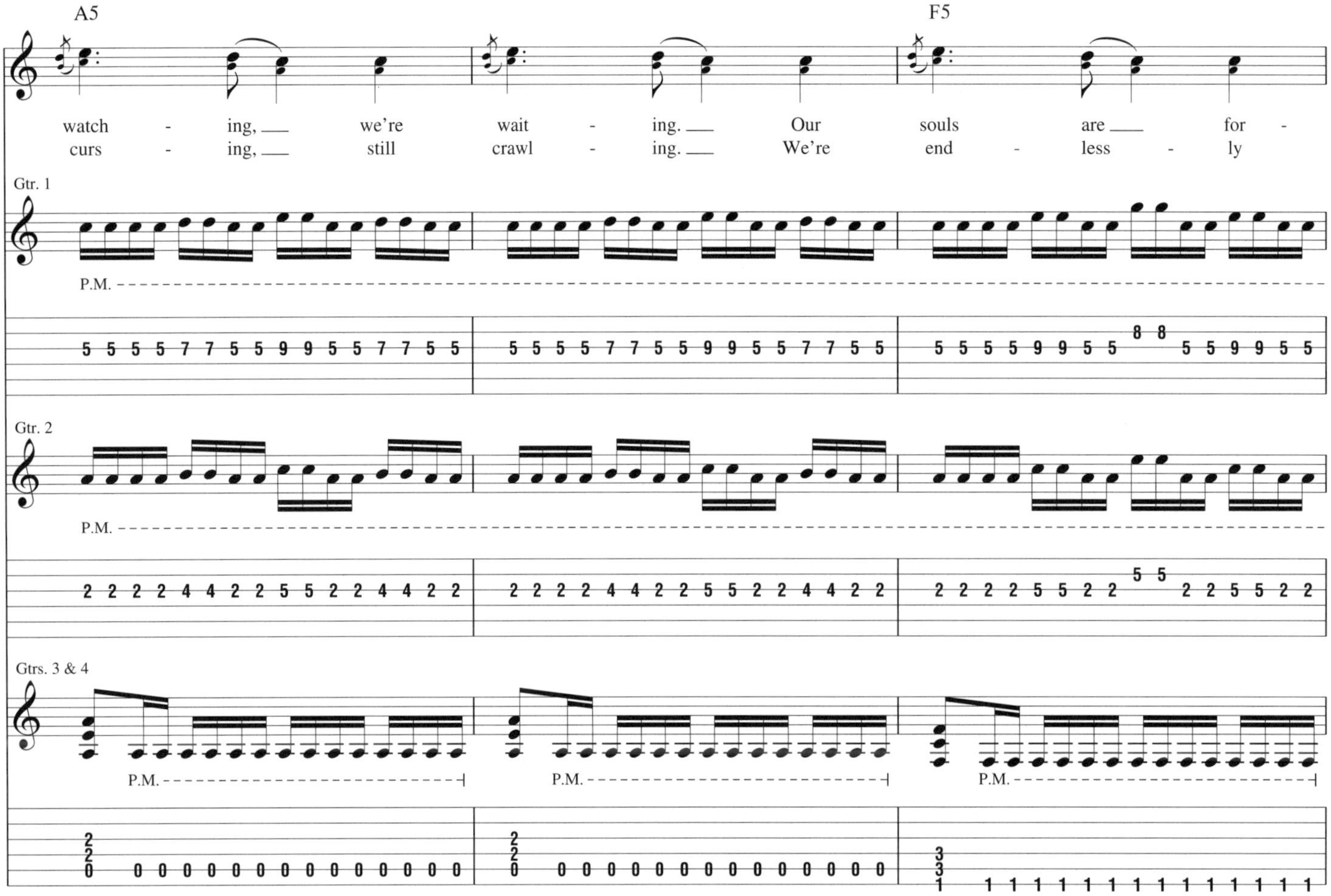

A5 F5

watch - ing, we're wait - ing. Our souls are for -
curs - ing, still crawl - ing. We're end - less - ly

Gtr. 1

P.M.

Gtr. 2

P.M.

Gtrs. 3 & 4

P.M. P.M. P.M.

Gtrs. 1 & 2 tacet

A5 C5

sak - en. The sign of the war - ri - ors, the
fall - ing. The down - fall of man - kind, the

P.M.

P.M.

P.M. P.M.

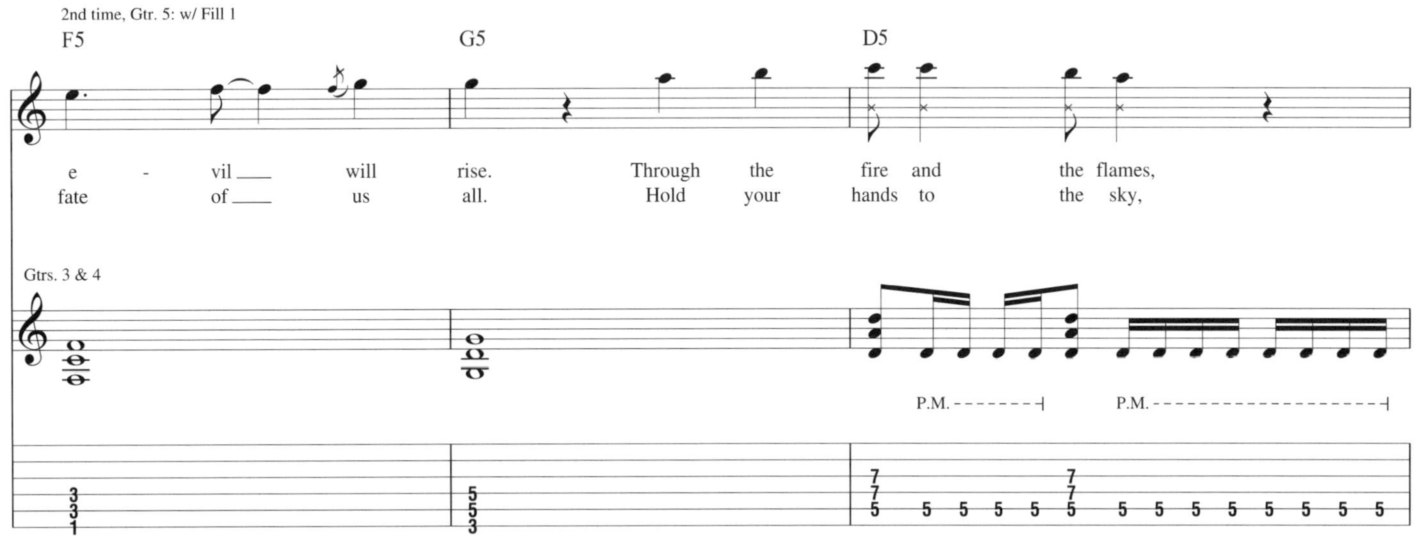
2nd time, Gtr. 5: w/ Fill 1
F5
G5
D5
e - vil will rise. Through the fire and the flames,
fate of us all. Hold your hands to the sky,
Gtrs. 3 & 4
P.M.
P.M.

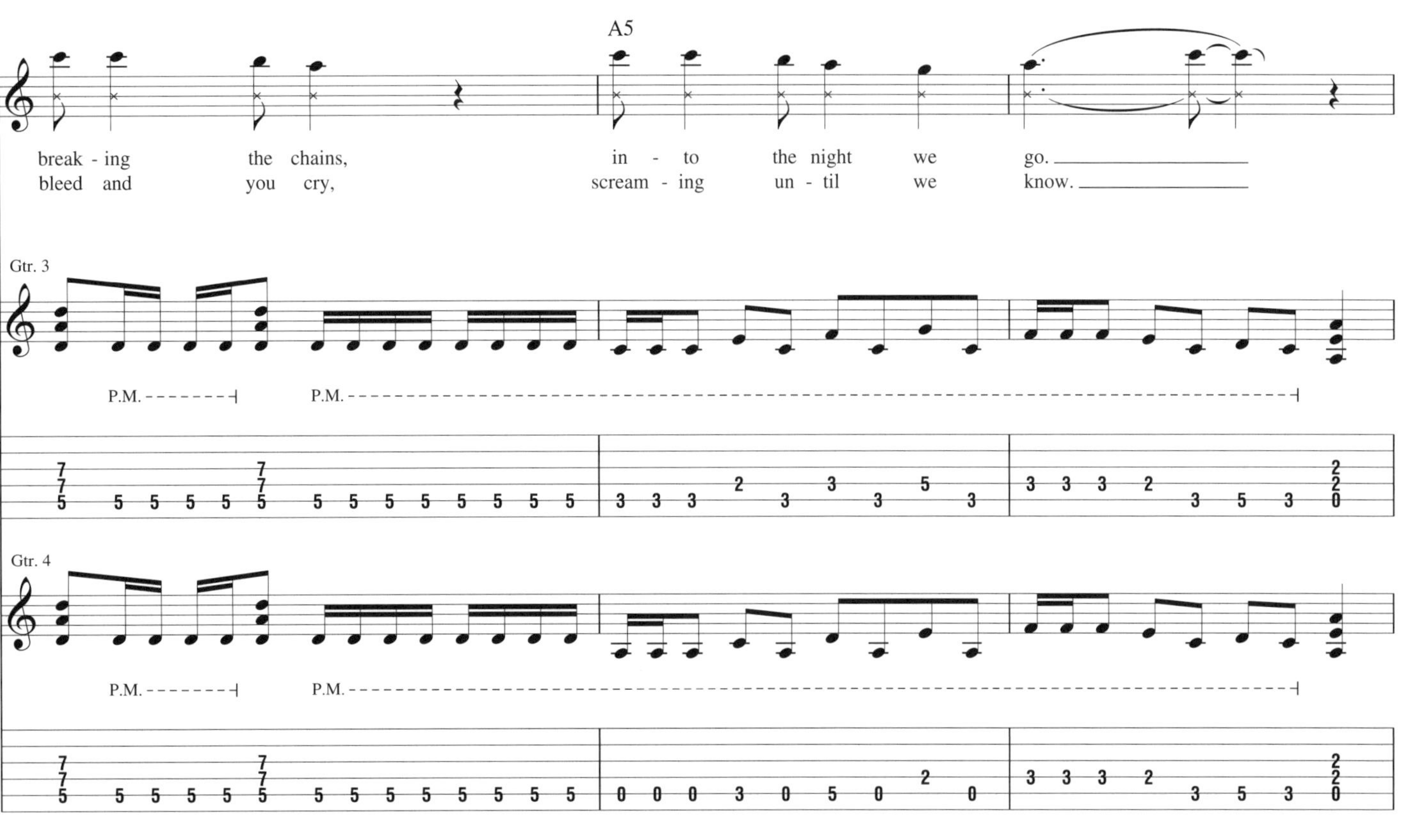
A5
break - ing the chains, in - to the night we go.
bleed and you cry, scream - ing un - til we know.
Gtr. 3
P.M.
P.M.
Gtr. 4
P.M.
P.M.

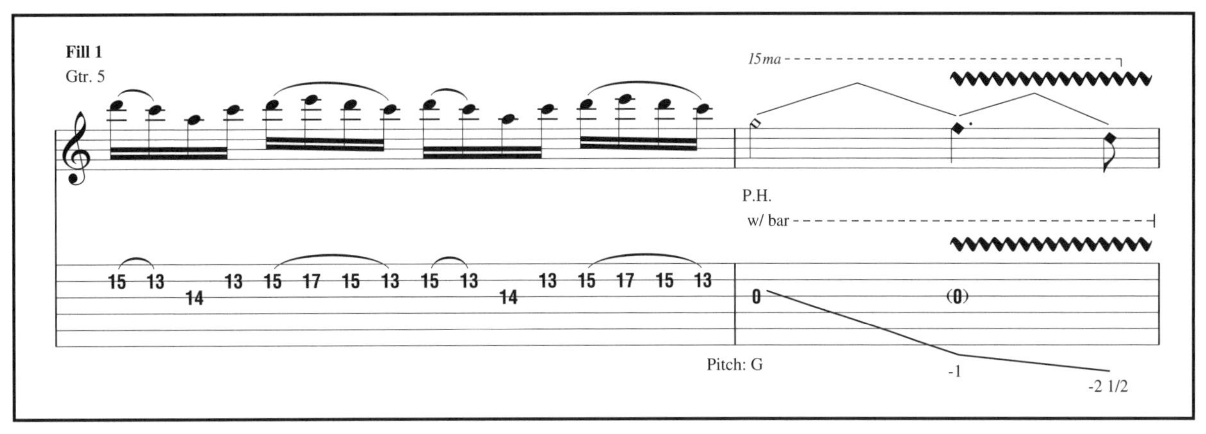
Fill 1
Gtr. 5
15ma
P.H.
w/ bar
Pitch: G
-1
-2 1/2

To Coda 1
D5
A5
Tor - ment and pain tram - ple the slain. Sol - diers of death, we
Dy - ing in pain a - gain and a - gain,
Gtr. 1
Gtr. 2
Gtrs. 3 & 4
P.M.
Pre-Chorus
G5
F5 N.C.
F5 N.C.
know. Our steel will shine for - ev - er
8va
*w/ DigiTech Whammy Pedal
w/ bar
*Set for one octave above when depressed (toe down).
Rhy. Fig. 3

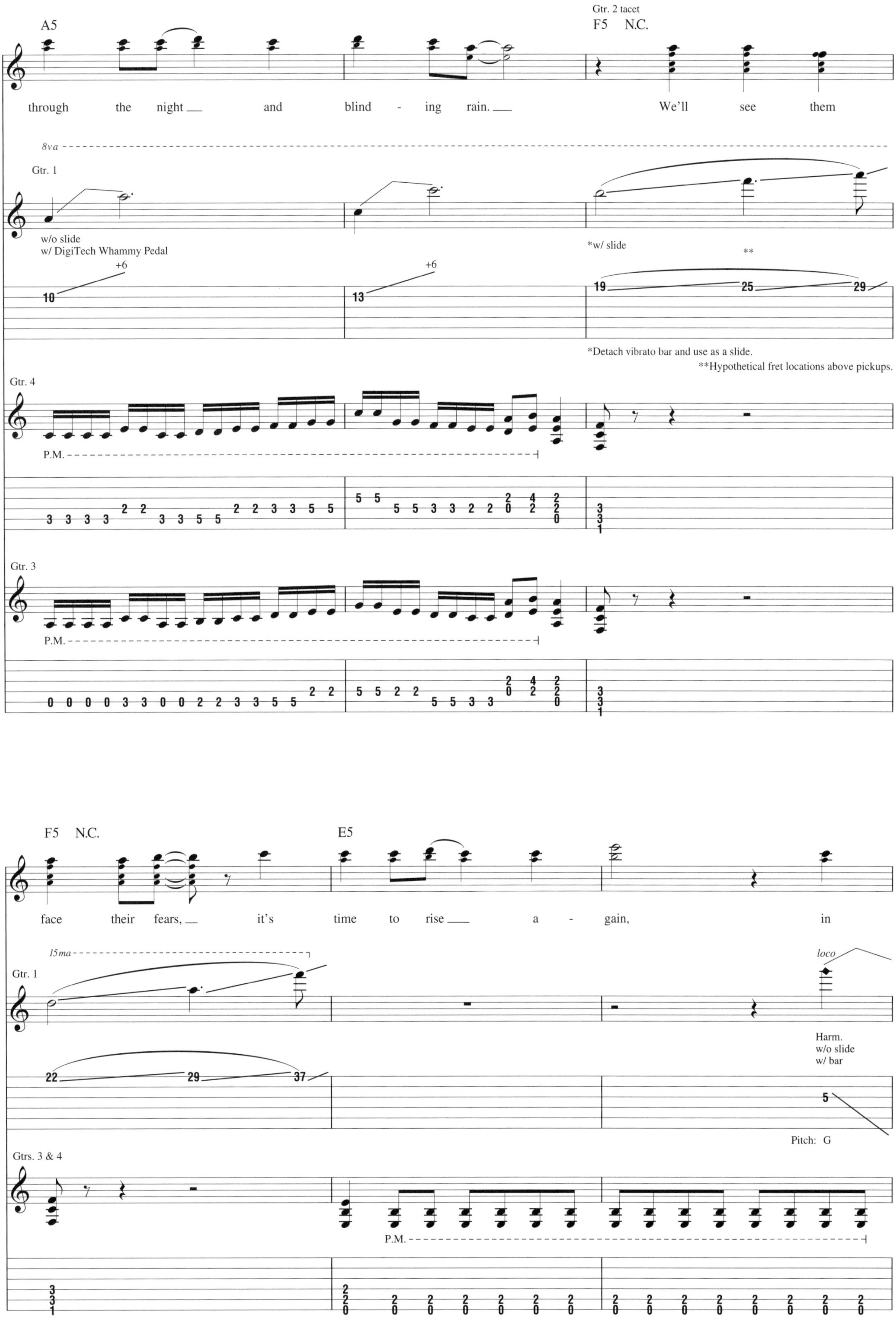

Gtr. 2 tacet

A5 F5 N.C.

through the night and blind - ing rain. We'll see them

8va

Gtr. 1

w/o slide
w/ DigiTech Whammy Pedal

+6 +6

*w/ slide

**

*Detach vibrato bar and use as a slide.
**Hypothetical fret locations above pickups.

Gtr. 4

P.M.

Gtr. 3

P.M.

Chorus
1st time, Gtrs. 1 & 2 tacet
3rd time, Gtrs. 1 & 2: w/ Fill 2
A5
ev - er - last - ing pain.
Fly
Gtr. 2
8va
P.S.
Gtr. 1
Harm.
w/ bar
Pitch: G
-1 1/2
-3 1/2
-5
Gtrs. 3 & 4
End Rhy. Fig. 3
P.M.
C5
G5
A5
F5
free for what we be - lieve. One thou - sand hearts
Gtrs. 3 & 4
Fill 2
Gtr. 1
8va
Gtr. 2
divisi
*Gtr. 1 to left of slash in tab.

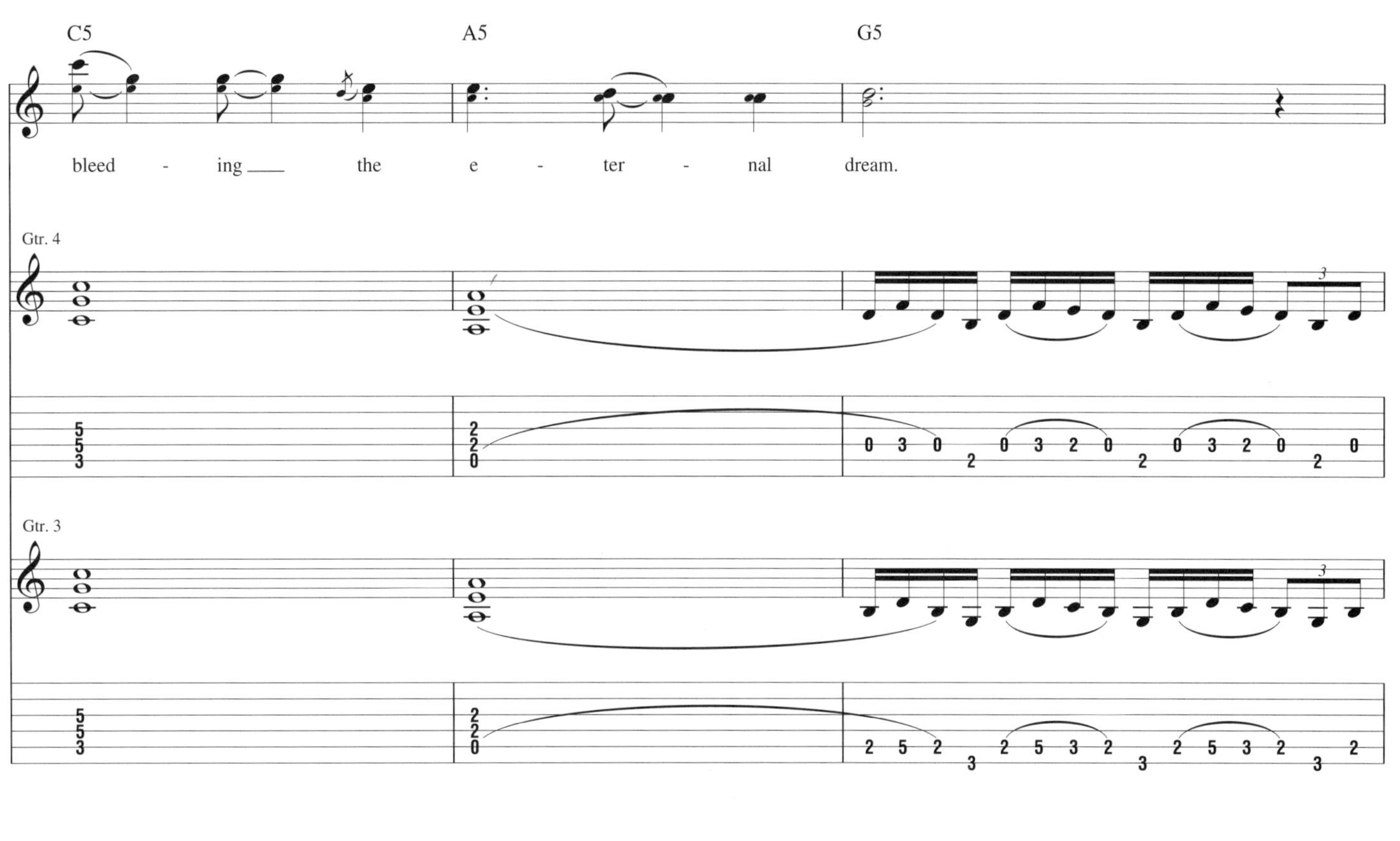
C5
A5
G5
bleed - ing the e - ter - nal dream.
Gtr. 4
Gtr. 3

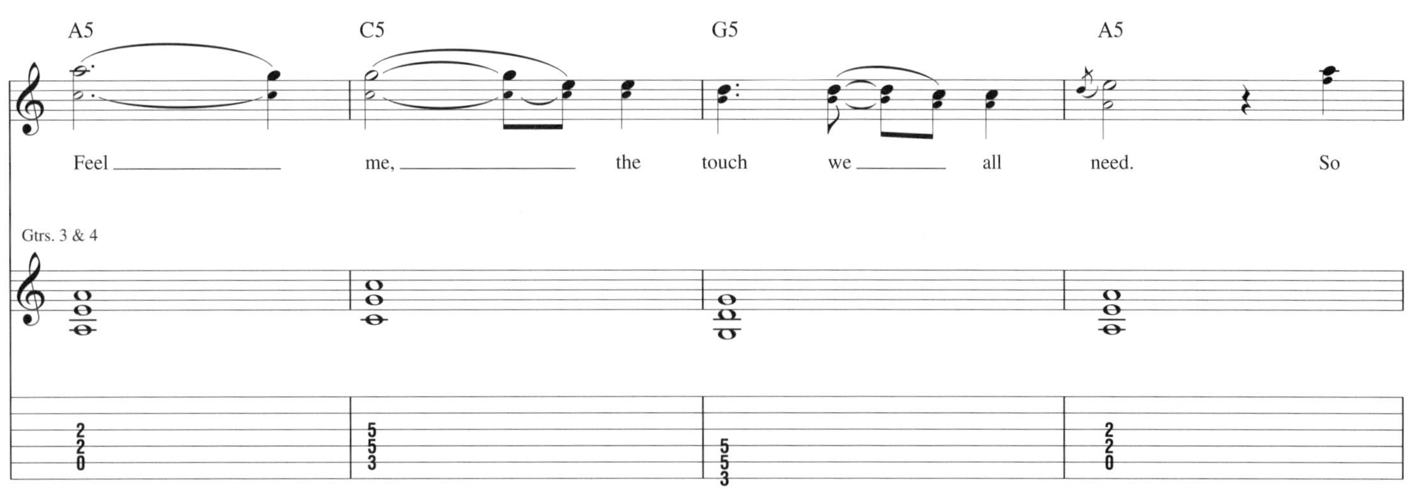
A5
C5
G5
A5
Feel me, the touch we all need. So
Gtrs. 3 & 4

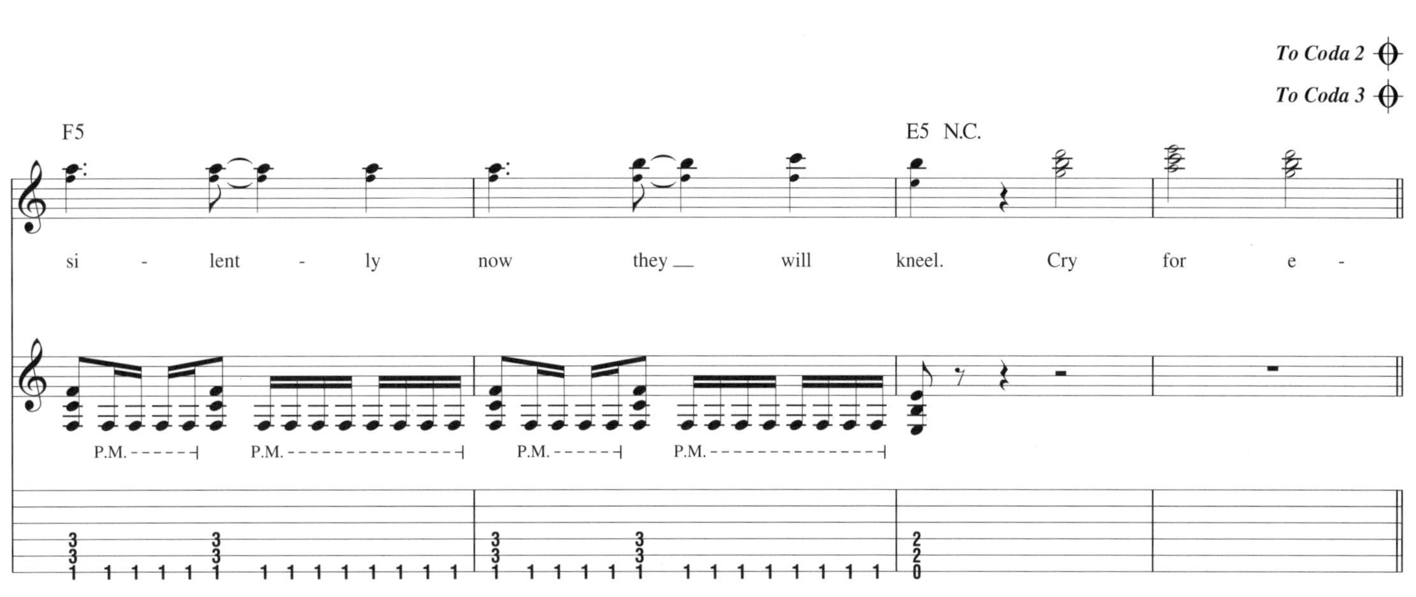
To Coda 2
To Coda 3
F5
E5 N.C.
si - lent - ly now they will kneel. Cry for e -
P.M.

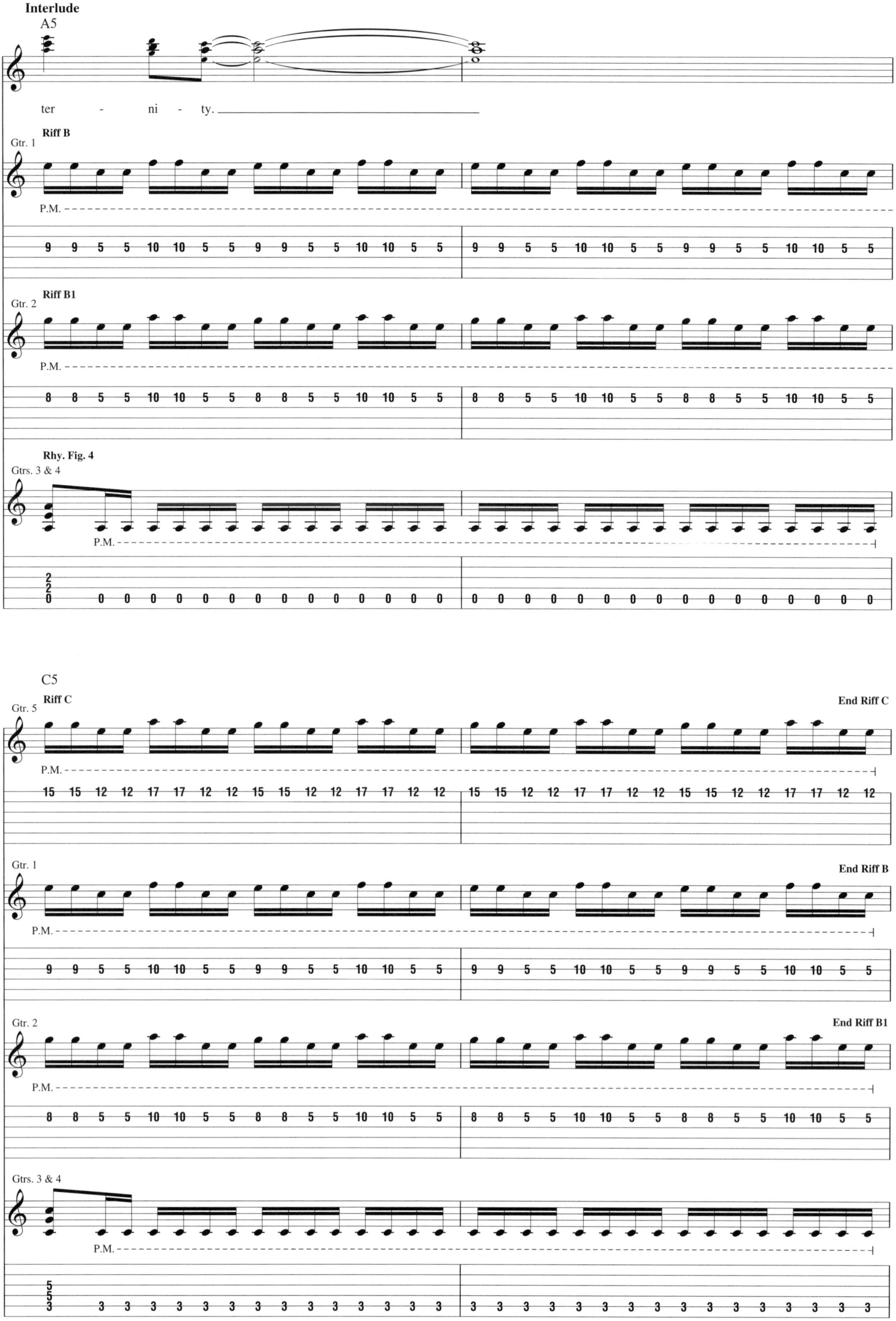

Interlude

A5

ter - ni - ty.

Riff B

Gtr. 1

P.M.

9 9 5 5 10 10 5 5 9 9 5 5 10 10 5 5 | 9 9 5 5 10 10 5 5 9 9 5 5 10 10 5 5

Riff B1

Gtr. 2

P.M.

8 8 5 5 10 10 5 5 8 8 5 5 10 10 5 5 | 8 8 5 5 10 10 5 5 8 8 5 5 10 10 5 5

Rhy. Fig. 4

Gtrs. 3 & 4

P.M.

2 2 0 / 0 0 0 0 0 0 0 0 0 0 0 0 0 0 | 0 0 0 0 0 0 0 0 0 0 0 0 0 0 0 0

C5

Riff C

Gtr. 5

End Riff C

P.M.

15 15 12 12 17 17 12 12 15 15 12 12 17 17 12 12 | 15 15 12 12 17 17 12 12 15 15 12 12 17 17 12 12

Gtr. 1

End Riff B

P.M.

9 9 5 5 10 10 5 5 9 9 5 5 10 10 5 5 | 9 9 5 5 10 10 5 5 9 9 5 5 10 10 5 5

Gtr. 2

End Riff B1

P.M.

8 8 5 5 10 10 5 5 8 8 5 5 10 10 5 5 | 8 8 5 5 10 10 5 5 8 8 5 5 10 10 5 5

Gtrs. 3 & 4

P.M.

5 5 3 / 3 3 3 3 3 3 3 3 3 3 3 3 3 3 | 3 3 3 3 3 3 3 3 3 3 3 3 3 3 3 3

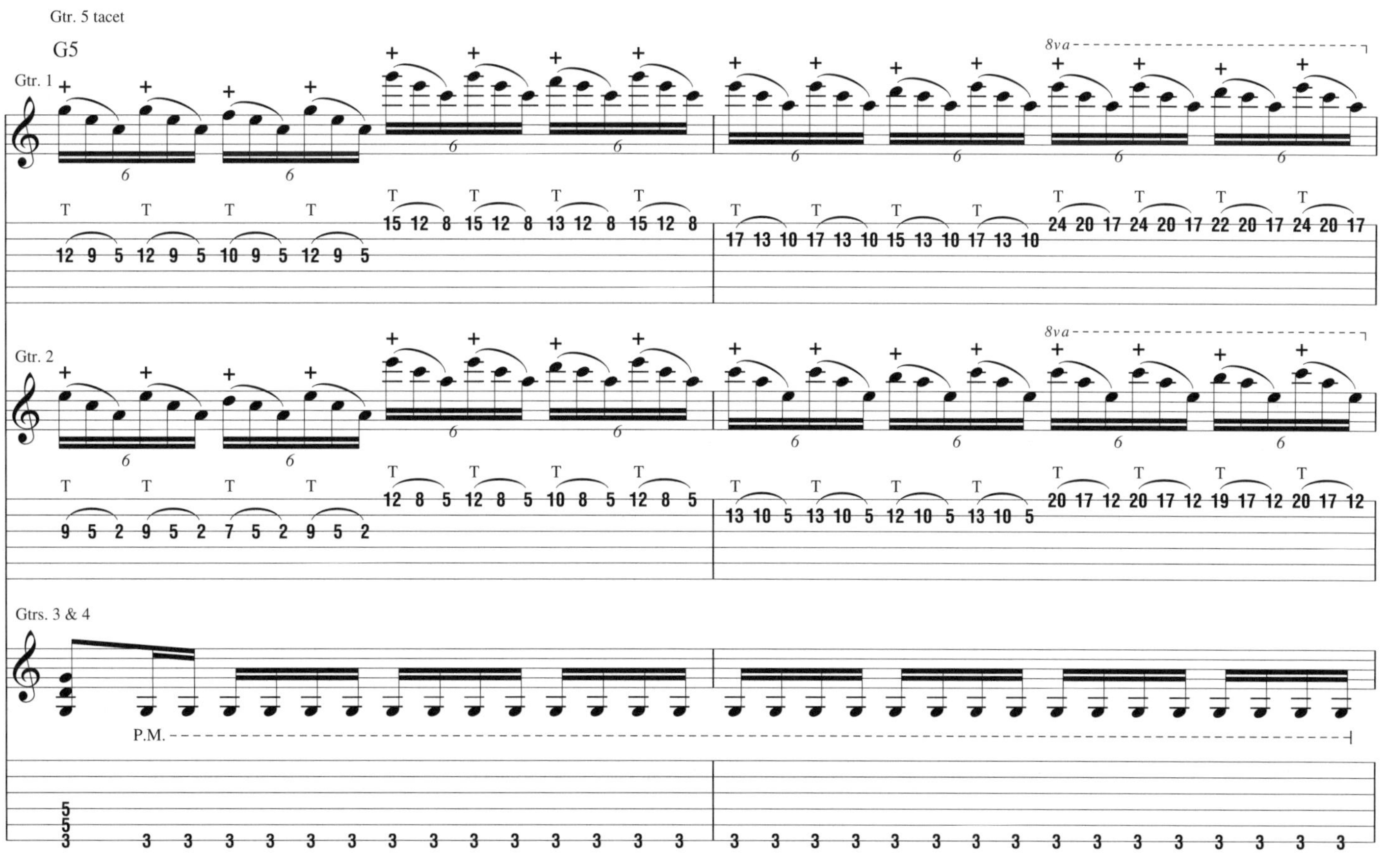

Gtrs. 3 & 4: w/ Rhy. Fig. 4 (1st 4 meas.)

E5 F5 E5 F5 G5 A5

Gtr. 1
loco
Riff D
w/ wah-wah
P.M.

Gtr. 2
loco
Riff D1
w/ wah-wah
P.M.

Gtr. 5
Riff D2
P.M.

Gtrs. 3 & 4
End Rhy. Fig. 4
P.M. P.M. P.M. P.M.

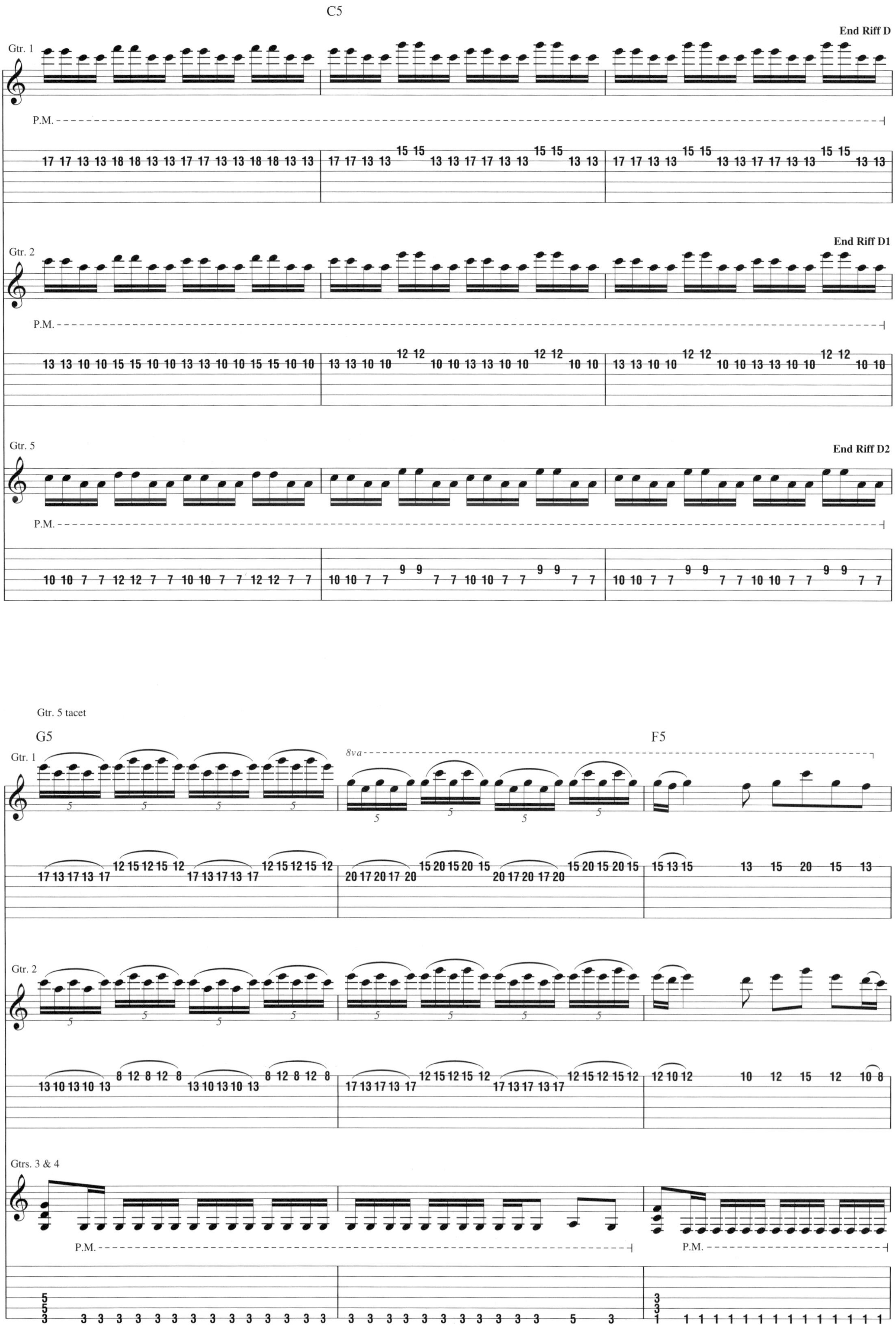

C5

End Riff D

Gtr. 1

P.M.

17 17 13 13 18 18 13 13 17 17 13 13 18 18 13 13 | 17 17 13 13 15 15 13 13 17 17 13 13 15 15 13 13 | 17 17 13 13 15 15 13 13 17 17 13 13 15 15 13 13

End Riff D1

Gtr. 2

P.M.

13 13 10 10 15 15 10 10 13 13 10 10 15 15 10 10 | 13 13 10 10 12 12 10 10 13 13 10 10 12 12 10 10 | 13 13 10 10 12 12 10 10 13 13 10 10 12 12 10 10

Gtr. 5

End Riff D2

P.M.

10 10 7 7 12 12 7 7 10 10 7 7 12 12 7 7 | 10 10 7 7 9 9 7 7 10 10 7 7 9 9 7 7 | 10 10 7 7 9 9 7 7 10 10 7 7 9 9 7 7

Gtr. 5 tacet

G5

F5

Gtr. 1

8va

5 5 5 5 | 5 5 5 5

17 13 17 13 17 12 15 12 15 12 17 13 17 13 17 12 15 12 15 12 | 20 17 20 17 20 15 20 15 20 15 20 17 20 17 20 15 20 15 20 15 | 15 13 15 13 15 20 15 13

Gtr. 2

5 5 5 5 | 5 5 5 5

13 10 13 10 13 8 12 8 12 8 13 10 13 10 13 8 12 8 12 8 | 17 13 17 13 17 12 15 12 15 12 17 13 17 13 17 12 15 12 15 12 | 12 10 12 10 12 15 12 10 8

Gtrs. 3 & 4

P.M.

P.M.

5 5 3 3 3 3 3 3 3 3 3 3 3 3 3 3 3 3 | 3 3 3 3 3 3 3 3 3 3 3 3 5 3 | 3 3 1 1 1 1 1 1 1 1 1 1 1 1 1 1 1 1 1

D.S. al Coda 1

Gtrs. 1 & 2 tacet
E5
A5
Gtrs. 3 & 4
(cont. in notation)
loco
semi-P.H.
Gtr. 5
8va
15ma
Harm. w/ bar
w/ bar
P.M.
(cont. in slashes)
Pitch: E B G
Coda 1
A5
G5
on - wards to hell be - low.
Gtr. 1
Gtr. 2
P.H. w/ bar
Gtrs. 3 & 4

Pre-Chorus

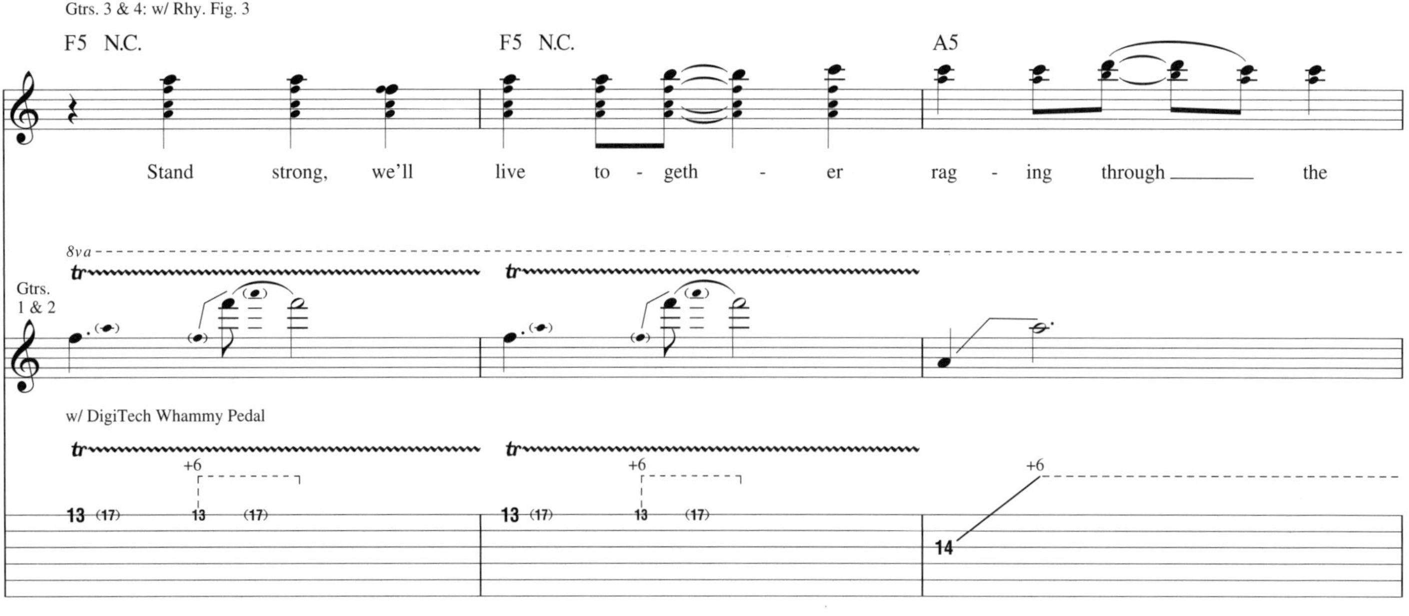

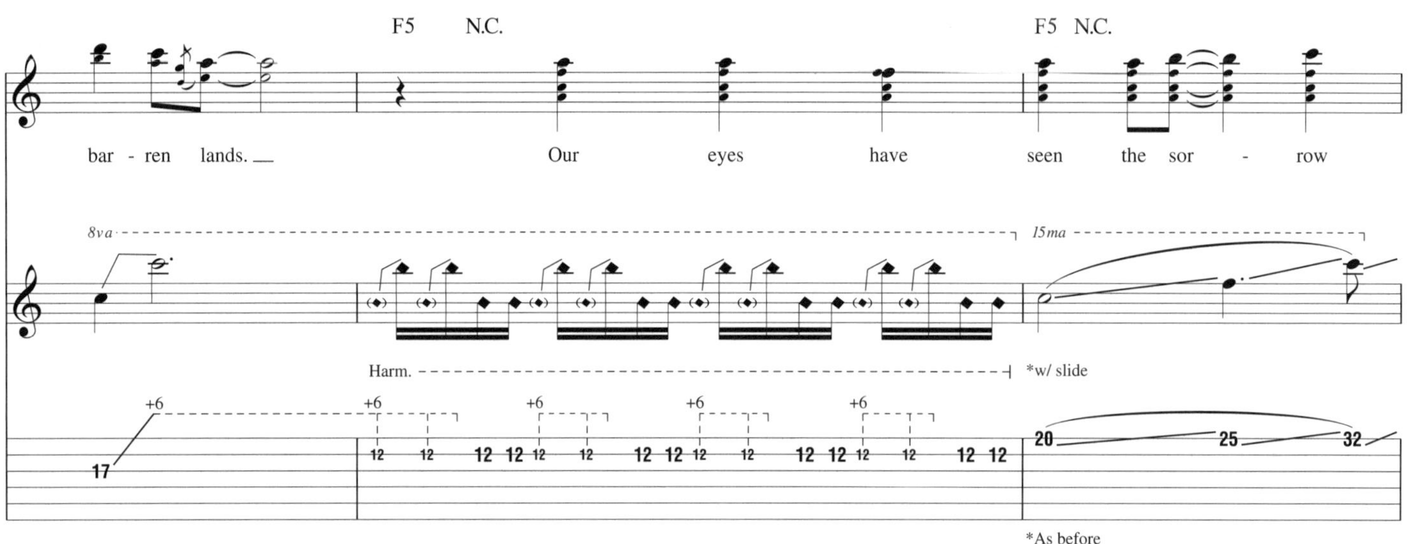

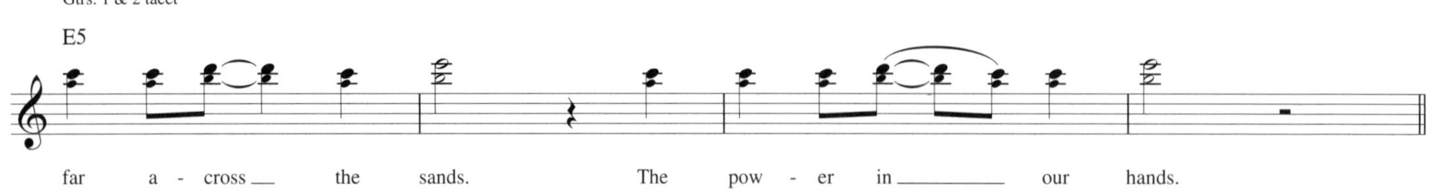

Coda 2

Interlude

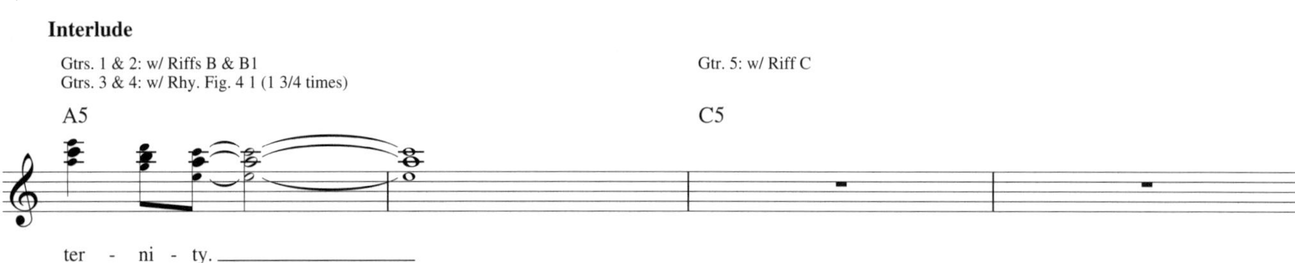

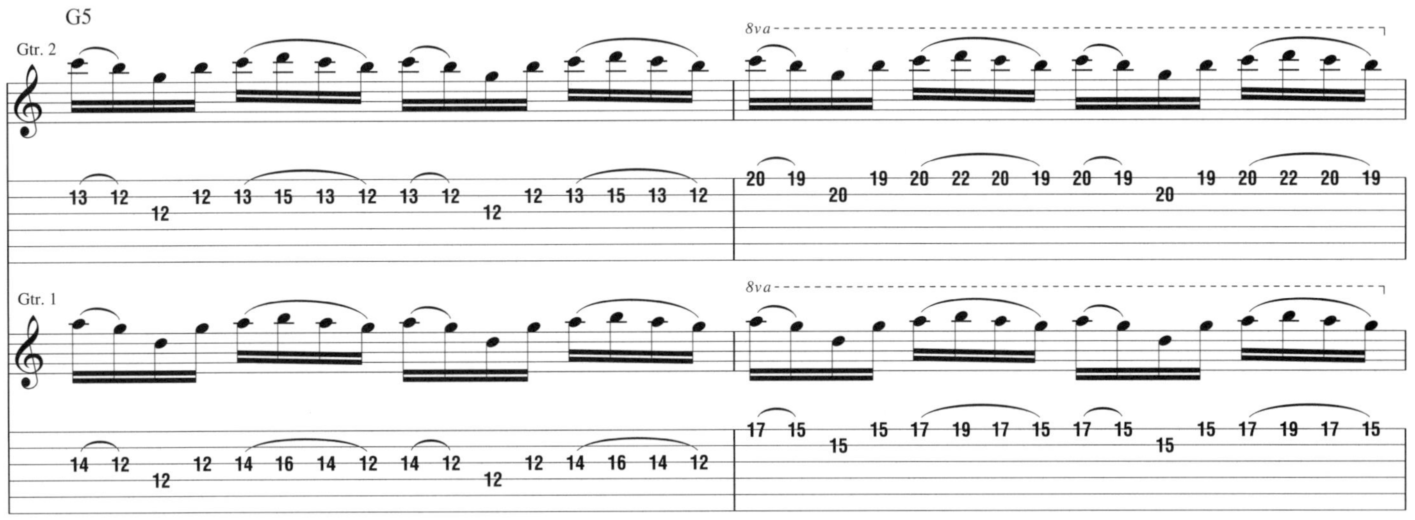
G5
Gtr. 2
8va
Gtr. 1
8va

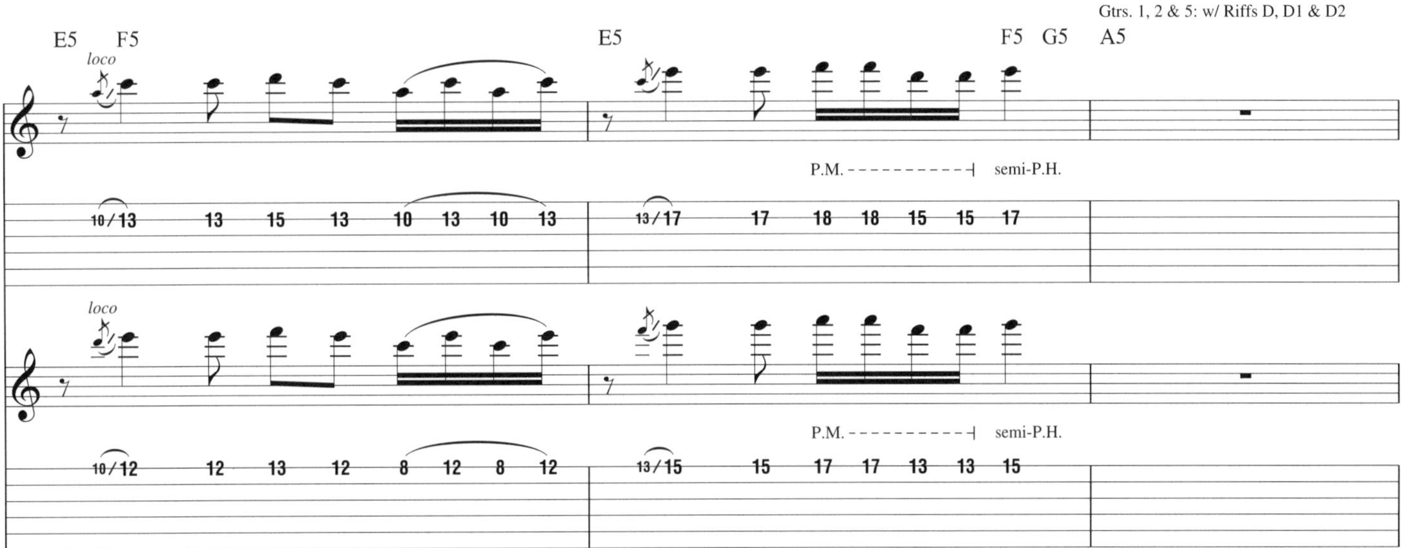
Gtrs. 1, 2 & 5: w/ Riffs D, D1 & D2
E5 F5
loco
E5
F5 G5 A5
P.M.
semi-P.H.
loco
P.M.
semi-P.H.

C5

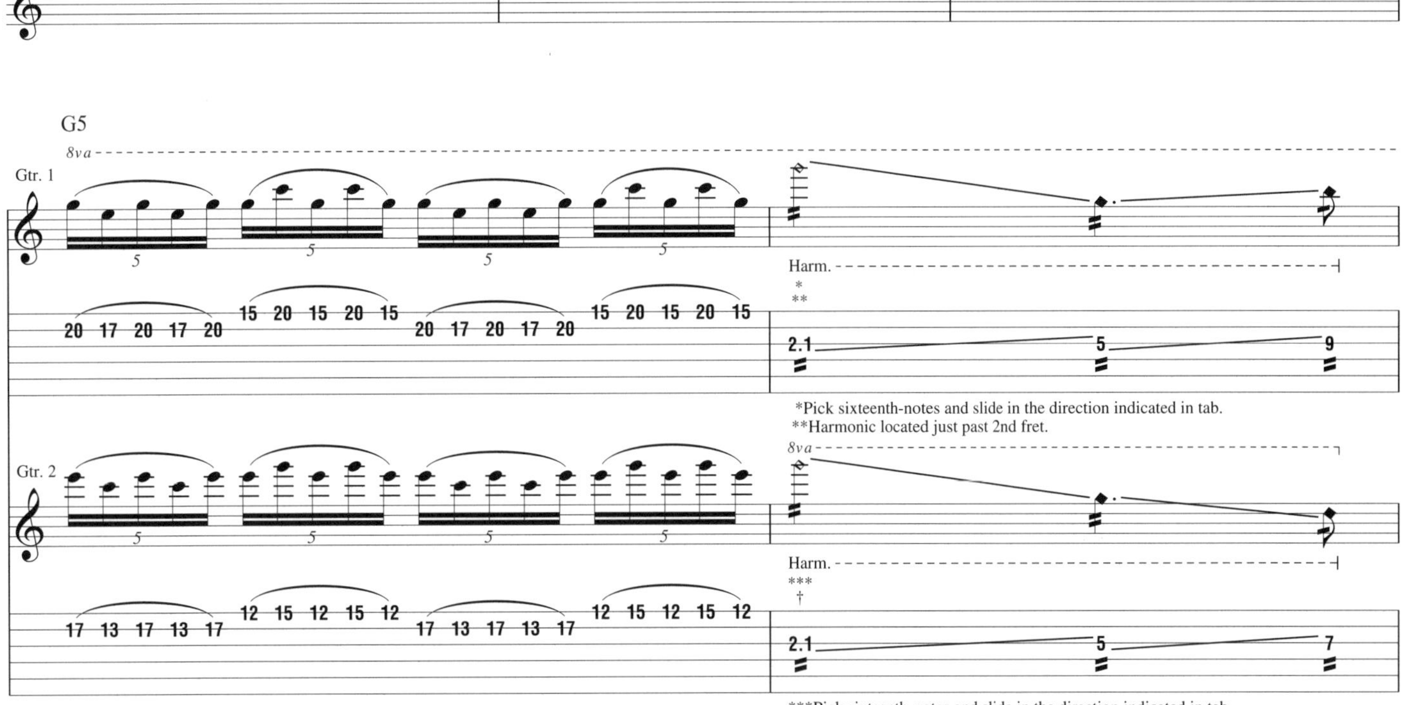
G5
8va
Gtr. 1
Harm.
*Pick sixteenth-notes and slide in the direction indicated in tab.
**Harmonic located just past 2nd fret.
Gtr. 2
8va
Harm.
***Pick sixteenth-notes and slide in the direction indicated in tab.
†Harmonic located just past 2nd fret.

End double-time feel
F5
E5
A5 N.C.
8va
loco
Gtr. 1
P.H.
Pitch: B
Gtr. 2
w/ bar
Pitch: E
Gtrs. 3 & 4
P.M.
Gtrs. 1-4 tacet
Am
G
F
G
A5
F5
Gtr. 2
P.M.
Gtr. 1
P.M.
Rhy. Fig. 5
End Rhy. Fig. 5
Gtrs. 3 & 4
P.M.

Gtrs. 3 & 4: w/ Rhy. Fig. 5 (3 times)

A5
F5
Gtr. 2
P.M.
Gtr. 1
P.M.

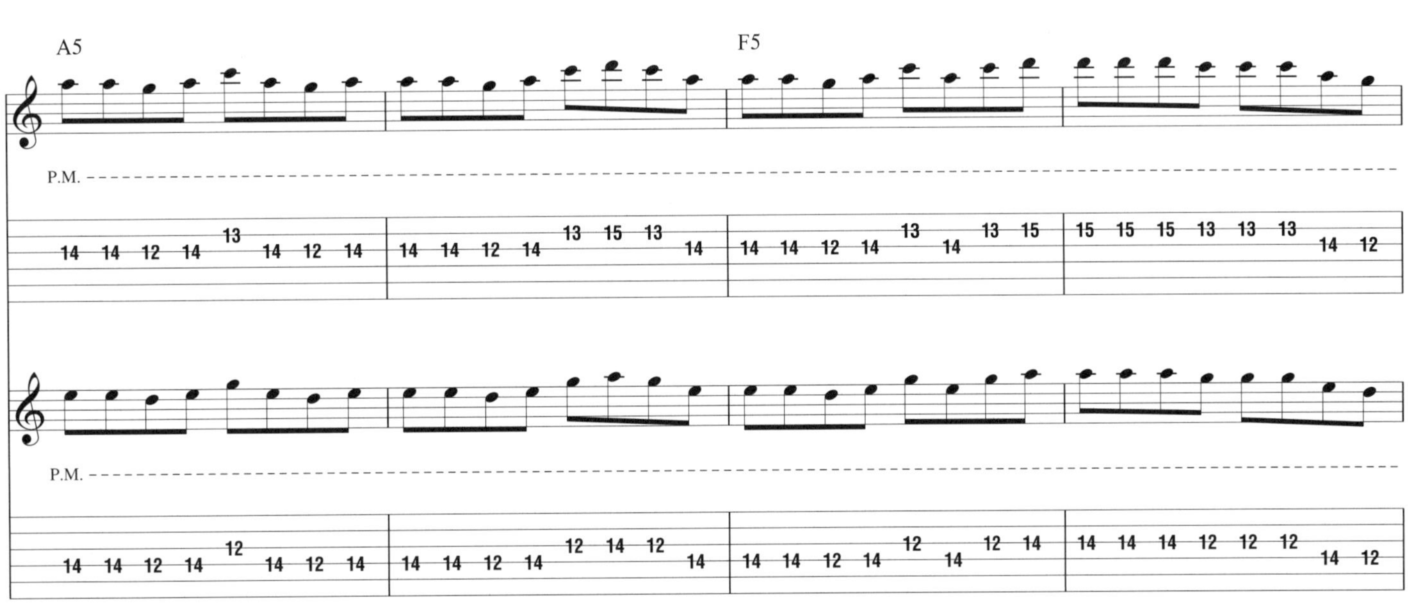
A5
F5
P.M.
P.M.

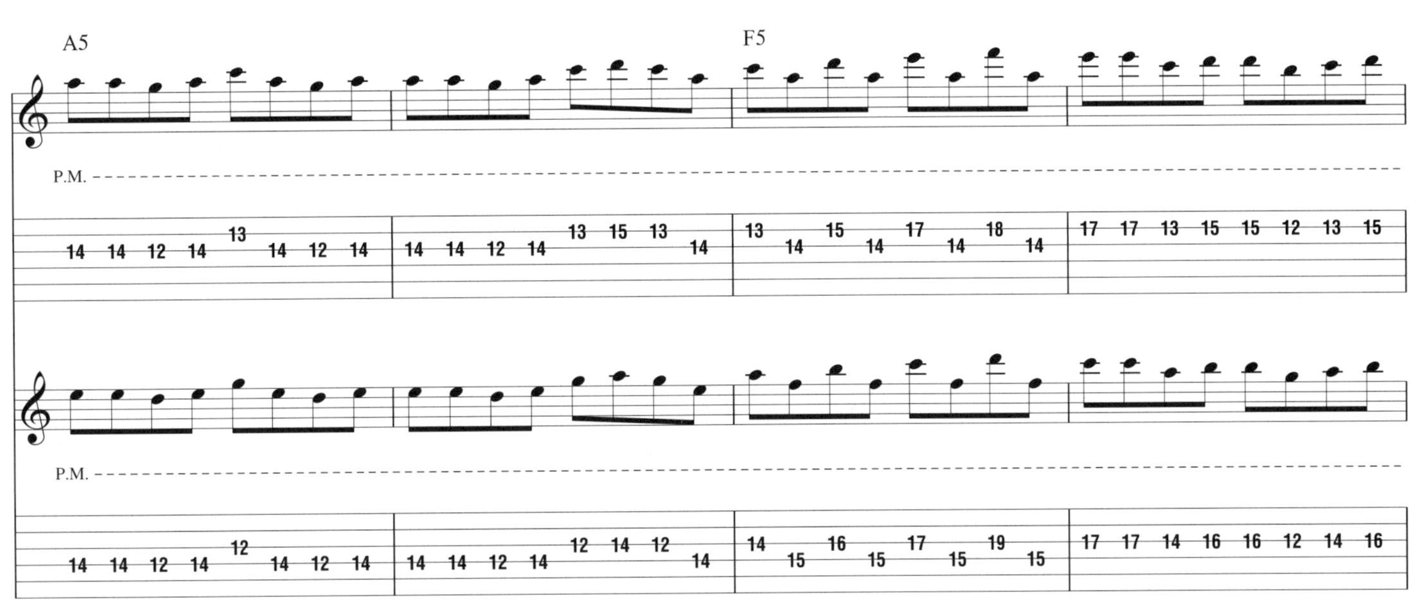
A5
F5
P.M.
P.M.

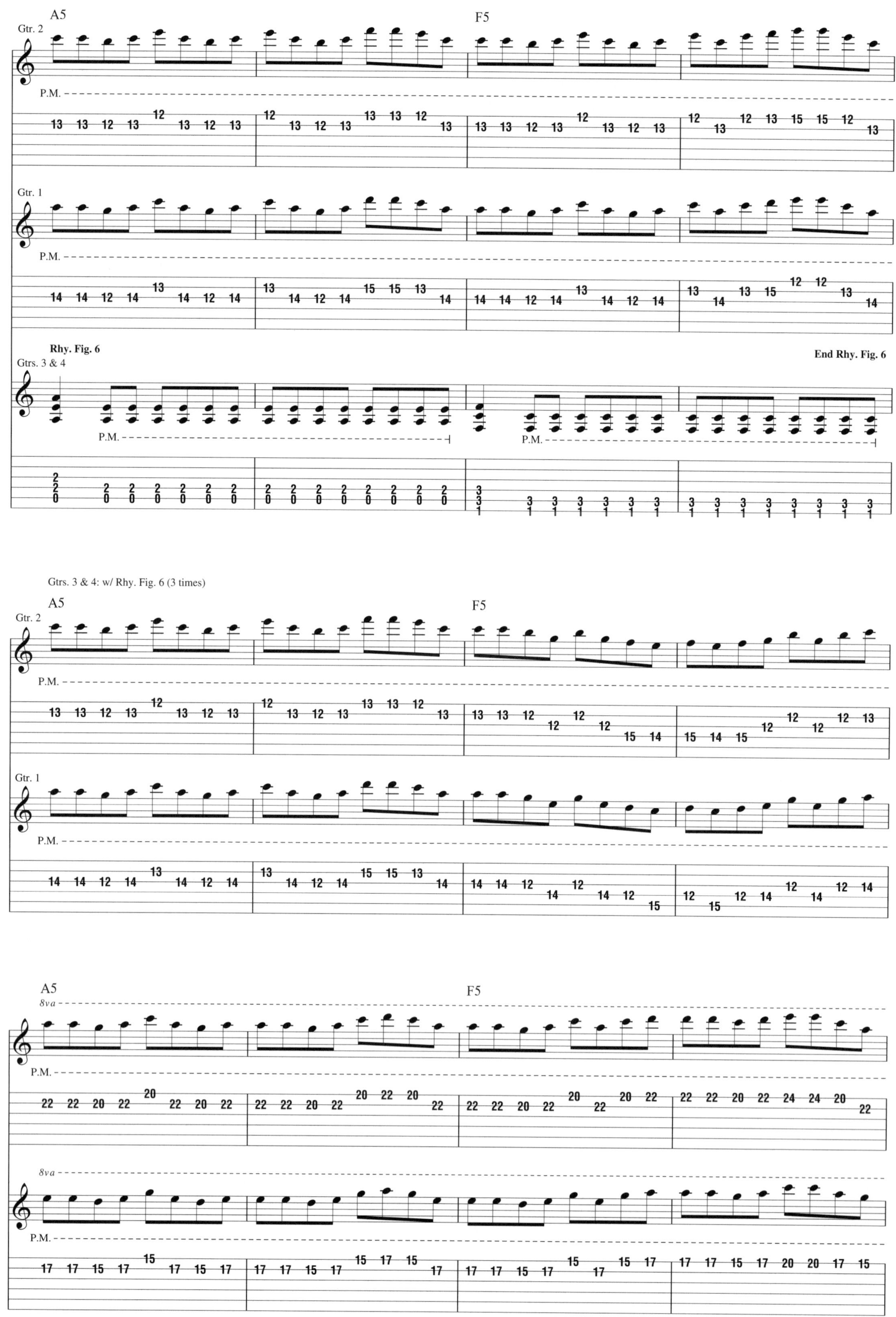
A5
F5
Gtr. 2
P.M.
Gtr. 1
P.M.
Rhy. Fig. 6
Gtrs. 3 & 4
End Rhy. Fig. 6
Gtrs. 3 & 4: w/ Rhy. Fig. 6 (3 times)
8va

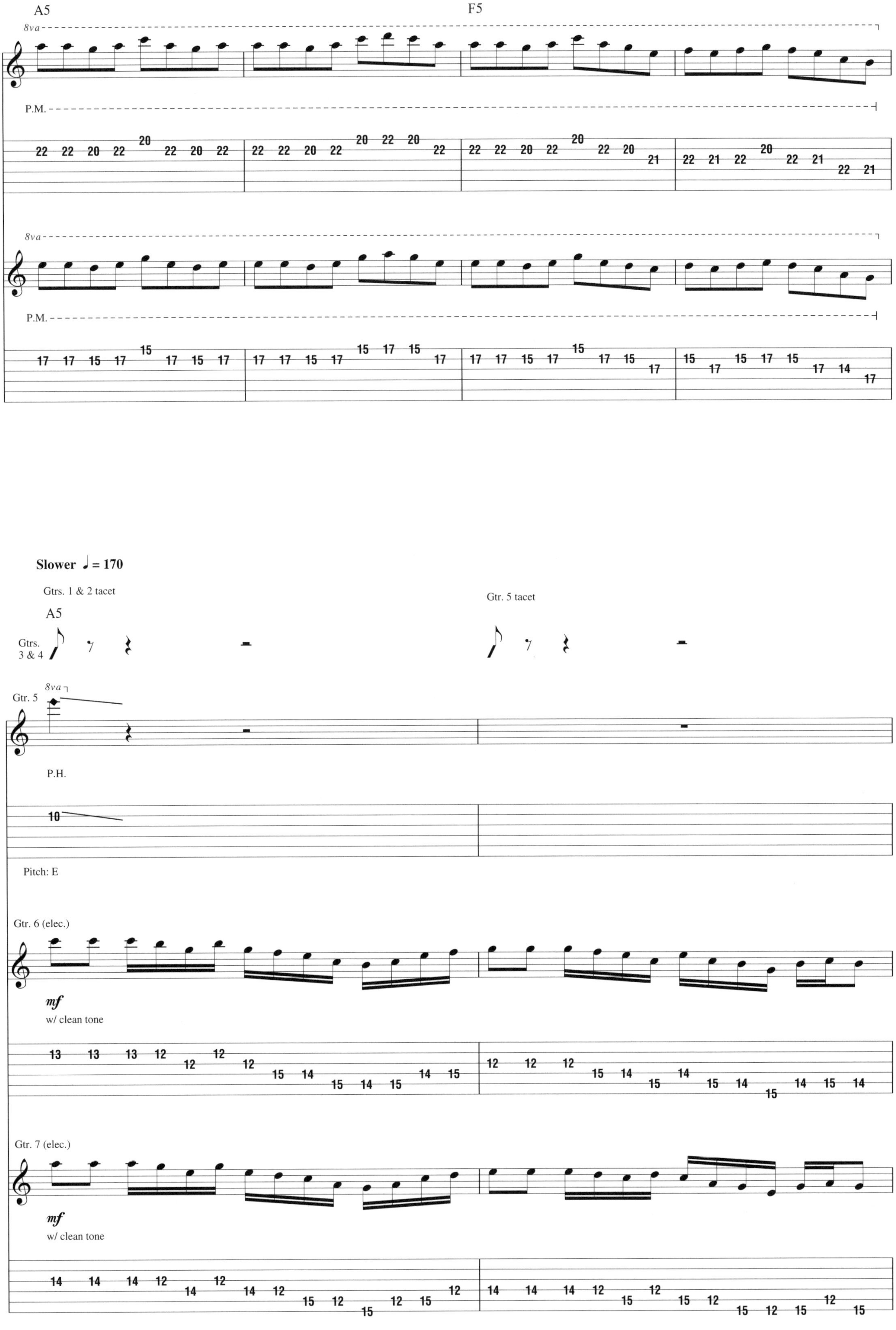

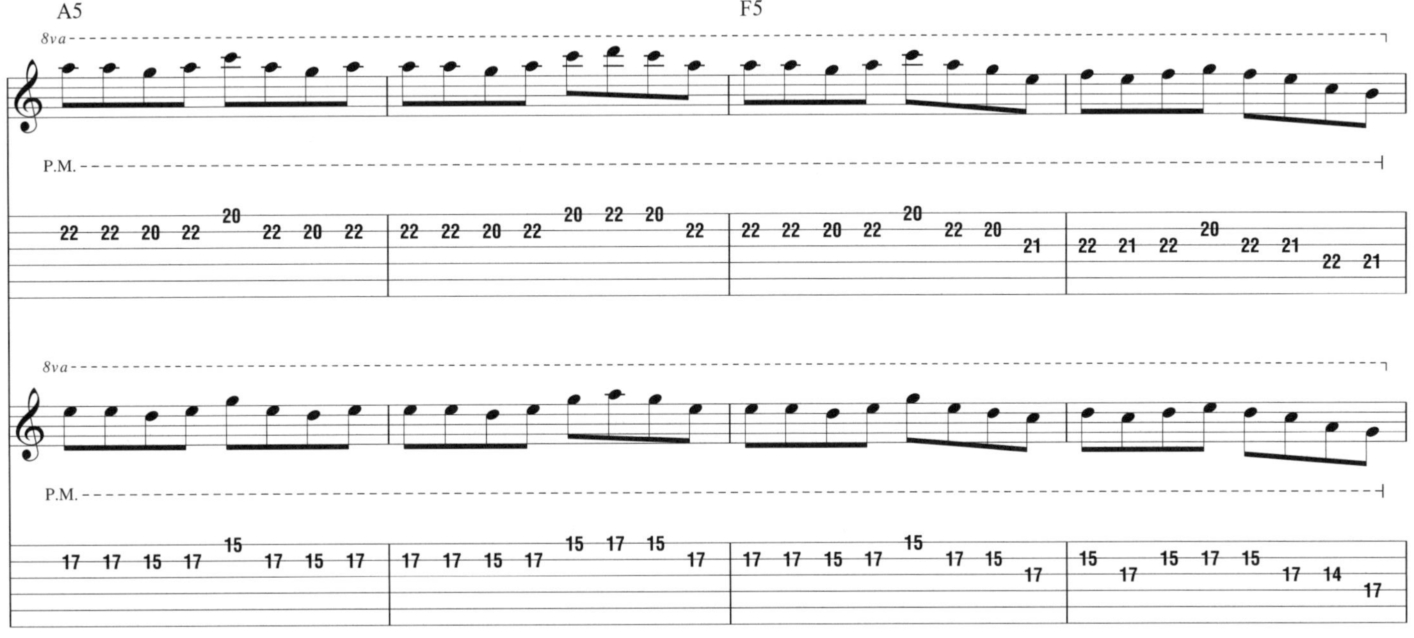

Slower ♩ = 170

Gtrs. 1 & 2 tacet

A5

Gtrs. 3 & 4

Gtr. 5 tacet

Gtr. 5

8va

P.H.

Pitch: E

Gtr. 6 (elec.)

mf

w/ clean tone

Gtr. 7 (elec.)

mf

w/ clean tone

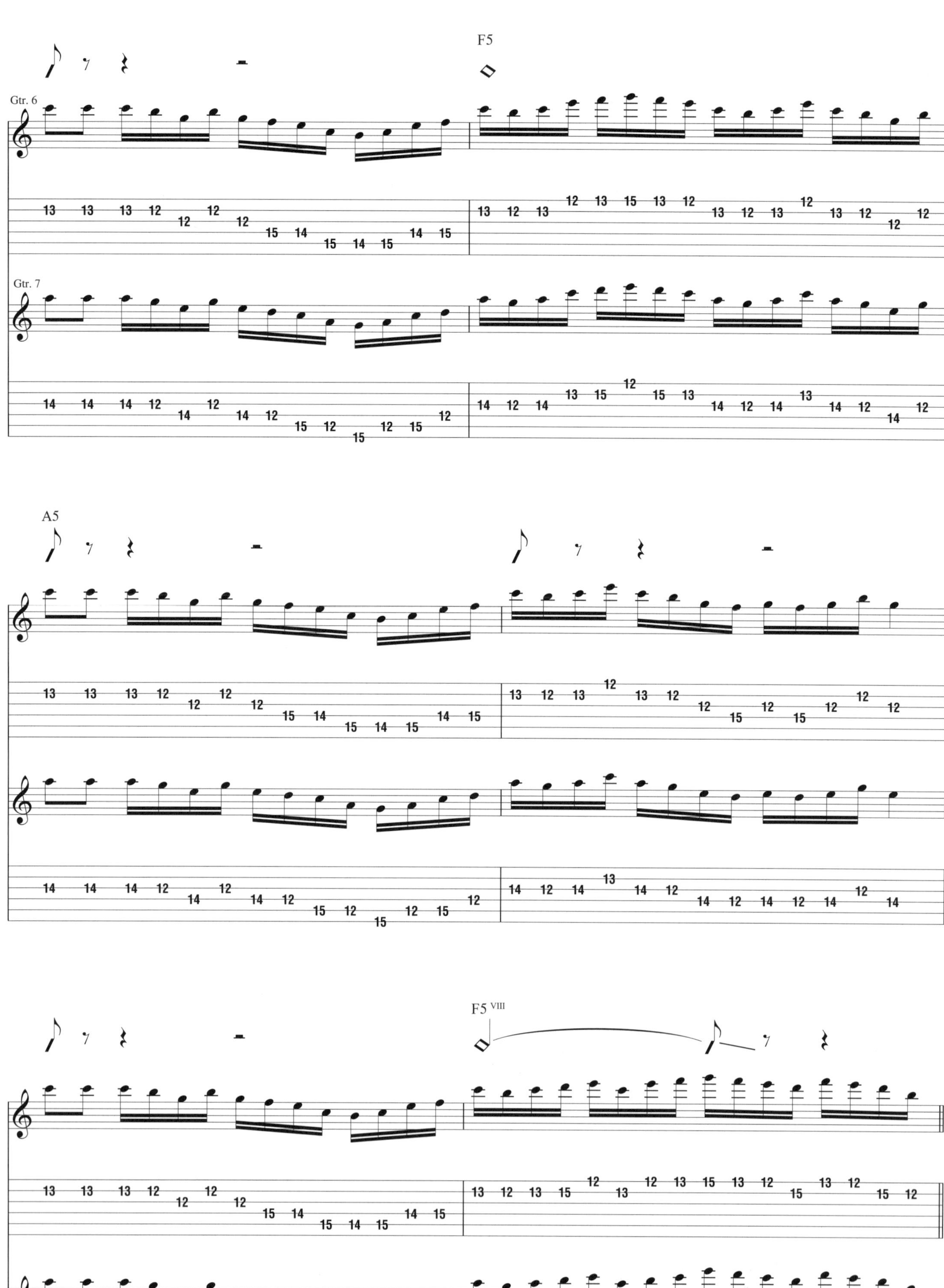
F5
Gtr. 6
Gtr. 7
A5
F5 VIII

Guitar Solo

Double-time feel

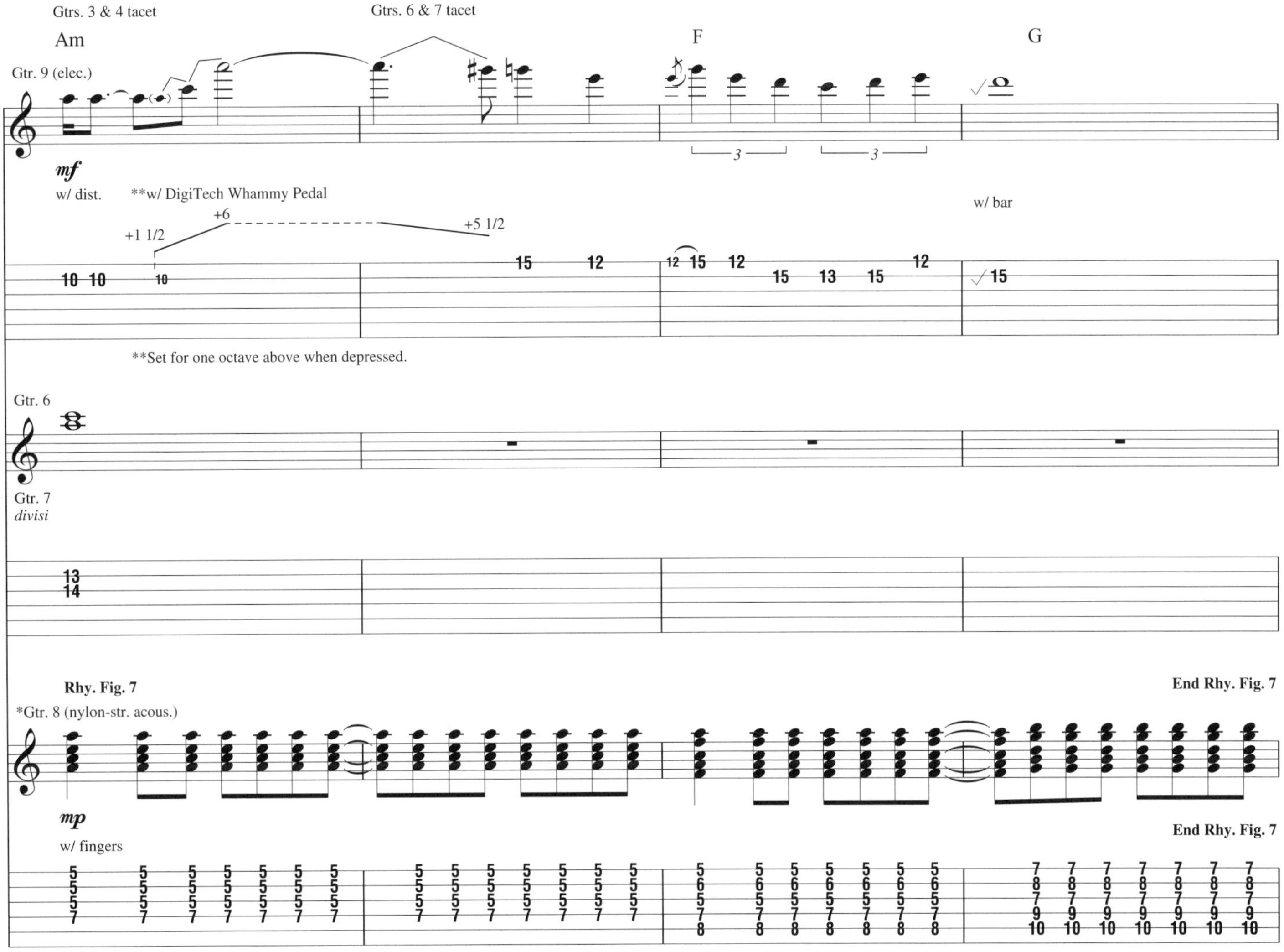

Gtrs. 3 & 4 tacet

Gtrs. 6 & 7 tacet

Am F G

Gtr. 9 (elec.)

mf

w/ dist. **w/ DigiTech Whammy Pedal

+1 1/2 +6 +5 1/2

w/ bar

**Set for one octave above when depressed.

Gtr. 6

Gtr. 7
divisi

Rhy. Fig. 7

*Gtr. 8 (nylon-str. acous.)

End Rhy. Fig. 7

mp

w/ fingers

End Rhy. Fig. 7

*Two gtrs. arr. for one.

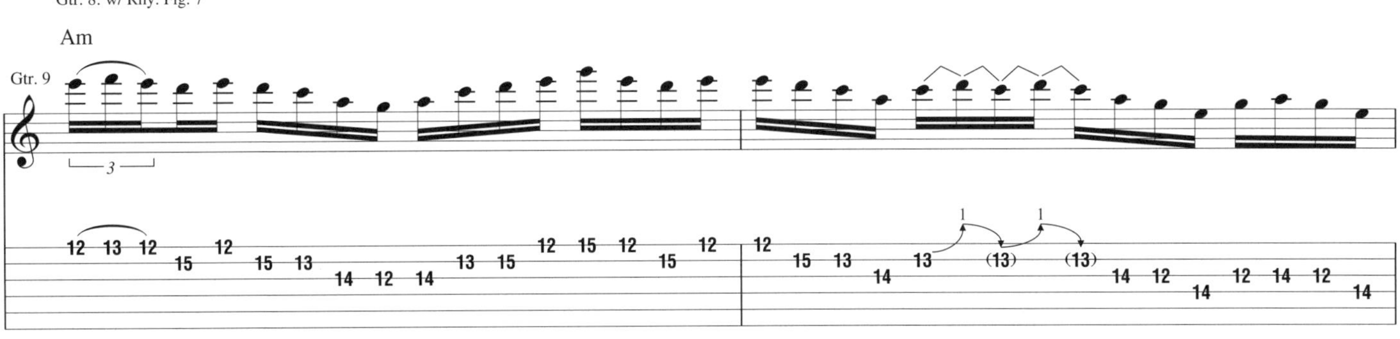

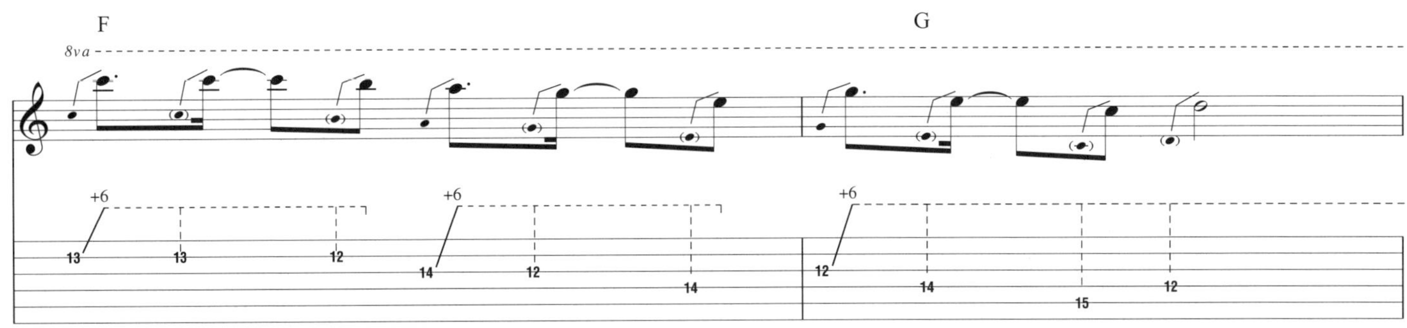

Am

8va

Gtr. 9

+6

8va

Gtr. 10 (elec.)

mf

w/ dist.

*w/ DigiTech Whammy Pedal

+6

*Set for one octave above when depressed.

Rhy. Fig. 8

Gtr. 8

C

G

8va

+6

8va

+6

End Rhy. Fig. 8

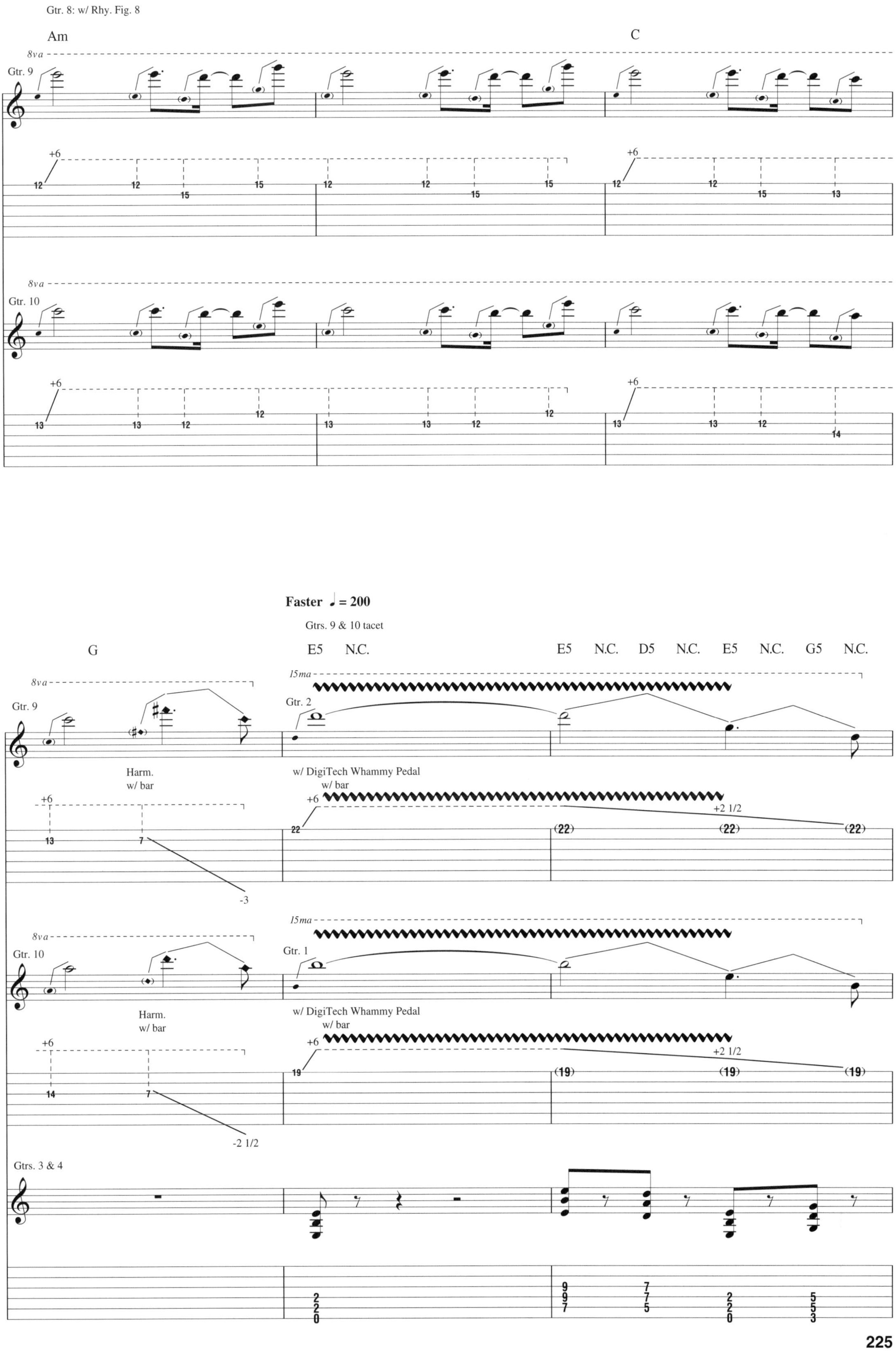

Gtr. 8: w/ Rhy. Fig. 8

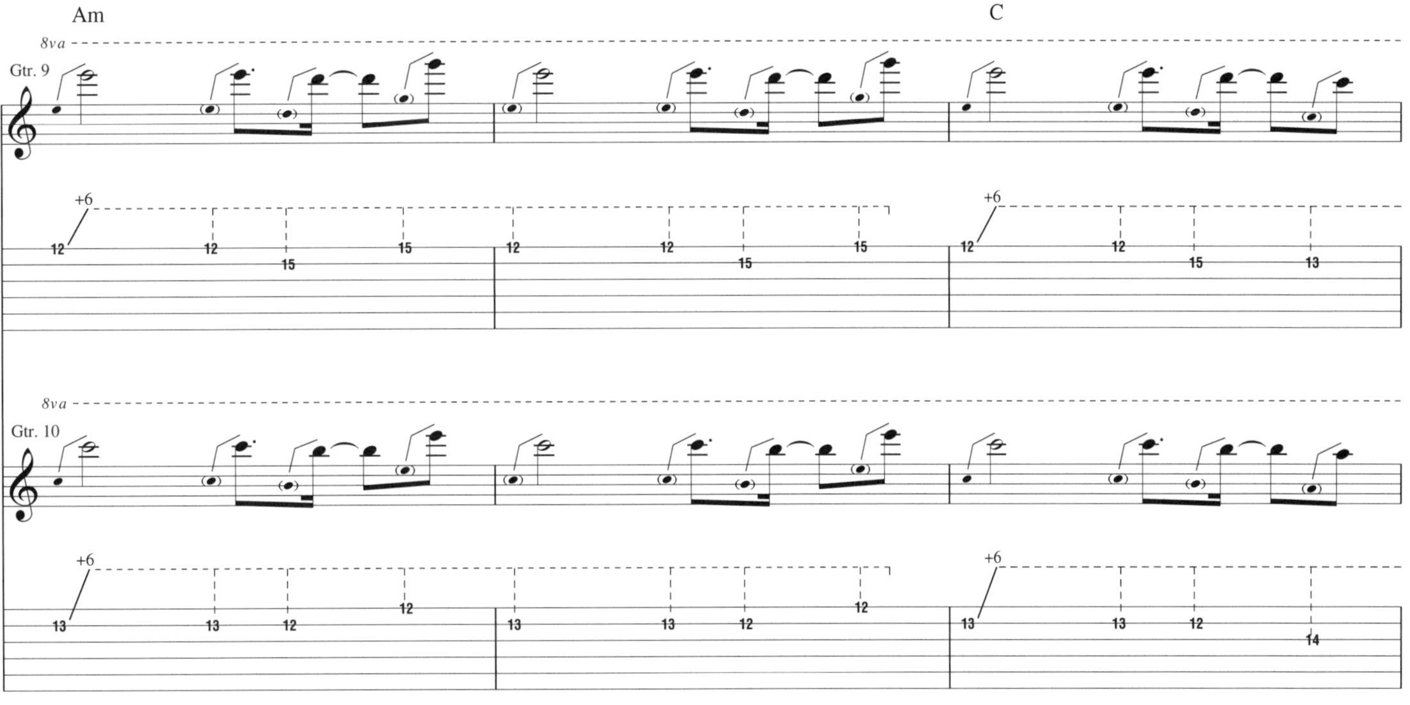

Faster ♩ = 200

Gtrs. 9 & 10 tacet

G E5 N.C. E5 N.C. D5 N.C. E5 N.C. G5 N.C.

8va

15ma

Gtr. 9

Gtr. 2

Harm.
w/ bar

w/ DigiTech Whammy Pedal
w/ bar

+6 +6 +2 1/2

-3

15ma

8va

Gtr. 10

Gtr. 1

Harm.
w/ bar

w/ DigiTech Whammy Pedal
w/ bar

+6 +6 +2 1/2

-2 1/2

Gtrs. 3 & 4

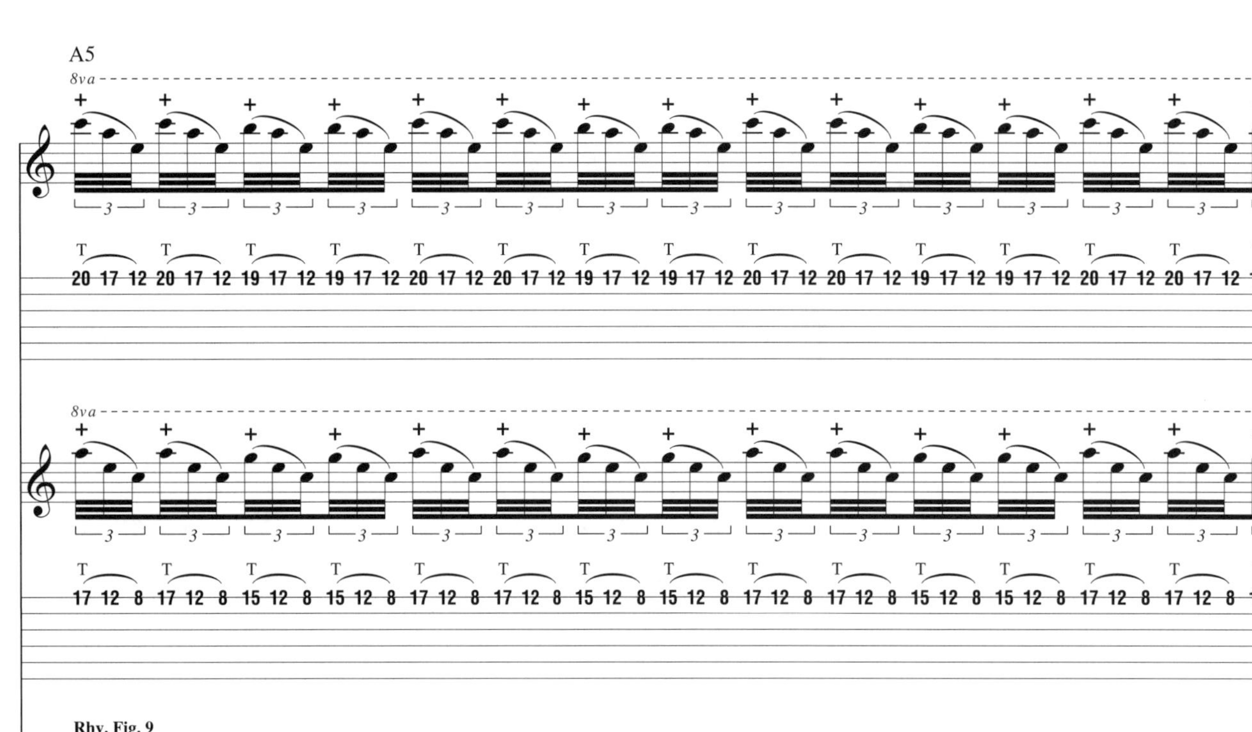

8va

20 17 12 20 17 12 24 17 12 24 17 12 20 17 12 20 17 12 24 17 12 24 17 12 20 17 12 20 17 12 24 17 12 24 17 12 20 17 12 20 17 12 24 17 12 24 17 12

8va

17 12 8 17 12 8 20 12 8 20 12 8 17 12 8 17 12 8 20 12 8 20 12 8 17 12 8 17 12 8 20 12 8 20 12 8 17 12 8 17 12 8 20 12 8 20 12 8

P.M.

5 5 5 5 5 5 5 5 5 5 5 5 5/3 7/5

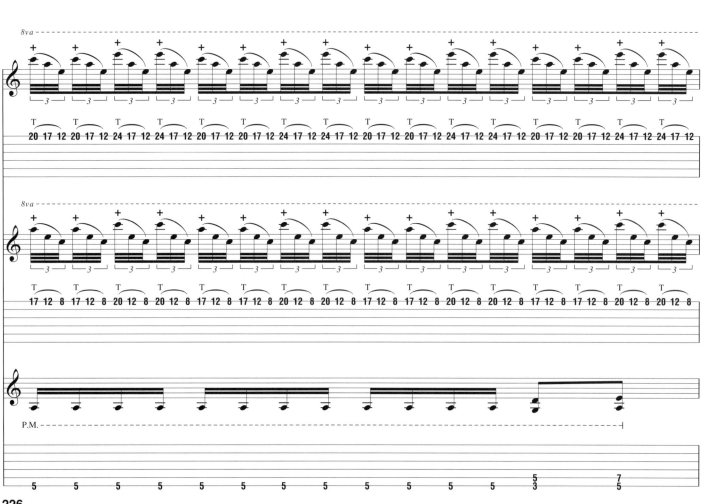

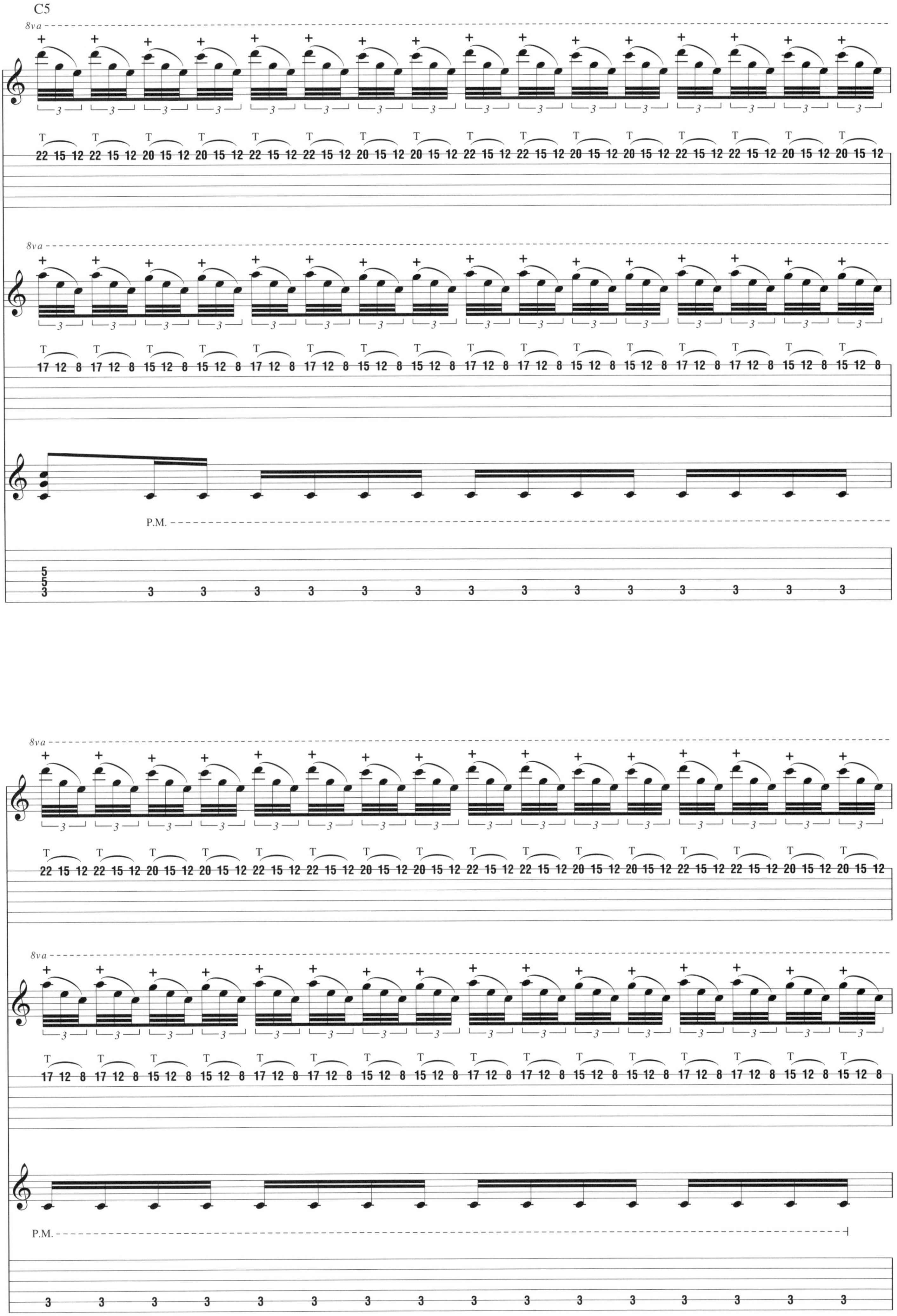

C5

8va

T T T T T T T T T T T T T T T T

22 15 12 22 15 12 20 15 12 20 15 12 22 15 12 22 15 12 20 15 12 20 15 12 22 15 12 22 15 12 20 15 12 20 15 12 22 15 12 22 15 12 20 15 12 20 15 12

8va

T T T T T T T T T T T T T T T T

17 12 8 17 12 8 15 12 8 15 12 8 17 12 8 17 12 8 15 12 8 15 12 8 17 12 8 17 12 8 15 12 8 15 12 8 17 12 8 17 12 8 15 12 8 15 12 8

P.M.

5
5
3 3 3 3 3 3 3 3 3 3 3 3 3 3 3 3

8va

T T T T T T T T T T T T T T T T

22 15 12 22 15 12 20 15 12 20 15 12 22 15 12 22 15 12 20 15 12 20 15 12 22 15 12 22 15 12 20 15 12 20 15 12 22 15 12 22 15 12 20 15 12 20 15 12

8va

T T T T T T T T T T T T T T T T

17 12 8 17 12 8 15 12 8 15 12 8 17 12 8 17 12 8 15 12 8 15 12 8 17 12 8 17 12 8 15 12 8 15 12 8 17 12 8 17 12 8 15 12 8 15 12 8

P.M.

3 3 3 3 3 3 3 3 3 3 3 3 3 3 3 3

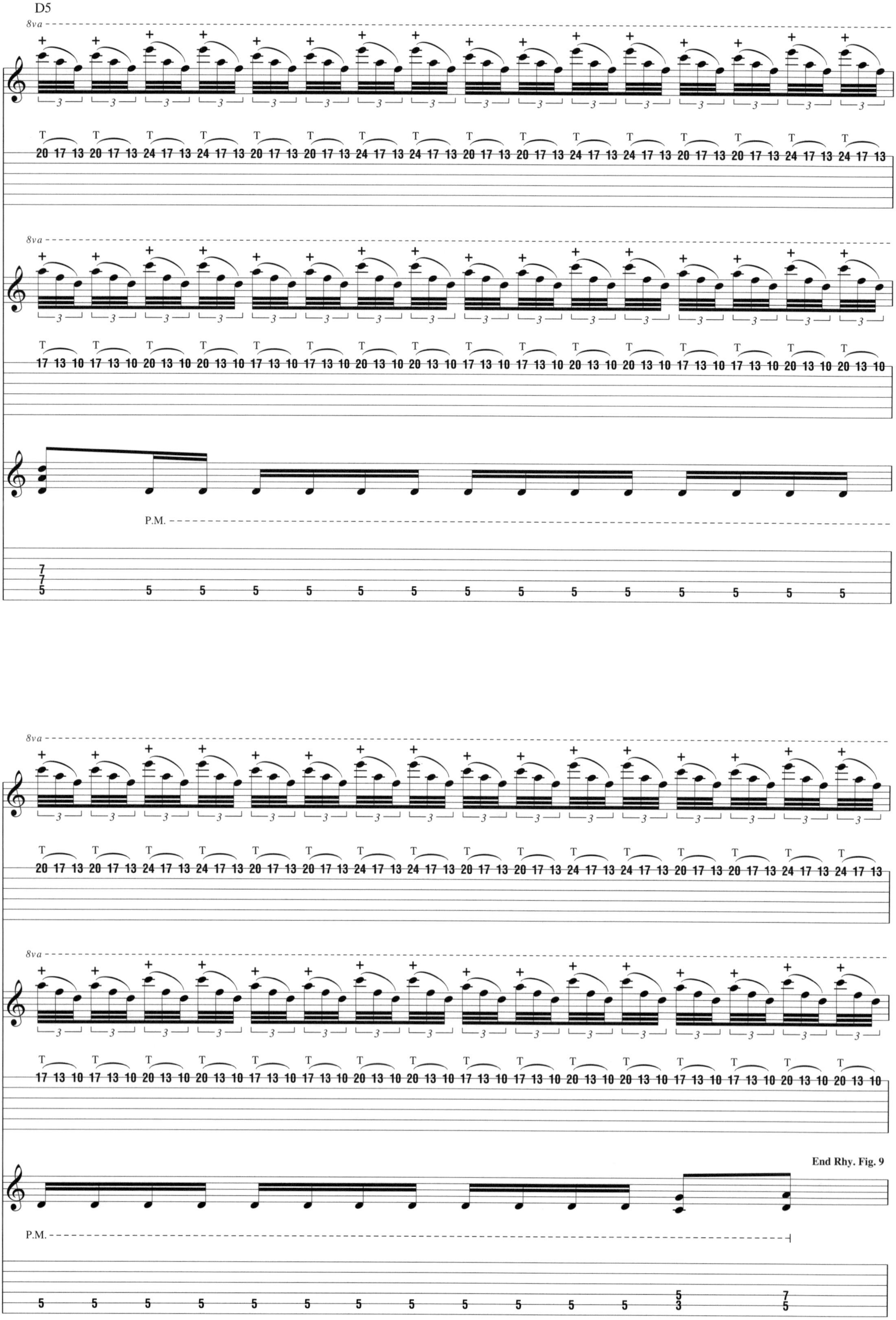

D5
8va
P.M.
End Rhy. Fig. 9

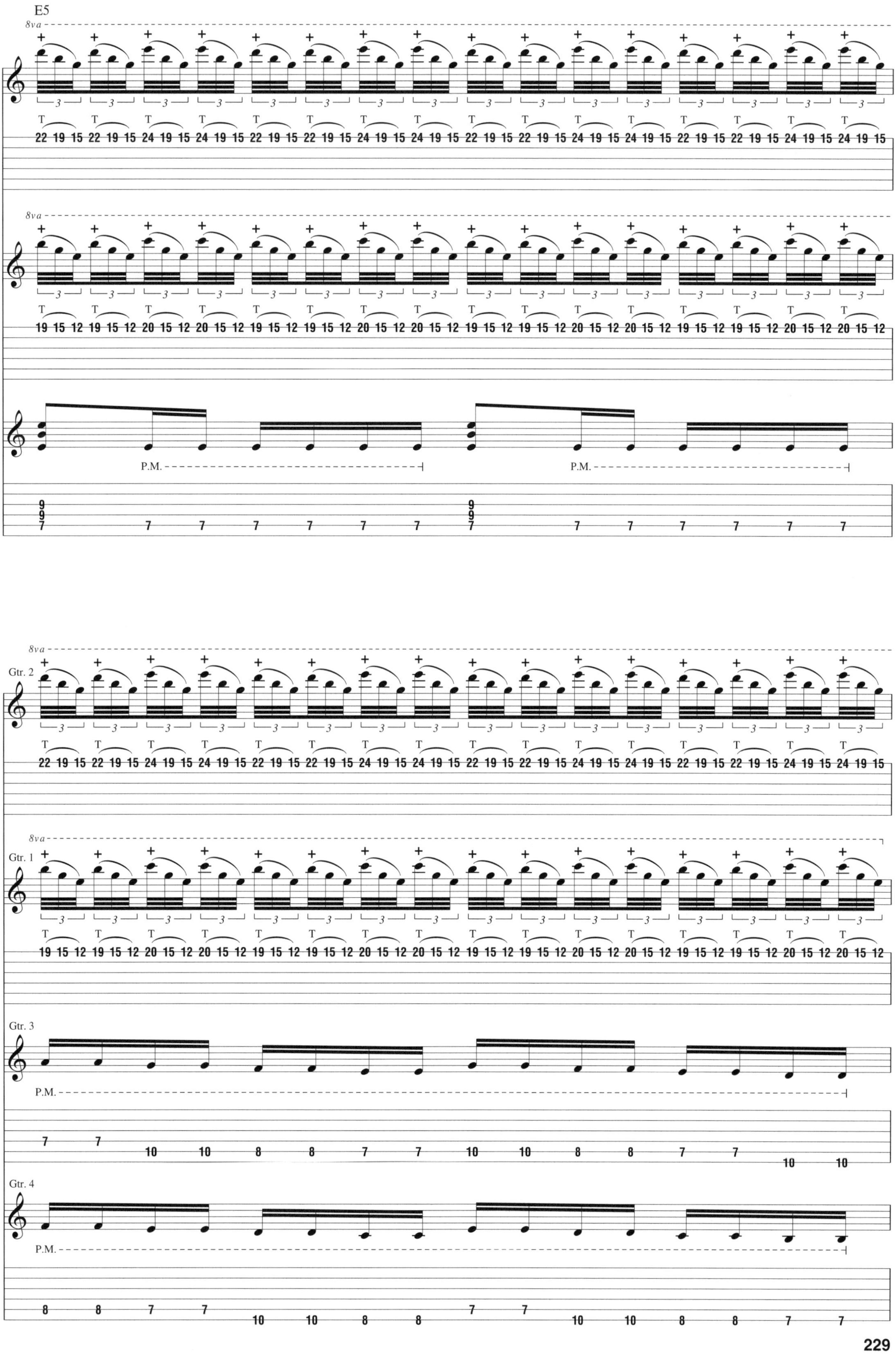

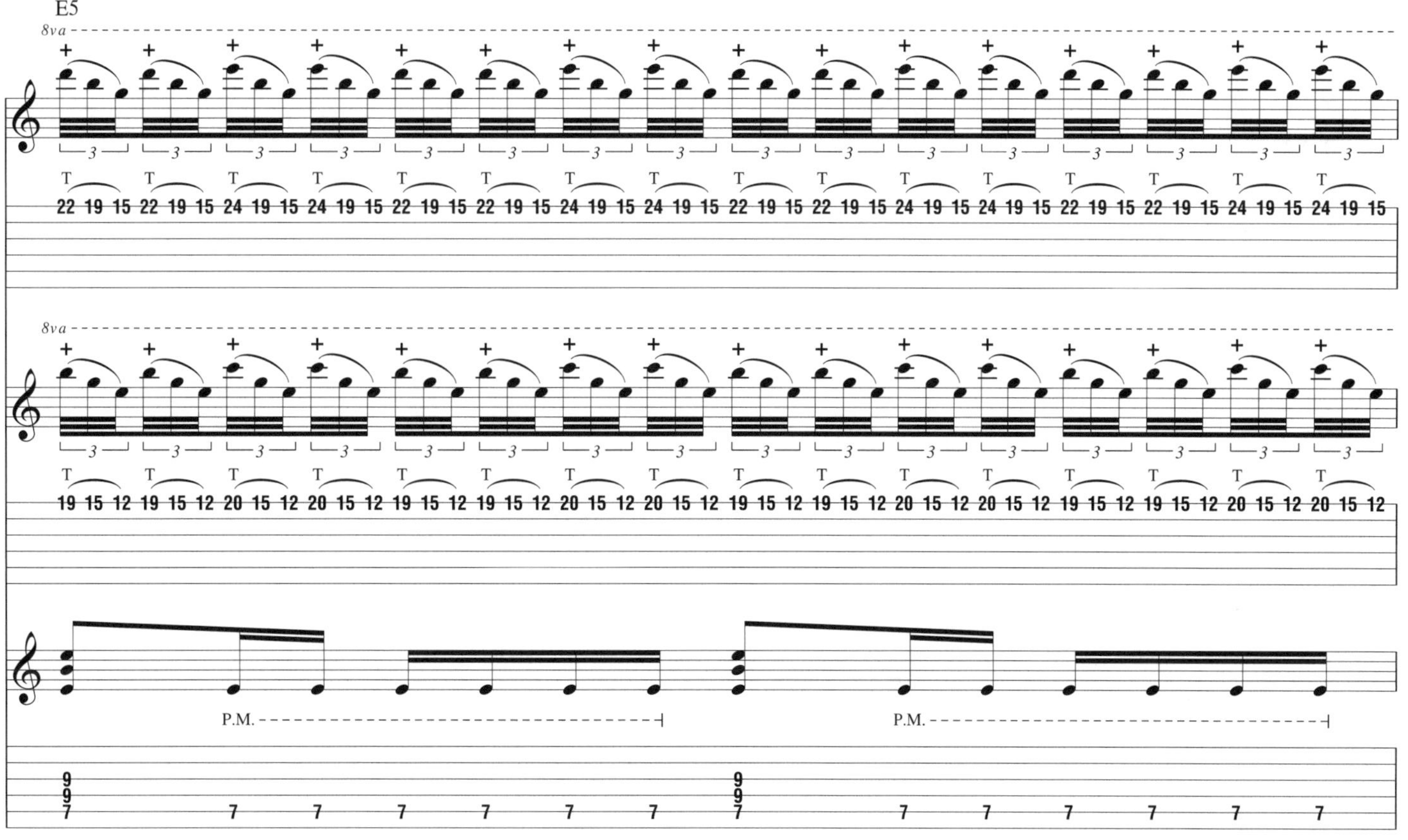

8va

Gtr. 2

T

22 19 15 22 19 15 24 19 15 24 19 15 22 19 15 22 19 15 24 19 15 24 19 15 22 19 15 22 19 15 24 19 15 24 19 15 22 19 15 22 19 15 24 19 15 24 19 15

8va

Gtr. 1

T

19 15 12 19 15 12 20 15 12 20 15 12 19 15 12 19 15 12 20 15 12 20 15 12 19 15 12 19 15 12 20 15 12 20 15 12 19 15 12 19 15 12 20 15 12 20 15 12

Gtr. 3

P.M.

7 7 10 10 8 8 7 7 10 10 8 8 7 7 10 10

Gtr. 4

P.M.

8 8 7 7 10 10 8 8 7 7 10 10 8 8 7 7

Gtrs. 3 & 4: w/ Rhy. Fig. 9
A5
8va
Gtr. 2
P.M.
Gtr. 1
loco

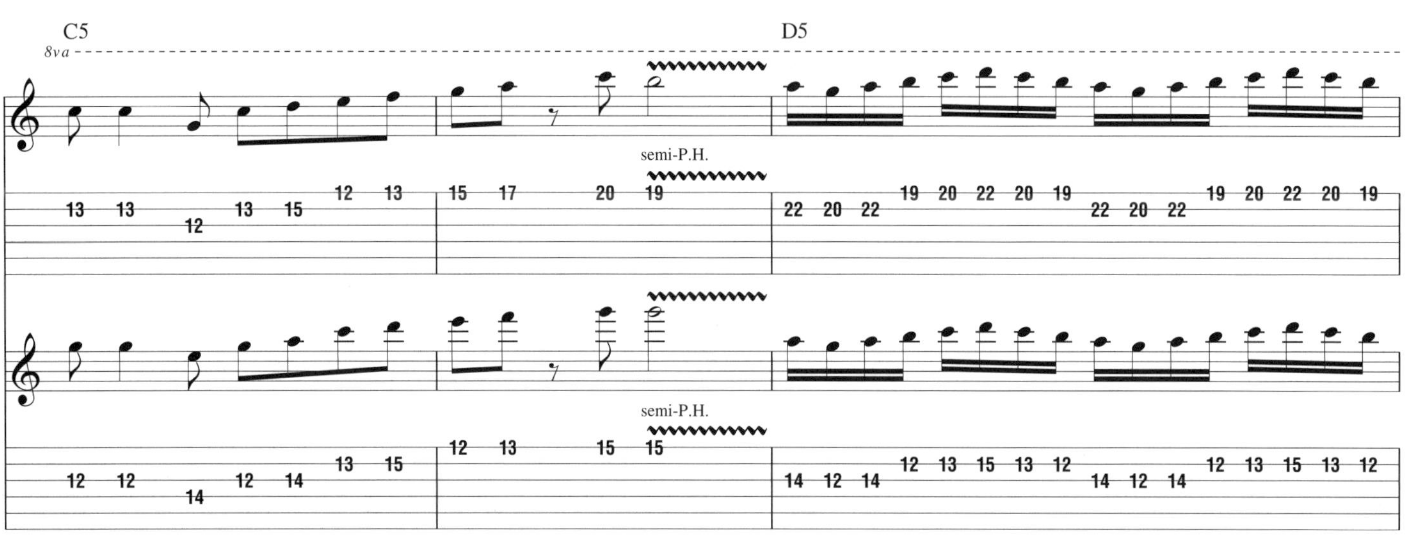
C5
D5
8va
semi-P.H.

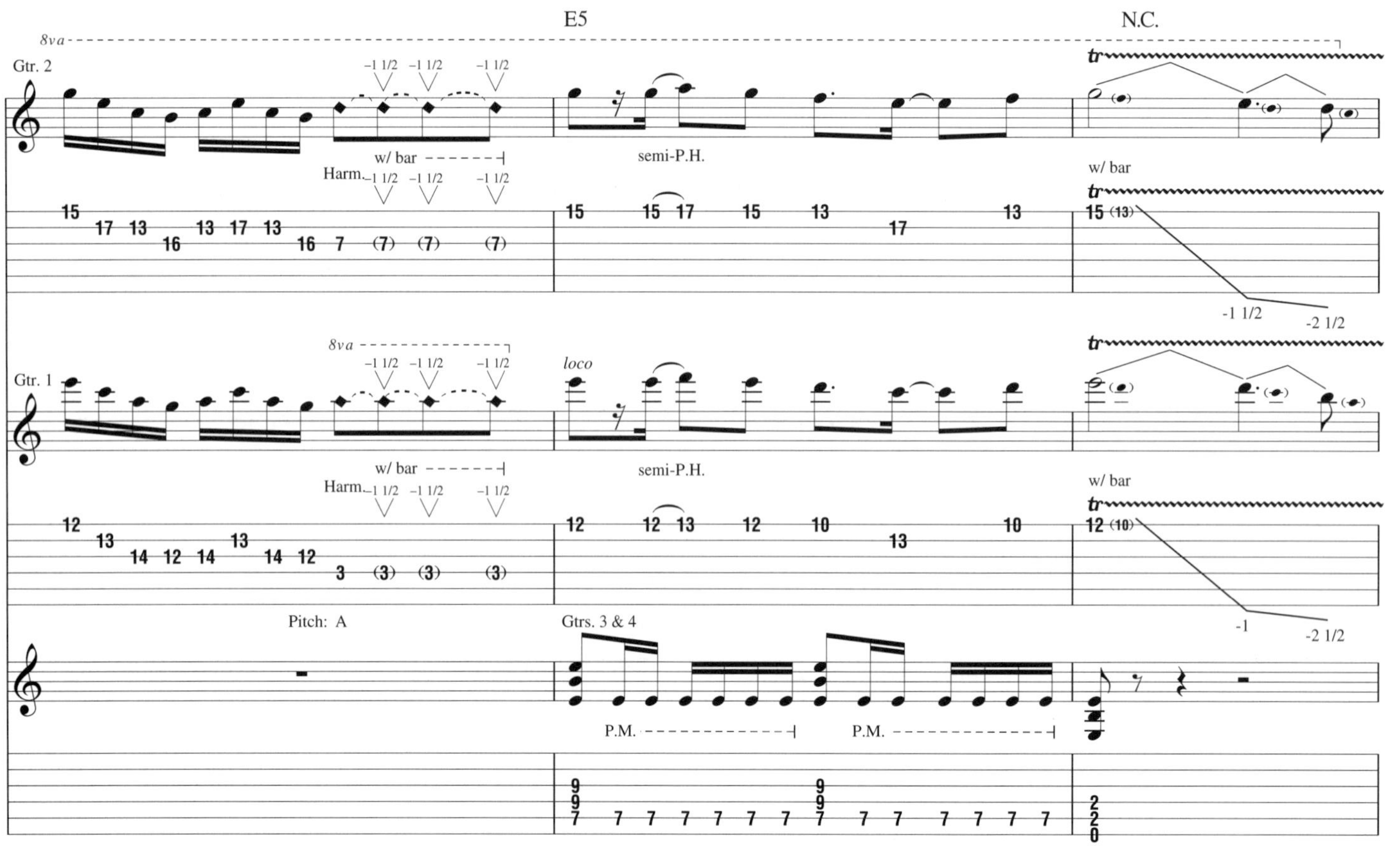
E5
N.C.
8va
Gtr. 2
w/ bar
Harm.
semi-P.H.
Gtr. 1
loco
Pitch: A
Gtrs. 3 & 4
P.M.

Gtrs. 1-4 tacet
Am
C
G
Gtr. 6

Am
F

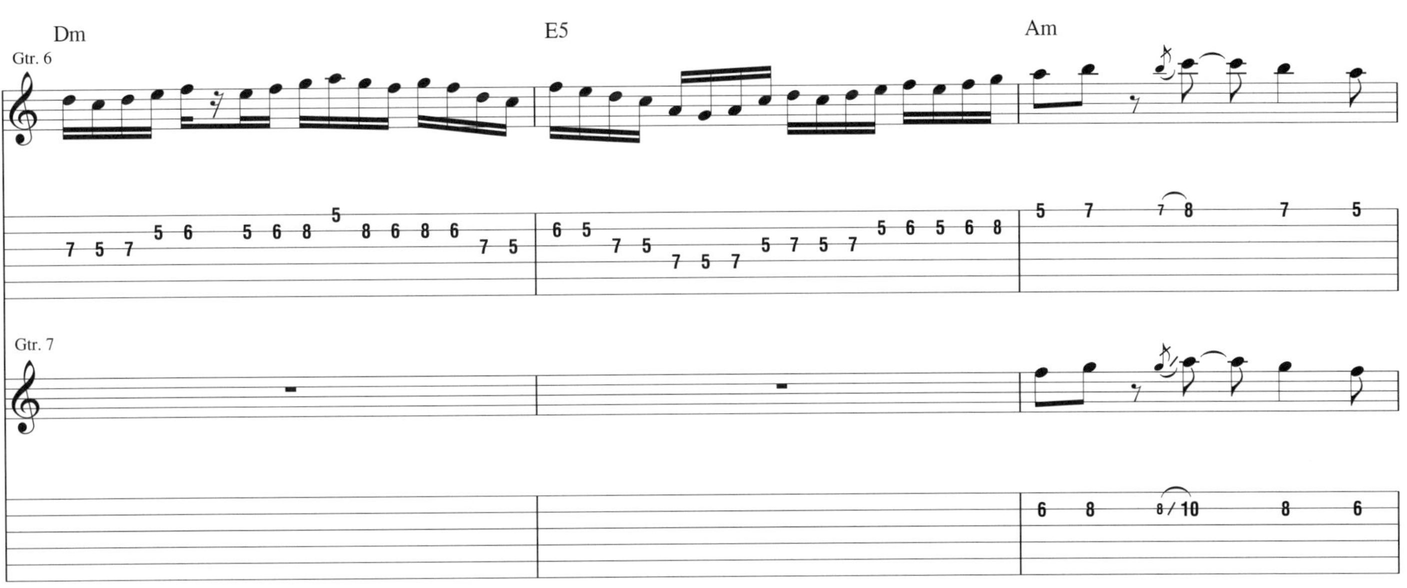
Dm
E5
Am
Gtr. 6
Gtr. 7

C
G
Am

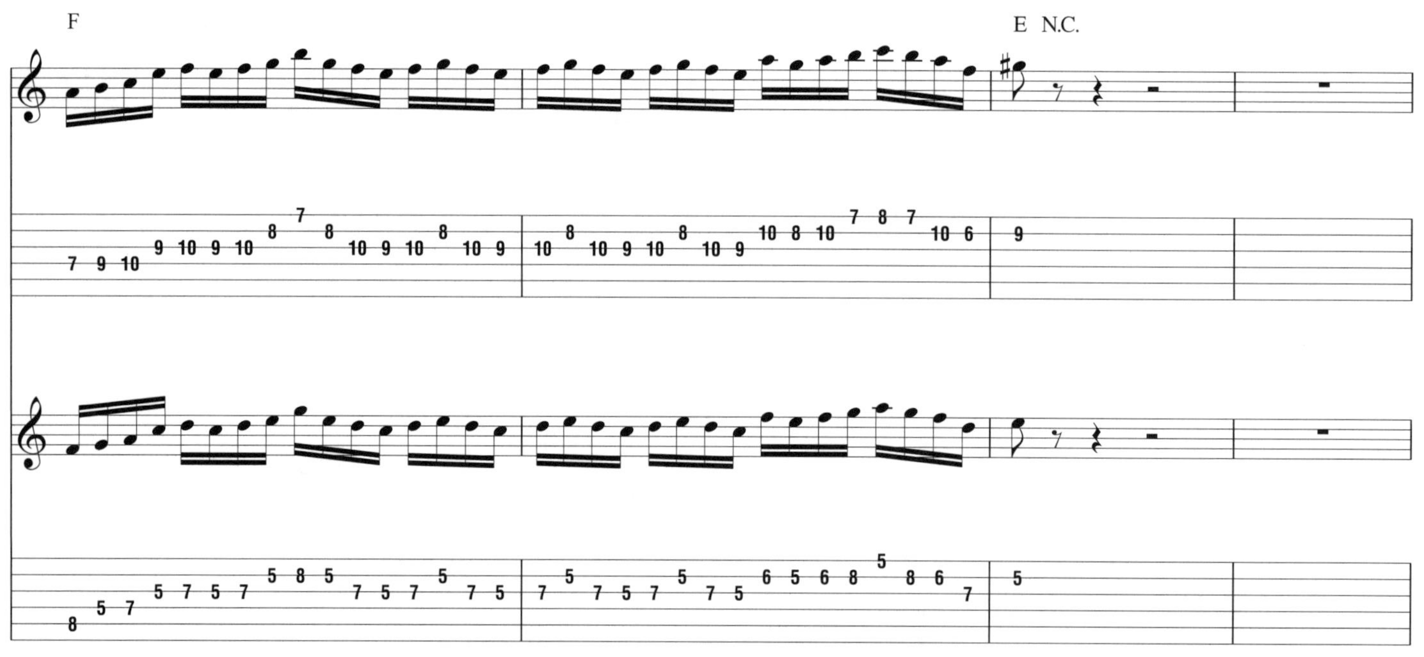

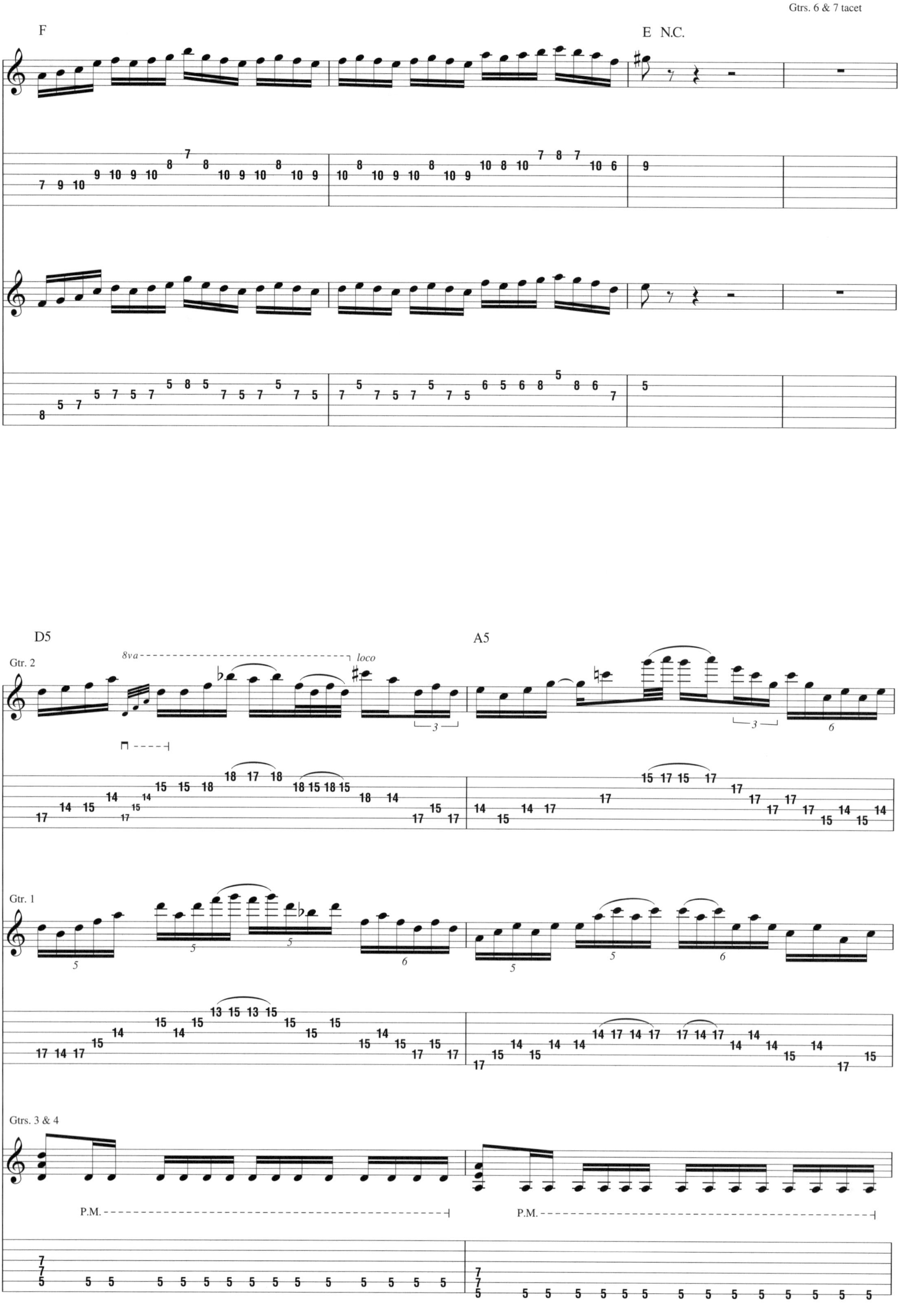

D5
A5

Gtr. 2

8va
loco

Gtr. 1

Gtrs. 3 & 4

P.M.
P.M.

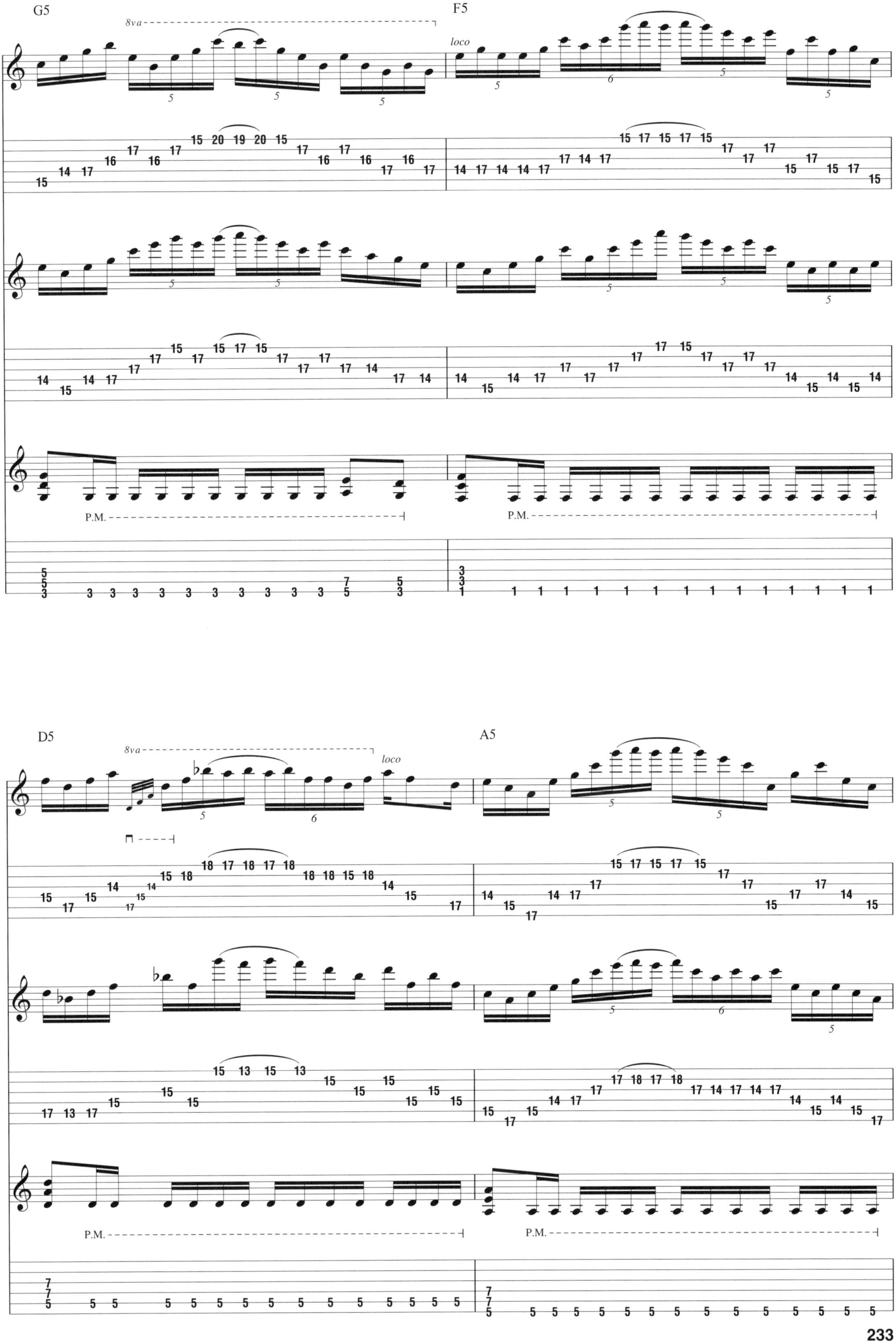

G5 *8va* F5 *loco*

P.M. P.M.

D5 *8va* *loco* A5

P.M. P.M.

F5
E5
G5
A5
8va
Harm.
w/ DigiTech Whammy Pedal
w/ bar
Pitch: G
15ma
Pitch: E
P.M.
(cont. in slashes)
C5
Gtrs. 3 & 4
Gtr. 2
Gtr. 1
Gtrs. 1 & 2
(cont. in notation)

Gtr. 2

8va

Gtrs. 1 & 2

(Gtr. 1, cont. in lower staff)

Gtr. 1

8va

Gtr. 4

(cont. in lower staff)

Gtr. 3

Gtrs. 3 & 4

C5

G5

8va

15ma

8va

A5

15ma

8va

15ma

P.M.

P.M.

E5

15ma

15ma

P.M.

P.M.

P.M.

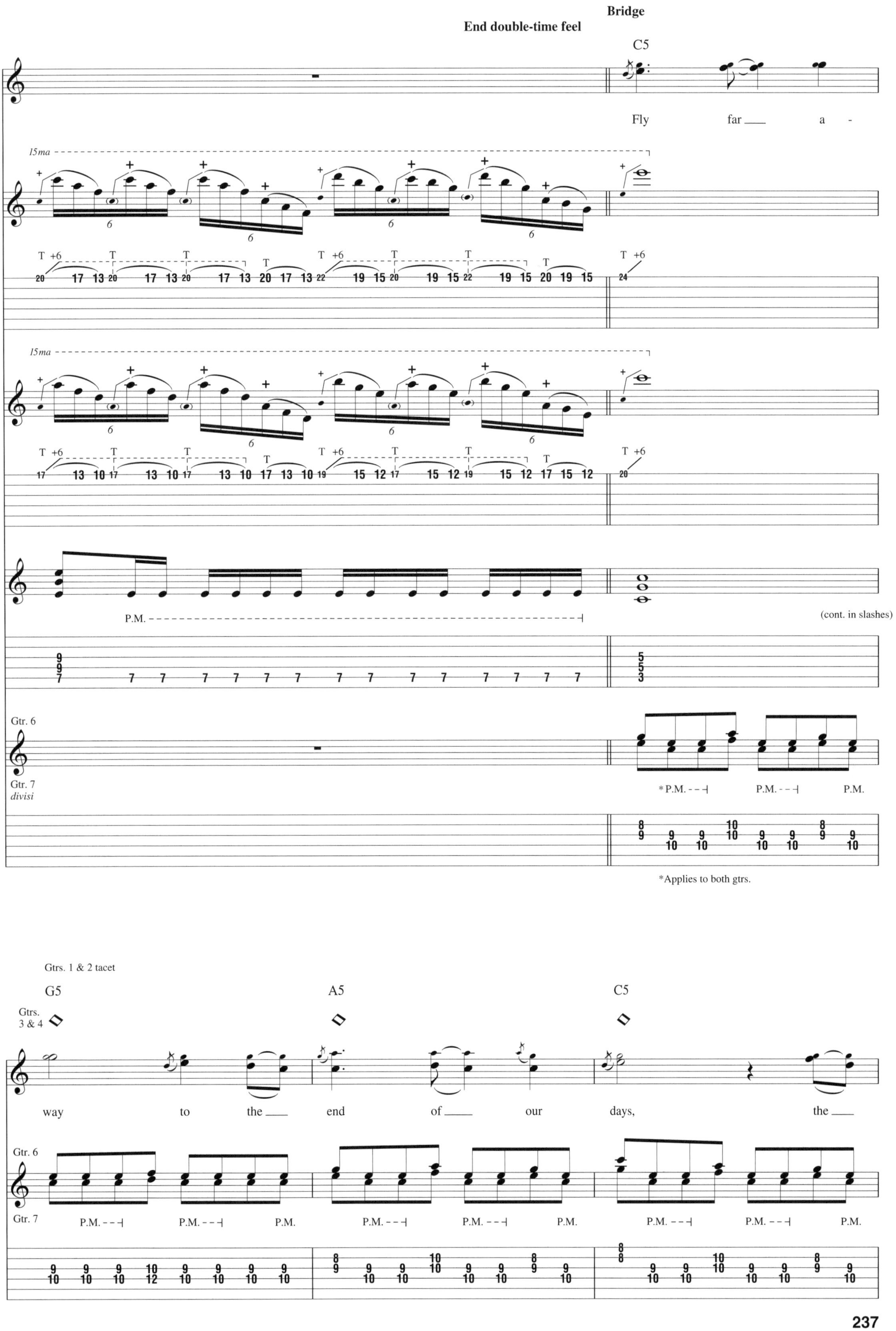

Bridge

End double-time feel

C5

Fly far a -

P.M.

(cont. in slashes)

Gtr. 6

Gtr. 7
divisi

*P.M. P.M. P.M.

*Applies to both gtrs.

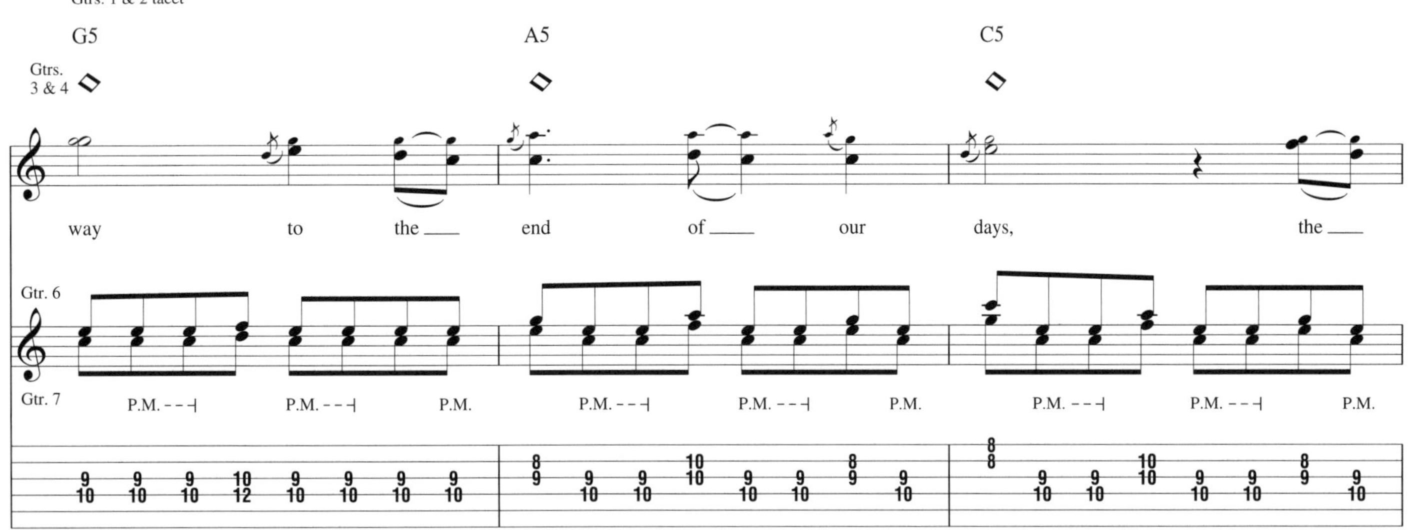

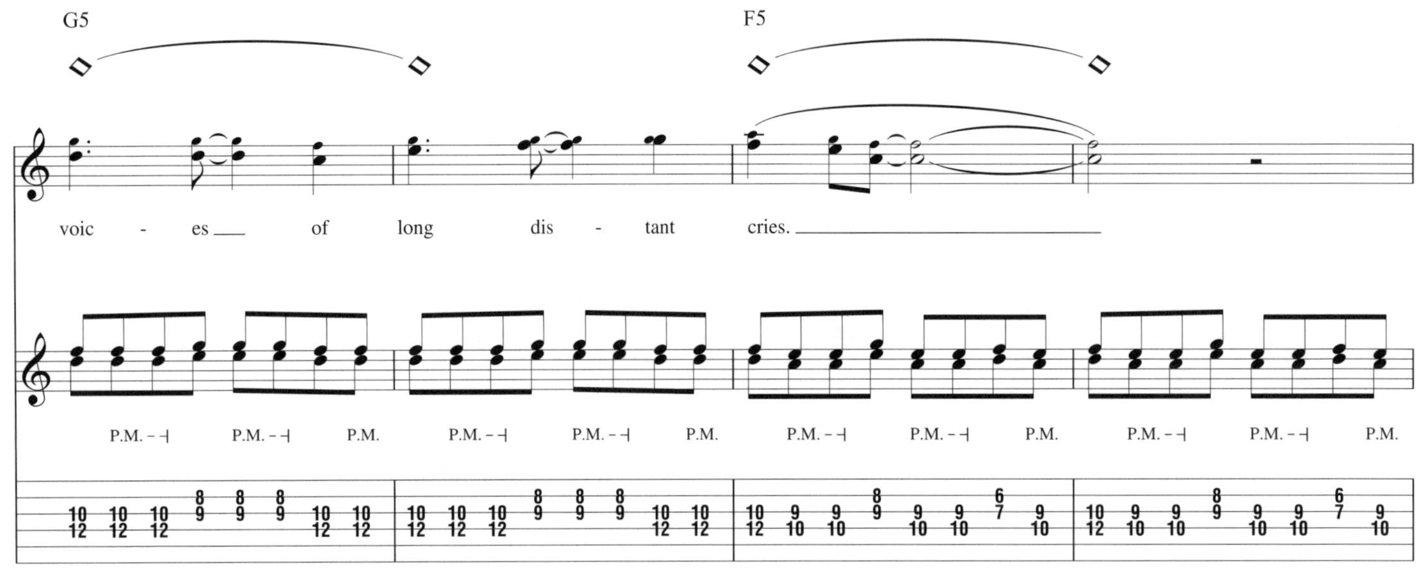
G5
F5
voic - es ___ of long dis - tant cries. ___
P.M.

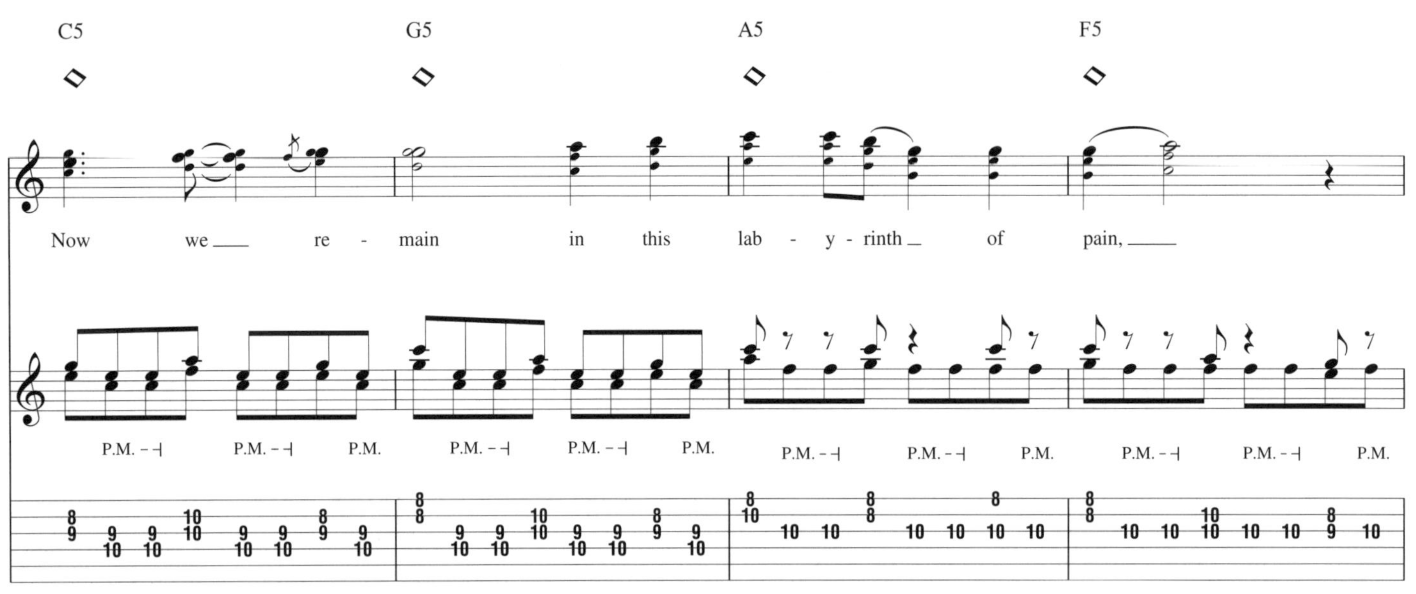
C5
G5
A5
F5
Now we ___ re - main in this lab - y - rinth ___ of pain, ___
P.M.

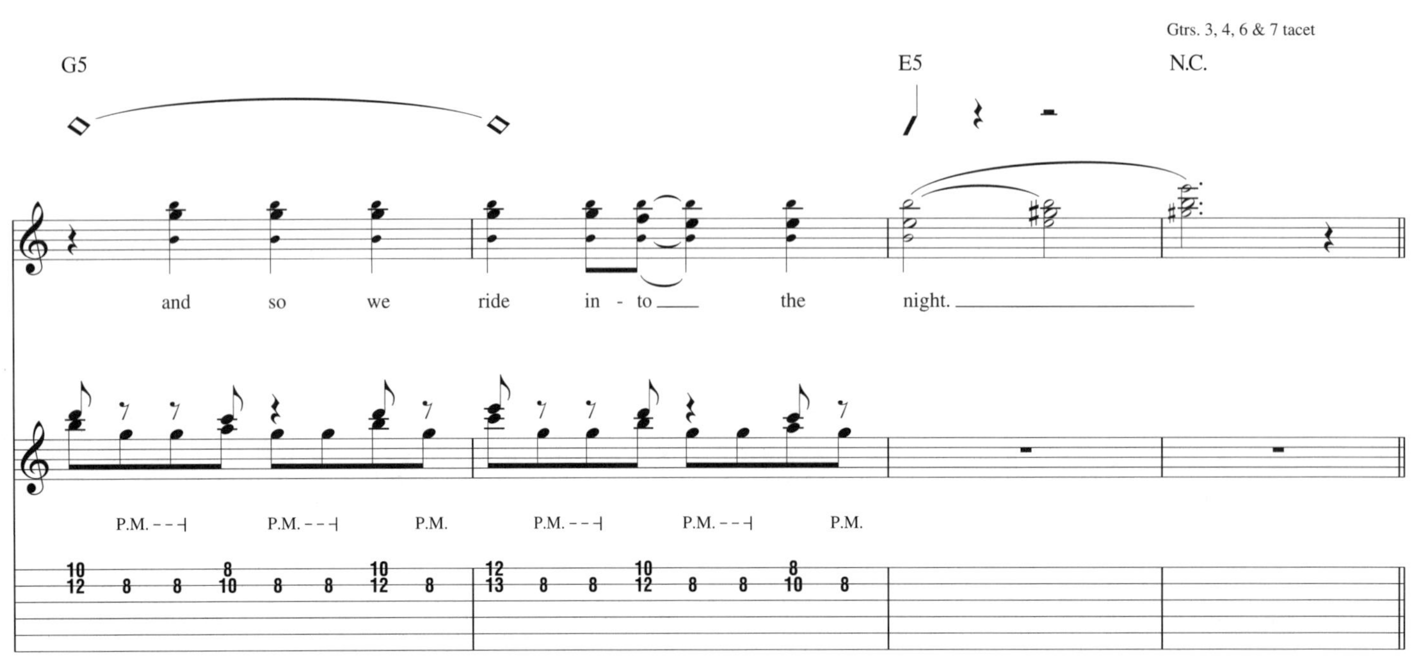
Gtrs. 3, 4, 6 & 7 tacet
G5
E5
N.C.
and so we ride in - to ___ the night. ___
P.M.

Pre-Chorus

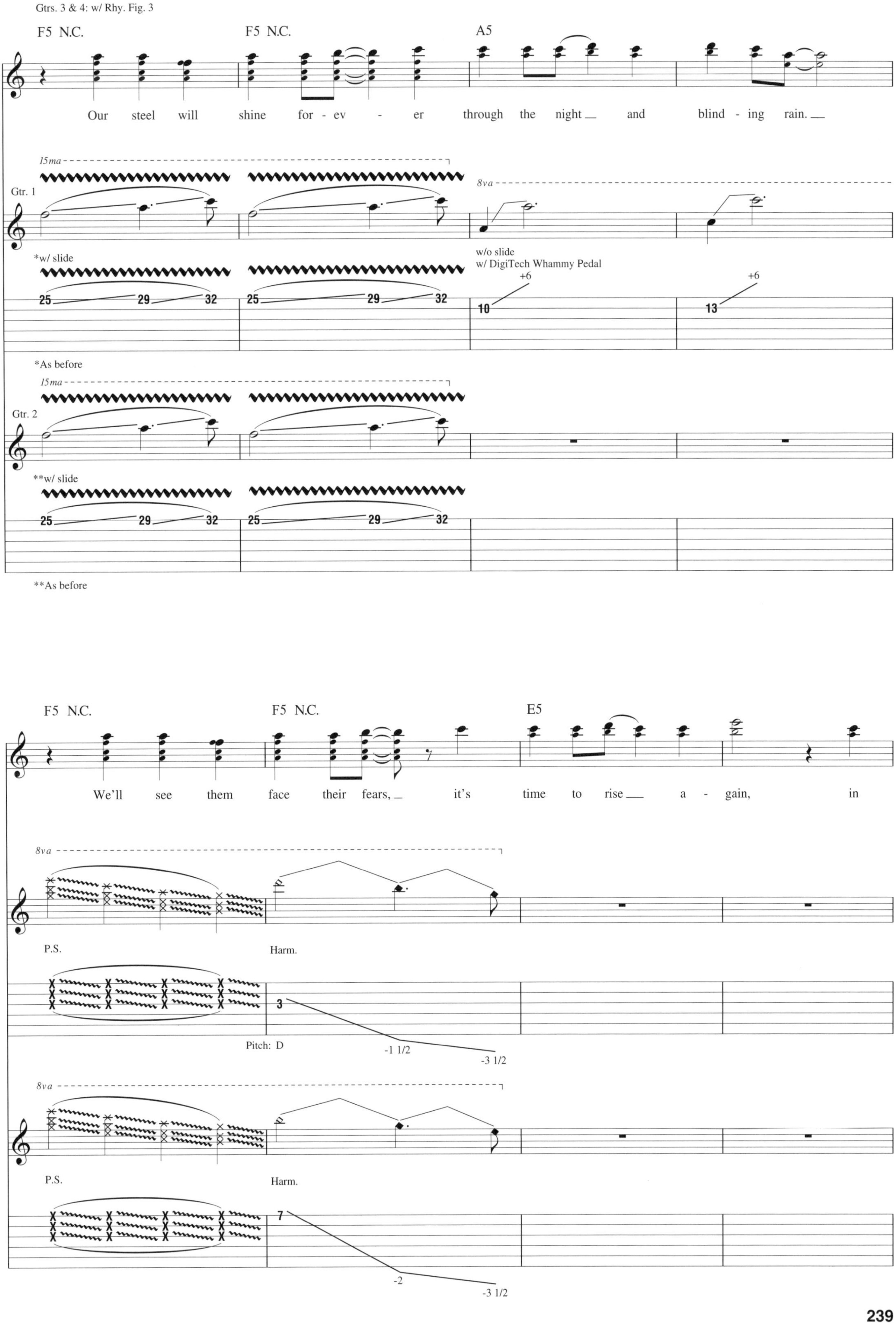

Gtrs. 3 & 4: w/ Rhy. Fig. 3

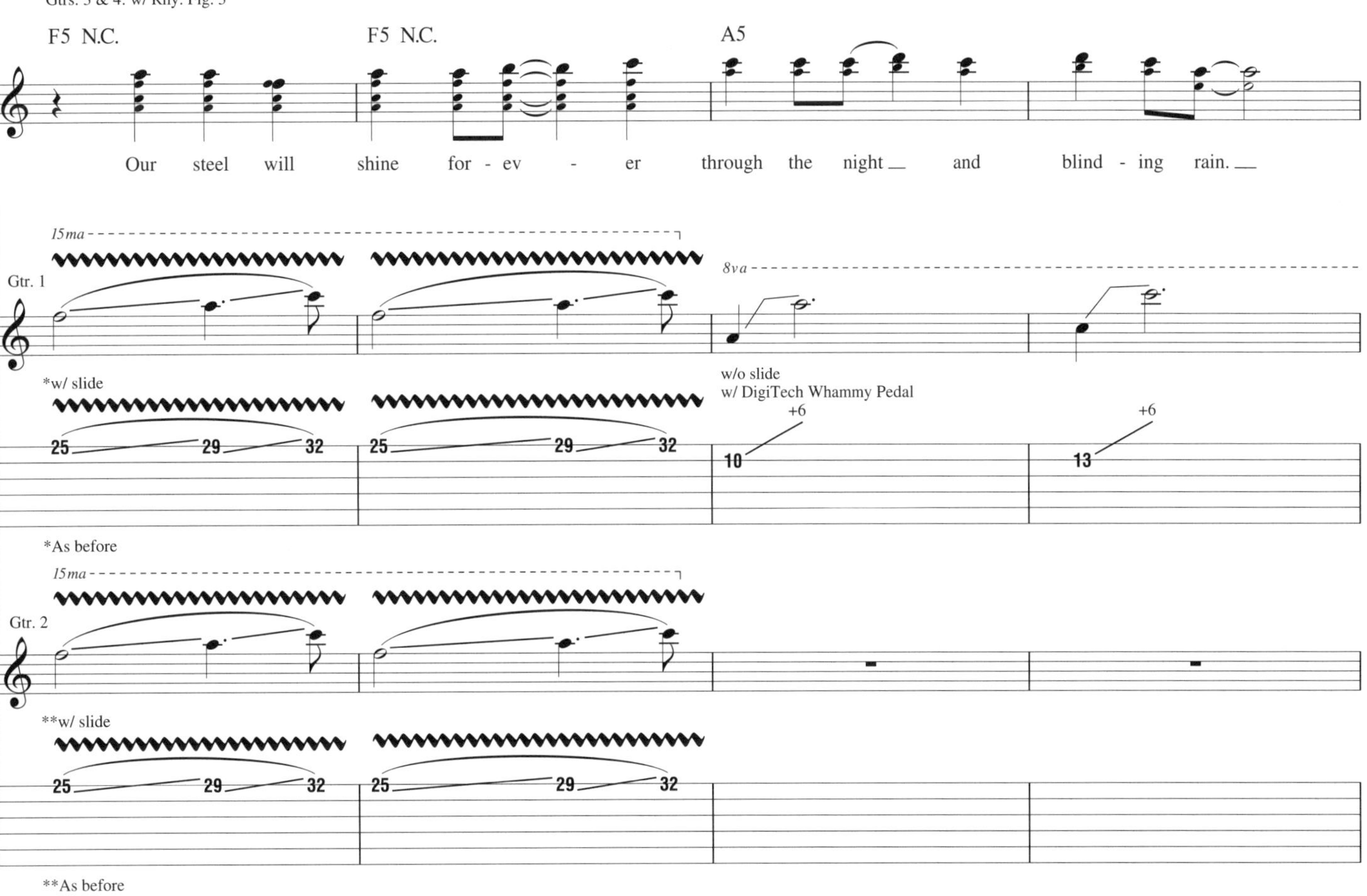

F5 N.C.
F5 N.C.
E5
We'll see them face their fears, __ it's time to rise __ a - gain, in
8va
P.S.
Harm.
3
Pitch: D
-1 1/2
-3 1/2
8va
P.S.
Harm.
7
-2
-3 1/2

D.S.S. al Coda 3
ev - er - last - ing pain.
8va
loco

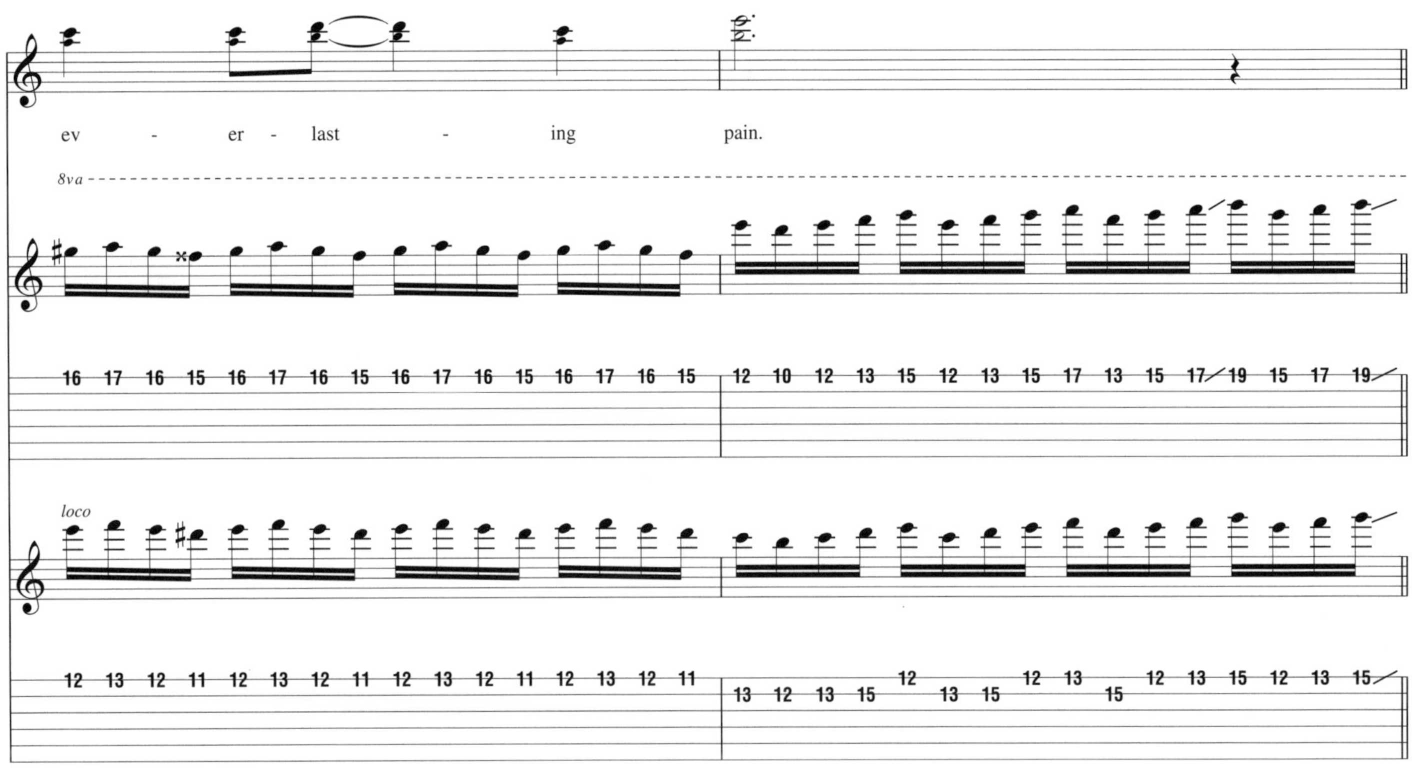

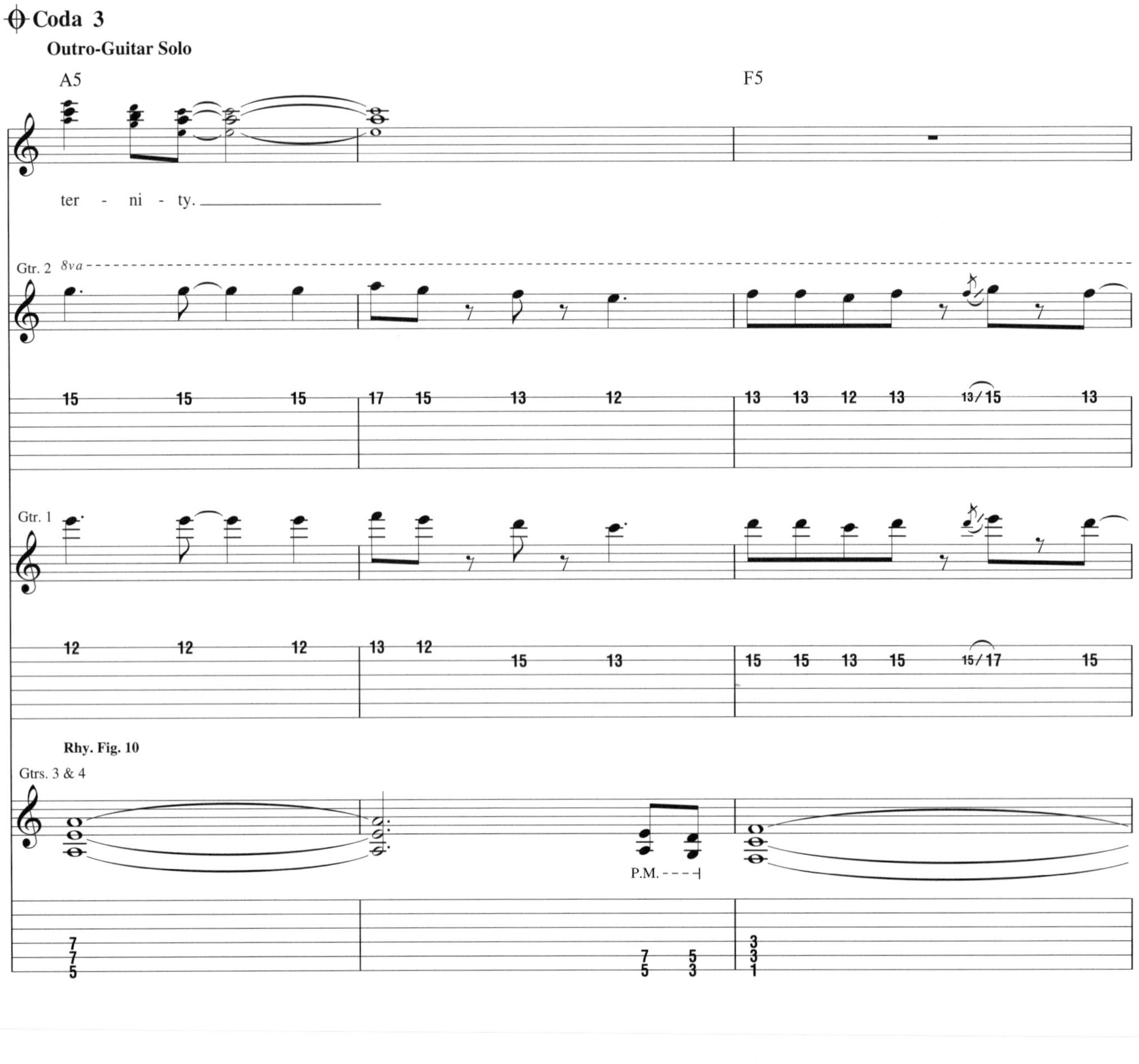

Coda 3
Outro-Guitar Solo
A5
F5
ter - ni - ty.
Gtr. 2
8va
Gtr. 1
Rhy. Fig. 10
Gtrs. 3 & 4
P.M.

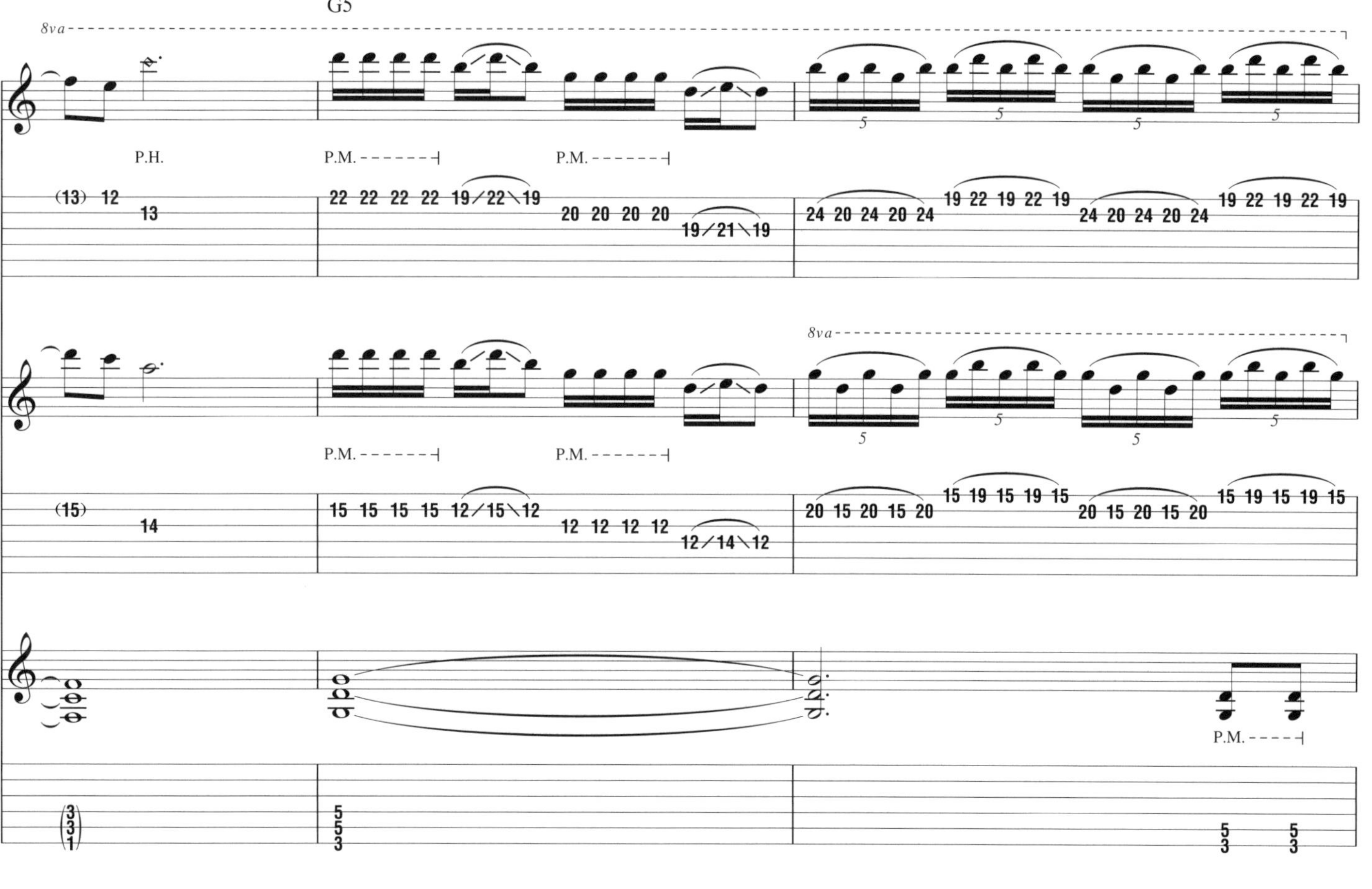

E5

C5

Cry for e -

loco

semi-P.H.

loco

semi-P.H.

End Rhy. Fig. 10

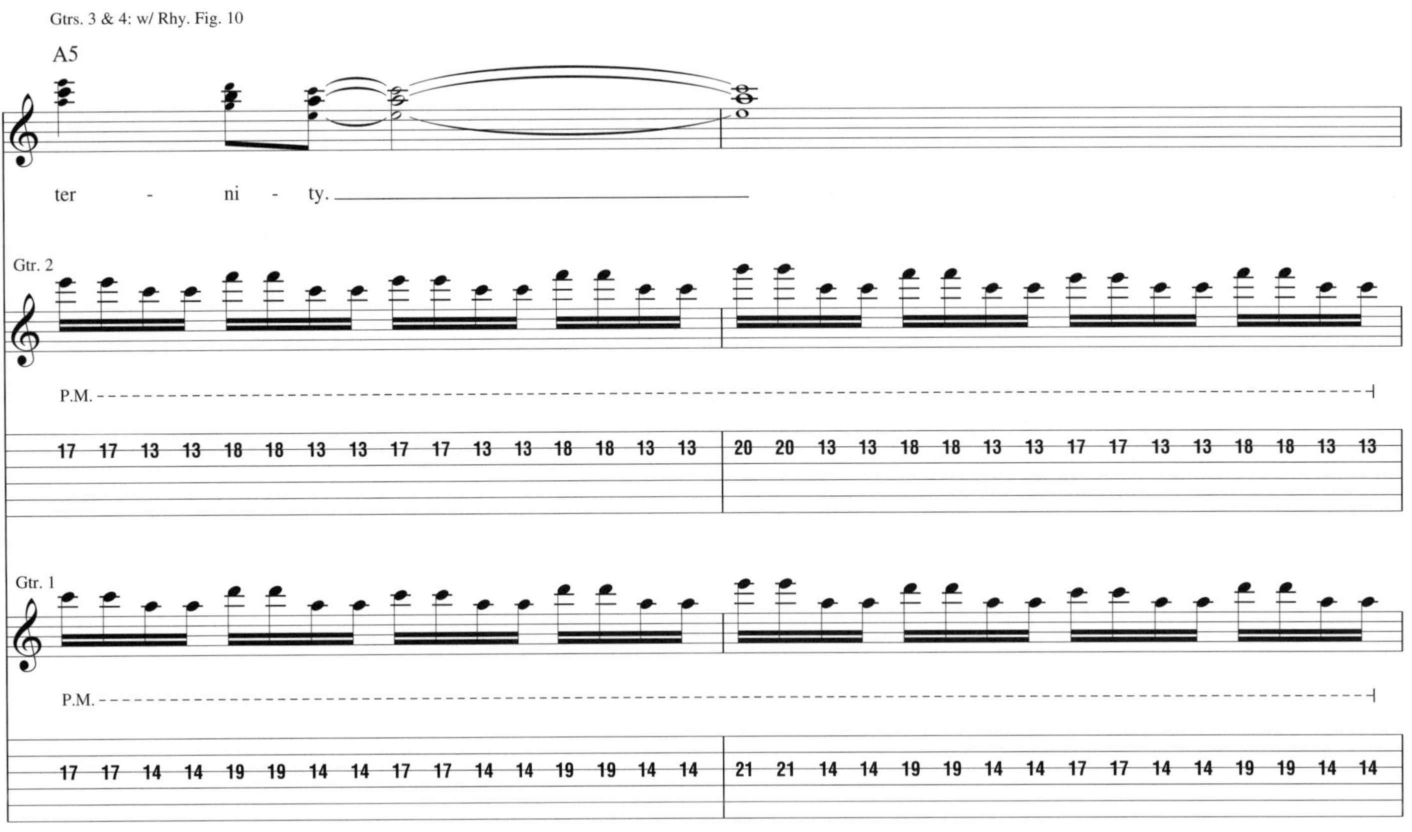

Gtrs. 3 & 4: w/ Rhy. Fig. 10
A5
ter - ni - ty.
Gtr. 2
P.M.
Gtr. 1
P.M.

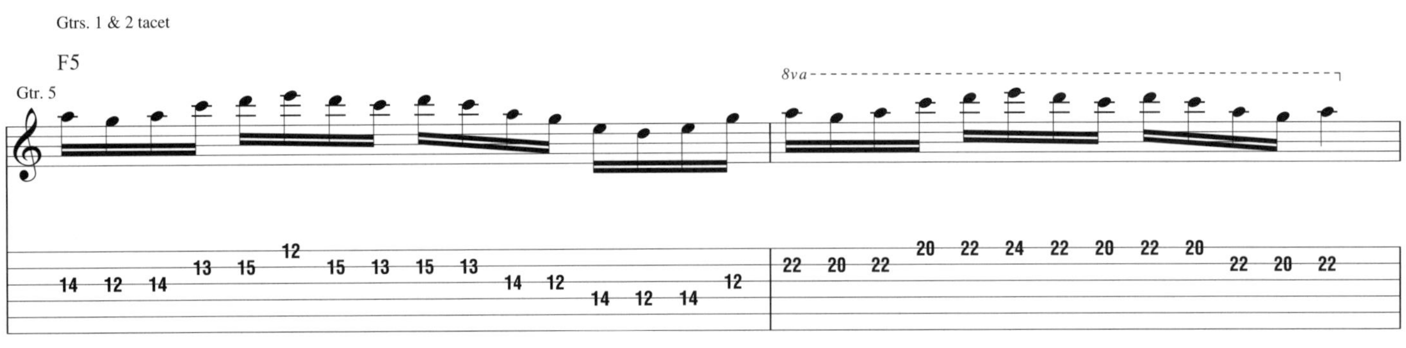

Gtrs. 1 & 2 tacet
F5
Gtr. 5
8va

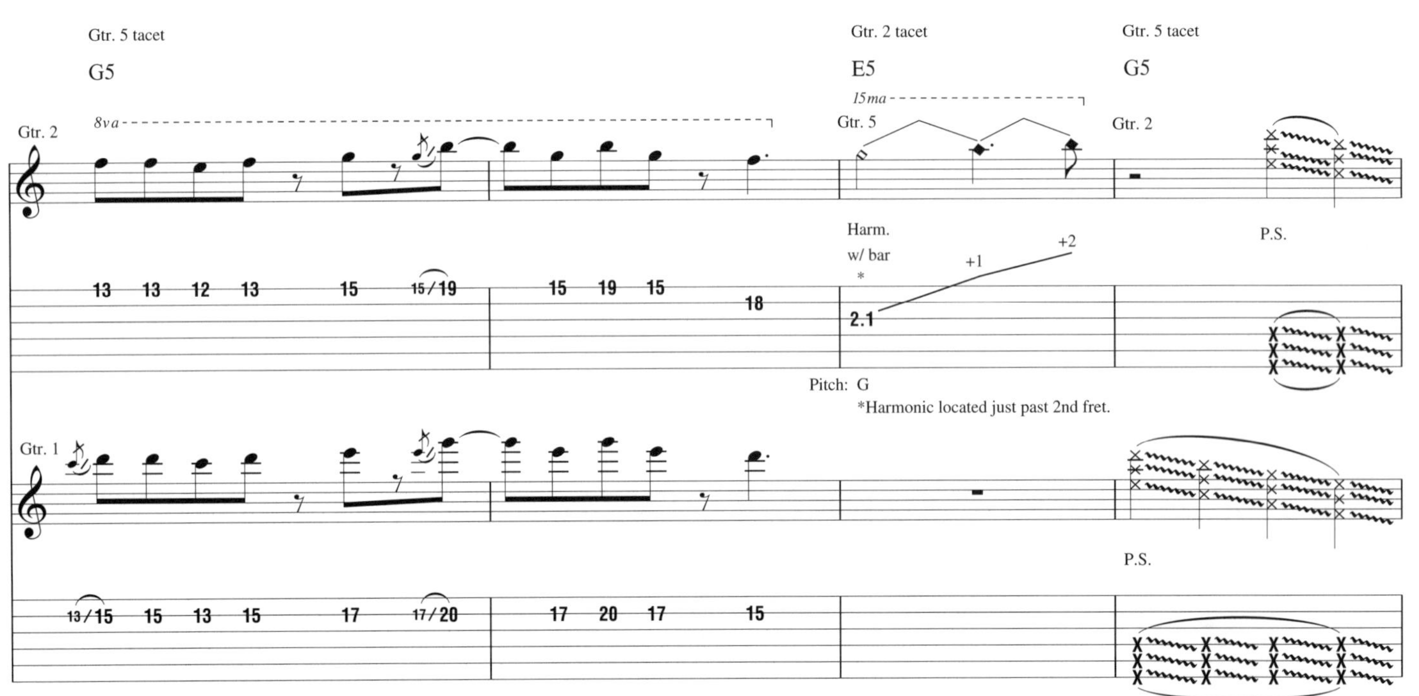

Gtr. 5 tacet
G5
Gtr. 2 tacet
E5
Gtr. 5 tacet
G5
Gtr. 2
8va
15ma
Gtr. 5
Gtr. 2
Harm.
w/ bar
+1
+2
P.S.
Pitch: G
*Harmonic located just past 2nd fret.
Gtr. 1
P.S.

A5

8va

Gtr. 5

Gtrs. 3 & 4

P.M.

C5

8va

P.M.

G5

loco

8va

P.M.

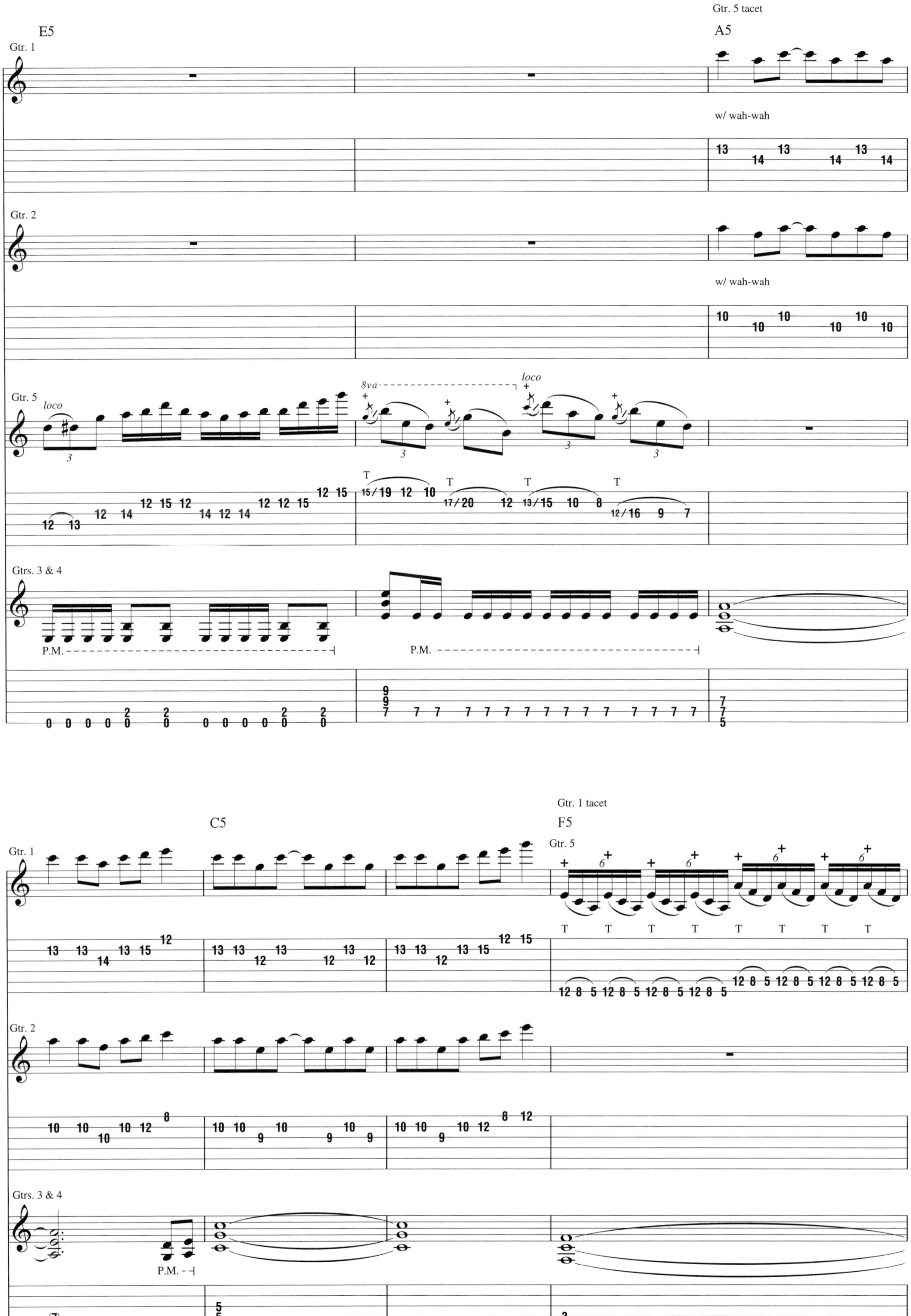

Gtr. 5 tacet

E5 A5

Gtr. 1

w/ wah-wah

Gtr. 2

w/ wah-wah

Gtr. 5

loco

8va

loco

Gtrs. 3 & 4

P.M.

P.M.

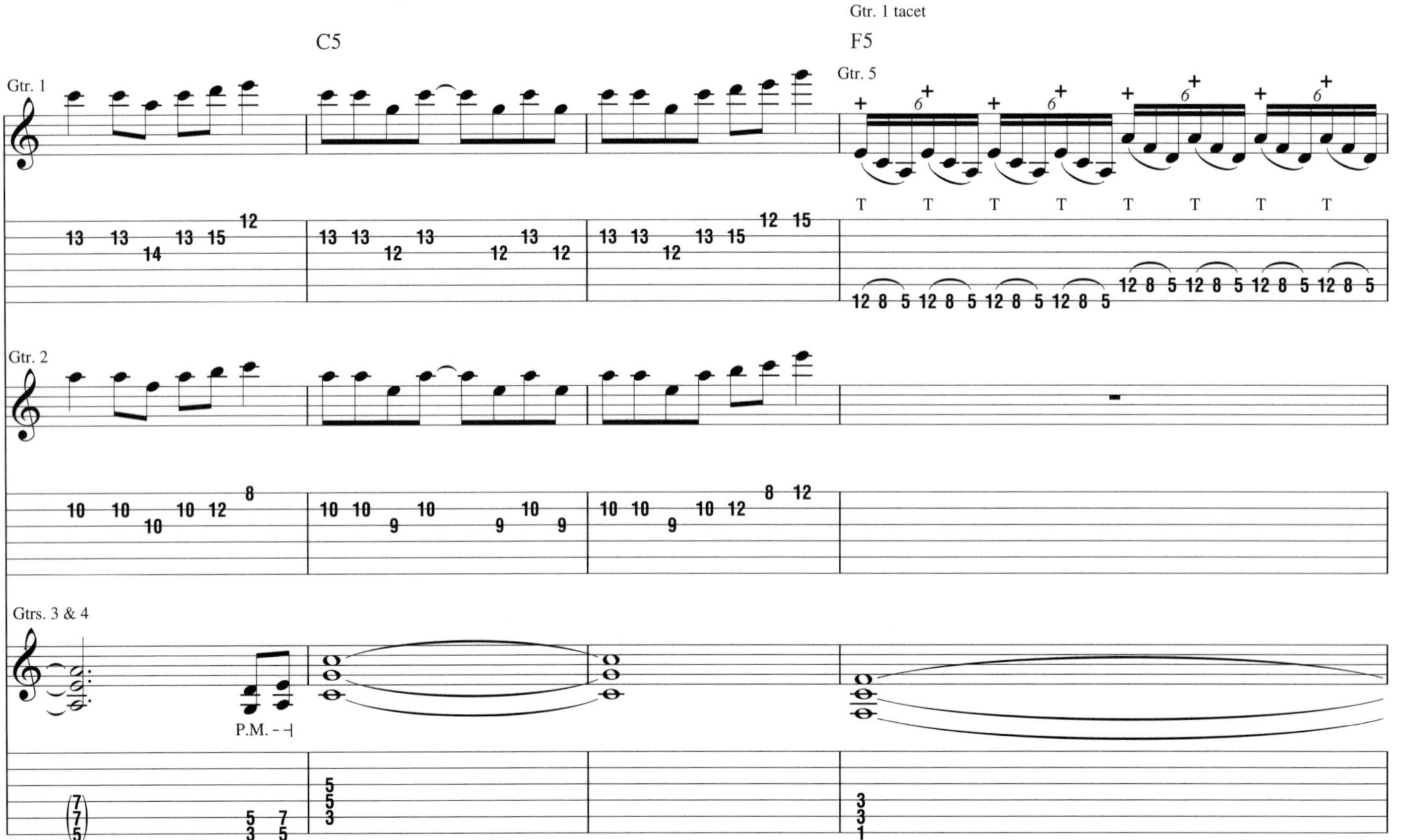

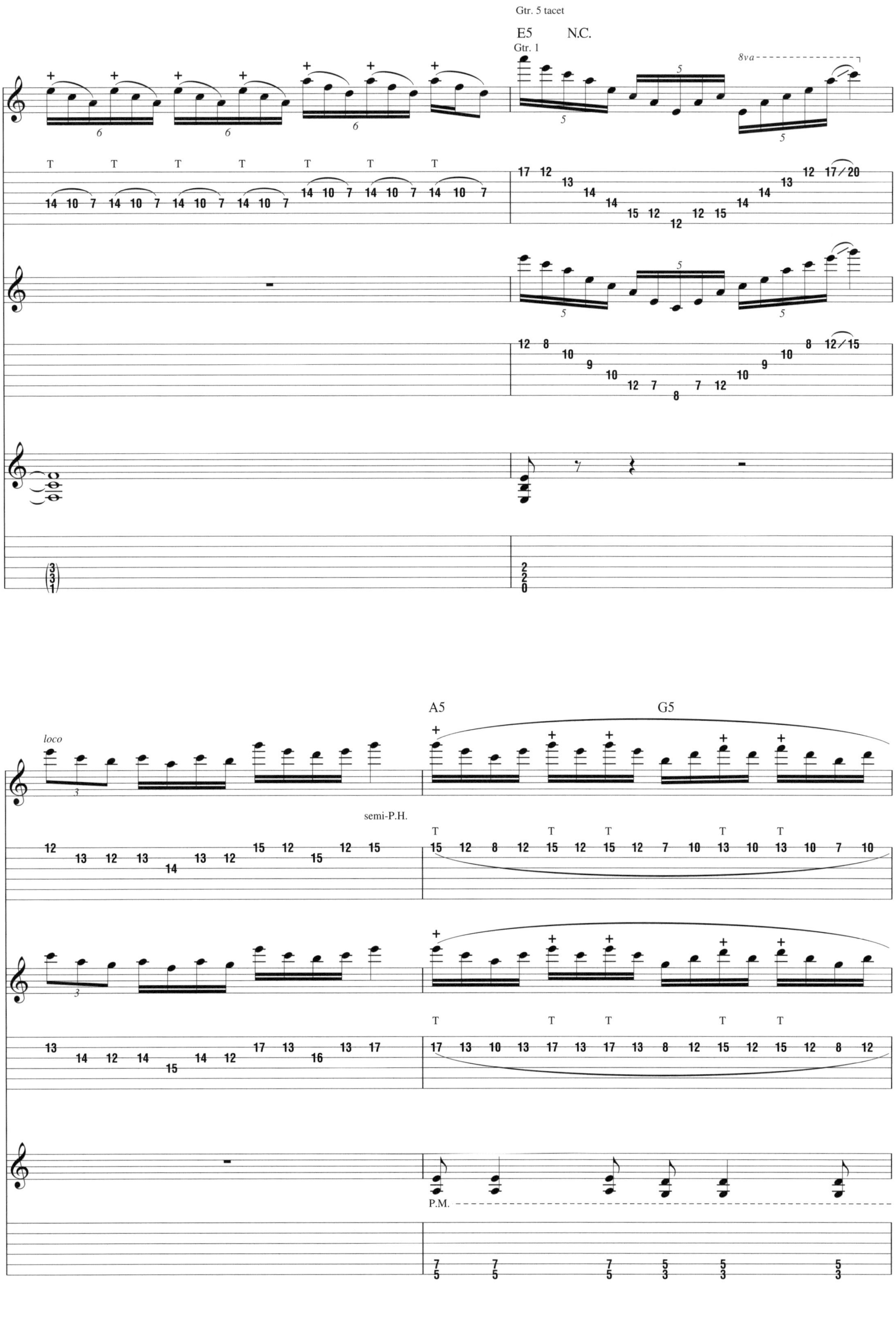

Gtr. 5 tacet

E5 N.C.

Gtr. 1

8va

T T T T T T T

14 10 7 14 10 7 14 10 7 14 10 7 14 10 7 14 10 7 14 10 7

17 12 13 14 14 15 12 12 12 15 14 14 13 12 17/20

12 8 10 9 10 12 7 8 7 12 10 9 10 8 12/15

3 3 1

2 2 0

loco

semi-P.H.

A5 G5

P.M.

T T T T T

12 13 12 13 14 13 12 15 12 15 12 15

15 12 8 12 15 12 15 12 7 10 13 10 13 10 7 10

13 14 12 14 15 14 12 17 13 16 13 17

17 13 10 13 17 13 17 13 8 12 15 12 15 12 8 12

7 5 7 5 7 5 5 3 5 3 5 3

F5 D5 E5

8va

w/ DigiTech Whammy Pedal

Harm.

Pitch: G

8va

w/ DigiTech Whammy Pedal

Harm.

P.M.

15ma

A5 N.C.

15ma

P.M.

The Flame of Youth

Words and Music by Herman Li, ZP Theart, Sam Totman and Vadim Pruzhanov

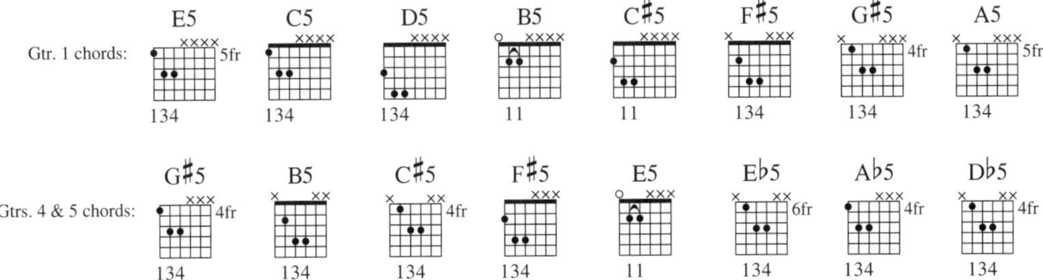

Gtr. 1: 7-string tuning:
(low to high) B-E-A-D-G-B-E

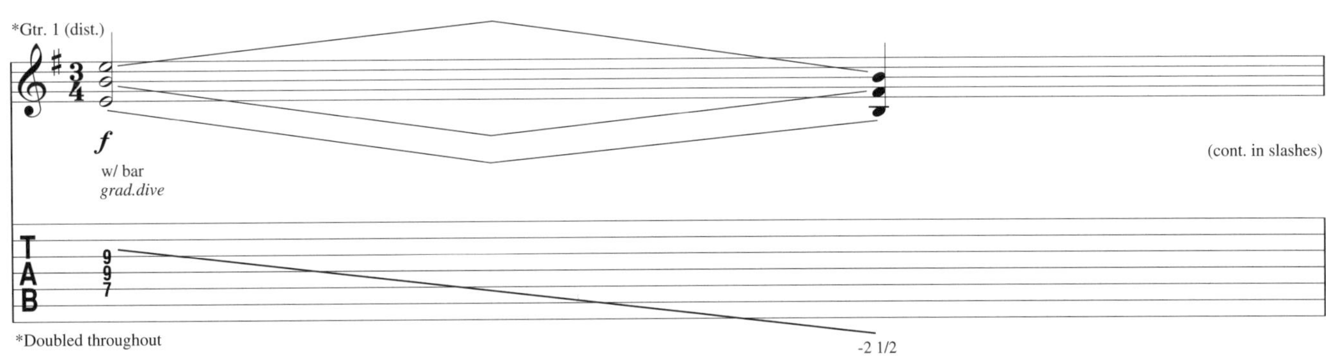

**Symbols in parentheses represent chord names respective to de-tuned guitar.
Symbols above represent actual sounding chords.
Chord symbols reflect overall harmony.

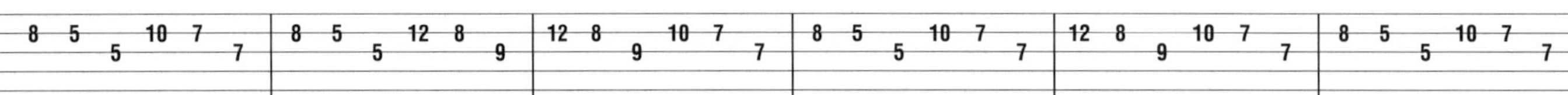

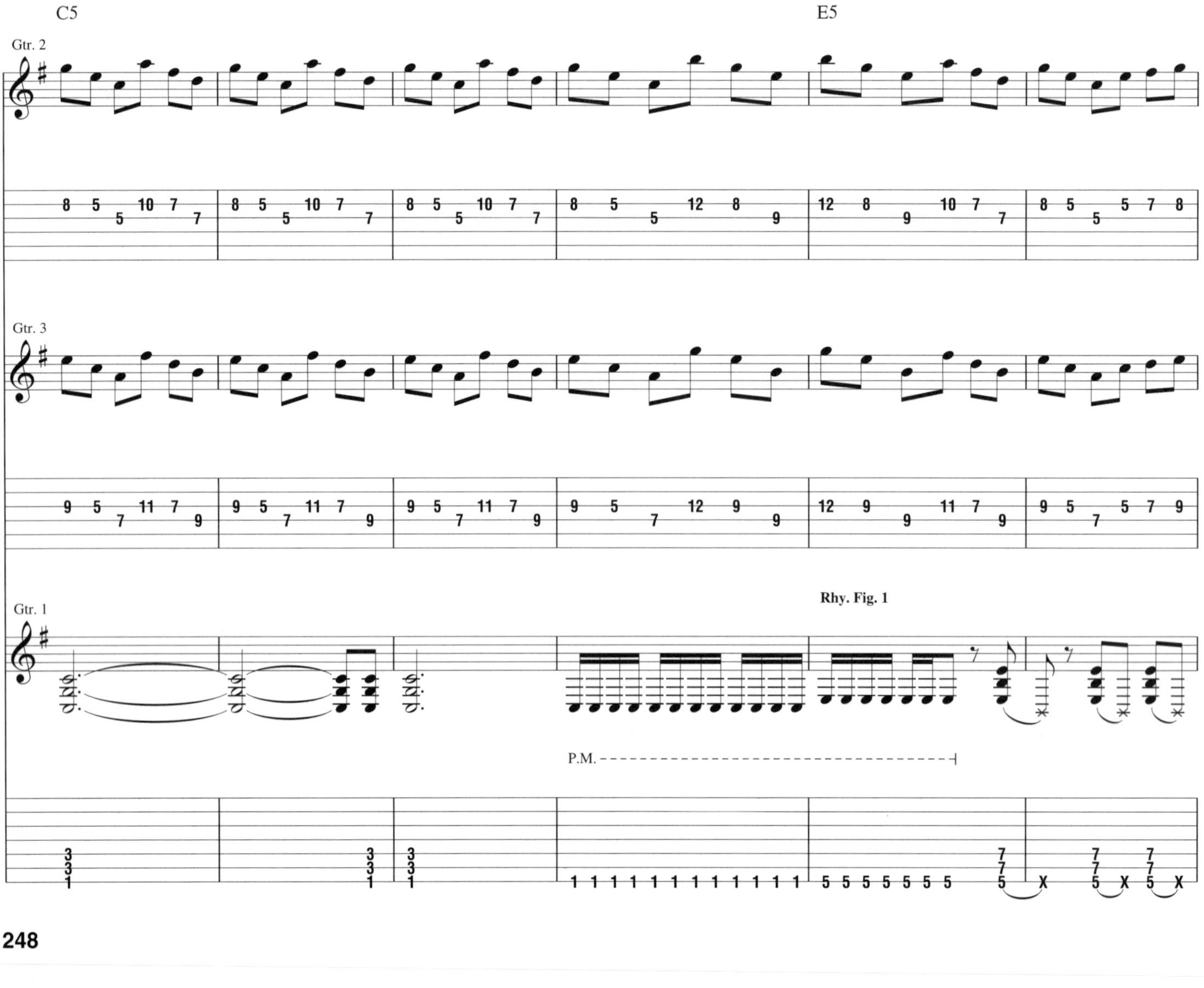

C5

E5

Gtr. 2

Gtr. 3

Gtr. 1

Rhy. Fig. 1

P.M.

C5
End Rhy. Fig. 1
P.M.
P.M.
P.M.

Gtr. 1: w/ Rhy. Fig. 1
E5
C5
Gtr. 2
semi-P.H.
semi-P.H.
Gtr. 3
semi-P.H.
semi-P.H.

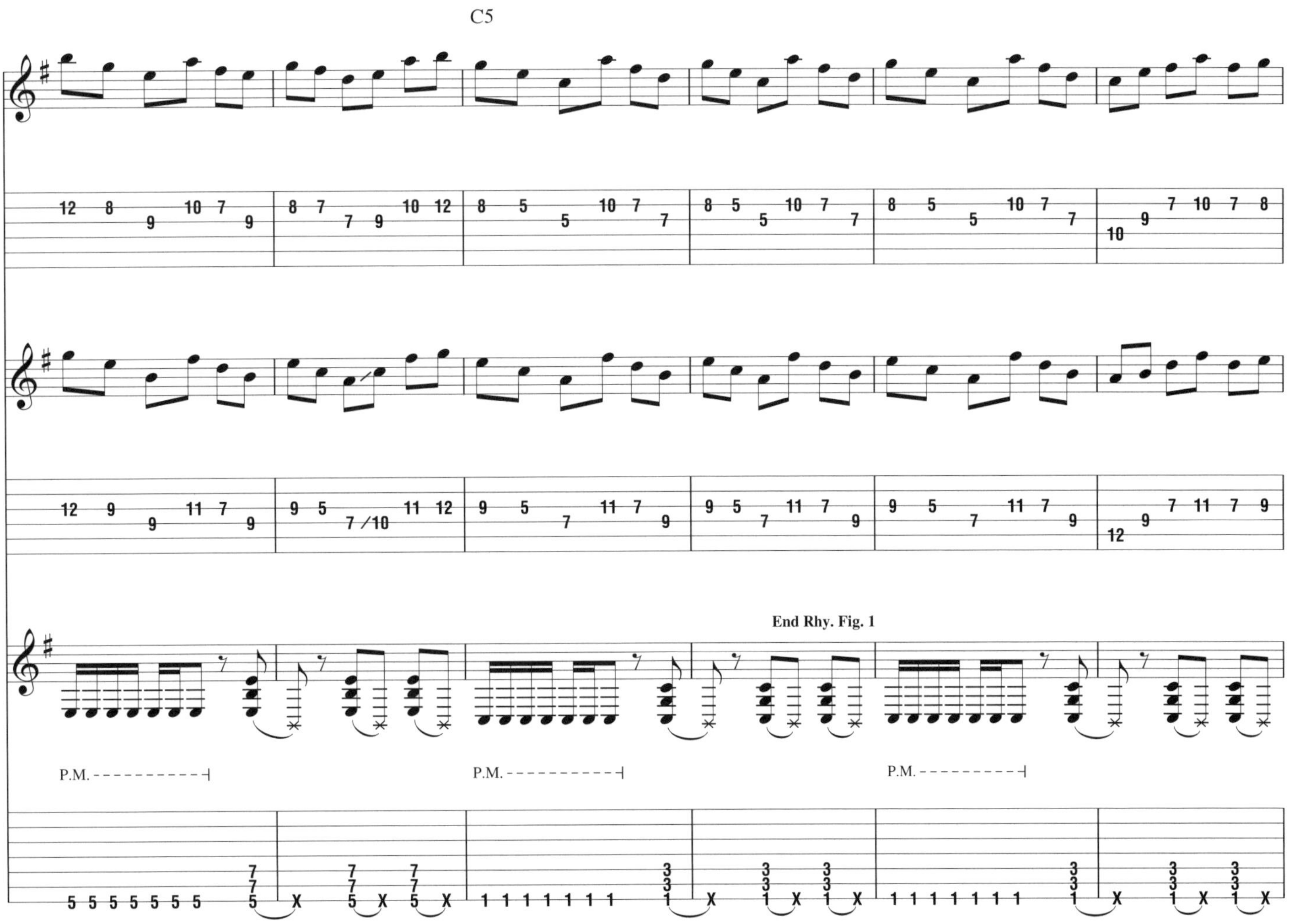

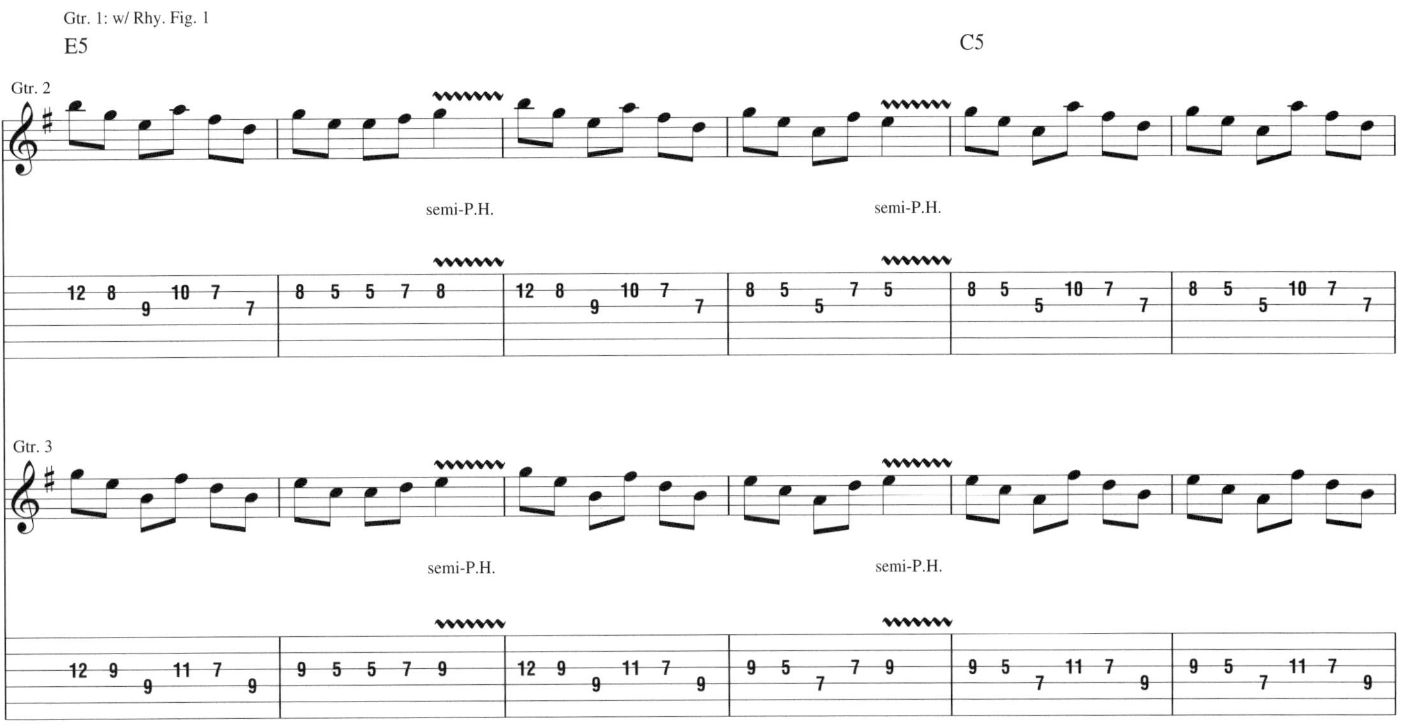

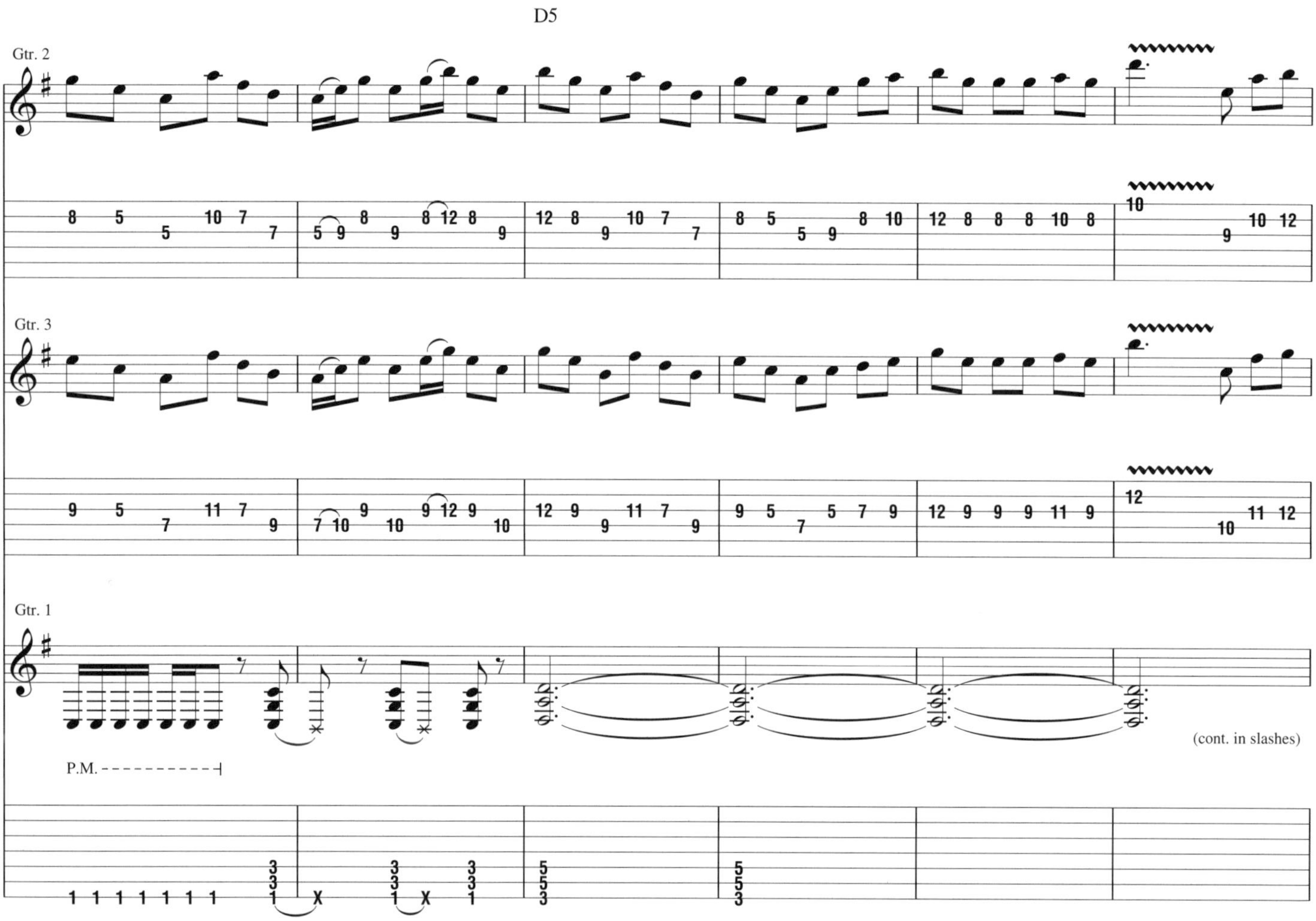

D5

Gtr. 2

Gtr. 3

Gtr. 1

P.M.

(cont. in slashes)

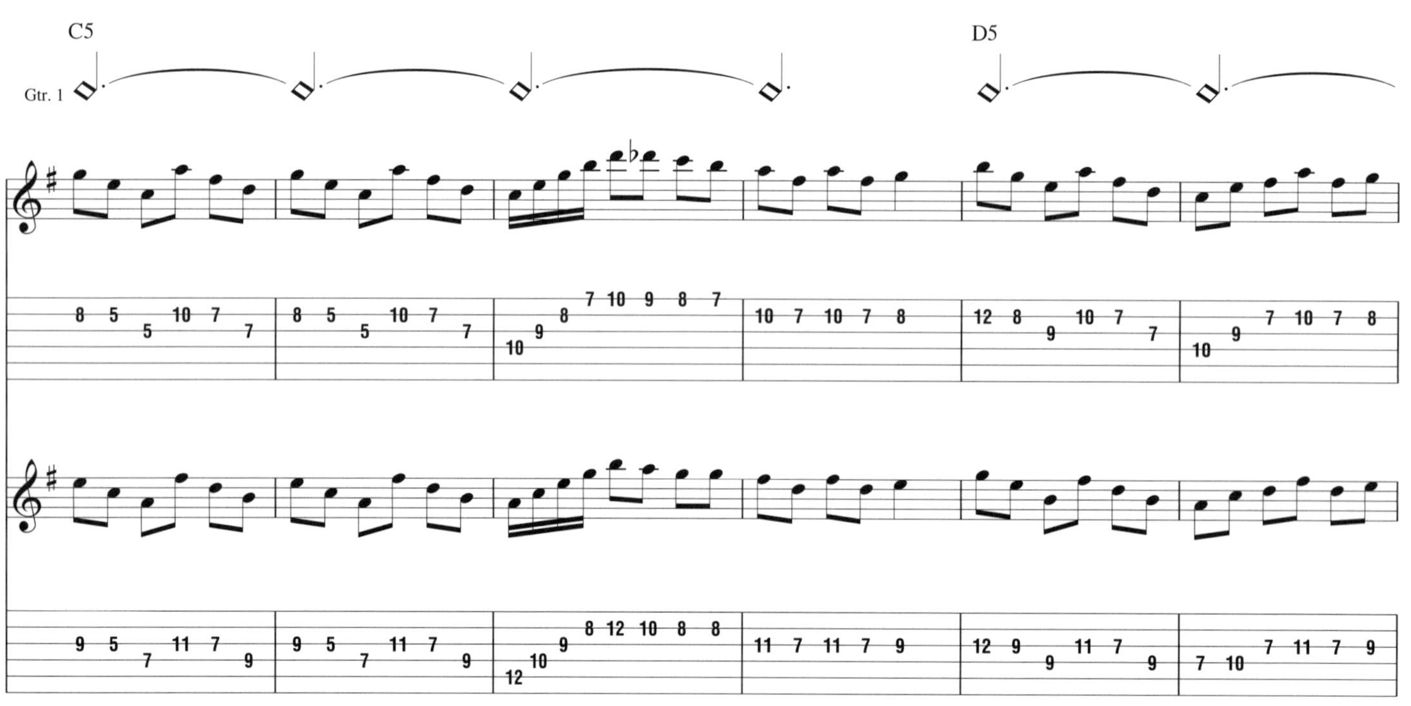

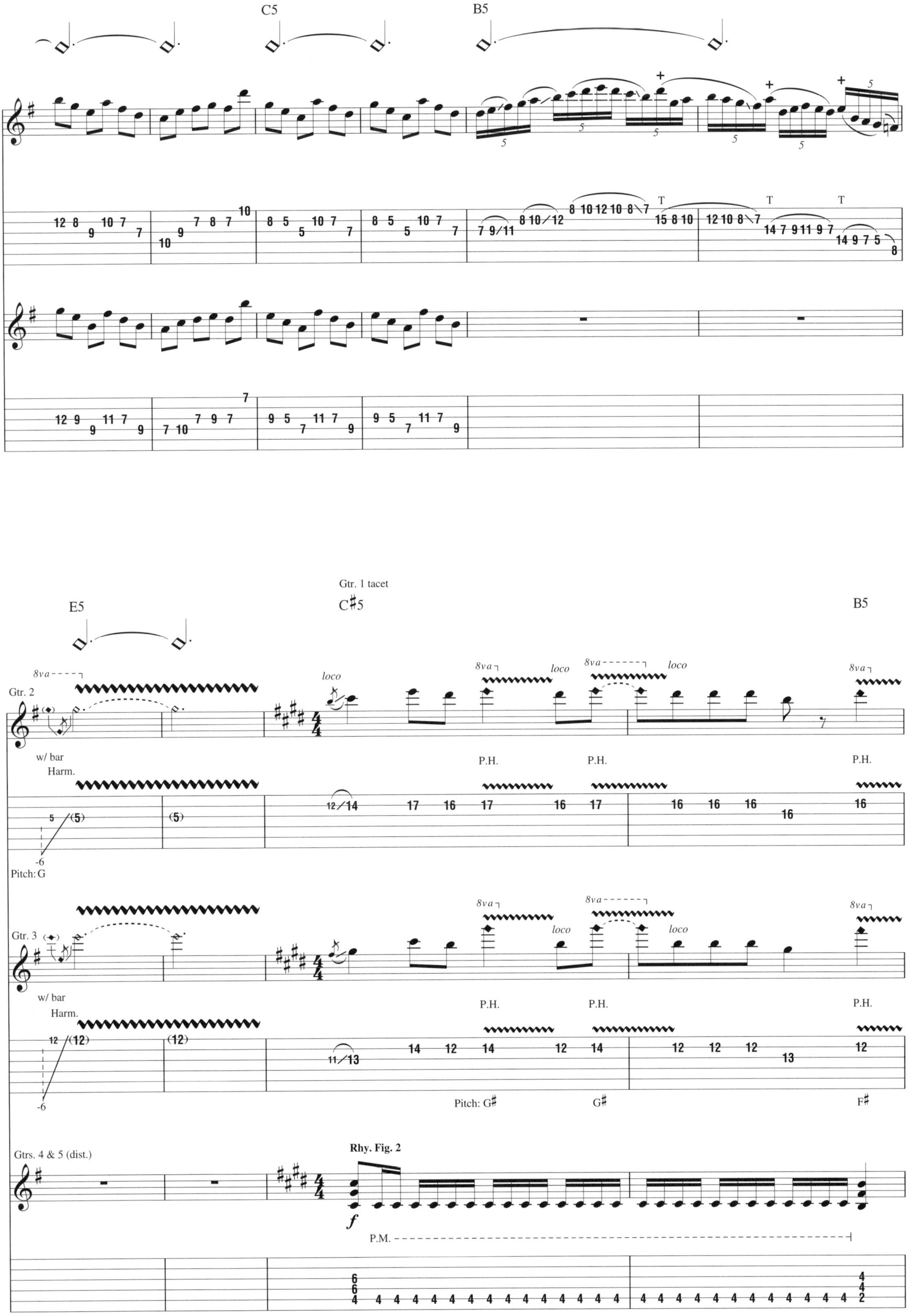

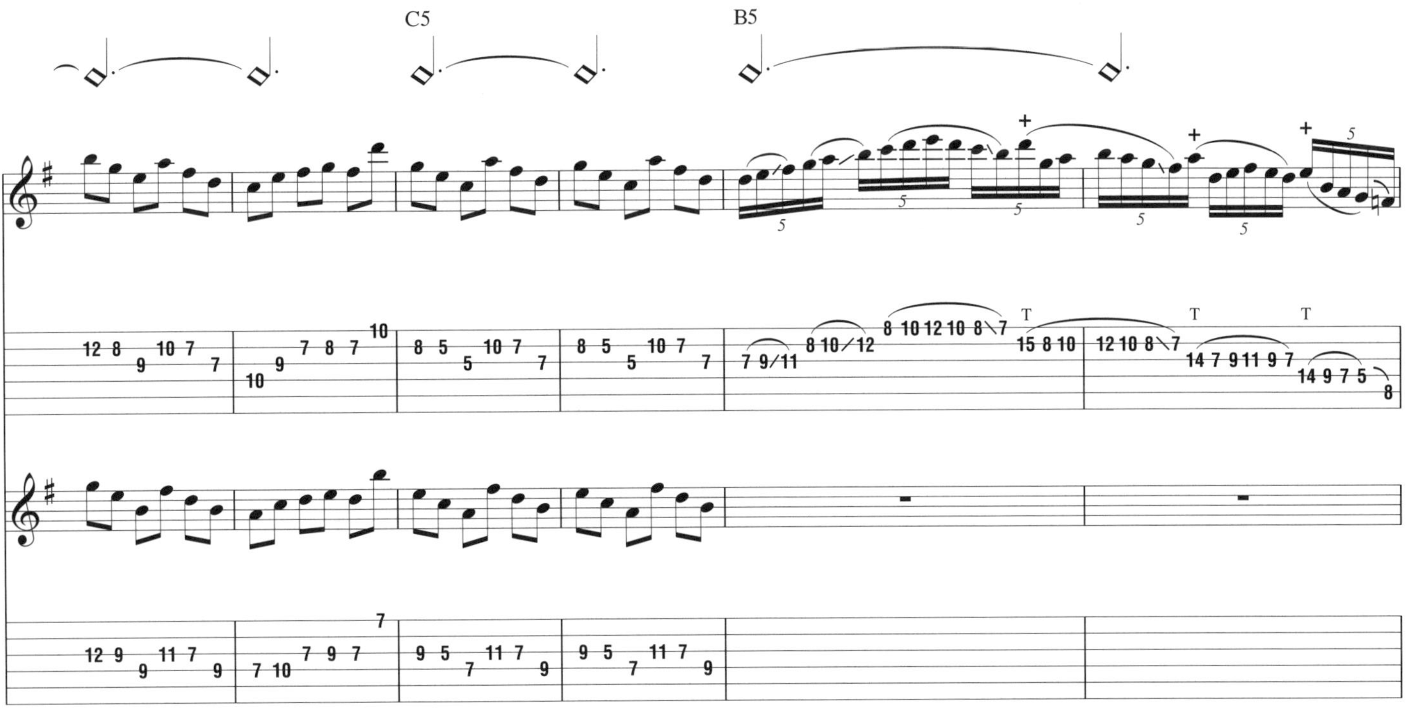

Gtr. 1 tacet

E5

C♯5

B5

8va

loco

Gtr. 2

w/ bar

Harm.

P.H.

Pitch: G

Gtr. 3

Pitch: G♯

G♯

F♯

Gtrs. 4 & 5 (dist.)

Rhy. Fig. 2

f

P.M.

C♯5 B5 A5

loco 8va loco 8va loco 8va

P.H. P.H. semi-P.H. P.H.

loco 8va loco 8va loco 8va loco 8va

P.H. P.H. semi-P.H. P.H. P.H.

Pitch: G♯ G♯ G♯ G♯

P.M. P.M.

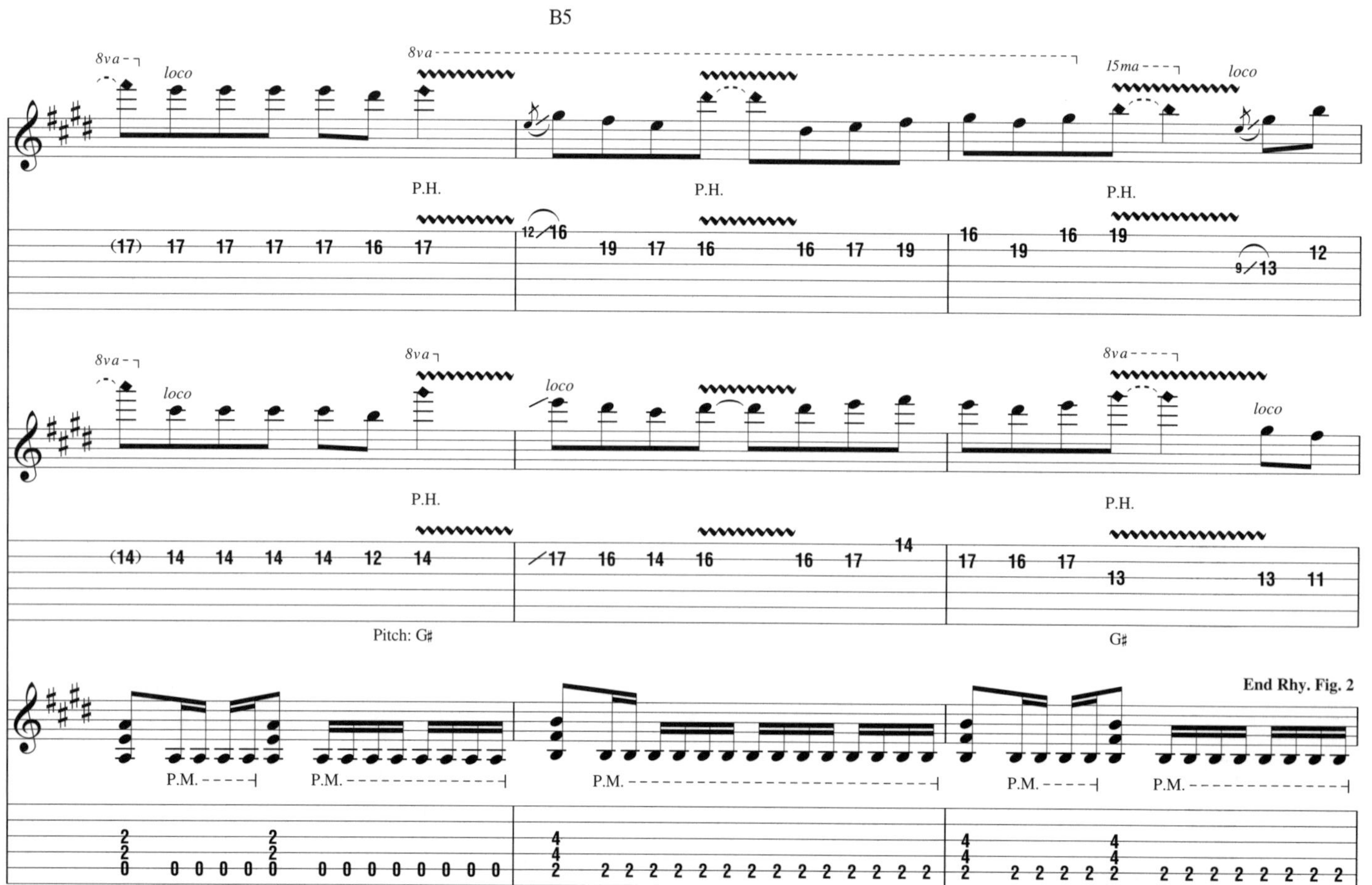

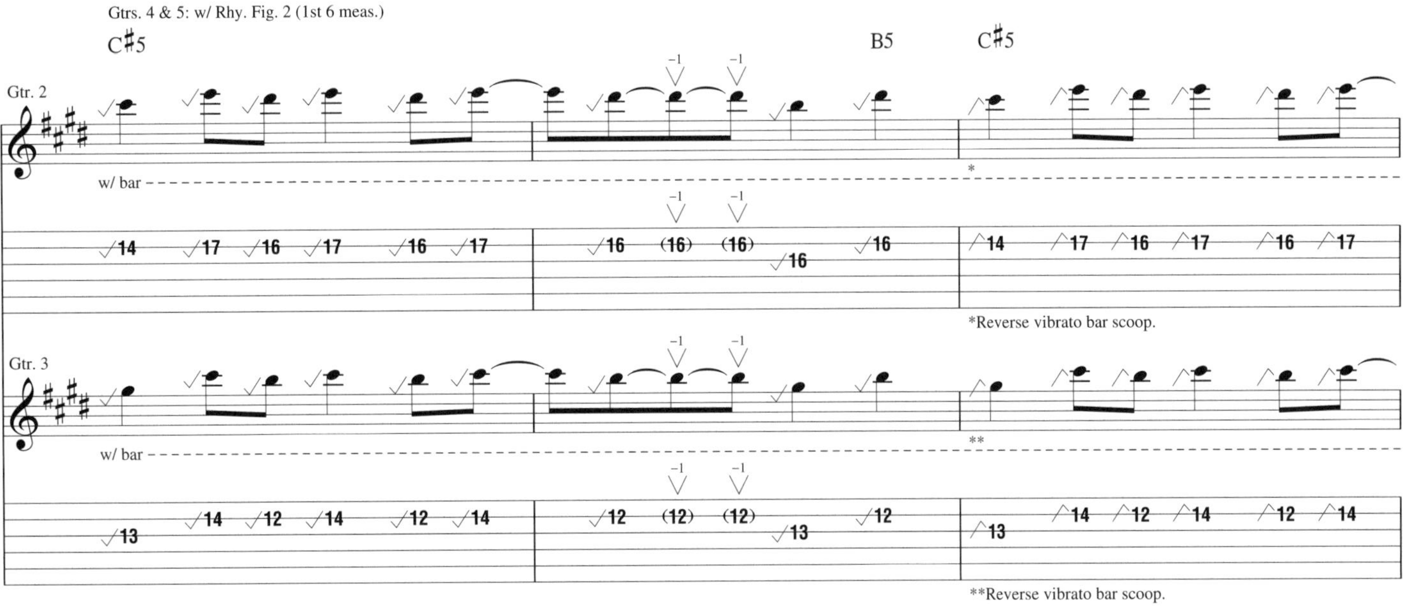
Gtrs. 4 & 5: w/ Rhy. Fig. 2 (1st 6 meas.)
C♯5
B5
C♯5
Gtr. 2
w/ bar
*Reverse vibrato bar scoop.
Gtr. 3
w/ bar
**Reverse vibrato bar scoop.

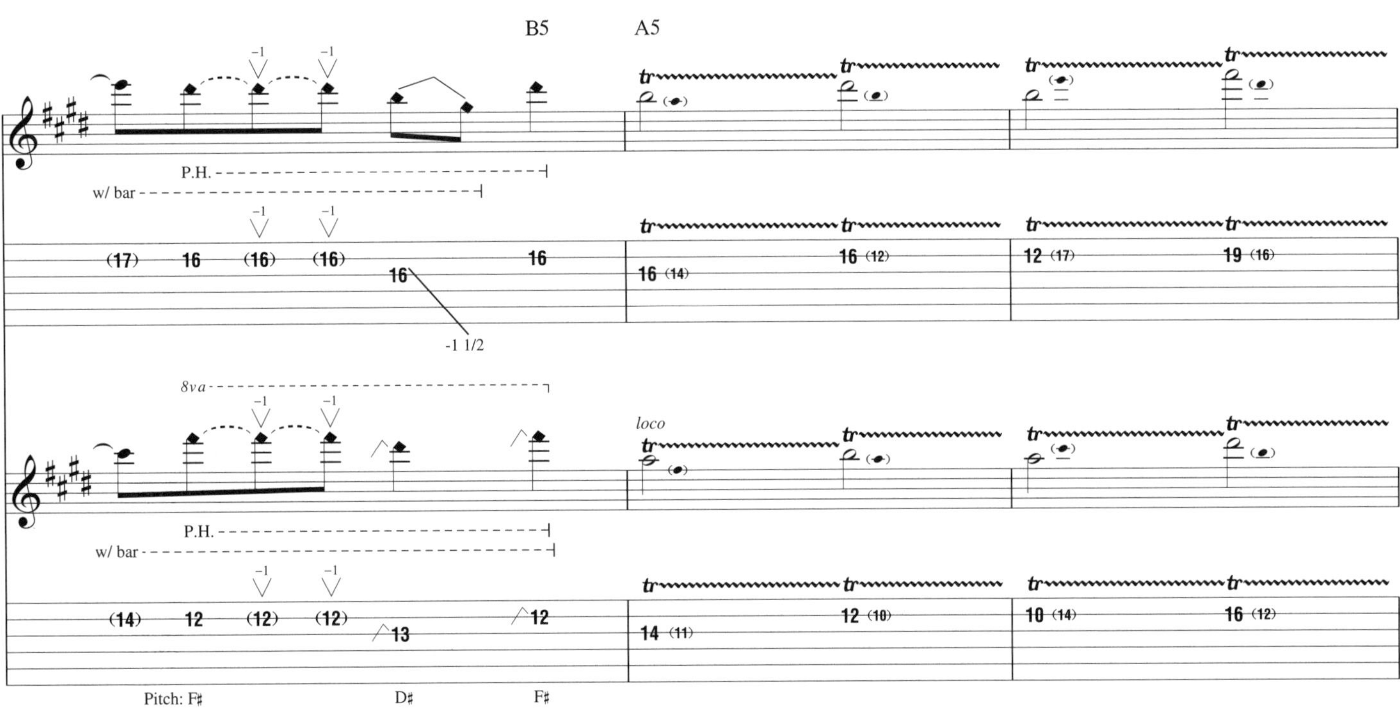
B5
A5
P.H.
w/ bar
-1 1/2
8va
loco
P.H.
w/ bar
Pitch: F♯
D♯
F♯

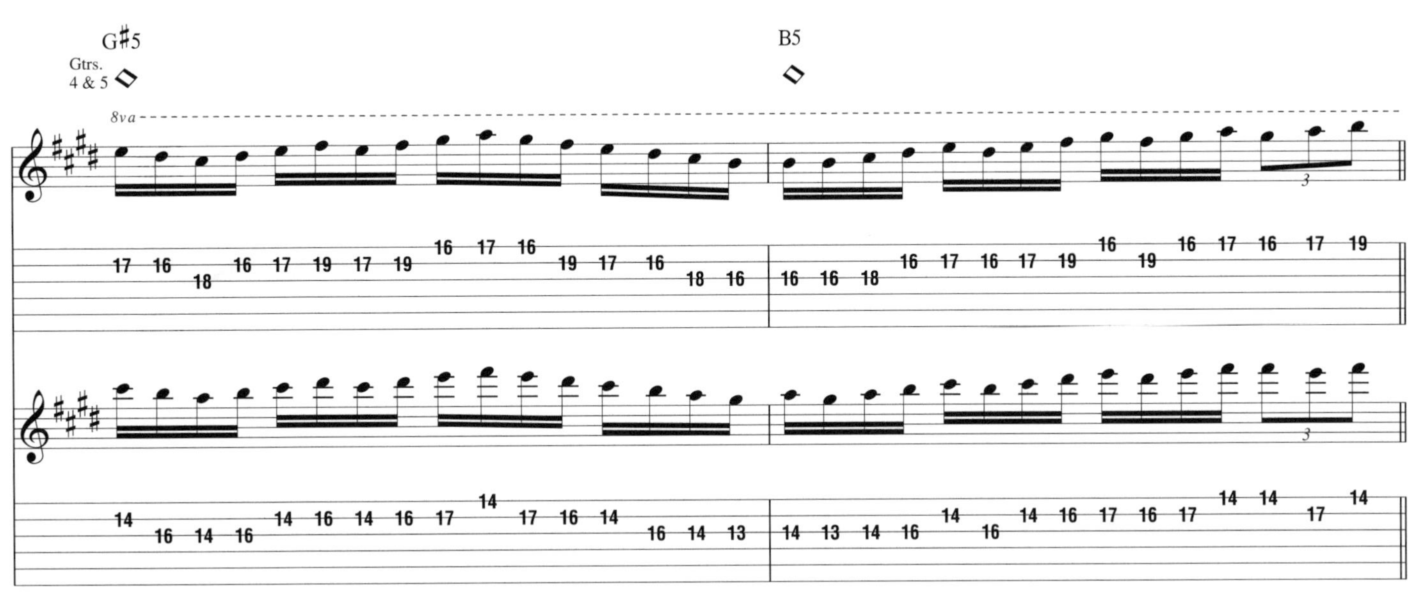
G♯5
B5
Gtrs. 4 & 5
8va

Verse

Gtrs. 2 & 3 tacet
C#5
N.C.
G#5
C#5
N.C.
(cont. in notation)
1. Close your eyes, hear the thun - der and rain. Fear in - side of the tor - tur - ing pain for the
8va
Gtrs. 4 & 5
steady gliss.
B5
A5
cries of the world, and the last lives re -
Gtrs. 4 & 5
P.M.
P.M.
P.M.
B5
C#5
G#5
C#5
Gtr. 4
(cont. in notation)
main. Chain your heart, swear to die for their gain. Deep in - side, slow - ly
Gtr. 5
(Gtr. 4, cont. in slashes)

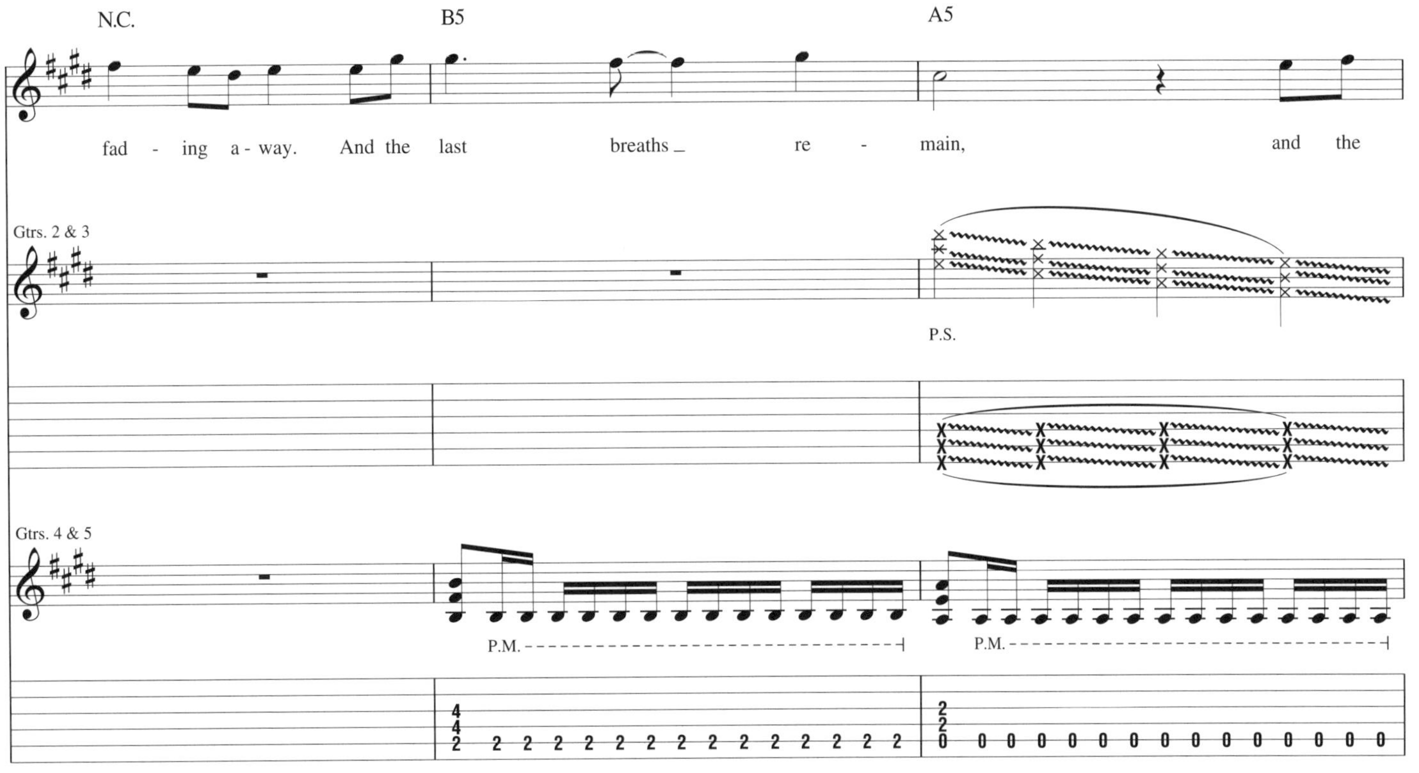
N.C.
B5
A5
fad - ing a - way. And the last breaths re - main, and the
Gtrs. 2 & 3
P.S.
Gtrs. 4 & 5
P.M.
P.M.

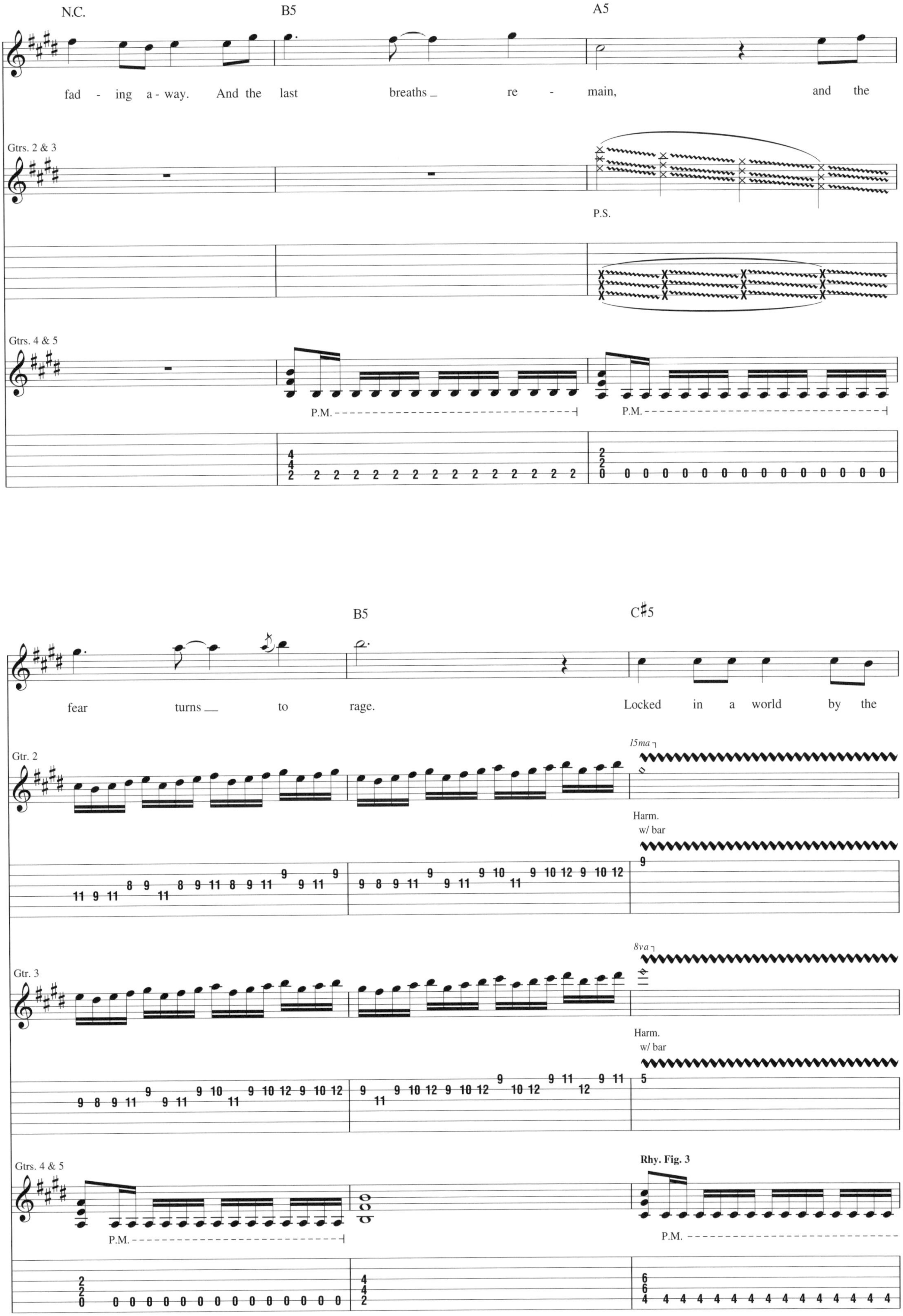

B5 C♯5

fear turns to rage. Locked in a world by the

Gtr. 2

15ma

Harm. w/ bar

Gtr. 3

8va

Harm. w/ bar

Gtrs. 4 & 5

Rhy. Fig. 3

P.M.

P.M.

Gtrs. 2 & 3 tacet

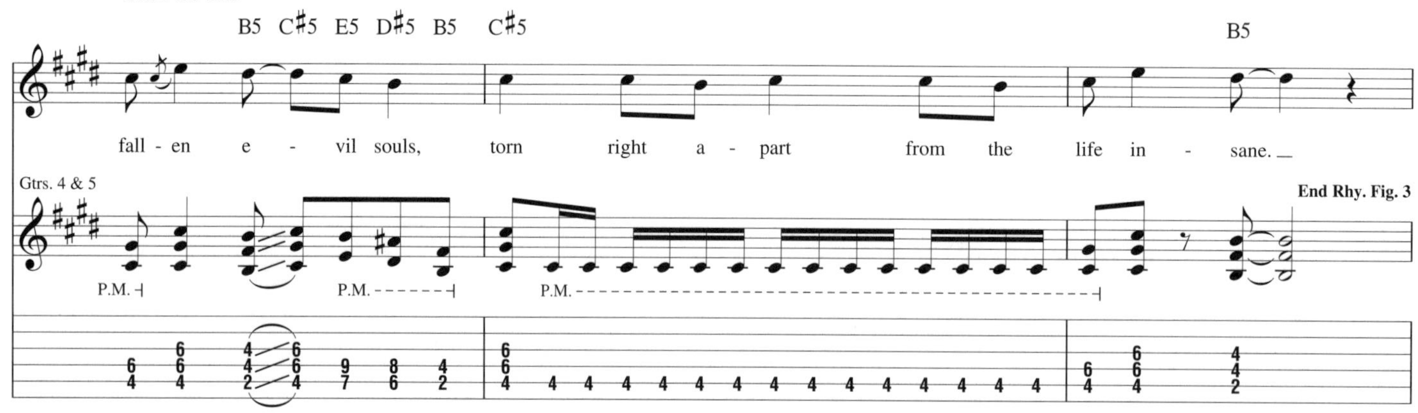
B5 C♯5 E5 D♯5 B5 C♯5
B5
fall - en e - vil souls, torn right a - part from the life in - sane.
Gtrs. 4 & 5
End Rhy. Fig. 3
P.M.
P.M.
P.M.

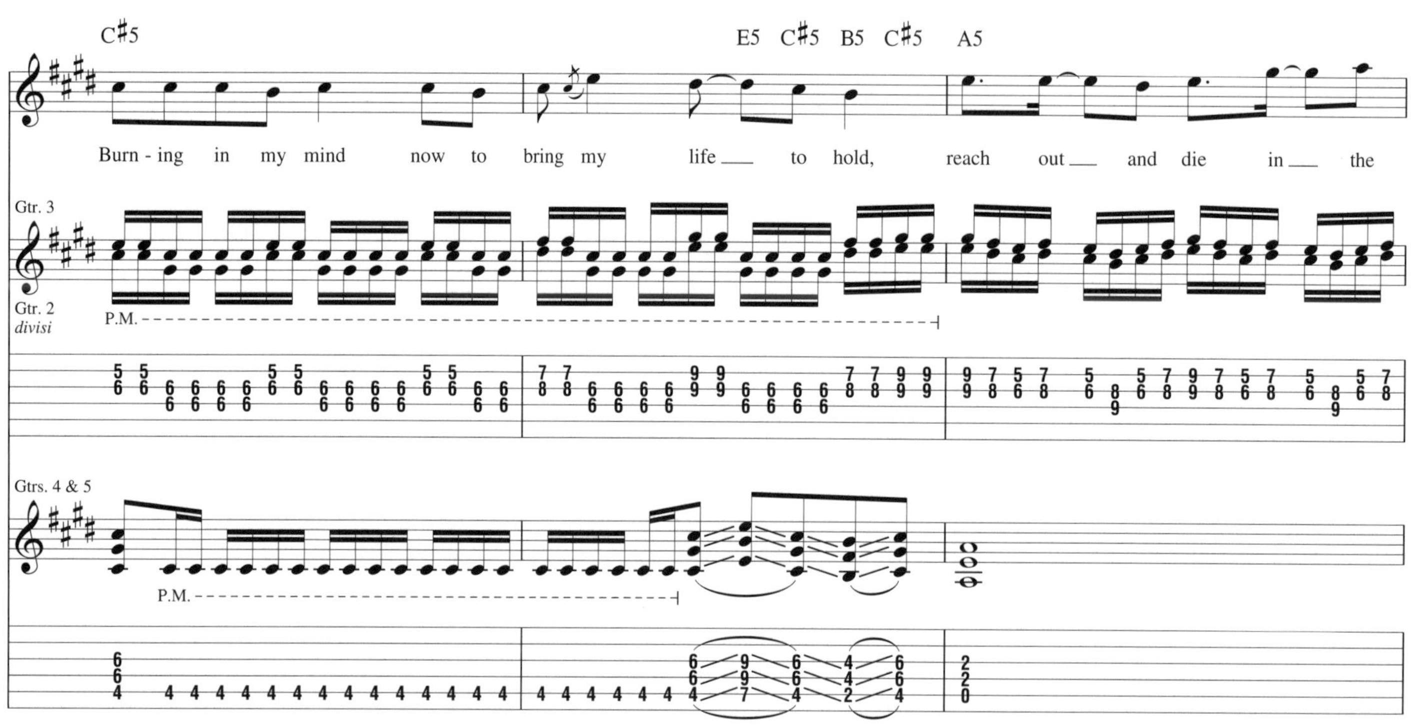
C♯5
E5 C♯5 B5 C♯5 A5
Burn - ing in my mind now to bring my life to hold, reach out and die in the
Gtr. 3
Gtr. 2
divisi
P.M.
Gtrs. 4 & 5
P.M.

B5
C♯5
Gtrs. 2 & 3 tacet
flames. See through the lies in their ev - er star - ing eyes,
8va
P.H.
P.M.

B5
C♯5
now is the time to de - fend your ground.
Des - ti - ny will call to re -
Gtrs. 4 & 5
Rhy. Fig. 4
P.M.

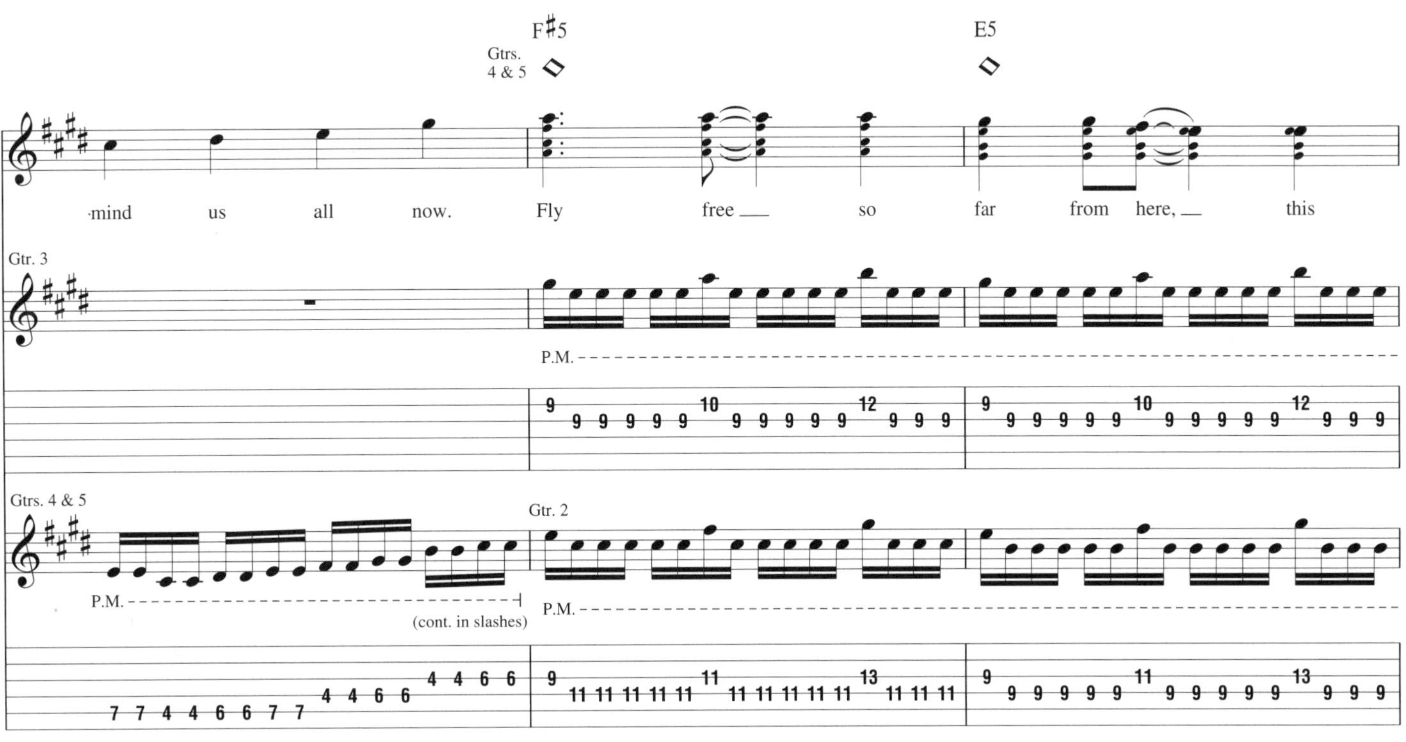
F♯5
E5
Gtrs. 4 & 5
mind us all now. Fly free so far from here, this
Gtr. 3
P.M.
Gtrs. 4 & 5
Gtr. 2
(cont. in slashes)

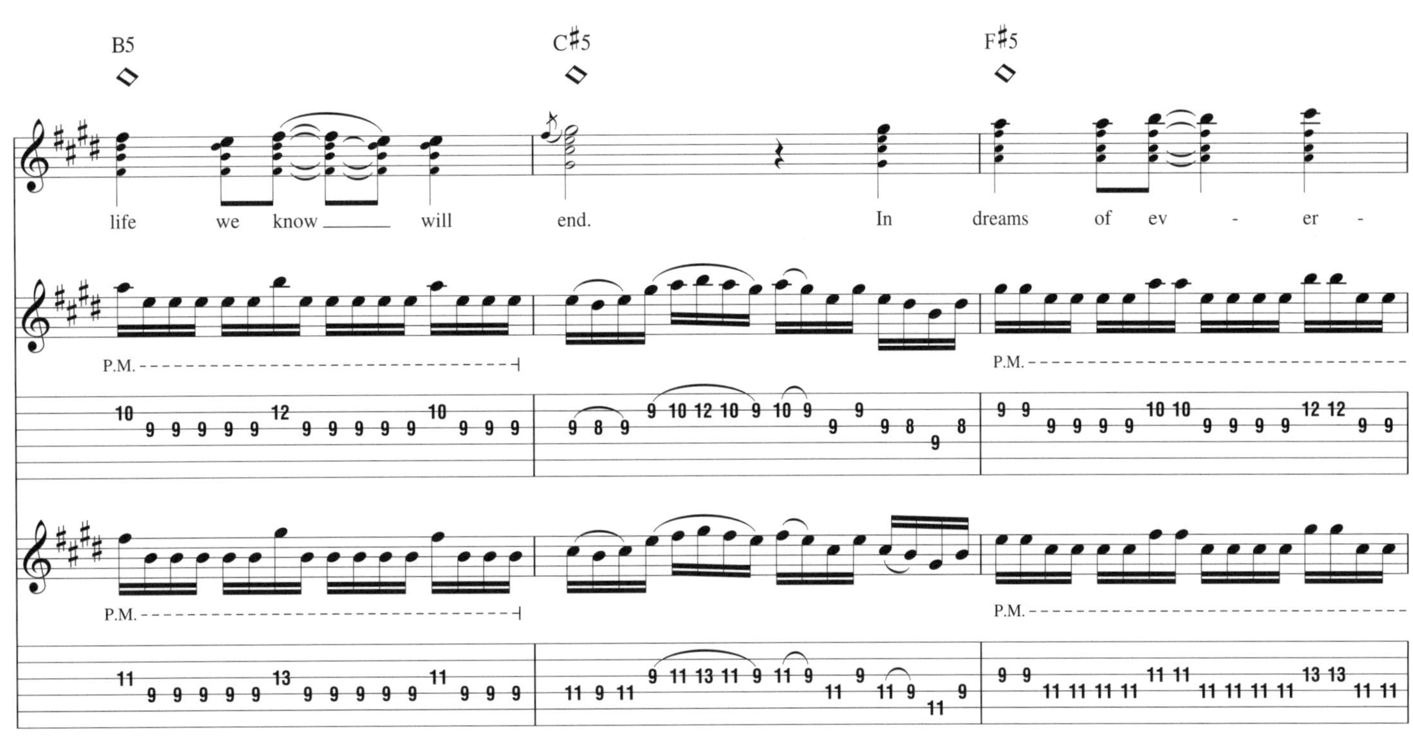
B5
C♯5
F♯5
life we know will end. In dreams of ev - er -
P.M.

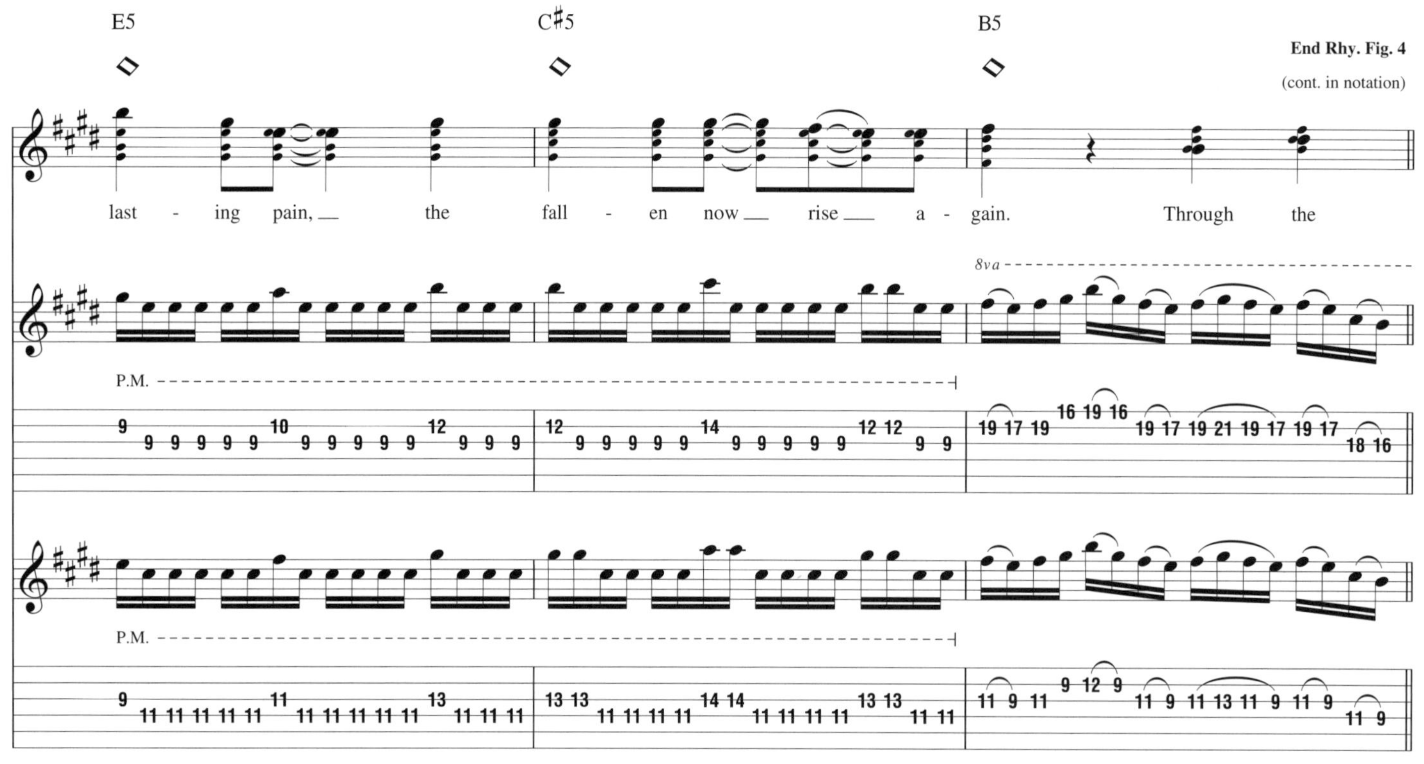

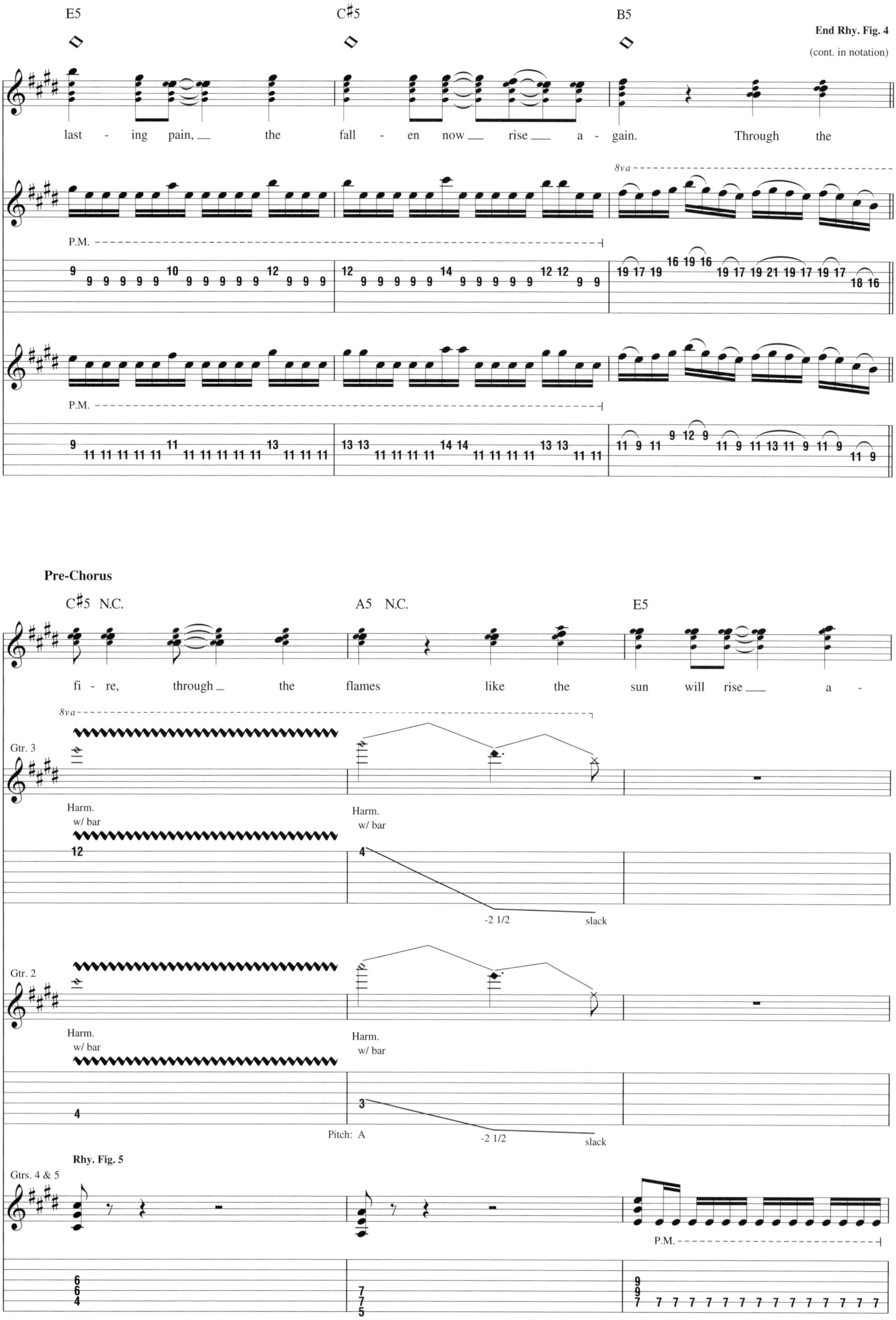

Pre-Chorus

C♯5 N.C. A5 N.C. E5

fi - re, through the flames like the sun will rise a -

8va

Gtr. 3

Harm. w/ bar

Harm. w/ bar

12

4

-2 1/2 slack

Gtr. 2

Harm. w/ bar

Harm. w/ bar

4

3

Pitch: A

-2 1/2 slack

Rhy. Fig. 5

Gtrs. 4 & 5

P.M.

B5
C♯5 N.C.
A5 N.C.
gain. Lost in time, lost in space to the
15ma
loco
*w/ slide
Harm.
***
Harm.
w/ bar
+1 1/2
+2 1/2
*Detach vibrato bar and use as slide.
***Hypothetical fret locations.
**w/ slide
Harm.
†
**Detach vibrato bar and use as slide.
†Hypothetical fret locations.
P.M.
E5
B5
C♯5
B5 C♯5
end of all their days. See their end-less ways, in-san-i-ty. The

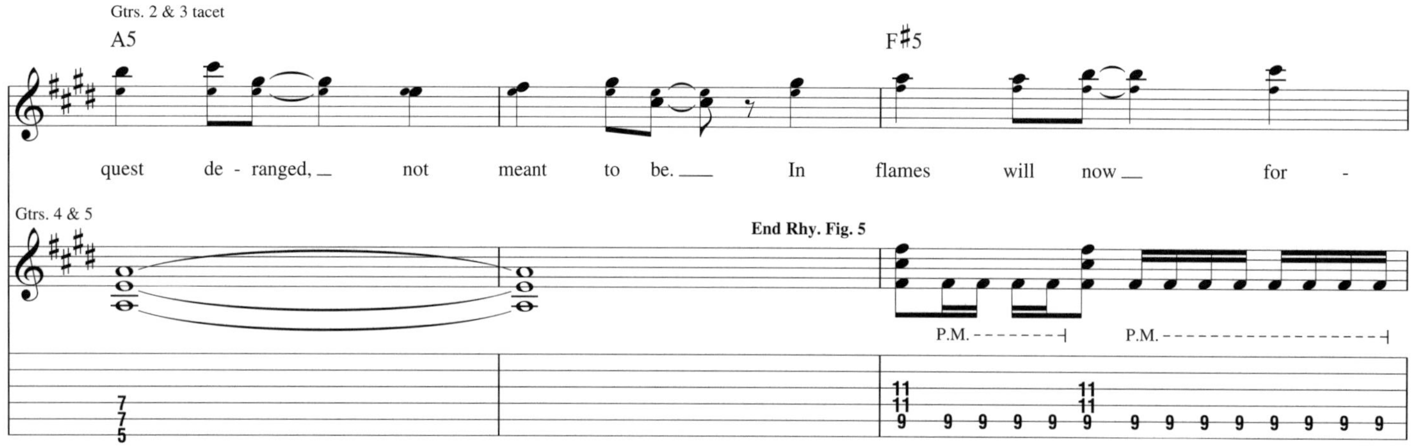
Gtrs. 2 & 3 tacet
A5
F♯5
quest de - ranged, not meant to be. In flames will now for -
Gtrs. 4 & 5
End Rhy. Fig. 5
P.M.
P.M.

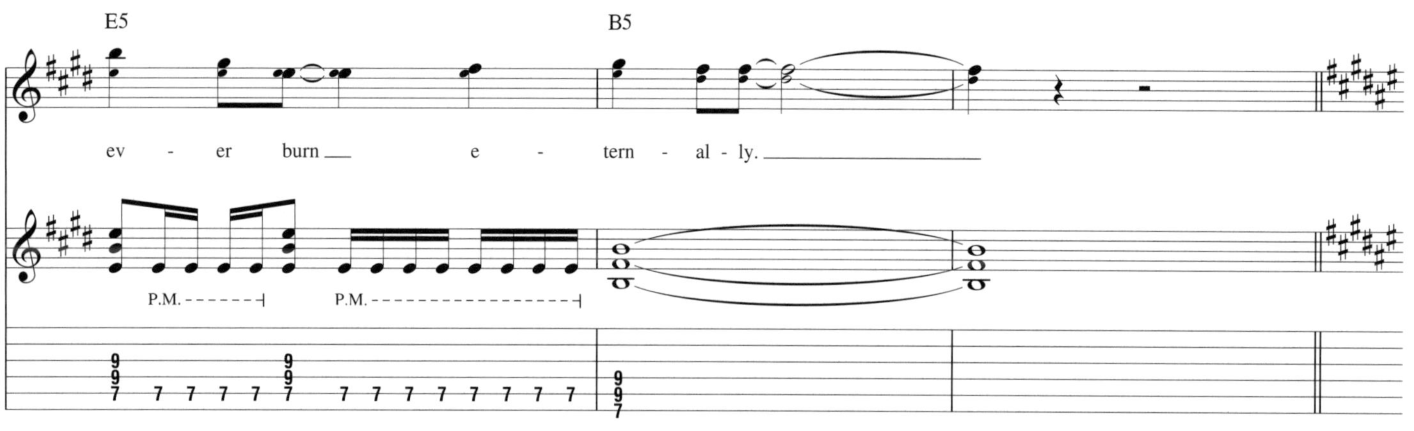
E5
B5
ev - er burn e - tern - al - ly.
P.M.
P.M.

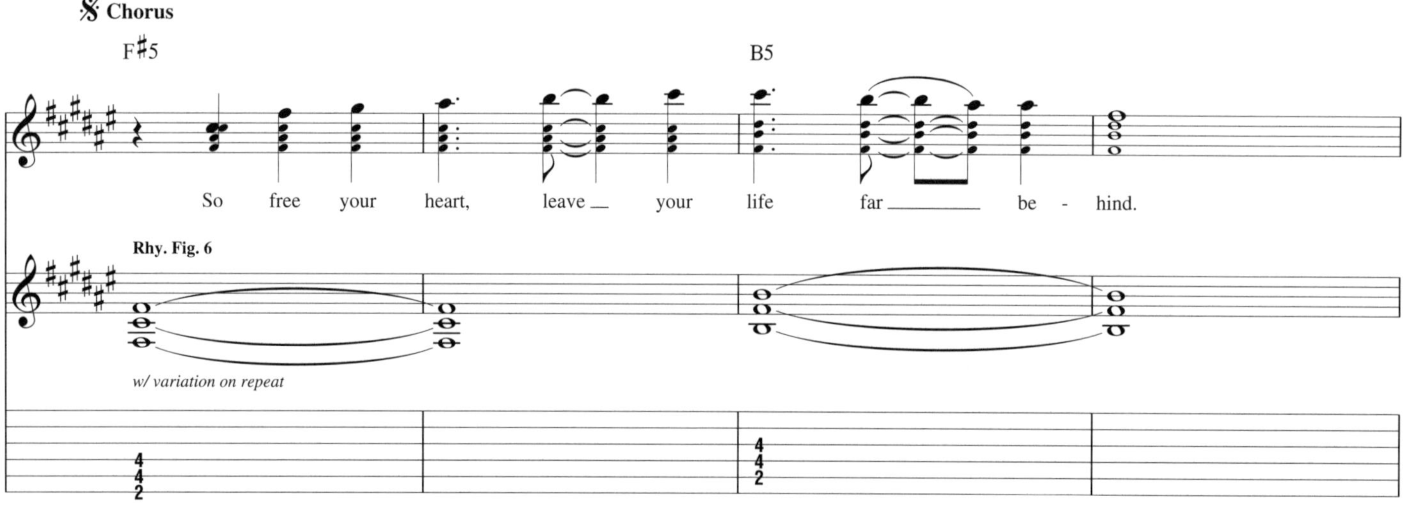
Chorus
F♯5
B5
So free your heart, leave your life far be - hind.
Rhy. Fig. 6
w/ variation on repeat

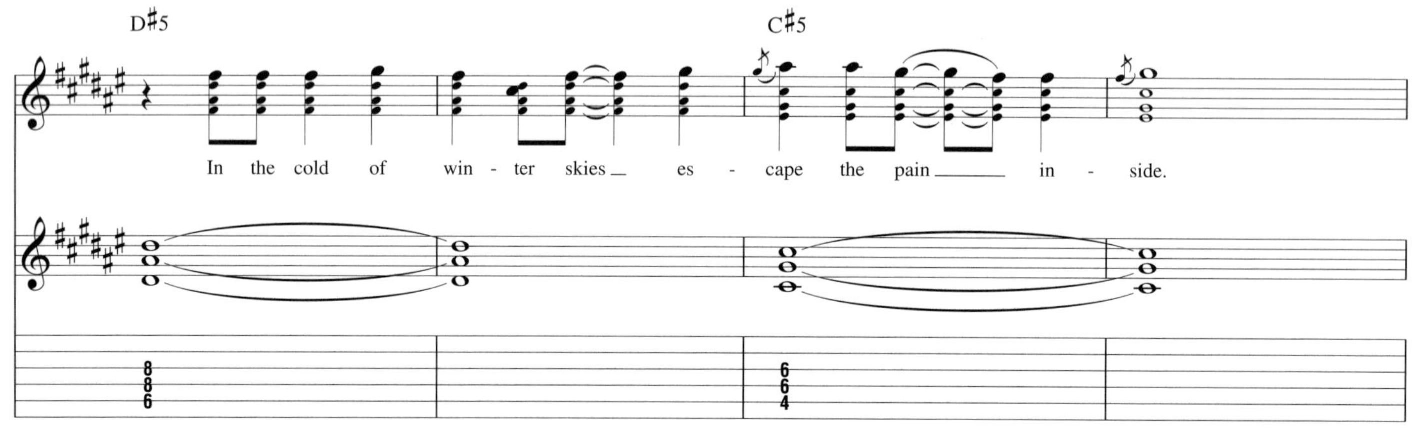
D♯5
C♯5
In the cold of win - ter skies es - cape the pain in - side.

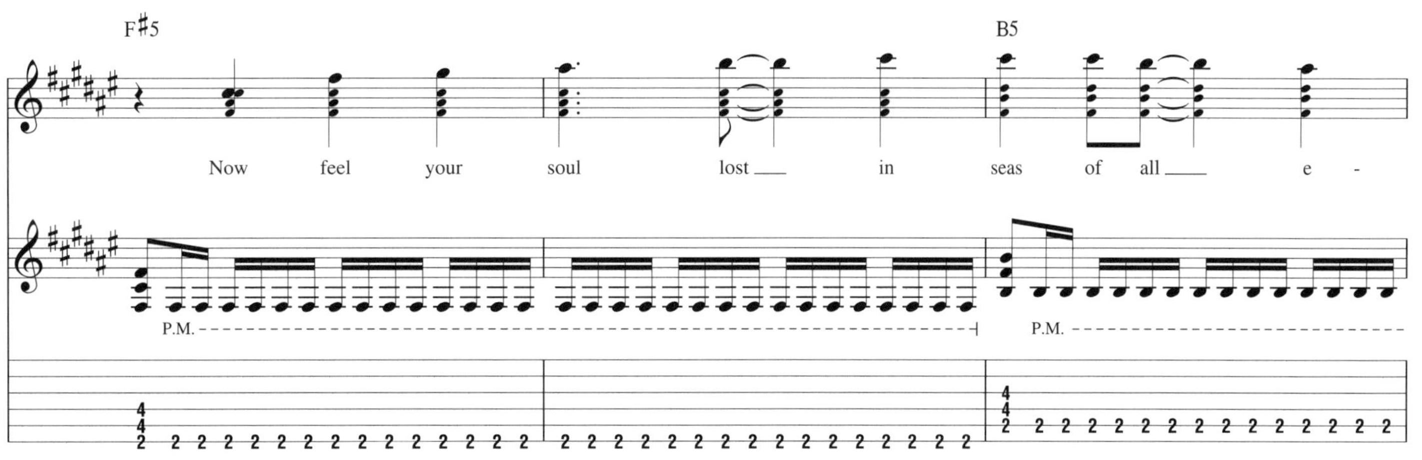
F#5
B5
Now feel your soul lost in seas of all e -
P.M.
P.M.

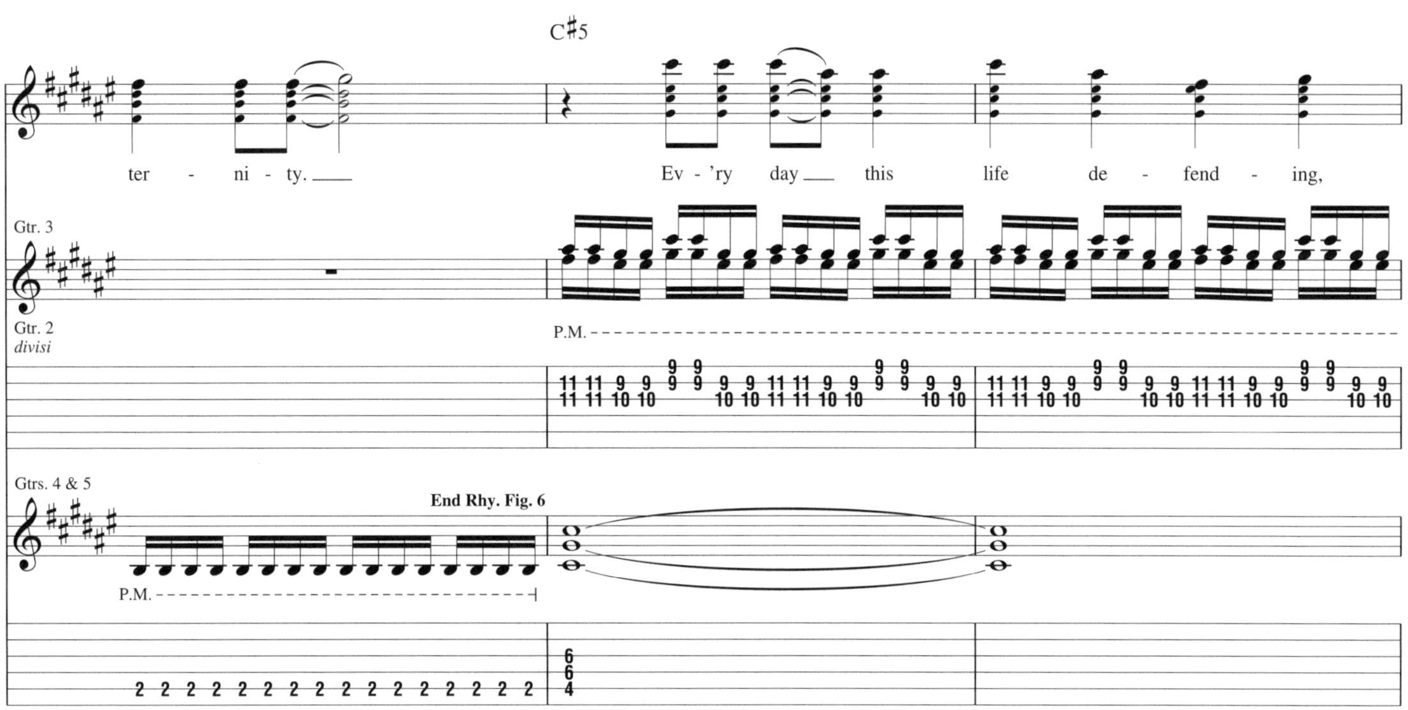
C#5
ter - ni - ty.
Ev - 'ry day this life de - fend - ing,
Gtr. 3
Gtr. 2
divisi
P.M.
Gtrs. 4 & 5
End Rhy. Fig. 6
P.M.

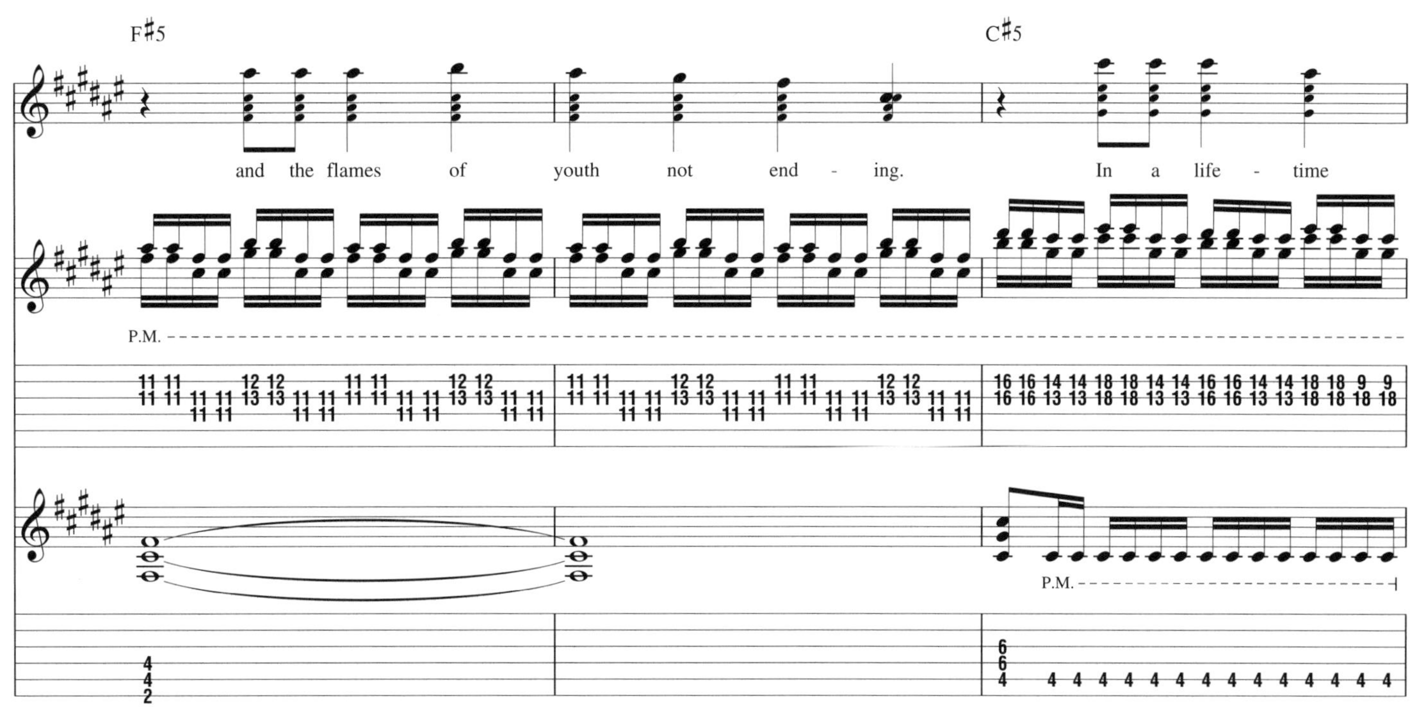
F#5
C#5
and the flames of youth not end - ing.
In a life - time
P.M.
P.M.

To Coda 𝄌

B5 N.C.

search - ing we must fight through ___ the e - ter - nal

Gtr. 3

P.M.

16 16 14 14 18 18 14 14 16 16 14 14 18 18 14 14 | 14 11 14 12 14 12 11 11 10 11 11 12 14 11 14 12 | 11 12 14 11 13 11 14 12 13 14 13 11 14 12 11 12

Gtr. 2

P.M.

16 16 13 13 18 18 13 13 16 16 13 13 18 18 13 13 | 11 12 11 13 11 13 11 13 11 13 11 13 11 12 11 13 | 13 11 13 11 12 14 12 11 12 14 11 14 12 11 13 11

Gtrs. 4 & 5

Rhy. Fig. 7

P.M. P.M.

6 6 4 4 4 4 4 6 6 4 4 4 4 4 4 4 4 4 | 4 4 2

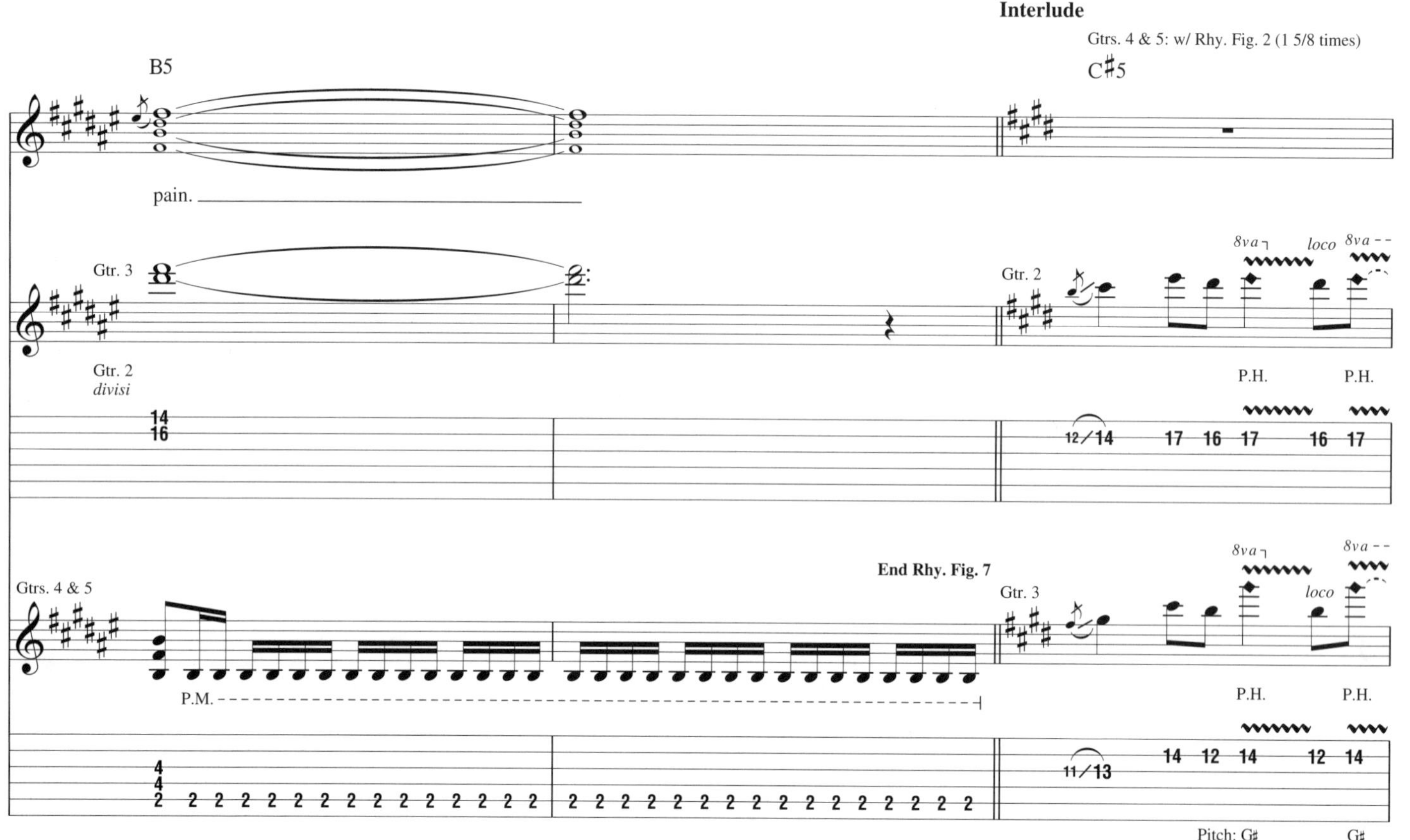

B5
C♯5
B5
8va
loco
P.H.
Pitch: F♯
G♯
G♯
F♯

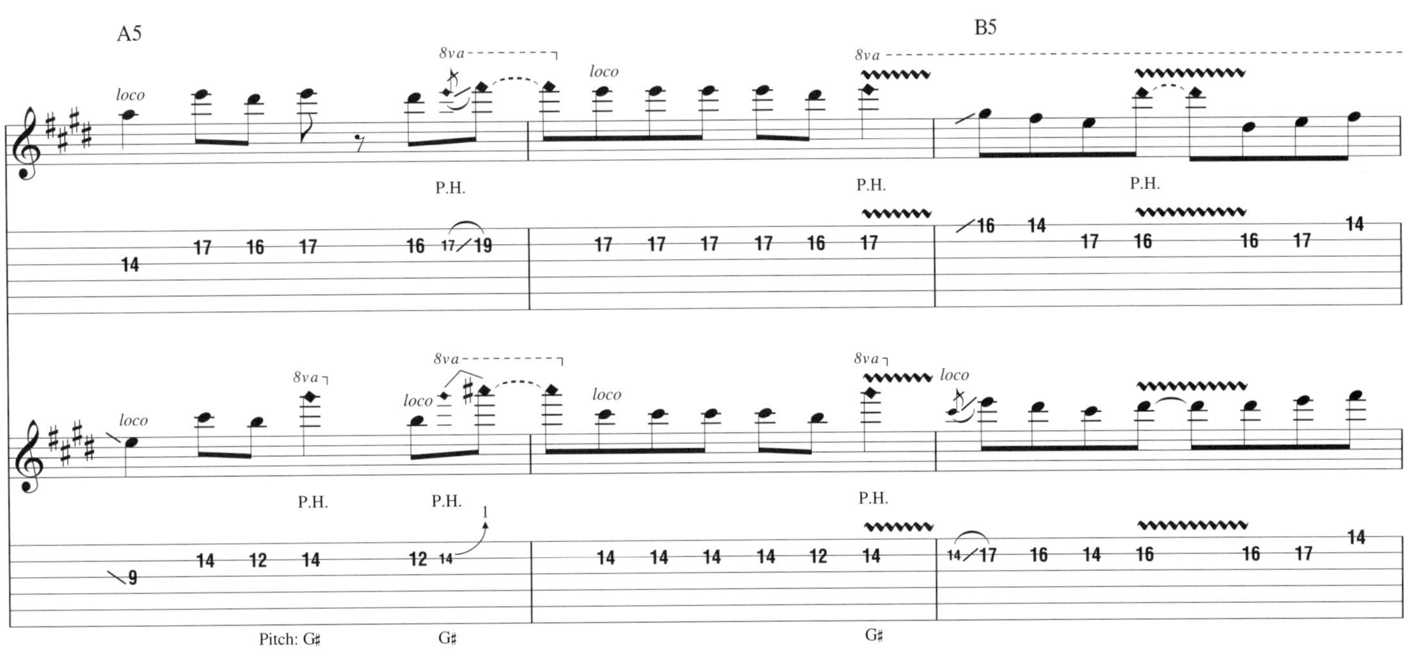
A5
B5
8va
loco
P.H.
Pitch: G♯
G♯
G♯

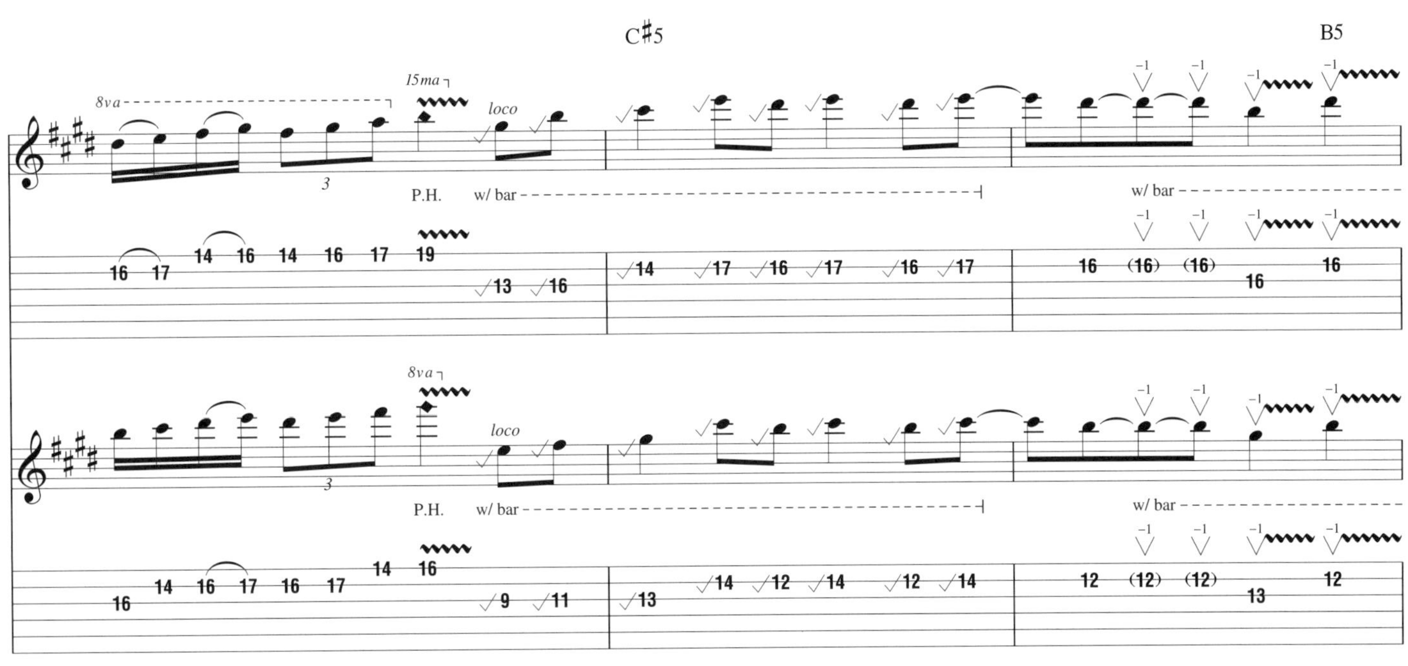
C♯5
B5
8va
15ma
loco
P.H.
w/ bar

C♯5
B5
A5
8va
loco
15ma
P.H.
w/ bar
P.M.
-1 1/2
8va
loco
8va
P.H.
w/ bar
P.M.
Pitch: F♯
D♯
F♯
F♯

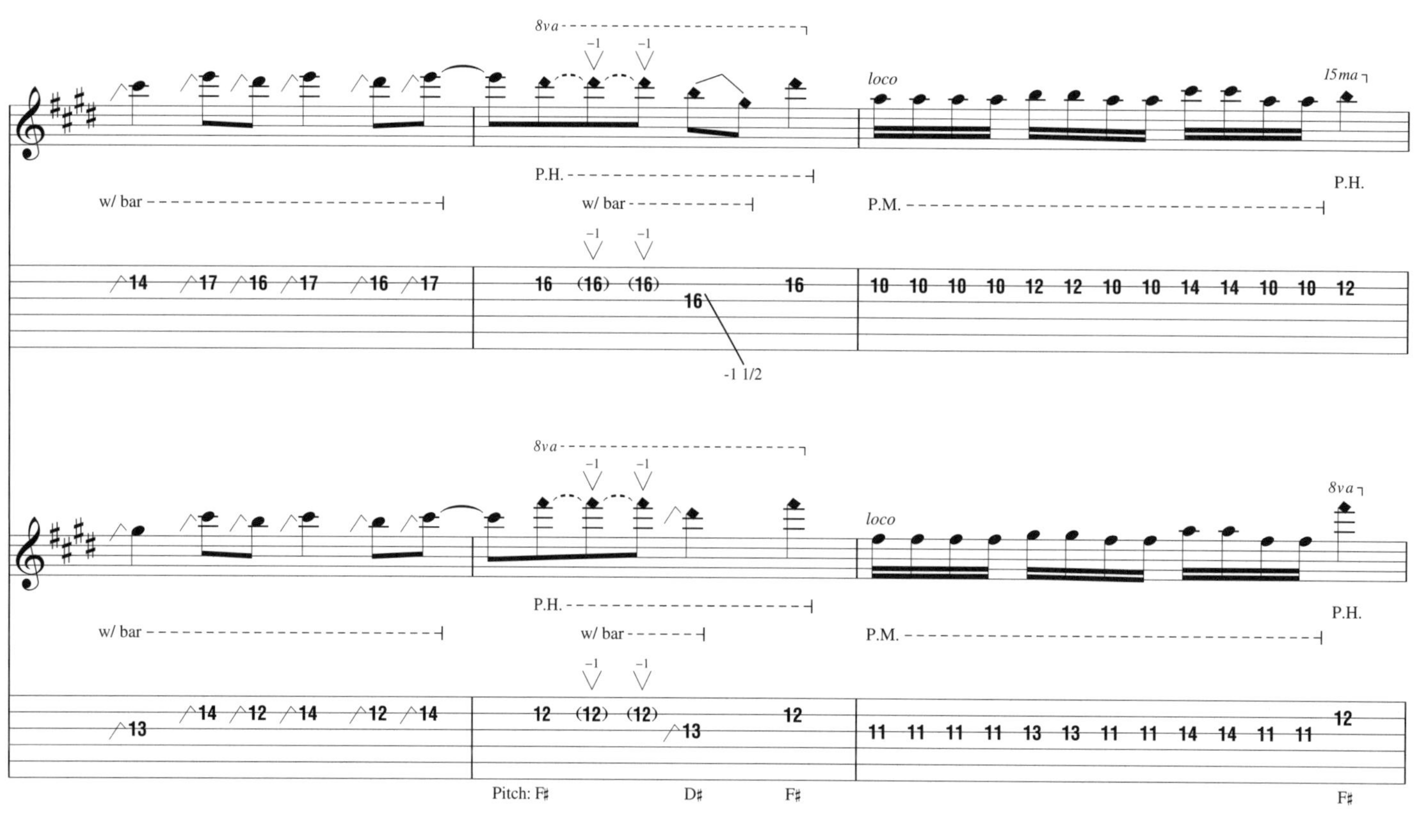

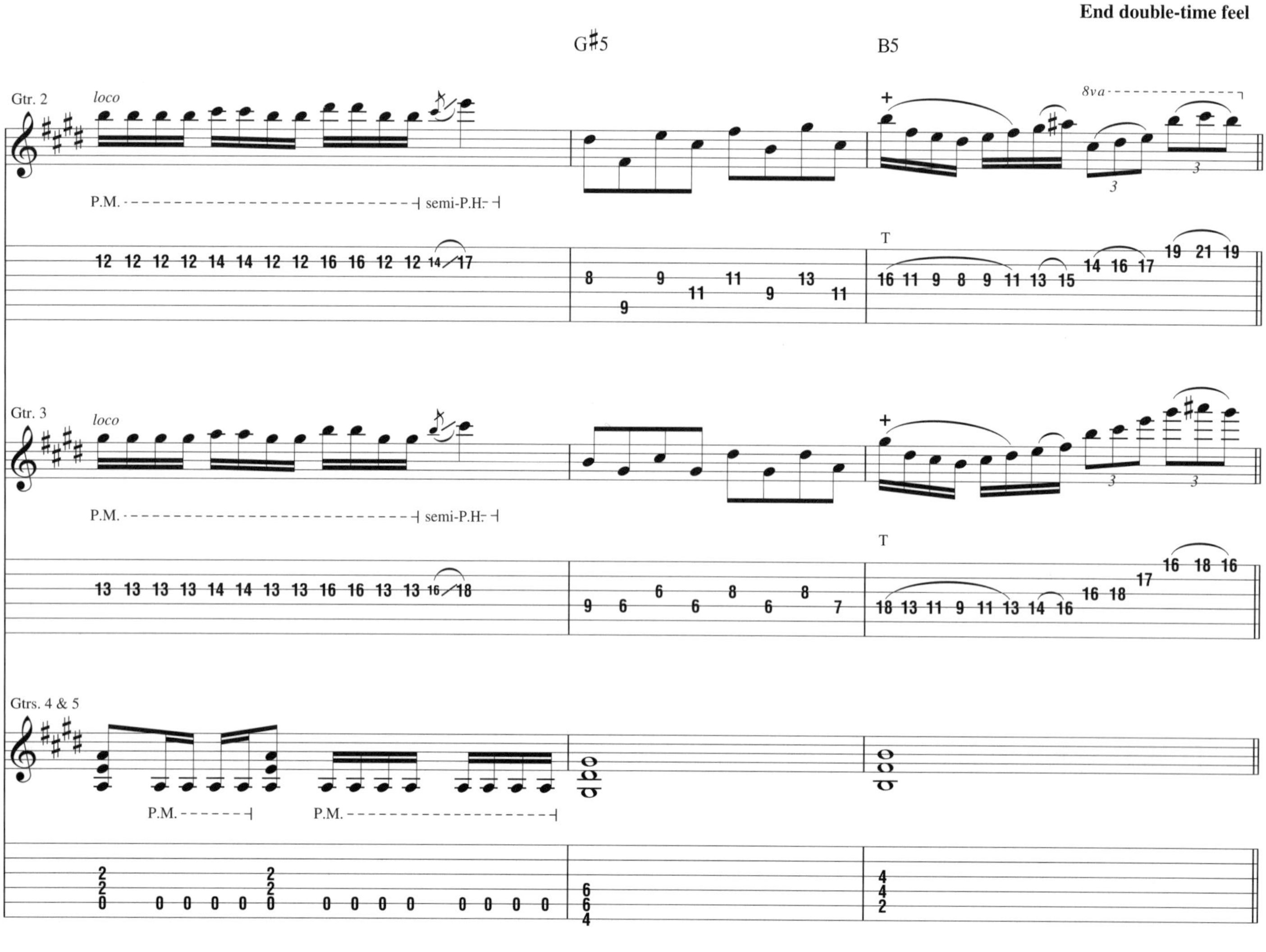

End double-time feel
G♯5
B5
Gtr. 2
loco
8va
P.M.
semi-P.H.
T
Gtr. 3
loco
P.M.
semi-P.H.
T
Gtrs. 4 & 5
P.M.
P.M.

Verse

Gtrs. 2 & 3 tacet
C♯5
2. So a - lone in a world far a - way. Mem - o - ries of a
loco
Gtr. 2
Gtr. 3
divisi
*Gtr. 2 to left of slash in tab.
Gtrs. 4 & 5
P.M.

B5
A5
dream will re - main as the world fall - ing calls and our
Gtrs. 4 & 5
P.M.

Double-time feel
Gtrs. 2 & 3 tacet
Gtrs. 4 & 5: w/ Rhy. Fig. 3
B5
Gtrs. 4 & 5
C♯5
B5 C♯5 E5 D♯5 B5
lives are in vain. Fi - re in my soul will for - ev - er rise a - gain,
Gtrs. 2 & 3
15ma
P.M.
Harm.
w/ bar
(cont. in slashes)

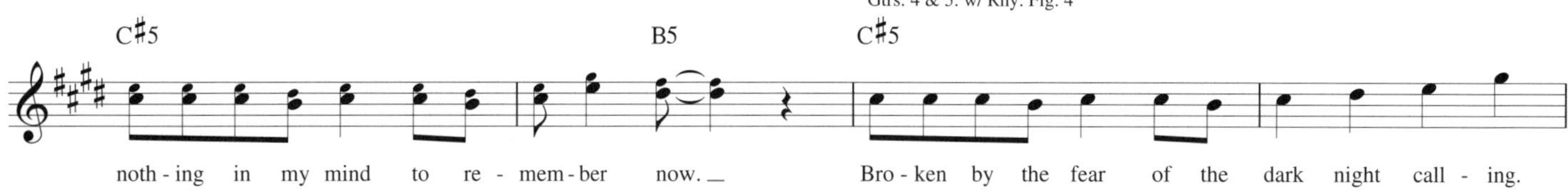
Gtrs. 4 & 5: w/ Rhy. Fig. 4
C♯5
B5
C♯5
noth - ing in my mind to re - mem - ber now.
Bro - ken by the fear of the dark night call - ing.

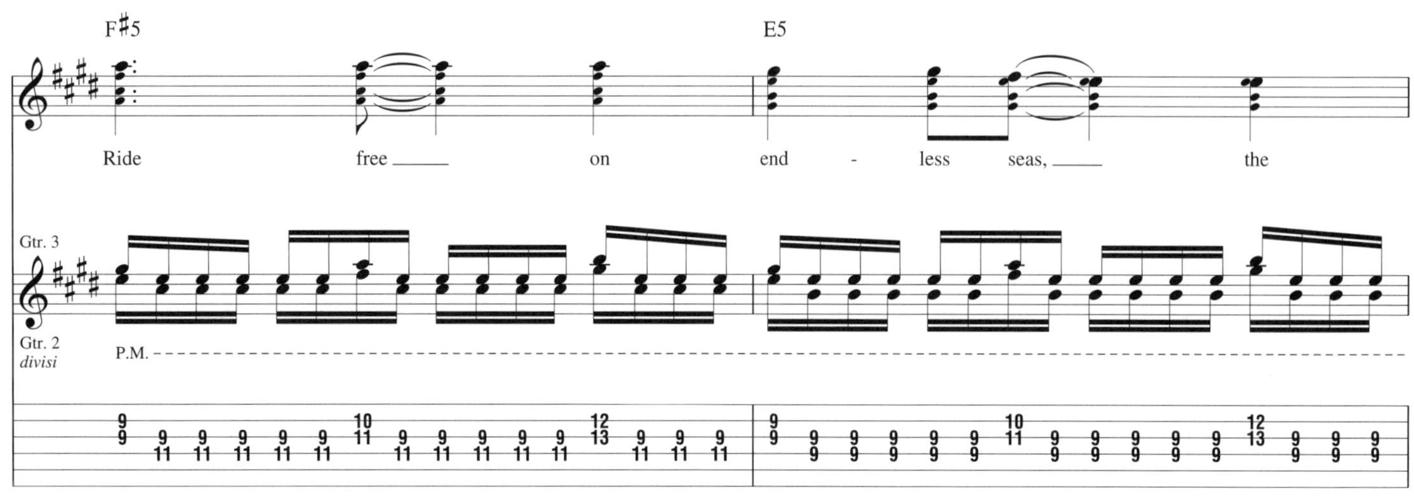
F♯5
E5
Ride free on end - less seas, the
Gtr. 3
Gtr. 2
divisi
P.M.

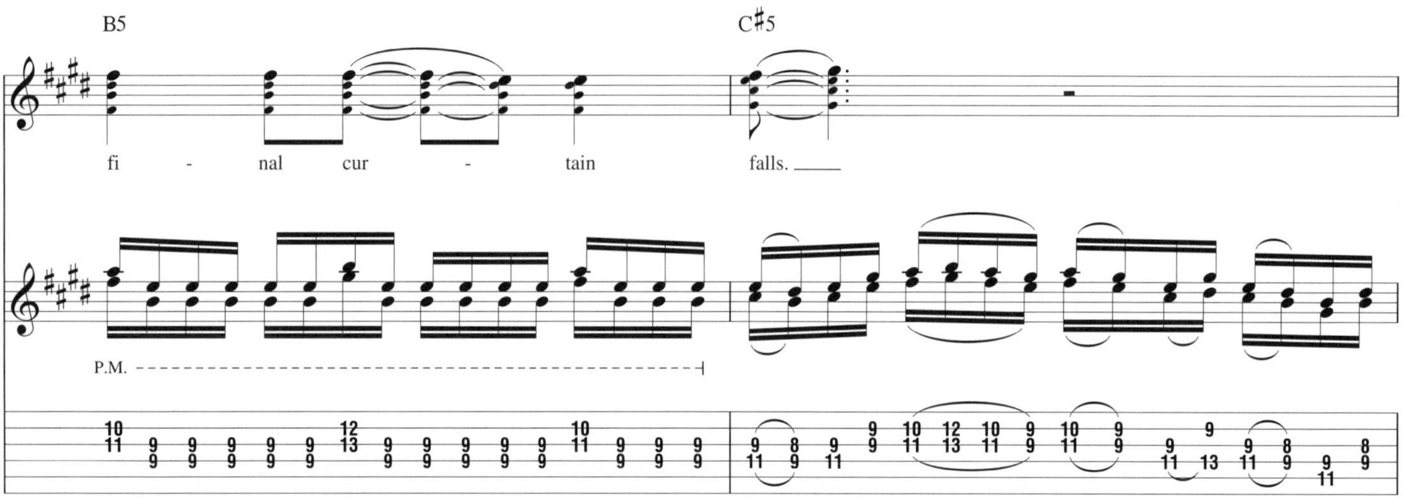
B5
C♯5
fi - nal cur - tain falls.
P.M.

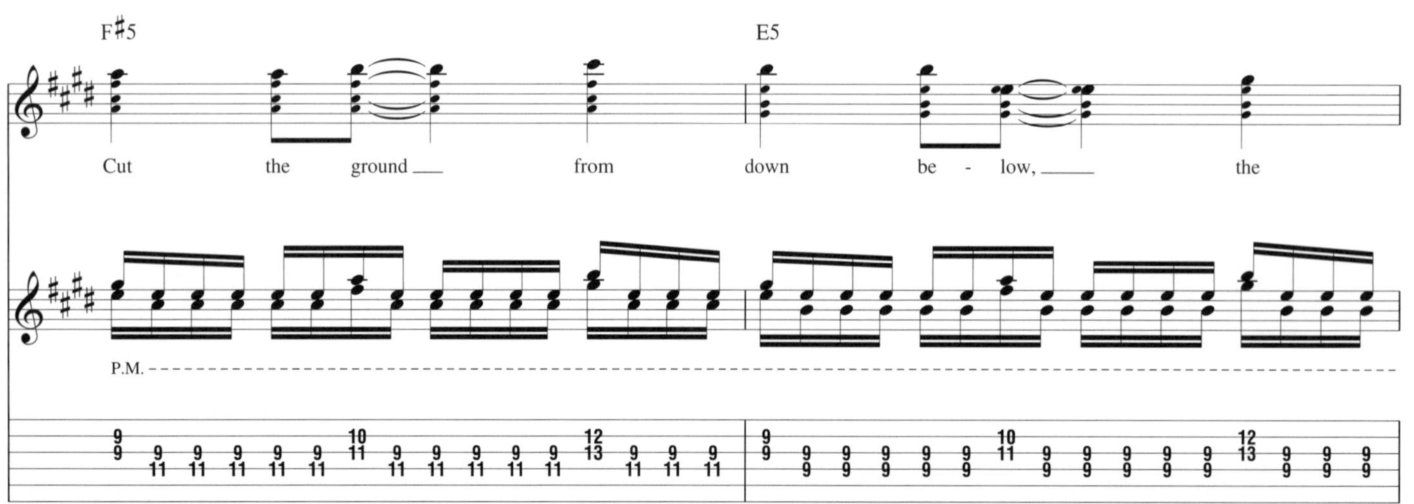
F♯5
E5
Cut the ground from down be - low, the
P.M.

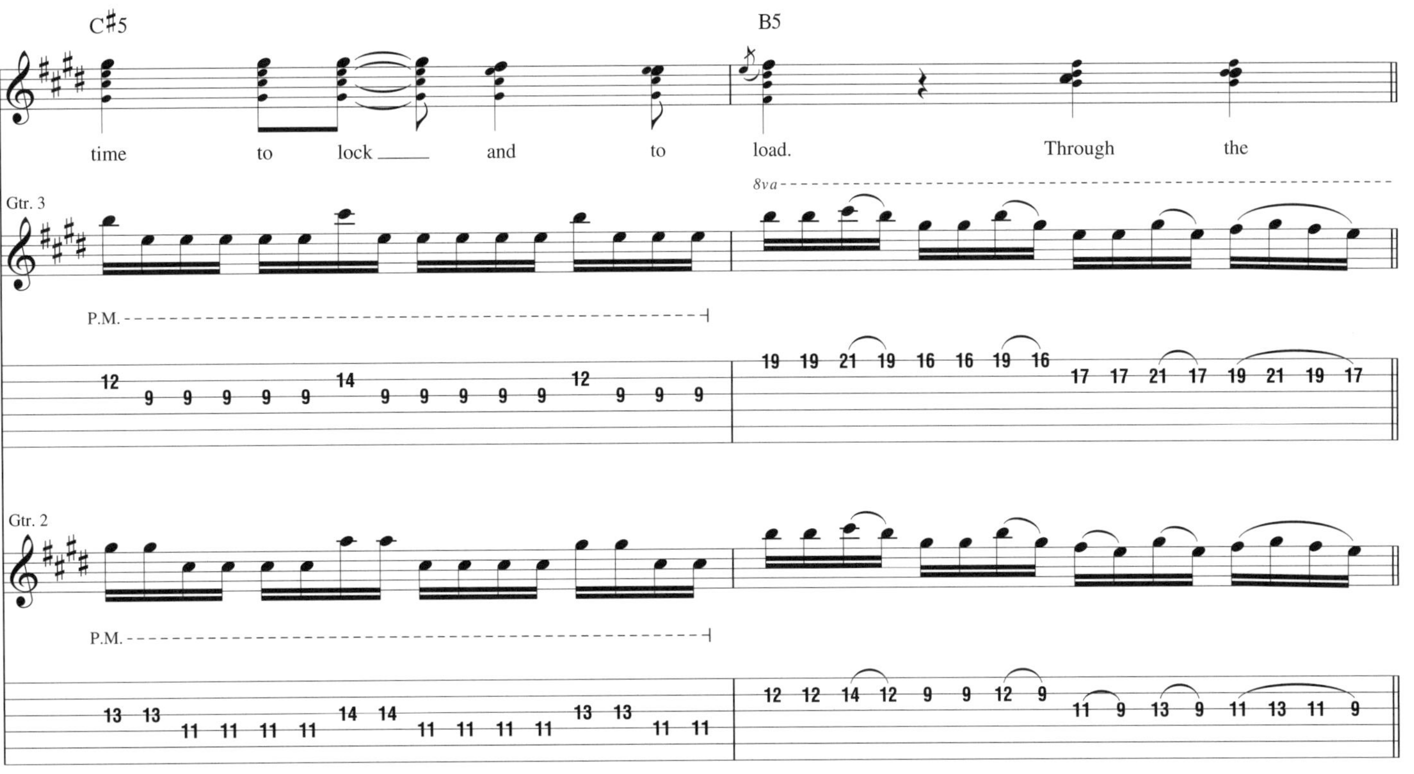

Pre-Chorus

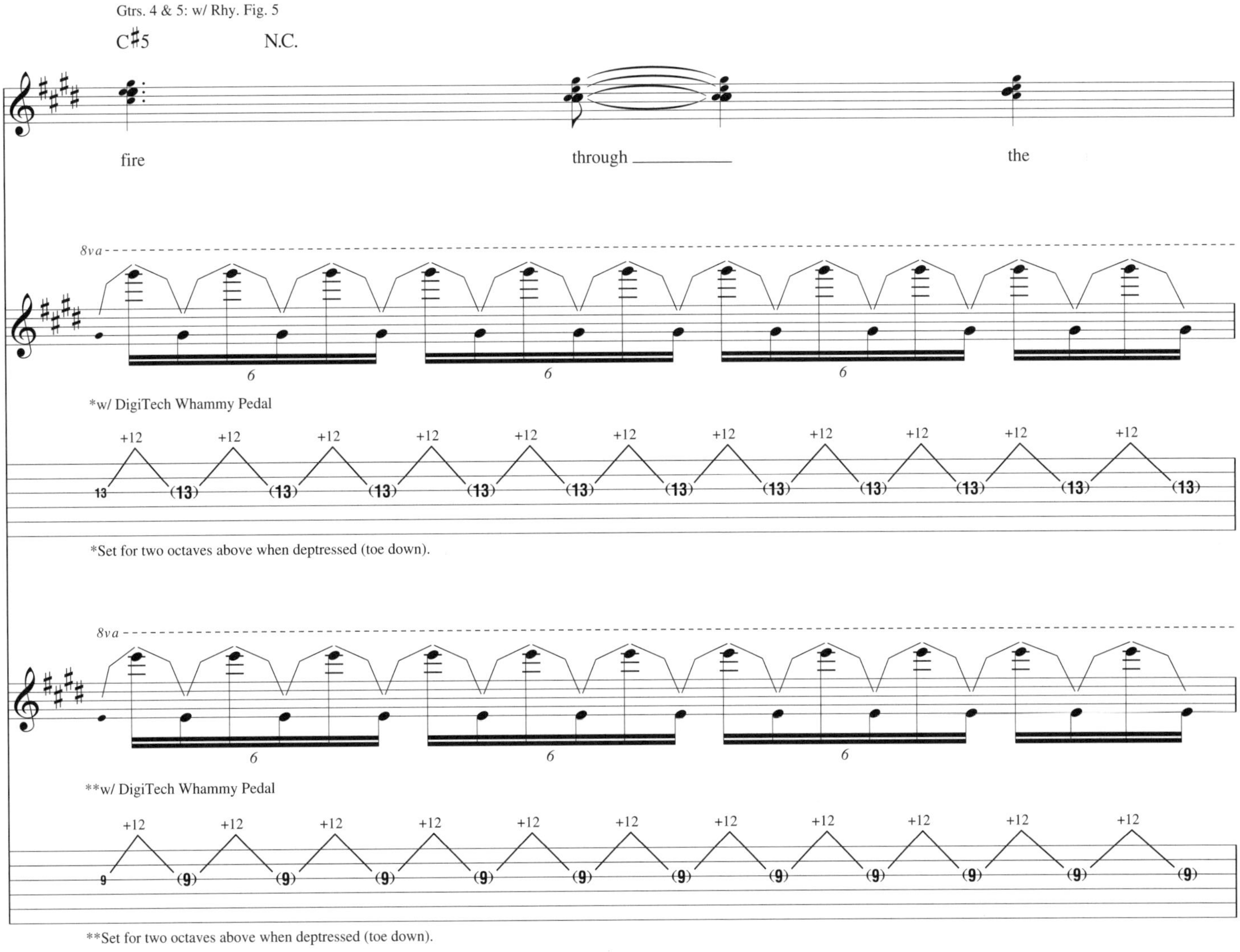

Gtrs. 4 & 5: w/ Rhy. Fig. 5

C#5 N.C.

fire through the

8va

6 6 6

*w/ DigiTech Whammy Pedal

+12 +12 +12 +12 +12 +12 +12 +12 +12 +12 +12

13 (13) (13) (13) (13) (13) (13) (13) (13) (13) (13) (13)

*Set for two octaves above when deptressed (toe down).

8va

6 6 6

**w/ DigiTech Whammy Pedal

+12 +12 +12 +12 +12 +12 +12 +12 +12 +12 +12

9 (9) (9) (9) (9) (9) (9) (9) (9) (9) (9) (9)

**Set for two octaves above when deptressed (toe down).

A5 N.C.
E5
rain, far a - cross the dis - tant
8va
+12 +12 +12 +12 +12
14 (14) (14) (14) (14) (14) (14)
8va
+12 +12 +12 +12 +12
11 (11) (11) (11) (11) (11) (11)

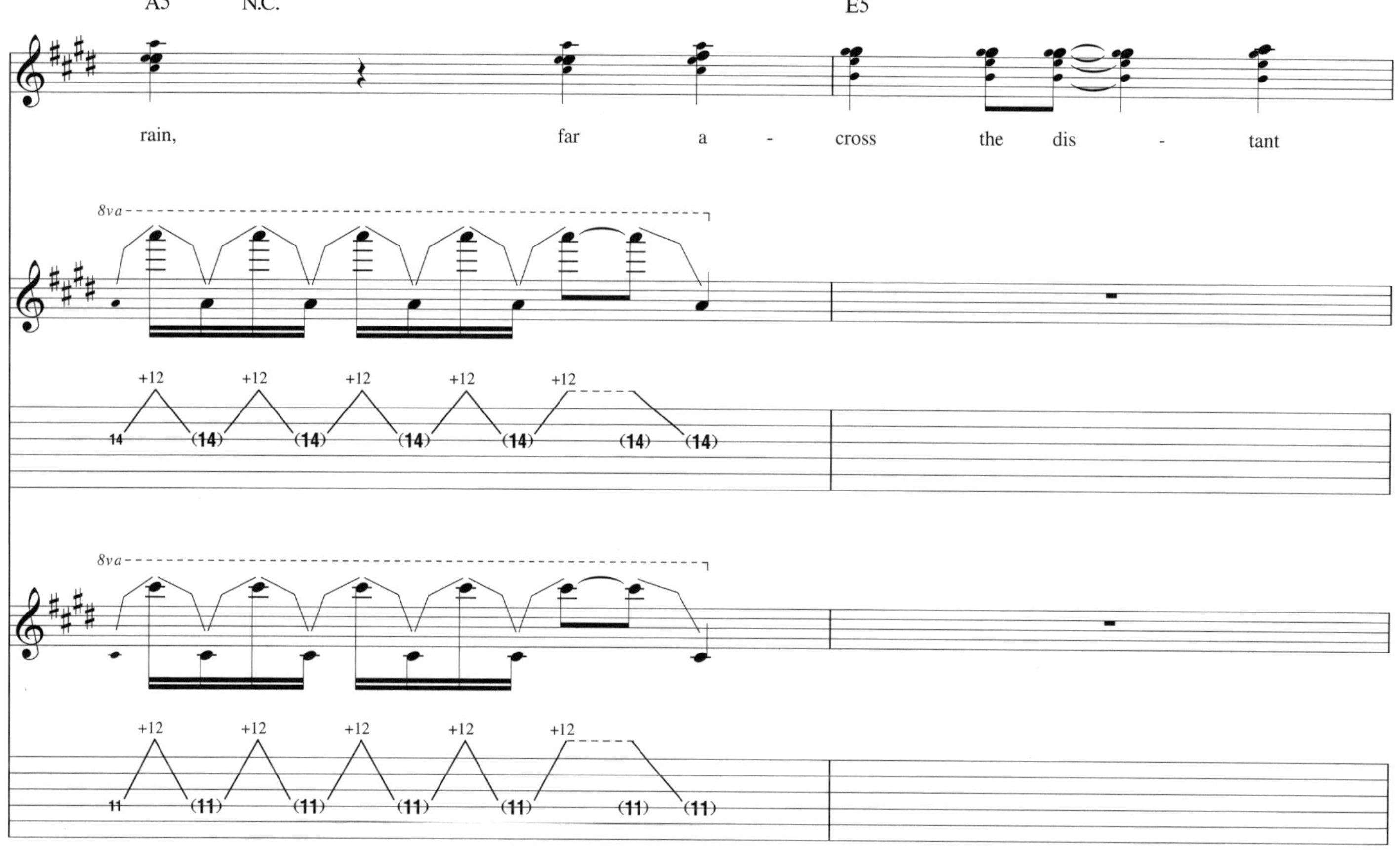

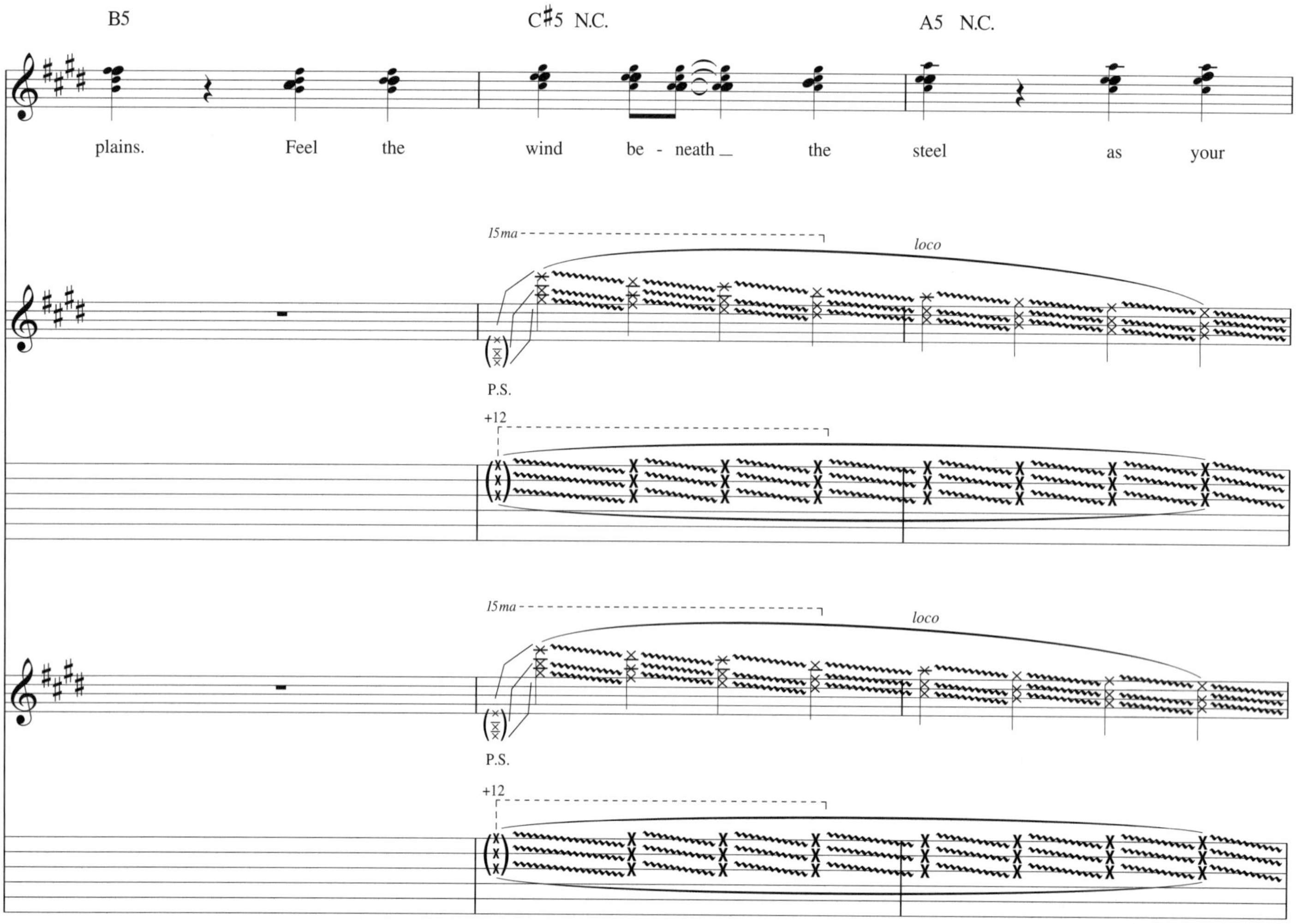

B5
C♯5 N.C.
A5 N.C.
plains. Feel the wind be - neath _ the steel as your
15ma
loco
P.S.
+12
15ma
loco
P.S.
+12

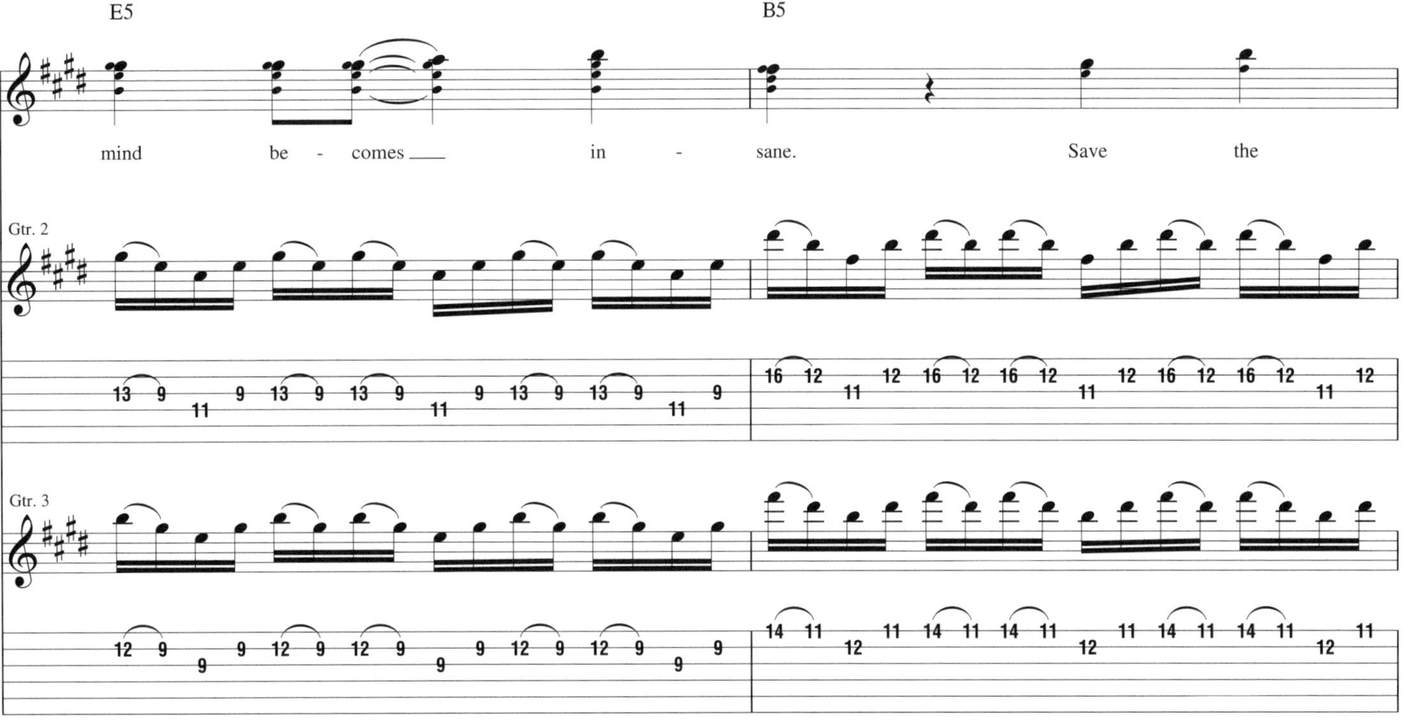
E5
B5
mind be - comes in - sane. Save the
Gtr. 2
Gtr. 3

Gtrs. 2 & 3 tacet
C♯5
B5 C♯5
A5
pain from all hu - man - i - ty that rides through-out our des - ti - ny. For
15ma
Gtr. 2
Gtr. 3
divisi
P.H.
w/ bar
*Gtr. 2 to left of slash in tab.

D.S. al Coda
F♯5
E5
B5
free - dom now we rise for all a - gain.
Gtrs. 4 & 5
P.M.
P.S.

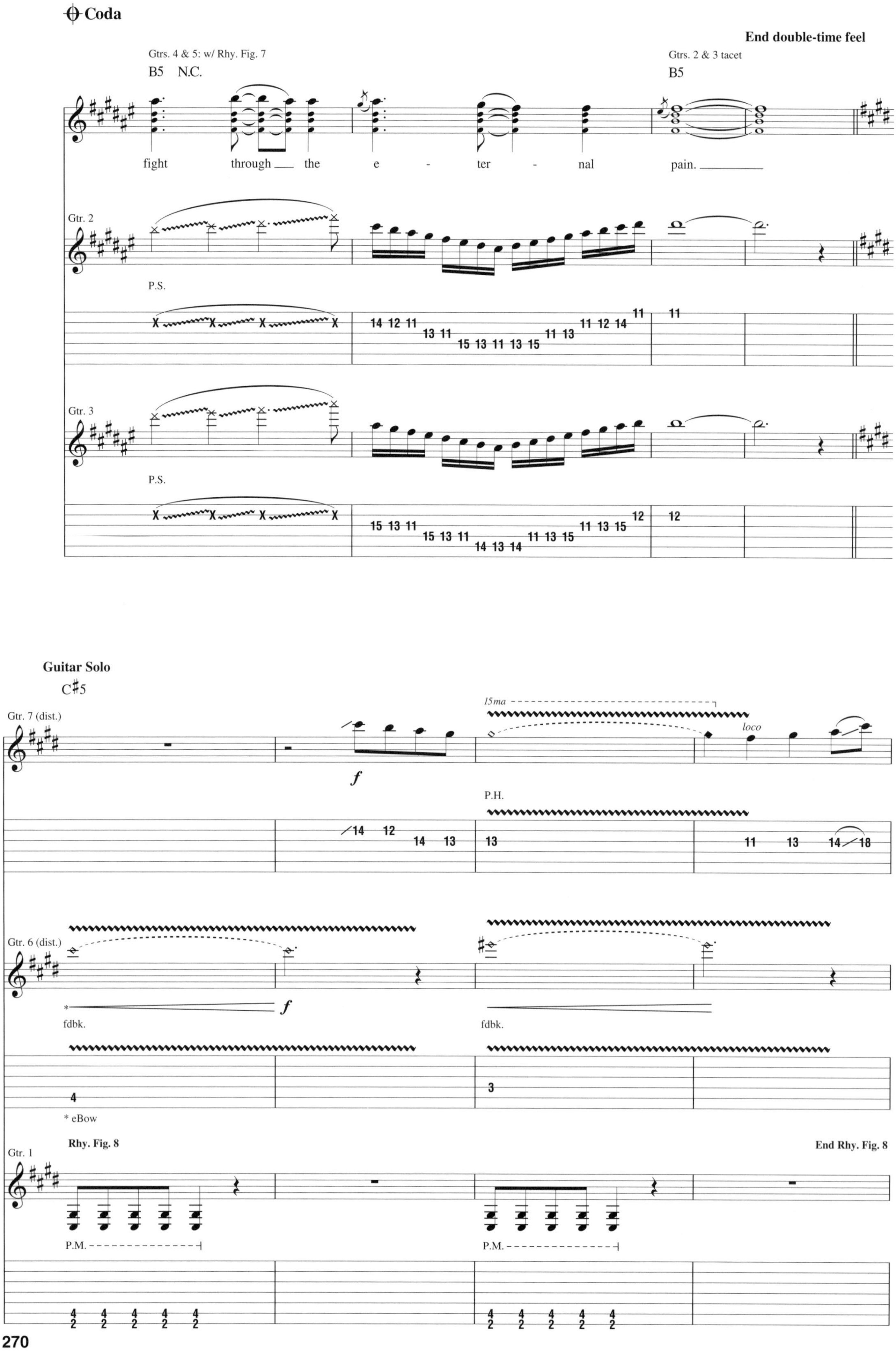

Coda

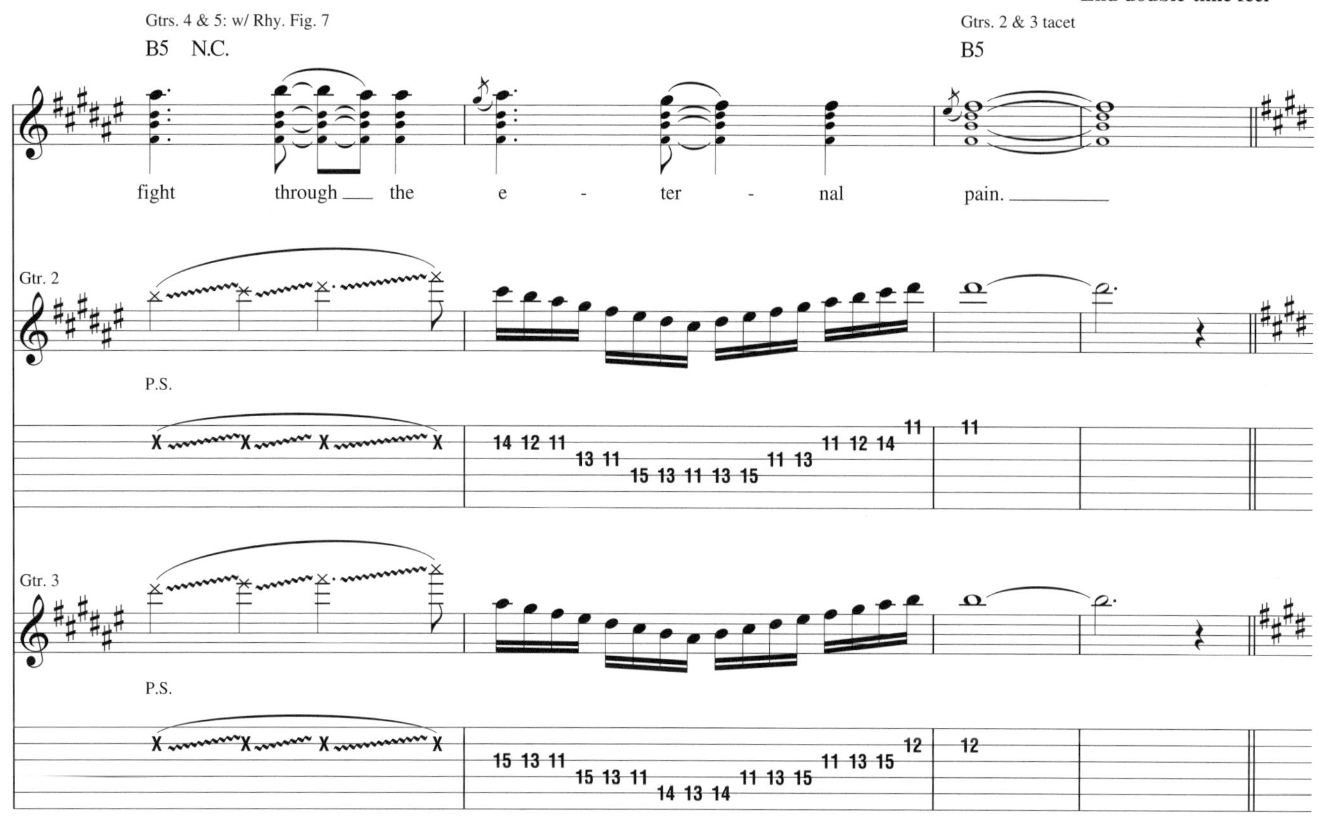

Guitar Solo

C♯5

Gtr. 7 (dist.)

f

15ma

loco

P.H.

Gtr. 6 (dist.)

f

fdbk.

fdbk.

* eBow

Gtr. 1

Rhy. Fig. 8

End Rhy. Fig. 8

P.M.

P.M.

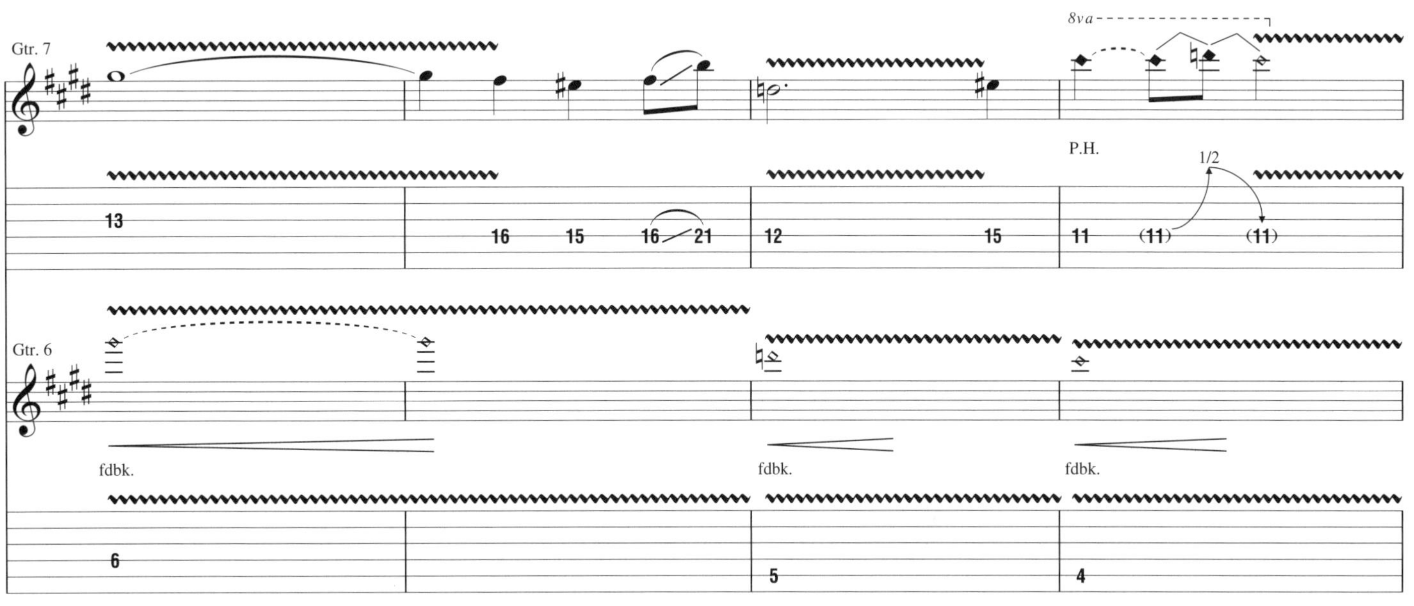
Gtr. 1: w/ Rhy. Fig. 8
Gtr. 7
8va
P.H.
1/2
Gtr. 6
fdbk.
fdbk.
fdbk.

Gtr. 6 tacet
Gtr. 7
Rhy. Fig. 9
End Rhy. Fig. 9
Gtr. 1
P.M.

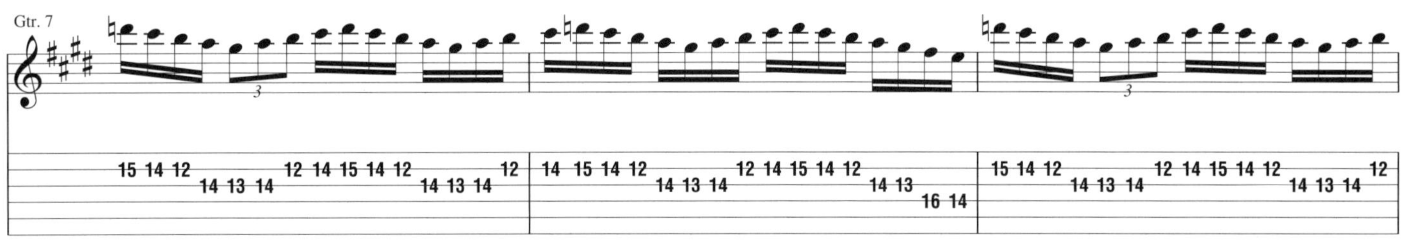
Gtr. 1: w/ Rhy. Fig. 9 (3 times)
Gtr. 7

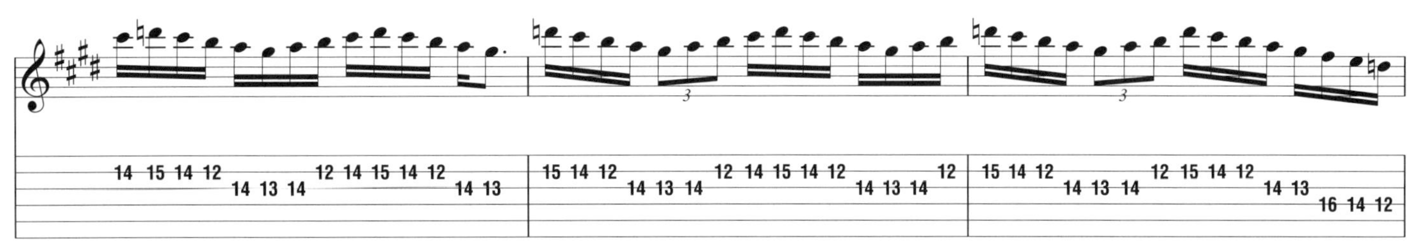

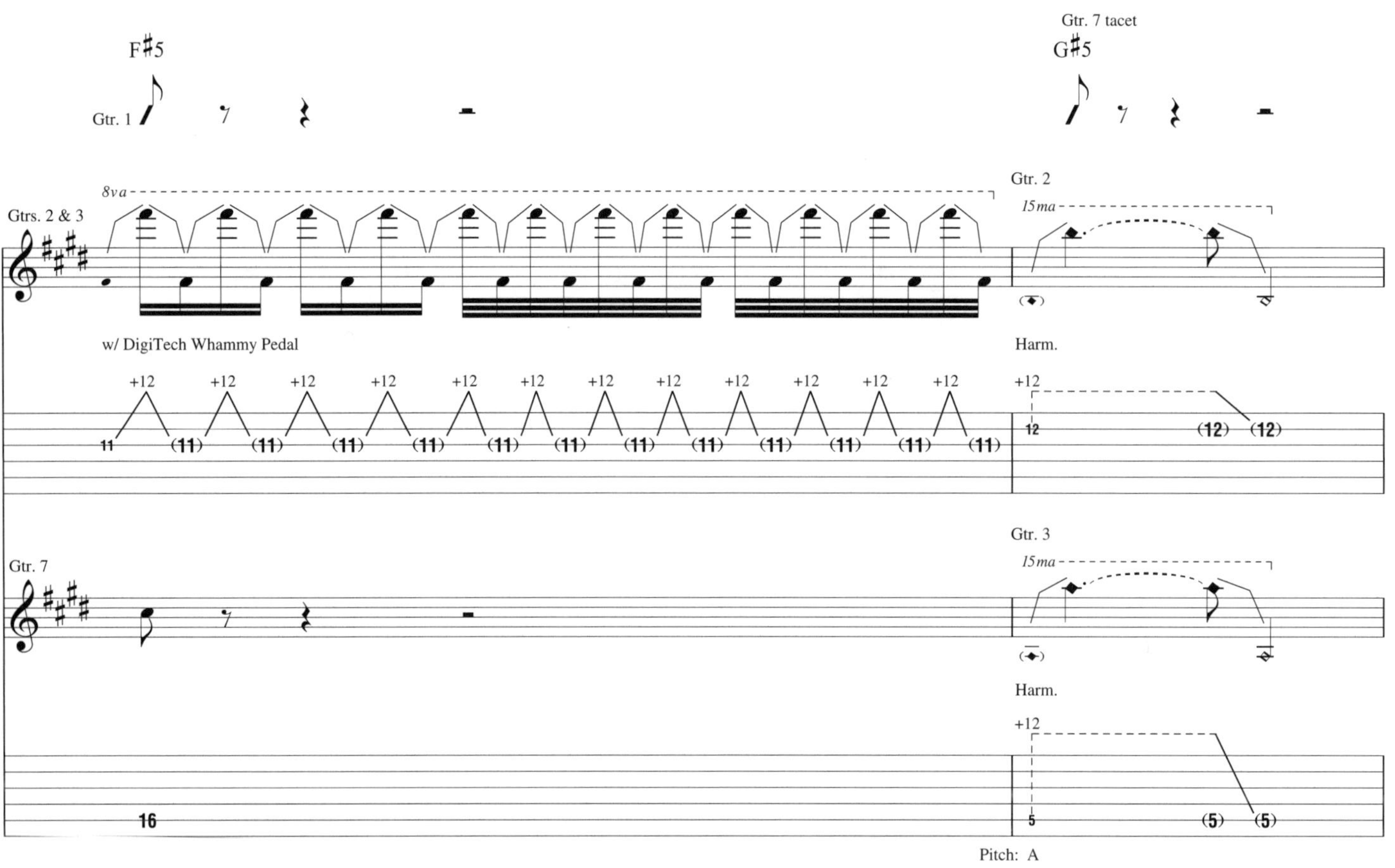

Double-time feel

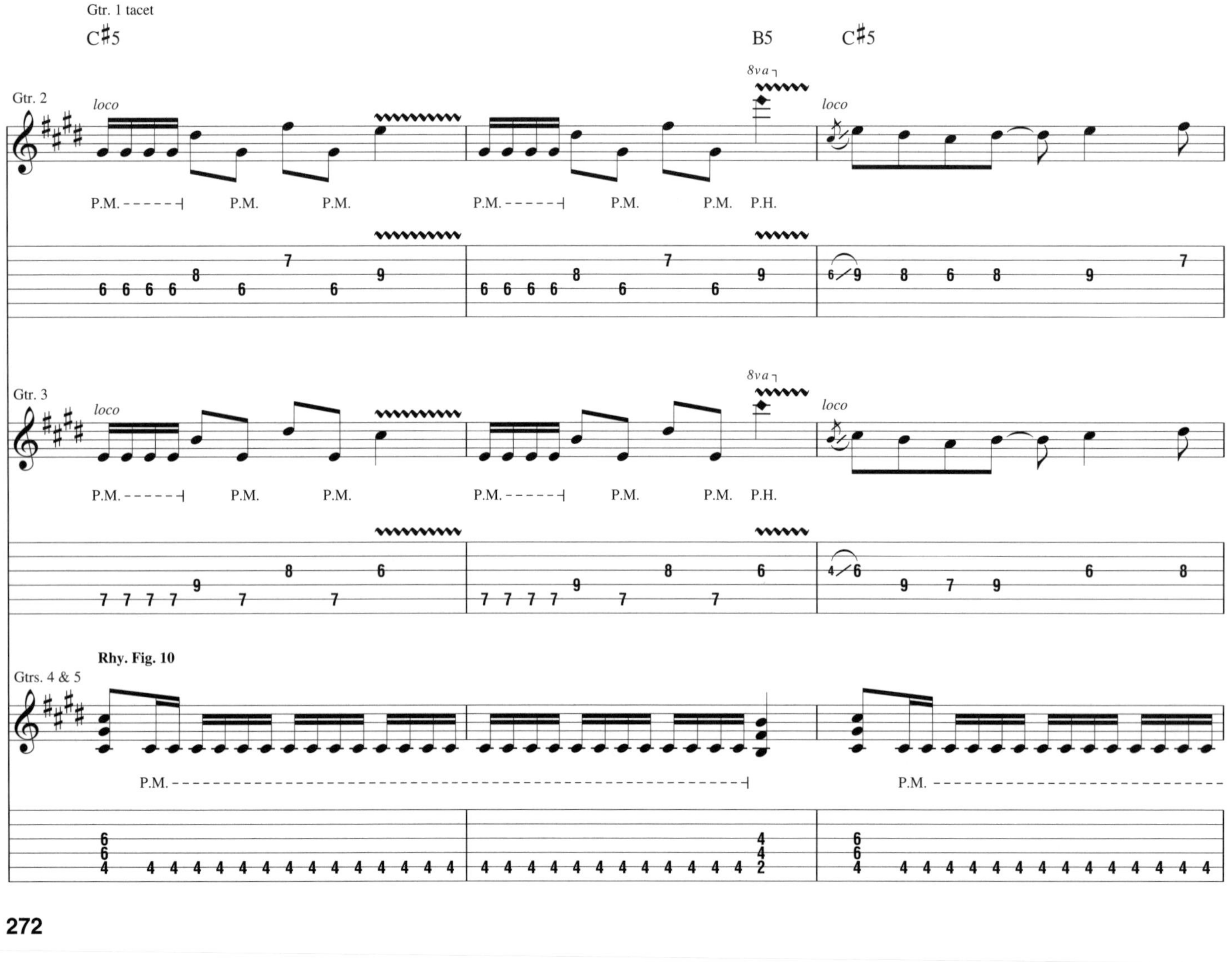

Gtr. 1 tacet

C♯5 B5 C♯5

Gtr. 2 loco 8va loco

P.M. P.M. P.M. P.M. P.M. P.M. P.H.

Gtr. 3 loco 8va loco

P.M. P.M. P.M. P.M. P.M. P.M. P.H.

Rhy. Fig. 10

Gtrs. 4 & 5

P.M. P.M.

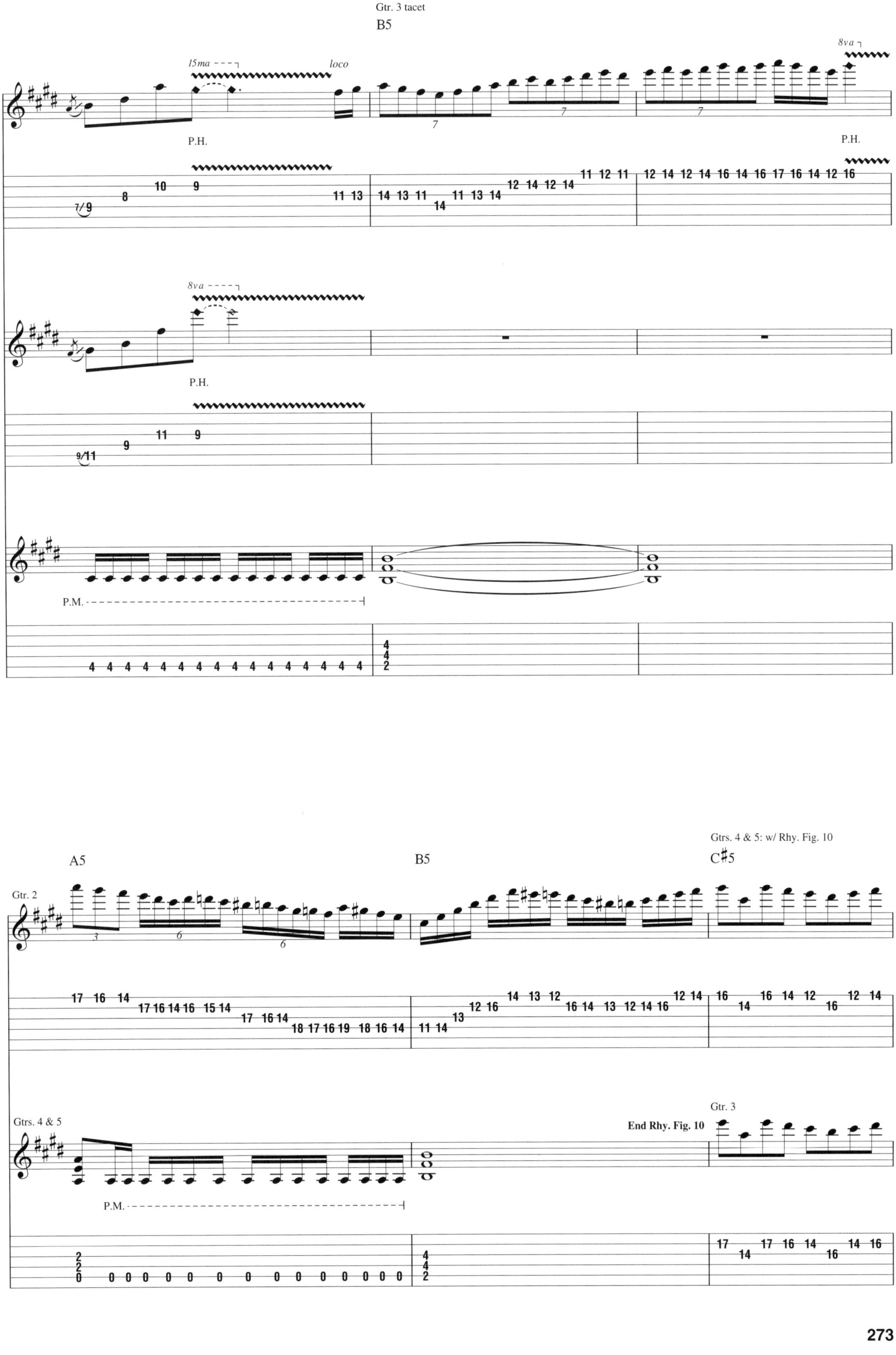

Gtr. 3 tacet

B5

15ma loco 8va

P.H.

8va

P.H.

P.M.

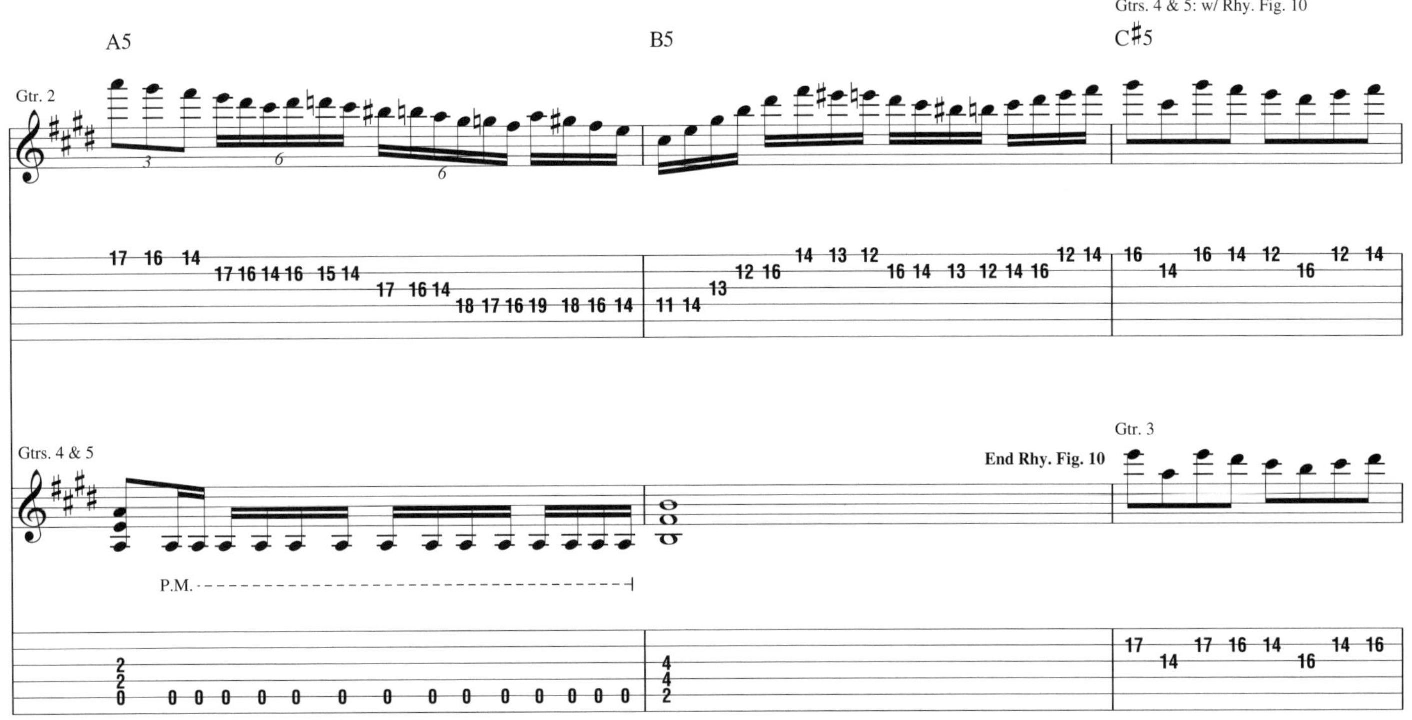

B5
C♯5

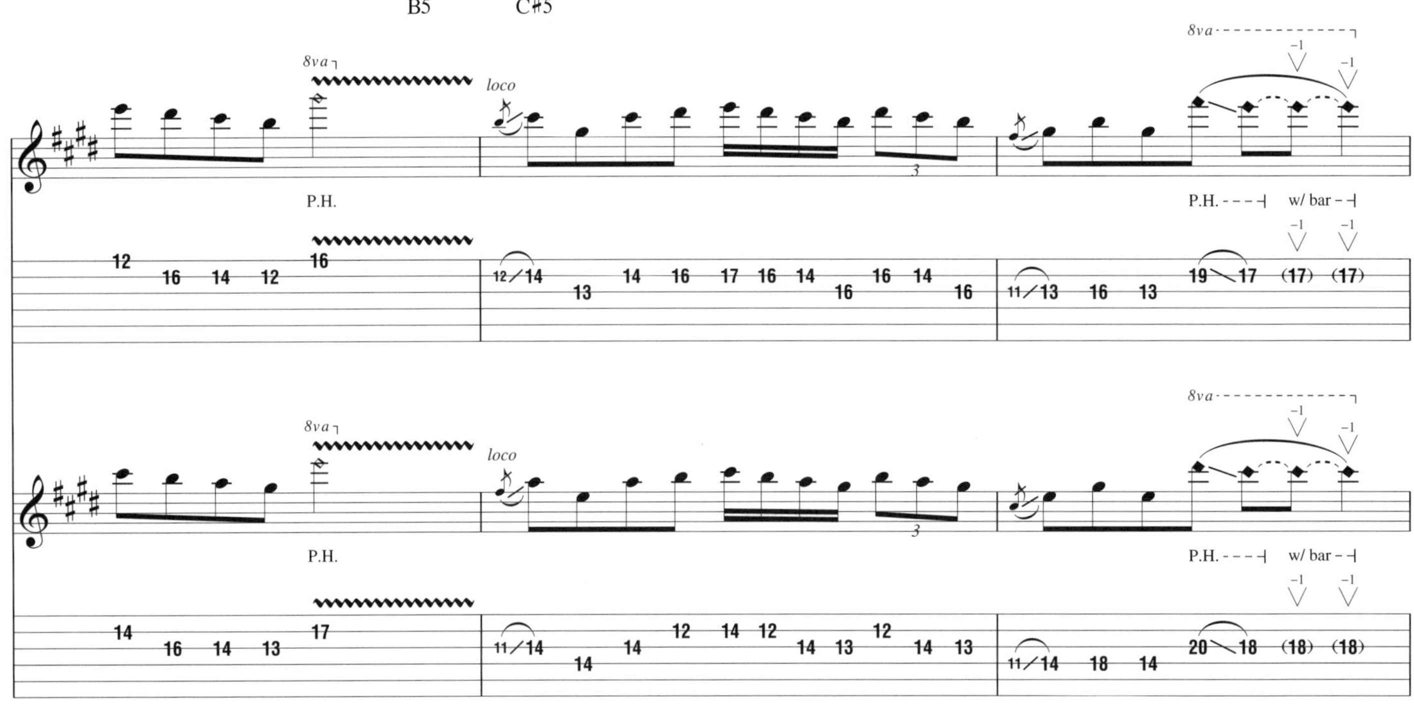
8va
loco
P.H.
w/ bar

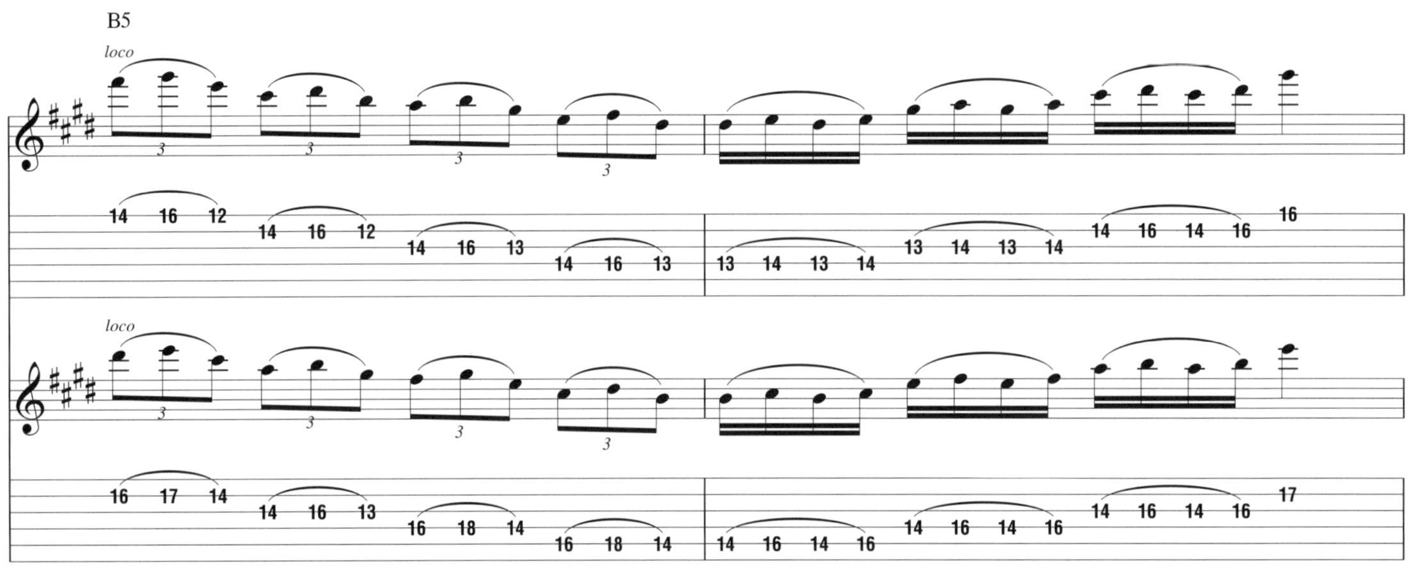
B5
loco

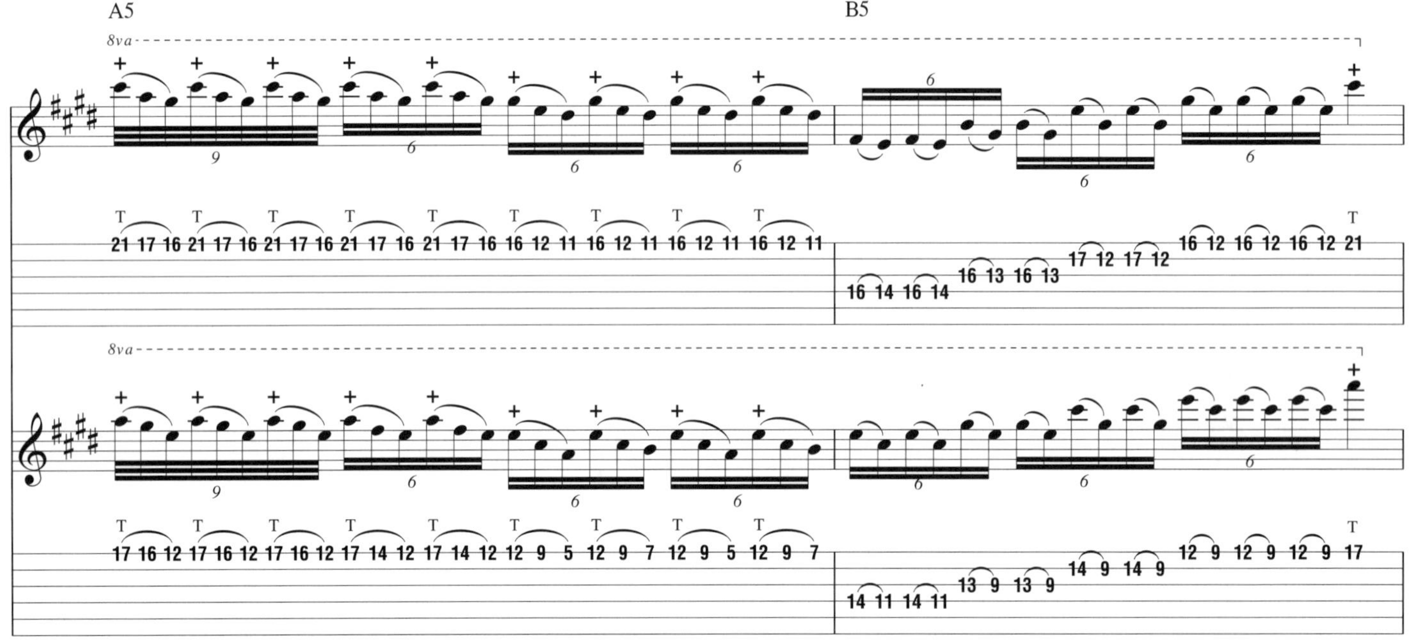
A5
B5
8va

F♯5 E5 B5

Gtr. 2
loco

w/ bar

−1 −1

14 13 14 13 14 14 15 17 15 14 | 14 (14) (14) 17 14 17 14 17 | 14 13 14 14 15 14 15 17 17 17 15 17 15 14 15 17

Gtr. 3
loco

w/ bar

−1 −1

11 9 11 9 11 10 12 14 12 10 | 11 (11) (11) 10 11 9 11 9 | 11 9 11 10 12 10 12 14 12 14 12 14 12 10 11 10

Gtrs. 4 & 5

4 4 2 | 2 2 0 | 4 4 2

C♯5 F♯5 E5

8va

w/ bar

−1 −1 −1 −1

17 15 13 16 | 9 10 9 10 9 9 10 9 10 9 10 10 | 16 17 16 17 21 16 17 21 22 21 22 17

8va

w/ bar

−1 −1 −1 −1

14 12 10 13 | 9 11 9 11 10 9 11 10 12 10 12 9 | 17 19 17 19 17 17 19 17 19 17 19 17

6 6 4 | 4 4 2 | 2 2 0

C#5 B5 A5

8va

loco

tr

w/ bar

-1 1/2

loco

tr

w/ bar

-1 1/2

P.M.

Gtr. 3 tacet

C#5

8va

P.H.

P.M. P.M. P.M. P.M. P.M.

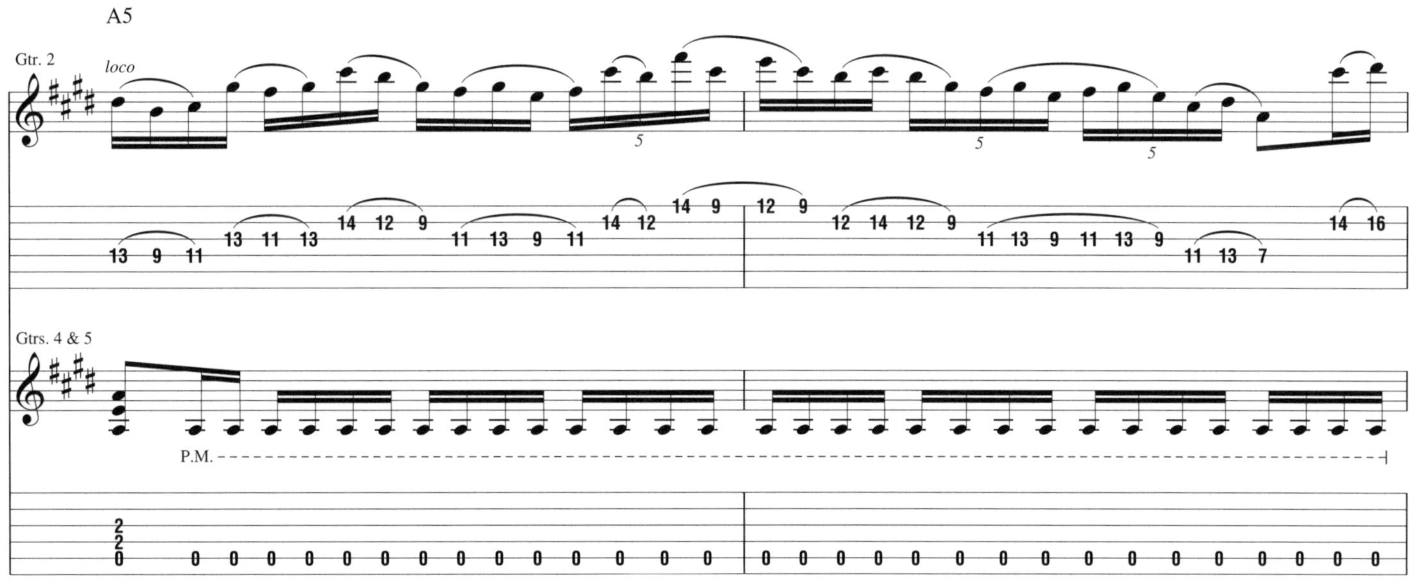

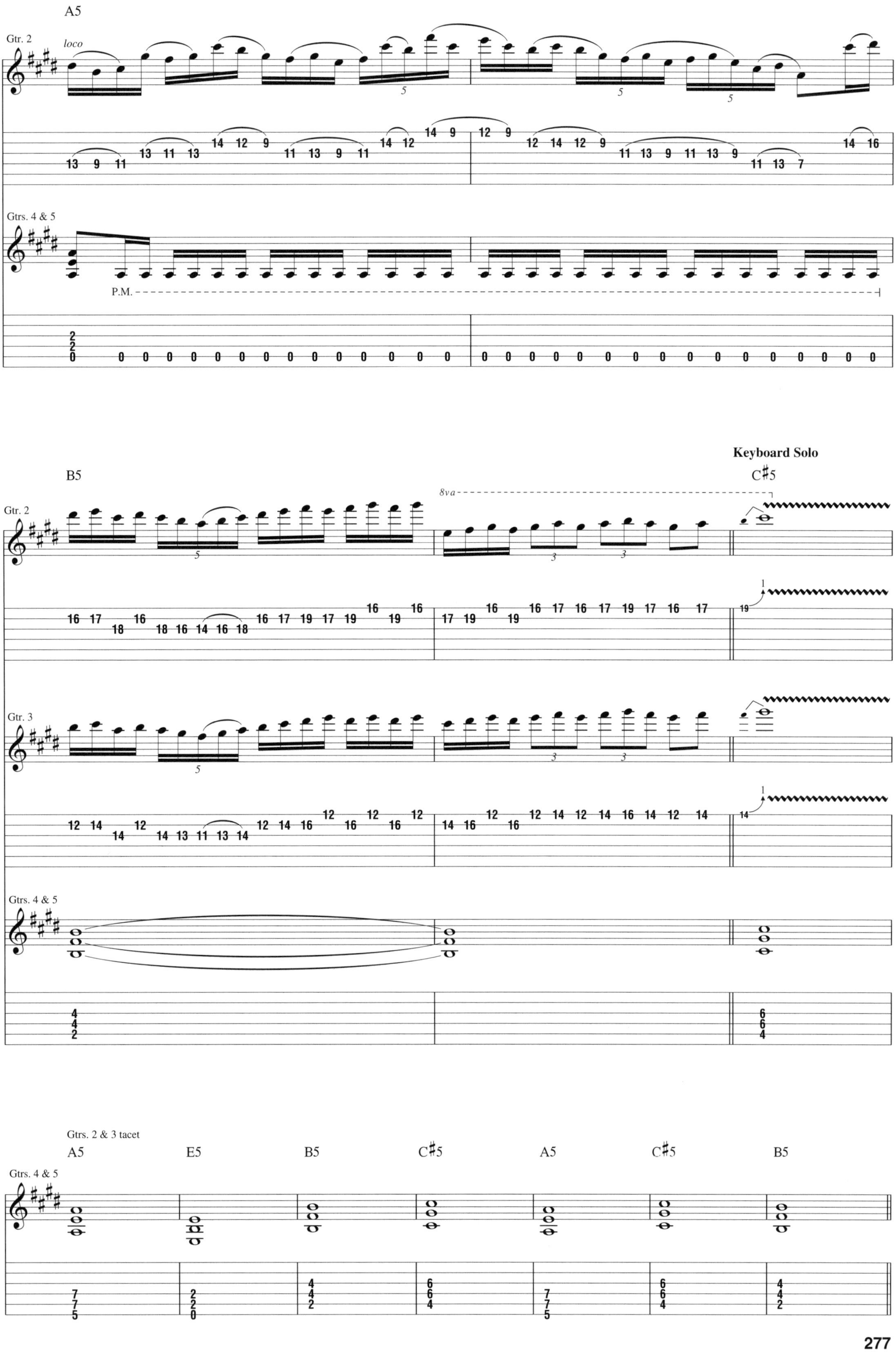

B5

Keyboard Solo

C#5

Gtr. 2

8va

Gtr. 3

Gtrs. 4 & 5

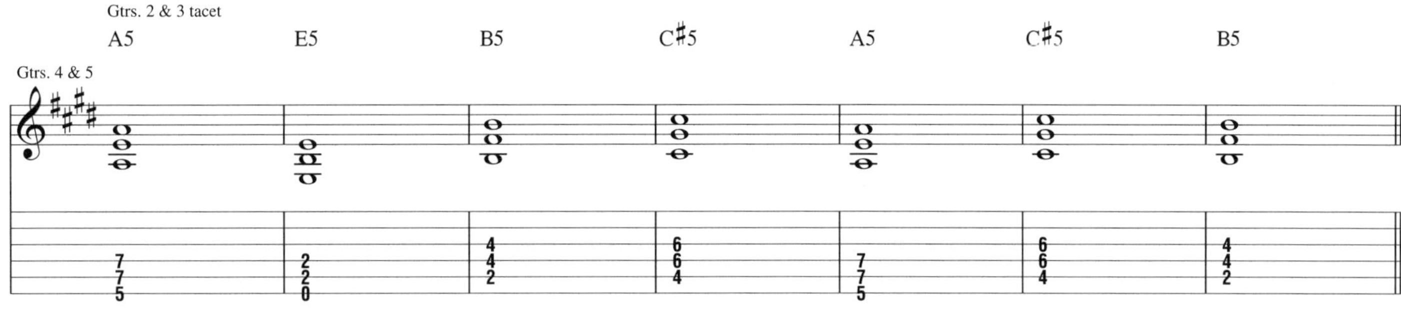

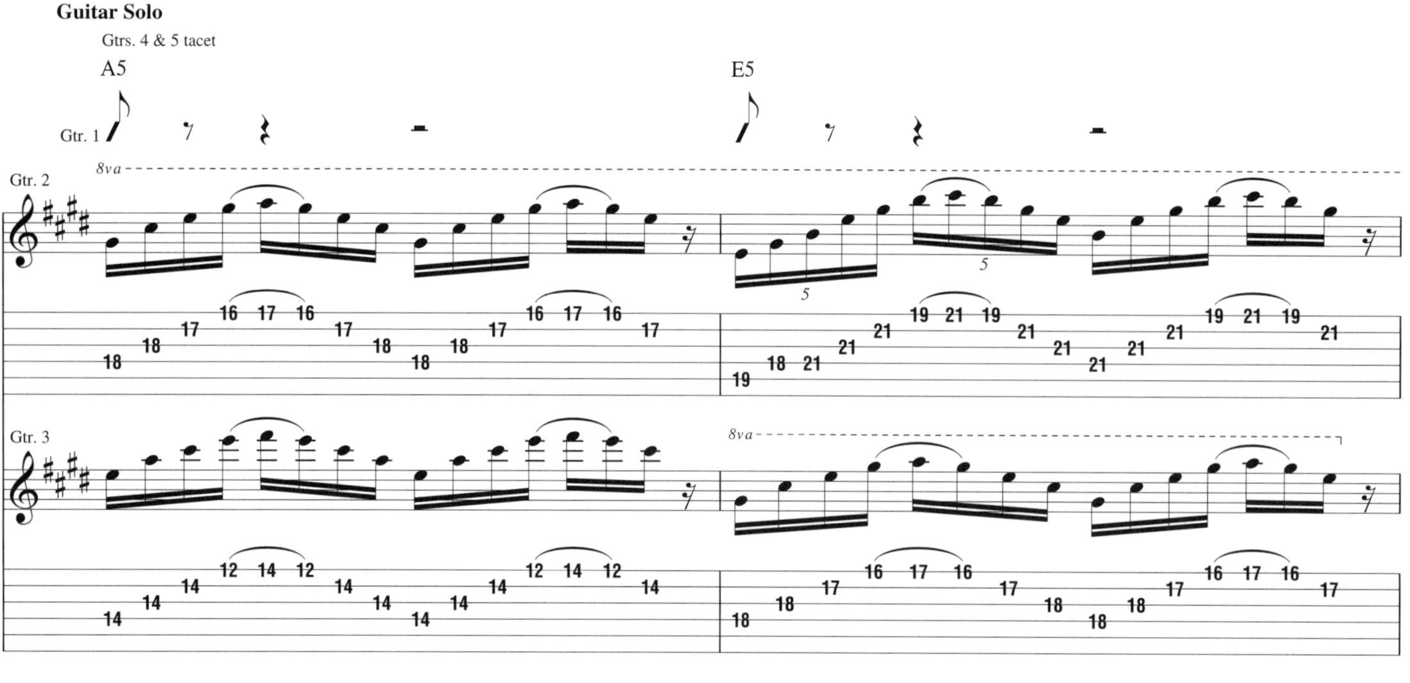
Guitar Solo
Gtrs. 4 & 5 tacet
A5
E5
Gtr. 1
Gtr. 2
8va
Gtr. 3
8va

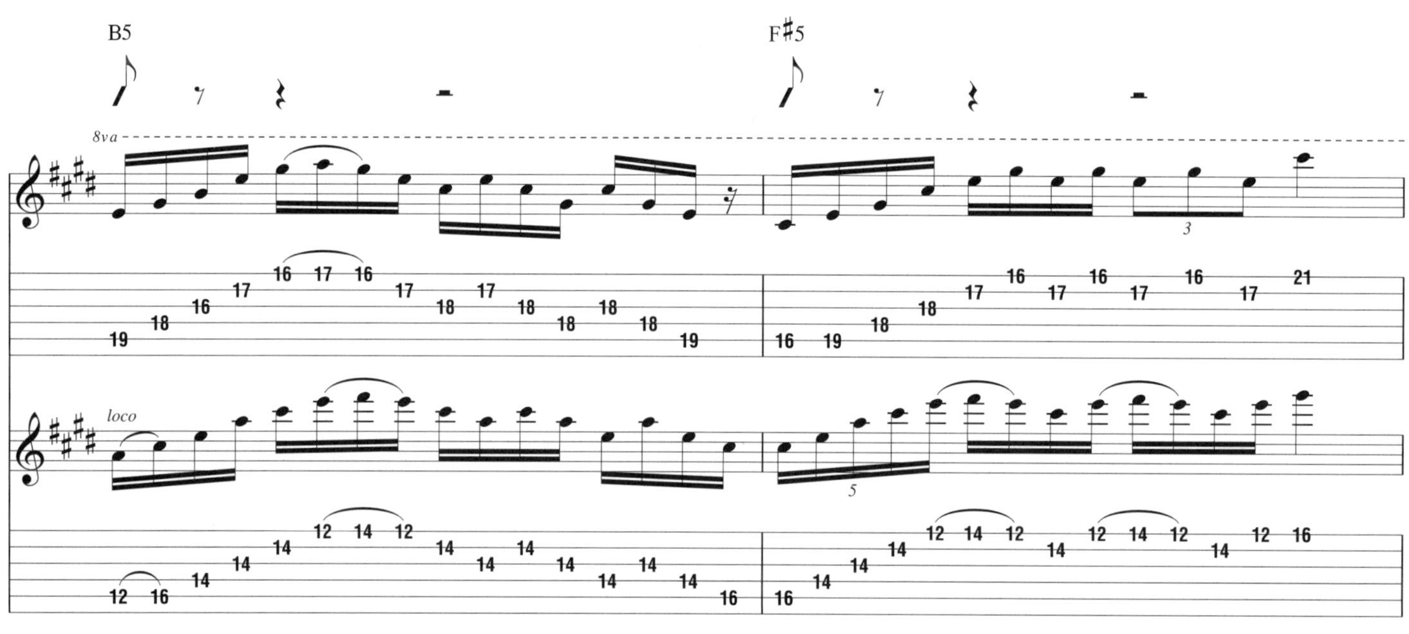
B5
F♯5
8va
loco

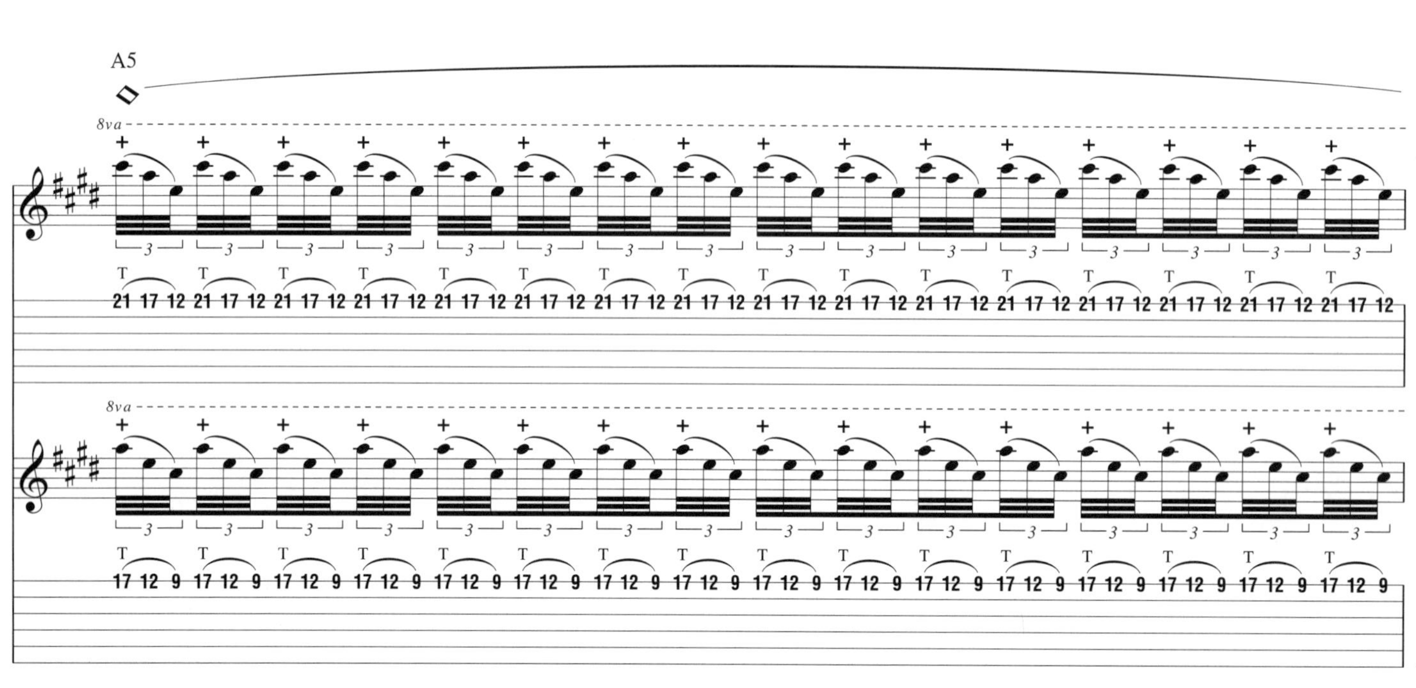
A5
8va
8va

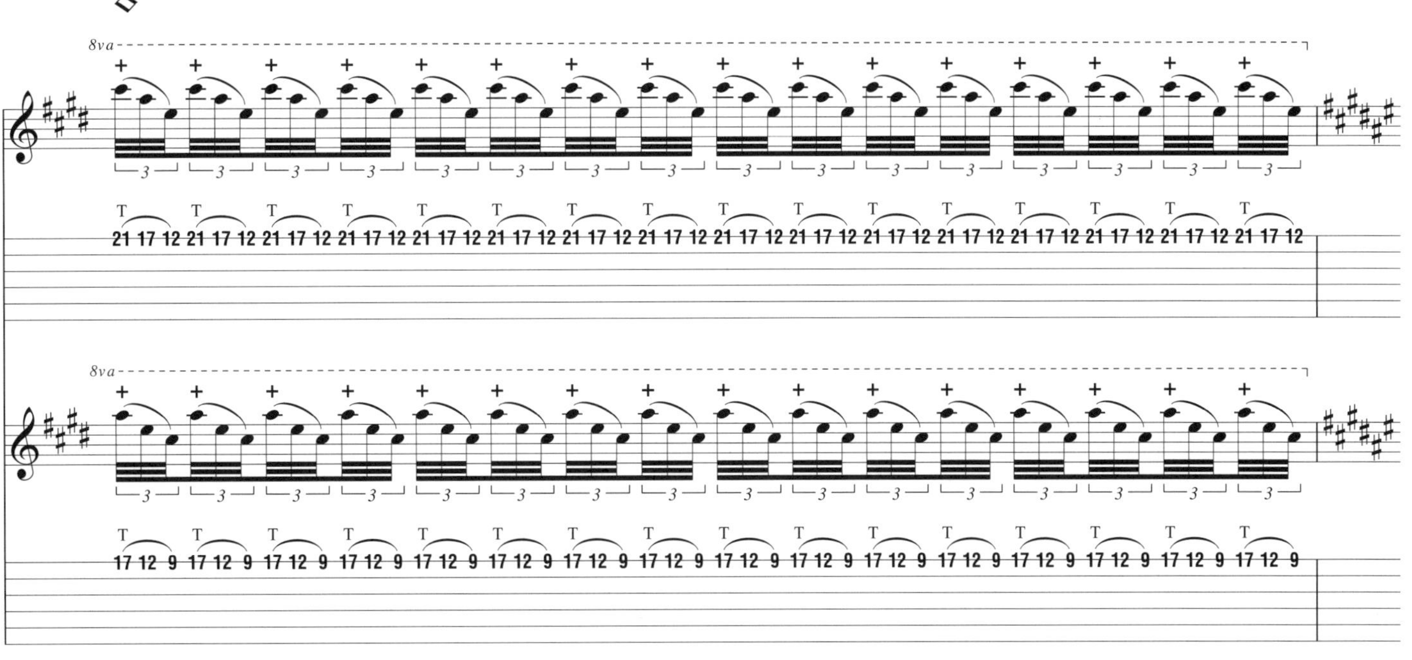
8va
8va

Gtr. 1 tacet
Gtrs. 4 & 5: w/ Rhy. Fig. 6
F♯5
B5
loco
8va
loco

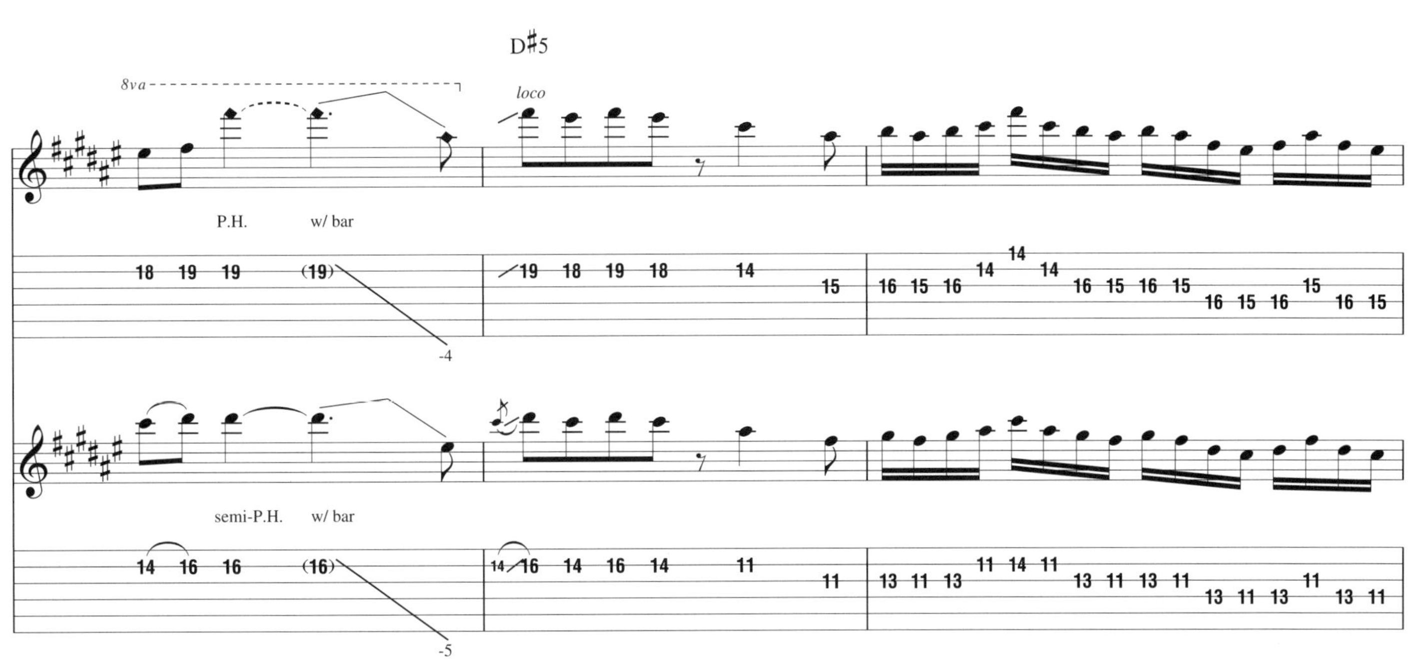
D♯5
8va
loco
P.H.
w/ bar
semi-P.H.
w/ bar

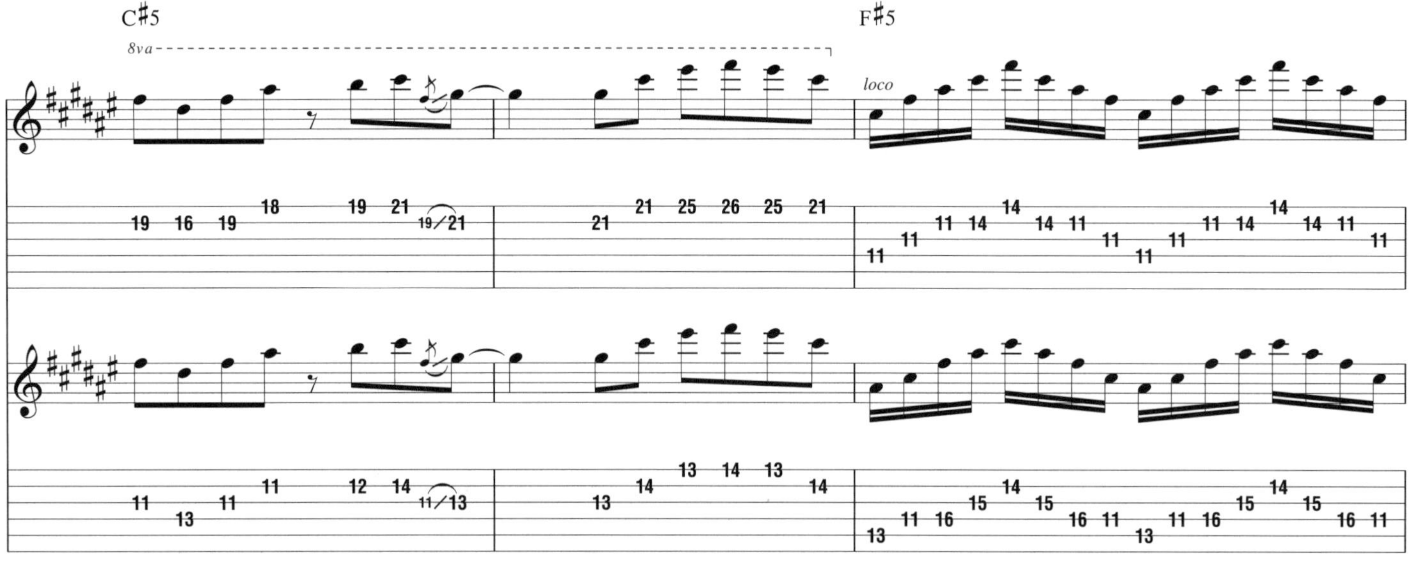
C#5
F#5
8va
loco

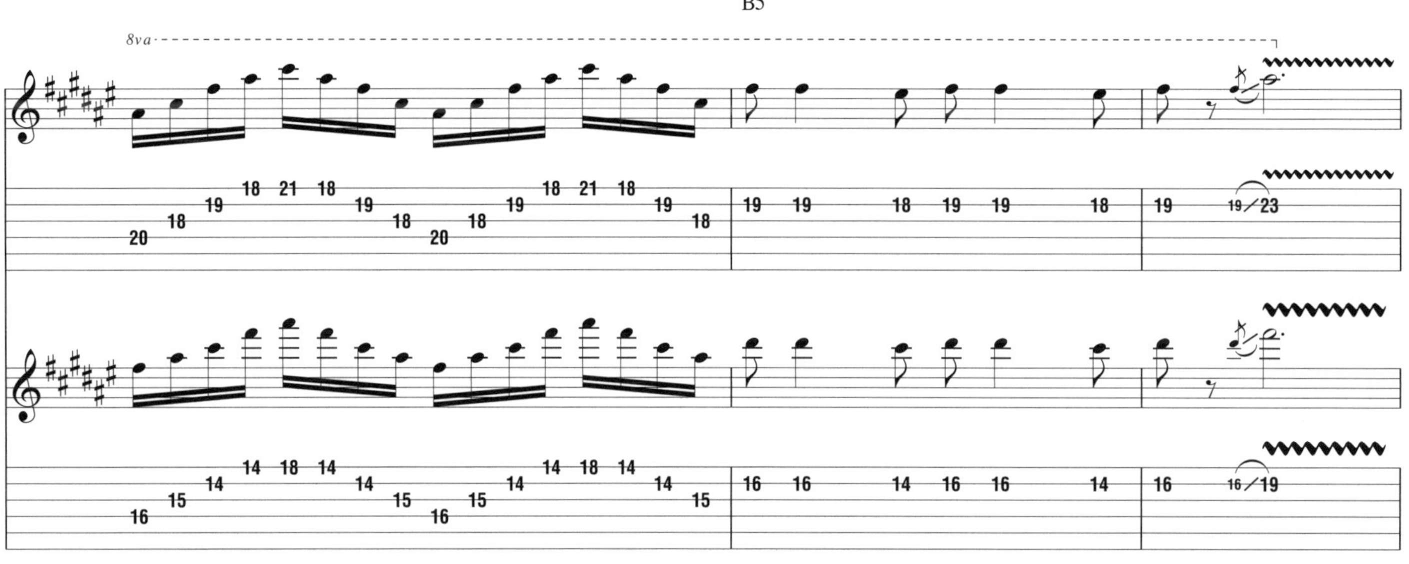
B5
8va

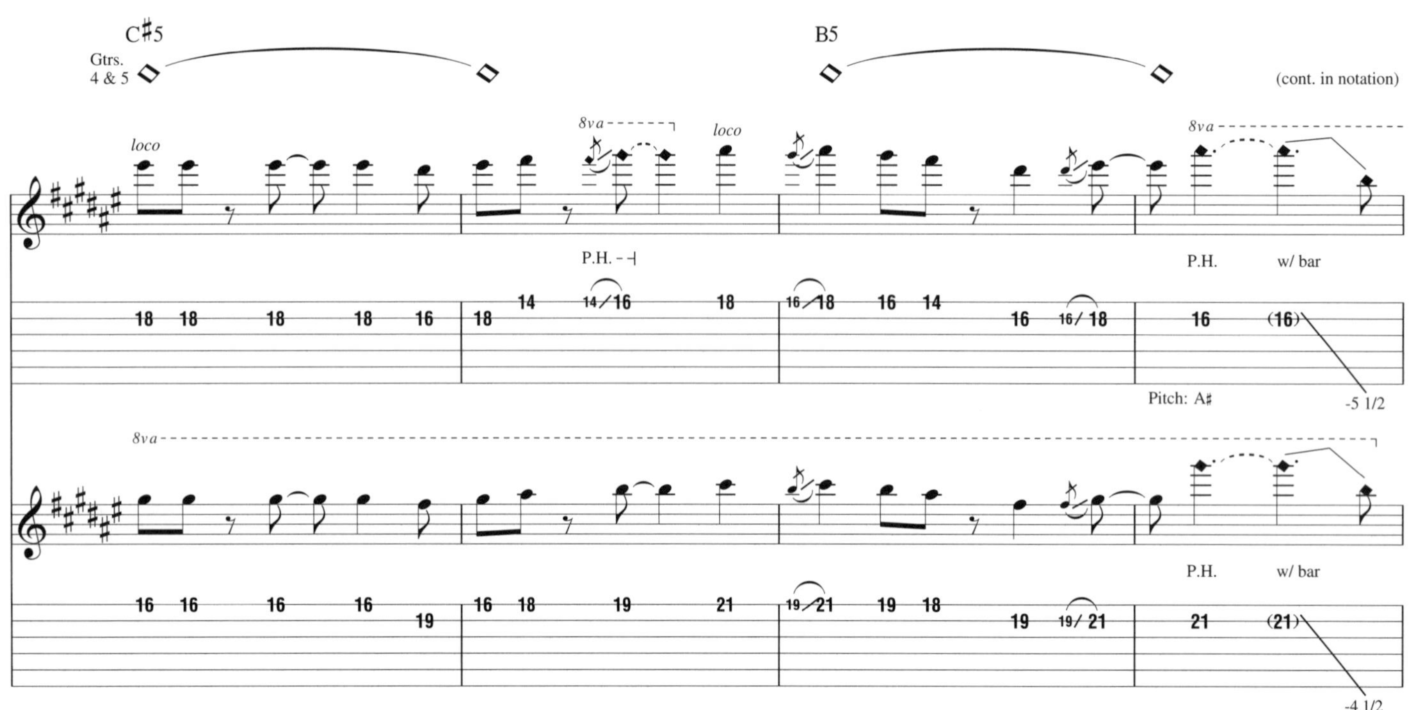
C#5
B5
Gtrs. 4 & 5
(cont. in notation)
8va
loco
P.H.
w/ bar
Pitch: A#
-5 1/2
-4 1/2

C♯5
B5
Gtr. 2
8va
loco
Gtr. 3
loco
8va
Gtrs. 4 & 5
P.M.
P.M.
P.M.
P.M.

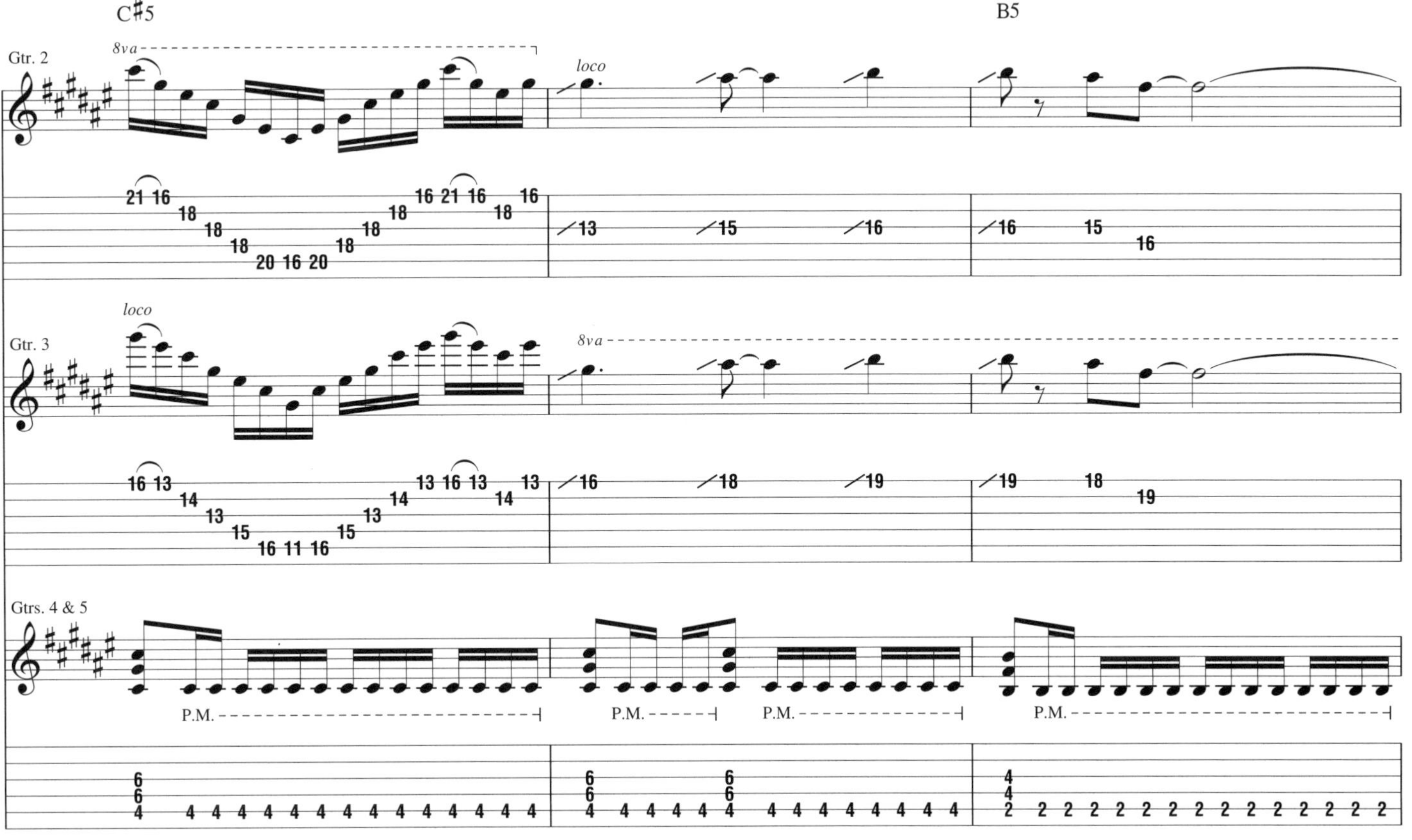

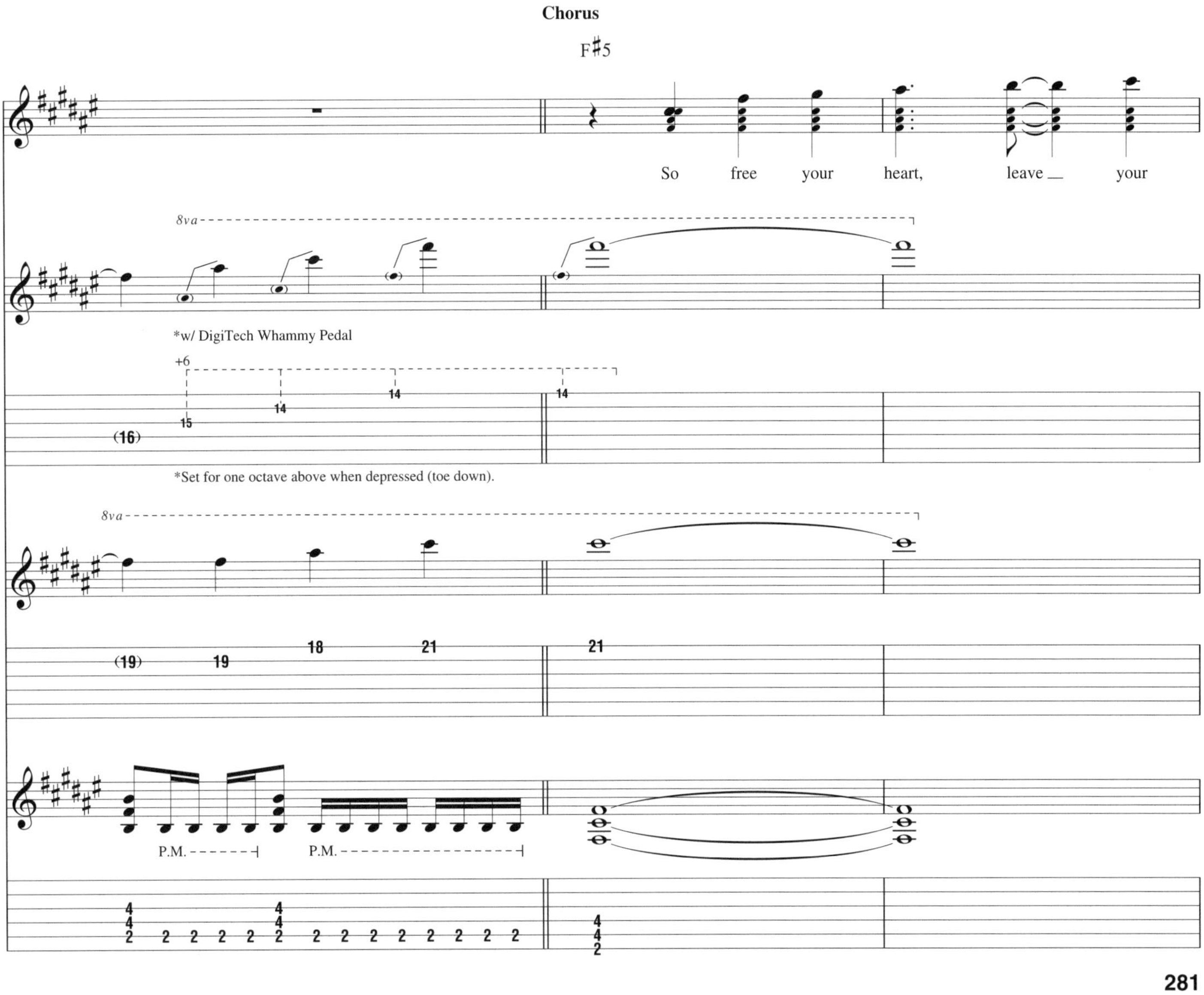

Chorus
F♯5
So free your heart, leave your
8va
*w/ DigiTech Whammy Pedal
+6
*Set for one octave above when depressed (toe down).
8va
P.M.
P.M.

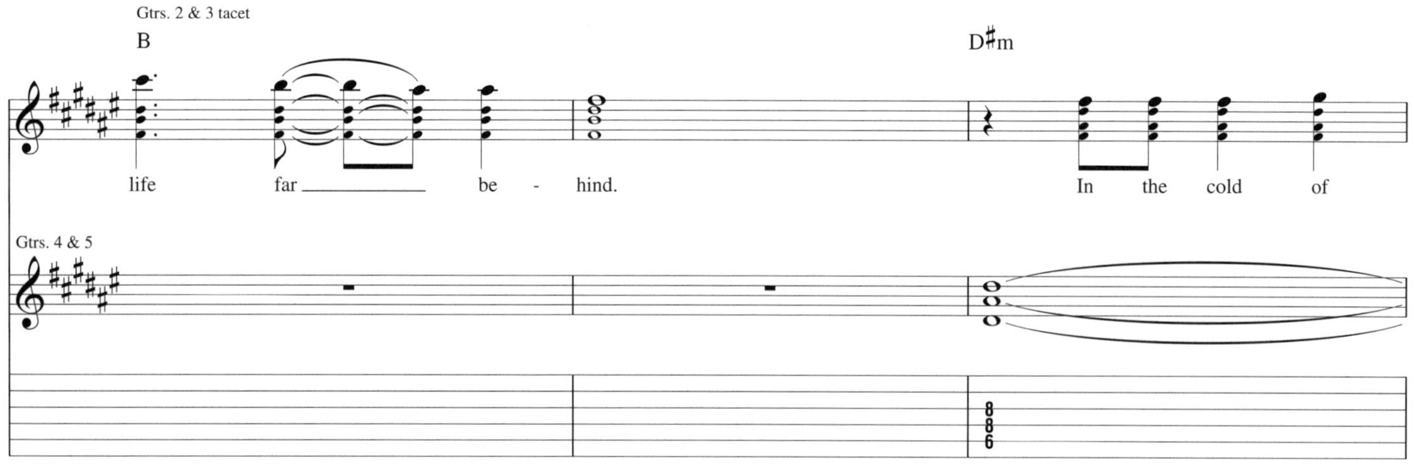
Gtrs. 2 & 3 tacet
B
D♯m
life far be - hind. In the cold of
Gtrs. 4 & 5

C♯
Gtrs. 4 & 5 tacet
win - ter skies es - cape the pain in - side.
Gtr. 2
15ma
w/ DigiTech Whammy Pedal
w/ bar
+6
21 (21)
Gtrs. 4 & 5
Gtr. 3
15ma
*w/ DigiTech Whammy Pedal
w/ bar
+6
21 (21)
*Set for one octave above when depressed (toe down).

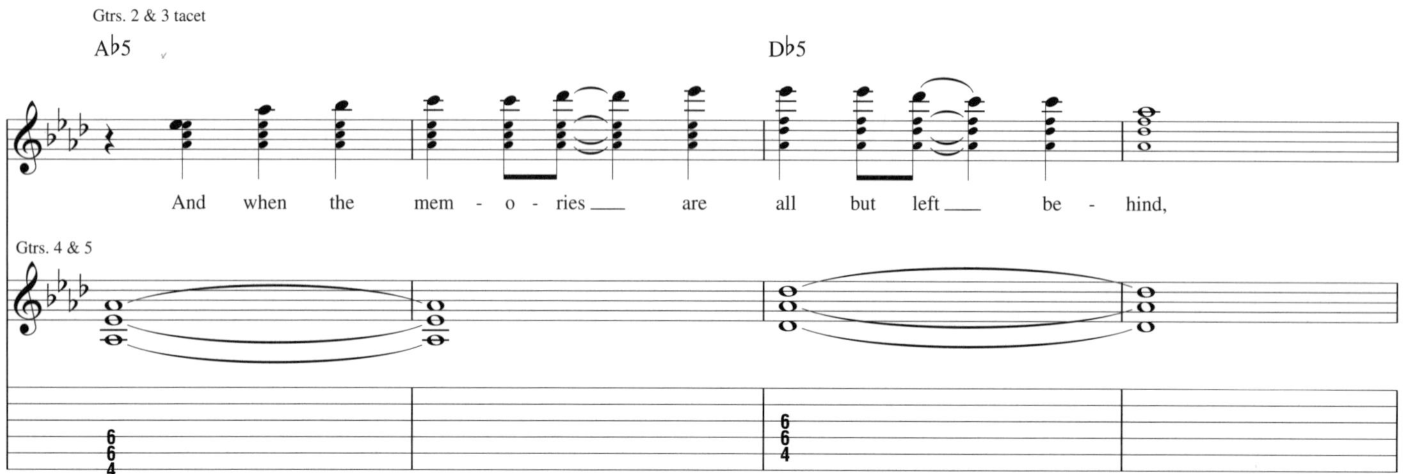
Gtrs. 2 & 3 tacet
A♭5
D♭5
And when the mem - o - ries are all but left be - hind,
Gtrs. 4 & 5

F5
E♭5
and the days have gone for - ev - er lost with - in my mind.
A♭5
D♭5
Now feel your soul burn in seas of all e -
P.M.
E♭5
Gtrs. 4 & 5
ter - ni - ty.
Ev - 'ry day this life de - fend - ing,
Gtr. 3
Gtrs. 4 & 5
Gtr. 2
(cont. in slashes)

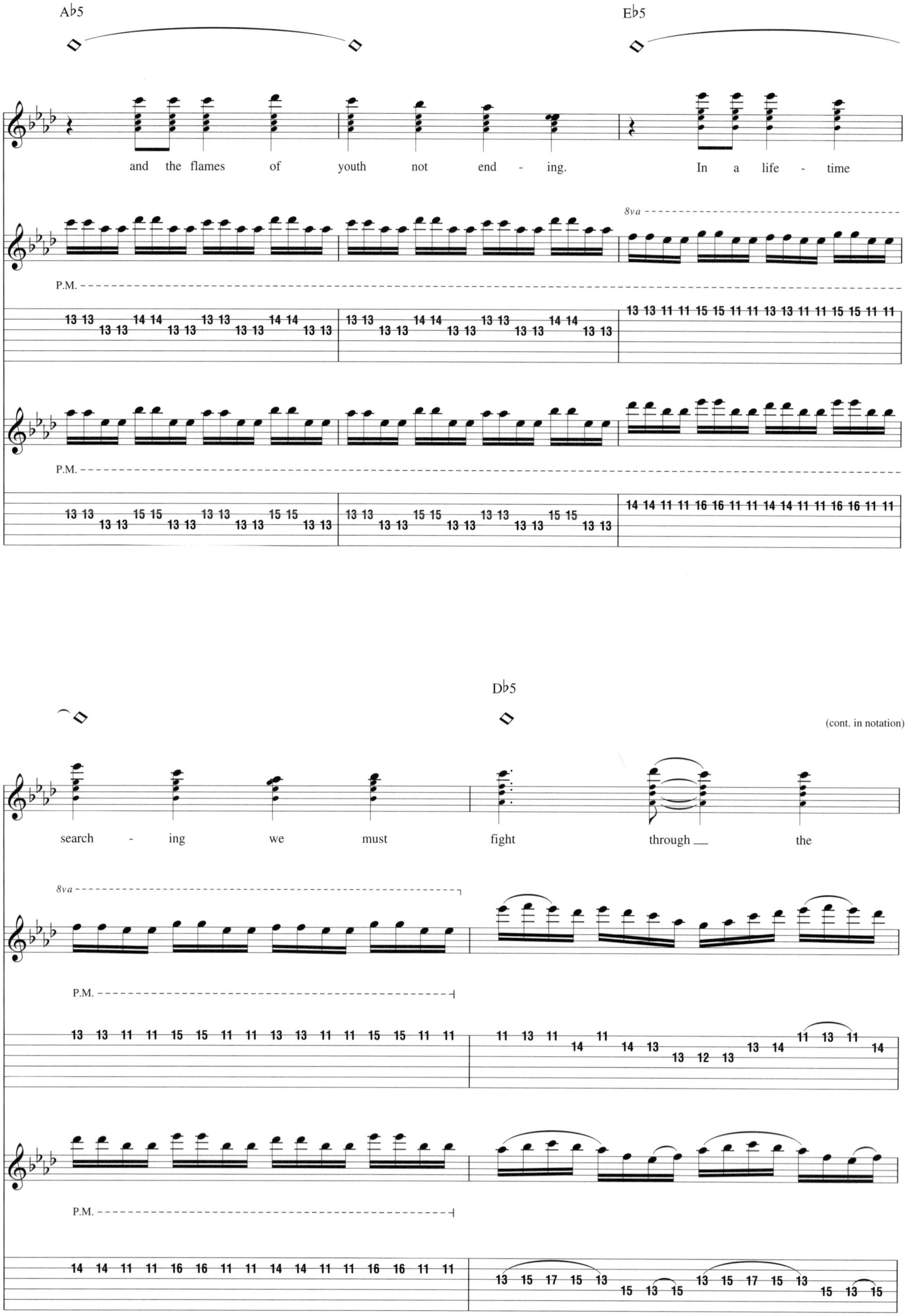

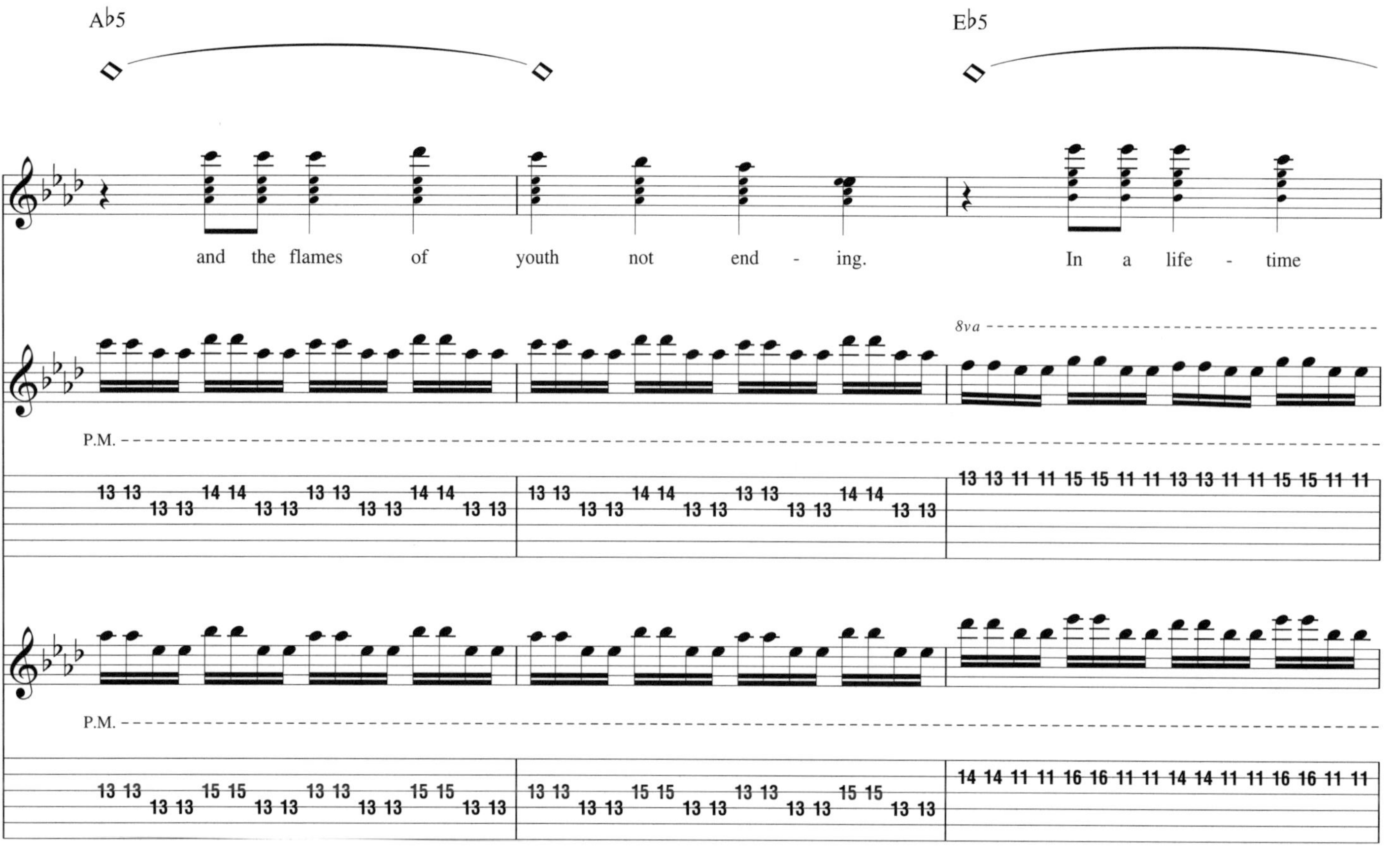

A♭5
E♭5
and the flames of youth not end - ing. In a life - time
8va
P.M.
13 13 13 13 14 14 13 13 13 13 13 13 14 14 13 13
13 13 13 13 14 14 13 13 13 13 13 13 14 14 13 13
13 13 11 11 15 15 11 11 13 13 11 11 15 15 11 11
P.M.
13 13 13 13 15 15 13 13 13 13 13 13 15 15 13 13
13 13 13 13 15 15 13 13 13 13 13 13 15 15 13 13
14 14 11 11 16 16 11 11 14 14 11 11 16 16 11 11
D♭5
(cont. in notation)
search - ing we must fight through the
8va
P.M.
13 13 11 11 15 15 11 11 13 13 11 11 15 15 11 11
11 13 11 14 11 14 13 13 12 13 13 14 11 13 11 14
P.M.
14 14 11 11 16 16 11 11 14 14 11 11 16 16 11 11
13 15 17 15 13 15 13 15 13 15 17 15 13 15 13 15

E♭5
D♭5
e - ter - nal pain.
8va
Gtr. 3
T
+6
8va
Gtr. 2
Gtrs. 4 & 5
P.M.

End double-time feel
D♭5 N.C.
8va
+6
+4
+4 1/2
P.M.

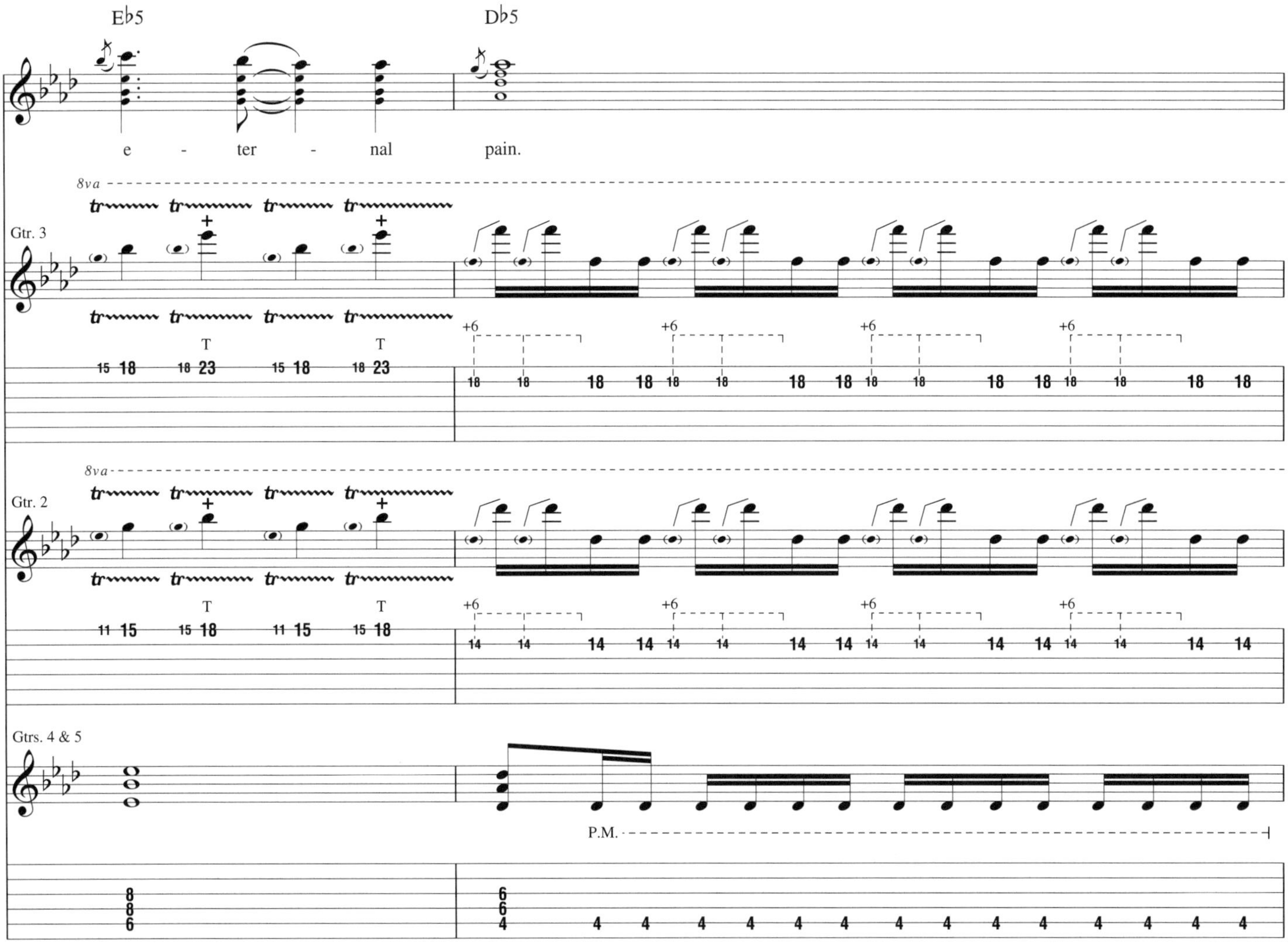

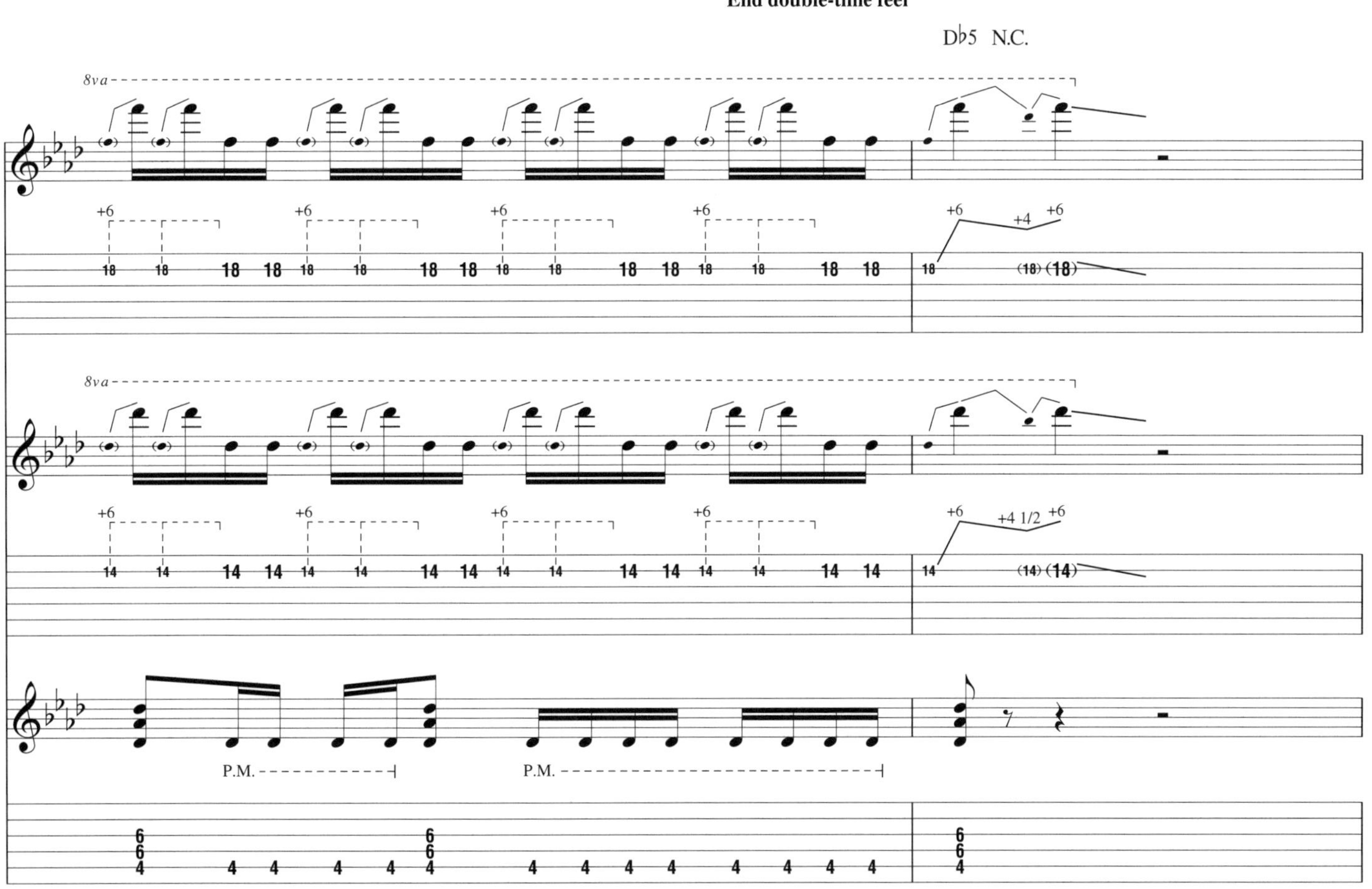

Gtrs. 2–5 tacet

Outro

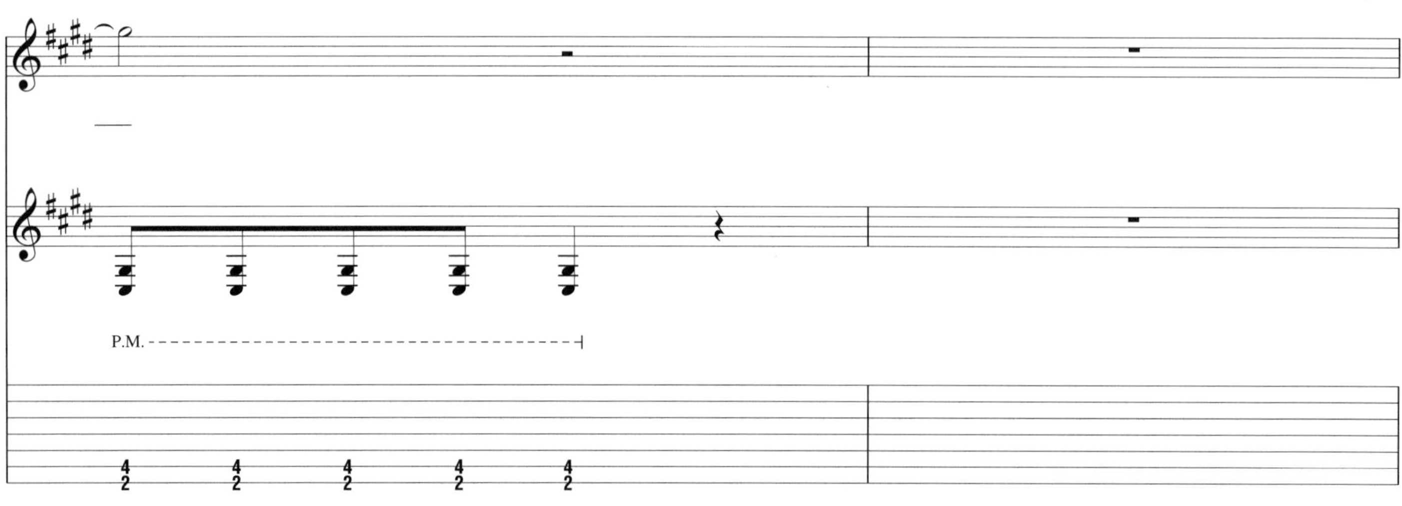

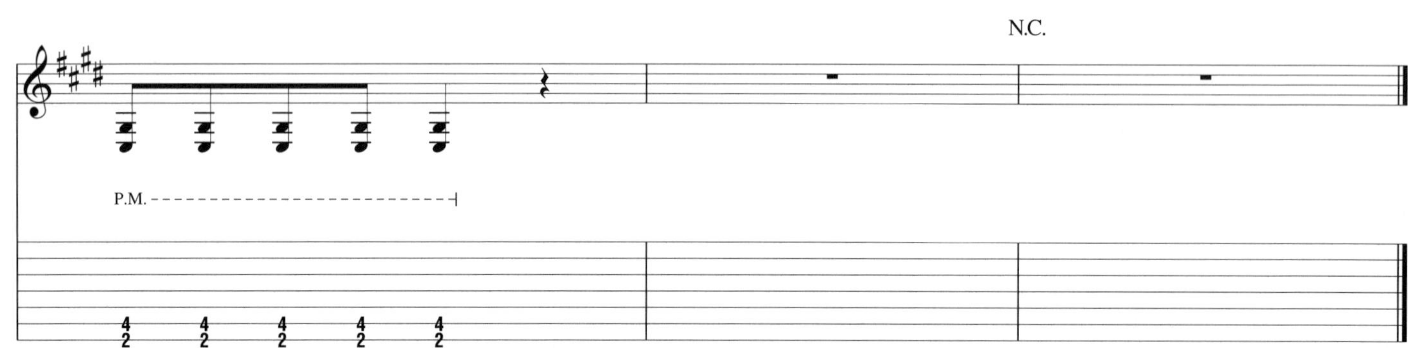

Trail of Broken Hearts

Words and Music by Herman Li, ZP Theart, Sam Totman and Vadim Pruzhanov

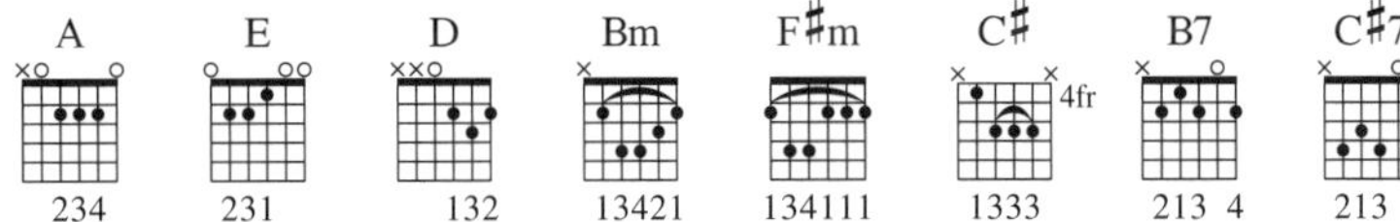

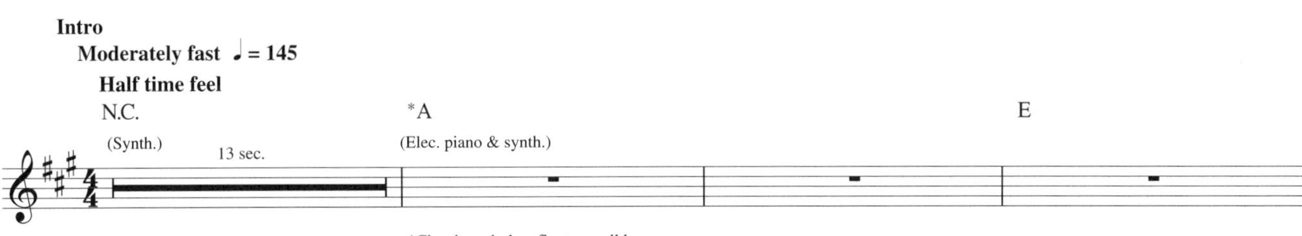

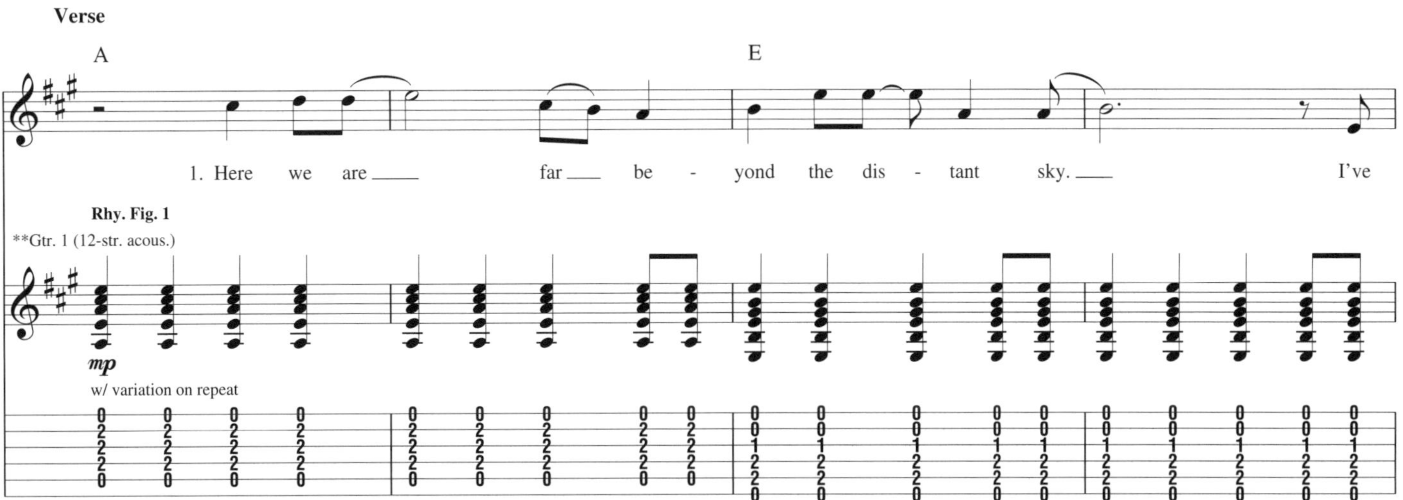

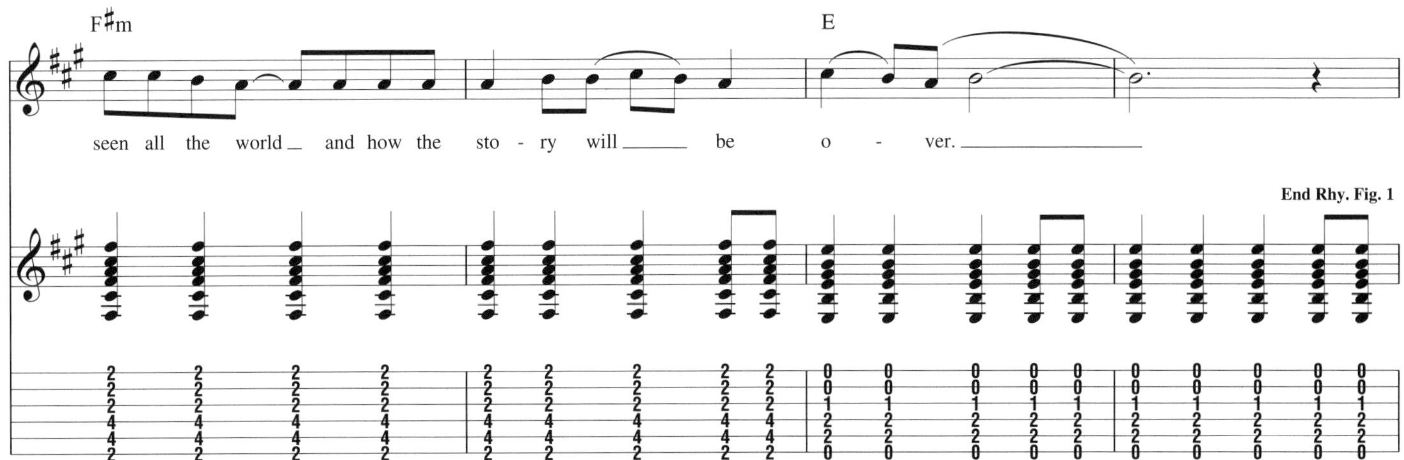

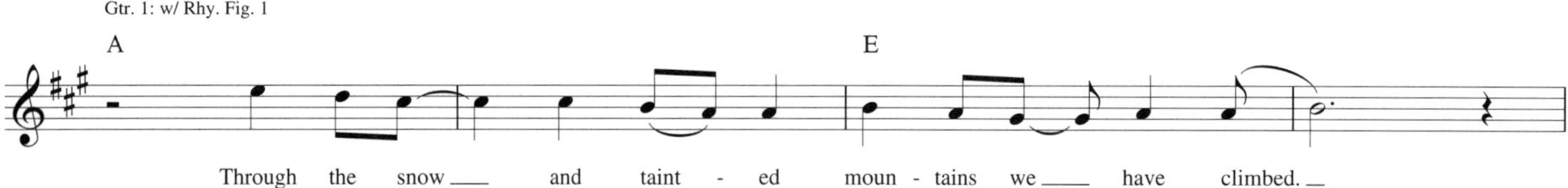

Gtr. 1: w/ Rhy. Fig. 1
A
E
Through the snow and taint - ed moun - tains we have climbed.

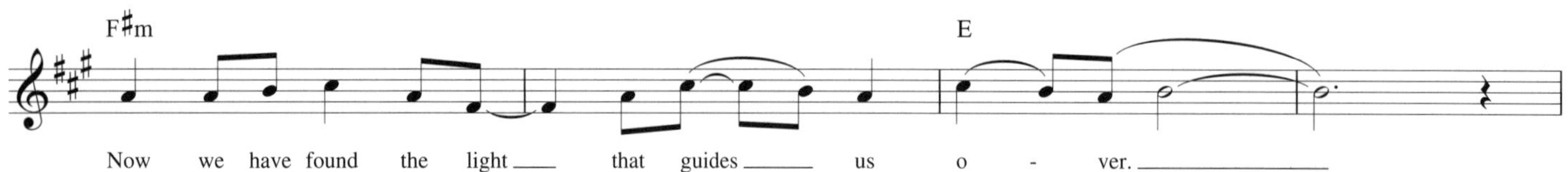

F♯m
E
Now we have found the light that guides us o - ver.

D
F♯m
E
Through the fall - ing rain we trav - elled far and wide.
Gtr. 1

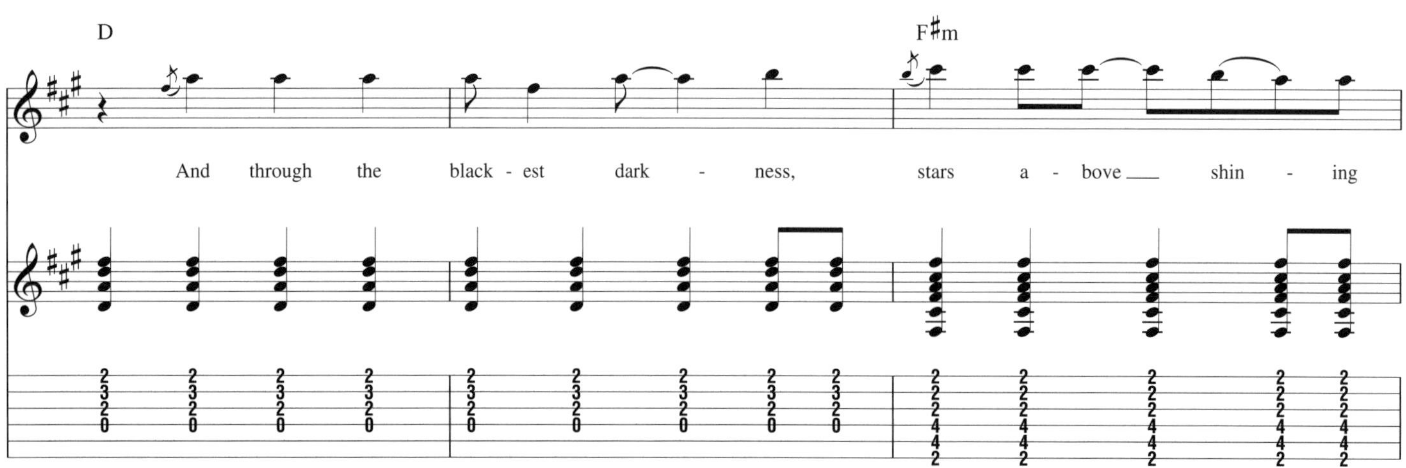

D
F♯m
And through the black - est dark - ness, stars a - bove shin - ing

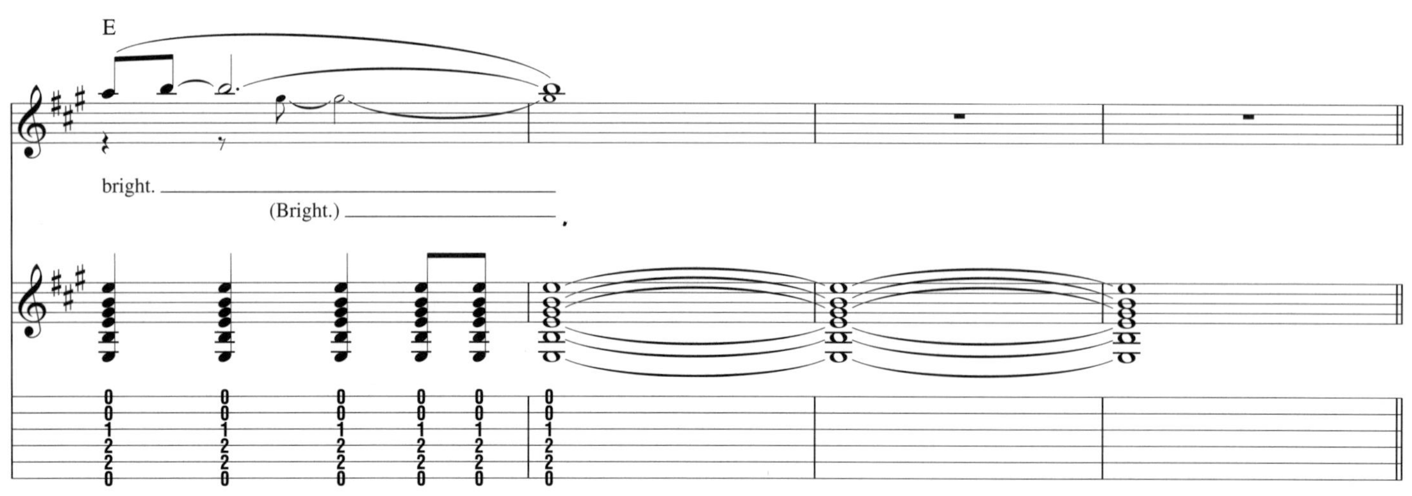

E
bright.
(Bright.)

Verse
Gtr. 1: w/ Rhy. Fig. 1 (2 times)
A
E
2. Through the sun and win - ter rain will fall. All our
Gtr. 2 (elec.)
f
w/ dist.
P.M.
Gtr. 3 (elec.)
f
w/ dist.
P.M.

F♯m
E
lives we all were wait-ing for a sign to call.
P.M.

A
E
We're walk - ing hand in hand ___ in dreams of end - less time. ___
3
P.M.
P.M.

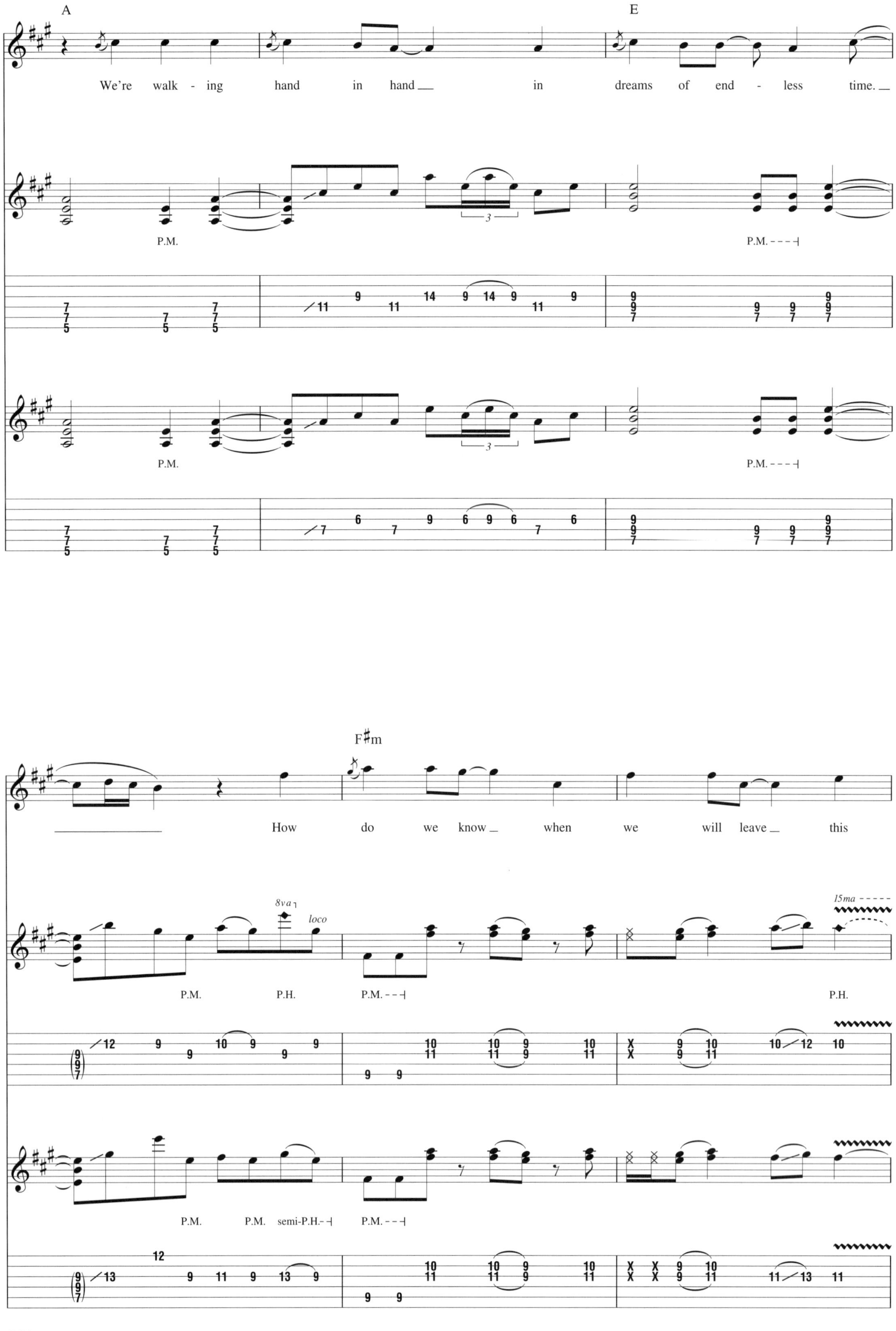

F♯m

How do we know ___ when we will leave ___ this

8va loco 15ma

P.M. P.H. P.M. P.H.

P.M. P.M. semi-P.H. P.M.

Pre-Chorus
E
D5
A5
life be - hind?
Stare at life through eyes of mine, the
15ma loco
Rhy. Fig. 2
P.M.

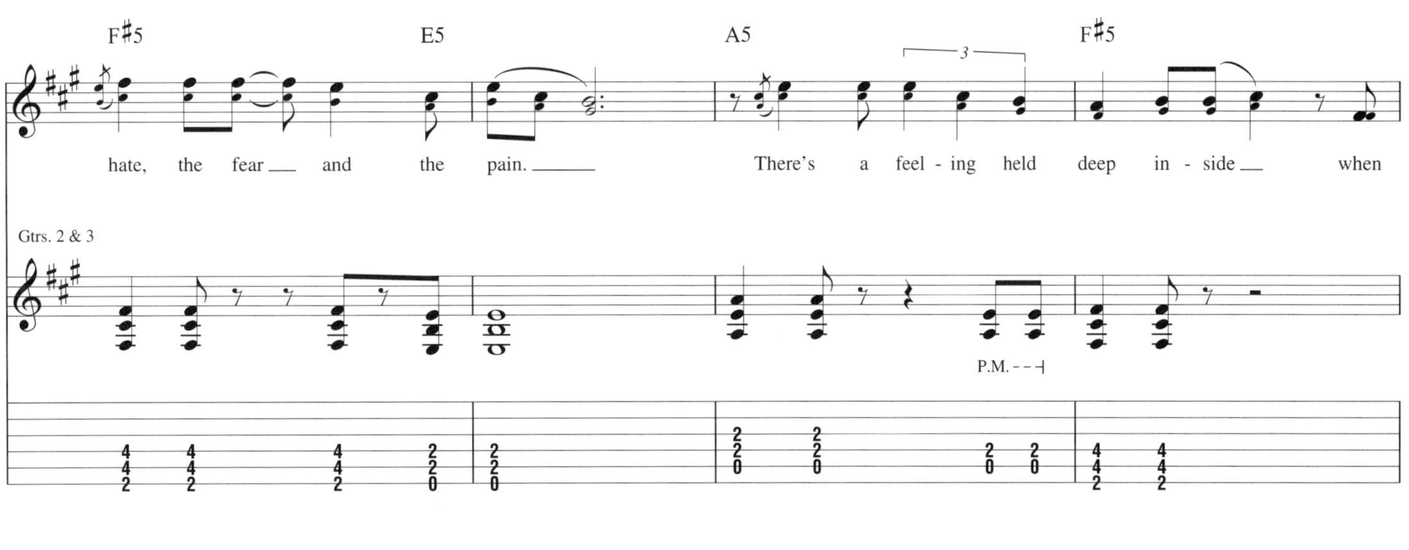
F♯5
E5
A5
F♯5
hate, the fear and the pain.
There's a feel - ing held deep in - side when
Gtrs. 2 & 3
P.M.

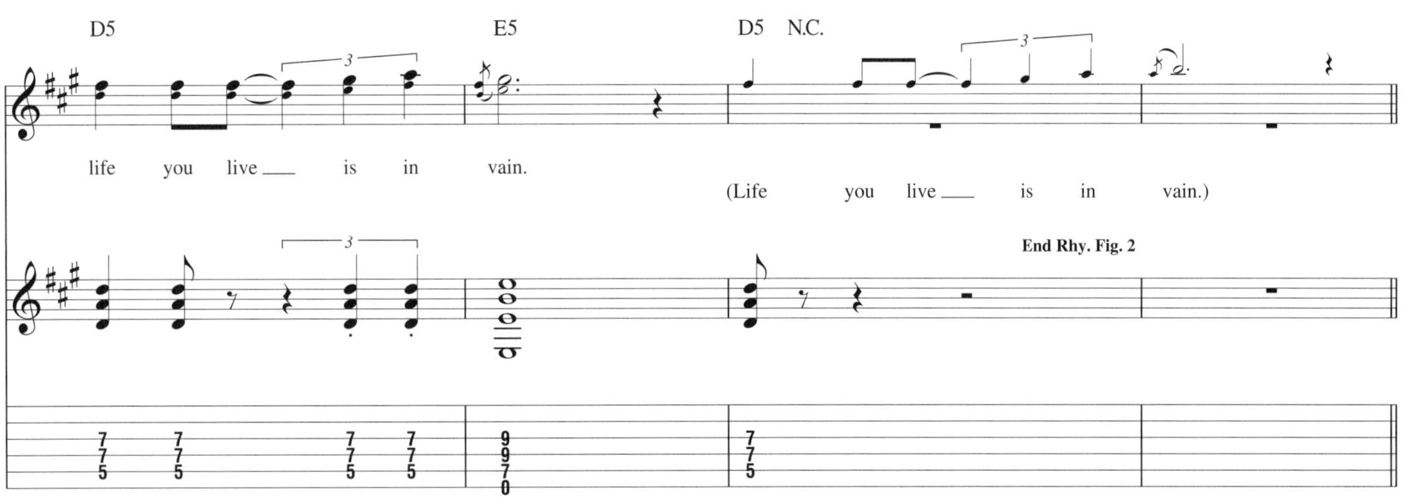
D5
E5
D5 N.C.
life you live is in vain.
(Life you live is in vain.)
End Rhy. Fig. 2

Chorus
3rd time, Gtrs. 4 & 5: w/ Fill 1
A
E
D
E
Gtr. 1
Fly a - way down the lone - ly roads of yes - ter - day.
(Ah, lone - ly roads of yes - ter - day.
Gtrs. 2 & 3
P.M.

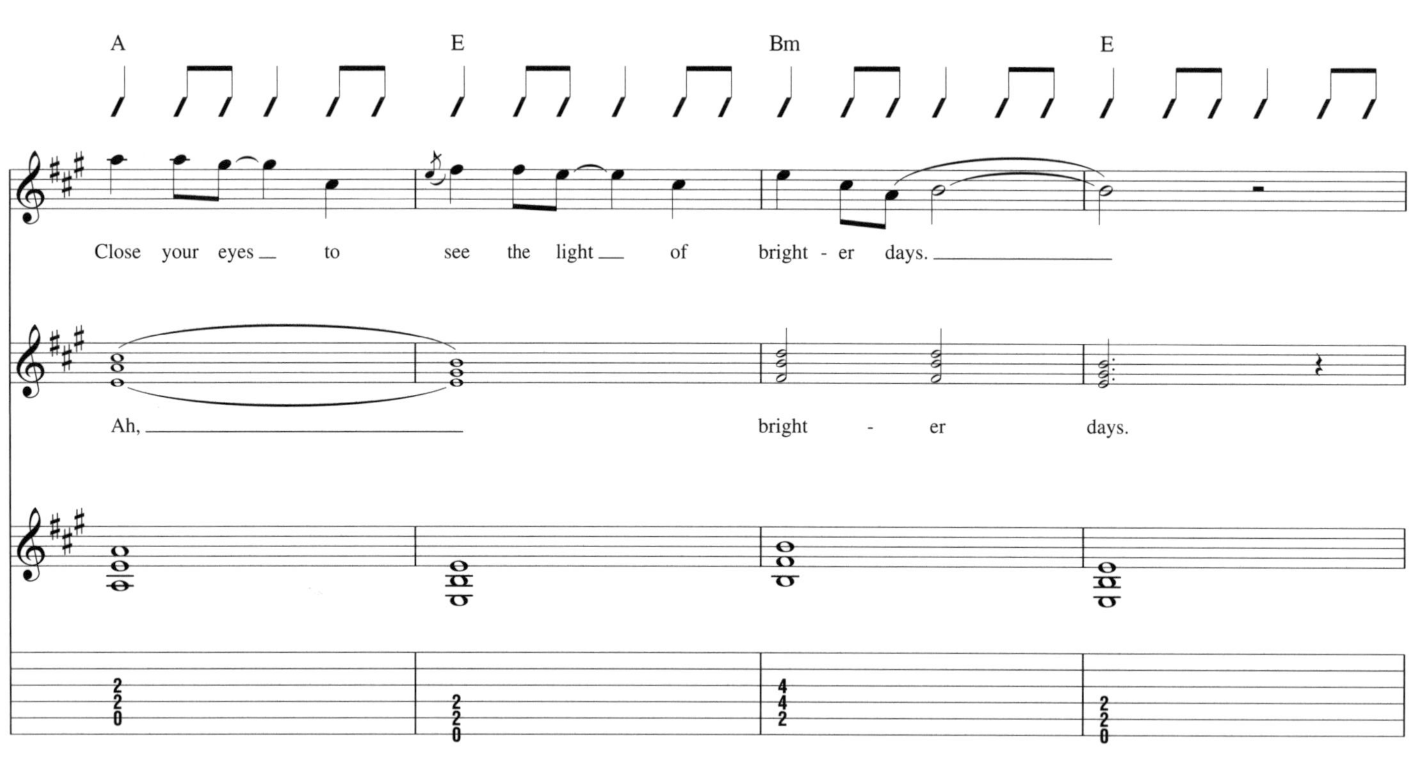
A
E
Bm
E
Close your eyes to see the light of bright - er days.
Ah, bright - er days.

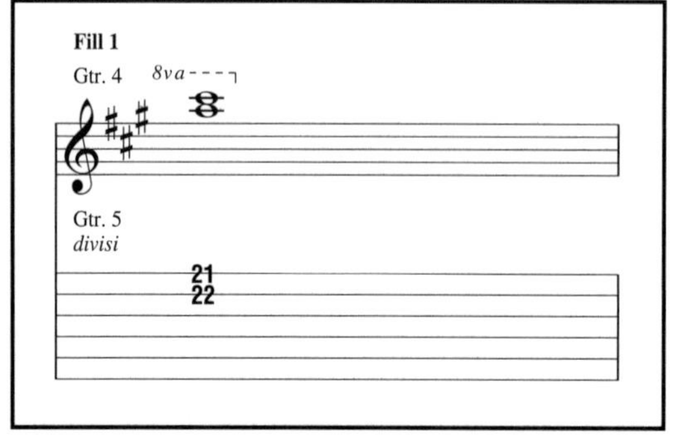
Fill 1
Gtr. 4
8va
Gtr. 5
divisi
21
22

To Coda 1
A
D
E
F♯m
And all a - lone we'll be where time can nev - er heal with the
Ah,
time can nev - er heal.
To Coda 2
D
E
A
trail of bro - ken hearts fly - ing free.
Trail of bro - ken hearts.)
Interlude
Gtr. 1 tacet
F♯m
D
E

Verse

Gtr. 1: w/ Rhy. Fig. 1 (2 times)

E
F♯m
what we left be - hind.
Re - live the dreams, the
P.M.
end - less screams of pain in - side.
15ma
P.H.
8va
loco
Pre-Chorus
Gtrs. 2 & 3: w/ Rhy. Fig. 2
D5
A5
F♯5
E5
Lives are filled with emp - ti - ness. The fear re - turns once a -
gain.
Search - ing end - less - ly, now we will see.
D.S. al Coda 1
N.C.
Drown your mind in the pain.
(Drown your mind in the pain.)

Coda 1
E
F♯m
D
time can nev - er heal with the trail of bro - ken
time can nev - er heal with the trail of bro - ken
E
A
F♯m
D
hearts fly - ing free.
The last temp - ta - tion will be
hearts fly - ing free.
The last temp - ta - tion will be
Bridge
E
C♯
Rhy. Fig. 3
D
all that's left for me,
yeah.
When I see those
all that's left for me,
yeah.)
(When I see those
Rhy. Fig. 4
P.M.
P.M.

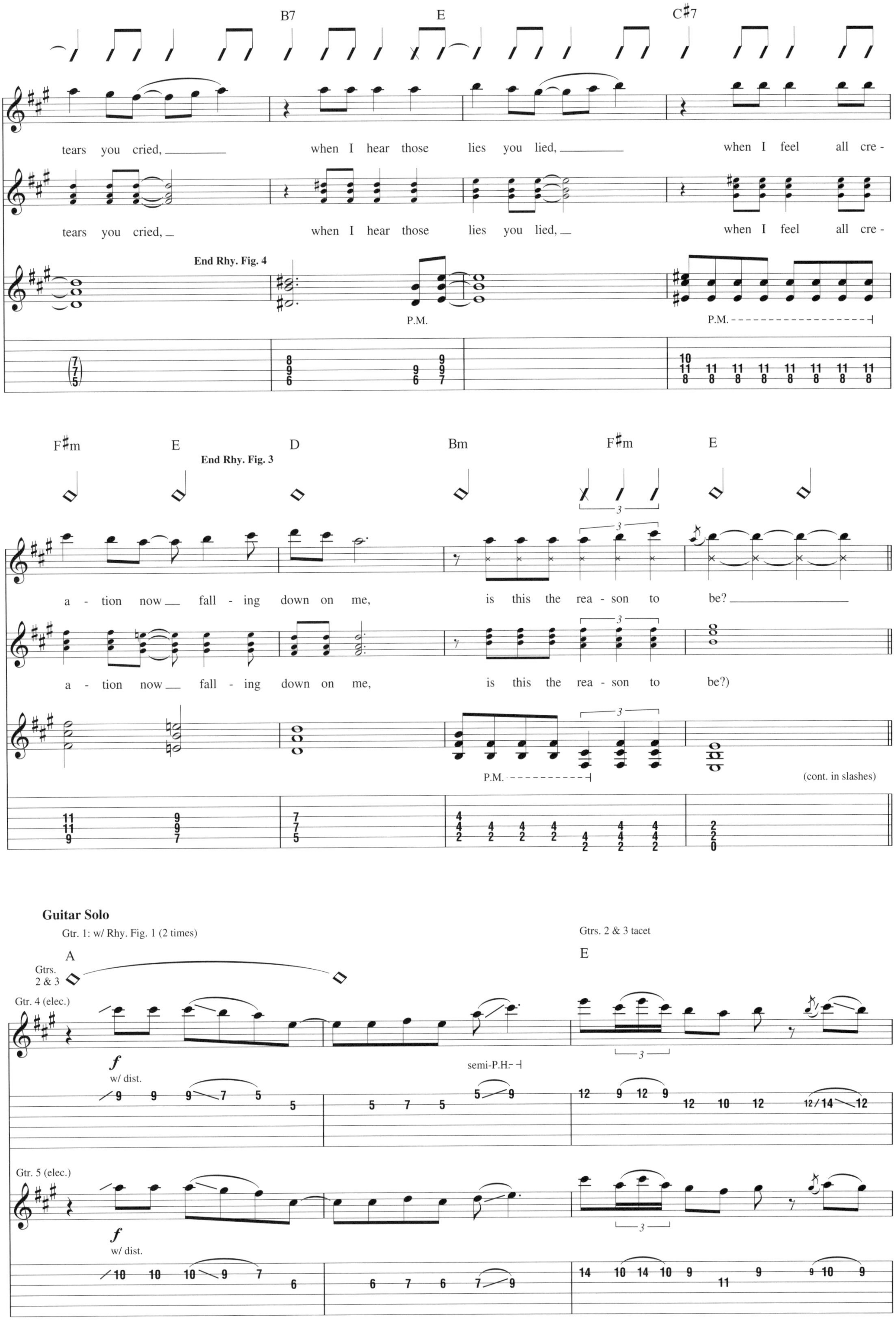

B7 E C♯7

tears you cried, when I hear those lies you lied, when I feel all cre -

tears you cried, when I hear those lies you lied, when I feel all cre -

End Rhy. Fig. 4

P.M. P.M.

F♯m E D Bm F♯m E

End Rhy. Fig. 3

a - tion now fall - ing down on me, is this the rea - son to be?

a - tion now fall - ing down on me, is this the rea - son to be?)

P.M.

(cont. in slashes)

Guitar Solo

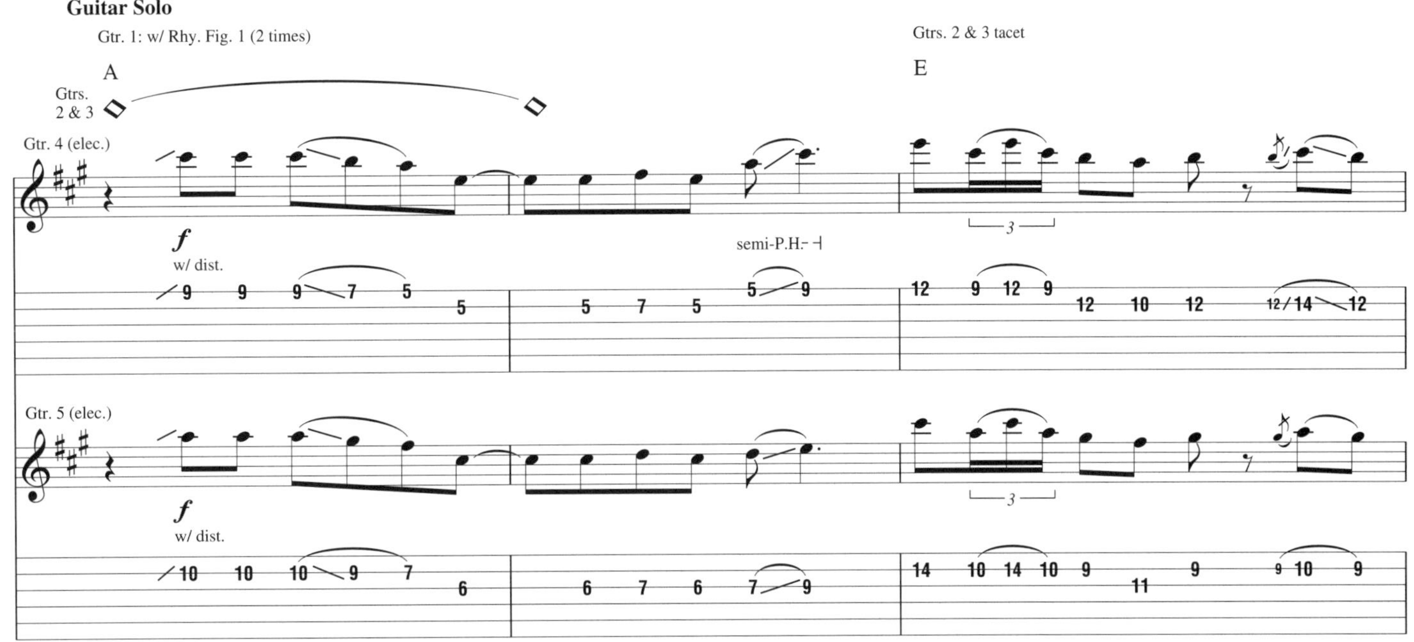

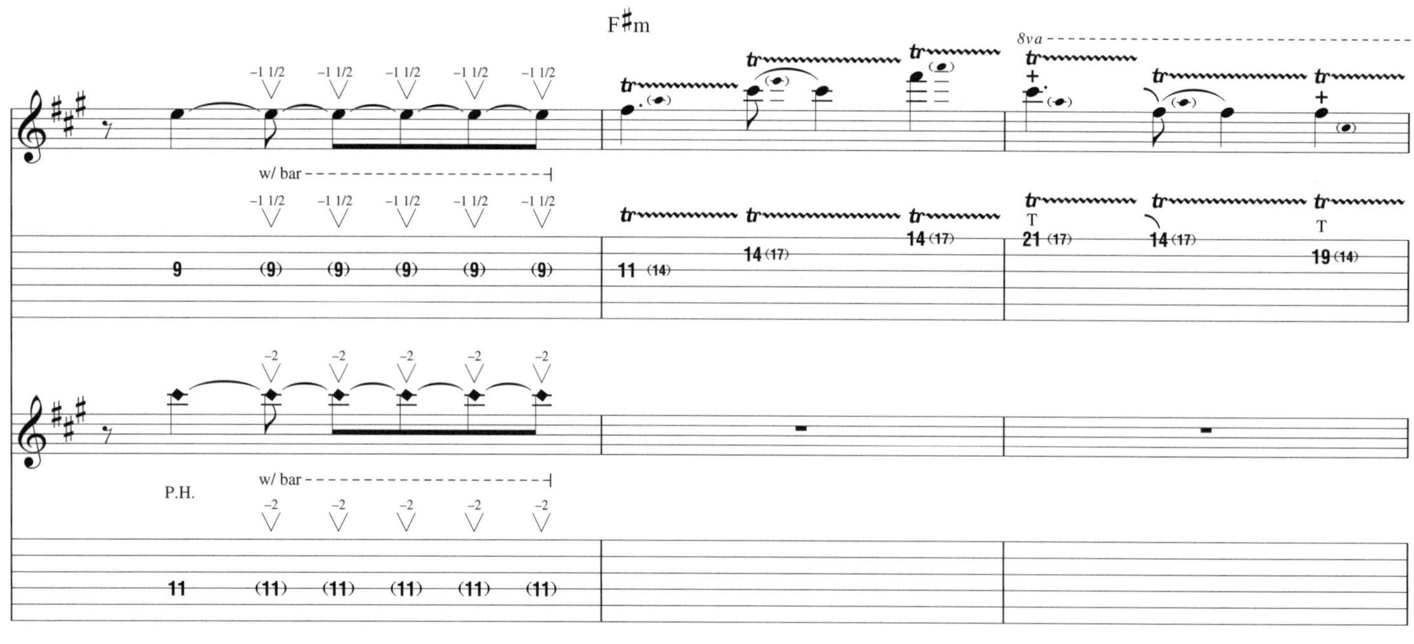
F♯m
8va
w/ bar
P.H.
w/ bar

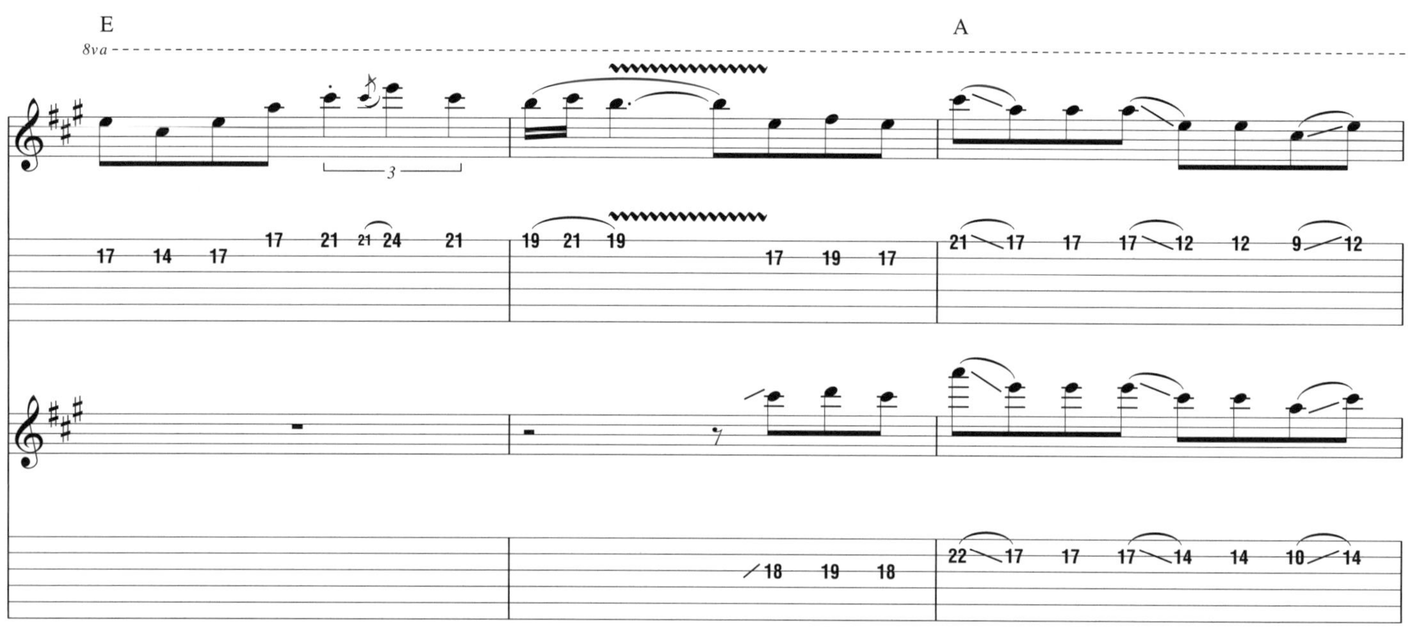
E
8va
A

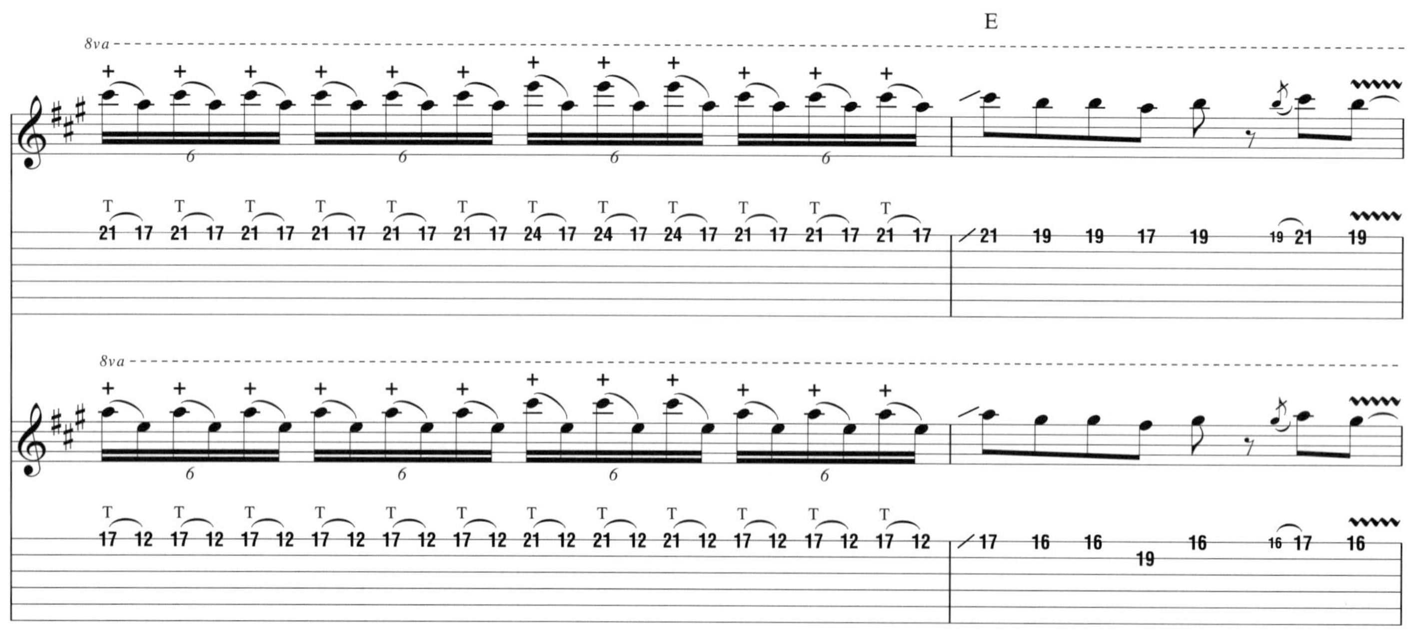
8va
E
8va

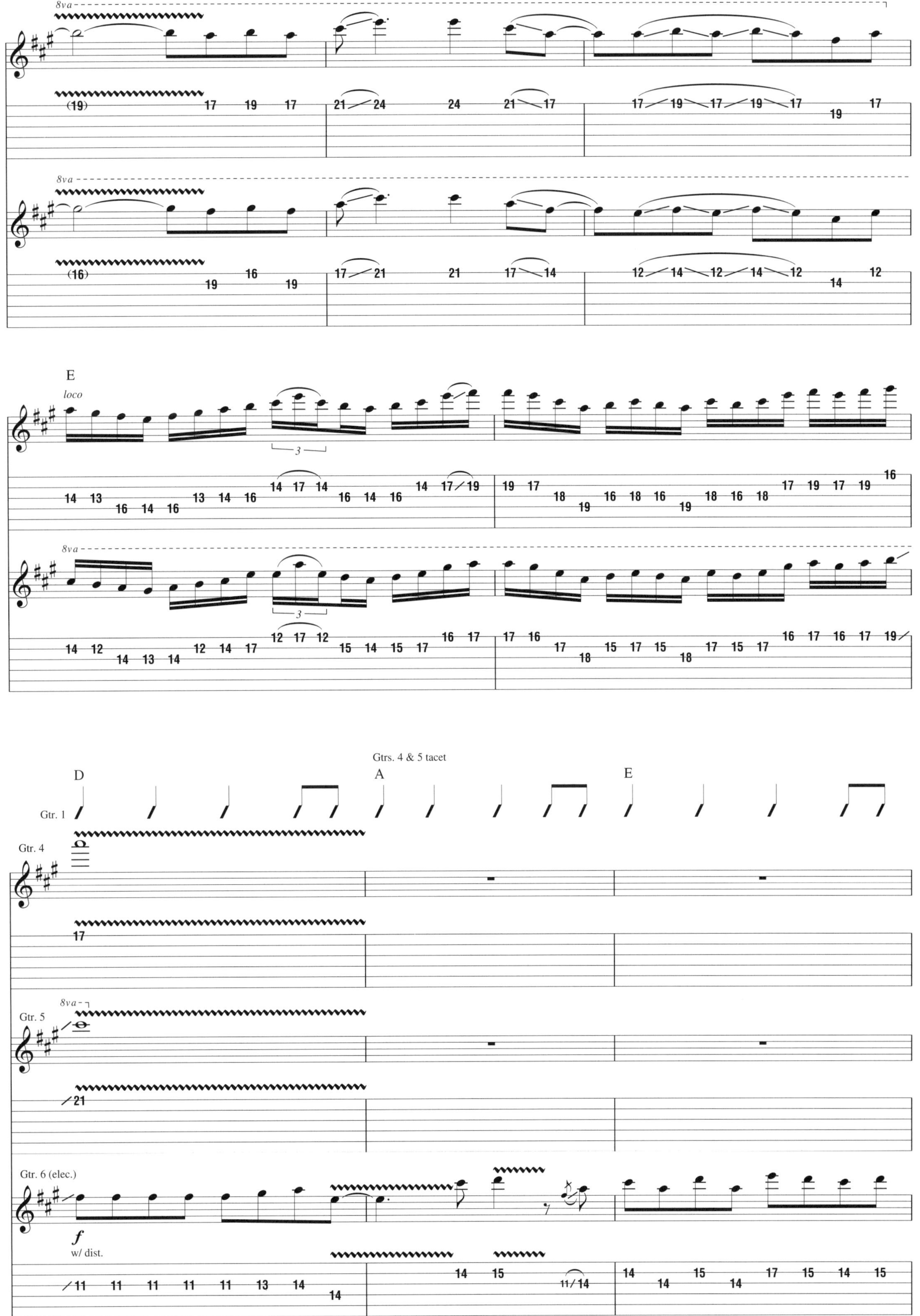

F♯m
8va
E
loco
8va
D
A
E
Gtrs. 4 & 5 tacet
Gtr. 1
Gtr. 4
Gtr. 5
8va
Gtr. 6 (elec.)
w/ dist.

F♯m
D
A
Gtr. 6
8va
F♯m
E
Gtr. 7 tacet
D
loco
P.H.
*Vol. swells
Gtr. 7 (elec.)
Pitch: A
w/ dist.
**Vol. swell
Gtrs. 2 & 3
P.M.
A
E
F♯m
Gtr. 6
Gtrs. 2 & 3

Bm
A
F♯m
Gtr. 6
8va
1
1 1/2
Gtr. 7
1/2
Gtrs. 2 & 3
Gtr. 1: w/ Rhy. Fig. 3
Gtrs. 2 & 3: w/ Rhy. Fig. 4
Gtr. 7 tacet
Gtr. 6 tacet
E
C♯
D
Gtr. 4
Gtr. 5

B7 E C♯7 F♯m E D

Gtr. 4

8va

Gtr. 5

8va

loco

P.H.

Pitch: E

Gtrs. 2 & 3

P.M.

P.M.

P.M.

D.S. al Coda 2

D Bm F♯m E

Gtr. 1

8va

8va

P.M.